The Kabbalistic Bible

Genesis

Technology for the Soul™

Edited by

RAV YEHUDA BERG

KABBALAH PUBLISHING™

www.kabbalah.com™

Published by
The Kabbalah Centre International Inc.

155 E. 48th St., New York, NY 10017
1062 S. Robertson Blvd., Los Angeles, CA 90035

Director Rav Berg

First Printing 2003

ISBN: 1-57189-230-3

Printed in USA

To merit one iota of the energy and beauty and redemption brought to this world by the Soul of Messiah that powered Rabbi Shimon Bar Yochai. I gratefully extend my patronage toward the printing, in English, of this, The Holy Grail, and inscribe the names of my beloved family.

Hannah-Elisiah, Leah, Miriam,

Yacov, Benjamin,

Yacov and Yacov

Special Readings

English Translation

Introduction

Whether you know it or not, you have just taken one of the most positive and momentous actions of your life: you have decided to open this book. There are a thousand reasons why you may have taken that action -- or why you think you took it -- but the real reason is much deeper, much more concealed, and infinitely more powerful. The action you've taken is an expression of your deepest desires as a human being. You may not realize that now, but when you reach the last page of the book you'll know it's true. In fact, even by the time you finish reading this Introduction, you'll see of the huge opportunity that this book represents and you'll be ready to take part in it to the fullest extent.

The book you've just opened is part of a very unique category. The Hebrew word for this kind of book is chumash, which is derived from the Hebrew word for five. The Five Books of Moses are inscribed into the scroll of the Torah; the chumash is a book version of the weekly Torah portions together with relevant commentary and interpretation. You may have seen other books of this kind, since there are many in the stores right now. Some chumash were composed hundreds of years ago, while others are very recent. With the recent upsurge of interest in spirituality, there are probably more books available in this category than at any other time in history.

But is chumash just another literary classification? Is it simply another genre that can continue indefinitely? Just as Hollywood turns out movies and music companies produce DVDs, can there be chumash forthcoming for many years?

The answer to this is most definitely no -- because chumash is not just an object made of ink and paper. In fact, it's nothing less than a spiritual tool for transforming yourself and the world.

This is a critically important point. It takes us to the heart of Kabbalistic wisdom about who we are, where we came from, and where we're going -- not just physically, but in the spiritual dimension that is the seed level of our existence. Grasping this begins with a single, fundamental insight: Kabbalah teaches that the universe and our lives in it have a direction. We're not here just to fill up time and space. In short, there is an end point and the purpose of our existence is to reach it.

What is that end point? There's a certain irony in the answer to that question, because understanding the end requires us to look at the beginning. The unity, the Oneness that existed between humanity and the Creator before the beginning of time is the goal that we're all striving to reach. Kabbalah calls

that original state of Oneness the Endless World, because it existed outside all the finite boundaries that we take for granted in our everyday lives.

In the Endless World there was no pain, no suffering, no illness, and most importantly, there was immortality. Death and every other kind of chaos had no place in our lives in the Endless World -- nor are they a necessary part of our lives today, despite the way things may seem. Chaos will remain with us only until we return to the Endless World through our spiritual work, though the tools and teachings of Kabbalah -- and most immediately, through the power of the book you're reading right now. This is not just a metaphor. In very practical terms, the end of all suffering; the end of all pain, even the end of death itself is in your grasp.

The ultimate purpose of the chumash is to bring about it's own end, to terminate our very need for it!

The whole history of humanity -- and, believe it or not, of your life as an individual human being -- is the story of our painstaking return to the Oneness with God that was ours in the Endless World. But when will that return be complete? When will the exile be over? The truth is, on one occasion we came very, very close to achieving that objective. This occurred at the foot of Mount Sinai, when Moses received the tablets inscribed by the Creator with the Ten Utterance, often mistakenly called the Ten Commandments. But the Utterances are much more than the list of "thou shalts" and "thou shalt nots" that we're so familiar with. In fact, even the term "Ten Utterances" is a coded message, and it refers to the ten dimensions that constitute total reality.

We live in the tenth and lowest dimension, the physical realm where darkness and despair constantly try to find their way into our lives. The hidden dimensions above us are an infinite pool of spiritual Light that can remove darkness from our own being and banish darkness from this world. They are the source of our joy, the root of our happiness and fountainhead of all wisdom. When we make contact with these hidden realms, we experience fulfillment. When we disconnect we experience chaos.

The tablets at Mount Sinai connected us to the full power of infinite Light swirling in these hidden realities. And they could have ignited a critical mass -- a spiritual explosion in which everything would have been fundamentally rebuilt, reconfigured, reconstructed, and reconstituted. In short, they could have brought us to the Endless World, heaven on earth. But only Moses held the Tablets! Only Moses possessed the Kabbalistic wisdom that gave access to all ten dimensions. The people as a whole excluded themselves by the sin of the Golden Calf, which caused Moses to shatter the tablets. So the

possibility for the ultimate transformation on Mount Sinai was now lost when Moses shattered the tablets.

But there was still hope!

What Moses achieved on Sinai was fundamentally similar to what modern science has been seeking for at least a century, since the beginning of the revolution that began with Albert Einstein's Theory of Relativity. Throughout his life, Einstein fervently believed in the existence of an even greater theory, the so-called "theory of everything" that would unite all scientific knowledge in a single all-inclusive explanation of the universe.

Here Einstein was simply expressing in physical terms the same quest for Oneness that Kabbalah understands to be fundamentally spiritual. Though Einstein never succeeded in his quest, he and others who came after him made great progress in that direction. Physics has shown that time, mass, and speed are all relative. If a mass attains a high enough speed, time stops. More recently, medicine and genetics are showing that aging, illness, and death are not inherently "necessary" and can be eliminated at the most basic biological levels. Science is correct in these insights. But what science is trying to achieve physically through genetic engineering or the construction of particle accelerators Moses achieved spiritually at Mount Sinai. The tablets had the power to take us beyond time and space, because they connected us to the infinite realm of Light, a reality without time and space. But when the Israelites built the Golden Calf, and the tablets were smashed "the clock started ticking again."

Thus, we lost the opportunity to replenish and restore the full power of the Light in one flashpoint, which Moses offered us on Sinai. Now, with time back in the picture, the work of regaining the Endless World would become an ongoing endeavor within the borders of time. Enter the weekly Chumash -- and this book in particular -- whose purpose is to activate the Kabbalistic technology utilized by Moses to connect the planet to the Light of the hidden dimensions.

Once this is understood, it's clear that the chumash you now hold in your hands is no ordinary book. The infinite energy of the Sinai's tablets is in these pages -- the power to connect us to ALL Ten Dimensions, the power to replenish ALL the Light we had on Sinai, the power to reveal ALL the infinite aspects of the divine that manifest throughout the universe. This infinitely diverse yet fundamentally unified energy is what the kabbalists refer to as the Creator's Light.

Consider, for example, what scientists refer to as "white light" -- the unfiltered

radiance that exists all around us during all our waking hours. Actually, this white light contains red, yellow, blue, green, and all the others colors of the spectrum. When these colors are combined as one, the result is white light. The Light of the Creator works in a similar fashion. Each dimension of the Light is another "color," -- another aspect of the Creator's Energy. Together, all the dimensions comprise the totality of the Creator's Light, which is pure, infinite, and all-encompassing.

Moses' tablets were a complete connection to the Light, all at once and instantly. Since the smashing of the tablets, we must reestablish that connection within the realm of time. That's exactly what the weekly chumash have done. But there will be an end point, a completion, a final chumash that ignites the critical mass that was just about to detonate at Sinai. This is the true meaning of the End of Days -- the revelation of Kabbalistic wisdom NOW, so that we can finish the job once and for all.

In the best and most positive sense of the term, this is truly "the end of the world." Not a radioactive mushroom cloud or a rapidly spreading epidemic, but a quantum change in the soul of humanity. That's what the term "Messiah" really means. It's the final redemption, that's the supreme transformation of all humanity.

You can experience this transformation by connecting with the energy of this book. Though science tells us that the speed of light can never be attained, you can absolutely gain the speed of Light -- the Creator's Light -- with the Kabbalistic tools and teachings in these pages. Be assured: this book is not just another example of biblical scholarship. Like Einstein's formula E = MC2, the Kabbalistic chumash reveals a new and higher reality. What's more, the chumash is also a tool for entering that reality. And now you are invited to step through that door.

Lesson of Beresheet

"In the beginning, God created the heaven and the earth"

Every year just after the High Holy Days, we start again to read the Torah with the portion of Beresheet. As we begin, we should ask ourselves one question: This year, how will things be different?

Over the past year, we heard the Torah read every week. Despite this, there may have been events in our lives that didn't turn out as we had hoped. Perhaps something very negative happened either to us or to someone we love. This, however, only means that we didn't really connect to the Torah readings. So if this year is to be different, it will be because of changes that we make in our inner selves.

In other words, if we want things to be different this year, it's our own consciousness that has to change. The Torah certainly doesn't need to change because the Torah exists in a dimension above and beyond everything: beyond death, beyond time, beyond negativity of any kind. For this reason, even though it may be ordained on Rosh Hashanah that negativity will occur in a certain week, listening to the reading of the Torah that week will protect us from the negativity - provided we really connect with what we hear and we enter the dimension of the Torah.

Every week, the Torah's protection is available to us, but this week in particular, we have a special opportunity. This week, we can connect with the power of Creation itself - with the energy that brought the world into being. The seed for that energy exists only in the Torah: As the Talmud explains, the Creator looked at the Torah and then created the world according to it. Without the spiritual power of the Torah, the material world and its physical laws would not exist. Even the principles of physics that cause the earth to travel around the sun exist because of the Torah. In fact, the earth and the sun themselves exist only because of the Torah.

Even our physical possessions - and the desire for them - are present in our lives because of the Torah's laws. For example, even though there is a spiritual law that prohibits us from taking other people's possessions, our negative nature causes us to desire the belongings of others. The whole purpose of this desire, and indeed, of physical possessions, is to give us an opportunity to restrict and overcome those wants. That's why the material world exists. We have the seed of all this in the story of Creation. By connecting with the energy of that story, we can literally become the center of the world, just as the Torah is the center of the world. Everything will revolve around us, just as the earth revolves around the sun. But we must listen and participate in the

reading with our whole heart and soul.

As we listen to the words in the portion describing the beginning of the world, it's important to realize how crucial every word - and even every letter - really is. Our sages tell us that before the world was created, each of the Hebrew letters came before God and said, “Why don't you create the world with me?" And the Creator explained to each letter why this couldn’t be done.

Finally the letter bet appeared before Him and said, "Master of the world, create the world with me. With me, all the blessings in the upper world and the lower world will come to you because I am the first letter of the Hebrew word bracha, or blessing.” And the Creator agreed. So the Torah - and the world itself - begins with bet, for blessing.

Rabbi Yehuda Ashlag was the teacher and master of Rabbi Yehuda Brandwein, who was in turn the Rav’s teacher. In his commentary on the Zohar entitled Sulam (Hebrew for “the ladder”), Rabbi Ashlag explains that negative forces cannot latch onto a blessing. Negativity can enter only where there's emptiness, and since the blessing of the Creator is present everywhere, in both the upper worlds and in the lower, there is no opening for the negative forces. But we can create an opening for negativity through our actions and our consciousness. By disconnecting from the Light and connecting to our ego desires, we offer a foothold to the negative side.

The choice is always ours. By tapping into the energy of this week’s portion and its description of the creation of the world, we can transport ourselves to the Tree of Life reality (as the Rav often refers to it) where everything is good. In the Tree of Life reality, no spiritual work is needed to bring us connection with the Creator. The connection is always there, constantly and continually. As long as we are still in a physical body, however, entering the Tree of Life reality is almost impossible. But through the power of this week's portion and through the connection to the Tree of Knowledge good and evil, we can begin to move in that direction.

Along with the story of the letter bet, there are other great teachings in this week’s portion. We learn that in the beginning, all of us were part of Adam. We were all one - all part of his infinite body and his soul. Nobody was smarter or less smart. Nobody was faster or slower, richer or poorer. There was just Adam, or in Hebrew, Adam Rishon, the first person.

Now, of course, everything is different. We were all part of one tree - the Tree of Life - but now an infinite number of trees bring forth an infinite number of different kinds of fruit. In a similar vein, all of us may listen to the Torah reading, but not all of us hear it the same way. Just as the fruits of different

trees exist in countless varieties, each of us connects with this week's portion in our own unique way. Just as some fruits have taste but no smell while some have smell with no taste, most of us are somewhere in the spiritual "middle." We're not wicked people, but we're not perfect. Sometimes, we care about others, and many times, we're most concerned about ourselves. But the important point is this: Everyone has within himself a spark of the Light of the Creator because in the beginning, we were all one endless manifestation of the Light.

For the final transformation of humanity to take place, we need to return to that unity consciousness - to the awareness of our Oneness through the Light and with the Light. No "I'm more than you are" or "I'm less than you." Everyone is essential, just as every brick in a house is essential even though some may look bigger and stronger than others.

There's a story about the Rav that illustrates this. Someone once suggested the Rav for the position of chief rabbi of Holland. The Rav was invited to Holland, and he asked if he could give a talk in the synagogue, which would be open to everyone in the community. A huge crowd turned out. There were more people at the synagogue than came even for Yom Kippur. The Rav spoke about Kabbalah with a little bit about physics thrown in, and the people loved it.

Later, the heads of the community came to the Rav and told him, "We definitely want you as our rabbi, but not the rabbi of the people who appear only on special occasions or once a year on the holidays." When he heard this, the Rav declined the position. If he couldn't be a teacher for everyone, he couldn't give himself to the task. Because the world can be transformed only when we consider the whole world as one.

The Creator doesn't recognize higher or lower. The blessing is always the same. But to connect with that blessing, we must become higher this year than we were in the year that just ended. As Reb Nachman of Breslev wrote: "If a person is not better today than yesterday, why does he need tomorrow?" We need tomorrow for the same reason we are in the world in the first place, which is to reveal the Light. From this week's reading, we can gain the power to fulfill that purpose by gaining the strength to change ourselves.

Synopsis of Beresheet

Deconstructing Genesis: The Seed

In essence, the biblical story of Creation pertains to the power of a seed. Just as an apple seed contains the entire tree from initial root to final fruit, the seed of Creation contains the entire spiritual evolution of humankind. Thus, Genesis holds within itself the final outcome of a perfected humanity, living in eternal bliss, unified with the Light of the Creator.

This is the magnitude of Light that is available to us in this portion.

Today our souls are born anew. Moreover, the spiritual energy of our entire year is contained within these opening verses. The seven readings are seedlings for the next twelve months. Accordingly, the Torah now bestows upon us the power to control the entire year, to determine the quality of our life, both individually and globally.

Kabbalistic Influence

This is the first time in history that the hidden insights of Kabbalah are shedding light on the secrets of Creation for all humanity. Hence, this Light nourishes the seed in a manner that is unprecedented in human history.

The spiritual DNA level of reality is altered. Our destiny is now transformed. The entire world undergoes a quantum shift towards a future that embodies an immediate and final perfection of humans with untold sweet mercy. As we open our hearts to these truths and arouse repentance in our souls, we control the conclusion to the drama of human existence and ensure a process filled with loving kindness.

The Light that shines from this portion exterminates the root of all evil. A deathblow is dealt to the Angel of Death himself, paving the way for immortality and endless fulfillment.

First Reading - Abraham - Chesed

א (א) בְּרֵאשִׁית בָּרָא (קנ"א ב"ן) אֱלֹהִים (ילה) אֵת הַשָּׁמַיִם (י"פ

The Torah expounds upon the seven days of Creation. In truth, the Creation process concerns the distance that we've placed between the Light and ourselves (and the souls of humanity). All of us seek, in every part of our lives, to remove this distance so that we may connect deeply with loved ones, friends, our own souls, and the source of all - the Light of the Creator.

The purpose of this reading is to bridge the gap, remove the space, eradicate the distance between us and the Light. We achieve this objective during this first aliyah, bringing family, friends, and the Creator close to our hearts.

In addition, when we set our hearts upon a goal, there is always a process we must endure before we can realize our objective. This process, however, creates an opening for negativity, obstacles, challenges, and turmoil.

בְּרֵאשִׁית - Here we remove the "process" from our lives. Time and space are eradicated as we complete our Final Redemption. This is the ultimate embryonic state, before the Sin of Adam. Everything is in a purified state of wholeness. This day is known as Day One, as opposed to the first day. The term "first" suggests more than one, whereas the word "one" implies oneness, wholeness, and exquisite unity.

Through this Torah reading, our cells and our souls revert to a state of oneness as we dip ourselves in the pure and pristine supernal waters that cleanse us of all negativity.

בְּרֵאשִׁית - The large Bet: The reason the world was created with the letter Bet, as opposed to the letter Aleph (or any other letter for that matter), is that Bet begins the Hebrew word Brachah ("blessing"). The inner significance of the word blessing includes the concept of free will and the

choices we make.
Blessing is our reward, our payback, the way we become the creators of our own fulfillment. When we resist our innate nature of ego and selfishness and choose not to react to chaos, we ignite blessings in our life. At the moment of Creation, all the blessings (the Light) were concealed, hidden away inside creation, waiting for man to reveal them through his own actions. Therefore, in truth, blessings embody all the joys and fulfillment that we seek in life, whatever form they may take. Just as white light contains all the colors of the rainbow, blessings contain all the kinds of delight we desire.

בְּרֵאשִׁית - The letter Vav begins each column of the Torah except for six places where a letter from a specific word is chosen to start the column. These six locations represent the six levels of Zeir Anpin. According to the Zohar, at the moment of Creation, six of the ten dimensions of The Tree of Life, called Sfirot compacted into one dimension known as Zeir Anpin. This left four dimensions, which allude to our three-dimensional world plus the fourth dimension of space-time. Now, some 2000 years after the ancient Kabbalists revealed that reality exists in ten dimensions - and that six of those dimensions are compacted into one - physicists have arrived at the same conclusion. This has come to be called the superstring theory.

According to this theory, our universe is built of tiny vibrating loops. Different vibrations create different particles of matter. Brian Greene, one of the leading superstring theorists, describes the theory in his book The Elegant Universe: Superstrings, Hidden Dimensions, and the Quest for the Ultimate Theory:

Just as the vibrational patterns of a violin string give rise to different musical notes, the different vibrational patterns of a fundamental string give rise to different masses and force charges. String theory also requires extra space dimensions that must be curled up to a very small size to be consistent with our never having seen them.

It turns out that the number of dimensions required to make the theory work (ten) and the number of dimensions that are curled up and compacted into one (six) are identical to the numbers given by the ancient Kabbalists.

(טל) וְאֵת הָאָרֶץ (מילוי אלהים ע"ה): (ב) וְהָאָרֶץ (מילוי אלהים ע"ה) הָיְתָה
תֹהוּ וָבֹהוּ וְחֹשֶׁךְ עַל־פְּנֵי (חכמה, בינה) תְהוֹם וְרוּחַ אֱלֹהִים (ילה)
מְרַחֶפֶת עַל־פְּנֵי (חכמה, בינה) הַמָּיִם: (ג) וַיֹּאמֶר אֱלֹהִים (ילה)
יְהִי אוֹר (רז) וַיְהִי־אוֹר (רז): (ד) וַיַּרְא אֱלֹהִים (ילה) אֶת־הָאוֹר
(רז) כִּי־טוֹב (והו) (אום) וַיַּבְדֵּל אֱלֹהִים (ילה) בֵּין הָאוֹר (רז) וּבֵין
הַחֹשֶׁךְ: (ה) וַיִּקְרָא אֱלֹהִים (ילה) | לָאוֹר (רז) יוֹם (נגד, זן) וְלַחֹשֶׁךְ
קָרָא לָיְלָה (מלה) וַיְהִי־עֶרֶב וַיְהִי־בֹקֶר יוֹם (נגד, זן) אֶחָד (אהבה):

Dr. Michio Kaku is an internationally recognized authority on theoretical physics and a leading proponent of superstring theory. In his book Hyperspace, Dr. Kaku writes:

When strings move in ten-dimensional space-time, they warp the space-time surrounding them in precisely the way predicted by general relativity. Physicists retrieve our more familiar four-dimensional Universe by assuming that, during the Big Bang, six of the ten dimensions curled up [or compacted] into a tiny ball, while the remaining four expanded explosively, giving us the universe we see.

(ו) וַיֹּאמֶר אֱלֹהִים (ילה) יְהִי רָקִיעַ בְּתוֹךְ הַמָּיִם וִיהִי מַבְדִּיל
בֵּין מַיִם לָמָיִם: (ז) וַיַּעַשׂ אֱלֹהִים (ילה) אֶת־הָרָקִיעַ וַיַּבְדֵּל
בֵּין הַמַּיִם אֲשֶׁר מִתַּחַת לָרָקִיעַ וּבֵין הַמַּיִם אֲשֶׁר מֵעַל (עלם)
לָרָקִיעַ וַיְהִי־כֵן: (ח) וַיִּקְרָא אֱלֹהִים (ילה) לָרָקִיעַ שָׁמָיִם (י״פ)
(טל) וַיְהִי־עֶרֶב וַיְהִי־בֹקֶר יוֹם (נגד, זן) שֵׁנִי: (ט) וַיֹּאמֶר אֱלֹהִים

וַיֹּאמֶר - Unlike Day One, which embodies a simple and elegant unity, the second day features the birth of separation. One becomes two. The unity is broken. Appropriately, Hell is created on this second day, signifying the dangers associated with disunity and disharmony between people. The Kabbalists teach us to never underestimate the perils of disunity.

Here, we ignite a unifying force of oneness, a splendid Light of unity to shine upon our world of many. We receive inspiration and wisdom to be both independent and interdependent souls. We acquire the ability to unify the parts into a whole, so they can retain their individuality but work together as a team to ensure there is no space for negative forces to enter.

The second day of Creation correlates to Monday. Hence, the sages advise us to avoid beginning a new enterprise on this fragmented day when there is an opening for negative forces to infect our ventures.

וַיֹּאמֶר - The third day corresponds to the creation of the Central Column force. According to Kabbalah, there are three primal forces at the heart of all existence: the Right, Left, and Central Columns.

- The Right Column corresponds to the positive (+) force of sharing (soul).
- The Left Column corresponds to the negative (–) force of receiving (ego).
- The Central Column corresponds to our free will that allows us to resist the selfish desires born from ego and to choose to live life according to the will of our soul.

(ילה) יִקָּווּ הַמַּיִם מִתַּחַת הַשָּׁמַיִם (י"פ טל) אֶל־מָקוֹם אֶחָד (אהבה)
וְתֵרָאֶה הַיַּבָּשָׁה וַיְהִי־כֵן: (י) וַיִּקְרָא אֱלֹהִים (ילה) | לַיַּבָּשָׁה
אֶרֶץ וּלְמִקְוֵה הַמַּיִם קָרָא יַמִּים (נלך) וַיַּרְא אֱלֹהִים (ילה) כִּי־
טוֹב (והו) (אום): (יא) וַיֹּאמֶר אֱלֹהִים (ילה) תַּדְשֵׁא הָאָרֶץ (מילוי אלהים
ע"ה) דֶּשֶׁא עֵשֶׂב (אותיות ע"ב שמות) מַזְרִיעַ זֶרַע עֵץ פְּרִי עֹשֶׂה פְּרִי
לְמִינוֹ אֲשֶׁר זַרְעוֹ־בוֹ עַל־הָאָרֶץ (מילוי אלהים ע"ה) וַיְהִי־כֵן: (יב)
וַתּוֹצֵא הָאָרֶץ (מילוי אלהים ע"ה) דֶּשֶׁא עֵשֶׂב (אותיות ע"ב שמות) מַזְרִיעַ
זֶרַע לְמִינֵהוּ וְעֵץ עֹשֶׂה־פְּרִי אֲשֶׁר זַרְעוֹ־בוֹ לְמִינֵהוּ וַיַּרְא
אֱלֹהִים (ילה) כִּי־טוֹב (והו) (אום): (יג) וַיְהִי־עֶרֶב וַיְהִי־בֹקֶר יוֹם
(נגד, זן) שְׁלִישִׁי: (יד) **וַיֹּאמֶר** אֱלֹהִים (ילה) יְהִי מְאֹרֹת בִּרְקִיעַ

The third day reading strengthens the free will in our consciousness so that we forever resist and triumph over our Left Column impulses (otherwise known as the Evil Inclination). Moreover, the collective consciousness of humankind is raised and fortified permanently, thus rejecting the seductive influences of the negative forces that dwell within the Left Column.

For this reason, the Torah states the following verse: “It was good.” We learn that Central Column - our willingness to reject selfish behavior - propagates goodness in life, both in our individual lives and all over the world.

From this reading, goodness emanates throughout all existence.

וַיֹּאמֶר - Here on the fourth day, we have the seed origin of the force known as jealousy, which Kabbalists identify as the root of all evil. We’re told that the moon and sun were once of equal importance and worth in the heavens. However, the moon was not satisfied with its stature. The moon desired to be greater than the sun, to be the single king of the cosmos.

הַשָּׁמַיִם (י"פ טל) לְהַבְדִּיל בֵּין הַיּוֹם (נגד, זן) וּבֵין הַלָּיְלָה (מלה) וְהָיוּ
לְאֹתֹת וּלְמוֹעֲדִים וּלְיָמִים (נלך) וְשָׁנִים: (טו) וְהָיוּ לִמְאוֹרֹת
בִּרְקִיעַ הַשָּׁמַיִם (י"פ טל) לְהָאִיר עַל־הָאָרֶץ (מילוי אלהים ע"ה)
וַיְהִי־כֵן: (טז) וַיַּעַשׂ אֱלֹהִים (ילה) אֶת־שְׁנֵי הַמְּאֹרֹת הַגְּדֹלִים
אֶת־הַמָּאוֹר הַגָּדֹל (להח, מבה עד"א) לְמֶמְשֶׁלֶת הַיּוֹם (נגד, זן) וְאֶת־
הַמָּאוֹר הַקָּטֹן לְמֶמְשֶׁלֶת הַלַּיְלָה (מלה) וְאֵת הַכּוֹכָבִים:
(יז) וַיִּתֵּן אֹתָם אֱלֹהִים (ילה) בִּרְקִיעַ הַשָּׁמָיִם (י"פ טל) לְהָאִיר
עַל־הָאָרֶץ (מילוי אלהים ע"ה): (יח) וְלִמְשֹׁל בַּיּוֹם (נגד, זן) וּבַלַּיְלָה

This scenario plays itself out each day of our lives. A man constantly casts a jealous eye towards the physical and spiritual assets of friends and neighbors, even though he may possess the very same treasures. Our nature is to blindly crave what others possess without ever thinking about the price they may have paid in life to acquire their possessions.

Here, we awaken the consciousness to understand that life is a package deal - that everything comes at a cost. Material possessions have the highest cost combined with the longest payment plan - a life that includes physical pain and emotional suffering - yet they yield the least amount of pleasure.

Spiritual treasures, however, are inexpensive - we pay only with our ego - but they endure eternally.

The Light cast from this fourth day eradicates envy from our nature. We uproot and exterminate the cosmic seed of jealousy, ending its rule over the hearts of humankind. Appreciation for our own lot in life blossoms forth, creating inner peace and contentment within our souls.

The Kabbalists advise us to not begin new ventures on this fourth day because evil was born during this period.

(מלה) וּלְהַבְדִּיל בֵּין הָאוֹר (רז) וּבֵין הַחֹשֶׁךְ וַיַּרְא אֱלֹהִים
(ילה) כִּי־טוֹב (והו) (אום): (יט) וַיְהִי־עֶרֶב וַיְהִי־בֹקֶר יוֹם (נגד, זן)
רְבִיעִי: (כ) **וַיֹּאמֶר** אֱלֹהִים (ילה) יִשְׁרְצוּ הַמַּיִם שֶׁרֶץ נֶפֶשׁ
חַיָּה וְעוֹף יְעוֹפֵף עַל־הָאָרֶץ (מילוי אלהים ע"ה) עַל־פְּנֵי (חכמה, בינה)
רְקִיעַ הַשָּׁמָיִם (י"פ טל): (כא) וַיִּבְרָא אֱלֹהִים (ילה) אֶת־הַתַּנִּינִם
הַגְּדֹלִים וְאֵת כָּל (ילי)־ נֶפֶשׁ הַחַיָּה | הָרֹמֶשֶׂת אֲשֶׁר שָׁרְצוּ
הַמַּיִם לְמִינֵהֶם וְאֵת כָּל (ילי)־עוֹף כָּנָף (ע"ה קנ"א) לְמִינֵהוּ וַיַּרְא
אֱלֹהִים (ילה) כִּי־טוֹב (והו) (אום): (כב) וַיְבָרֶךְ (עסמ"ב) אֹתָם אֱלֹהִים
(ילה) לֵאמֹר פְּרוּ וּרְבוּ וּמִלְאוּ אֶת־הַמַּיִם בַּיַּמִּים (נלך) וְהָעוֹף
יִרֶב בָּאָרֶץ: (כג) וַיְהִי־עֶרֶב וַיְהִי־בֹקֶר יוֹם (נגד, זן) חֲמִישִׁי: (כד)
וַיֹּאמֶר אֱלֹהִים (ילה) תּוֹצֵא הָאָרֶץ (מילוי אלהים ע"ה) נֶפֶשׁ חַיָּה

וַיֹּאמֶר - According to the Zohar, the fifth day connects us to the true Light of the Torah. This band of Light is our umbilical cord to the Creator throughout the coming year. It enriches and strengthens our connection to the infinite emanation of Divine Energy as we toil in this darkened dimension of physicality.

וַיֹּאמֶר - Man is created on this sixth day. The Light that radiates here empowers us with the divine gift of free will. We acquire the wisdom and strength to make the correct choices in life. We can choose to grow spiritually through the subjugation of our ego, or we can choose to take the path of pain and suffering, which also cleanses us of our egocentric behavior. The choice is always ours. When we choose spiritual deeds to elevate our souls, we elevate all Creation along with ourselves.

לְמִינָ֔הּ בְּהֵמָה֙ (לכב) וָרֶ֛מֶשׂ וְחַֽיְתוֹ־אֶ֖רֶץ לְמִינָ֑הּ וַֽיְהִי־כֵֽן׃ (כה)

וַיַּ֣עַשׂ אֱלֹהִים֮ (ילה) אֶת־חַיַּ֣ת הָאָ֜רֶץ (מילוי אלהים ע״ה) לְמִינָהּ֙ וְאֶת־

הַבְּהֵמָה֙ (לכב) לְמִינָ֔הּ וְאֵ֛ת כָּל־ (ילי) רֶ֥מֶשׂ הָֽאֲדָמָ֖ה לְמִינֵ֑הוּ

וַיַּ֥רְא אֱלֹהִ֖ים (ילה) כִּי־ טֽוֹב (והו) (אום)׃ (כו) וַיֹּ֣אמֶר אֱלֹהִ֗ים (ילה)

נַֽעֲשֶׂ֤ה אָדָם֙ (מ״ה) בְּצַלְמֵ֣נוּ כִּדְמוּתֵ֔נוּ וְיִרְדּוּ֩ בִדְגַ֨ת הַיָּ֜ם (ילי)

וּבְע֣וֹף הַשָּׁמַ֗יִם (י״פ טל) וּבַבְּהֵמָה֙ (לכב) וּבְכָל־הָאָ֔רֶץ (מילוי

אלהים ע״ה) וּבְכָל־ (לכב) הָרֶ֖מֶשׂ הָֽרֹמֵ֥שׂ עַל־הָאָֽרֶץ (מילוי אלהים ע״ה)׃

(כז) וַיִּבְרָ֨א אֱלֹהִ֤ים (ילה) אֶת־הָֽאָדָם֙ (מ״ה) בְּצַלְמ֔וֹ בְּצֶ֥לֶם

אֱלֹהִ֖ים (ילה) בָּרָ֣א (קנ״א ב״ן) אֹת֑וֹ זָכָ֥ר וּנְקֵבָ֖ה בָּרָ֥א (קנ״א ב״ן)

אֹתָֽם׃ (כח) וַיְבָ֣רֶךְ (עסמ״ב) אֹתָם֮ אֱלֹהִים֒ (ילה) וַיֹּ֨אמֶר לָהֶ֜ם

אֱלֹהִ֗ים (ילה) פְּר֥וּ וּרְב֛וּ וּמִלְא֥וּ אֶת־הָאָ֖רֶץ (מילוי אלהים ע״ה)

וְכִבְשֻׁ֑הָ וּרְד֞וּ בִּדְגַ֤ת הַיָּם֙ (ילי) וּבְע֣וֹף הַשָּׁמַ֔יִם (י״פ טל) וּבְכָל־

(לכב) חַיָּ֖ה הָֽרֹמֶ֥שֶׂת עַל־הָאָֽרֶץ (מילוי אלהים ע״ה)׃ (כט) וַיֹּ֣אמֶר

אֱלֹהִ֗ים (ילה) הִנֵּה֩ נָתַ֨תִּי לָכֶ֜ם אֶת־כָּל־ (ילי) עֵ֣שֶׂב (אותיות ע״ב שמות)

זֹרֵ֣עַ זֶ֗רַע אֲשֶׁר֙ עַל־פְּנֵ֣י (וכמה, בינה) כָל־ (ילי) הָאָ֔רֶץ (מילוי אלהים

ע״ה) וְאֶת־כָּל־ (ילי) הָעֵ֛ץ אֲשֶׁר־בּ֥וֹ פְרִי־ עֵ֖ץ זֹרֵ֣עַ זָ֑רַע לָכֶ֥ם

יִֽהְיֶ֖ה (ייי) לְאָכְלָֽה׃ (ל) וּֽלְכָל־ (יה אדני) חַיַּ֣ת הָ֠אָרֶץ (מילוי אלהים

ע״ה) וּלְכָל־ (יה אדני) ע֨וֹף הַשָּׁמַ֜יִם (י״פ טל) וּלְכֹ֣ל ׀ (יה אדני) רוֹמֵ֣שׂ

עַל־הָאָ֗רֶץ (מילוי אלהים ע״ה) אֲשֶׁר־בּוֹ֙ נֶ֣פֶשׁ חַיָּ֔ה אֶת־כָּל־ (ילי) יֶ֥רֶק

עֵשֶׂב (אותיות ע"ב שמות) לְאָכְלָה וַיְהִי־כֵן׃ (לא) וַיַּרְא אֱלֹהִים (ילה)
אֶת־כָּל (ילי)־אֲשֶׁר עָשָׂה וְהִנֵּה־טוֹב (והו) מְאֹד וַיְהִי־עֶרֶב
וַיְהִי־בֹקֶר יוֹם (נגד, זן) הַשִּׁשִּׁי׃ ב (א) וַיְכֻלּוּ (ע"ב) הַשָּׁמַיִם (י"פ
טל) וְהָאָרֶץ (מילוי אלהים ע"ה) וְכָל (ילי)־צְבָאָם׃ (ב) וַיְכַל אֱלֹהִים (ילה)
בַּיּוֹם (נגד, זן) הַשְּׁבִיעִי מְלַאכְתּוֹ אֲשֶׁר עָשָׂה וַיִּשְׁבֹּת בַּיּוֹם (נגד,
זן) הַשְּׁבִיעִי מִכָּל (ילי)־מְלַאכְתּוֹ אֲשֶׁר עָשָׂה׃ (ג) וַיְבָרֶךְ (עסמ"ב)
אֱלֹהִים (ילה) אֶת־יוֹם (נגד, זן) הַשְּׁבִיעִי וַיְקַדֵּשׁ אֹתוֹ כִּי בוֹ שָׁבַת
מִכָּל (ילי)־מְלַאכְתּוֹ אֲשֶׁר־בָּרָא (קנ"א ב"ן) אֱלֹהִים (ילה) לַעֲשׂוֹת׃

Second Reading - Issac - Gvurah

(ד) אֵלֶּה תוֹלְדוֹת הַשָּׁמַיִם (י"פ טל) וְהָאָרֶץ (מילוי אלהים ע"ה)

וַיְכֻלּוּ - The concept of a Day of Rest on the Shabbat is a code. The word "rest" alludes to a realm of no time, space, or motion: a dimension of infinite stillness, wholeness, and exquisite unity. This blessed realm is the embodiment of spiritual Light. On the Shabbat, our souls ascend into this reality so that we may cleanse and purify ourselves, eradicating the negativity that we've accumulated in both this and past lives. Each Shabbat, we continue to cleanse and thus evolve along our spiritual path. Accordingly, the Shabbat, rather than being a "day of rest," is actually the one day of the week when we work the hardest, identifying and uprooting egocentric qualities from our nature.

As we read about the Shabbat here on this Shabbat Day, we can arouse repentance and admit our jealousies and character faults to ourselves. This difficult action will repair our iniquities and purify our souls by summoning the Light of all the Sabbatot throughout history.

אֵלֶּה - In Genesis, we find the only verses in the Torah where only

בְּהִבָּרְאָם בְּיוֹם (נגד, זן) עֲשׂוֹת יְהֹוָהאדניאהדונהי אֱלֹהִים (ילה)
אֶרֶץ וְשָׁמָיִם (י"פ טל): (ה) וְכֹל (ילי) | שִׂיחַ הַשָּׂדֶה טֶרֶם יִהְיֶה

goodness and Light are mentioned, verses that precede the Sin of Adam and the sin of the Golden Calf. Accordingly, by following these verses of Scripture, we further the goal of the Final Correction. We repair all our sins committed in this and past lives - along with all the iniquities of the human race - bringing us to our final perfection in a process that embodies incredible soft-heartedness. .

בְּהִבָּרְאָם - In Genesis 2:4, we find the verse: "When they were created." In Hebrew, this verse is written "BEHEI BARAM". Here we find a small version of the Hebrew letter Hei. This phrase contains the same letters that spell out be'Abraham, which means "for the sake of Abraham." Thus, the Midrash teaches us that the world was created for the sake of Abraham. This small Hei will eventually appear in the name of Abraham (Lech Lecha 17:5) when it changes from Abram to Abraham. This Hei represents the divinity imbued in Abraham's nature. Our goal in life is to transform ourselves from selfish reactive individuals into people who receive for the sake of sharing, thus personifying the unconditional sharing nature of our patriarch Abraham. Abraham is our seed. Just as the final fruit is contained within the seed, our final perfected state of sharing is contained within Abraham. Accordingly, the small Hei in the Torah is now implanted in our soul, igniting a spark of divinity within us. We are empowered with the courage to seek spiritual transformation, to share, to resist self-seeking desires - in short, to become like Abraham.

אֶרֶץ - There are two aspects to Creation: the metaphysical blueprint and the physical manifestation where humans make their appearance on the stage of the material world. This second aspect unfolds in this portion.

The Garden of Eden comes into existence and represents the concept of parallel universes: the realm of the Tree of Life and the domain of the Tree of Knowledge of Good and Evil.

The Tree of Life corresponds to the 99 per cent of reality that we do not

perceive with our five senses. This is a place where there is perfect order, bliss, harmony, and enlightenment. All the joy and wisdom of the world flows from this 99 per cent reality.

The Tree of Knowledge of Good and Evil corresponds to our one per cent world, which represents only a tiny fraction of true reality. It is our physical dimension of darkness, disorder, and sudden chaos.

Both worlds exist side by side. When a scientist makes a startling discovery, he has made contact with the 99 per cent world. Similarly, when parents feel pleasure from the hugs of their child, their joy originates and flows from the 99 per cent world.

All our pleasurable and tranquil moments in life signify our connection to the Tree of Life. When our consciousness is positive and strong - when we feel the truth of the Creator in our hearts - we are connected to the Tree of Life realm.

When, however, we are in doubt or are overcome with sadness, depression, or selfishness, we have severed our connection to the Tree of Life. We are now floundering in the dimension of the Tree of Knowledge of Good and Evil. Unfortunately, this is where people dwell most of their lives.

Looking for solutions to our problems in the Tree of Knowledge of Good and Evil realm is an impossible task. It can be likened to a man sinking in quicksand. It is futile for him to try to pull himself out by tugging on his own collar. The only escape is to reach upwards to grab a branch of a nearby tree. Likewise, we must ascend into the Tree of Life realm to climb out of the mud and to effect positive change in our physical world.

This is our only hope, according to Kabbalah.

Here we achieve the authentic great escape. A branch of Light extending from the Tree of Life shines upon us in this portion of the Torah. We are lifted out of the world of chaos and placed gently into a world of perfection. And as we meditate to share this Light with our fellow human beings, we initiate our Final Redemption in a most merciful manner. Kabbalistic learning engenders a deep connection to the Tree of Life, according to the most learned sages.

(ייי) בָּאָרֶץ וְכָל (ילי)־עֵשֶׂב (אותיות ע״ב שמות) הַשָּׂדֶה טֶרֶם יִצְמָח
כִּי לֹא הִמְטִיר יְהֹוָהאדניאהדונהי אֱלֹהִים (ילה) עַל־הָאָרֶץ (מילוי
אלהים ע״ה) וְאָדָם (מ״ה) אַיִן לַעֲבֹד אֶת־הָאֲדָמָה׃ (ו) וְאֵד יַעֲלֶה
מִן־הָאָרֶץ (מילוי אלהים ע״ה) וְהִשְׁקָה אֶת־כָּל (ילי)־פְּנֵי (חכמה, בינה)
הָאֲדָמָה׃ (ז) וַיִּיצֶר יְהֹוָהאדניאהדונהי אֱלֹהִים (ילה) אֶת־הָאָדָם
(מ״ה) עָפָר מִן־הָאֲדָמָה וַיִּפַּח בְּאַפָּיו נִשְׁמַת חַיִּים (בינה ע״ה) וַיְהִי
הָאָדָם (מ״ה) לְנֶפֶשׁ חַיָּה׃ (ח) וַיִּטַּע יְהֹוָהאדניאהדונהי אֱלֹהִים (ילה)
גַּן־בְּעֵדֶן מִקֶּדֶם וַיָּשֶׂם שָׁם אֶת־הָאָדָם (מ״ה) אֲשֶׁר יָצָר׃
(ט) וַיַּצְמַח יְהֹוָהאדניאהדונהי אֱלֹהִים (ילה) מִן־הָאֲדָמָה כָּל (ילי)־
עֵץ נֶחְמָד לְמַרְאֶה וְטוֹב (והו) לְמַאֲכָל וְעֵץ הַחַיִּים (בינה ע״ה)
בְּתוֹךְ הַגָּן וְעֵץ הַדַּעַת טוֹב (והו) וָרָע׃ (י) וְנָהָר יֹצֵא מֵעֵדֶן
לְהַשְׁקוֹת אֶת־הַגָּן וּמִשָּׁם יִפָּרֵד וְהָיָה (יהה) (יהוה) לְאַרְבָּעָה
רָאשִׁים׃ (יא) שֵׁם הָאֶחָד (אהבה) פִּישׁוֹן הוּא הַסֹּבֵב אֵת כָּל
(ילי)־ אֶרֶץ הַחֲוִילָה אֲשֶׁר־שָׁם הַזָּהָב (וזהו)׃ (יב) וּזֲהַב הָאָרֶץ
(מילוי אלהים ע״ה) הַהִוא טוֹב (והו) שָׁם הַבְּדֹלַח וְאֶבֶן הַשֹּׁהַם׃ (יג)
וְשֵׁם־הַנָּהָר הַשֵּׁנִי גִּיחוֹן הוּא הַסּוֹבֵב אֵת כָּל (ילי)־אֶרֶץ
כּוּשׁ׃ (יד) וְשֵׁם־הַנָּהָר הַשְּׁלִישִׁי חִדֶּקֶל הוּא הַהֹלֵךְ (מיה)
קִדְמַת אַשּׁוּר וְהַנָּהָר הָרְבִיעִי הוּא פְרָת׃ (טו) וַיִּקַּח (חעם)
יְהֹוָהאדניאהדונהי אֱלֹהִים (ילה) אֶת־הָאָדָם (מ״ה) וַיַּנִּחֵהוּ בְגַן־עֵדֶן

לְעָבְדָהּ וּלְשָׁמְרָהּ׃ (טז) וַיְצַו יְהוָה יאהדונהי אֱלֹהִים (ילה)
עַל־הָאָדָם (מ״ה) לֵאמֹר מִכֹּל (ילי) עֵץ־הַגָּן אָכֹל תֹּאכֵל׃ (יז)
וּמֵעֵץ הַדַּעַת טוֹב (והו) וָרָע לֹא תֹאכַל מִמֶּנּוּ כִּי בְּיוֹם (נגד, זן)
אֲכָלְךָ מִמֶּנּוּ מוֹת תָּמוּת׃ (יח) וַיֹּאמֶר יְהוָה יאהדונהי אֱלֹהִים
(ילה) לֹא־טוֹב (והו) הֱיוֹת הָאָדָם (מ״ה) לְבַדּוֹ (מ״ב) אֶעֱשֶׂה־לּוֹ
עֵזֶר כְּנֶגְדּוֹ (זן, מזבח)׃ (יט) וַיִּצֶר יְהוָה יאהדונהי אֱלֹהִים (ילה) מִן־
הָאֲדָמָה כָּל (ילי)־חַיַּת הַשָּׂדֶה וְאֵת כָּל (ילי)־עוֹף הַשָּׁמַיִם
(י״פ טל) וַיָּבֵא אֶל־הָאָדָם (מ״ה) לִרְאוֹת מַה (מ״ה)־יִּקְרָא־לוֹ וְכֹל
(ילי) אֲשֶׁר יִקְרָא־לוֹ הָאָדָם (מ״ה) נֶפֶשׁ חַיָּה הוּא שְׁמוֹ (מהש ע״ה)׃

וְכֹל - The Torah tells us that Adam bestowed names upon all the creatures. A name is composed of letters derived from an alphabet. Kabbalistically, this correlates to the concept of DNA, which is based on a genetic alphabet.

DNA is best described as an instruction manual for our cells. All cells begin in an undifferentiated state. Our DNA then determines which cells will evolve to become internal organs, bone, brain matter, or other tissues. Like all instruction manuals, DNA is written in a language utilizing an alphabet. In the late 1950s, geneticists cracked the genetic code of life and determined that the DNA alphabet is composed of four "letters," which they designated A, T, C, and G.

A, T, C, and G refer to four different kinds of nucleotides. These four nucleotides combine to create twenty amino acids, which produce the "words" and "sentences" that make up the genetic code of every individual. Human beings have about three billion letters in our genetic codes. The differences between individuals lie in the combination and sequences of these four nucleotides.

Third Reading - Jacob - Tiferet

(כ) וַיִּקְרָא הָאָדָם (מ"ה) שֵׁמוֹת לְכָל (יה אדני) ־הַבְּהֵמָה (לכב)
וּלְעוֹף הַשָּׁמַיִם (י"פ טל) וּלְכֹל (יה אדני) חַיַּת הַשָּׂדֶה וּלְאָדָם
(מ"ה) לֹא־מָצָא עֵזֶר כְּנֶגְדּוֹ (זן, מזבח)׃ (כא) וַיַּפֵּל יְהֹוָהאדניאהדונהי
אֱלֹהִים (ילה) | תַּרְדֵּמָה עַל־הָאָדָם (מ"ה) וַיִּישָׁן וַיִּקַּח (וזעם) אַחַת
מִצַּלְעֹתָיו וַיִּסְגֹּר בָּשָׂר תַּחְתֶּנָּה׃ (כב) וַיִּבֶן יְהֹוָהאדניאהדונהי

Biblical names, therefore, are concern with the spiritual genetic essence of a life-form - the raw spiritual elements that are configured in various combinations to conceive and give birth to a given entity in this dimension of existence.

The names of the great Patriarchs and other noble biblical characters represent the DNA of their soul, their respective spiritual attributes.

Thus, a person's name holds great significance in relation to his or her soul. The Kabbalists advise us to name our children after the great men and women of the Bible so that we can imbue our offspring with the same characteristics and qualities of these majestic figures.

Moreover, this passage helps us strengthen our own connection to our names, instilling us with divinity and Light, and awakening the power of our soul.

וַיִּבֶן - The Torah tells us that God created Eve from Adam. This is the beginning, the seed level of all male and female relationships destined to occur in our world.

According to Kabbalists, the phrase "Adam and Eve" is a code, a metaphor that refers to a single, unified soul that existed before our universe came into

אֱלֹהִים (ילה) | אֶת־הַצֵּלָע אֲשֶׁר־לָקַח מִן־הָאָדָם (מ"ה)
לְאִשָּׁה וַיְבִאֶהָ אֶל־הָאָדָם (מ"ה): (כג) וַיֹּאמֶר הָאָדָם (מ"ה)
זֹאת הַפַּעַם (מנק) עֶצֶם מֵעֲצָמַי וּבָשָׂר מִבְּשָׂרִי לְזֹאת יִקָּרֵא
אִשָּׁה כִּי מֵאִישׁ לֻקֳחָה־זֹּאת: (כד) עַל־כֵּן יַעֲזָב־אִישׁ אֶת־
אָבִיו וְאֶת־אִמּוֹ וְדָבַק בְּאִשְׁתּוֹ וְהָיוּ לְבָשָׂר אֶחָד (אהבה): (כה)
וַיִּהְיוּ שְׁנֵיהֶם עֲרוּמִּים הָאָדָם (מ"ה) וְאִשְׁתּוֹ וְלֹא יִתְבֹּשָׁשׁוּ:

existence. This infinitely large soul is called a Vessel, and all the souls of mankind - including yours - were contained within this one entity, just as all the colors of a rainbow exist within a single beam of sunlight.

Imagine a spattering of tiny water droplets. Each individual bead of water represents another individual soul of humanity. If we gather all the single drops together, they form a single pool of water, the Vessel.

This Vessel has two aspects or two polarities: a positive (+) and a negative (–) pole, just as a battery has a plus and minus charge. Adam corresponds to the positive charge. Eve corresponds to the negative charge. All the female souls who have roamed this physical planet throughout history are bound up as one unified whole in Eve. Likewise, all the male souls who have sauntered through this earthly terrain are bound up as one unified whole within Adam.

Thus, we learn that we are all of the same stock and source. No man or woman is higher or lower than another. We are, in truth, all one - and thus, interdependent with one another.

The Light radiating from the reading of these verses enriches all of our relationships with members of the opposite sex, while engendering unity among all of humanity.

ג (א) וְהַנָּחָשׁ הָיָה (יהה) עָרוּם מִכֹּל (ילי) חַיַּת הַשָּׂדֶה אֲשֶׁר
עָשָׂה יְהוָֹהאדניאהדונהי אֱלֹהִים (ילה) וַיֹּאמֶר אֶל־הָאִשָּׁה אַף כִּי־
אָמַר אֱלֹהִים (ילה) לֹא תֹאכְלוּ מִכֹּל (ילי) עֵץ הַגָּן׃ (ב) וַתֹּאמֶר
הָאִשָּׁה אֶל־הַנָּחָשׁ מִפְּרִי עֵץ־הַגָּן נֹאכֵל׃ (ג) וּמִפְּרִי הָעֵץ
אֲשֶׁר בְּתוֹךְ־הַגָּן אָמַר אֱלֹהִים (ילה) לֹא תֹאכְלוּ מִמֶּנּוּ וְלֹא
תִגְּעוּ בּוֹ פֶּן־תְּמֻתוּן׃ (ד) וַיֹּאמֶר הַנָּחָשׁ אֶל־הָאִשָּׁה לֹא־מוֹת
תְּמֻתוּן׃ (ה) כִּי יֹדֵעַ אֱלֹהִים (ילה) כִּי בְּיוֹם (נגד, זן) אֲכָלְכֶם מִמֶּנּוּ
וְנִפְקְחוּ עֵינֵיכֶם (מ"ה בריבוע) וִהְיִיתֶם כֵּאלֹהִים (ילה) יֹדְעֵי טוֹב (והו)
וָרָע׃ (ו) וַתֵּרֶא הָאִשָּׁה כִּי טוֹב (והו) (אום) הָעֵץ לְמַאֲכָל וְכִי

וְהַנָּחָשׁ - The concept of the negative Satan is introduced into the world for the first time in the Torah. The Satan is both a personal attribute and a global phenomenon. As a personal attribute, the Satan manifests as the human ego. As a global phenomenon, the Satan is the force of chaos and the occurrence of turmoil in our world. Our individual egos are the life-force of the global Satan. In other words, he feeds off our personal destructive deeds. The Satan uses the negative energy arising from our hateful actions to create turmoil in the world. These destructive forces are also the source of our personal chaos. Here, in Beresheet, we conquer our ego and in turn, deplete the global Satan of his energy and influence upon humanity.

וַתֵּרֶא - Before the creation of the world, Adam and Eve were spiritual beings who incorporated all the souls of humanity. We were all like cells that formed the body of these supernal beings. Adam and Eve collectively are known as the Vessel.

In the traditional biblical story of Creation, we're told that after creating

the other living things on Earth, God created Adam, the first man. But not wanting Adam to be alone, God took Adam's rib and made him a partner. This was Eve, the first woman. God left the couple in the Garden of Eden with the instruction that while they could partake of all the delights they found there, including fruit from the Tree of Life, they were forbidden to eat from the Tree of Knowledge of Good and Evil for the fruits were unripe and they would surely die.

But someone else happened to be in the Garden - the infamous serpent (the Satan). Urged on by the seductive encouragement of the snake, Eve disobeyed God. She plucked an apple from the forbidden tree and ate it. Then she offered the apple to Adam, enticing him to eat it along with her. He did, and with that, their fleeting age of innocence was over.

On another level of spiritual understanding, Adam and Eve's bite of the fruit indicates a sexual connection between the original Vessel and the serpent. In other words, the very act of succumbing to the deceitful prodding of the serpent also denotes a sexual union between them - a merging of their consciousnesses.

The negative Satan has two aspects, Male and Female. The Male aspect is known as (do not pronounce his name) Samael. The Female aspect is known as (do not pronounce her name) Lilit. Thus, the Vessel submitting to the temptation of the serpent also means, from our perspective in this realm, that Lilit copulated with Adam and Samael copulated with Eve. In spiritual terms, this implies that the consciousnesses of Adam and Eve were lowered and thus tainted by the negative angels.

Moreover, this sexual union - or the merging of the two consciousnesses - mutated the nature of the Vessel. In the language of genetics, the act of sexual connection between the Vessel and the serpent altered the Vessel's DNA from a desire to receive to the more selfish desire to receive for the self alone. Consequently, every cell (our souls) in the cosmic body of Adam and Eve had its DNA recombined with the DNA (consciousness) of the serpent. This is the birth of our "selfish gene" - the ego, the dark side of man's nature.

The Vessel then shattered into individual souls. Adam and Eve became countless sparks of souls, who descended into this physical world and assumed the garment of physical bodies. Adam and Eve were then

תַּאֲוָה־הוּא לָעֵינַיִם (מ"ה בריבוע) וְנֶחְמָד הָעֵץ לְהַשְׂכִּיל וַתִּקַּח
מִפִּרְיוֹ וַתֹּאכַל וַתִּתֵּן (ב"פ כהת) גַּם־לְאִישָׁהּ עִמָּהּ וַיֹּאכַל׃ (ז)
וַתִּפָּקַחְנָה עֵינֵי (מ"ה בריבוע) שְׁנֵיהֶם וַיֵּדְעוּ כִּי עֵירֻמִּם הֵם
וַיִּתְפְּרוּ עֲלֵה תְאֵנָה וַיַּעֲשׂוּ לָהֶם חֲגֹרֹת׃ (ח) וַיִּשְׁמְעוּ אֶת־
קוֹל יְהֹוָהאדניאהדונהי אֱלֹהִים (ילה) מִתְהַלֵּךְ (מיה) בַּגָּן לְרוּחַ הַיּוֹם
(נגד, זן) וַיִּתְחַבֵּא הָאָדָם (מ"ה) וְאִשְׁתּוֹ מִפְּנֵי יְהֹוָהאדניאהדונהי אֱלֹהִים
(ילה) בְּתוֹךְ עֵץ הַגָּן׃ (ט) וַיִּקְרָא יְהֹוָהאדניאהדונהי אֱלֹהִים (ילה) אֶל־
הָאָדָם (מ"ה) וַיֹּאמֶר לוֹ אַיֶּכָּה׃ (י) וַיֹּאמֶר אֶת־קֹלְךָ שָׁמַעְתִּי בַּגָּן
וָאִירָא כִּי־עֵירֹם אָנֹכִי (אי"ע) וָאֵחָבֵא׃ (יא) וַיֹּאמֶר מִי (ילי) הִגִּיד
לְךָ כִּי עֵירֹם אָתָּה הֲמִן־הָעֵץ אֲשֶׁר צִוִּיתִיךָ לְבִלְתִּי אֲכָל־
מִמֶּנּוּ אָכָלְתָּ׃ (יב) וַיֹּאמֶר הָאָדָם (מ"ה) הָאִשָּׁה אֲשֶׁר נָתַתָּה

empowered with the task of eradicating the negative consciousness from their own nature and reuniting all the scattered pieces of the one fractured soul back into a single unified whole. This is the purpose of our lives.

The dark and egocentric aspect of human nature was born from this union between the Vessel and the serpent. All of our egoistic character traits, jealousies, and overall negative behaviors are rooted in this original Sin.

From this story, we acquire the spiritual power to eradicate Satan's influence, both externally and internally, from our consciousness. Our ego is herewith subjugated. Our soul's radiance is unleashed. Selfishness is purged from our nature, and unconditional love for our fellow man blossoms forth.

וַיֹּאמֶר - After the Sin, God asks Adam why he sinned. Adam's response is to blame Eve. Before us is a lesson concerning our own failure to take

עִמָּדִי הִוא נָתְנָה־לִּי מִן־הָעֵץ וָאֹכֵל׃ (יג) וַיֹּאמֶר יְהֹוָהאדניאהדונהי
אֱלֹהִים (ילה) לָאִשָּׁה מַה (מ״ה) ־זֹּאת עָשִׂית וַתֹּאמֶר הָאִשָּׁה
הַנָּחָשׁ הִשִּׁיאַנִי וָאֹכֵל׃ (יד) וַיֹּאמֶר יְהֹוָהאדניאהדונהי אֱלֹהִים (ילה)
| אֶל־הַנָּחָשׁ כִּי עָשִׂיתָ זֹּאת אָרוּר אַתָּה מִכָּל (ילי) ־הַבְּהֵמָה
(לכב) וּמִכֹּל (ילי) חַיַּת הַשָּׂדֶה עַל־גְּחֹנְךָ תֵלֵךְ וְעָפָר תֹּאכַל
כָּל (ילי) ־יְמֵי חַיֶּיךָ׃ (טו) וְאֵיבָה | אָשִׁית בֵּינְךָ וּבֵין הָאִשָּׁה
וּבֵין זַרְעֲךָ וּבֵין זַרְעָהּ הוּא יְשׁוּפְךָ רֹאשׁ וְאַתָּה תְּשׁוּפֶנּוּ
עָקֵב (ב״פ מום)׃ ס (טז) אֶל־הָאִשָּׁה אָמַר הַרְבָּה אַרְבֶּה (יצחק)
עִצְּבוֹנֵךְ וְהֵרֹנֵךְ בְּעֶצֶב תֵּלְדִי בָנִים וְאֶל־אִישֵׁךְ תְּשׁוּקָתֵךְ

responsibility for the chaos and strife that befall us. Our natural inclination is to point the finger of blame when things go wrong in our lives. And when things go very wrong, many of us point heavenward. What's more, the Creator often seems painfully indifferent to human pleas for help. We now discover a long-hidden Kabbalistic truth: God doesn't answer our prayers - we do!

Any turmoil in our lives is a direct result of some negative action we've committed in this or a past life. Our prayers and the Light of Torah are activated only when we fully acknowledge our personal responsibility for the pain and suffering we endure. Prayers ascend heavenward when we relinquish our victim mindset. Conversely, when we're in denial and when our hearts are filled with self-pity, prayer and Torah become worthless tools, even fruitless symbols of tradition, instead of awesome instruments of power.

Listening to this reading arouses remorse in our hearts and awakens the consciousness of accountability within us. In turn, our sins are corrected as the Light of the Torah purifies our soul and cleanses the world of its iniquities.

וְהוּא יִמְשָׁל־בָּךְ׃ ס (יז) וּלְאָדָם (מ"ה) אָמַר כִּי־שָׁמַעְתָּ לְקוֹל
אִשְׁתֶּךָ וַתֹּאכַל מִן־הָעֵץ אֲשֶׁר צִוִּיתִיךָ לֵאמֹר לֹא תֹאכַל
מִמֶּנּוּ אֲרוּרָה הָאֲדָמָה בַּעֲבוּרֶךָ בְּעִצָּבוֹן תֹּאכֲלֶנָּה כֹּל (יל"י)
יְמֵי חַיֶּיךָ׃ (יח) וְקוֹץ וְדַרְדַּר תַּצְמִיחַ לָךְ וְאָכַלְתָּ אֶת־עֵשֶׂב
הַשָּׂדֶה׃ (אותיות ע"ב שמות) (יט) בְּזֵעַת אַפֶּיךָ תֹּאכַל לֶחֶם (ג' הויות) עַד

וּלְאָדָם - The Torah tells us that Adam, Eve, and the serpent Satan all receive punishment following the Sin. The snake is condemned to roam the earth on its belly and eat of the dust. Women are destined to endure the pain of childbirth; before the Sin, there was no menstrual period, and child-bearing was an immediate phenomenon. Adam is forced to work the field, to strive for food, and to labor for the Light. Here, once again, we have a metaphor that conceals deeper spiritual truths.

The concepts of punishment and reward have no basis in spirituality. If we inadvertently or even purposely touch a burning coal and injure ourselves, we do not profess to have been punished by the fiery ember. Conversely, if we use this coal to heat our home, cook our family's food, or bathe ourselves in warmed waters, we do not construe this as a reward. It is our knowledge (or lack of knowledge) of the properties of the coal that actually determines the coal's influence in our life.

God does not punish. The Creator does not reward. And the Lord does not command. When Adam (we, the Vessel) was initially created by God to receive endless fulfillment and joy, Adam inherited a trait, a "gene" from this Divine Force. He received the DNA of being Godlike. Adam (and we, the Vessel) wanted to be the creator of our own Light. Being a creator is the greatest fulfillment of all.

But just as candlelight has no genuine value in the presence of the sun, Adam

שׁוּבְךָ֙ אֶל־הָ֣אֲדָמָ֔ה כִּ֥י מִמֶּ֖נָּה לֻקָּ֑חְתָּ כִּֽי־עָפָ֣ר אַ֔תָּה וְאֶל־
עָפָ֖ר תָּשֽׁוּב׃ (כ) וַיִּקְרָ֧א הָֽאָדָ֛ם (מ"ה) שֵׁ֥ם אִשְׁתּ֖וֹ חַוָּ֑ה כִּ֣י הִ֥וא
הָֽיְתָ֖ה אֵ֥ם (יוהך) כָּל (ילי)־חָֽי (חיים, בינה ע"ה)׃ (כא) וַיַּ֩עַשׂ֩ יְהֹוָ֨האדניאהדונהי
אֱלֹהִ֜ים (ילה) לְאָדָ֧ם (מ"ה) וּלְאִשְׁתּ֛וֹ כָּתְנ֥וֹת ע֖וֹר וַיַּלְבִּשֵֽׁם׃

(we) left the luminous perfection of the Garden of Eden (a dimension of pure Light) to enter our disordered dimension of darkness, where the Light is concealed. But Man, through his own labor and effort, can now rekindle the Light, and thus share in the divine act of Creation: He (we) becomes responsible for creating Heaven on Earth and, in turn, becomes Godlike!

Thus, it was Adam's decision to come to this world. It was not a punishment decreed by God. We chose to enter a domain of darkness, with a consciousness tainted with ego (the Satan), so that we could work hard to triumph over our selfish impulses and to strive to bring perfection to the world.

This satisfies our deepest need, our most profound yearning - the desire to be the cause and creators of our own fulfillment. The snake does not have this opportunity. The serpent can never evolve or appreciate the divine joy associated with creating Light.

The underlying lesson in this portion concerns the value of appreciation. When paradise is handed to us freely, without any notion of having to earn it or any knowledge of darkness, we can never truly grasp or appreciate the treasures of Light that are in our possession.

Thus, our spiritual work concerns appreciating all that we have, and striving to create order out of chaos by conquering our self-centered qualities born of ego. This supreme objective is attained in the here-and-now by virtue of this reading combined with our awareness of these penetrating Kabbalistic insights.

Fourth Reading - Moses - Netzach

(כב) וַיֹּאמֶר | יְהֹוָאדהנויה אהדונהי אֱלֹהִים (ילה) הֵן הָאָדָם (מ"ה) הָיָה
(יהה) כְּאַחַד (אהבה) מִמֶּנּוּ לָדַעַת טוֹב (והו) וָרָע וְעַתָּה | פֶּן־יִשְׁלַח
יָדוֹ וְלָקַח גַּם מֵעֵץ הַחַיִּים (בינה ע"ה) וְאָכַל וָחַי לְעֹלָם (ס"ג ברבוע
עם י' אותיות): (כג) וַיְשַׁלְּחֵהוּ יְהֹוָאדהנויה אהדונהי אֱלֹהִים (ילה) מִגַּן־עֵדֶן
לַעֲבֹד אֶת־הָאֲדָמָה אֲשֶׁר לֻקַּח מִשָּׁם: (כד) וַיְגָרֶשׁ אֶת־
הָאָדָם (מ"ה) וַיַּשְׁכֵּן מִקֶּדֶם לְגַן־עֵדֶן אֶת־הַכְּרֻבִים וְאֵת לַהַט
הַחֶרֶב הַמִּתְהַפֶּכֶת לִשְׁמֹר אֶת־דֶּרֶךְ (ב"פ יב"ק) עֵץ הַחַיִּים (בינה

וַיֹּאמֶר - After committing the Sin, Adam is expelled from the Garden of Eden. In truth, Adam did not possess the trait of free will during the actual act of sinning. The Kabbalists tell us that the Sin is code for a stage of development, a phase in the process of creation. The Torah, speaking in the cryptic language of metaphor, is telling us that there was no authentic act of disobedience or misdeed by Adam. Rather, the story concerns man's evolution to a higher level where he was endowed with the gift of free will. Man, at his own request, would now become accountable for the amount of Light he receives in life. This is the inner meaning behind Adam's sin and his expulsion from Eden.

The expulsion has additional meaning and relevance to our lives. People on the spiritual path often tend to fall into complacency when learning wisdom such as Kabbalah. Studying from holy books is a noble gesture, but true growth occurs only in the real world of hardship. Each day of our lives, we must leave the Garden (that is, complacency, our comfort zone, even our spiritual study sessions) to enter into the chaos of life where we can transform our reactive nature and rise above the primal impulses of our ego, learning to love our friends and foes unconditionally. This is the place where true spiritual greatness is found. And this is the ultimate objective of life on earth.

(ע"ה) : ס ד (א) וְהָאָדָם (מ"ה) יָדַע אֶת-חַוָּה אִשְׁתּוֹ וַתַּהַר וַתֵּלֶד
אֶת-קַיִן וַתֹּאמֶר קָנִיתִי אִישׁ אֶת-יְהֹוָהאדניאהדונהי: (ב) וַתֹּסֶף
לָלֶדֶת אֶת-אָחִיו אֶת-הָבֶל וַיְהִי-הֶבֶל רֹעֵה צֹאן וְקַיִן הָיָה
(יהה) עֹבֵד אֲדָמָה: (ג) וַיְהִי מִקֵּץ (מנק) יָמִים (נלך) וַיָּבֵא קַיִן מִפְּרִי
הָאֲדָמָה מִנְחָה (ע"ה ב"פ ב"ן) לַיהֹוָהאדניאהדונהי: (ד) וְהֶבֶל הֵבִיא
גַם-הוּא מִבְּכֹרוֹת צֹאנוֹ וּמֵחֶלְבֵהֶן וַיִּשַׁע יְהֹוָהאדניאהדונהי

יָדַע - We are told that Adam knew Eve, and then Eve gave birth to Cain. The Zohar asks why the Torah uses the word "knew" to imply a sexual connection between man and woman. Once again, we have a verse of Torah couched in metaphor.

The pleasure derived from sex - along with all the joys of life - originates from the 99 per cent realm of spiritual Light. We receive this Light whenever there is a union, a connection between the Lower World (the one per cent realm) and the Upper World (the 99 per cent realm). The Torah is telling us that "knowledge" (from the word "knew") is our connection to the 99 per cent realm. When we acquire the Kabbalistic knowledge that reveals the true meaning of the Torah's verses, we can then connect to and mate with the Upper World of endless Light.

Herein lies the ultimate purpose of these insights. Knowledge is the key to spiritual transformation. Knowledge is our means of access to spiritual Light.

Now that we possess the knowledge about the secrets of knowledge itself, all the portions inscribed in the parchment of the Torah scroll shine more brightly than a galaxy of stars. We activate and "switch on" the greatest power generator in the universe - the instrument of the Torah.

וְהֶבֶל - The Torah states that Abel "also brought" a sacrifice. The word

אֶל־הֶבֶל וְאֶל־מִנְחָתוֹ׃ (ה) וְאֶל־קַיִן וְאֶל־מִנְחָתוֹ לֹא שָׁעָה
וַיִּחַר לְקַיִן מְאֹד וַיִּפְּלוּ פָּנָיו׃ (ו) וַיֹּאמֶר יְהֹוָהאדניאהדונהי אֶל־
קָיִן לָמָּה חָרָה לָךְ וְלָמָּה נָפְלוּ פָנֶיךָ (סמ"ב)׃ (ז) הֲלוֹא אִם
(יוהך)־תֵּיטִיב שְׂאֵת וְאִם (יוהך) לֹא תֵיטִיב לַפֶּתַח חַטָּאת
רֹבֵץ וְאֵלֶיךָ תְּשׁוּקָתוֹ וְאַתָּה תִּמְשָׁל־בּוֹ׃ (ח) וַיֹּאמֶר קַיִן
אֶל־הֶבֶל אָחִיו וַיְהִי בִּהְיוֹתָם בַּשָּׂדֶה וַיָּקָם קַיִן אֶל־הֶבֶל
אָחִיו וַיַּהַרְגֵהוּ׃ (ט) וַיֹּאמֶר יְהֹוָהאדניאהדונהי אֶל־קַיִן אֵי הֶבֶל

"also" indicates that Abel's consciousness was not focused directly and solely upon the sacrifice. This created an opening for negativity to enter his life - namely, his slaying at the hand of his brother Cain.

When we connect to the Light, we must ensure that our effort, desire, and certainty are 100 per cent, lest we leave an opening for negative energy to contaminate our lives. When we sacrifice our ego, we must let go absolutely. The Light cast through the story of Cain and Abel empowers us with the courage to surrender completely and giving up our negative traits from our nature. This "sacrifice" is herewith performed.

וַיַּהַרְגֵהוּ - The Zohar reveals extraordinary insights into the story of Cain and Abel that concern the host of demons who dwell among us, the sexual seduction that takes place both when we are awake and during our sleep, and the root cause behind the premature death of children.

The Zohar says that demonic angels (negative intelligent forces of energy) originate from the time of Cain:

Rabbi Yitzchak said that from the time that Cain killed Abel, Adam separated from his wife. Two female spirits used to come and mate with him. And he bore from them spirits and demons that roam around the world.
- Zohar, Volume II, 62:346

אָחִיךָ וַיֹּאמֶר לֹא יָדַעְתִּי הֲשֹׁמֵר אָחִי אָנֹכִי (אי"ע): (י) וַיֹּאמֶר
מֶה (מ"ה) עָשִׂיתָ קוֹל דְּמֵי אָחִיךָ צֹעֲקִים אֵלַי מִן־הָאֲדָמָה:
(יא) וְעַתָּה אָרוּר אָתָּה מִן־הָאֲדָמָה אֲשֶׁר פָּצְתָה אֶת־פִּיהָ
לָקַחַת אֶת־דְּמֵי אָחִיךָ מִיָּדֶךָ: (יב) כִּי תַעֲבֹד אֶת־הָאֲדָמָה
לֹא־תֹסֵף תֵּת־כֹּחָהּ לָךְ נָע וָנָד תִּהְיֶה בָאָרֶץ: (יג) וַיֹּאמֶר
קַיִן אֶל־יְהֹוָאדהנויאהדונהי גָּדוֹל (להח, מבה עד"א) עֲוֹנִי מִנְּשֹׂא: (יד) הֵן
גֵּרַשְׁתָּ אֹתִי הַיּוֹם (נגד, זן) מֵעַל (עלם) פְּנֵי (חכמה, בינה) הָאֲדָמָה
וּמִפָּנֶיךָ (סמ"ב) אֶסָּתֵר (ב"פ מצר) וְהָיִיתִי נָע וָנָד בָּאָרֶץ וְהָיָה
(יהה) (יהוה) כָל (ילי)־מֹצְאִי יַהַרְגֵנִי: (טו) וַיֹּאמֶר לוֹ יְהֹוָאדהנויאהדונהי

Though we cannot observe these negative forces with our physical senses, they are as influential as the unseen force of gravity and as real as the invisible atoms in the air.

These negative forces are the root cause of the ailments that afflict our children and the negative, selfish, sexual impulses that fester within us.

Rabbi Shimon, the author of the Zohar, states:
Woe to the sons of man, for they are not aware and do not take heed nor search for knowledge. They are all blindfolded and do not know how full the world is with strange and invisible creatures and things. If permission were to be given to the eye to see, people would wonder greatly as to how it is possible to survive in this world.
- Zohar, Volume II, 62:356

Through the story of Cain and Abel, the Torah and the Zohar are empower us with the Light necessary to eliminate all demons and evil forces from existence. And this occurs now: Children are healed, diseases are eradicated, and we correct the sexual sins of man throughout history.

לָכֵן כָּל (ילי)-הֹרֵג קַיִן שִׁבְעָתַיִם **יֻקָּם** וַיָּשֶׂם יְהֹוָאדניאהדונהי

יֻקָּם - In this verse, the Torah says the phrase Yukam (Eng. 'be raised') Cain. The word YuKaM is an acronym for Yitro, Korach and Mitriz all of which, the Zohar explains, were reincarnations of Cain. It is a clever but simple code. The Yud in YuKaM stands for Yitro (Jethro), who becomes Moses's father-in-law. Jethro is Cain reincarnated. The Zohar reveals that Moses is the reincarnation of Cain's brother, Abel. The Zohar also reveals that Abel is known as flesh, as stated in a verse of Torah (Genesis 6:13). The word flesh, the Zohar explains, is also a secret code for Moses.

Thus, Jethro and Moses (Cain and Abel) are able to resolve age-old karmic obligations when Jethro gives Moses his daughter's hand in marriage. In their original incarnation, Jethro (Cain) took Moses's (Abel's) life. In the later incarnation, Jethro provides Moses with a wife.

The "K" alludes to Korach, who rises up to challenge Moses's leadership in a later story. Korach fails in his bid to overthrow Moses and is swallowed up by the Earth. The "M" refers to an Egyptian named Mitriz, whom Moses had slain.

These three incarnations of Cain allowed him to correct his sin, complete his act of repentance, and make amends with his brother Abel. According to the Zohar, Moses used the two of the 72 Names of God to slay the Egyptian Mitriz:

- Caf, Hei, Tav - **כהת**
- Yud, Caf, Shin - **יכש**

This portion, combined with these potent meditations, now slay the Cain within each of us. We correct all our sins from this and past lives. Moreover, the Light of these letters now rectifies the iniquities of all the generations who have descended from Cain in a manner that embodies infinite mercy as opposed to harsh judgment. This merciful path is made available to us in the present moment by virtue of the Zohar's divine insights and the Divine Energy radiating from the scroll.

לְקַיִן **אוֹת** לְבִלְתִּי הַכּוֹת־אֹתוֹ כָּל (ילי) ־מֹצְאוֹ׃ (טז) וַיֵּצֵא
קַיִן מִלִּפְנֵי יְהֹוָהאדניאהדונהי וַיֵּשֶׁב בְּאֶרֶץ־נוֹד קִדְמַת־עֵדֶן׃ (יז)
וַיֵּדַע קַיִן אֶת־אִשְׁתּוֹ וַתַּהַר וַתֵּלֶד אֶת־חֲנוֹךְ וַיְהִי בֹּנֶה עִיר
(סוזוךר, סנדלפון, ערי) וַיִּקְרָא שֵׁם הָעִיר (סוזוךר, סנדלפון, ערי) כְּשֵׁם בְּנוֹ
חֲנוֹךְ׃ (יח) וַיִּוָּלֵד לַחֲנוֹךְ אֶת־עִירָד וְעִירָד יָלַד אֶת־מְחוּיָּאֵל
וּמְחִיָּיאֵל יָלַד אֶת־מְתוּשָׁאֵל וּמְתוּשָׁאֵל יָלַד אֶת־לָמֶךְ׃

אוֹת - Cain knows that he will be murdered by the people of his generation in response to his slaying his brother, Abel. Cain understands the law of cause and effect and knows that the energy emanating from him radiates his sin to anyone in his presence. Cain then makes an attempt to deeply repent for his sin.

According to the Zohar, God inscribed the Hebrew Letter Vav onto the forehead of Cain. The letter Vav connects to the Sfirat Yesod, which signifies the Covenant between God and the Israelites. Because Cain sincerely repents for the murder of his brother, the letter Vav protects him from the murderous hands of the people who were aroused against him by the spiritual law of cause and effect.

Here we learn that if Cain is able to repent for the reprehensible act of murder, then all of us can repent for our own sins - if, that is, we truly desire to change our ways forever.

As Adam states in the Zohar:
The strength of repentance is so great and powerful…
- Zohar, Volume II, 62:345

By meditating upon the letter Vav during this reading and with great remorse in our hearts, we receive protection from any decrees of judgment. Moreover, the energy emanating here destroys the negative angel (do not pronounce his name) Samael and corrects the roots of all sins.

Fifth Reading - Aaron - Hod

(יט) וַיִּקַּח (ווּעם)-לוֹ לֶמֶךְ שְׁתֵּי נָשִׁים שֵׁם הָאַחַת עָדָה
(סיט) וְשֵׁם הַשֵּׁנִית צִלָּה: (כ) וַתֵּלֶד עָדָה (סיט) אֶת־יָבָל
הוּא הָיָה (יהה) אֲבִי יֹשֵׁב אֹהֶל וּמִקְנֶה: (כא) וְשֵׁם אָחִיו
יוּבָל הוּא הָיָה (יהה) אֲבִי כָּל (ילי)-תֹּפֵשׂ כִּנּוֹר וְעוּגָב: (כב)
וְצִלָּה גַם־הִוא יָלְדָה אֶת־תּוּבַל קַיִן לֹטֵשׁ כָּל (ילי)-חֹרֵשׁ
נְחֹשֶׁת וּבַרְזֶל (ר"ת בלהה רחל זילפה לאה) וַאֲחוֹת תּוּבַל־קַיִן נַעֲמָה:

Sixth Reading - Yosef HaTzadik

(כג) וַיֹּאמֶר לֶמֶךְ לְנָשָׁיו עָדָה (סיט) וְצִלָּה שְׁמַעַן קוֹלִי נְשֵׁי
לֶמֶךְ הַאְזֵנָּה (יוד הי ואו הה) אִמְרָתִי כִּי אִישׁ הָרַגְתִּי לְפִצְעִי וְיֶלֶד
לְחַבֻּרָתִי: (כד) כִּי שִׁבְעָתַיִם יֻקַּם־קָיִן וְלֶמֶךְ שִׁבְעִים וְשִׁבְעָה:

הָרַגְתִּי - Lemech is a blind man who accidentally kills his great, great grandfather (seven generations past), who is Cain. Because of his blindness, Lemech could not see the mark on Cain's head.

We learn from this story that each of us is responsible for all of our actions, both positive and negative. Moreover, our state of consciousness and our awareness of spiritual laws determine whether or not we plant positive seeds or negative seeds in life. Ignorance of the law is no excuse. Whether we touch a frayed wire purposely or inadvertently, we still receive a painful shock in either case. If our consciousness is negative and if we are blind to the spiritual laws that govern our reality, our good intentions will still lead us into chaos and short-circuits.

The truth of the law of cause and effect and of accountability for our actions is etched into our hearts and minds during this reading.

(כה) וַיֵּדַע אָדָם (מ"ה) עוֹד אֶת־אִשְׁתּוֹ וַתֵּלֶד בֵּן וַתִּקְרָא אֶת־
שְׁמוֹ (מהש ע"ה) שֵׁת כִּי שָׁת־לִי אֱלֹהִים (כוק) (ילה) זֶרַע אַחֵר תַּחַת
הֶבֶל כִּי הֲרָגוֹ קָיִן׃ (כו) וּלְשֵׁת גַּם־הוּא יֻלַּד־בֵּן וַיִּקְרָא אֶת־
שְׁמוֹ (מהש ע"ה) אֱנוֹשׁ אָז הוּחַל לִקְרֹא בְּשֵׁם יְהֹוָהאדניאהדונהי׃ ס
ה (א) זֶה סֵפֶר תּוֹלְדֹת אָדָם (מ"ה) בְּיוֹם (נגד, זן) בְּרֹא (קנ"א ב"ן)

אָז - Although it is not explicitly mentioned in the Torah, this reading speaks of the destruction of a third of the world's population in what's known as dor ("the generation") of Enosh.

The sages teach us that the people of this era tried to use another medium, a cosmic detour to connect to the Divine Energy, so they could avoid having to take responsibility for their actions. This is also the underlying secret of the Golden Calf, which will be explored in a later portion.

A desire to be held accountable for our actions stirs within us, in turn, giving us the power to repent and thus control our destiny.

זֶה - Concerning The Book of Adam, the Zohar states the following:

[God says,] "This is the Book of the generations of Adam," and there literally is such a book. We have already explained that when Adam was in the Garden of Eden, the Holy One, blessed be He, sent a book down to him with Raziel, the holy angel who is in charge of the supernal sacred secrets.
- Zohar, Volume II, 63:361

The Book of Adam is the original book of Kabbalah, and it contains all the secrets of our universe as well as all the sublime mysteries of the supernal worlds above. The Book of Adam is the DNA code of the cosmos, the most powerful book in existence. The Zohar, along with all Kabbalistic wisdom, is encoded in its cryptic texts.

It is a formula much like Einstein's formula $E=mc^2$, whose five simple

אֱלֹהִים (ילה) אָדָם (מ״ה) בִּדְמוּת אֱלֹהִים (ילה) עָשָׂה אֹתוֹ: (ב)
זָכָר וּנְקֵבָה בְּרָאָם וַיְבָרֶךְ (עסמ״ב) אֹתָם וַיִּקְרָא אֶת־שְׁמָם

characters conceal all the mathematical equations that define time, space, matter, and energy.

Likewise, The Book of Adam is a concise formula that conceals all the spiritual equations that define absolute reality. Moreover, this Book holds the glorious Light of Creation, the endless joy and boundless bliss embodied by the Garden of Eden. It represents our world in its perfected form, its destined state of greatness. When Adam sinned, the book flew away from him, and Adam was anguished.

The Zohar states that:

Adam used to beat upon his head and weep. He went into the waters of the River Gichon up to his neck, because he repented and mortified himself, until his body became wrinkled and porous and his radiance changed.
- Zohar, Volume II 63:364

Our own repentance rekindles the Light that shines from The Book of Adam. Our heartfelt meditation upon its letters awakens untold greatness within ourselves. It ignites our Final Redemption with an abundance of mercy and commences the Age of Messiah with immeasurable kindheartedness. With it, we create the Garden of Eden within us and around us. This book, the Zohar tells us, helped Enoch (in Hebrew, Chanoch) become a heavenly angel known as Metatron, who represents eternal youth and immortality. Thus, through The Book of Adam, Enoch, and Metatron, we bring immortality to all mankind. Heaven on earth now becomes our new reality.

מבש	עוי	מיץ
גרג	ווה	יצד
דצב	זדו	היי
לקו	שוה	ונך

אָדָם (מ"ה) בְּיוֹם (נגד, זן) הִבָּרְאָם: (ג) וַיְחִי אָדָם (מ"ה) שְׁלֹשִׁים
וּמְאַת שָׁנָה וַיּוֹלֶד בִּדְמוּתוֹ כְּצַלְמוֹ וַיִּקְרָא אֶת־שְׁמוֹ (מהש ע"ה)
שֵׁת: (ד) וַיִּהְיוּ יְמֵי־אָדָם (מ"ה) אַחֲרֵי הוֹלִידוֹ אֶת־שֵׁת שְׁמֹנֶה
מֵאֹת שָׁנָה וַיּוֹלֶד בָּנִים וּבָנוֹת: (ה) וַיִּהְיוּ כָּל (ילי)־יְמֵי אָדָם (מ"ה)
אֲשֶׁר־חַי תְּשַׁע מֵאוֹת שָׁנָה וּשְׁלֹשִׁים שָׁנָה וַיָּמֹת: ס (ו) וַיְחִי־
שֵׁת חָמֵשׁ שָׁנִים וּמְאַת שָׁנָה וַיּוֹלֶד אֶת־אֱנוֹשׁ: (ז) וַיְחִי־שֵׁת
אַחֲרֵי הוֹלִידוֹ אֶת־אֱנוֹשׁ שֶׁבַע שָׁנִים וּשְׁמֹנֶה מֵאוֹת שָׁנָה
וַיּוֹלֶד בָּנִים וּבָנוֹת: (ח) וַיִּהְיוּ כָּל (ילי)־יְמֵי־שֵׁת שְׁתֵּים עֶשְׂרֵה

וַיְחִי - We learn that there are ten generations from Adam to Noah. The "ten generations" is a code alluding to the Ten Sfirot, the ten dimensions that comprise all reality. The Light of the Creator must flow through these ten dimensions enroute to our world.

For that reason, ten men are required in a prayer service, each soul connecting to one of the dimensions, to ensure the complete revelation of Light. These verses of Torah establish our connection to the Ten Sfirot so that we may be plugged into all the dimensions, securing for us and the world a total manifestation of Divine Energy and Light here on this Shabbat day.

תְּשַׁע - We learn that Adam, his children, and his grandchildren lived for centuries, some as long as 900 years. The underlying significance of this story is to kindle the Light of life, longevity, and even immortality so that it may radiate in our souls. Here in Genesis, we achieve this profound effect. Moreover, the Angel of Death meets his own demise the moment we meditate to share this Light aroused by Genesis with all mankind.

שָׁנָה וּתְשַׁע מֵאוֹת שָׁנָה וַיָּמֹת: ס (ט) וַיְחִי אֱנוֹשׁ תִּשְׁעִים
שָׁנָה וַיּוֹלֶד אֶת־קֵינָן: (י) וַיְחִי אֱנוֹשׁ אַחֲרֵי הוֹלִידוֹ אֶת־קֵינָן
חֲמֵשׁ עֶשְׂרֵה שָׁנָה וּשְׁמֹנֶה מֵאוֹת שָׁנָה וַיּוֹלֶד בָּנִים וּבָנוֹת:
(יא) וַיִּהְיוּ כָּל (ילי)־יְמֵי אֱנוֹשׁ חָמֵשׁ שָׁנִים וּתְשַׁע מֵאוֹת שָׁנָה
וַיָּמֹת: ס (יב) וַיְחִי קֵינָן שִׁבְעִים שָׁנָה וַיּוֹלֶד אֶת־מַהֲלַלְאֵל:
(יג) וַיְחִי קֵינָן אַחֲרֵי הוֹלִידוֹ אֶת־מַהֲלַלְאֵל אַרְבָּעִים שָׁנָה
וּשְׁמֹנֶה מֵאוֹת שָׁנָה וַיּוֹלֶד בָּנִים וּבָנוֹת: (יד) וַיִּהְיוּ כָּל (ילי)־
יְמֵי קֵינָן עֶשֶׂר שָׁנִים וּתְשַׁע מֵאוֹת שָׁנָה וַיָּמֹת: ס (טו) וַיְחִי
מַהֲלַלְאֵל חָמֵשׁ שָׁנִים וְשִׁשִּׁים שָׁנָה וַיּוֹלֶד אֶת־יָרֶד: (טז)
וַיְחִי מַהֲלַלְאֵל אַחֲרֵי הוֹלִידוֹ אֶת־יֶרֶד שְׁלֹשִׁים שָׁנָה
וּשְׁמֹנֶה מֵאוֹת שָׁנָה וַיּוֹלֶד בָּנִים וּבָנוֹת: (יז) וַיִּהְיוּ כָּל (ילי)־יְמֵי
מַהֲלַלְאֵל חָמֵשׁ וְתִשְׁעִים שָׁנָה וּשְׁמֹנֶה מֵאוֹת שָׁנָה וַיָּמֹת:
ס (יח) וַיְחִי־יֶרֶד שְׁתַּיִם וְשִׁשִּׁים שָׁנָה וּמְאַת שָׁנָה וַיּוֹלֶד אֶת־
חֲנוֹךְ: (יט) וַיְחִי־יֶרֶד אַחֲרֵי הוֹלִידוֹ אֶת־חֲנוֹךְ שְׁמֹנֶה מֵאוֹת
שָׁנָה וַיּוֹלֶד בָּנִים וּבָנוֹת: (כ) וַיִּהְיוּ כָּל (ילי)־יְמֵי־יֶרֶד שְׁתַּיִם
וְשִׁשִּׁים שָׁנָה וּתְשַׁע מֵאוֹת שָׁנָה וַיָּמֹת: ס (כא) וַיְחִי חֲנוֹךְ
חָמֵשׁ וְשִׁשִּׁים שָׁנָה וַיּוֹלֶד אֶת־מְתוּשָׁלַח: (כב) וַיִּתְהַלֵּךְ (מיה)
חֲנוֹךְ אֶת־הָאֱלֹהִים (ילה) אַחֲרֵי הוֹלִידוֹ אֶת־מְתוּשֶׁלַח שְׁלֹשׁ
מֵאוֹת שָׁנָה וַיּוֹלֶד בָּנִים וּבָנוֹת: (כג) וַיְהִי כָּל (ילי)־יְמֵי חֲנוֹךְ

וְחָמֵשׁ וְשִׁשִּׁים שָׁנָה וּשְׁלֹשׁ מֵאוֹת שָׁנָה: (כד) וַיִּתְהַלֵּךְ (מ״ה)
חֲנוֹךְ אֶת־הָאֱלֹהִים (ילה) וְאֵינֶנּוּ כִּי־לָקַח אֹתוֹ אֱלֹהִים (ילה): ס

Seventh Reading - David - Malchut

(כה) וַיְחִי מְתוּשֶׁלַח שֶׁבַע וּשְׁמֹנִים שָׁנָה וּמְאַת שָׁנָה וַיּוֹלֶד
אֶת־לָמֶךְ: (כו) וַיְחִי מְתוּשֶׁלַח אַחֲרֵי הוֹלִידוֹ אֶת־לֶמֶךְ
שְׁתַּיִם וּשְׁמוֹנִים שָׁנָה וּשְׁבַע מֵאוֹת שָׁנָה וַיּוֹלֶד בָּנִים
וּבָנוֹת: (כז) וַיִּהְיוּ כָּל (ילי)־יְמֵי מְתוּשֶׁלַח תֵּשַׁע וְשִׁשִּׁים שָׁנָה

וְאֵינֶנּוּ - The biblical character Enoch is the first person to become an actual angel, attaining the prominent position of king of all angels. Angels are above the constraints of time and space. Hence, they can perceive the future consequences of all their deeds. For this reason, they never commit wrongful acts.

We all have the power to become like angels - to foresee future repercussions associated with our actions of the present moment, to avoid mistakes and evade pitfalls, and in turn, to experience true miracles. This power of elevated consciousness is bestowed upon us through the vocalization and vibrations of the Hebrew letters adorning this portion of the Torah.

מְתוּשֶׁלַח - Enoch's son Methuselah lived longer then any person in the world - 969 years. He was a truly righteous person and embodies the concept of mind over matter. Methuselah received the wisdom of Kabbalah from his father and used it to attain control over the physical world. This is reflected by his long life and by the fact that the Flood did not occur during his lifetime or for seven days after his passing.

Here the Torah's words bestow the power of mind over matter upon us so that we can halt all acts of destruction decreed upon the world. We ignite the Light of healing as well as its ultimate benefit - the immortality of mankind.

וּתְשַׁע מֵאוֹת שָׁנָה וַיָּמֹת׃ ס (כח) וַיְחִי־לֶמֶךְ שְׁתַּיִם וּשְׁמֹנִים
שָׁנָה וּמְאַת שָׁנָה וַיּוֹלֶד בֵּן׃ (כט) וַיִּקְרָא אֶת־שְׁמוֹ (מהש ע"ה) נֹחַ
לֵאמֹר זֶה יְנַחֲמֵנוּ מִמַּעֲשֵׂנוּ וּמֵעִצְּבוֹן יָדֵינוּ מִן־הָאֲדָמָה
אֲשֶׁר אֵרְרָהּ יְהֹוָהאדניאהדונהי׃ (ל) וַיְחִי־לֶמֶךְ אַחֲרֵי הוֹלִידוֹ
אֶת־נֹחַ חָמֵשׁ וְתִשְׁעִים שָׁנָה וַחֲמֵשׁ מֵאֹת שָׁנָה וַיּוֹלֶד
בָּנִים וּבָנוֹת׃ (לא) וַיְהִי כָּל (ילי)־יְמֵי־לֶמֶךְ שֶׁבַע וְשִׁבְעִים
שָׁנָה וּשְׁבַע מֵאוֹת שָׁנָה וַיָּמֹת׃ ס (לב) וַיְהִי־נֹחַ בֶּן־חֲמֵשׁ
מֵאוֹת שָׁנָה וַיּוֹלֶד נֹחַ אֶת־שֵׁם אֶת־חָם וְאֶת־יָפֶת׃ ו (א)
וַיְהִי כִּי־הֵחֵל הָאָדָם (מ"ה) לָרֹב עַל־פְּנֵי (חכמה, בינה) הָאֲדָמָה

וַיְהִי־נֹחַ - In Genesis, we read about all the generations from Adam to Noah. This passing of generations alludes to mankind's gradual separation from the realm of Endless Light and our journey to this physical world.

The last three generations leading to Noah connect us to the three Sfirot (spiritual dimensions) known as Hod, Yesod, and our physical realm of existence Malchut. We learn that as we draw closer to the physical domain, spiritual work becomes more difficult.

Meditating high on a mountaintop, according to Kabbalah, is not the path or method for achieving spiritual greatness. Rather, spiritual greatness is found in the turmoil of physical existence, through our efforts at transforming chaos into order, pain into pleasure, and strife into serenity. Thus, we must embrace the obstacles of life, realizing that they contain the seeds of our spiritual majesty. This is the underlying purpose of our descent from the higher spiritual dimensions into the lower material world.

וַיִּרְאוּ - It is commonly said that only human beings possess the free will to choose negative or positive behavior. However, the Torah tells us that

וּבָנוֹת יֻלְּדוּ לָהֶם׃ (ב) **וַיִּרְאוּ** בְנֵי־הָאֱלֹהִים (ילה) אֶת־בְּנוֹת
הָאָדָם (מ״ה) כִּי טֹבֹת הֵנָּה וַיִּקְחוּ לָהֶם נָשִׁים מִכֹּל (ילי) אֲשֶׁר
בָּחָרוּ׃ (ג) וַיֹּאמֶר יְהֹוָהאדניאהדונהי לֹא־יָדוֹן רוּחִי בָאָדָם (מ״ה)
לְעֹלָם (ס״ג בריבוע עם י׳ אותיות) בְּשַׁגַּם הוּא בָשָׂר וְהָיוּ יָמָיו מֵאָה
וְעֶשְׂרִים שָׁנָה׃ (ד) הַנְּפִלִים הָיוּ בָאָרֶץ בַּיָּמִים (נלך) הָהֵם וְגַם
אַחֲרֵי־כֵן אֲשֶׁר יָבֹאוּ בְּנֵי הָאֱלֹהִים (ילה) אֶל־בְּנוֹת הָאָדָם
(מ״ה) וְיָלְדוּ לָהֶם הֵמָּה הַגִּבֹּרִים אֲשֶׁר מֵעוֹלָם אַנְשֵׁי הַשֵּׁם׃

negative angels have, in fact, engaged in illicit sexual relations with women of this world.

According to biblical teachings, angels are not supposed to eat, drink, or partake of any activity in this mundane level of existence. Thus, we learn that angels do indeed possess an aspect of free will. However, angels are above the limitations of time and space because they are close to the Light of the Creator - a realm without time. For this reason, angels can observe the "future" repercussions of their deeds, so they find it easy to behave according to spiritual law. This is, to a lesser degree, a form of free will, but certainly not of the same magnitude as our free will.

וַיַּרְא - In truth, God does not punish. God does not destroy. Nor does God reward. The Kabbalists tell us that man, by nature, is a reactive creature. Our unique purpose in this world is to nullify this trait; to transform ourselves into proactive, spiritual people; to rise above our own human nature and, in turn, acquire control over Mother Nature.

The root of our reactive impulses is the human ego. We must understand this truth and strive to eradicate egocentric qualities from our being. This is what constitutes spiritual work, and it is the purpose of our existence. Ignorance

Maftir

(ה) וַיַּרְא יְהֹוָהאהדונהי כִּי רַבָּה רָעַת הָאָדָם (מ״ה) בָּאָרֶץ וְכָל
(ילי)־יֵצֶר מַחְשְׁבֹת לִבּוֹ רַק רַע כָּל (ילי)־הַיּוֹם (נגד, זן)׃ (ו) וַיִּנָּחֶם
יְהֹוָהאהדונהי כִּי־עָשָׂה אֶת־הָאָדָם (מ״ה) בָּאָרֶץ וַיִּתְעַצֵּב אֶל־
לִבּוֹ׃ (ז) וַיֹּאמֶר יְהֹוָהאהדונהי אֶמְחֶה אֶת־הָאָדָם (מ״ה) אֲשֶׁר־
בָּרָאתִי מֵעַל (עלם) פְּנֵי (חכמה, בינה) הָאֲדָמָה מֵאָדָם (מ״ה) עַד־
בְּהֵמָה (לכב) עַד־רֶמֶשׂ וְעַד־עוֹף הַשָּׁמָיִם (י״פ טל) כִּי נִחַמְתִּי כִּי
עֲשִׂיתִם׃ (ח) וְנֹחַ מָצָא חֵן (מוחי) בְּעֵינֵי (מ״ה בריבוע) יְהֹוָהאהדונהי׃ פפפ

of this truth and failure to effect this transformation causes continued destruction, chaos, and turmoil in our lives and in the world.

The Light of these sacred words enlightens us to the meaning of our existence, instilling within us a deep sense of responsibility for our selfish and intolerant ways. Moreover, our awareness of these kabbalistic insights during this reading cleanses negative characteristics from our nature. In turn, we prevent acts of devastation from occurring in the world.

The Haftarah of Beresheet

The Haftarah of Beresheet talks about the process of creation. The energy of this Haftarah is the energy that came to Moses, and it is of an extremely high level. We can connect with it through someone who is a channel, like a prophet. This powerful Light must come to us through the filter of a righteous person, rather than in a concentrated form directly from the source. Thus, we read these Haftarahs through the prophet Isaiah, in the Book of Isaiah.

ישעיהו פרק מב

(ה) כֹּה־אָמַר הָאֵל (לאה) | יְהֹוָה בּוֹרֵא הַשָּׁמַיִם (כוזו, י"פ טל) וְנוֹטֵיהֶם
רֹקַע הָאָרֶץ וְצֶאֱצָאֶיהָ נֹתֵן (ושר, אבג יתץ, אהבת חנם) נְשָׁמָה (יוד הא ואו הא) לָעָם
עָלֶיהָ (עלם) וְרוּחַ (פהל) לַהֹלְכִים בָּהּ: (ו) אֲנִי (אני) יְהֹוָה קְרָאתִיךָ
בְצֶדֶק וְאַחְזֵק (פהל) בְּיָדֶךָ וְאֶצָּרְךָ וְאֶתֶּנְךָ לִבְרִית עָם לְאוֹר
(רז, אין סוף) גּוֹיִם: (ז) לִפְקֹחַ עֵינַיִם עִוְרוֹת לְהוֹצִיא מִמַּסְגֵּר אַסִּיר
מִבֵּית (ב"פ ראה) כֶּלֶא יֹשְׁבֵי חֹשֶׁךְ: (ח) אֲנִי (אני) יְהֹוָה הוּא (מום) שְׁמִי
וּכְבוֹדִי לְאַחֵר לֹא־אֶתֵּן וּתְהִלָּתִי לַפְּסִילִים: (ט) הָרִאשֹׁנוֹת
הִנֵּה־בָאוּ וַחֲדָשׁוֹת אֲנִי (אני) מַגִּיד בְּטֶרֶם תִּצְמַחְנָה אַשְׁמִיעַ
אֶתְכֶם: {פ}

(י) שִׁירוּ לַיהֹוָה שִׁיר חָדָשׁ תְּהִלָּתוֹ מִקְצֵה הָאָרֶץ
יוֹרְדֵי הַיָּם (ילי) וּמְלֹאוֹ אִיִּים וְיֹשְׁבֵיהֶם: (יא) יִשְׂאוּ מִדְבָּר
וְעָרָיו חֲצֵרִים תֵּשֵׁב קֵדָר יָרֹנּוּ יֹשְׁבֵי סֶלַע מֵרֹאשׁ
הָרִים יִצְוָחוּ: (יב) יָשִׂימוּ לַיהֹוָה כָּבוֹד וּתְהִלָּתוֹ בָּאִיִּים
יַגִּידוּ: (ייי) (יג) יְהֹוָה כַּגִּבּוֹר יֵצֵא כְּאִישׁ מִלְחָמוֹת יָעִיר קִנְאָה

(יוסף, ציון) יָרִ֙יעַ֙ אַף־יַצְרִ֔יחַ עַל־אֹיְבָ֖יו יִתְגַּבָּֽר׃ {ס}

(יד) הֶחֱשֵׁ֙יתִי֙ מֵֽעוֹלָ֔ם אַחֲרִ֖ישׁ אֶתְאַפָּ֑ק כַּיּוֹלֵדָ֣ה אֶפְעֶ֔ה

אֶשֹּׁ֥ם וְאֶשְׁאַ֖ף יָֽחַד׃ (טו) אַחֲרִ֤יב הָרִים֙ וּגְבָע֔וֹת וְכָל־עֶשְׂבָּ֖ם

אוֹבִ֑ישׁ וְשַׂמְתִּ֤י נְהָרוֹת֙ לָֽאִיִּ֔ים וַאֲגַמִּ֖ים אוֹבִֽישׁ׃ (טז) וְהוֹלַכְתִּ֣י

עִוְרִ֗ים בְּדֶ֙רֶךְ֙ (ב"פ יב"ק) לֹ֣א יָדָ֔עוּ בִּנְתִיב֥וֹת לֹֽא־יָדְע֖וּ אַדְרִיכֵ֑ם

אָשִׂים֩ (ילי) מַחְשָׁ֙ךְ לִפְנֵיהֶ֤ם לָאוֹר֙ (ר"ז, אין סוף) וּמַֽעֲקַשִּׁים֙ לְמִישׁ֔וֹר

אֵ֚לֶּה הַדְּבָרִ֔ים עֲשִׂיתִ֖ם וְלֹ֥א עֲזַבְתִּֽים׃ (יז) נָסֹ֤גוּ אָחוֹר֙ יֵבֹ֣שׁוּ

בֹ֔שֶׁת הַבֹּטְחִ֖ים בַּפָּ֑סֶל הָאֹמְרִ֥ים לְמַסֵּכָ֖ה אַתֶּ֥ם אֱלֹהֵֽינוּ (רמב,

ילה)׃ {פ}

(יח) הַחֵרְשִׁ֖ים שְׁמָ֑עוּ וְהַעִוְרִ֖ים הַבִּ֥יטוּ לִרְאֽוֹת׃ (יט) מִ֤י (ילי) עִוֵּר֙

כִּ֣י אִם־עַבְדִּ֔י וְחֵרֵ֖שׁ כְּמַלְאָכִ֣י אֶשְׁלָ֑ח מִ֤י (ילי) עִוֵּר֙ כִּמְשֻׁלָּ֔ם

וְעִוֵּ֖ר כְּעֶ֥בֶד יְהוָֽה׃ (כ) רָא֥וֹת (כתיב: ראית) רַבּ֖וֹת וְלֹ֣א תִשְׁמֹ֑ר

פָּק֥וֹחַ אָזְנַ֖יִם (נגד, מזבח) וְלֹ֣א יִשְׁמָֽע׃ (כא) יְהוָ֥ה חָפֵ֖ץ לְמַ֣עַן צִדְק֑וֹ

יַגְדִּ֥יל תּוֹרָ֖ה (ציית) וְ|(אבגיתץ ועיר – אהבת חינם)יַאְדִּֽיר׃ (הרי)

Lesson of Noach

The secret of the Flood

This week's reading concerns one of the most horrific episodes in the whole Torah. Only a thousand years after creating the world, the Creator brings a flood that destroys virtually the entire human race. What does this teach us? What can we learn from the fact that a general cleansing was necessary even though the world had been in existence for only a short time?
First, we should learn that from the moment we come out of the womb, the negative force is waiting for us. This is true not only for individual human beings, but also for humanity as a whole. It is said that when children are born, their hands are clenched like fists, as if to say, "I am coming only to take." But this intention isn't limited to the very young. Most of the world is governed by desire to receive for the self alone. Although there hasn't been another great flood since Noah's time, it is not because we are such righteous people; after all, the two Temples were destroyed as a result of hatred for no reason. No, there hasn't been a flood simply because the Creator promised that there wouldn't be one. Instead, He made the rainbow, which signifies that the world should be destroyed, but won't be. God's mercy has given us another opportunity to become better human beings.

There is only one period of time that the rainbow did not appear, and that was while Rabbi Shimon was in the world. From Creation until the transformation of the world (hopefully soon), the lifetime of Rabbi Shimon was the only time that the world did not deserve to be cleansed.
Just as Noah had the ark during the Great Flood, we have the Zohar every day of our lives. Only through the power of the Zohar can we be saved from the danger that surrounds us, whether it is damage to the environment, or wars and terrorism, or epidemics and diseases. The Zohar can protect us, but it is up to us to create a real connection with it. We need to read and scan the Zohar every single day. Our reading can last for three minutes or two minutes or even one minute, but there must be a personal and individual contact. This is the only way we can be saved from "the flood" as it exists in our time.

The Torah tells us that Noah was a righteous man in his generation. What does this mean? According to one interpretation, there were so many wicked people in Noah's time that it's remarkable a man of his righteousness could even exist in such an environment. Noah's connection with the Light of the Creator was so strong that no evil person could sway him to the other side. Therefore, if he had lived in the time of Abraham when there were larger numbers of righteous people, Noah would have been an even greater tzadik (Eng. 'righteous').

Another interpretation takes the opposite view. Only in a generation of wicked people was Noah righteous. He was not fundamentally different from those individuals; he just was just a little better, so he is considered a righteous person within his very negative generation. Had he lived in the time of Abraham, he would have been just an average person, not noteworthy for his virtue.

The Torah passage concerning Noah's righteousness has been debated for centuries. But the really important thing is this: We have to view people individually, as themselves and not in relation to others. Are we righteous or are we not? Are we connected to the Light of the Creator or not?

This is an important lesson of this week's portion, but it is not the only lesson. Every year, the portion of Noach teaches us that whoever looks for a merely comfortable life will never achieve it. Conversely, those who challenge themselves will gain true joy and fulfillment in this world and in the next. Thus, a Midrash in the portion of Vayeshev says: "And Jacob sat." Jacob wanted to live out his remaining years in comfort. He wanted to study all day, quietly. He had gone through so much with his brother, Esau, and with his father-in-law, Laban.

Jacob wanted a little comfort. Why was this so bad? The answer, as King Solomon wrote, is that everything under the sky has a time, and the time for comfort is not in this world. Here we are in battle every second against the desire to receive for ourselves alone. Ours is a lifetime of tests. We can't say to ourselves, "I am comfortable. I don't have to battle any more". We have to constantly strive not to let our consciousness fall as a result of our tests. We have to know that true comfort is in the Light we receive and in the fulfillment that we achieve. Comfort is not something we should go looking for.
This lesson is not to judge Jacob, but to learn from him. If we believe that our tests are over and think, "I have reached where I am supposed to reach. I reached the peak. That is the end. I have finished my Tikun (Eng. 'correction')", we will find out differently. At least, we should find out differently because in this world, "I did enough" is never a real option. If we are still in the physical realm, chances are that we have much more to do.

There are people who will begin studying at the Kabbalah Centre, and then suddenly stop. Perhaps they tell themselves, "Well, now I know more than when I came here. So maybe that's enough." But it is not enough. There are endless things we have to do, and someone who just looks for rest is losing the battle with his personal correction. If you really want to change and grow, do not seek what's comfortable, and then, paradoxically, you will find the real comfort on a much higher level. Then you will have happiness, health, financial support, success, and protection in all that you do.

Synopsis of Noach

Appreciation and the Covenant

One portion has now elapsed from the creation of our beautiful and glorious world. Already, the negative actions of mankind have destroyed all that was beautiful. Man, by nature, is seduced by immediate gratification of the ego, and thus he appreciates his spiritual treasures only when they are taken from him. In this portion we receive the Light to awaken a genuine appreciation for all the good things in our lives so that we do not have to lose them in order to cherish their value and importance.

This portion also pertains to the covenant between Noah and God. This covenant relates to sexual misdeeds and the wanton spilling of a man's seed for selfish, indulgent pleasure as opposed to sharing and the creation of life.

In this portion, we cleanse the world of sexual sins. We destroy the negative forces and beings that are created from the wasting of a man's sperm. We imbue our own sexual relationships with divinity. We abolish all of our selfish desires while unleashing the will of our souls, thus meriting a portion in the World to Come.

Kabbalistically, the World to Come refers to the spiritual realm of Binah. Binah is vastly important, being a boundless bank of Light from which we draw the beneficence of the Creator.

Through the covenant and our desire to observe it, we now connect to the Light of Binah to banish all negative forces, thus preventing corruption and destruction in our world. By virtue of this connection to Binah, the World to Come becomes our world, in the here and now, because iniquity and darkness .cannot prevail in the presence of Binah's Light

First Reading - Abraham - Chesed

(ט) אֵלֶּה תּוֹלְדֹת נֹחַ נֹחַ אִישׁ צַדִּיק תָּמִים הָיָה (יהה)
בְּדֹרֹתָיו אֶת־הָאֱלֹהִים (ילה) הִתְהַלֶּךְ (מיה)־נֹחַ: (י) וַיּוֹלֶד נֹחַ

נֹחַ - In Hebrew, the name Noach (in English, "Noah") also means "to be comfortable." All of our problems in life occur when we remain within our comfort zone, when we look for the easy way out, gratifying our ego instead of yielding to the longings of our soul.

In this verse, we receive the courage and might to pursue the often-uncomfortable spiritual path that inevitably leads us to enduring fulfillment.

נֹחַ - The sages teach us that Noah had the regrettable distinction of having this portion of the destruction of the world named after him because he failed to feel the pain of his fellow beings who were destined to die in the flood. Noah knew intellectually that his prayers and tears would not alter the fate of mankind because of the lack of righteous souls in his generation. Nevertheless, if he had truly felt the pain of others and the pain of the world, he would have cried out, regardless, on their behalf.

Hence, we learn that spiritual growth entails feeling the pain of others. If we genuinely experience the anguish of those around us, we could never inflict harm upon them. The Light cast from these verses opens our hearts to the suffering of the world and in turn enlightens us to the senselessness of hurting another human being.

בְּדֹרֹתָיו - Noah did not attain the same spiritual heights as Moses or Abraham because he dwelt in a generation of negative, corrupt people. The sages teach us that environment is an integral factor in determining our level of spiritual growth. When we surround ourselves with negative people, we are eventually dragged down and we fall. Jealousy and speaking evil of others are just some of the ways we defile our souls and the world. According to the sages, airborne diseases and other maladies are born from these negative relationships, from the very words that speak ill of others.

שְׁלֹשָׁה בָנִים אֶת־שֵׁם אֶת־חָם וְאֶת־יָפֶת׃ (יא) וַתִּשָּׁחֵת
הָאָרֶץ (מילוי אלהים ע"ה) לִפְנֵי הָאֱלֹהִים (ילה) וַתִּמָּלֵא הָאָרֶץ (מילוי
אלהים ע"ה) חָמָס׃ (יב) וַיַּרְא אֱלֹהִים (ילה) אֶת־הָאָרֶץ (מילוי אלהים
ע"ה) וְהִנֵּה נִשְׁחָתָה כִּי־הִשְׁחִית כָּל (ילי)־בָּשָׂר אֶת־דַּרְכּוֹ

For that reason, it is in our own interest to surround ourselves with spiritual people in a loving, positive environment.

Through the name of Noah, we meditate to imbue our environment with Light and positivity, bringing an end to airborne disease and human suffering.

הִשְׁחִית - Sexual immorality was a major source of negativity during this generation. Moreover, the Zohar explains that this verse also pertains to the wicked people who caused living creatures to mix and mate with other species, thus altering the God-given genetic code of each breed of creature.

Today we find the same phenomenon occurring. Sexual indulgence is rampant. The spiritual insights and purpose of intimate relations between a husband and wife have been lost.

What's more, in medical science's attempts to search out solutions to disease, cloning, animal-to-human transplants, and genetic engineering are altering the make-up of both human and animal. According to the Zohar, the cures for all our ailments are to be found in the spiritual domain, not through physical means, which can only treat symptoms.

Now, just as in the time of Noah, water and the remainder of our planet's natural environment are fighting back. Pollution, strains of bacteria and viruses, and toxic wastes are destroying our drinking water, air, agricultural land, and our own immune systems. This portion remedies these afflictions on a spiritual seed level. And because the actions of a few righteous individuals can outweigh all the negative deeds of the wicked who are many, we can now use this portion to purify our souls and the entire planet.

A flood of Light - as opposed to a flood of water - engulfs our planet. For us,

עַל-הָאָרֶץ (מילוי אלהים ע"ה) סּ: (יג) וַיֹּאמֶר אֱלֹהִים (ילה) לְנֹחַ קֵץ
(מנק) כָּל (ילי)-בָּשָׂר בָּא לְפָנַי כִּי-מָלְאָה הָאָרֶץ (מילוי אלהים ע"ה)
חָמָס מִפְּנֵיהֶם וְהִנְנִי מַשְׁחִיתָם אֶת-הָאָרֶץ (מילוי אלהים ע"ה):
(יד) עֲשֵׂה לְךָ תֵּבַת עֲצֵי-גֹפֶר קִנִּים תַּעֲשֶׂה אֶת-הַתֵּבָה

these rays of Light are pleasurable, warm, and cleansing for the soul. For the truly wicked, the soulless beings who propagate only evil, these sparks of Light are the fires of Hell itself. But both pleasure and pain can purify; and therefore, the entire world is now prepared for the Final Redemption.

עֲשֵׂה - Kabbalistically, the story of Noah and the ark is a code:

• Noah is a metaphor for the Upper World dimension known as Yesod. This Upper World is our source and the fountainhead for all the spiritual Light that flows into our life.

• The ark is a code for the realm known as Malchut, which is our physical existence.

• The wicked men of Noah's generation represent the egocentric traits that taint our own souls, the dark side of human nature.

When the Upper and Lower Worlds are linked (metaphorically described as Noah entering into the ark), the Light is free to flow into our world, bringing protection, untold joy, and serenity to life. When, however, these two realms are disconnected, the Light is cut off, leaving our dimension in a chaotic sea of darkness, which is the birthplace of destruction and suffering.

Our own sins, born of ego, cause disconnection between the Upper and Lower Worlds. This is the root cause behind any destruction that befalls mankind.

In truth, God does not penalize, nor does the Creator decree judgments upon humanity. Our own actions either unite us with the source of all Light or sever our connection to the Realm of Infinite Bliss. We have the free will to

וְכָפַרְתָּ אֹתָהּ מִבַּיִת (ב"פ ראה) וּמִחוּץ בַּכֹּפֶר׃ (טו) וְזֶה אֲשֶׁר
תַּעֲשֶׂה אֹתָהּ שְׁלֹשׁ מֵאוֹת אַמָּה אֹרֶךְ הַתֵּבָה חֲמִשִּׁים
אַמָּה רָחְבָּהּ וּשְׁלֹשִׁים אַמָּה קוֹמָתָהּ׃ (טז) צֹהַר | תַּעֲשֶׂה
לַתֵּבָה וְאֶל־אַמָּה תְּכַלֶּנָּה מִלְמַעְלָה וּפֶתַח הַתֵּבָה בְּצִדָּהּ
תָּשִׂים תַּחְתִּיִּם שְׁנִיִּם וּשְׁלִשִׁים תַּעֲשֶׂהָ׃ (יז) וַאֲנִי (אני) הִנְנִי
מֵבִיא אֶת־הַמַּבּוּל מַיִם עַל־הָאָרֶץ (מילוי אלהים ע"ה) לְשַׁחֵת
כָּל (ילי)־בָּשָׂר אֲשֶׁר־בּוֹ רוּחַ חַיִּים (בינה ע"ה) מִתַּחַת הַשָּׁמָיִם
(י"פ טל) כֹּל (ילי) אֲשֶׁר־בָּאָרֶץ יִגְוָע׃ (יח) וַהֲקִמֹתִי אֶת־בְּרִיתִי
אִתָּךְ וּבָאתָ אֶל־הַתֵּבָה אַתָּה וּבָנֶיךָ וְאִשְׁתְּךָ וּנְשֵׁי־בָנֶיךָ
אִתָּךְ׃ (יט) וּמִכָּל (ילי)־הָחַי מִכָּל (ילי)־בָּשָׂר שְׁנַיִם מִכֹּל

choose our behavioral actions.

This portion combined with this Kabbalistic understanding repairs the sins of mankind throughout time by linking the Upper and Lower Worlds. Just as Noah entered the ark, the Light now enters Malchut - our world - to amend our iniquities, perfect our souls, and forever protect us against judgment.

In the same way that the wicked people of Noah's generation were destroyed by the Flood, our negative traits meet their destruction as a flood of Light cleanses us forever of self-love and self-indulgence.

וּמִכָּל - The Creator saved every animal on Earth, indicating the interconnectedness and sacredness of all life-forms. When a species is lost from this world, the natural balance, complexity, and sanctity of our world is diminished because the creature's Light is gone forever.

Our planet and all of her creatures are healed through this reading.

(ילי) תָּבִיא אֶל־הַתֵּבָה לְהַחֲיֹת אִתָּךְ זָכָר וּנְקֵבָה יִהְיוּ׃ (כ)

מֵהָעוֹף לְמִינֵהוּ וּמִן־הַבְּהֵמָה (לכב) לְמִינָהּ מִכֹּל (ילי) רֶמֶשׂ

הָאֲדָמָה לְמִינֵהוּ שְׁנַיִם מִכֹּל (ילי) יָבֹאוּ אֵלֶיךָ לְהַחֲיוֹת׃ (כא)

וְאַתָּה קַח־לְךָ מִכָּל (ילי) ־מַאֲכָל אֲשֶׁר יֵאָכֵל וְאָסַפְתָּ אֵלֶיךָ

וְהָיָה (יהה) (יהוה) לְךָ וְלָהֶם לְאָכְלָה׃ (כב) וַיַּעַשׂ נֹחַ כְּכֹל (ילי)

אֲשֶׁר צִוָּה אֹתוֹ אֱלֹהִים (ילה) כֵּן עָשָׂה׃ ס

Second Reading - Issac - Gvurah

ז (א) וַיֹּאמֶר יְהוָה(אדני אהדונהי) לְנֹחַ בֹּא־אַתָּה וְכָל (ילי) ־בֵּיתְךָ

וְאַתָּה - The Creator instructs Noah to gather enough food for the ark to feed everyone throughout the entire ordeal. The lesson concerns care. When we care with all of our hearts and souls for others, miracles take place and the end results always manage to turn out positive.

In this portion, we ignite concern and care in our hearts for our fellow human beings. In turn, this action ensures the healing of our land and the rehabilitation of our water, so food will always be plentiful for all of God's children. This same effect holds true with spiritual nourishment as endless Light now rains down upon us to nourish our souls forever.

וַיֹּאמֶר - The great Kabbalist Rabbi Shimon Bar bar Yochai revealed that the ark is a code, a metaphor signifying protection and well-being for man during times of severe judgment. Moreover, the Kabbalists have explained that in our present generation, this ark would once again appear in the world. The ark, according to Rabbi Shimon, is the holy Zohar.

In response, the Satan uses every means at his disposal to prevent the broad dissemination of this sacred book. His prime objective is to flood the world with reckless behavior and turmoil so that man drowns in a sea of chaos. The

(ב״פ ראה) אֶל־הַתֵּבָה כִּי־אֹתְךָ רָאִיתִי צַדִּיק לְפָנַי בַּדּוֹר
הַזֶּה (והו): (ב) מִכֹּל (ילי) | הַבְּהֵמָה (לכב) הַטְּהוֹרָה תִּקַּח־לְךָ
שִׁבְעָה שִׁבְעָה אִישׁ וְאִשְׁתּוֹ וּמִן־הַבְּהֵמָה (לכב) אֲשֶׁר לֹא
טְהֹרָה הִוא שְׁנַיִם אִישׁ וְאִשְׁתּוֹ: (ג) גַּם מֵעוֹף הַשָּׁמַיִם (י״פ
טל) שִׁבְעָה שִׁבְעָה זָכָר וּנְקֵבָה לְחַיּוֹת זֶרַע עַל־פְּנֵי (חכמה, בינה)
כָל (ילי)־הָאָרֶץ (מילוי אלהים ע״ה): (ד) כִּי לְיָמִים (נלך) עוֹד שִׁבְעָה
אָנֹכִי (איע) מַמְטִיר עַל־הָאָרֶץ (מילוי אלהים ע״ה) אַרְבָּעִים יוֹם (נגד,
זן) וְאַרְבָּעִים לָיְלָה (מלה) וּמָחִיתִי אֶת־כָּל (ילי)־הַיְקוּם אֲשֶׁר
עָשִׂיתִי מֵעַל (עלם) פְּנֵי (חכמה, בינה) הָאֲדָמָה: (ה) וַיַּעַשׂ נֹחַ כְּכֹל (ילי)

Zohar is our protection, our ark. The Zohar safeguards us from judgment if we possess a desire to change our ways.

Unlike Noah, we must cry out in pain for others who have not yet found the ark. We must feel the anguish of the world, using all of our powers to share the Zohar with our fellow human beings.

Usually judgments are not calamitous global events such as the flooding of the Earth. The Satan is far more subtle. Our rivers, lakes, and groundwater have become contaminated, destroying agricultural land and drinking water, and poisoning us without our ever realizing the toxins we ingest through our consumption of fruits, vegetables, and liquids.

The Zohar's Light, combined with this Torah portion, protects us from these unseen dangers. Through the verses that speak of the ark, we reverse judgments decreed upon the world. We purify and cleanse the water on our planet, including the water that comprises over 65 per cent of the human body.

אֲשֶׁר־צִוָּהוּ יְהֹוָהאדניאהדונהי: (ו) וְנֹחַ בֶּן־שֵׁשׁ מֵאוֹת שָׁנָה
וְהַמַּבּוּל הָיָה (יהה) מַיִם עַל־הָאָרֶץ (מילוי אלהים ע"ה): (ז) וַיָּבֹא
נֹחַ וּבָנָיו וְאִשְׁתּוֹ וּנְשֵׁי־בָנָיו אִתּוֹ אֶל־הַתֵּבָה מִפְּנֵי מֵי (ילי)
הַמַּבּוּל: (ח) מִן־הַבְּהֵמָה (לכב) הַטְּהוֹרָה וּמִן־הַבְּהֵמָה (לכב)
אֲשֶׁר אֵינֶנָּה טְהֹרָה וּמִן־הָעוֹף וְכֹל (ילי) אֲשֶׁר־רֹמֵשׂ עַל־
הָאֲדָמָה: (ט) שְׁנַיִם שְׁנַיִם בָּאוּ אֶל־נֹחַ אֶל־הַתֵּבָה זָכָר
וּנְקֵבָה כַּאֲשֶׁר צִוָּה אֱלֹהִים (ילה) אֶת־נֹחַ: (י) וַיְהִי לְשִׁבְעַת
הַיָּמִים (נלך) וּמֵי (ילי) הַמַּבּוּל הָיוּ עַל־הָאָרֶץ (מילוי אלהים ע"ה): (יא) **בִּשְׁנַת**

וְהַמַּבּוּל - Before the Flood, water possessed an intrinsic capacity to wash away both the physical dirt of the body and the spiritual negativity of the soul. Water was a natural healing agent. For this reason, the people of the generations before Noah lived for hundreds of years.

In truth, the Flood effected a dramatic change in water's molecular and spiritual structure. Water lost its power to heal and nourish as it had done before the deluge. Though H_2O is still the lifeblood of the planet, it can no longer regenerate both our cells and our souls.

This portion, combined with our meditation, restores the water of our planet to its antediluvian state. Water is now empowered with the Divine Force of healing, helping us achieve the ultimate objective - eternal life. It is interesting to note that the molecular weight of water is 18eighteen, the same numerical value as the Hebrew word chai, which means "life."

בִּשְׁנַת - The Flood occurred during the month of Scorpio, one of the most negative months of the year. Abraham the Patriarch, writing in his Kabbalistic treatise The Book of Formation, calls this month "bitter Cheshvan." The Zohar, however, reveals that we live in a reality of perfect balance. Hence, wherever we encounter the greatest volume of darkness, we

שֵׁשׁ־מֵאוֹת שָׁנָה לְחַיֵּי־נֹחַ בַּחֹדֶשׁ (י״ב הויות) הַשֵּׁנִי בְּשִׁבְעָה־
עָשָׂר יוֹם (נגד, זן) לַחֹדֶשׁ (י״ב הויות) בַּיּוֹם (נגד, זן) הַזֶּה (והו) נִבְקְעוּ
כָּל (ילי)־מַעְיְנוֹת תְּהוֹם רַבָּה וַאֲרֻבֹּת הַשָּׁמַיִם (י״פ טל) נִפְתָּחוּ:
(יב) וַיְהִי הַגֶּשֶׁם (י״פ אל ל״ב נתיבות החכמה ע״ה) עַל־הָאָרֶץ (מילוי אלהים ע״ה)
אַרְבָּעִים יוֹם (נגד, זן) וְאַרְבָּעִים לָיְלָה (מלה): (יג) בְּעֶצֶם הַיּוֹם (נגד,
זן) הַזֶּה (והו) בָּא נֹחַ וְשֵׁם־וְחָם וָיֶפֶת בְּנֵי־נֹחַ וְאֵשֶׁת נֹחַ וּשְׁלֹשֶׁת
נְשֵׁי־בָנָיו אִתָּם אֶל־הַתֵּבָה: (יד) הֵמָּה וְכָל (ילי)־הַחַיָּה לְמִינָהּ
וְכָל (ילי)־הַבְּהֵמָה (לכב) לְמִינָהּ וְכָל (ילי)־הָרֶמֶשׂ הָרֹמֵשׂ עַל־
הָאָרֶץ (מילוי אלהים ע״ה) לְמִינֵהוּ וְכָל (ילי)־הָעוֹף לְמִינֵהוּ כֹּל (ילי)
צִפּוֹר כָּל (ילי)־כָּנָף (ע״ה קנ״א): (טו) וַיָּבֹאוּ אֶל־נֹחַ אֶל־הַתֵּבָה
שְׁנַיִם שְׁנַיִם מִכָּל (ילי)־הַבָּשָׂר אֲשֶׁר־בּוֹ רוּחַ חַיִּים (בינה ע״ה):
(טז) וְהַבָּאִים זָכָר וּנְקֵבָה מִכָּל (ילי)־בָּשָׂר בָּאוּ כַּאֲשֶׁר צִוָּה
אֹתוֹ אֱלֹהִים (ילה) וַיִּסְגֹּר יְהוָֹאדנָיאהדונהי בַּעֲדוֹ:

will also find the potential for the greatest amount of spiritual Light.

A tremendous quantity of Light now shines upon us, illuminating the entire world as we reflect upon Kabbalistic concept during the reading. The darkness in our world is, at last, transformed into Light. Personally, each of us can look inward to identify our darkest traits, allowing this Divine Light to banish forever these negative and careless qualities from our being.

וַיִּזְכֹּר - The Great Flood also ceased during the month of Scorpio.

Third Reading - Jacob - Tiferet

(יז) וַיְהִי הַמַּבּוּל אַרְבָּעִים יוֹם (נגד, זן) עַל־הָאָרֶץ (מילוי אלהים ע"ה)
וַיִּרְבּוּ הַמַּיִם וַיִּשְׂאוּ אֶת־הַתֵּבָה וַתָּרָם מֵעַל (עלם) הָאָרֶץ (מילוי
אלהים ע"ה): (יח) וַיִּגְבְּרוּ הַמַּיִם וַיִּרְבּוּ מְאֹד עַל־הָאָרֶץ (מילוי אלהים
ע"ה) וַתֵּלֶךְ הַתֵּבָה עַל־פְּנֵי (חכמה, בינה) הַמָּיִם: (יט) וְהַמַּיִם גָּבְרוּ
מְאֹד מְאֹד עַל־הָאָרֶץ (מילוי אלהים ע"ה) וַיְכֻסּוּ כָּל (ילי)־הֶהָרִים
הַגְּבֹהִים אֲשֶׁר־תַּחַת כָּל (ילי)־ הַשָּׁמָיִם (י"פ טל): (כ) חֲמֵשׁ
עֶשְׂרֵה אַמָּה מִלְמַעְלָה גָּבְרוּ הַמָּיִם וַיְכֻסּוּ הֶהָרִים: (כא)
וַיִּגְוַע כָּל (ילי)־בָּשָׂר | הָרֹמֵשׂ עַל־הָאָרֶץ (מילוי אלהים ע"ה) בָּעוֹף
וּבַבְּהֵמָה (לכב) וּבַחַיָּה וּבְכָל (לכב)־הַשֶּׁרֶץ הַשֹּׁרֵץ עַל־הָאָרֶץ
(מילוי אלהים ע"ה) וְכֹל (ילי) הָאָדָם (מ"ה): (כב) כֹּל (ילי) אֲשֶׁר נִשְׁמַת־
רוּחַ חַיִּים (בינה ע"ה) בְּאַפָּיו מִכֹּל (ילי) אֲשֶׁר בֶּחָרָבָה מֵתוּ: (כג)
וַיִּמַח אֶת־כָּל (ילי)־הַיְקוּם | אֲשֶׁר | עַל־פְּנֵי (חכמה, בינה) הָאֲדָמָה
מֵאָדָם (מ"ה) עַד־בְּהֵמָה (לכב) עַד־רֶמֶשׂ וְעַד־עוֹף הַשָּׁמַיִם (י"פ
טל) וַיִּמָּחוּ מִן־הָאָרֶץ (מילוי אלהים ע"ה) וַיִּשָּׁאֶר אַךְ (אהיה)־נֹחַ וַאֲשֶׁר
אִתּוֹ בַּתֵּבָה: (כד) וַיִּגְבְּרוּ הַמַּיִם עַל־הָאָרֶץ (מילוי אלהים ע"ה)
חֲמִשִּׁים וּמְאַת יוֹם (נגד, זן): ח (א) וַיִּזְכֹּר (יהי אור ע"ה) אֱלֹהִים (ילה)

Dates and time frames in the Torah are never given arbitrarily. Every date represents a window of opportunity, a opening, skylight to the Upper World

אֶת־נֹחַ וְאֵת כָּל (ילי) ־הַחַיָּה וְאֶת־כָּל (ילי) ־הַבְּהֵמָה (לכב) אֲשֶׁר
אִתּוֹ בַּתֵּבָה וַיַּעֲבֵר אֱלֹהִים (ילה) רוּחַ עַל־הָאָרֶץ (מילוי אלהים ע"ה)
וַיָּשֹׁכּוּ הַמָּיִם׃ (ב) וַיִּסָּכְרוּ מַעְיְנֹת תְּהוֹם וַאֲרֻבֹּת הַשָּׁמָיִם
(י"פ טל) וַיִּכָּלֵא הַגֶּשֶׁם (י"פ אל ל"ב נתיבות החכמה ע"ה) מִן־הַשָּׁמָיִם (י"פ טל)׃
(ג) וַיָּשֻׁבוּ הַמַּיִם מֵעַל (עלם) הָאָרֶץ (מילוי אלהים ע"ה) הָלוֹךְ וָשׁוֹב
וַיַּחְסְרוּ הַמַּיִם מִקְצֵה חֲמִשִּׁים וּמְאַת יוֹם (נגד, זן)׃ (ד) וַתָּנַח
הַתֵּבָה בַּחֹדֶשׁ (י"ב הויות) הַשְּׁבִיעִי בְּשִׁבְעָה־עָשָׂר יוֹם (נגד, זן)
לַחֹדֶשׁ (י"ב הויות) עַל הָרֵי אֲרָרָט׃ (ה) וְהַמַּיִם הָיוּ הָלוֹךְ וְחָסוֹר
עַד הַחֹדֶשׁ (י"ב הויות) הָעֲשִׂירִי בָּעֲשִׂירִי בְּאֶחָד (אהבה) לַחֹדֶשׁ
(י"ב הויות) נִרְאוּ רָאשֵׁי הֶהָרִים׃ (ו) וַיְהִי מִקֵּץ (מנק) אַרְבָּעִים

through which a particular spiritual influence flows into our world. This explains the critical importance attached to the dates in our lives. Planting seeds at the correct time is how one realizes the sweetest fruits. The negative angel, the Satan, who appears in our world as the ego, constantly compels us through our impatience to choose the wrong dates - planting a seed too early or waiting too long through procrastination, thus missing important opportunities.

These emotional urges are so strong within us that we must use every tool at our disposal to keep them at bay. Beginning a marriage, launching a new business venture, or selecting a date to move into a new home are some of the activities that are substantially affected by the cosmic timetable. The Kabbalistic calendar and the insights of the Torah provide us with the appropriate time frames for engaging in or refraining from the various activities of daily life.

יוֹם (נגד, זן) וַיִּפְתַּח נֹחַ אֶת־חַלּוֹן (מנזר) הַתֵּבָה אֲשֶׁר עָשָׂה: (ז) וַיְשַׁלַּח
אֶת־הָעֹרֵב וַיֵּצֵא יָצוֹא וָשׁוֹב עַד־יְבֹשֶׁת הַמַּיִם מֵעַל (עלם)
הָאָרֶץ (מילוי אלהים ע״ה): (ח) וַיְשַׁלַּח אֶת־הַיּוֹנָה מֵאִתּוֹ לִרְאוֹת
הֲקַלּוּ הַמַּיִם מֵעַל (עלם) פְּנֵי (חכמה, בינה) הָאֲדָמָה: (ט) וְלֹא־

חַלּוֹן - When the floodwaters subside, Noah first opens a window before he leaves the ark. When a man is attempting to free himself from difficult circumstances, he must open a window in his soul, thus creating an opening in a heart that has been blocked and boxed in by ego.

Often, this entails a willingness to ask for help - sometimes from another person, sometimes from the Light of the Creator, whichever causes pain to our ego the most.

The spiritual influences arising from this portion diminish our ego in a merciful fashion. These forces create an opening within the soul of all mankind. A global window is opened to the heavens, allowing the Light of the Creator to radiate throughout existence, commencing our Final Redemption.

וַיְשַׁלַּח - Noah sends forth a raven and a dove to see if it is safe to leave the ark. This action speaks to the importance of signs in our life - through birds or other "messengers" - that can provide us with guidance.

In order to perceive signs, we must be open and never disregard any event in our life, no matter how small or insignificant it might appear to be.

What's more, because this part of the Torah portion is now empowered with these insights from the Zohar, the holy words of the Torah become a sign for us - a sign that judgment is now over and that all the world's chaos, disease, pollution, personal suffering, corruption, and turmoil are now ending through the merit of the Zohar and the righteous souls, whose shoulders we stand upon.

מָצְאָה הַיּוֹנָה מָנוֹחַ לְכַף־רַגְלָהּ וַתָּשָׁב אֵלָיו אֶל־הַתֵּבָה
כִּי־מַיִם עַל־פְּנֵי (חכמה, בינה) כָל (ילי) ־הָאָרֶץ (מילוי אלהים ע״ה) וַיִּשְׁלַח
יָדוֹ וַיִּקָּחֶהָ וַיָּבֵא אֹתָהּ אֵלָיו אֶל־הַתֵּבָה׃ (י) וַיָּחֶל עוֹד שִׁבְעַת
יָמִים (נלך) אֲחֵרִים וַיֹּסֶף (ציון) שַׁלַּח אֶת־ הַיּוֹנָה מִן־הַתֵּבָה׃ (יא)
וַתָּבֹא אֵלָיו הַיּוֹנָה לְעֵת עֶרֶב וְהִנֵּה עֲלֵה־זַיִת טָרָף בְּפִיהָ
וַיֵּדַע נֹחַ כִּי־קַלּוּ הַמַּיִם מֵעַל (עלם) הָאָרֶץ (מילוי אלהים ע״ה)׃ (יב)
וַיִּיָּחֶל עוֹד שִׁבְעַת יָמִים (נלך) אֲחֵרִים וַיְשַׁלַּח אֶת־הַיּוֹנָה וְלֹא
יָסְפָה שׁוּב־אֵלָיו עוֹד׃ (יג) וַיְהִי בְּאַחַת וְשֵׁשׁ־מֵאוֹת שָׁנָה
בָּרִאשׁוֹן בְּאֶחָד (אהבה) לַחֹדֶשׁ (י״ב הויות) חָרְבוּ (רי״ו) הַמַּיִם מֵעַל
(עלם) הָאָרֶץ (מילוי אלהים ע״ה) וַיָּסַר נֹחַ אֶת־מִכְסֵה הַתֵּבָה וַיַּרְא
וְהִנֵּה חָרְבוּ (רי״ו) פְּנֵי (חכמה, בינה) הָאֲדָמָה׃ (יד) וּבַחֹדֶשׁ (י״ב הויות)
הַשֵּׁנִי בְּשִׁבְעָה וְעֶשְׂרִים יוֹם (נגד, זן) לַחֹדֶשׁ (י״ב הויות) יָבְשָׁה
הָאָרֶץ (מילוי אלהים ע״ה)׃ ס

Fourth Reading - Moses - Netzach

(טו) וַיְדַבֵּר (ראה) אֱלֹהִים (ילה) אֶל־נֹחַ לֵאמֹר׃ (טז) צֵא מִן־

צֵא - Noah's leaving the Ark pertains to our leaving the comforts and trappings of our material, self-indulgent existence to embrace the spiritual work that must be accomplished in our lifetime.

Spirituality, according to Kabbalah, is not about trekking up a mountain to commune with God and nature while meditating alongside a clear stream as

הַתֵּבָה אַתָּה וְאִשְׁתְּךָ וּבָנֶיךָ וּנְשֵׁי־בָנֶיךָ אִתָּךְ׃ (יז) כָּל
(ילי)־הַחַיָּה אֲשֶׁר־אִתְּךָ מִכָּל (ילי)־בָּשָׂר בָּעוֹף וּבַבְּהֵמָה (לכב)
וּבְכָל (לכב)־הָרֶמֶשׂ הָרֹמֵשׂ עַל־הָאָרֶץ (מילוי אלהים ע"ה) הַיְצֵא
(הַוְצֵא כתיב) אִתָּךְ וְשָׁרְצוּ בָאָרֶץ וּפָרוּ וְרָבוּ עַל־הָאָרֶץ (מילוי
אלהים ע"ה)׃ (יח) וַיֵּצֵא־נֹחַ וּבָנָיו וְאִשְׁתּוֹ וּנְשֵׁי־בָנָיו אִתּוֹ׃ (יט) כָּל
(ילי)־הַחַיָּה כָּל (ילי)־ הָרֶמֶשׂ וְכָל (ילי)־הָעוֹף כֹּל (ילי) רוֹמֵשׂ

the birds sing of the beauty of the world. That makes for a poetic scene, but it is not the purpose of our lives. Nor is divorcing ourselves from the physical world, secluding ourselves up on a mountaintop contemplating the majesty of nature or furthering our intellectual pursuits. According to Kabbalah, these are not effective ways to achieve spiritual growth.

We came down from the mountain, so to speak, to enter the world of chaos, hardship, turmoil, and burden so that we could confront the triggers that ignite primal reactions. Each trigger gives us an opportunity to transform our reactive behavior, allowing us to become the cause of our fulfillment. Through transformation, we create heaven on earth and become God-like. As an old proverb says: "Smooth seas do not make skillful sailors."

In truth, our positive traits do not win us any points in life. Our wonderful characteristics and endearing qualities serve no practical purpose when it comes to awakening new levels of fulfillment and Light in our lives. Those traits are already in a proactive state. On the contrary, it is our negative characteristics and traits that actually give us the opportunity to effect a true transformation of character.

We came to this world to create positive change within ourselves and in the world around us. Positive change will encounter resistance, conflict, and obstacles. We must embrace these difficult situations.

The Torah in this portion imbues us with the courage and fortitude to accomplish our personal spiritual mission and achieve transformation.

עַל־הָאָרֶץ (מילוי אלהים ע״ה) לְמִשְׁפְּחֹתֵיהֶם יָצְאוּ מִן־הַתֵּבָה׃
(כ) וַיִּבֶן נֹחַ מִזְבֵּחַ (זן) לַיהוָה אדני יאהדונהי וַיִּקַּח (ווע״ם) מִכֹּל (ילי) |
הַבְּהֵמָה (לכב) הַטְּהֹרָה וּמִכֹּל (ילי) הָעוֹף הַטָּהֹר וַיַּעַל עֹלֹת
(אבג יתץ, ושר, אהבת חנם) בַּמִּזְבֵּחַ (זן)׃ (כא) וַיָּרַח יְהוָה אדני יאהדונהי אֶת־
רֵיחַ הַנִּיחֹחַ וַיֹּאמֶר יְהוָה אדני יאהדונהי אֶל־לִבּוֹ לֹא אֹסִף לְקַלֵּל
עוֹד אֶת־הָאֲדָמָה בַּעֲבוּר הָאָדָם (מ״ה) כִּי יֵצֶר לֵב הָאָדָם
(מ״ה) רַע מִנְּעֻרָיו וְלֹא־אֹסִף עוֹד לְהַכּוֹת אֶת־כָּל (ילי) ־חַי (וזיים,
בינה ע״ה) כַּאֲשֶׁר עָשִׂיתִי׃ (כב) עֹד כָּל (ילי) ־יְמֵי הָאָרֶץ (מילוי אלהים
ע״ה) זֶרַע וְקָצִיר וְקֹר וָחֹם וְקַיִץ וָחֹרֶף וְיוֹם (נגד, זן) וָלַיְלָה (מלה)
לֹא יִשְׁבֹּתוּ׃ ט (א) וַיְבָרֶךְ (עסמ״ב) אֱלֹהִים (ילה) אֶת־נֹחַ וְאֶת־

וַיִּבֶן - Upon leaving the ark, Noah offers sacrifices to thank the Creator. According to the ancient Kabbalists, the concept of sacrifices pertains to the sacrificing of our own negative attributes. Offering thanks concerns the awakening of appreciation - not for the sake of the Creator, who has absolutely no need for thanks or appreciation - but for ourselves. Appreciation is an actual spiritual force, a packet of energy that protects all that we hold dear in our hearts. Offering thanks is a tool for us to safeguard the joy and treasures that we possess.

וַיְבָרֶךְ - God bestows a blessing upon Noah and his sons by telling them to "be fruitful and multiply, and replenish the Earth."

Bearing children and teaching them spiritual values is the most potent way to bring Light to our own lives and to the entire planet. Each new soul that enters our world to walk the spiritual path is akin to lighting another candle in a darkened room. Each new Light diminishes the darkness, eventually banishing it completely. Thus, the phrase "replenish the Earth" refers to the

בָּנָיו וַיֹּאמֶר לָהֶם פְּרוּ וּרְבוּ וּמִלְאוּ אֶת־הָאָרֶץ (מילוי אלהים
ע"ה): (ב) וּמוֹרַאֲכֶם וְחִתְּכֶם יִהְיֶה (ייי) עַל כָּל (ילי) (עמם)־חַיַּת
הָאָרֶץ (מילוי אלהים ע"ה) וְעַל כָּל (ילי) (עמם)־עוֹף הַשָּׁמָיִם (י"פ טל)
בְּכֹל (לכב) אֲשֶׁר תִּרְמֹשׂ הָאֲדָמָה וּבְכָל (לכב)־דְּגֵי הַיָּם (ילי)
בְּיֶדְכֶם נִתָּנוּ: (ג) כָּל (ילי)־רֶמֶשׂ אֲשֶׁר הוּא־חַי לָכֶם יִהְיֶה (ייי)
לְאָכְלָה כְּיֶרֶק עֵשֶׂב (אותיות ע"ב שמות) נָתַתִּי לָכֶם אֶת־כֹּל (ילי):
(ד) אַךְ (אהיה)־בָּשָׂר בְּנַפְשׁוֹ דָמוֹ לֹא תֹאכֵלוּ: (ה) וְאַךְ (אהיה)
אֶת־דִּמְכֶם לְנַפְשֹׁתֵיכֶם אֶדְרֹשׁ מִיַּד כָּל (ילי)־חַיָּה אֶדְרְשֶׁנּוּ
וּמִיַּד הָאָדָם (מ"ה) מִיַּד אִישׁ אָחִיו אֶדְרֹשׁ אֶת־נֶפֶשׁ הָאָדָם
(מ"ה): (ו) **שֹׁפֵךְ** דַּם הָאָדָם (מ"ה) בָּאָדָם (מ"ה) דָּמוֹ יִשָּׁפֵךְ כִּי

replenishment of the Light that was hidden at the time of Creation. Here, we receive blessings to help us bear children. We can meditate to share these blessings with others who are also seeking to create a family.

What's more, those people with whom we share the wisdom of Kabbalah are considered to be our spiritual children. Thus, the concept of being fruitful and multiplying also pertains to the ever-widening dissemination of this spiritual wisdom. God's blessing to Noah is bestowed upon us here so that we may become beacons of Light for all the people we encounter.

שֹׁפֵךְ - God warns Noah about the ramifications associated with the sin of bloodshed and murder. Murder does not refer exclusively to cold-blooded killing. We commit murder when we publicly or privately disgrace or humiliate others, causing the blood to rush to their faces out of embarrassment. The Kabbalists tell us that we can either kill someone either physically or emotionally and spiritually. We can assassinate a person's body and we can also assassinate a person's character. We can destroy

בְּצֶלֶם אֱלֹהִים (ילה) עָשָׂה אֶת־הָאָדָם (מ״ה)׃ (ז) וְאַתֶּם פְּרוּ
וּרְבוּ שִׁרְצוּ בָאָרֶץ וּרְבוּ־בָהּ׃ ס

Fifth Reading - Aaron - Hod

(ח) וַיֹּאמֶר אֱלֹהִים (ילה) אֶל־נֹחַ וְאֶל־בָּנָיו אִתּוֹ לֵאמֹר׃ (ט)
וַאֲנִי (אני) הִנְנִי מֵקִים אֶת־ בְּרִיתִי אִתְּכֶם וְאֶת־זַרְעֲכֶם
אַחֲרֵיכֶם׃ (י) וְאֵת כָּל (ילי)־נֶפֶשׁ הַחַיָּה אֲשֶׁר אִתְּכֶם בָּעוֹף
בַּבְּהֵמָה (לכב) וּבְכָל (לכב)־חַיַּת הָאָרֶץ (מילוי אלהים ע״ה) אִתְּכֶם
מִכֹּל (ילי) יֹצְאֵי הַתֵּבָה לְכֹל (יה אדני) חַיַּת הָאָרֶץ (מילוי אלהים ע״ה)׃
(יא) וַהֲקִמֹתִי אֶת־בְּרִיתִי אִתְּכֶם וְלֹא־יִכָּרֵת כָּל (ילי)־בָּשָׂר

someone's relationships and we can also ruin their livelihood.

As we read this passage and recall past events when we have shamed another person or committed the sin of spiritual murder, we correct our iniquities and remove hatred from the collective heart of humanity.

בְּרִיתִי - The Creator makes a covenant with mankind. More important than the details of this divine contract is the notion that we require the Light of the Creator in our lives if we are to truly achieve both personal and global transformation. Our ego (the Satan) creates the intellectually driven illusion that we live in a Godless world and that we alone are the architects and masterminds of our good fortune.

וַהֲקִמֹתִי - After the floodwaters subside, God promises Noah that He will not curse the world with another flood. However, whereas water once healed the body and soul of man, thus ensuring long life, the water of our planet, after the Flood, lost this intrinsic divine power.

Our spiritual work entails restoring the water of our planet - and of our

עוֹד מִמֵּי (ילי) הַמַּבּוּל וְלֹא־יִהְיֶה (ייי) עוֹד מַבּוּל לְשַׁחֵת
הָאָרֶץ (מילוי אלהים ע"ה): (יב) וַיֹּאמֶר אֱלֹהִים (ילה) זֹאת אוֹת־
הַבְּרִית אֲשֶׁר־אֲנִי (אני) נֹתֵן (אבג יתץ, ושר, אהבת חנם) בֵּינִי וּבֵינֵיכֶם
וּבֵין כָּל (ילי)־נֶפֶשׁ חַיָּה אֲשֶׁר אִתְּכֶם לְדֹרֹת עוֹלָם: (יג) אֶת־קַשְׁתִּי
נָתַתִּי בֶּעָנָן וְהָיְתָה לְאוֹת בְּרִית בֵּינִי וּבֵין הָאָרֶץ (מילוי אלהים
ע"ה): (יד) וְהָיָה (יהה) (יהוה) בְּעַנְנִי עָנָן עַל־הָאָרֶץ (מילוי אלהים ע"ה)

physical body - to its antediluvian state. These verses accomplish this very act. Each pair of eyes that reads this portion and each set of ears that listens to this reading ignites the rehabilitation of the Earth's waters so that they may once again possess the power to heal, rejuvenate, and regenerate the cells of the body and the souls of human beings.

קַשְׁתִּי - The rainbow is a code for the seven Sfirot (dimensions) that directly influence our physical dimension. The complete Ten Sfirot are structured as follows:

The upper three realms are closest to the Light of the Creator and do not exert any direct influence over our world. The lower seven, however, have a direct impact on our lives: For this reason, we have seven colors in a rainbow, seven diatonic musical notes, seven major continents, seven seas, seven days in a week, and so on.

Although there are seven Sfirot (or dimensions), an exquisite unity underlies this structure. Just as a single band of white sunlight contains the seven colors of the rainbow, the Light of the Creator is embodied by the seven Sfirot. In other words, our world represents the refraction of this single shaft of Light into all the "colors" that comprise Creation.

The rainbow spoken of in this portion now connects us to the full measure of Light that we may use to restore the waters back to their pre-Flood structure. The water of our planet is now empowered to heal and inspire the immortality of mankind.

וְנִרְאֲתָה הַקֶּשֶׁת בֶּעָנָן׃ (טו) וְזָכַרְתִּי אֶת־בְּרִיתִי אֲשֶׁר בֵּינִי
וּבֵינֵיכֶם וּבֵין כָּל (ילי) ־נֶפֶשׁ חַיָּה בְּכָל (לכב) ־בָּשָׂר וְלֹא־יִהְיֶה
(ייי) עוֹד הַמַּיִם לְמַבּוּל לְשַׁחֵת כָּל (ילי) ־בָּשָׂר׃ (טז) וְהָיְתָה
הַקֶּשֶׁת בֶּעָנָן וּרְאִיתִיהָ לִזְכֹּר (יהי אור ע"ה) בְּרִית עוֹלָם בֵּין
אֱלֹהִים (ילה) וּבֵין כָּל (ילי) ־נֶפֶשׁ חַיָּה בְּכָל (לכב) ־בָּשָׂר אֲשֶׁר
עַל־הָאָרֶץ (מילוי אלהים ע"ה)׃ (יז) וַיֹּאמֶר אֱלֹהִים (ילה) אֶל־נֹחַ זֹאת
אוֹת־הַבְּרִית אֲשֶׁר הֲקִמֹתִי בֵּינִי וּבֵין כָּל (ילי) ־בָּשָׂר אֲשֶׁר
עַל־הָאָרֶץ (מילוי אלהים ע"ה)׃ פ

Sixth Reading - Joseph - Yesod

(יח) וַיִּהְיוּ בְנֵי־נֹחַ הַיֹּצְאִים מִן־הַתֵּבָה שֵׁם וְחָם וָיָפֶת וְחָם
הוּא אֲבִי כְנָעַן׃ (יט) שְׁלֹשָׁה אֵלֶּה בְּנֵי־נֹחַ וּמֵאֵלֶּה נָפְצָה
כָל (ילי) ־הָאָרֶץ (מילוי אלהים ע"ה)׃ (כ) וַיָּחֶל נֹחַ אִישׁ הָאֲדָמָה וַיִּטַּע
כָּרֶם׃ (כא) וַיֵּשְׁתְּ מִן־הַיַּיִן (מלה) וַיִּשְׁכָּר וַיִּתְגַּל בְּתוֹךְ אָהֳלֹה׃

וַיֵּשְׁתְּ - The intoxication of Noah. The Zohar explains that both Noah and Adam sinned under the influence of wine. Kabbalah teaches that wine is a powerful tool, an antenna for drawing in Light, just as the grape is a potent conduit of spiritual energy. Wine is therefore used as a tool in blessings to reveal God's Light into our physical world. When in the absence of a blessing we do not prepare a large enough Vessel to hold this Energy or if we consume wine for reasons not related to spirituality, the torrent of Light aroused causes an uncontrollable awakening of our dark side. This is the mystery that explains wine's ability to induce intoxicated behavior.

How does the most spiritual person on the planet suddenly fall into a state of drunkenness? Noah, after experiencing the ultimate in trying times - watching the world being destroyed before his very eyes - believes his spiritual work is finally over. The pain has ended. The suffering has subsided.

However, experiencing hardship without the knowledge of its root cause turns into needless suffering if the lesson is not taken in by the sufferer. Hence, pain will not purify. Suffering will not sanctify. And catastrophe will not cleanse.

Here we learn that we must probe to identify the cause behind our afflictions. To put an end to our own pain in life, we must become accountable and let go of our victim mindset. Moreover, we must delve deeply within ourselves to uproot those flaws in our past behavior that brought about our current misfortune.

Thankfully, our embracing of these very insights is the first step in understanding that we alone are responsible for the world's afflictions. Through this understanding, we correct the sins of the past generations so that all the suffering throughout history now has spiritual value and a purifying effect on the world. Humanity is herewith cleansed of all iniquities, past and present.

The Zohar offers us a still deeper understanding of Noah's drunkenness. Noah received the wisdom of Kabbalah from God and used it to build the ark and protect the creatures of the world. Noah entering into the ark is a symbol for our world connecting to the Upper Realm known as Yesod, the source of our Light and Divine Energy.

After the waters had subsided, Noah uses Kabbalah to ascend into even higher spiritual realms in an attempt to examine the Sin of Adam and Eve. He does so with the intent of not repeating the Sin but rather of making reparations in the world.

This higher spiritual realm that Noah entered is the inner meaning behind the vineyard and grapes that caused Noah to become drunk.

• The vineyard is a metaphor alluding to a higher spiritual dimension.
• The grapes pertain to the intoxicating energy that swirls in this supernal realm.

The spiritual energy radiating in this higher dimension is far too potent for Noah to handle. He has not yet purged all the negative desires from his being. His connection to this higher realm is premature, so the energy proves lethal.

The effect is similar to what happens to a person who ingests a potent narcotic, such as crack-cocaine, intending it as a one-time experiment only. The energy, however, is too intense and overwhelming, and causes an immediate addiction because of the body's weakness to the drug. The lesson emerging from this Kabbalistic insight concerns our own good intentions. As the old adage states: "The road to hell is paved with good intentions."

We repeatedly with good intentions seek out enjoyment from life, but the pleasure we receive often awakens selfish desires in the process. This occurs because there is an aspect of our ego that partakes of the joy we acquire. This gratification strengthens the dark side of our nature and its hold over us. We become intoxicated, drunk with self-indulgence. We become addicted to the incessant cravings of our ego. Pleasure has become poison.

All of us must learn how to receive pleasure and fulfillment for the purpose of sharing with others. We must be watchful that no trace of selfishness exists within us when we set and achieve goals in life. This is a lifelong task and the basis of all spiritual work. This portion of the Torah detoxifies us, making us spiritually sober. We connect safely to the highest levels of spiritual Light for the purpose of sharing it with others. This immediately sets the Age of Messiah into motion.

עֶרְוַת - Noah's son Ham rapes his father while Noah is intoxicated. The lesson of this difficult section concerns the power of the negative side, the Satan. If there is even the slightest opening in our lives (signified by Noah's drunken state or our ego out of control), we become vulnerable to any negative forces around us.

Our closest friends and family members can be the cause of our misfortune if we allow even the smallest conflicts or problems to fester or inflame our ego. We must make every effort to block all openings for negativity in our

(כב) וַיַּרְא חָם אֲבִי כְנַעַן אֵת עֶרְוַת אָבִיו וַיַּגֵּד לִשְׁנֵי־אֶחָיו
בַּחוּץ׃ (כג) וַיִּקַּח (וזעם) שֵׁם וָיֶפֶת אֶת־הַשִּׂמְלָה וַיָּשִׂימוּ עַל־
שְׁכֶם שְׁנֵיהֶם וַיֵּלְכוּ אֲחוֹרַנִּית וַיְכַסּוּ אֵת עֶרְוַת אֲבִיהֶם

relationships. We must completely shut down our own Evil Inclination and place all of our relationships upon a spiritual foundation.

On a deeper level of understanding, the rape of Noah is connected to the sexual relations that took place between Adam and the negative angel (do not pronounce her name) Lilit and Eve with the negative angel (do not pronounce his name) Samael. In other words, Adam and Eve listened to and followed the instructions of the serpent to eat from the Tree of Knowledge of Good and Evil, which is equivalent to our listening to our own ego telling us to eat the fruit of overindulgence.

Moreover, the sexual connection between Adam and Eve and the serpent can also be understood as the Vessel (the collective souls of man) connecting to a higher level of energy prematurely, before the Vessel's selfish reactive consciousness has been fully purged from its being.

This concept relates to the power of patience, of waiting, of restricting our need to have it all now. We need the patience to subdue our self-absorbed desires before we have any chance for receiving any form of joy. When we set out to procure physical or spiritual pleasure for selfish reasons, without any regard to the other people in our life, we have been seduced and raped by our own ego - the negative force called the Satan.

In effect, the rape of Noah is akin to the serpent - our ego - raping our own souls. The illuminating verses that speak of this story kindle a Light that seals up any openings through which negative influences can attempt to seduce and violate us. The covetousness in our nature is eliminated. The negative angels (do not pronounce their names) Samael and Lilit are banished from our existence, and ancient wounds are healed as we achieve a renewed state of purity.

וּפְנֵיהֶם אֲחֹרַנִּית וְעֶרְוַת אֲבִיהֶם לֹא רָאוּ׃ (כד) וַיִּיקֶץ נֹחַ
מִיֵּינוֹ וַיֵּדַע אֵת אֲשֶׁר־עָשָׂה לוֹ בְּנוֹ הַקָּטָן׃ (כה) וַיֹּאמֶר
אָרוּר כְּנָעַן עֶבֶד עֲבָדִים יִהְיֶה (ייי) לְאֶחָיו׃ (כו) וַיֹּאמֶר בָּרוּךְ
יְהֹוָה{אדני־אהדונהי} אֱלֹהֵי (דמב) שֵׁם וִיהִי כְנַעַן עֶבֶד לָמוֹ׃ (כז) יַפְתְּ
אֱלֹהִים (ילה) לְיֶפֶת וְיִשְׁכֹּן בְּאָהֳלֵי־שֵׁם וִיהִי כְנַעַן עֶבֶד לָמוֹ׃
(כח) וַיְחִי־נֹחַ אַחַר הַמַּבּוּל שְׁלֹשׁ מֵאוֹת שָׁנָה וַחֲמִשִּׁים שָׁנָה׃
(כט) וַיְהִי כָּל (ילי) יְמֵי־נֹחַ תְּשַׁע מֵאוֹת שָׁנָה וַחֲמִשִּׁים שָׁנָה
וַיָּמֹת׃ פ י (א) וְאֵלֶּה תּוֹלְדֹת בְּנֵי־נֹחַ שֵׁם חָם וָיָפֶת וַיִּוָּלְדוּ
לָהֶם בָּנִים אַחַר הַמַּבּוּל׃ (ב) בְּנֵי יֶפֶת גֹּמֶר וּמָגוֹג וּמָדַי וְיָוָן
וְתֻבָל וּמֶשֶׁךְ וְתִירָס׃ (ג) וּבְנֵי גֹּמֶר אַשְׁכְּנַז וְרִיפַת וְתֹגַרְמָה׃
(ד) וּבְנֵי יָוָן אֱלִישָׁה וְתַרְשִׁישׁ כִּתִּים וְדֹדָנִים׃ (ה) מֵאֵלֶּה

וְאֵלֶּה - Tremendous growth now occurs within the generations of the sons of Noah. As the population rises, separation and division takes place between individuals, nations, and the land.

This story conceals a lesson pertaining to the perils of disunity. Disunity is the root cause of all chaos - be it in health, relationships, finances, or global turmoil. This story represents the seed and birth of disunity, which in turn creates disunity in the cells of our body, among family members, in our communities, and in our world.

This reading banishes the barriers that have created separation and conflict among people throughout history. A great Light of unity shines upon us, healing and uniting us into one true global village. This healing extends to the very cells of our body, engendering health and well-being.

נִפְרְד֞וּ אִיֵּ֤י הַגּוֹיִם֙ בְּאַרְצֹתָ֔ם אִ֖ישׁ לִלְשֹׁנ֑וֹ לְמִשְׁפְּחֹתָ֖ם בְּגֽוֹיֵהֶֽם: (ו) וּבְנֵ֣י חָ֔ם כּ֥וּשׁ וּמִצְרַ֖יִם (מצר) וּפ֥וּט וּכְנָֽעַן: (ז) וּבְנֵ֣י כ֔וּשׁ סְבָא֙ וַֽחֲוִילָ֔ה וְסַבְתָּ֥ה וְרַעְמָ֖ה וְסַבְתְּכָ֑א וּבְנֵ֥י רַעְמָ֖ה שְׁבָ֥א וּדְדָֽן: (ח) וְכ֖וּשׁ יָלַ֣ד אֶת־נִמְרֹ֑ד ה֣וּא הֵחֵ֔ל לִֽהְי֥וֹת גִּבֹּ֖ר בָּאָֽרֶץ: (ט) ה֤וּא־הָיָה (יהה) גִבֹּֽר־צַ֨יִד֙ לִפְנֵ֣י יְהֹוָ֔הֆ עַל־כֵּן֙ יֵֽאָמַ֔ר כְּנִמְרֹ֛ד גִּבּ֥וֹר צַ֖יִד לִפְנֵ֥י יְהֹוָֽהֆ (י) וַתְּהִ֨י רֵאשִׁ֤ית מַמְלַכְתּוֹ֙ בָּבֶ֔ל וְאֶ֖רֶךְ וְאַכַּ֣ד וְכַלְנֵ֑ה בְּאֶ֖רֶץ שִׁנְעָֽר: (יא) מִן־הָאָ֥רֶץ (מילוי אלהים ע"ה) הַהִ֖וא יָצָ֣א אַשּׁ֑וּר וַיִּ֨בֶן֙ אֶת־נִ֣ינְוֵ֔ה וְאֶת־רְחֹבֹ֥ת עִ֖יר (מזוזך, סנדלפון, ערי) וְאֶת־כָּֽלַח: (יב) וְֽאֶת־רֶ֔סֶן בֵּ֥ין נִֽינְוֵ֖ה וּבֵ֣ין כָּ֑לַח הִ֖וא הָעִ֥יר (מזוזך, סנדלפון, ערי) הַגְּדֹלָֽה: (יג) וּמִצְרַ֡יִם (מצר) יָלַ֣ד אֶת־לוּדִ֧ים וְאֶת־עֲנָמִ֛ים וְאֶת־לְהָבִ֖ים וְאֶת־נַפְתֻּחִֽים: (יד) וְֽאֶת־פַּתְרֻסִ֞ים וְאֶת־ כַּסְלֻחִים֙ אֲשֶׁ֨ר יָצְא֤וּ מִשָּׁם֙ פְּלִשְׁתִּ֔ים וְאֶת־כַּפְתֹּרִֽים:ס (טו) וּכְנַ֗עַן יָלַ֛ד אֶת־צִידֹ֥ן בְּכֹר֖וֹ וְאֶת־חֵֽת: (טז) וְאֶת־הַיְבוּסִי֙ וְאֶת־הָ֣אֱמֹרִ֔י וְאֵ֖ת הַגִּרְגָּשִֽׁי: (יז) וְאֶת־הַֽחִוִּ֥י וְאֶת־הָֽעַרְקִ֖י וְאֶת־הַסִּינִֽי:

וּבְנֵי חָם - The majority of the world's population emerged from the sons of Ham, including Egypt and China. Relevant to us is the interconnectedness of all humanity. As we meditate to inject all the nations of the world with Light, we crush the seeds of intolerance and propagate lasting peace throughout existence. The concept of "love thy neighbor" is achieved in our day.

(יח) וְאֶת־הָאַרְוָדִי וְאֶת־הַצְּמָרִי וְאֶת־הַחֲמָתִי וְאַחַר נָפֹצוּ
מִשְׁפְּחוֹת הַכְּנַעֲנִי׃ (יט) וַיְהִי גְּבוּל הַכְּנַעֲנִי מִצִּידֹן בֹּאֲכָה
גְרָרָה עַד־עַזָּה בֹּאֲכָה סְדֹמָה וַעֲמֹרָה וְאַדְמָה וּצְבֹיִם עַד־
לָשַׁע׃ (כ) אֵלֶּה בְנֵי־חָם לְמִשְׁפְּחֹתָם לִלְשֹׁנֹתָם בְּאַרְצֹתָם
בְּגוֹיֵהֶם׃ ס (כא) וּלְשֵׁם יֻלַּד גַּם־הוּא אֲבִי כָּל (ילי) בְּנֵי־עֵבֶר
אֲחִי יֶפֶת הַגָּדוֹל (להוז, מבה עד״א)׃ (כב) בְּנֵי שֵׁם עֵילָם וְאַשּׁוּר
וְאַרְפַּכְשַׁד וְלוּד וַאֲרָם׃ (כג) וּבְנֵי אֲרָם עוּץ וְחוּל וְגֶתֶר
וָמַשׁ׃ (כד) וְאַרְפַּכְשַׁד יָלַד אֶת־שָׁלַח וְשֶׁלַח יָלַד אֶת־עֵבֶר׃
(כה) וּלְעֵבֶר יֻלַּד שְׁנֵי בָנִים שֵׁם הָאֶחָד (אהבה) פֶּלֶג כִּי בְיָמָיו
נִפְלְגָה הָאָרֶץ (מילוי אלהים ע״ה) וְשֵׁם אָחִיו יָקְטָן׃ (כו) וְיָקְטָן
יָלַד אֶת־אַלְמוֹדָד וְאֶת־שָׁלֶף וְאֶת־חֲצַרְמָוֶת וְאֶת־יָרַח׃
(כז) וְאֶת־הֲדוֹרָם וְאֶת־אוּזָל וְאֶת־דִּקְלָה׃ (כח) וְאֶת־עוֹבָל
וְאֶת־אֲבִימָאֵל וְאֶת־שְׁבָא׃ (כט) וְאֶת־אוֹפִר וְאֶת־חֲוִילָה
וְאֶת־יוֹבָב כָּל (ילי) אֵלֶּה בְּנֵי יָקְטָן׃ (ל) וַיְהִי מוֹשָׁבָם מִמֵּשָׁא
בֹּאֲכָה סְפָרָה הַר הַקֶּדֶם׃ (לא) אֵלֶּה בְנֵי־שֵׁם לְמִשְׁפְּחֹתָם
לִלְשֹׁנֹתָם בְּאַרְצֹתָם לְגוֹיֵהֶם׃ (לב) אֵלֶּה מִשְׁפְּחֹת בְּנֵי־נֹחַ
לְתוֹלְדֹתָם בְּגוֹיֵהֶם וּמֵאֵלֶּה נִפְרְדוּ הַגּוֹיִם בָּאָרֶץ אַחַר
הַמַּבּוּל׃ פ

Seventh Reading - David - Malchut

יא (א) וַיְהִי כָל (ילי) ־הָאָרֶץ (מילוי אלהים ע״ה) שָׂפָה אֶחָת וּדְבָרִים

שָׂפָה אֶחָת - We are told by the Torah that the whole Earth was of "one language" and that the people of this generation used brick and stone to build "a city and a tower" that reached up to Heaven. According to the Zohar, there are two parallel worlds in existence - the pure and the impure, the holy and the evil. Just as there are Ten Sfirot within the holy and pure side, there are also Ten Sfirot on the side of the evil world.

The city and the tower that reached to Heaven actually refer to the Ten Sfirot of the impure world. The city correlates to the realm of Chochmah on the evil side. The tower correlates to the realm of Binah on the dark side.

The bricks and stones used to build the "city and tower" are the letters of the Hebrew alphabet. This is also the "one language" of the Earth that is spoken of by the Torah. The verse "Let us make ourselves a name" is another reference to the wondrous power of the Hebrew letters.

The Zohar explains that the people of this generation were spiritually advanced but wicked, drawn to the dark influences of the Other Side. They discovered the secret wisdom of Kabbalah left behind by Noah and used it to gain control over the world.

Through the power of the Hebrew letters and through that people's unbroken unity, these negative souls ascended into the highest spiritual worlds - Chochmah and Binah of the Dark Side - to use this negative energy for evil purposes. They intended to challenge God and seek world domination.

Unity, being the most powerful force in existence, made it impossible even for God to stop them. Thus, the Zohar states:

And if they, because they were of one heart and one desire, all spoke the Holy Language, it is written: "Nothing that they have planned to do will be withheld from them...."
- Zohar, Volume II, Noach, 42:386

We learn that unified evil will always be able to defeat and conquer the side

(ראה) אֲחָדִים׃ (ב) וַיְהִי בְּנָסְעָם מִקֶּדֶם וַיִּמְצְאוּ בִקְעָה בְּאֶרֶץ
שִׁנְעָר וַיֵּשְׁבוּ שָׁם׃ (ג) וַיֹּאמְרוּ אִישׁ אֶל־רֵעֵהוּ הָבָה נִלְבְּנָה
לְבֵנִים וְנִשְׂרְפָה לִשְׂרֵפָה וַתְּהִי לָהֶם הַלְּבֵנָה לְאָבֶן וְהַחֵמָר

of good if disunity exists among the good people. The only way to defeat unified evil is through total unity on the side of good.

Consequently, God was forced to create disunity to break this rebellious people. For that reason, He confused their language, creating seventy other tongues and thereby severing their lines of communication. Over the generations up to this very day, the power and purpose of Hebrew has been lost to humanity.

In our current generation, however, wrote the sainted Kabbalist Rav Yehuda Ashlag, evil people will no longer seek out Kabbalah, for they will have been seduced by the material world and all of its illusionary riches. Only the good will embrace this wisdom, and thus the Kabbalistic secrets of the letters can now again be revealed to the world.

All these magnificent forces are now available for our use, which is the underlying purpose of this book. This awesome spiritual power is herewith placed in your hands. Through meditation, we demolish the "city" and tear down the "tower" of the negative forces, forever freeing ourselves from its evil influences. As the Zohar states so emphatically:

Like the Holy Side, the Other Side has no power to rule in the world without a city and a tower.
- Zohar, Volume II, Noach, 42:351

Through Kabbalah and Torah, we bring the Age of Messiah upon us immediately, in a kindhearted, compassionate manner, minus any judgment, for the Zohar states:
For us, and the friends who occupy themselves with the Torah and are of one heart and one desire…. Nothing that we want to do will be withheld from us.
- Zohar, Volume II, Noach, 42:386

הָיָה (יהה) לָהֶם לַחֹמֶר: (ד) וַיֹּאמְרוּ הָבָה | נִבְנֶה־לָּנוּ (מום) עִיר
וּמִגְדָּל וְרֹאשׁוֹ בַשָּׁמַיִם (י"פ טל) וְנַעֲשֶׂה־לָּנוּ (מום)
(סנזופך, סנדלפון, ערי)
שֵׁם פֶּן־נָפוּץ עַל־פְּנֵי (וחכמה, בינה) כָל (ילי) ־הָאָרֶץ (מילוי אלהים ע"ה): (ה)
וַיֵּרֶד (ריי) יְהֹוָאדניאהדונהי לִרְאֹת אֶת־הָעִיר (סנזופך, סנדלפון, ערי) וְאֶת־
הַמִּגְדָּל אֲשֶׁר בָּנוּ בְּנֵי הָאָדָם (מ"ה): (ו) וַיֹּאמֶר יְהֹוָאדניאהדונהי הֵן
עַם אֶחָד (אהבה) וְשָׂפָה אַחַת לְכֻלָּם וְזֶה הַחִלָּם לַעֲשׂוֹת וְעַתָּה
לֹא־יִבָּצֵר מֵהֶם כֹּל (ילי) אֲשֶׁר יָזְמוּ לַעֲשׂוֹת: (ז) הָבָה נֵרְדָה
וְנָבְלָה שָׁם שְׂפָתָם אֲשֶׁר לֹא יִשְׁמְעוּ אִישׁ שְׂפַת רֵעֵהוּ: (וז)
וַיָּפֶץ יְהֹוָאדניאהדונהי אֹתָם מִשָּׁם עַל־פְּנֵי (וחכמה, בינה) כָל (ילי) ־
הָאָרֶץ (מילוי אלהים ע"ה) וַיַּחְדְּלוּ לִבְנֹת הָעִיר (סנזופך, סנדלפון, ערי): (ט)
עַל־כֵּן קָרָא שְׁמָהּ בָּבֶל כִּי־שָׁם בָּלַל יְהֹוָאדניאהדונהי שְׂפַת
כָּל (ילי) ־הָאָרֶץ (מילוי אלהים ע"ה) וּמִשָּׁם הֱפִיצָם יְהֹוָאדניאהדונהי עַל־
פְּנֵי (וחכמה, בינה) כָּל (ילי) ־הָאָרֶץ (מילוי אלהים ע"ה): פ (י) אֵלֶּה תּוֹלְדֹת

אֵלֶּה - The generations from Noah to Abraham are ten, the same number of generations as between Adam and Noah. The Kabbalists reveal that this indicates the cyclical structure of our universe. Moreover, according to the Kabbalists, reality is composed of ten dimensions. The Kabbalists refer to these as the Ten Sfirot, meaning "ten emanations" of Light. These ten dimensions were formed when the infinite Divine Force of Energy, which kabbalists call the Light, contracted itself. This contraction created a tiny, microscopic point of darkness into which our universe was born.

Sixteenth-century Kabbalist Rabbi Isaac Luria (the Ari) revealed that six

of the ten dimensions compacted and enfolded into one super-dimension known as Zeir Anpin. Centuries after the ancient kabbalists revealed that reality exists in ten dimensions and that six of those dimensions are folded into one, modern physicists have arrived at the same conclusion with the emergence of superstring theory.

Dr. Michio Kaku is an internationally recognized authority in theoretical physics and a leading proponent of superstring theory. In his book Hyperspace, Dr. Kaku writes:

The Universe is a symphony of vibrating strings. And when strings move in ten-dimensional space-time, they warp the space-time surrounding them in precisely the way predicted by general relativity. Physicists retrieve our more familiar four-dimensional Universe by assuming that, during the Big Bang, six of the ten dimensions curled up (or "compactified") into a tiny ball, while the remaining four expanded explosively, giving us the Universe we see.

Those six dimensions that lie just beyond our perception are the source and fountainhead of all the knowledge and fulfillment that appear in our world. This is the realm that Plato wrote about—the timeless world of Ideas or Forms that exists beyond the physical world of the five senses.

Sir Isaac Newton, considered to be the one of the greatest scientists ever, wrote:

Plato, traveling to Egypt when the Jews were numerous in that country, learnt there his metaphysical opinions about the superior beings and formal causes of all things, which he calls Ideas and which the Kabbalists call Sfirot.... (MS. Yahuda, 15.7, p. 137v)

Connection with this multi-dimensional realm is the key to genuine control and fulfillment in life. But it's not easy to do. Therefore, we have the Torah and other Kabbalistic tools such as the Zohar to help us bridge the physical with the spiritual realms.

Whenever the Torah alludes to the Ten Sfirot in a coded fashion, such as the Ten Generations, it is an indication that we are making contact with these supernal spheres. In accordance, Light flows into our world, creating

שֵׁם בֶּן־מְאַת שָׁנָה וַיּוֹלֶד אֶת־אַרְפַּכְשָׁד שְׁנָתַיִם
אַחַר הַמַּבּוּל: (יא) וַיְחִי־שֵׁם אַחֲרֵי הוֹלִידוֹ אֶת־אַרְפַּכְשָׁד
חֲמֵשׁ מֵאוֹת שָׁנָה וַיּוֹלֶד בָּנִים וּבָנוֹת: ס (יב) וְאַרְפַּכְשַׁד חַי
חָמֵשׁ וּשְׁלֹשִׁים שָׁנָה וַיּוֹלֶד אֶת־שָׁלַח: (יג) וַיְחִי אַרְפַּכְשַׁד
אַחֲרֵי הוֹלִידוֹ אֶת־שֶׁלַח שָׁלֹשׁ שָׁנִים וְאַרְבַּע מֵאוֹת שָׁנָה
וַיּוֹלֶד בָּנִים וּבָנוֹת: ס (יד) וְשֶׁלַח חַי שְׁלֹשִׁים שָׁנָה וַיּוֹלֶד אֶת־
עֵבֶר: (טו) וַיְחִי־שֶׁלַח אַחֲרֵי הוֹלִידוֹ אֶת־עֵבֶר שָׁלֹשׁ שָׁנִים
וְאַרְבַּע מֵאוֹת שָׁנָה וַיּוֹלֶד בָּנִים וּבָנוֹת: ס (טז) וַיְחִי־עֵבֶר
אַרְבַּע וּשְׁלֹשִׁים שָׁנָה וַיּוֹלֶד אֶת־פָּלֶג: (יז) וַיְחִי־עֵבֶר אַחֲרֵי
הוֹלִידוֹ אֶת־פֶּלֶג שְׁלֹשִׁים שָׁנָה וְאַרְבַּע מֵאוֹת שָׁנָה וַיּוֹלֶד
בָּנִים וּבָנוֹת: ס (יח) וַיְחִי־פֶלֶג שְׁלֹשִׁים שָׁנָה וַיּוֹלֶד אֶת־רְעוּ:
(יט) וַיְחִי־פֶלֶג אַחֲרֵי הוֹלִידוֹ אֶת־רְעוּ תֵּשַׁע שָׁנִים וּמָאתַיִם

order out of chaos, as it helps us correct our iniquities and hasten our Final Redemption.

וַיְחִי - During the ten generations leading to Noah, the average lifespan of humans was approximately 300 years. During the generations leading to Abraham, the average lifespan fell to approximately 100 years. As we journey further away from the time of Adam and the Garden of Eden—where immortality was the reality—death becomes a stronger force in the world.

Using the Zohar, Kabbalah-water, and the Torah, we can "travel back" to the Garden and recapture the Light of Immortality. Moreover, we can now use as an antidote to death those verses in the Torah that speak of all the generations, reversing the aging process and hastening the arrival of immortality in our lifetime.

שָׁנָה וַיּוֹלֶד בָּנִים וּבָנוֹת: ס (כ) וַיְחִי רְעוּ שְׁתַּיִם וּשְׁלֹשִׁים
שָׁנָה וַיּוֹלֶד אֶת־שְׂרוּג: (כא) וַיְחִי רְעוּ אַחֲרֵי הוֹלִידוֹ אֶת־
שְׂרוּג שֶׁבַע שָׁנִים וּמָאתַיִם שָׁנָה וַיּוֹלֶד בָּנִים וּבָנוֹת: ס (כב)
וַיְחִי שְׂרוּג שְׁלֹשִׁים שָׁנָה וַיּוֹלֶד אֶת־ נָחוֹר: (כג) וַיְחִי שְׂרוּג
אַחֲרֵי הוֹלִידוֹ אֶת־נָחוֹר מָאתַיִם שָׁנָה וַיּוֹלֶד בָּנִים וּבָנוֹת:ס
(כד) וַיְחִי נָחוֹר תֵּשַׁע וְעֶשְׂרִים שָׁנָה וַיּוֹלֶד אֶת־תָּרַח: (כה)
וַיְחִי נָחוֹר אַחֲרֵי הוֹלִידוֹ אֶת־תֶּרַח תְּשַׁע־ עֶשְׂרֵה שָׁנָה
וּמְאַת שָׁנָה וַיּוֹלֶד בָּנִים וּבָנוֹת:ס (כו) וַיְחִי־תֶרַח שִׁבְעִים
שָׁנָה וַיּוֹלֶד אֶת־אַבְרָם אֶת־נָחוֹר וְאֶת־הָרָן: (כז) וְאֵלֶּה
תּוֹלְדֹת תֶּרַח תֶּרַח הוֹלִיד אֶת־ אַבְרָם אֶת־נָחוֹר וְאֶת־הָרָן
וְהָרָן הוֹלִיד אֶת־לוֹט: (כח) וַיָּמָת הָרָן עַל־פְּנֵי (חכמה, בינה) תֶּרַח

אַבְרָם - In a story told in the Midrash, Abram is thrown into an oven by Nimrod. Abram is not burned or hurt and escapes unharmed. Abram employed the instrument of the 72 Names of God, which imbued him with the power of mind over matter to achieve this miracle. Through the name of Abraham and the Light of this portion, we can tap into the 72 Names and attain a state of mind over matter. When problems heat up our lives and we find ourselves tossed into the "fire," we can overcome and triumph over the physical world of chaos. It begins with our having total certainty regarding the Light and with our resisting our natural [negative] reflexive responses. [Possessing] these two traits are [will effect] a miraculous change of human nature and in turn will ignite miracles of Mother Nature.

All humanity is herewith empowered with the ability to attain mind over matter and absolute control over the physical world.

אָבִ֑יו בְּאֶ֥רֶץ מוֹלַדְתּ֖וֹ בְּא֥וּר כַּשְׂדִּֽים׃

Maftir

(כט) וַיִּקַּ֨ח (וזעם) אַבְרָ֧ם וְנָח֛וֹר לָהֶ֖ם נָשִׁ֑ים שֵׁ֤ם אֵֽשֶׁת־אַבְרָם֙
שָׂרָ֔י וְשֵׁ֤ם אֵֽשֶׁת־נָחוֹר֙ מִלְכָּ֔ה בַּת־הָרָ֥ן אֲבִֽי־מִלְכָּ֖ה וַאֲבִ֥י
יִסְכָּֽה׃ (ל) וַתְּהִ֥י שָׂרַ֖י עֲקָרָ֑ה אֵ֥ין לָ֖הּ וָלָֽד׃ (לא) וַיִּקַּ֨ח (וזעם)
תֶּ֜רַח אֶת־אַבְרָ֣ם בְּנ֗וֹ וְאֶת־ל֤וֹט בֶּן־הָרָן֙ בֶּן־בְּנ֔וֹ וְאֵת֙ שָׂרַ֣י
כַּלָּת֔וֹ אֵ֖שֶׁת אַבְרָ֣ם בְּנ֑וֹ וַיֵּצְא֨וּ אִתָּ֜ם מֵא֣וּר כַּשְׂדִּ֗ים לָלֶ֙כֶת֙
אַ֣רְצָה כְּנַ֔עַן וַיָּבֹ֥אוּ עַד־חָרָ֖ן וַיֵּ֥שְׁבוּ שָֽׁם׃ (לב) וַיִּהְי֣וּ יְמֵי־תֶ֔רַח
חָמֵ֥שׁ שָׁנִ֖ים וּמָאתַ֣יִם שָׁנָ֑ה וַיָּ֥מָת תֶּ֖רַח בְּחָרָֽן׃ פפפ

The Haftarah of Noach

This Haftarah refers to "Noach's Flood." When Sodom and Gomorrah were destined to be destroyed, Abraham prayed for them. But Noach didn't pray for the people who would perish in the flood. He himself was righteous, but he didn't have the extra care for those around him. Isaiah is telling us that Noach did not cause the Flood, but he did not try to avoid it either.

ישעיהו פרק נד

(א) רָנִּי עֲקָרָה לֹא יָלָדָה פִּצְחִי רִנָּה וְצַהֲלִי לֹא־חָלָה
(להח) כִּי־רַבִּים בְּנֵי־שׁוֹמֵמָה מִבְּנֵי בְעוּלָה אָמַר יְהוָה׃ (ב)
הַרְחִיבִי ׀ מְקוֹם אָהֳלֵךְ וִירִיעוֹת מִשְׁכְּנוֹתַיִךְ יַטּוּ אַל־
תַּחְשֹׂכִי הַאֲרִיכִי מֵיתָרַיִךְ וִיתֵדֹתַיִךְ חַזֵּקִי (פהל)׃ (ג) כִּי־יָמִין
וּשְׂמֹאול תִּפְרֹצִי וְזַרְעֵךְ גּוֹיִם יִירָשׁ וְעָרִים נְשַׁמּוֹת יוֹשִׁיבוּ׃ (ד)
אַל־תִּירְאִי כִּי־לֹא תֵבוֹשִׁי וְאַל־תִּכָּלְמִי כִּי לֹא תַחְפִּירִי כִּי
בֹשֶׁת עֲלוּמַיִךְ תִּשְׁכָּחִי וְחֶרְפַּת אַלְמְנוּתַיִךְ לֹא תִזְכְּרִי־עוֹד׃
(ה) כִּי בֹעֲלַיִךְ עֹשַׂיִךְ יְהוָה צְבָאוֹת (פני שכינה) שְׁמוֹ (מהש) וְגֹאֲלֵךְ
קְדוֹשׁ יִשְׂרָאֵל אֱלֹהֵי (רמב, ילה) כָל־הָאָרֶץ יִקָּרֵא׃ (ו) כִּי־כְאִשָּׁה
עֲזוּבָה וַעֲצוּבַת רוּחַ קְרָאָךְ יְהוָה וְאֵשֶׁת נְעוּרִים כִּי תִמָּאֵס
אָמַר אֱלֹהָיִךְ׃ (רמב, ילה) (ז) בְּרֶגַע קָטֹן עֲזַבְתִּיךְ וּבְרַחֲמִים
גְּדֹלִים אֲקַבְּצֵךְ׃ (ח) בְּשֶׁצֶף קֶצֶף הִסְתַּרְתִּי פָנַי רֶגַע מִמֵּךְ
וּבְחֶסֶד (ע"ב, יוד הי ויו הי, י יה יהו יהוה) עוֹלָם רִחַמְתִּיךְ אָמַר גֹּאֲלֵךְ
יְהוָה׃ {ס}

(ט) כִּי־מֵי ^(ילי) נֹחַ' זֹאת לִי אֲשֶׁר נִשְׁבַּ֫עְתִּי מֵעֲבֹ֫ר מֵי^(ילי)־נֹחַ

עוֹד עַל־הָאָ֫רֶץ כֵּן נִשְׁבַּ֫עְתִּי מִקְּצֹף עָלַ֫יִךְ וּמִגְּעָר־בָּֽךְ: ^(י)

כִּי הֶהָרִים' יָמ֫וּשׁוּ וְהַגְּבָעוֹת תְּמוּטֶ֫ינָה וְחַסְדִּי ^{(ע״ב, יוד הי ויו הי,}

^{י ה יהו יהוה)} מֵאִתֵּךְ לֹא־יָמ֫וּשׁ וּבְרִית שְׁלוֹמִי' לֹא תָמ֫וּט אָמַר

מְרַחֲמֵךְ יְהֹוָֽה: {ס}

Lesson of Lech Lecha

"Get thee out of thy country, and from thy kindred, and from thy father's house."

This week's portion begins with the Creator telling Abraham to leave his home, to leave everything he has, and to go to a land that the Creator will identify to him.

Abraham's journey refers to more than everyday traveling.

God tells Abraham: "Go out from your homeland. Leave the place you were born. Leave your father's house." What does this tell us? Our sages explain that God is telling Abraham to begin an internal journey as well as a physical one.

It is human nature to stay with what we are used to, to keep doing what we have always done and what our friends and family are doing. This includes sticking with not only the restaurants and ballgames everyone is attending, but also with what's spiritually "in vogue." If it is "in" to be spiritual, many people say, "Well, I'll be spiritual." But the hardest thing–and the most rewarding–in spiritual work is to do what most people don't do. That's why the Creator states the "going out" of Abraham in so many different ways and why the physical act of leaving was only one element in Abraham's test.

Abraham understood all this. He knew he had to undertake an inner change, and he chose to do so–to be totally with the Light. Abraham completely "left" the desire to receive for the self alone. Whoever chooses to go against ego-driven desires merits the Creator's presence all the time. Because of Abraham's choice, the Creator told him, "Whoever blesses you is blessed. Whoever curses you is cursed. And with you, everyone will be blessed." In the same way, when we sincerely choose to embark on our spiritual journey, we can also bring blessing to the whole world.

Abraham is a symbol of conquering the desire to receive for the self alone. When a person reaches that level–at that precise second that he decides to go against the desire to receive for the self alone–that's when God connects to him. When Abraham made that decision, he instantly became holy. Therefore, what God is really asking of us is not to become righteous in one day, but to decide that we want to leave behind the desire of the ego.

It is not easy. Breaking away from the life we are used to is very difficult. But this is exactly why we gain so much by doing so. Whenever people stop

themselves, for example, from speaking with malice or from showing anger, they receive so much Light that even angels can't fathom the amount. We learn from Abraham that the world is blessed only as a result of the effort of people who leave their ego-desires. As the Vilna Gaon wrote, conquering those desires is the most important work we have in this world. Once again, we don't have to become righteous in a second; we just have to make the decision to want to become righteous, and in that second that we decide, we open ourselves to receive the Light.

More on Lech Lecha.

Regarding the portion of Lech Lecha, the great Reb Zusha explained that when it says "Leave your land," the portion refers to our personal dirt. When it says to leave your birthplace, it refers to the negativity that came through our mother–the baggage in our souls that is part of us at birth because we did not take care of it the last time we were here. And when the passage says, "Your father's house," it is referring to the negativity that came through our father from our last life. Only when we've left those negative elements behind are we able to go to the land where all the Light comes from.

The Nes Aschar, Rabbi Tzvi Elimelech Obdinov, reveals another very important teaching in this portion. Life is not just a matter of finding ways to make money or to have fun. We should be aware that in every moment and in every circumstance, the Creator is giving us an opportunity to find what we need. The real opportunity is not in what we do or don't do, but in the connection to the Light that is there for us.

If we have a little headache, for example, it is exactly what we need and deserve. It is based on what we did or perhaps what we could have done and should have done. Everything is weighed on the scale, and everything that results is measure for measure correct. But it is not for us to figure out what that judgment should be. We have to be aware that the Creator sees the whole picture even if we can't see it ourselves. It's not good enough to do good things. Sometimes, there are bad reasons why we do good things. Someone could be a very giving person, but only to gain power and control or perhaps so that everyone will see how good he is. Then, if there's a judgment in his life, he thinks, "I did so much good, but why is the Creator not accepting that good? How could He do this to me?"

If we can just understand that we don't see everything, then we'll see more.

There is a story that happened in the time of the Ari, Rabbi Isaac Luria, that can help us understand this. One Friday afternoon, a thought came to a baker. He wanted to give a sacrifice to the Creator. He baked the most

fragrant, heavenly bread he had ever baked.

He came to the synagogue with the bread. He didn't know exactly what to do, so he went to the Ark and opened it. He said, "God, please accept this sacrifice. I want to be closer to you." Then he put the bread inside the Ark, closed it, and left.

Five minutes later, a beggar came into the synagogue. He'd begged for food his whole life. He went to the Ark and began to cry, pleading, "Please, God, help me." He opened the Ark and inside were two loaves of bread God gave him. He beamed with joy, not only for the bread itself but for the miracle that the Creator deemed him worthy to receive.

The next morning, the baker who had placed the bread in the Ark looked to see if God had accepted his sacrifice. Ah, the bread was gone! He was the happiest person alive. He went to his wife, hugged and kissed her and started dancing with her, and she didn't know why.

A week later, he thought, "You know, maybe God will accept another sacrifice." He brought the bread to the Ark–and again, the same thing happened! The beggar took the loaves. This went on, week after week, year after year. Fourteen whole years passed.

Then one Friday afternoon, the rabbi of the synagogue fell asleep in his office. Suddenly, he heard someone at the Ark mumbling some words about some sacrifice. Very quietly, the rabbi looked into the synagogue and saw the baker put bread into the Ark and leave. A few minutes later, the beggar entered and pleaded, "God, please give me some food." Then he took the loaves out the ark, beamed with joy, and ran away.

The rabbi said, "I have to fix this." The following day, he called both baker and beggar into his office. He said, "I don't know what you think is going on here. You say you are giving God a sacrifice. You say God's giving you food. But there's no such thing happening. One of you puts the bread in, the other one takes it out. God is not in on it.
That very second, in walked Rabbi Isaac Luria. He said to the rabbi, "Rabbi, prepare yourself to die. You are going to leave this world before the end of the day."

The rabbi was astonished and terrified. "What did I do? Why me? Why?"

Rabbi Isaac Luria said, "Of course, God is in on it. Don't you think it is a miracle that for fourteen years the baker arrived just before the beggar? Not even once did they miss each other in fourteen years. The Creator had such

joy and happiness that this was taking place that the Angel of Death could not enter your synagogue. God has many ways of receiving a sacrifice. One of His ways is by giving it to the needy. The happiness the Creator had is what kept you alive for these fourteen years. You were supposed to leave this world on that Friday when this beautiful story began, and you would have died then except for the happiness that God was receiving–just as this beggar would have died if he had not received the bread."

Not everything we think is real is real. Some of the things we think are real are the most unreal things in the world, and those are the things we need to leave behind. We can learn that from this week's portion.

Synopsis of Lech Lecha

Israel: A State of Mind, a State of Spirituality

The name of this portion is Lech Lecha, which means "going out." The basic thought and spiritual influence behind this week's Torah portion is to help us go out of ourselves - to escape the bonds of our ego, to break free of self-interest and emancipate ourselves from our illusionary comfort zone. True spiritual Light is only found outside the box in which we live physically, emotionally, and spiritually.

Abram is told to migrate to Israel. Israel is a code word symbolizing a higher level of spiritual existence. According to the Zohar, this higher level spirituality corresponds to the Sfirat Chesed, which embodies the energy of mercy.

This was Abram's destiny - to be the channel and conduit bringing kindhearted mercy into our physical world for all generations to sweeten [CF1] the judgments set forth against us by our own negative deeds.

To do so, Abram is required to leave his country, his birthplace and his father's house, all of which are metaphors for his lower state of consciousness. In effect, Abram must shed the shells of negativity that engulf him. He must raise his consciousness and elevate his headspace to a higher level of spirituality.

Each of us has the same mission and destiny as Abram. All of us are commanded to migrate to Israel - Israel being a state of mind, a level of spirituality, and a deeper connection to the Light of the Creator.

To move to Israel means to move from being a reactive individual to a person

who is deeply proactive, spiritual and loving.

Through the merit of Abraham, we achieve this growth in a merciful manner as opposed to through the path of torment. (Tragedies that befall us in life occur solely to correct past negative deeds and to motivate us onto the spiritual path.)

Going out of our country, our birthplace, and the house of our father means that we must let go of our ego, our old ways of thinking, and our negative habitual behavioral patterns if we are to connect to the Light and find positive, eternal fulfillment.

The sacred words that tell this story remove the shells and blockages in our consciousness so that we can attain the state of Israel within our own soul.

The Light flowing through these letters softens our resolve in situations where our stubbornness and ego prevent us from embracing spiritual change.

First Reading - Abraham - Chesed

יב (א) וַיֹּאמֶר יְהֹוָהאדניאהדונהי אֶל־אַבְרָם לֶךְ־לְךָ מֵאַרְצְךָ

וַיֹּאמֶר - The Zohar tells us that Abram became wise in the ways of the supernal worlds. He studied the Ten Sfirot and the spiritual and physical subatomic realms of reality. He mastered the wisdom of the stars, the planets, and the signs of the zodiac. However, the Zohar states that "get you out" also meant that Abram should not have concerned himself with horoscopes, the idea being that human beings have the ability to rise above planetary influences and become the captains of their own fate.

Here in this portion, we ascend above the plane of the planets and their negative influences.

וַיֹּאמֶר - The story of Abram's migration to Israel is a metaphor concealing an even deeper concept. It pertains to the journey of our own soul as it leaves the Upper World (our Father's house) and begins its sojourn in our earthly realm, where it is given the garment of a human body to utilize in its quest to achieve spiritual transformation.

Spiritual transformation, in essence, concerns the nullification of our ego and the subjugation of the body's reactive, impulsive nature. In turn, we unleash the will and power of our soul, which inspires proactive behavior and unconditional love for others.

Our soul is part of God, a spark of our supernal Father. Thus, our soul is the true father and governor of our body. This truth is found in the name of Abram.

Av is Hebrew for "father," while Ram is Hebrew for "supernal."
Thus, God speaking to Abram is a code for God speaking to our divine supernal soul. In this way, Abram's task is our task. The phrase "Get you out…" actually refers to liberating our soul from the prison and bonds of our physical body.

לֶךְ־לְךָ - Before the soul leaves the Upper World, it stands before the Creator and swears to pursue the spiritual path and achieve transformation.

וּמִמּוֹלַדְתְּךָ וּמִבֵּית (ב״פ ראה) אָבִיךָ אֶל־הָאָרֶץ (מילוי אלהים ע״ה)
אֲשֶׁר אַרְאֶךָּ׃ (ב) וְאֶעֶשְׂךָ לְגוֹי גָּדוֹל (להח, מבה עד״א) וַאֲבָרֶכְךָ
וַאֲגַדְּלָה שְׁמֶךָ וֶהְיֵה (יהה) (יהוה) בְּרָכָה׃ (ג) וַאֲבָרְכָה מְבָרְכֶיךָ
וּמְקַלֶּלְךָ אָאֹר וְנִבְרְכוּ (יהוה ריבוע יהוה ריבוע מ״ה) בְךָ כֹּל (ילי) מִשְׁפְּחֹת
הָאֲדָמָה׃ (ד) וַיֵּלֶךְ (כלי) אַבְרָם כַּאֲשֶׁר דִּבֶּר (ראה) אֵלָיו
יְהוָהאדניאהדונהי וַיֵּלֶךְ (כלי) אִתּוֹ לוֹט **וְאַבְרָם** בֶּן־חָמֵשׁ שָׁנִים

However, the perpetual pull and tug of the material world is so powerful that we forget our true purpose in life as we succumb to the seductive illusions of physical existence. Power, prestige, greed, monetary wealth, and self-indulgence are powerful enticements that lead us astray as we mature into adulthood.
Hence, we need the Light of this portion to reawaken our desire to remain true to our own soul's original commitment to pursue the spiritual path.

The act of connecting to this Torah portion is a part of the act of spiritual transformation. Thus, we are achieving our life's purpose in the here-and-now, especially when we share this Light with others through our kind behavior and selfless actions during the week.

וְאַבְרָם - Each of us is required to begin this task of spiritual transformation at age thirteen. This is when the power of our soul and the power of our free will are activated.
The Zohar states:
The soul will not start fulfilling the mission it was commanded to perform until it has completed thirteen years in this world. Because from the twelfth year onward, the soul is aroused to fulfill its task.
- Zohar, Volume III, 8:42

Abram, we're told in the Torah, is 75 years old when he leaves the country of Charan. Charan signifies both the negative physical world and the ego.

The Zohar says that Abram's age when he left his home is a code, alluding to ourselves: 7 + 5 = 12.

וְשִׁבְעִים שָׁנָה בְּצֵאתוֹ מֵחָרָן׃ (ה) וַיִּקַּח (וזעם) אַבְרָם אֶת־
שָׂרַי אִשְׁתּוֹ וְאֶת־לוֹט בֶּן־אָחִיו וְאֶת־כָּל (ילי) ־רְכוּשָׁם אֲשֶׁר
רָכָשׁוּ וְאֶת־הַנֶּפֶשׁ אֲשֶׁר־ עָשׂוּ בְחָרָן וַיֵּצְאוּ לָלֶכֶת אַרְצָה
כְּנַעַן וַיָּבֹאוּ אַרְצָה כְּנָעַן׃ (ו) וַיַּעֲבֹר (רפ״ח) אַבְרָם בָּאָרֶץ עַד
מְקוֹם שְׁכֶם עַד אֵלוֹן מוֹרֶה וְהַכְּנַעֲנִי אָז בָּאָרֶץ׃ (ז) וַיֵּרָא

During our first twelve years of life, we live within the domain of negativity without the ability to transform. At age thirteen, we have the power to go outside the desires of our body, just as Abram went out of Charan.

שְׁכֶם - At this point in time, the city of Sh'chem is not a significant or sacred landmark. However, the righteous sage Joseph is eventually buried there, transforming the city into a known spiritual landmark. Joseph's presence serves as a reservoir of spiritual Light that mankind has utilized to this very day.

However, through the eyes of the Kabbalist, Sh'chem is not a holy site because it became Joseph's resting place. Rather, Sh'chem was already a holy site; it was - and is - always an energy center, and for that very reason, Joseph found burial there. This Kabbalistic insight holds true for the city of Jerusalem as well. Since Jerusalem is the energy center and spiritual storehouse for the entire world, the Temple must reside there. Jerusalem is not holy because of the Temple's presence, but rather, the Temple resides in Jerusalem because the land itself is holy and divine.

Joseph, the Zohar tells us, represents the source of sustenance for our entire world. He corresponds to the Sfirat Yesod, the portal through which all Light and energy flow into our world. Thus, in this portion, we summon forth the power of Joseph and Sh'chem to eradicate poverty and purge darkness from the landscape of civilization. We draw down spiritual and physical sustenance for ourselves and for all humankind.

יְהֹוָאדניאהדונהי אֶל־אַבְרָם וַיֹּאמֶר לְזַרְעֲךָ אֶתֵּן אֶת־הָאָרֶץ
(מילוי אלהים ע"ה) הַזֹּאת וַיִּבֶן שָׁם מִזְבֵּחַ (זן) לַיהֹוָאדניאהדונהי הַנִּרְאֶה
אֵלָיו׃ (וז) וַיַּעְתֵּק מִשָּׁם הָהָרָה מִקֶּדֶם לְבֵית (ב"פ ראה) ־אֵל וַיֵּט
אָהֳלֹה בֵּית (ב"פ ראה) ־אֵל מִיָּם (ילי) וְהָעַי מִקֶּדֶם וַיִּבֶן־שָׁם
מִזְבֵּחַ (זן) לַיהֹוָאדניאהדונהי וַיִּקְרָא בְּשֵׁם יְהֹוָאדניאהדונהי׃ (ט)
וַיִּסַּע אַבְרָם הָלוֹךְ וְנָסוֹעַ הַנֶּגְבָּה׃
(י) וַיְהִי רָעָב בָּאָרֶץ וַיֵּרֶד (רי"י) אַבְרָם מִצְרַיְמָה (מצר) לָגוּר

וַיְהִי רָעָב - Any form of plague, be it hunger or disease, occurs through the collective negative actions of people. Each of us can be a carrier of plague, spiritually speaking, if we speak evil of friends or foes or if we consort with others who commit egocentric deeds, display intolerance, or bear hatred in their hearts for others. The Light cast here in this verse expels hatred and intolerance from our own hearts so that we may protect ourselves from disease and from being carriers of plagues. This Light abolishes plagues and disease from our planet and inspires gladness of heart in all mankind.

מִצְרַיְמָה - The Zohar reveals that Egypt is a code word for the depths of man's own negativity into which the divine sparks of Light have fallen. The great spiritual leaders of history often descended into these negative regions to retrieve and elevate the sparks trapped within the dark recesses of our being.

However, it goes against the grain of human nature to look inward and reflect upon one's own immoral attributes. Our five senses and ego are constantly tuned into the external environment around us. The introspection and self-scrutiny performed by Abram serve as a timeless repository of energy that is available to us through the sounds and vibrations that ignite at the reading of this portion.

שָׁם כִּי־כָבֵד הָרָעָב בָּאָרֶץ׃ (יא) וַיְהִי כַּאֲשֶׁר הִקְרִיב
לָבוֹא מִצְרָיְמָה (מצר) וַיֹּאמֶר אֶל־שָׂרַי אִשְׁתּוֹ הִנֵּה־נָא יָדַעְתִּי
כִּי אִשָּׁה יְפַת־מַרְאֶה אָתְּ׃ (יב) וְהָיָה (יהה) (יהוה) כִּי־יִרְאוּ אֹתָךְ
הַמִּצְרִים (מצר) וְאָמְרוּ אִשְׁתּוֹ זֹאת וְהָרְגוּ אֹתִי וְאֹתָךְ יְחַיּוּ׃ (יג)
אִמְרִי־נָא אֲחֹתִי אָתְּ לְמַעַן יִיטַב־לִי בַעֲבוּרֵךְ וְחָיְתָה נַפְשִׁי
בִּגְלָלֵךְ׃

The Light we now receive shines deep into our inner self, expelling the hardhearted qualities of our character from our being. The energy arising here elevates all the sparks that have fallen into matter. The Egypt within us and around us is conquered at last. Freedom and Light now radiate throughout the cosmos.

אִמְרִי־נָא - The Zohar teaches us that because it is forbidden to lie, Abram was not lying when he referred to his wife, Sarai, as his sister. Abram and Sarai are soul-mates. Therefore, Sarai represents the Shechinah, the female divine presence that shines in this world, and Abram represents the male divine presence. The Shechinah, according to the Zohar, is considered to be a sister to each of us. On the surface, Sarai is the wife of Abram, but Kabbalistically, Sarai is also the sister of Abram and thus sister to us all. So on a deeper spiritual level, Abram's words were true.

The sages of Kabbalah teach us never to take the Torah at face value - that any contradiction, paradox, or seemingly unspiritual event always conceals within itself a deeper truth and lesson for life. Therein lies the purpose of the Zohar and the wisdom of Kabbalah.

Moreover, Kabbalist Rav Yehuda Ashlag teaches us that even the smallest of our white lies prevents us from evolving spiritually. We must be truthful to others and, more importantly (and more difficult to achieve), we must be painfully truthful to ourselves. The courage to speak - and hear - the truth is summoned forth through the words spoken and heard in this portion.

Second Reading - Issac - Gvurah

(יד) וַיְהִי כְּבוֹא אַבְרָם מִצְרָיְמָה (מצר) וַיִּרְאוּ הַמִּצְרִים (מצר)
אֶת־הָאִשָּׁה כִּי־יָפָה הִוא מְאֹד: (טו) וַיִּרְאוּ אֹתָהּ שָׂרֵי
פַרְעֹה וַיְהַלְלוּ (ללה) אֹתָהּ אֶל־פַּרְעֹה וַתֻּקַּח הָאִשָּׁה בֵּית
(ב"פ ראה) פַּרְעֹה: (טז) וּלְאַבְרָם הֵיטִיב בַּעֲבוּרָהּ וַיְהִי־לוֹ
צֹאן וּבָקָר וַחֲמֹרִים וַעֲבָדִים וּשְׁפָחֹת וַאֲתֹנֹת וּגְמַלִּים:
(יז) וַיְנַגַּע יְהֹוָהאדניאהדונהי | אֶת־פַּרְעֹה נְגָעִים גְּדֹלִים וְאֶת־

וַיְנַגַּע - Abram, we are told, goes down into Egypt. Spiritually, the purpose of his journey was to plant the seed for the eventual redemption of the Israelites from Egypt during the time of Moses, which would take place many centuries later.

During this visit, Sarai, the wife of Abram, is abducted by the king of Egypt. Abram and Sarai are subsequently able to gain control over the king and win Sarai's freedom by utilizing the tools of the Torah and Kabbalah.

This event held cosmic significance for future generations. The action of gaining control over the king of Egypt and over the negative cosmic forces he represented created the system that would be used again, five generations later, when the Israelites would be freed from bondage in Egypt.

Moreover, the plagues that occur in this portion are the very seeds of the ten plagues that will occur later in Exodus. In truth, we achieve our own spiritual growth only because we stand on the shoulders of giants. The Light that shines in our world today was lit by the hands of generations past. Similarly, our actions of the present moment not only assist us, but they also serve and support future generations.

Thus, the entire chain of human existence is forever interconnected, each link requiring all the others. Upon the merit and work of Abraham, Moses,

בֵּיתוֹ (ב"פ ראה) עַל־דְּבַר (ראה) שָׂרַי אֵשֶׁת אַבְרָם׃ (יח) וַיִּקְרָא
פַרְעֹה לְאַבְרָם וַיֹּאמֶר מַה (מ"ה)־זֹּאת עָשִׂיתָ לִּי לָמָּה לֹא־
הִגַּדְתָּ לִּי כִּי אִשְׁתְּךָ הִוא׃ (יט) לָמָה אָמַרְתָּ אֲחֹתִי הִוא
וָאֶקַּח אֹתָהּ לִי לְאִשָּׁה וְעַתָּה הִנֵּה אִשְׁתְּךָ קַח וָלֵךְ׃ (כ)
וַיְצַו עָלָיו פַּרְעֹה אֲנָשִׁים וַיְשַׁלְּחוּ אֹתוֹ וְאֶת־אִשְׁתּוֹ וְאֶת־כָּל
(ילי)־אֲשֶׁר־לוֹ׃ יג (א) וַיַּעַל מִמִּצְרַיִם (מצר) הוּא וְאִשְׁתּוֹ וְכָל
(ילי)־אֲשֶׁר־לוֹ וְלוֹט עִמּוֹ הַנֶּגְבָּה׃ (ב) וְאַבְרָם כָּבֵד מְאֹד
בַּמִּקְנֶה בַּכֶּסֶף וּבַזָּהָב׃ (ג) וַיֵּלֶךְ (כלי) לְמַסָּעָיו מִנֶּגֶב וְעַד־
בֵּית (ב"פ ראה)־אֵל עַד־הַמָּקוֹם אֲשֶׁר־הָיָה (יהה) שָׁם אָהֳלֹה
בַּתְּחִלָּה בֵּין בֵּית (ב"פ ראה)־אֵל וּבֵין הָעָי׃ (ד) אֶל־מְקוֹם
הַמִּזְבֵּחַ (זן) אֲשֶׁר־עָשָׂה שָׁם בָּרִאשֹׁנָה וַיִּקְרָא שָׁם אַבְרָם
בְּשֵׁם יְהֹוָאדניאהדונהי׃

and Rabbi Shimon bar Yochai, we achieve what no other generation has achieved: the Final Redemption and freedom from Egypt and Pharaoh. We can now escape the darkness of our world and of our self-destructive ego.

וַיַּעַל - After leaving Egypt, Abram returns to Israel. Whenever we reveal Light in a place, we should always return to maintain our connection. If a person experiences a miracle in a particular locale, the person should revisit that place to tap into this miraculous energy and keep it alive in his life.

Through Abram's actions, we revisit Israel - which signifies the great spiritual elevation that Abram had attained - and we capture this Light to elevate and achieve a miraculous and peaceful transformation of our world.

Third Reading - Jacob - Tiferet

(ה) וְגַם־לְלוֹט הַהֹלֵךְ (מ״ה) אֶת־אַבְרָם הָיָה (יהה) צֹאן־וּבָקָר
וְאֹהָלִים׃ (ו) וְלֹא־נָשָׂא אֹתָם הָאָרֶץ (מילוי אלהים ע״ה) לָשֶׁבֶת
יַחְדָּו כִּי־הָיָה (יהה) רְכוּשָׁם רָב וְלֹא יָכְלוּ לָשֶׁבֶת יַחְדָּו׃
(ז) וַיְהִי־רִיב בֵּין רֹעֵי מִקְנֵה־אַבְרָם וּבֵין רֹעֵי מִקְנֵה־לוֹט
וְהַכְּנַעֲנִי וְהַפְּרִזִּי אָז יֹשֵׁב בָּאָרֶץ׃ (ח) וַיֹּאמֶר אַבְרָם אֶל־
לוֹט אַל־נָא תְהִי מְרִיבָה בֵּינִי וּבֵינֶךָ וּבֵין רֹעַי וּבֵין רֹעֶיךָ
כִּי־אֲנָשִׁים אַחִים אֲנָחְנוּ׃ (ט) הֲלֹא כָל (ילי)־הָאָרֶץ (מילוי אלהים
ע״ה) לְפָנֶיךָ (סמ״ב) הִפָּרֶד נָא מֵעָלָי אִם (יוהך)־הַשְּׂמֹאל וְאֵימִנָה

הִפָּרֶד - The Torah states that strife arose between the herdsmen of Abram's cattle and the herdsmen of Lot's cattle. The Zohar reveals that this conflict is a code for Lot's desire to return to idol-worshipping. Whenever we allow an external object or situation to control our behavior, our thoughts, or our emotions, we are committing the sin of idol-worshipping. Many people, for example, worship the idol of money; they are disciples of their businesses. Others are ruled by appearances of those around them. Or they bow down before the icons and images of our culture, including the self-image they feel they must convey to others. The moment we allow the external world to control our hearts and minds, we become idol-worshippers.

When Abram discovered that Lot, his nephew, was again engaging in idol-worshipping, Abram knew immediately that he had to separate and disconnect himself completely from Lot. Lot then chose to go to Sodom and Gomorrah, while Abram chose the land of Israel.

This story concerns the influence that our immediate environment exerts upon us. All of us should associate with people who are sincere in their desire for spiritual growth. Although our own intentions may be pure,

וְאִם (יוהך)-הַיָּמִין וְאַשְׂמְאִילָה׃ (י) וַיִּשָּׂא-לוֹט אֶת-עֵינָיו (מ"ה
בריבוע) וַיַּרְא אֶת-כָּל (ילי)-כִּכַּר הַיַּרְדֵּן (י' הויות וד' אותיות) כִּי כֻלָּהּ
מַשְׁקֶה לִפְנֵי | שַׁחֵת יְהֹוָהאדניאהדונהי אֶת-סְדֹם וְאֶת-עֲמֹרָה
כְּגַן-יְהֹוָהאדניאהדונהי כְּאֶרֶץ מִצְרַיִם (מצר) בֹּאֲכָה צֹעַר׃ (יא)
וַיִּבְחַר-לוֹ לוֹט אֵת כָּל (ילי)-כִּכַּר הַיַּרְדֵּן (י' הויות וד' אותיות) וַיִּסַּע
לוֹט מִקֶּדֶם וַיִּפָּרְדוּ אִישׁ מֵעַל (עלם) אָחִיו׃ (יב) אַבְרָם יָשַׁב

the influences that surround us inevitably affect our consciousness and behavior, and negative people in our life will inevitably bring us down. As the Zohar states:

Whoever accompanies a wicked person shall eventually follow in his steps....
 - Zohar, Volume III, 20:176

Second, we learn that like attracts like. Abram, being pure and positive, naturally moved to Israel. Lot, who possessed negative traits, automatically gravitated towards Sodom and Gomorrah. Thus, if we behave positively and resist our avaricious tendencies, we will naturally attract the Light of the Creator into our lives. Instead of receiving short-term pleasure followed by chaos, we will attract long-term fulfillment.

Through the verses that tell this story, we gain the power to separate ourselves from our own negative desires. In effect, we part ways with our rash impulses and self-indulgent urges born of ego, just as Abram parted company with Lot.

Moreover, this Light and Divine Power extend to the entire world - right now - via our meditation. Lot, the Zohar reveals, is also a code for the serpent, or the Satan, who cursed our world with death and destruction. This secret is found within the name Lot, which means "curse" in Aramaic. Hence, this reading separates the serpent - the Satan and death itself - from this physical world, banishing them forever from our lives.

בְּאֶרֶץ־כְּנָעַן וְלוֹט יָשַׁב בְּעָרֵי הַכִּכָּר וַיֶּאֱהַל עַד־סְדֹם׃
(יג) וְאַנְשֵׁי סְדֹם רָעִים וְחַטָּאִים לַיהוָאדניאהדונהי מְאֹד׃ (יד)
וַיהוָאדניאהדונהי אָמַר אֶל־אַבְרָם אַחֲרֵי הִפָּרֶד־לוֹט מֵעִמּוֹ
שָׂא נָא עֵינֶיךָ (ע"ה קס"א) וּרְאֵה (ראה) מִן־הַמָּקוֹם אֲשֶׁר־אַתָּה
שָׁם צָפֹנָה (ע"ה עסמ"ב) וָנֶגְבָּה וָקֵדְמָה וָיָמָּה׃ (טו) כִּי אֶת־כָּל
(ילי)־הָאָרֶץ (מילוי אלהים ע"ה) אֲשֶׁר־אַתָּה רֹאֶה (ראה) לְךָ אֶתְּנֶנָּה
וּלְזַרְעֲךָ עַד־עוֹלָם׃ (טז) וְשַׂמְתִּי אֶת־זַרְעֲךָ כַּעֲפַר הָאָרֶץ
(מילוי אלהים ע"ה) אֲשֶׁר | אִם (יוהך)־יוּכַל אִישׁ לִמְנוֹת אֶת־עֲפַר
הָאָרֶץ (מילוי אלהים ע"ה) גַּם־זַרְעֲךָ יִמָּנֶה׃ (יז) קוּם הִתְהַלֵּךְ (מיה)
בָּאָרֶץ לְאָרְכָּהּ וּלְרָחְבָּהּ כִּי לְךָ אֶתְּנֶנָּה׃ (יח) וַיֶּאֱהַל אַבְרָם
וַיָּבֹא וַיֵּשֶׁב בְּאֵלֹנֵי מַמְרֵא אֲשֶׁר בְּחֶבְרוֹן וַיִּבֶן־שָׁם מִזְבֵּחַ
(זן) לַיהוָאדניאהדונהי׃ פ

Fourth Reading - Moses - Netzach

יד (א) וַיְהִי בִּימֵי אַמְרָפֶל מֶלֶךְ־שִׁנְעָר אַרְיוֹךְ מֶלֶךְ

וַיְהִי - War breaks out in what is now the Middle East between five nations and four other nations. During this reading, we meditate on peace in the Middle East today. Ironically, all the wars of the Middle East throughout history were caused by religion. Eminent Kabbalist Rav Yehuda Brandwein writes that the Kabbalah Centre was established to promote unity and tolerance among all people. Religion, Rav Brandwein points out, has been used to create separation, division, and conflict, as opposed to unity and tolerance among all God's children.

אֶלָּסָר כְּדָרְלָעֹמֶר מֶלֶךְ עֵילָם וְתִדְעָל מֶלֶךְ גּוֹיִם׃ (ב) עָשׂוּ
מִלְחָמָה אֶת־בֶּרַע מֶלֶךְ סְדֹם וְאֶת־בִּרְשַׁע מֶלֶךְ עֲמֹרָה
שִׁנְאָב | מֶלֶךְ אַדְמָה וְשֶׁמְאֵבֶר מֶלֶךְ צְבוֹיִם (צְבֹיִים כתיב)
וּמֶלֶךְ בֶּלַע הִיא־צֹעַר׃ (ג) כָּל (ילי) ־אֵלֶּה חָבְרוּ אֶל־עֵמֶק
הַשִּׂדִּים הוּא יָם (ילי) הַמֶּלַח׃ (ד) שְׁתֵּים עֶשְׂרֵה שָׁנָה עָבְדוּ
אֶת־כְּדָרְלָעֹמֶר וּשְׁלֹשׁ־עֶשְׂרֵה שָׁנָה מָרָדוּ׃ (ה) וּבְאַרְבַּע
עֶשְׂרֵה שָׁנָה בָּא כְדָרְלָעֹמֶר וְהַמְּלָכִים אֲשֶׁר אִתּוֹ וַיַּכּוּ
אֶת־רְפָאִים בְּעַשְׁתְּרֹת קַרְנַיִם וְאֶת־הַזּוּזִים בְּהָם וְאֵת
הָאֵימִים בְּשָׁוֵה קִרְיָתָיִם׃ (ו) וְאֶת־הַחֹרִי בְּהַרְרָם שֵׂעִיר עַד
אֵיל פָּארָן אֲשֶׁר עַל־הַמִּדְבָּר׃ (ז) וַיָּשֻׁבוּ וַיָּבֹאוּ אֶל־עֵין (מ"ה
בריבוע) מִשְׁפָּט (ע"ה ה"פ אלהים) הִוא קָדֵשׁ וַיַּכּוּ אֶת־כָּל (ילי) ־שְׂדֵה
הָעֲמָלֵקִי וְגַם אֶת־הָאֱמֹרִי הַיֹּשֵׁב בְּחַצְצֹן תָּמָר׃ (ח) וַיֵּצֵא
מֶלֶךְ־סְדֹם וּמֶלֶךְ עֲמֹרָה וּמֶלֶךְ אַדְמָה וּמֶלֶךְ צְבוֹיִם (צְבֹיִים
כתיב) וּמֶלֶךְ בֶּלַע הִוא־צֹעַר וַיַּעַרְכוּ אִתָּם מִלְחָמָה בְּעֵמֶק

Hence, Kabbalah's aim is not to preach, convert, or convince, but rather to arouse respect for each person's path to the Light by fostering tolerance among people. Until each member of each religion treats everyone with nothing less than human dignity, a lasting peace cannot come to pass.

Here, our meditation engenders love among and for people of all faiths.

הַשִּׂדִּים׃ (ט) אֵת כְּדָרְלָעֹמֶר מֶלֶךְ עֵילָם וְתִדְעָל מֶלֶךְ גּוֹיִם
וְאַמְרָפֶל מֶלֶךְ שִׁנְעָר וְאַרְיוֹךְ מֶלֶךְ אֶלָּסָר אַרְבָּעָה מְלָכִים
אֶת־הַחֲמִשָּׁה׃ (י) וְעֵמֶק הַשִּׂדִּים בֶּאֱרֹת בֶּאֱרֹת חֵמָר וַיָּנֻסוּ
מֶלֶךְ־סְדֹם וַעֲמֹרָה וַיִּפְּלוּ־שָׁמָּה וְהַנִּשְׁאָרִים הֶרָה נָּסוּ׃ (יא)
וַיִּקְחוּ אֶת־כָּל־רְכֻשׁ סְדֹם וַעֲמֹרָה וְאֶת־כָּל־אָכְלָם
וַיֵּלֵכוּ׃ (יב) וַיִּקְחוּ אֶת־לוֹט וְאֶת־רְכֻשׁוֹ בֶּן־אֲחִי אַבְרָם וַיֵּלֵכוּ
וְהוּא יֹשֵׁב בִּסְדֹם׃ (יג) וַיָּבֹא הַפָּלִיט וַיַּגֵּד לְאַבְרָם הָעִבְרִי

וַיָּבֹא - The five kings fall to defeat at that hands of the four kings. In the process, the four kings capture Lot. One of Lot's men escapes to tell Abram about Lot's capture. Abram then assembles 318 armed servants to fight the army of the four kings, defeating them.

Clearly, a small band of men cannot overpower the armies of four nations. The secret to their victory, however, is found in the number 318, the numerical value of the Hebrew word siach, which means "speech." Kabbalist Rav Berg reveals that siach refers to the speech of the angels. These angels, or packets of energy, are the 72 Names of God, which consist of 72 three-letter sequences of Hebrew letters. These sequences are the angelic forces that give us the power of mind over matter. Abram used these Names to conquer the four nations.

Spiritually, these four nations denote our own Evil Inclination - our dark tendencies and self-destructive traits. Through the 72 Names, we can achieve mind over matter. We can perform miracles of human nature - eliminating our negative qualities - which, in turn, summon forth miracles of Mother Nature.

The Zohar offers another insight into the capture of Lot. Lot, the Zohar explains, was similar in appearance to Abram. When the kings captured Lot, they believed mistakenly that they had actually apprehended Abram, which was the actual purpose behind the war.

וְהוּא שֹׁכֵן בְּאֵלֹנֵי מַמְרֵא הָאֱמֹרִי אֲחִי אֶשְׁכֹּל וַאֲחִי עָנֵר
וְהֵם בַּעֲלֵי בְרִית־אַבְרָם׃ (יד) וַיִּשְׁמַע אַבְרָם כִּי נִשְׁבָּה
אָחִיו וַיָּרֶק אֶת־חֲנִיכָיו יְלִידֵי בֵיתוֹ (כ״פ ראה) שְׁמֹנָה עָשָׂר
וּשְׁלֹשׁ מֵאוֹת וַיִּרְדֹּף עַד־דָּן׃ (טו) וַיֵּחָלֵק עֲלֵיהֶם ׀ לַיְלָה
הוּא וַעֲבָדָיו וַיַּכֵּם וַיִּרְדְּפֵם עַד־חוֹבָה אֲשֶׁר מִשְּׂמֹאל (מלה)
לְדַמָּשֶׂק׃ (טז) וַיָּשֶׁב אֵת כָּל (ילי)־הָרְכֻשׁ וְגַם אֶת־לוֹט אָחִיו
וּרְכֻשׁוֹ הֵשִׁיב וְגַם אֶת־הַנָּשִׁים וְאֶת־הָעָם׃ (יז) וַיֵּצֵא מֶלֶךְ־
סְדֹם לִקְרָאתוֹ אַחֲרֵי שׁוּבוֹ מֵהַכּוֹת אֶת־כְּדָרְלָעֹמֶר וְאֶת־
הַמְּלָכִים אֲשֶׁר אִתּוֹ אֶל־עֵמֶק שָׁוֵה הוּא עֵמֶק הַמֶּלֶךְ׃ (יח)
וּמַלְכִּי (נלך)־צֶדֶק מֶלֶךְ שָׁלֵם הוֹצִיא לֶחֶם (ג׳ הויות) וָיָיִן (מ״כ, י״פ

The kings wanted to slay Abram because he had enlightened the people, leading them away from the futility of idol-worshipping.

We learn that people like Abram, who dare to initiate positive change and help others in their spiritual awakening, always encounter opposition from the dark forces who seek to propagate chaos and ignorance for their own personal gain.

Throughout human history, any major advance in civilization was first met with opposition, defiance, and scorn from those who would not benefit from the betterment of the human condition. This represents a spiritual principle that holds true in our personal lives. As opportunities for spiritual advancement present themselves to us, we will encounter obstacles and opposition - from our own ego and from people around us. This Torah passage overthrows the forces that attempt to impede our spiritual progress.

(האא) וְהוּא כֹהֵן (מלה) לְאֵל עֶלְיוֹן׃ (יט) וַיְבָרְכֵהוּ וַיֹּאמַר בָּרוּךְ
אַבְרָם לְאֵל עֶלְיוֹן קֹנֵה שָׁמַיִם (י"פ טל) וָאָרֶץ׃ (כ) וּבָרוּךְ אֵל
עֶלְיוֹן אֲשֶׁר־מִגֵּן צָרֶיךָ בְּיָדֶךָ וַיִּתֶּן־לוֹ מַעֲשֵׂר מִכֹּל (יל"י)׃

וַיִּתֶּן־לוֹ - After the war, Melchizedek, king of Salem, offers Abram the spoils of war. Abram refuses to partake and tithes it all away instead.

Kabbalistically, money possesses Light and energy that can influence our life in unseen ways. Hence, we should be careful to handle and keep money that is derived only through positive and honest labor. Money gained through illicit means possesses no Light. It might generate temporary financial or material gain, but eventually darkness and negativity will enter our life.

The Zohar also reveals a secret concerning the power of tithing. Because we live in a physical world, the negative force Satan is allowed nourishment while he carries out his task of testing us and tempting us into sin via our ego. Thus, all the financial sustenance we earn is tainted by his presence. By tithing a portion of our money, we sever the Satan's influence in our life.

Regarding the amount of a tithe, the Zohar states:

It is one out of ten, and ten out of a hundred....
- Zohar, Volume III, 25:257

Hence, we learn that we must tithe ten per cent of our money to disconnect our livelihood from the influence of the Satan. By giving away ten per cent, we actually create an opening to receive even greater sustenance. Conversely, by not tithing, we save ten per cent in the short term, but now the Satan has gained access into our lives where he causes ten times more chaos, be it in the area of finance, health, relationships, or our emotional well-being.

Moreover, the sages teach us that whatever annual income we earn, regardless of how large or small, the Light always bestows upon us an extra ten per cent for us to tithe. This is a tool for us to use to prevent the Satan from entering our lives. For this reason, tithing is not considered charity but rather protection from the Satan. It is the next ten per cent that we may

Fifth Reading - Aaron - Hod

(כא) וַיֹּאמֶר מֶלֶךְ־סְדֹם אֶל־אַבְרָם תֶּן־לִי הַנֶּפֶשׁ וְהָרְכֻשׁ
קַח־לָךְ׃ (כב) וַיֹּאמֶר אַבְרָם אֶל־מֶלֶךְ סְדֹם הֲרִימֹתִי יָדִי
אֶל־יְהֹוָהאדניאהדונהי אֵל עֶלְיוֹן קֹנֵה שָׁמַיִם (י״פ טל) וָאָרֶץ׃ (כג) אִם
(יוהך)־מִחוּט וְעַד שְׂרוֹךְ־נַעַל וְאִם (יוהך)־אֶקַּח מִכָּל (ילי)־אֲשֶׁר־
לָךְ וְלֹא תֹאמַר אֲנִי (אני) הֶעֱשַׁרְתִּי אֶת־אַבְרָם׃ (כד) בִּלְעָדַי
רַק אֲשֶׁר אָכְלוּ הַנְּעָרִים וְחֵלֶק הָאֲנָשִׁים אֲשֶׁר הָלְכוּ
אִתִּי עָנֵר אֶשְׁכֹּל וּמַמְרֵא הֵם יִקְחוּ חֶלְקָם׃ ס טו (א) אַחַר |
הַדְּבָרִים (ראה) הָאֵלֶּה הָיָה (יהה) דְבַר (ראה)־יְהֹוָהאדניאהדונהי אֶל־
אַבְרָם בַּמַּחֲזֶה לֵאמֹר אַל־תִּירָא אַבְרָם אָנֹכִי (איע) מָגֵן
(מיכאל גבריאל נוריאל) לָךְ שְׂכָרְךָ הַרְבֵּה מְאֹד׃ (ב) וַיֹּאמֶר אַבְרָם
אֲדֹנָי יֱהֹוִהאדניאהדונהי מַה (מ״ה)־תִּתֶּן (ב״פ כהת)־לִי וְאָנֹכִי (איע) הוֹלֵךְ
עֲרִירִי וּבֶן־מֶשֶׁק בֵּיתִי (ב״פ ראה) הוּא דַּמֶּשֶׂק אֱלִיעֶזֶר׃ (ג)

choose to give, over and above the original tithe, that is considered an act of true charity.

Abram, by tithing away all the physical possessions procured from the war, received eternal spiritual blessings in return, which ensured his immortality.

For that reason, upon Abram's merit, we, his descendents, summon the Light of Immortality into our world, cutting off forever the influence of the Angel of Death.

וַיֹּאמֶר אַבְרָם הֵן לִי לֹא נָתַתָּה זָרַע וְהִנֵּה בֶן־בֵּיתִי (כ"פ ראה)
יוֹרֵשׁ אֹתִי׃ (ד) וְהִנֵּה דְבַר (ראה) יְהֹוָאדניאהדונהי אֵלָיו לֵאמֹר
לֹא יִירָשְׁךָ זֶה כִּי־אִם (יוהך) אֲשֶׁר יֵצֵא מִמֵּעֶיךָ הוּא יִירָשֶׁךָ׃
(ה) **וַיּוֹצֵא** אֹתוֹ הַחוּצָה וַיֹּאמֶר הַבֶּט־נָא הַשָּׁמַיְמָה וּסְפֹר
הַכּוֹכָבִים אִם (יוהך) תּוּכַל לִסְפֹּר אֹתָם וַיֹּאמֶר לוֹ כֹּה (הי)
יִהְיֶה (ייי) זַרְעֶךָ׃ (ו) וְהֶאֱמִן בַּיהֹוָאדניאהדונהי וַיַּחְשְׁבֶהָ לּוֹ צְדָקָה
(ע"ה אלהים בריבוע)׃

וַיּוֹצֵא - Abram cries out to God, lamenting his inability to have children, for he saw in the stars that he was not destined to father a child. The Creator explains that all people have certain judgments hanging over them from previous deeds committed in this or past lives. These decrees of judgment are then visible to us through the influence of the stars and planets.

However, God tells Abram that it is up to him to rise above these planetary influences by transforming his very nature through the Light of the Creator.

This secret is revealed in the Zohar:

The Holy One, blessed be He, said to him, "Do not look to this - THE WISDOM OF THE STARS - but rather to the secret of My Name, WHICH IS THE NUKVA. You shall father a son!"
- Zohar, Volume III, 30:322

When a man changes his internal nature, The physical world mirrors that action – the power of mind over matter is activated and judgments are removed. A man can rise above planetary influences. In fact, it is his duty. By empowering Abram with this wisdom, God has, in effect, taken Abram out from under the influence of his astrological sign.
Here we learn that each of us has the power to change anything and everything in our lives. Judgments set forth against us because of our actions

Sixth Reading - Joseph - Yesod

(ז) וַיֹּאמֶר אֵלָיו אֲנִי (אני) יְהֹוָהאדניאהדונהי אֲשֶׁר הוֹצֵאתִיךָ מֵאוּר
כַּשְׂדִּים לָתֶת לְךָ אֶת־הָאָרֶץ (מילוי אלהים ע"ה) הַזֹּאת לְרִשְׁתָּהּ׃
(ח) וַיֹּאמַר אֲדֹנָי יֱהֹוִהאדניאהדונהי בַּמָּה אֵדַע כִּי אִירָשֶׁנָּה׃
(ט) וַיֹּאמֶר אֵלָיו קְחָה לִי עֶגְלָה מְשֻׁלֶּשֶׁת וְעֵז מְשֻׁלֶּשֶׁת
וְאַיִל מְשֻׁלָּשׁ וְתֹר וְגוֹזָל׃ (י) וַיִּקַּח (וזעם)־לוֹ אֶת־כָּל (ילי)־אֵלֶּה
וַיְבַתֵּר אֹתָם בַּתָּוֶךְ וַיִּתֵּן אִישׁ־בִּתְרוֹ לִקְרַאת רֵעֵהוּ וְאֶת־

in this or past lives can be removed if we remove the negative trait that caused the misdeed in the first place.

Through these verses, we and all the world overcome the influence of the planets in our lives. As we reflect upon and admit to our own negative traits now, we immediately shift our lives as well as the collective destiny of mankind to a future that embodies an immediate, gentle Redemption and the arrival of the Messiah - the Messiah within us and in the world at large.

וַיֹּאמֶר - After God takes Abram out of Ur of the Chaldeans, the first bond between the Creator and human beings is born (Genesis 15:7).

We are all a part of God. Each of us is a divine spark of Light. However, humans never had a physical connection to God until this first bond was created. It infused humanity with the divine power to be God-like on a physical level. However, there is a prerequisite for activating this inherited divine trait: We must emulate Abram, who embodies the ideal both of unconditional caring for others and of imparting Light to one's fellow human beings. Failure to live in this manner disconnects us from the Creator and the God-like feature instilled within our soul.

These particular verses of Torah strengthen our bond to the Light of the Creator and awaken our desire to share with others.

הַצִּפֹּר לֹא בָתָר׃ (יא) וַיֵּרֶד (רי"ו) הָעַיִט עַל־הַפְּגָרִים וַיַּשֵּׁב
אֹתָם אַבְרָם׃ (יב) וַיְהִי הַשֶּׁמֶשׁ לָבוֹא וְתַרְדֵּמָה נָפְלָה
עַל־אַבְרָם וְהִנֵּה אֵימָה חֲשֵׁכָה גְדֹלָה נֹפֶלֶת עָלָיו׃ (יג)
וַיֹּאמֶר לְאַבְרָם יָדֹעַ תֵּדַע כִּי־גֵר | יִהְיֶה (ייי) זַרְעֲךָ בְּאֶרֶץ
לֹא לָהֶם וַעֲבָדוּם וְעִנּוּ אֹתָם אַרְבַּע מֵאוֹת שָׁנָה׃ (יד)
וְגַם אֶת־הַגּוֹי אֲשֶׁר יַעֲבֹדוּ דָּן אָנֹכִי (אי"ע) וְאַחֲרֵי־כֵן יֵצְאוּ
בִּרְכֻשׁ גָּדוֹל (להח, מבה עד"א)׃ (טו) וְאַתָּה תָּבוֹא אֶל־אֲבֹתֶיךָ
בְּשָׁלוֹם תִּקָּבֵר בְּשֵׂיבָה טוֹבָה (אכא)׃ (טז) וְדוֹר (רי"ו) רְבִיעִי
יָשׁוּבוּ הֵנָּה כִּי לֹא־שָׁלֵם עֲוֹן הָאֱמֹרִי עַד־הֵנָּה׃ (יז) וַיְהִי
הַשֶּׁמֶשׁ בָּאָה וַעֲלָטָה הָיָה (יהה) וְהִנֵּה תַנּוּר עָשָׁן וְלַפִּיד
אֵשׁ אֲשֶׁר עָבַר בֵּין הַגְּזָרִים הָאֵלֶּה׃ (יח) בַּיּוֹם (נגד, זן) הַהוּא
כָּרַת יְהֹוָאדני אהדונהי אֶת־אַבְרָם בְּרִית לֵאמֹר לְזַרְעֲךָ נָתַתִּי
אֶת־הָאָרֶץ (מילוי אלהים ע"ה) הַזֹּאת מִנְּהַר מִצְרַיִם (מצר) עַד־הַנָּהָר
הַגָּדֹל (להח, מבה עד"א) נְהַר־פְּרָת׃ (יט) אֶת־הַקֵּינִי וְאֶת־הַקְּנִזִּי
וְאֵת הַקַּדְמֹנִי׃ (כ) וְאֶת־הַחִתִּי וְאֶת־הַפְּרִזִּי וְאֶת־הָרְפָאִים׃
(כא) וְאֶת־הָאֱמֹרִי וְאֶת־הַכְּנַעֲנִי וְאֶת־הַגִּרְגָּשִׁי וְאֶת־הַיְבוּסִי׃
ס טז (א) וְשָׂרַי אֵשֶׁת אַבְרָם לֹא יָלְדָה לוֹ וְלָהּ שִׁפְחָה

וְשָׂרַי - Abram's wife, Sarai, is unable to bear children. Sarai tells Abram to father a child through their Egyptian maidservant, Hagar. Abram agrees,

מִצְרִית (מצר) וּשְׁמָהּ הָגָר׃ (ב) וַתֹּאמֶר שָׂרַי אֶל־אַבְרָם הִנֵּה־
נָא עֲצָרַנִי יְהֹוָה (אדני אהדונהי) מִלֶּדֶת בֹּא־נָא אֶל־שִׁפְחָתִי אוּלַי
(אום) אִבָּנֶה מִמֶּנָּה וַיִּשְׁמַע אַבְרָם לְקוֹל שָׂרָי׃ (ג) וַתִּקַּח שָׂרַי
| אֵשֶׁת אַבְרָם אֶת־הָגָר הַמִּצְרִית (מצר) שִׁפְחָתָהּ מִקֵּץ (מנק)
עֶשֶׂר שָׁנִים לְשֶׁבֶת אַבְרָם בְּאֶרֶץ כְּנָעַן וַתִּתֵּן (כ״פ כהת) אֹתָהּ
לְאַבְרָם אִישָׁהּ לוֹ לְאִשָּׁה׃ (ד) וַיָּבֹא אֶל־הָגָר וַתַּהַר וַתֵּרֶא
כִּי הָרָתָה וַתֵּקַל גְּבִרְתָּהּ בְּעֵינֶיהָ (מ״ה בריבוע)׃ (ה) וַתֹּאמֶר שָׂרַי
אֶל־אַבְרָם חֲמָסִי עָלֶיךָ אָנֹכִי (איע) נָתַתִּי שִׁפְחָתִי בְּחֵיקֶךָ
וַתֵּרֶא כִּי הָרָתָה וָאֵקַל בְּעֵינֶיהָ (מ״ה בריבוע) יִשְׁפֹּט יְהֹוָה (אדני אהדונהי) בֵּינִי
וּבֵינֶיךָ׃ (ו) וַיֹּאמֶר אַבְרָם אֶל־שָׂרַי הִנֵּה שִׁפְחָתֵךְ בְּיָדֵךְ

and through this union, Ishmael, the seed and father of all the Arab nations, is born. Ishmael and Abram's future son, Isaac, are the seed [root] of all conflict and strife between Jews and Arabs, yet the two brothers and their descendents share one common seed.

The Light emanating from this story engenders unconditional love and respect for human dignity between Jews and Moslems and within the entire family of humanity. Intolerance is hereby banished from the hearts of humans. Racial and religious barriers dissolve into nothingness.

וּבֵינֶיךָ - Whenever a dot appears above a word in the Torah, it signifies an additional emanation of a particular spiritual force into our life. Here we receive protection from evil eye.

Evil eye pertains to the negative glances and resentful looks that we receive from those who may harbor envious feelings or ill will towards us. The Kabbalist attributes the majority of common ailments and misfortunes to evil eye. Moreover, when we cast an evil eye towards others, we create

עֲשִׂי־לָהּ הַטּוֹב (והו) בְּעֵינָיִךְ (ע״ה קס״א) וַתְּעַנֶּהָ שָׂרַי וַתִּבְרַח
מִפָּנֶיהָ׃ (ז) וַיִּמְצָאָהּ מַלְאַךְ יְהֹוָה(אדני)אהדונהי עַל־עֵין (מ״ה בריבוע)
הַמַּיִם בַּמִּדְבָּר עַל־הָעַיִן (מ״ה בריבוע) בְּדֶרֶךְ (ב״פ יב״ק) שׁוּר (אבג
יתץ, ושר, אהבת חנם)׃ (ח) וַיֹּאמַר הָגָר שִׁפְחַת שָׂרַי אֵי־מִזֶּה בָאת
וְאָנָה תֵלֵכִי וַתֹּאמֶר מִפְּנֵי שָׂרַי גְּבִרְתִּי אָנֹכִי (איע) בֹּרַחַת׃
(ט) וַיֹּאמֶר לָהּ מַלְאַךְ יְהֹוָה(אדני)אהדונהי שׁוּבִי אֶל־גְּבִרְתֵּךְ
וְהִתְעַנִּי תַּחַת יָדֶיהָ׃ (י) וַיֹּאמֶר לָהּ מַלְאַךְ יְהֹוָה(אדני)אהדונהי
הַרְבָּה אַרְבֶּה (יצחק) אֶת־זַרְעֵךְ וְלֹא יִסָּפֵר מֵרֹב׃ (יא) וַיֹּאמֶר
לָהּ מַלְאַךְ יְהֹוָה(אדני)אהדונהי הִנָּךְ הָרָה וְיֹלַדְתְּ בֵּן וְקָרָאת שְׁמוֹ
(מהש ע״ה) יִשְׁמָעֵאל כִּי־שָׁמַע יְהֹוָה(אדני)אהדונהי אֶל־עָנְיֵךְ (מ״ה בריבוע)׃
(יב) וְהוּא יִהְיֶה (ייי) פֶּרֶא אָדָם (מ״ה) יָדוֹ בַכֹּל (לכב) וְיַד כֹּל (ילי)
בּוֹ וְעַל־פְּנֵי (חכמה, בינה) כָל (ילי)־אֶחָיו יִשְׁכֹּן׃ (יג) וַתִּקְרָא שֵׁם־
יְהֹוָה(אדני)אהדונהי הַדֹּבֵר (ראה) אֵלֶיהָ אַתָּה אֵל רֳאִי כִּי אָמְרָה
הֲגַם הֲלֹם רָאִיתִי אַחֲרֵי רֹאִי׃ (יד) עַל־כֵּן קָרָא לַבְּאֵר (קנ״א

an opening within ourselves that attracts even more negative glances. We ourselves become more vulnerable to its effects, and a vicious circle is created. This action brings equal harm to both the bearer of evil eye and to the recipient.

The dot eradicates the envy and ill-will that we harbor towards other people, in turn generating a field of protection around us so that we are shielded from the effects of evil eye directed at us by others.

ב"ן) בְּאֵ֗ר (קנ"א ב"ן) לַחַ֣י רֹאִ֑י הִנֵּ֥ה בֵין־קָדֵ֖שׁ וּבֵ֥ין בָּֽרֶד׃ (טו)
וַתֵּ֨לֶד הָגָ֤ר לְאַבְרָם֙ בֵּ֑ן וַיִּקְרָ֨א אַבְרָ֧ם שֶׁם־בְּנ֛וֹ אֲשֶׁר־
יָלְדָ֥ה הָגָ֖ר יִשְׁמָעֵֽאל׃ (טז) וְאַבְרָ֕ם בֶּן־שְׁמֹנִ֥ים שָׁנָ֖ה וְשֵׁ֣שׁ
שָׁנִ֑ים בְּלֶֽדֶת־הָגָ֥ר אֶת־יִשְׁמָעֵ֖אל לְאַבְרָֽם׃ ס יז (א) וַיְהִ֣י
אַבְרָ֔ם בֶּן־תִּשְׁעִ֥ים שָׁנָ֖ה וְתֵ֣שַׁע שָׁנִ֑ים וַיֵּרָ֨א יְהֹוָ֜ה אדני אהדונהי
אֶל־אַבְרָ֗ם וַיֹּ֤אמֶר אֵלָיו֙ אֲנִי (אני) ־אֵ֣ל שַׁדַּ֔י (מהש) הִתְהַלֵּ֥ךְ (מ"ה)
לְפָנַ֖י וֶהְיֵ֥ה (יהה) (יהוה) תָמִֽים׃ (ב) וְאֶתְּנָ֥ה בְרִיתִ֖י בֵּינִ֣י וּבֵינֶ֑ךָ
וְאַרְבֶּ֥ה (יצחק) אוֹתְךָ֖ בִּמְאֹ֥ד מְאֹֽד׃ (ג) וַיִּפֹּ֥ל אַבְרָ֖ם עַל־פָּנָ֑יו
וַיְדַבֵּ֥ר (ראה) אִתּ֛וֹ אֱלֹהִ֖ים (ילה) לֵאמֹֽר׃ (ד) אֲנִ֕י (אני) הִנֵּ֥ה בְרִיתִ֖י
אִתָּ֑ךְ וְהָיִ֕יתָ לְאַ֖ב הֲמ֥וֹן גּוֹיִֽם׃ (ה) וְלֹא־יִקָּרֵ֥א ע֛וֹד אֶת־שִׁמְךָ֖
אַבְרָ֑ם וְהָיָ֤ה (יהה) (יהוה) שִׁמְךָ֙ אַבְרָהָ֔ם (רמ"ח) כִּ֛י אַב־הֲמ֥וֹן

אַבְרָהָם - While he was under the influence of the stars, Abraham was called Abram. Once he underwent spiritual transformation, the Hebrew letter Hei was added to his name, changing it from Abram to Abraham.

The profound Kabbalistic concept of altering a person's name alphabetically can be compared to the science of genetic engineering, in which the genetic code of a person is altered to reduce a genetic predisposition to various diseases and ailments. Interestingly, all DNA is structured and consequently classified alphabetically. Our genetic code is written out using four chemical letters or nucleotides known as A, T, C, and G.

Just as our traits can be changed if our DNA is altered, Abram's traits are changed when his spiritual DNA is altered. When his name is changed to Abraham, so is his entire being. The ancient kabbalists tell us that our

גּוֹיִם נְתַתִּיךָ׃ (ו) וְהִפְרֵתִי אֹתְךָ בִּמְאֹד מְאֹד וּנְתַתִּיךָ לְגוֹיִם
וּמְלָכִים מִמְּךָ יֵצֵאוּ׃

Seventh Reading - David - Malchut

(ז) וַהֲקִמֹתִי אֶת־בְּרִיתִי בֵּינִי וּבֵינֶךָ וּבֵין זַרְעֲךָ אַחֲרֶיךָ
לְדֹרֹתָם לִבְרִית עוֹלָם לִהְיוֹת לְךָ לֵאלֹהִים (ילה) וּלְזַרְעֲךָ

Hebrew name is the spiritual genetic code of our soul.

The spiritual influences arising in this passage imbue us with the power to alter our spiritual DNA, thereby changing our destiny. By transforming the negative aspects of our nature, we rise above cosmic influences, remove judgments that may be hanging over us, and evolve to higher levels of spirituality.

The numeric value of Abraham's new name is 248, the same number as the bones and bone segments in our body. This connection allows the Light of healing, generated through the Light and mercy that shine from Abraham, to heal our entire body.

The concept of a Hebrew name is critically important, according to Kabbalah. A Hebrew name transfers traits and qualities associated with that particular name to a person's soul. For this reason, we are advised to name our children after the great figures of the Torah so that we imbue our loved ones with their noble traits.

If our children are named after a relative who experienced various hardships in life, be they health-related, financial, or marital, the spiritual traits and karmic debts of the relative are often passed onto the children. Thus, we are advised to change a child's name to connect the child to the people of the Bible. For example, we can change the DNA of the current name of a living person who was named after his grandfather David by redirecting the name from the grandfather to King David. The name remains the same, but the DNA of the name has been switched through meditation and other spiritual tools to that of King David.

אַחֲרֶיךָ: (ח) וְנָתַתִּי לְךָ וּלְזַרְעֲךָ אַחֲרֶיךָ אֵת | אֶרֶץ מְגֻרֶיךָ
אֵת כָּל (ילי) ־אֶרֶץ כְּנַעַן לַאֲחֻזַּת עוֹלָם וְהָיִיתִי לָהֶם לֵאלֹהִים
(ילה): (ט) וַיֹּאמֶר אֱלֹהִים (ילה) אֶל־אַבְרָהָם (רמ״ח) וְאַתָּה אֶת־
בְּרִיתִי תִשְׁמֹר אַתָּה וְזַרְעֲךָ אַחֲרֶיךָ לְדֹרֹתָם: (י) זֹאת בְּרִיתִי
אֲשֶׁר תִּשְׁמְרוּ בֵּינִי וּבֵינֵיכֶם וּבֵין זַרְעֲךָ אַחֲרֶיךָ הִמּוֹל לָכֶם
כָּל (ילי) ־זָכָר: (יא) וּנְמַלְתֶּם אֵת בְּשַׂר עָרְלַתְכֶם וְהָיָה (יהה) (יהוה)

וּנְמַלְתֶּם - The male sexual organ corresponds to the spiritual world of Yesod, which is located directly above our world. Yesod is a vast reservoir into which the eight Upper Worlds that exist above Yesod pour their individual spiritual forces.

Yesod is the portal and the funnel through which all this positive spiritual energy flows into our own dimension. This great Light is responsible for the miracle of procreation and the pleasure derived from it.

Countless negative forces hover around Yesod to try to capture the positive Light that flows from there.

This situation is reflected in our world as well. Negative forces manifest and attach themselves to the male sexual organ (the physical embodiment of Yesod) the moment a male child comes into this world. Circumcision removes these spiritually harmful forces from the baby and has the same effect on and benefit for the world at large.

Circumcision, performed properly with Kabbalistic mediation, removes all negativity from both the child and the world. According to Kabbalah, it also strengthens the immune system. Performing this ancient ritual can reduce many disease risks, including cancer.

In regards to circumcision, which is the sign of the Covenant, the Zohar states:

לְאוֹת בְּרִית בֵּינִי וּבֵינֵיכֶם׃ (יב) וּבֶן־שְׁמֹנַת יָמִים (נלך) יִמּוֹל
לָכֶם כָּל (ילי)־זָכָר לְדֹרֹתֵיכֶם יְלִיד בָּיִת (ב״פ ראה) וּמִקְנַת־כֶּסֶף
מִכֹּל (ילי) בֶּן־נֵכָר אֲשֶׁר לֹא מִזַּרְעֲךָ הוּא׃ (יג) הִמּוֹל | יִמּוֹל
יְלִיד בֵּיתְךָ (ב״פ ראה) וּמִקְנַת כַּסְפֶּךָ וְהָיְתָה בְרִיתִי בִּבְשַׂרְכֶם
לִבְרִית עוֹלָם׃ (יד) וְעָרֵל | זָכָר אֲשֶׁר לֹא־יִמּוֹל אֶת־בְּשַׂר
עָרְלָתוֹ וְנִכְרְתָה הַנֶּפֶשׁ הַהִוא מֵעַמֶּיהָ אֶת־בְּרִיתִי הֵפַר׃
ס (טו) וַיֹּאמֶר אֱלֹהִים (ילה) אֶל־אַבְרָהָם (רמ״ח) שָׂרַי אִשְׁתְּךָ
לֹא־תִקְרָא אֶת־שְׁמָהּ שָׂרָי כִּי **שָׂרָה** שְׁמָהּ׃ (טז) וּבֵרַכְתִּי

Whoever retains this sign shall not go down to Gehenom (Hell) as long as he preserves it properly….
- Zohar, Volume III, 36:385

Here we purify the realm of Yesod - above and below - as we strengthen the Covenant and prevent our souls from experiencing any form of hell.

שָׂרָה - Sarai was unable to bear children. So her name was changed from Sarai to Sarah, indicating a spiritual genetic change, so that she could bring forth children.

Many women in our day have difficulty bearing children. A name change can assist in removing the spiritual and physical obstacles. A woman's name not only affects her soul but the souls of her children as well. For that reason, a woman should choose a name from the Torah to ensure that both she and her children can benefit from the most positive attributes and noble traits.

We meditate to share this Light with the women in our world who are having difficulty bringing forth children. The Light of this verse destroys all the blockages and ailments that prevent healthy conception and child-birth.

אֹתָהּ וְגַם נָתַתִּי מִמֶּנָּה לְךָ בֵּן וּבֵרַכְתִּיהָ וְהָיְתָה לְגוֹיִם
מַלְכֵי (נלך) עַמִּים מִמֶּנָּה יִהְיוּ׃ (יז) וַיִּפֹּל אַבְרָהָם (רמ"ח) עַל־פָּנָיו
וַיִּצְחָק (ר"פ ב"ן) וַיֹּאמֶר בְּלִבּוֹ הַלְּבֶן מֵאָה־שָׁנָה יִוָּלֵד וְאִם
(יוהך)־שָׂרָה הֲבַת־תִּשְׁעִים שָׁנָה תֵּלֵד׃ (יח) וַיֹּאמֶר אַבְרָהָם
(רמ"ח) אֶל־הָאֱלֹהִים (ילה) לוּ יִשְׁמָעֵאל יִחְיֶה לְפָנֶיךָ (סמ"ב)׃
(יט) וַיֹּאמֶר אֱלֹהִים (ילה) אֲבָל שָׂרָה אִשְׁתְּךָ יֹלֶדֶת לְךָ
בֵּן וְקָרָאתָ אֶת־שְׁמוֹ (מהש ע"ה) יִצְחָק (ר"פ ב"ן) וַהֲקִמֹתִי אֶת־
בְּרִיתִי אִתּוֹ לִבְרִית עוֹלָם לְזַרְעוֹ אַחֲרָיו׃ (כ) וּלְיִשְׁמָעֵאל
שְׁמַעְתִּיךָ הִנֵּה | בֵּרַכְתִּי אֹתוֹ וְהִפְרֵיתִי אֹתוֹ וְהִרְבֵּיתִי אֹתוֹ
בִּמְאֹד מְאֹד שְׁנֵים־עָשָׂר נְשִׂיאִם יוֹלִיד וּנְתַתִּיו לְגוֹי גָּדוֹל
(להח, מבה עד"א)׃ (כא) וְאֶת־בְּרִיתִי אָקִים אֶת־יִצְחָק (ר"פ ב"ן) אֲשֶׁר

וַיֹּאמֶר - Abraham was one hundred years old and Sarah, his wife, was ninety when the Creator informed Abraham that he and Sarah would become the parents of a male child in one year. God revealed this information far in advance of the birth to plant a seed of certainty within the consciousness of both Abraham and Sarah. Without this seed of certainty entrenched in their minds, the birth could never have taken place.

The Torah reveals a lesson concerning the power of mind over matter, demonstrating that consciousness is 99 per cent of reality while the physical world represents a scant one per cent.

Our own consciousness is fortified and elevated throughout this portion so that we and all humanity can finally achieve mind over matter and absolute control over our physical existence.

תֵּלֵד לְךָ שָׂרָה לַמּוֹעֵד הַזֶּה (והו) בַּשָּׁנָה הָאַחֶרֶת׃ (כב) וַיְכַל
לְדַבֵּר (ראה) אִתּוֹ וַיַּעַל אֱלֹהִים (ילה) מֵעַל (עלם) אַבְרָהָם (רמ״ח)׃
(כג) וַיִּקַּח (וזעם) אַבְרָהָם (רמ״ח) אֶת־יִשְׁמָעֵאל בְּנוֹ וְאֵת כָּל
(ילי)־יְלִידֵי בֵיתוֹ (כ״פ ראה) וְאֵת כָּל (ילי)־מִקְנַת כַּסְפּוֹ כָּל (ילי)־זָכָר
בְּאַנְשֵׁי בֵּית (כ״פ ראה) אַבְרָהָם (רמ״ח) וַיָּמָל אֶת־בְּשַׂר עָרְלָתָם
בְּעֶצֶם הַיּוֹם (נג״ד, זן) הַזֶּה (והו) כַּאֲשֶׁר דִּבֶּר (ראה) אִתּוֹ אֱלֹהִים
(ילה)׃

Maftir

(כד) וְאַבְרָהָם (רמ״ח) בֶּן־תִּשְׁעִים וָתֵשַׁע שָׁנָה בְּהִמֹּלוֹ בְּשַׂר
עָרְלָתוֹ׃ (כה) וְיִשְׁמָעֵאל בְּנוֹ בֶּן־שְׁלֹשׁ עֶשְׂרֵה שָׁנָה בְּהִמֹּלוֹ
אֵת בְּשַׂר עָרְלָתוֹ׃ (כו) בְּעֶצֶם הַיּוֹם (נג״ד, זן) הַזֶּה (והו) נִמּוֹל
אַבְרָהָם (רמ״ח) וְיִשְׁמָעֵאל בְּנוֹ׃ (כז) וְכָל (ילי)־אַנְשֵׁי בֵיתוֹ (כ״פ
ראה) יְלִיד בָּיִת (כ״פ ראה) וּמִקְנַת־כֶּסֶף מֵאֵת בֶּן־נֵכָר נִמֹּלוּ אִתּוֹ׃
פפפ

The Haftarah of Lech Lecha

Isaiah describes the war between Abraham and the kings, and how Abraham defeated them. The Creator is always with us in our battles, but if we think we can gain victory by ourselves, we will most certainly lose. Like Abraham, we must to surrender to the fact that we need the power of God.

ישעיהו פרק מ

(כז) לָמָּה תֹאמַר (יוהך) יַעֲקֹב (יאהדונהי אידהנויה) וּתְדַבֵּר (ראה) יִשְׂרָאֵל
(יא"י מילוי דס"ג) נִסְתְּרָה (ב"פ מצר) דַרְכִּי (ב"פ יב"ק) מֵיְהֹוָה וּמֵאֱלֹהַי (דמב,
ילה) מִשְׁפָּטִי יַעֲבוֹר (רפ"ח): (כח) הֲלוֹא יָדַעְתָּ אִם (יוהך)-לֹא שָׁמַעְתָּ
אֱלֹהֵי (דמב, ילה) עוֹלָם | יְהֹוָה בּוֹרֵא קְצוֹת הָאָרֶץ לֹא יִיעַף
וְלֹא יִיגָע אֵין חֵקֶר לִתְבוּנָתוֹ: (כט) נֹתֵן (ושר, אבג יתץ, אהבת חנם)
לַיָּעֵף כֹּחַ וּלְאֵין אוֹנִים עָצְמָה יַרְבֶּה: (ל) וְיִעֲפוּ נְעָרִים וְיִגָעוּ
וּבַחוּרִים כָּשׁוֹל יִכָּשֵׁלוּ: (לא) וְקוֹיֵ יְהֹוָה יַחֲלִיפוּ כֹחַ יַעֲלוּ
אֵבֶר כַּנְּשָׁרִים יָרוּצוּ וְלֹא יִיגָעוּ יֵלְכוּ (כלי) וְלֹא יִיעָפוּ: {ס}
(א) הַחֲרִישׁוּ אֵלַי אִיִּים וּלְאֻמִּים יַחֲלִיפוּ כֹחַ יִגְּשׁוּ אָז יְדַבֵּרוּ
(ראה) יַחְדָּו לַמִּשְׁפָּט נִקְרָבָה: (ב) מִי (ילי) הֵעִיר (ערי, סוזחך, סנדלפון)
מִמִּזְרָח צֶדֶק יִקְרָאֵהוּ (ראה) לְרַגְלוֹ יִתֵּן לְפָנָיו גּוֹיִם וּמְלָכִים
יַרְדְּ יִתֵּן כֶּעָפָר חַרְבּוֹ (רי"ו, גבורה) כְּקַשׁ נִדָּף קַשְׁתּוֹ: (ג) יִרְדְּפֵם
יַעֲבוֹר (רפ"ח) שָׁלוֹם אֹרַח בְּרַגְלָיו לֹא יָבוֹא: (ד) מִי (ילי)-פָעַל
וְעָשָׂה קֹרֵא הַדֹּרוֹת מֵרֹאשׁ אֲנִי (אני) יְהֹוָה רִאשׁוֹן וְאֶת-

אַחֲרֹנִים אֲנִי(אני)־הוּא(מום): (ה) רָאוּ אִיִּים וְיִירָאוּ קְצוֹת הָאָרֶץ
יֶחֱרָדוּ קָרְבוּ וַיֶּאֱתָיוּן: (ו) אִישׁ אֶת־רֵעֵהוּ (רהע) יַעְזֹרוּ וּלְאָחִיו
יֹאמַר חֲזָק (פהל): (ז) וַיְחַזֵּק (פהל) חָרָשׁ אֶת־צֹרֵף מַחֲלִיק פַּטִּישׁ
אֶת־הוֹלֶם פָּעַם (מנק) אֹמֵר לַדֶּבֶק טוֹב (והו) הוּא (מום) וַיְחַזְּקֵהוּ
(פהל) בְמַסְמְרִים לֹא יִמּוֹט: {ס} (ח) וְאַתָּה יִשְׂרָאֵל (יא״י מילוי דס״ג)
עַבְדִּי יַעֲקֹב (יאהדונהי אידהנויה) אֲשֶׁר בְּחַרְתִּיךָ זֶרַע אַבְרָהָם
אֹהֲבִי: (ט) אֲשֶׁר הֶחֱזַקְתִּיךָ (פהל) מִקְצוֹת הָאָרֶץ (מילוי אלהים
(יא״י מילוי דס״ג) וּמֵאֲצִילֶיהָ קְרָאתִיךָ וָאֹמַר לְךָ עַבְדִּי־אַתָּה
בְּחַרְתִּיךָ וְלֹא מְאַסְתִּיךָ: (י) אַל־תִּירָא כִּי עִמְּךָ־אָנִי (אני)
אַל־תִּשְׁתָּע כִּי־אֲנִי (אני) אֱלֹהֶיךָ (דמב, ילה) אִמַּצְתִּיךָ אַף־עֲזַרְתִּיךָ
(מיכאל, מלכיאל, שנדיאל) אַף־תְּמַכְתִּיךָ בִּימִין צִדְקִי: (יא) הֵן יֵבֹשׁוּ
וְיִכָּלְמוּ כֹּל (ילי) הַנֶּחֱרִים בָּךְ יִהְיוּ כְאַיִן וְיֹאבְדוּ אַנְשֵׁי רִיבֶךָ:
(יב) תְּבַקְשֵׁם וְלֹא תִמְצָאֵם אַנְשֵׁי מַצֻּתֶךָ יִהְיוּ כְאַיִן וּכְאֶפֶס
אַנְשֵׁי מִלְחַמְתֶּךָ: (יג) כִּי אֲנִי (אני) יְהוָה אֱלֹהֶיךָ(דמב, ילה) מַחֲזִיק
יְמִינֶךָ הָאֹמֵר לְךָ אַל־תִּירָא אֲנִי (אני) עֲזַרְתִּיךָ (מיכאל, מלכיאל, שנדיאל)
: {ס} (יד) אַל־תִּירְאִי תּוֹלַעַת יַעֲקֹב (יאהדונהי אידהנויה) מְתֵי יִשְׂרָאֵל
אֲנִי (אני) עֲזַרְתִּיךְ (מיכאל, מלכיאל, שנדיאל) נְאֻם־יְהוָה וְגֹאֲלֵךְ קְדוֹשׁ
יִשְׂרָאֵל: (טו) הִנֵּה שַׂמְתִּיךְ לְמוֹרַג חָרוּץ חָדָשׁ בַּעַל פִּיפִיּוֹת
תָּדוּשׁ הָרִים וְתָדֹק וּגְבָעוֹת כַּמֹּץ תָּשִׂים: (טז) תִּזְרֵם וְרוּחַ

תִּשָּׂאֵם וּסְעָרָה תָּפִיץ אוֹתָם וְאַתָּה תָּגִיל בַּיהוָה בִּקְדוֹשׁ
יִשְׂרָאֵל (ייא״י מילוי דס״ג) תִּתְהַלָּל׃ (ללה, אדני) {ס}

Lesson of Vayera

Regarding the welcoming in of guests

This portion begins on the third day after Abraham's circumcision. For an infant, this is said to be the most painful day, and Abraham was hardly an infant. He was 99 years old, so we can assume the pain was even greater. Yet the Creator knew that even in the midst of his pain, Abraham's nature would remain unchanged. He would be generous, hospitable, and giving. He would welcome any travelers on the road as his honored guests.

It is always hot in the desert, but the Creator made the day even hotter than usual. As Rashi puts it: "God took the sun out of its pocket." What a strange phrase! What is the sun's pocket? Actually, the phrase refers to the ozone layer that surrounds the earth and protects us from the ultraviolet radiation of the sun. In hearing and making a connection to this portion, therefore, we can gain protection from holes in the ozone layer. If, God forbid, the ozone were to disappear, this Torah reading will give us the same protection.

Scientists explain that the destruction of the ozone layer could potentially contaminate our food and water, making the world itself unfit for human life. Our connection with the Zohar, with Rabbi Shimon Bar Yochai, and with the Torah reading can protect us from all of this.

In spite of his pain and the heat, the Torah tells us that Abraham stayed outside, sitting in the doorway of his tent. His giving nature was such that he was not troubled by either his physical pain or the soaring temperature. Instead, he was distraught that he had no guest to welcome. Therefore, the Creator sent him three angels.

Think of the high spiritual level that Abraham had reached. What makes him different (and more) than we are? Is there any way we can reach his spiritual level?

Most of the time, we are not in physical pain, nor is the temperature outside 120 degrees. Yet unlike Abraham, we are too busy or too preoccupied to be concerned with anyone but ourselves. A first lesson we can learn from Abraham is to think of caring for others, even when we ourselves are in pain. When each of us, at our own level, makes that kind of effort, Abraham will help us. If we follow his path even a little way, he will be there for us. It does not matter how far we go as long as we go a little further today than yesterday. If every day we do even a bit more than previously, Abraham will be with us.

The Gemara reveals other lessons about Abraham. We learn, for example, that

welcoming guests is greater than welcoming the face of the Creator. When the Creator came to Abraham during his sickness, Abraham still rose to welcome his guests. And remember, Abraham kept all the Mitzvot of the Torah. He received and knew the Mitzvot through divine inspiration even before the Torah was given to the people of Israel. And the principle of welcoming guests–which is so important that it represents a higher level of consciousness than welcoming the face of the Creator–originates with this story of Abraham. How did Abraham himself know this was the right thing to do?

In The Torah of Rabbi Zusha, the rabbi explains that Abraham blessed all 249 parts of his body and all 365 ligaments, with the intention that they should always fulfill the desire of the Creator. He intended that his body should never do anything against God's desire. Therefore, when the Creator came to visit Abraham at the opening of his tent, Abraham knew that the matter of welcoming guests was a hugely important one simply because of his body's responses. His muscles gave him the strength to rise, and his feet had the power to run. Had this been against the Creator's will, Abraham could never have moved an inch for he had blessed every part of his body to never do such a thing. From this, we can understand that welcoming guests is a spiritually higher action than welcoming the face of the Creator.

We can further understand from Rabbi Zusha that Abraham was on a very high spiritual level, not only because of his hospitality but because in everything he did, his existence was directly connected to the Creator. Every breath he took, every step he walked was exactly what the Creator wanted him to do at that exact moment. Abraham's hands and feet sometimes would lead him into actions without his knowing why or what, but he always had the certainty that this was what the Creator wanted him to do.

We are not required to attain the spiritual level of Abraham. After all, almost everything we do is directed by our desire to receive for ourselves alone and not from our connection with the Creator. However, we do have to reach the level where our own spiritual potential is totally fulfilled. As Rabbi Zusha said: "I am not afraid if they will ask me in heaven why wasn't I like Abraham because I will answer that I did not have Godly powers like Abraham. But I am afraid that they will ask me why I wasn't like Zusha. Why was I not on the spiritual level that Zusha was supposed to reach?" Every person is committed to work for the Creator according to his own level and traits–not more than himself, but rather like himself.

So how do we start reaching a level where our body will be connected to the Light of the Creator and we can reach our spiritual potential? There is a story about Rabbi Elimelech and Rabbi Zusha that can help us to understand the way.

Once Rabbi Zusha was arguing with his brother, Rabbi Elimelech. One of them said that the most important thing for a person to know is how low he is, and from this will come an understanding of the greatness of the Creator. The other said the opposite: A person should look first at the greatness of the Creator, and only by seeing this will he understand how low he really is. The Maggid, our teacher Rabbi Dov, was asked to decide who was correct. And Rabbi Dov said they were both right in his eyes: that both these lessons were from God and were both true. But a person who thinks of himself as low before the Creator is at a higher level. Further, Rabbi Ya'akov Yitzchak from Lublin once said that he had heard from Rabbi Zusha that the most important thing with regards to his own spiritual work was to see how low he was. Rabbi Zusha said that if a person thinks of himself as small, he cannot deceive himself, and that is surely the true and right way of serving the Creator.

We can understand from what Rabbi Zusha said that what we need to do, so that everything we do will come from the desire of the Creator, is to make ourselves smaller–to grasp how much we do not understand, how much more there is than what we think there is. The more we do this, the closer we get to the Creator.

This week's reading also connects us with the power of the dots over the three letters, Aleph, Yud and Vav in the sentence: "And he said to him, where (Heb. ayeh, Aleph, Yud, Hei) is Sarah?" There is a connection between Aleph, Yud, Vav and Aleph, Yud, Hei or between our world of Malchut (Aleph, Yud, Hei) and the upper world (Aleph, Yud, Vav). Our world can be like the upper world only if we make ourselves smaller. The dots in the portion help us reduce our desire to receive for the self alone to the size of a dot.

As Rav Berg often says, if we want to shorten the process of transformation, we can do so only by connecting the two worlds, the upper world and the lower. The best way to achieve this is by making ourselves smaller: not physically smaller, but by shrinking our desire for ourselves alone. The dots in the portion help us to do this. They are also connected to the three angels that came to Abraham.

There are so many ways to further this process. We should never think, for example, that our own opinions are the only ones that have value; we must listen to others and be open to their thoughts. We shouldn't assume that we know what the Creator wants from us because maybe He wants something else. Maybe there is a business opportunity that can bring us more money and success than our current work, or maybe we need to experience some difficult financial times to learn an important lesson that we can take with us for the rest of our lives. We need to "shrink" our sense of self-importance. As

it is written: "Open for me an opening the size of the head of a needle, and I will give you the upper world." To really make this opening, we need to reduce our egos to that minute size.

It's not by coincidence that we also read of the binding of Isaac in this week's portion. What is the importance of this story? The Creator obviously did not need Abraham to bring him a sacrifice, nor did Creator need to see if Abraham loved Him. The Creator, after all, already knows our thoughts and feelings. Moreover, why is this even considered a test for Abraham? The responsibility was not exclusively on him. Isaac was 37 years old and was therefore responsible for whatever happened to him.

The Kabbalists explain that in this episode, Abraham created an opening for everyone: That if there are any judgments against any of us, we can overcome them as a result of the spiritual structure created by Abraham's binding of Isaac. We connect to the binding of Isaac by binding our own egos, by shrinking our egos and the ways we think of ourselves.

Finally, this week's reading is the only portion in which dots appear in two different places. The second occasion is on the word Ve'bakoma (Eng. 'when she rose'). When Lot was with his two daughters, it is written that he was drunk and they raped him. What is the connection to the dots? This is an act that cannot be easily understood: not just a rape, but the rape by daughters on their father.

We know that King David was descended from Ruth the Moabite, who was descended from the son who was born as a result of the rape of Lot by his daughter. Through the presence of the dots, the Torah teaches us that even the worst situation can have the Light of the Creator. There is no person so corrupt that he cannot connect to the Light! King David is a descendant of that unholy union of Lot and his daughter, and King David is the channel of Malchut for the whole world. What's more, we know also that Messiah, the final transformation, will come from David and Ruth. From every person in this world, from every situation in this world, we can and must reveal the Light of the Creator.

Synopsis of Vayera

This portion is deeply layered with meaning, offering us numerous lessons and spiritual Light for our lives. A single verse may be deciphered and studied for years but still not be mined of all its spiritual treasures and sparkling gems of wisdom.

It is the third day - the most painful - following Abraham's circumcision. Abraham waits outside his home with a single intent: to invite opportunities into his life that will allow him to perform acts of unconditional sharing. Instead of convalescing, he sacrifices all of his desires for comfort. This action merits him the visitation of three men. The Zohar states:

And even though he was in pain because of the circumcision, he ran forth to greet them, so that he would not miss anything and would not behave differently than before his circumcision -- as he always accepted and welcomed new guests.
- Zohar, Volume III, 7:95

The three men are actually angels sent to Abraham by the Creator to allow him to express his desire to share. These angels bestow various blessings upon Abraham, and it is these blessings that help us create life and prevent the loss of life as we read this portion. We learn that performing acts of charity and going outside our comfort zone have the power to reverse any sentence of death decreed against us and our loves ones. This Light and power shine upon us now, helping to protect us and our fellow man because of the merit of Abraham's charitable actions.

As the Holy Zohar states:

When harsh Judgment hangs over the world, the Holy One, blessed be He, remembers the charitable deeds that men performed.... As it is written: "But charity (righteousness) delivers from death."

- Zohar, Volume III, 12:169

While discoursing on this portion, the Zohar explains that there are times when the collective misdeeds of human beings reach such epic proportions that the Angel of Destruction is allowed to unleash a torrent of chaos so devastating that even the innocent and righteous are swallowed up in the process:

When the Angel of Destruction is granted permission to destroy, the righteous are in as much danger as the wicked.
- Zohar, Volume III, 26:369

However, the reverse is also true, which is why the Zohar devotes sacred space upon its pages to explain this matter. When the Zohar's Light is brought to bear, as it is now, even the unworthy are saved; they are purified by our efforts today, for that is the power of this holy book and of the sharing actions of Abraham our Patriarch.

First Reading - Abraham - Chesed

יוז (א) וַיֵּרָא אֵלָיו יְהוָֹה אדניאהדונהי בְּאֵלֹנֵי מַמְרֵא וְהוּא יֹשֵׁב פֶּתַח

מַמְרֵא - The Zohar reveals a secret about Mamre, telling us that Mamre is actually Jacob. In a later Torah story, Jacob is born to Isaac, the future son of Abraham. The Zohar is clearly discoursing in a spiritual realm beyond the concepts of time and space.

The Zohar states:

This is Ya'akov (Jacob) WHO IS CALLED MAMRE.
- Zohar, Volume III, 2:26

With regard to Jacob, the Zohar further states:

The Holy One, blessed be He, established a covenant with Jacob alone, more than THE COVENANT HE ESTABLISHED with all his fathers.
- Zohar, Volume III, 2:22

A striking statement is made here by the Zohar that pertains to the illumination of both spiritual Light and the simple light of the sun.

The Zohar explains that the Three Columns of spiritual forces must be present to generate an actual radiance of spiritual Light. These Three Columns correspond to Abraham (Right Column), Isaac (Left Column), and Jacob (Central Column). The Zohar ascribes additional importance to Jacob without whom Light cannot illuminate. The Zohar states:

ABRAHAM AND ISAAC ARE NOT ABLE TO SHINE WITHOUT HIM.
- Zohar, Volume III, 2:22

This spiritual truth is seen in our mundane world:

• The sun, which emanates a constant stream of rays, corresponds to Abraham. This is the positive Right Column of sharing. These rays of sunlight do not shine in the vacuum of space because there is no daylight above the earth's atmosphere in spite of the presence of the sun's photons in

this black void. So sunlight remains unmanifest, unobservable.

• The earth, or any physical object for that matter, corresponds to the receiver, the recipient that catches the sun's rays. This is Isaac, the negative Left Column of receiving. Though the earth may be designated as the recipient of the sunlight, there is still no illumination during this stage of receiving.

• The earth, however, reflects the sunlight entering the atmosphere. At the point of reflection, an immediate radiance occurs. This concept of resistance correlates to Jacob, the Central Column of resistance. It is this act of reflection and resistance that causes the rays of the sun to illuminate our world as shining light.

Without reflection and resistance, sunlight remains unmanifest and invisible to the naked eye. Darkness prevails. For this reason, Abraham and Isaac require the reflective powers of Jacob to express the Divine Energy that they embody, thus allowing it to illuminate in its entire splendor our material plane of existence.

A household light bulb operates under the same principle. The bulb possesses both a positive and a negative pole - Abraham and Isaac, or the Right and Left Column forces, respectively. However, the bulb requires a third and Central Column force of resistance to produce illumination. Herein lies the function of the filament, which resists the electrical current flowing between the negative and positive poles in the bulb. At the instance of resistance (Jacob, the Central Column), the light bulb brings forth light that illuminates a room. In the atom, these Three Columns correlate to the proton which is right column, the electron which is left column, and the neutron which is central column, respectively.

This wonderful model has practical applications for our own lives:
- Our soul correlates to Abraham and our willingness to share.
- Our ego correlates to Isaac and our self-seeking desires.
- Our free will to resist the selfish impulses of our ego and allow the will of our souls to guide our life correlates to Jacob.

Thus, we learn that only through free will - which is defined as resisting our Evil Inclination or resisting our ego - can we ever ignite spiritual Light in our life. If we allow our ego to control our behavior and govern our lives, then just as the sun's photons are present but unseen in the vacuum of space, the

Light of God, although ever-present, will remain hidden and unmanifest.

By virtue of Jacob (Mamre), this portion empowers us with the courage to exercise free will every day and to triumph over all of our desires borne of ego. In turn, intolerance, greed, impatience, jealousy, and anxiety are banished from our hearts.

The final letters of the Hebrew alphabet also correlate to Mamre. The five final letters (plus the oneness of the Creator) add up to 281, the same numerical value of Mamre.

The five final letters also correlate to the Messiah and the concept of Resurrection of the Dead. Hence, through the word Mamre, we bring about the arrival of the Messiah and the Resurrection of the Dead in our day. The Resurrection of the Dead includes any area of our lives that has undergone death, be it a business, a relationship, a marriage, or our inner peace and happiness.

פֶּתַח - The Torah states that Abraham is "sitting at the door of the tent in the heat of the day." The Zohar explains that the door of the tent is a code signifying a doorway to the Upper Worlds, which Abraham was able to ascend to by virtue of his circumcision.

We are then told that when Abraham looked up, he saw three men standing near him. These three men represent the three spiritual realms in the Upper World known as Chesed, Gvurah and Tiferet; these realms will eventually express themselves in our physical dimension as the patriarchs Abraham, Isaac, and Jacob.

The phrase "in the heat of the day" correlates to the realm of Chesed, whose particular wavelength of spiritual Light embodies the concept of mercy. This is the realm that Abraham connected to; and therefore, Abraham is the vehicle through which mercy enters into our world.

The spiritual force known as mercy sweetens the judgments pronounced upon us because of our unkind, intolerant actions. Mercy, Kabbalistically speaking, is also defined as time. Mercy offers us extra time to genuinely repent and change our ways, so we may repeal any decrees set forth against us by the universal karmic law of cause and effect.

-הָאֹהֶל **כְּחֹם** הַיּוֹם (נגד, זן): (ב) וַיִּשָּׂא עֵינָיו (מ"ה בריבוע) וַיַּרְא וְהִנֵּה

When we rise above physical and emotional pain and direct our consciousness towards helping others as Abraham did, we connect ourselves to the spiritual realms. We arouse untold blessings from the Upper Worlds, igniting a bounty of Light and mercy in our dimension.

As our ears catch the sound waves arising from this reading, boundless blessings ignite throughout existence. The verses instill us with courage, strength, and valor to transcend all forms of physical discomfort. We are inspired to share and care unconditionally for others, especially during the times when we are most self-involved. And because mercy is now in such abundance, we [should] use this time to forever transform our nature and revoke the judgments that hang over the world.

כְּחֹם - According to the Zohar, the phrase "heat of the day" refers to a particular ray of Light radiating from the supernal realm known as Chochmah. To the wicked, this Light condemns and burns. For the righteous, however, this same Light heals and regenerates.

Moreover, the Zohar states that the phrase "heat of the day" refers to the end of time - our time - when the greatest revelation of Light occurs:

This is the Day of Judgment that burns like a furnace in order to separate the soul from the body.
- Zohar, Volume III, 2:30

Thus, if we are spiritual, this Light will elevate us into joy. On the other hand, if we are imprisoned - which is, of course, by our own choosing - inside the material world, our path to the Light will be one of torment and suffering.

Each of us possesses traits of both the wicked and the righteous. This reading of the Torah connects us in a merciful manner to the profusion of Light so that its rays soothe and heal both us and all humanity. This Divine Radiance gently vanquishes our darkest traits while ensuring a Final Redemption that is free of judgment and overflowing with kindheartedness.

שְׁלֹשָׁה אֲנָשִׁים נִצָּבִים עָלָיו וַיַּרְא וַיָּרָץ לִקְרָאתָם מִפֶּתַח
הָאֹהֶל וַיִּשְׁתַּחוּ אָרְצָה: (ג) וַיֹּאמַר אֲדֹנָי אִם (יוהך) נָא
מָצָאתִי חֵן (מוזי) בְּעֵינֶיךָ (ע"ה קס"א) אַל־נָא תַעֲבֹר מֵעַל (עלם)
עַבְדֶּךָ (פוי): (ד) יֻקַּח (וזעם) נָא מְעַט מַיִם וְרַחֲצוּ רַגְלֵיכֶם וְהִשָּׁעֲנוּ

שְׁלֹשָׁה - Abraham made sure that there were four entrances to his tent so that visitors could enter from every corner. He opened himself up to the spiritual world, so he would not miss any opportunities to encounter angelic forces. We meet angels every day; however, we are usually blocked both spiritually and emotionally and therefore fail to perceive the sacred entities in our midst.

Sometimes, a child can be a channel for an angel. Events or unique circumstances that seemingly appear out of nowhere often signify that an angel is sending us a message. The more we are open to listening to the messages from people around us, the more the angels will tell us. If we are closed to messages, opinions, and viewpoints of friends and foes alike, we in turn close ourselves off to the angels and their profound messages for our life.

וְרַחֲצוּ רַגְלֵיכֶם - The Zohar teaches us that water corresponds to the purifying Light of the Creator and feet correspond to the Sfirat Malchut, which is our material plane of existence. Therefore, through the concealed words that speak these truths, Abraham washing the feet of the angels (that is, the three men) alludes to the power of Abraham's Light to purify and heal our world right now. Abraham and Sarah taught the people of their generation the importance of ritual immersion in water to cleanse the entire body and soul of impurities.

Here, we personally receive cleansing and purification by the Light through the immense caring of Abraham and Sarah, whose love for mankind is as constant and ageless as the shining sun.

וְהִשָּׁעֲנוּ - Abraham invites the three men to sit under a tree while he fetches them food. The tree of Abraham, according to the Zohar, possessed

special properties:

Whoever was pure was accepted by the tree. But whoever was impure was not accepted. Abraham then knew IF A PERSON WAS UNCLEAN. If this was the case, he purified him with water.
- Zohar, Volume III, 7:111

If the person who sat under the tree was a positive human being, the tree would stretch out its branches to offer cool shade and protection from the harmful rays of the sun. If the person was negative, the tree would shrink, denying the person shelter.

Abraham, therefore, knew who was pure and connected to the true Light of the Creator, and who was impure and connected to idol-worshipping. Idolatry does not refer simply to man-made statues and anthropomorphic icons before which we bow down. An idol is Kabbalistically defined as any material possession or external situation that controls our emotions and behavior. Our negative tendencies lead us to become worshippers of wealth and disciples of decadence. We are adorers of images - both the images and icons of our culture and the self-image we feel we must project to others.

Should any of these determine or influence our degree of contentment and joy of life, then we have surrendered control. We have severed our connection to our soul and its God-given ability to generate happiness from within ourselves. This is why Abraham would offer the impure person the opportunity to cleanse him- or herself through the power of water.

Often, we associate with the wrong people in life, duped by physical appearances. This reading raises our consciousness so that we may discern between the negative and positive people we encounter.

The Tree of Abraham also pertains both to the Tree of Life and to the Tree of Knowledge of Good and Evil. The Tree of Life is a flawless reality, a realm of perfect order, bliss, and infinite wisdom. This realm, which is the source of all human happiness, is imperceptible to our five senses. There are times, however, when we glimpse this reality through intuition or dreams.

The Tree of Knowledge of Good and Evil refers to our physical dimension of death and disorder. This is the world we perceive and experience through

תַּחַת הָעֵץ: (ה) וְאֶקְחָה פַת־לֶחֶם (ג' הויות) וְסַעֲדוּ לִבְּכֶם
אַחַר תַּעֲבֹרוּ כִּי־עַל־כֵּן עֲבַרְתֶּם עַל־עַבְדְּכֶם וַיֹּאמְרוּ
כֵּן תַּעֲשֶׂה כַּאֲשֶׁר דִּבַּרְתָּ (ראה): (ו) וַיְמַהֵר אַבְרָהָם (רמ"ח)
הָאֹהֱלָה אֶל־שָׂרָה וַיֹּאמֶר מַהֲרִי שְׁלֹשׁ סְאִים קֶמַח סֹלֶת
לוּשִׁי וַעֲשִׂי עֻגוֹת: (ז) וְאֶל־הַבָּקָר רָץ אַבְרָהָם (רמ"ח) וַיִּקַּח

our five senses.

When we behave with intolerance, insensitivity, and blatant disregard for the welfare of others, we find ourselves languishing in the reality of the Tree of Knowledge of Good and Evil, without any protection or shelter from negative forces. Consequently, turmoil eventually finds its way into our life, affecting our prosperity, relationships, and physical health and emotional well-being.

Our efforts today, through invoking the liberating Light of the Creator and the spiritual purity of Abraham, remove the power and allure of the "idols" that control us.

As Abraham used water to cleanse others, we now dip ourselves into the pristine waters of pure Light to wash away our sins and the reckless traits that initially brought about our misdeeds.

We add ourselves to the Tree of Life reality. This Divine Tree casts a protective shadow of Light over us, banishing darkness and death from our midst while engendering perfection, joy, and immortality all over the earth.

וְאֶל - Abraham fetches bread, meat, and other food to feed the three men who came to visit him. Abraham's unconditional caring is seen by his willingness to retrieve the food himself. He did not assign this task to someone else, even though he was still suffering the pain of circumcision. He took responsibility for feeding his guests, personally making sure that the job was completed.

(וזעם) בֶּן־בָּקָר רַךְ וָטוֹב (והו) וַיִּתֵּן אֶל־הַנַּעַר וַיְמַהֵר לַעֲשׂוֹת
אֹתוֹ׃ (ח) וַיִּקַּח (וזעם) חֶמְאָה וְחָלָב וּבֶן־הַבָּקָר אֲשֶׁר עָשָׂה
וַיִּתֵּן לִפְנֵיהֶם וְהוּא עֹמֵד עֲלֵיהֶם תַּחַת הָעֵץ וַיֹּאכֵלוּ׃ (ט)
וַיֹּאמְרוּ אֵלָיו אַיֵּה שָׂרָה אִשְׁתֶּךָ וַיֹּאמֶר הִנֵּה בָאֹהֶל׃

Often, we fail to follow through on our own spiritual goals and daily mundane responsibilities. We pass off work to another person, becoming complacent in our role as the conceiver of an idea or planner of a project.

Here, we receive fortitude, perseverance, and care to follow through with and complete all of our actions, carrying out even tedious tasks whenever possible, for it is these small actions that usually arouse the greatest blessings and Light.

אֵלָיו - In ten specific locations in the Torah, a dot or a set of dots is inscribed onto the parchment. Though tiny, these dots are potent forces of energy, each signifying an additional lesson and a unique ray of Light that is being emitted by the particular reading of the scroll.

In this portion, we find three dots in the word elav ("to him"), which appears in the verse "and they said to him" (Genesis 13:9). The letters with dots are Aleph, Yud and Vav אליו.

The three dots indicate that three angels came to visit Abraham.

These three angels - Michael, Raphael, and Gabriel - are the three men who stood near the patriarch outside his tent, as the Zohar reveals:

The verse, "And lo, three men" refers to the three angels - messengers who clothe themselves with air and come down to this world in a human image.
- Zohar, Volume III, 5:52

The Zohar then goes on to reveal the function of these angels:
And each OF THE THREE ANGELS served a different purpose. Raphael,

who governs the power to heal, helped Abraham recover from the circumcision. Another, Michael, who came to inform Sarah that she shall bear a son, rules over the right side. All the abundance and the blessings of the right side are handed over to him.

And Gabriel, who came to overturn Sodom, rules over the left side and is responsible for all Judgments in the world, AS JUDGMENTS COME from the left side. And the execution is done by the Angel of Death, THE KING'S CHIEF BAKER, who executes THE SENTENCES THAT ARE PASSED UNDER GABRIEL'S RULE.

- Zohar Volume III, 5:54–55

Michael - Abraham, the sages teach us, was sterile, and Sarah had already passed into menopause. Thus, bearing a child at Sarah's age, considering Abraham's physical condition, was unimaginable.
The angel Michael, who correlates to Sfirat Chesed, which is mercy and sharing, blesses Abraham and Sarah so that they can bring forth a child within one year.

Michael therefore embodies the power of sharing and the concept of mind over matter.

Our own sharing actions, when they are difficult to perform, imbue us with the ability to achieve mind over matter by virtue of our connection to Michael in this passage. Through the angel Michael, we receive control over the material world, including our physical bodies. This control increases with each difficult act of sharing that we perform.

Gabriel. Gabriel's role was to channel the energy of judgment into our dimension to destroy the corrupt, negative power centers of the world - the cities of Sodom and Gomorrah. Gabriel corresponds to the Sfirat Gvurah, which is judgment.

In our personal lives, we must also employ the power of judgment with spiritual discretion tempered with mercy. For instance, when we invoke judgment judiciously and proactively, it's akin to disciplining a child who misbehaves. This form of judgment is rooted in love and concern for the welfare of the child, not in our own frustration or reactive anger.

(י) וַיֹּאמֶר שׁוֹב אָשׁוּב אֵלֶיךָ כָּעֵת חַיָּה וְהִנֵּה־בֵן לְשָׂרָה

This is a difficult state of mind to achieve. However, we have Gabriel to elevate our consciousness through this reading, so we can always judge from a place of compassion and tenderness.

What's more, the Light cast through Gabriel uproots and abolishes the Sodom and Gomorrah within us - that is, the negative impulses that tempt us to indulgently gratify our own ego at the expense of others. The Light softens our heart so that we never judge people with excessive severity.

Raphael is the conduit through which healing enters our lives. He healed Abraham's circumcision and saved Abraham's nephew Lot when Sodom and Gomorrah were destroyed. Raphael signifies the energy of balance, the Sfirat Tiferet.

When we lack spiritual balance and are inclined towards physical pleasure and material illusion, an opening is created for physical illness to enter our system.

Here, we achieve balance, courtesy of Raphael. A yearning for spirituality blossoms within both us and the entire world. Human civilization, which is dangerously steeped in materialism, is corrected and balanced through our collective meditation during this reading.

וַיֹּאמֶר - The angels tell Abraham that Sarah will give birth to a son within the year. Abraham's unconditional act of sharing is a key factor in helping him and Sarah achieve mind over matter through the blessings of the angel Michael.

Most people usually offer charity or perform acts of kindness with a hidden agenda, sometimes consciously, sometimes unconsciously. These acts do not arouse blessings in our life. True sharing occurs only when we have no expectations. This secret is revealed in the following text of Zohar:

Come and behold: It was very polite and proper that they (the angels) said nothing to Abraham before he invited them to eat. This way, it did not seem that he invited them to eat because of the good news they brought him.

אִשְׁתֶּךָ וְשָׂרָה שֹׁמַעַת פֶּתַח הָאֹהֶל וְהוּא אַחֲרָיו: (יא) וְאַבְרָהָם
(רמ"ז) וְשָׂרָה זְקֵנִים בָּאִים בַּיָּמִים (נלך) חָדַל לִהְיוֹת לְשָׂרָה
אֹרַח כַּנָּשִׁים: (יב) וַתִּצְחַק שָׂרָה בְּקִרְבָּהּ לֵאמֹר אַחֲרֵי

Therefore, only after the verse stated "and they ate" did they inform him about the good news.
- Zohar, Volume III, 7:102

Here we learn that we must first perform unconditional, positive actions before blessings are returned to us and before any miracles can take place. If we expect blessings - or if we calculate and count on miracles because of our positive actions - in no way will they occur. If, however, we let go and give purely and unconditionally, we can then receive everything. This is the divine paradox of true spirituality.

A miracle, a wonder of nature, is essentially a mirror reflecting a profound spiritual change within human nature. Because our natural inclination is self-indulgence at the expense of others, the Light of this passage gives us the strength to overpower our natural tendencies and to apportion part of our life to the service of others, as exemplified by Abraham. When a person dedicates his or her life to sharing with others, the Creator causes great wonders to be revealed.

וַתִּצְחַק - A literal reading of Genesis 18:12 seems to indicate that Sarah doubts the wonders of God and the possibility of giving birth at her advanced age. Sarah's response seems to verge on cynicism and arrogance. A deeper analysis of the verse, however, reveals some compelling Kabbalistic secrets that have a dramatic impact on both us and the world the moment we become aware of them.

Sarah's first child will be named Isaac. The Hebrew word Isaac means "he will laugh." This is quite profound. Kabbalistically, the verse "Sarah laughed within herself" pertains to her son Isaac through the word "laughed." It means that the spiritual seed of Isaac was implanted within Sarah in that moment. Sarah laughing within herself alludes to the gift of childbirth being

בִּלֹתִ֤י הָיְתָה־לִּי֙ עֶדְנָ֔ה וַֽאדֹנִ֖י זָקֵֽן: (יג) וַיֹּ֥אמֶר יְהֹוָ֖הֿ֞אַדֹנִ֞יֿ֞אֲדֹנָֽי

אֶל־אַבְרָהָ֑ם (רמ"ז) לָ֣מָּה זֶּה֩ צָחֲקָ֨ה שָׂרָ֜ה לֵאמֹ֗ר הַאַ֥ף אֻמְנָ֛ם

אֵלֵ֖ד וַאֲנִ֥י (אני) זָקַֽנְתִּי: (יד) הֲיִפָּלֵ֥א מֵיְהֹוָֿ֞הֿ֞אֲדֹנָֿ֞יֿ֞אֲדֹנָ֖י דָּבָ֑ר (ראה)

לַמּוֹעֵ֞ד אָשׁ֥וּב אֵלֶ֛יךָ כָּעֵ֥ת חַיָּ֖ה וּלְשָׂרָ֥ה בֵֽן:

bestowed upon her.

Moreover, her apparent cynicism is our cynicism concerning the truth of the Creator and the ability of man to achieve mind over matter. The prerequisite for each and every miracle of nature is absolute certainty and trust. Our ego (the Satan) constantly implants doubts and cynical thoughts in our minds. Spiritual work entails transcending these artificial uncertainties. Our newfound awareness of this truth allows us to achieve this spiritual objective during this reading.

In addition, the miracle of childbirth is bestowed upon women who are having difficulty conceiving. This miracle is implanted within us the moment these particular verses are recited. Finally, the Zohar points out that the name Isaac is the same in Hebrew as the word for laughter. This laughter refers to the joy and delight we will experience in the Age of Messiah. Thus, these words of the Torah implant the seed of the Messiah in our world at this very moment, so we can give birth to endless laughter and joy in our lives.

הֲיִפָּלֵא - In response to Sarah's laughter and her doubts that she will ever bear a son, God says the above verse to Abraham (Genesis 18:14). The Zohar explains that this verse conceals secrets concerning the Resurrection of the Dead and the Age of Messiah:

What is meant by "the time appointed"? This is the time that is known to Me for the resurrection of the dead.
- Zohar, Volume III, 7:135

The Zohar continues in another verse:
I will return to you that same body which is sacred, renewed as before,

Second Reading - Issac - Gvurah

(טו) וַתְּכַחֵשׁ שָׂרָה | לֵאמֹר לֹא צָחַקְתִּי כִּי | יָרֵאָה (רי"ו)

(ראה) וַיֹּאמֶר | לֹא כִּי צָחָקְתְּ׃ (טז) וַיָּקֻמוּ מִשָּׁם הָאֲנָשִׁים

because you are like the holy angels. And that day shall be merry before Me and I shall rejoice in them…
- Zohar, Volume III, 7:137

Here we invoke the power of the Resurrection of the Dead - the dawning of the age that embodies immortality, boundless joy, and laughter - so that it will appear in our own day. Reinforcing this mystery, the Zohar offers this remarkable insight:

When the body exists in this world, it has not yet reached perfection. After it becomes righteous, walks the paths of honesty, and dies in its righteousness, then it is called "Sarah" (lit. "provided what is necessary"), as it has been perfected. When it reaches the Resurrection of the Dead, it is still called Sarah, so that nobody will say that the Holy One, blessed be He, has revived a different body. And after it becomes alive and rejoices with the Shechinah; and the Holy One, blessed be He, has wiped all distress from the world, as it is written: "He will swallow up death forever, and Hashem Elohim will wipe away tears from off all faces" (Yeshayah 25:8); then it shall be called Yitzchak [Isaac] (lit. "[to] be [laughter]"), because of the laughter and happiness of the righteous in the future.
- Zohar, Volume III 29:401

The Zohar is telling us that the word Sarah is a metaphor for mankind after it has completed its work of spiritual transformation. Man's ego is dead and buried. Her son Isaac is a metaphor pertaining to the dawn of the Resurrection of the Dead, the rebirth of spiritual man in a world that features endless joy and laughter. Therefore, the seed for the Resurrection of the Dead and the Age of Messiah is planted in the world through these verses. Our meditation nourishes this seed so that it blossoms in our day by virtue of the birth of Isaac, which occurs later in this portion. Our ego is laid to rest, and our soul - our true self - is reborn through the Light of this reading.

וַיַּשְׁקִפוּ עַל־פְּנֵי (חכמה, בינה) סְדֹם וְאַבְרָהָם (רמ"ח) הֹלֵךְ (מ"ה)
עִמָּם לְשַׁלְּחָם: (יז) וַיהֹוָ֘אדני֘אהדונהי אָמָר הַמְכַסֶּה אֲנִי (אני)
מֵאַבְרָהָם (רמ"ח) אֲשֶׁר אֲנִי (אני) עֹשֶׂה: (יח) וְאַבְרָהָם (רמ"ח) הָיוֹ
יִהְיֶה (יי) לְגוֹי גָּדוֹל (להח, מבה עד"א) וְעָצוּם וְנִבְרְכוּ (יהוה ריבוע יהוה ריבוע
מ"ה)־בוֹ כֹּל (ילי) גּוֹיֵי הָאָרֶץ (מילוי אלהים ע"ה): (יט) כִּי יְדַעְתִּיו לְמַעַן
אֲשֶׁר יְצַוֶּה אֶת־בָּנָיו וְאֶת־בֵּיתוֹ (ב"פ ראה) אַחֲרָיו וְשָׁמְרוּ דֶּרֶךְ
יְהֹוָ֘אדני֘אהדונהי (ב"פ יב"ק) לַעֲשׂוֹת צְדָקָה (ע"ה אלהים בריבוע) וּמִשְׁפָּט
(ע"ה ה"פ אלהים) לְמַעַן הָבִיא יְהֹוָ֘אדני֘אהדונהי עַל־אַבְרָהָם (רמ"ח) אֵת
אֲשֶׁר־דִּבֶּר (ראה) עָלָיו: (כ) וַיֹּאמֶר יְהֹוָ֘אדני֘אהדונהי זַעֲקַת סְדֹם
וַעֲמֹרָה כִּי־רָבָּה וְחַטָּאתָם כִּי כָבְדָה מְאֹד: (כא) אֵרֲדָה־
נָּא וְאֶרְאֶה הַכְּצַעֲקָתָהּ הַבָּאָה אֵלַי עָשׂוּ | כָּלָה וְאִם
(יוהך)־לֹא אֵדָעָה: (כב) וַיִּפְנוּ מִשָּׁם הָאֲנָשִׁים וַיֵּלְכוּ סְדֹמָה

וַיֹּאמֶר - Perhaps surprisingly to us, Abraham pleads to God for the salvation of Sodom and Gomorrah, the most negative centers of corruption and evil in the world. Abraham understood that regardless of how wicked or mean-spirited a person is, each individual in the world possesses a spark of God - each is a child of Creation.

If Abraham found it within himself to plead on behalf of the most negative people on Earth, imagine how much more tolerant and sensitive we would be towards our own friends, family, acquaintances, and foes - especially when we find ourselves casualties of their negative behavior - if we were to have the same positive inclinations towards others as Abraham did. Accordingly, tolerance and forbearance are awakened in our hearts through the reading of this section.

וְאַבְרָהָם (רמ"ח) עוֹדֶנּוּ עֹמֵד לִפְנֵי יְהֹוָהאדניאהדונהי: (כג) וַיִּגַּשׁ
אַבְרָהָם (רמ"ח) וַיֹּאמַר הַאַף תִּסְפֶּה צַדִּיק עִם־רָשָׁע: (כד)
אוּלַי (אום) יֵשׁ חֲמִשִּׁים צַדִּיקִם בְּתוֹךְ הָעִיר (סוזפך, סנדלפון, ערי)
הַאַף תִּסְפֶּה וְלֹא־תִשָּׂא לַמָּקוֹם לְמַעַן חֲמִשִּׁים הַצַּדִּיקִם
אֲשֶׁר בְּקִרְבָּהּ: (כה) חָלִלָה לְּךָ מֵעֲשֹׂת | כַּדָּבָר (ראה) הַזֶּה
(והו) לְהָמִית צַדִּיק עִם־רָשָׁע וְהָיָה (יהה) (יהוה) כַצַּדִּיק כָּרָשָׁע
חָלִלָה לָּךְ הֲשֹׁפֵט כָּל (ילי)־הָאָרֶץ (מילוי אלהים ע"ה) לֹא יַעֲשֶׂה
מִשְׁפָּט (ע"ה ה"פ אלהים): (כו) וַיֹּאמֶר יְהֹוָהאדניאהדונהי אִם (יוהך)־אֶמְצָא
בִסְדֹם חֲמִשִּׁים צַדִּיקִם בְּתוֹךְ הָעִיר (סוזפך, סנדלפון, ערי) וְנָשָׂאתִי
לְכָל (יה אדני)־הַמָּקוֹם בַּעֲבוּרָם: (כז) וַיַּעַן אַבְרָהָם (רמ"ח)
וַיֹּאמַר הִנֵּה־נָא הוֹאַלְתִּי לְדַבֵּר (ראה) אֶל־אֲדֹנָי וְאָנֹכִי (אי"ע)
עָפָר וָאֵפֶר: (כח) אוּלַי (אום) יַחְסְרוּן חֲמִשִּׁים הַצַּדִּיקִם חֲמִשָּׁה
הֲתַשְׁחִית בַּחֲמִשָּׁה אֶת־כָּל (ילי)־הָעִיר (סוזפך, סנדלפון, ערי) וַיֹּאמֶר
לֹא אַשְׁחִית אִם (יוהך)־אֶמְצָא שָׁם אַרְבָּעִים וַחֲמִשָּׁה: (כט)
וַיֹּסֶף (ציון) עוֹד לְדַבֵּר (ראה) אֵלָיו וַיֹּאמַר אוּלַי (אום) יִמָּצְאוּן שָׁם
אַרְבָּעִים וַיֹּאמֶר לֹא אֶעֱשֶׂה בַּעֲבוּר הָאַרְבָּעִים: (ל) וַיֹּאמֶר
אַל־נָא יִחַר לַאדֹנָי וַאֲדַבֵּרָה (ראה) אוּלַי (אום) יִמָּצְאוּן שָׁם
שְׁלֹשִׁים וַיֹּאמֶר לֹא אֶעֱשֶׂה אִם (יוהך)־אֶמְצָא שָׁם שְׁלֹשִׁים:
(לא) וַיֹּאמֶר הִנֵּה־נָא הוֹאַלְתִּי לְדַבֵּר (ראה) אֶל־אֲדֹנָי אוּלַי

(אום) יִמָּצְאוּן שָׁם עֶשְׂרִים וַיֹּאמֶר לֹא אַשְׁחִית בַּעֲבוּר
הָעֶשְׂרִים: (לב) וַיֹּאמֶר אַל־נָא יִחַר לַאדֹנָי וַאֲדַבְּרָה (ראה)
אַךְ (אהיה)־הַפַּעַם (מנק) אוּלַי (אום) יִמָּצְאוּן שָׁם עֲשָׂרָה וַיֹּאמֶר
לֹא אַשְׁחִית בַּעֲבוּר הָעֲשָׂרָה: (לג) וַיֵּלֶךְ (כלי) יְהֹוָהאדניאהדונהי
כַּאֲשֶׁר כִּלָּה לְדַבֵּר (ראה) אֶל־אַבְרָהָם (רמ"ח) וְאַבְרָהָם (רמ"ח)
שָׁב לִמְקֹמוֹ:

Third Reading - Jacob - Tiferet

יט (א) וַיָּבֹאוּ שְׁנֵי הַמַּלְאָכִים סְדֹמָה בָּעֶרֶב וְלוֹט יֹשֵׁב
בְּשַׁעַר־סְדֹם וַיַּרְא־לוֹט וַיָּקָם לִקְרָאתָם וַיִּשְׁתַּחוּ אַפַּיִם
אָרְצָה: (ב) וַיֹּאמֶר הִנֶּה נָּא־אֲדֹנַי סוּרוּ נָא אֶל־בֵּית (ב"פ)

וַיָּבֹאוּ - Sodom and Gomorrah represent the unveiling of the lowest level of human nature, where evil runs amok and man's darkest, most barbaric traits reign supreme. To civilized sensibilities, the cities of Sodom and Gomorrah were inverted, a world gone topsy-turvy. For instance, people who performed acts of kindness were immediately slain. Abraham's nephew, Lot, had a daughter who was caught giving bread to a beggar. She was covered with honey by the townspeople and left bound on a rooftop where she was stung to death by bees. Guards would even stand at the gates of the city to prevent hospitable people from taking others into their home for the night.

What's more, sexual perversion was rampant. Bestiality, rape, incest, and molestation were all accepted forms of behavior and were prevalent throughout both cities.

וַיֹּאמֶר - Sharing saves. Two angels, the Torah tells us, came to earth destroy Sodom and Gomorrah. When Lot observed them entering into the

עֲבָדְכֶם וְלִינוּ וְרַחֲצוּ רַגְלֵיכֶם וְהִשְׁכַּמְתֶּם וַהֲלַכְתֶּם (רֹאה)
לְדַרְכְּכֶם וַיֹּאמְרוּ לֹא כִּי בָרְחוֹב נָלִין: (ג) וַיִּפְצַר־בָּם
(מ"ב) מְאֹד וַיָּסֻרוּ אֵלָיו וַיָּבֹאוּ אֶל־בֵּיתוֹ (כ"פ ראה) וַיַּעַשׂ לָהֶם
מִשְׁתֶּה וּמַצּוֹת אָפָה וַיֹּאכֵלוּ: (ד) טֶרֶם יִשְׁכָּבוּ וְאַנְשֵׁי הָעִיר
(מזֹזֶּךְ, סנדלפון, עֲרִי) אַנְשֵׁי סְדֹם נָסַבּוּ עַל־הַבַּיִת (כ"פ ראה) מִנַּעַר
וְעַד־זָקֵן כָּל (יל"י) הָעָם מִקָּצֶה: (ה) וַיִּקְרְאוּ אֶל־לוֹט וַיֹּאמְרוּ

city, he ran over to invite them into his home, even though death was the prescribed punishment for hospitable behavior.

The Zohar explains Lot's motive: Abraham appeared to Lot in a vision, telling him to warmly welcome those visitors or else suffer death. This act of sharing, of welcoming the visitors into his home, is what saved Lot's life. This is why two angels arrived in the city - one came to destroy Sodom and Gomorrah, and the other came to save Lot.

Before any judgments are executed in this physical world, each of us is given an opportunity to sweeten or annul the judgment through an act of sharing. These opportunities are sent to us by the Creator. However, we generally do not recognize these chances because we are consumed by self-interest. Consequently, pain and turmoil (judgment) inevitably ensue.

The Light radiating through this story elevates our consciousness so that we can identify those moments for sharing in our life. Instead of passing these opportunities by - and rationalizing our behavior in the process - we are deeply inspired to embrace charitable deeds and acts of kindness with the knowledge that we are altering our personal destiny in a profoundly positive fashion.

Moreover, the Light of this passage repeals all guilty verdicts that have been found against humanity as a result of our past intolerant and negative deeds. For this gift, we must awaken untold gratitude for our forefather Abraham.

לוֹ אַיֵּה הָאֲנָשִׁים אֲשֶׁר־בָּאוּ אֵלֶיךָ הַלָּיְלָה (מלה) הוֹצִיאֵם
אֵלֵינוּ וְנֵדְעָה אֹתָם׃ (ו) וַיֵּצֵא אֲלֵהֶם לוֹט הַפֶּתְחָה וְהַדֶּלֶת
סָגַר אַחֲרָיו׃ וַיֹּאמַר אַל־נָא אַחַי תָּרֵעוּ׃ (ח) הִנֵּה־נָא לִי
שְׁתֵּי בָנוֹת אֲשֶׁר לֹא־יָדְעוּ אִישׁ אוֹצִיאָה־נָּא אֶתְהֶן אֲלֵיכֶם
וַעֲשׂוּ לָהֶן כַּטּוֹב (והו) בְּעֵינֵיכֶם (מ"ה בריבוע) רַק לָאֲנָשִׁים הָאֵל
(לאה) אַל־תַּעֲשׂוּ דָבָר (ראה) כִּי־עַל־כֵּן בָּאוּ בְּצֵל קֹרָתִי׃
(ט) וַיֹּאמְרוּ ׀ גֶּשׁ־הָלְאָה וַיֹּאמְרוּ הָאֶחָד (אהבה) בָּא־לָגוּר
וַיִּשְׁפֹּט שָׁפוֹט עַתָּה נָרַע לְךָ מֵהֶם וַיִּפְצְרוּ בָאִישׁ בְּלוֹט
מְאֹד וַיִּגְּשׁוּ לִשְׁבֹּר הַדָּלֶת׃ (י) **וַיִּשְׁלְחוּ** הָאֲנָשִׁים אֶת־יָדָם
וַיָּבִיאוּ אֶת־לוֹט אֲלֵיהֶם הַבָּיְתָה (ב"פ ראה) וְאֶת־הַדֶּלֶת סָגָרוּ׃
(יא) וְאֶת־הָאֲנָשִׁים אֲשֶׁר־פֶּתַח הַבַּיִת (ב"פ ראה) הִכּוּ בַּסַּנְוֵרִים

וַיִּשְׁלְחוּ - Protection. When the angels were in Lot's home, the citizens of Sodom surrounded the house, demanding that Lot remove the visitors from his home. Lot stood at the entrance of his door and pleaded with the men of city, but to no avail. They started to move towards Lot.

Suddenly the angels dragged Lot back into the house and created a glaring shield so that the men of Sodom were blinded.

This story speaks to the importance of spiritual protection when we find ourselves in a perilous and hostile environment from associating with negative people.

Accordingly, the Light of the angels filters through to us via this Torah reading, blanketing us with a protective shield of Light. Those who seek to wreak havoc in this world are blinded to our presence.

מִקָּטֹן וְעַד־גָּדוֹל (להח, מבה עד"א) וַיִּלְאוּ לִמְצֹא הַפָּתַח׃ (יב)
וַיֹּאמְרוּ הָאֲנָשִׁים אֶל־לוֹט עֹד מִי (ילי)־ לְךָ פֹה (ע"ה מום) חָתָן
וּבָנֶיךָ וּבְנֹתֶיךָ וְכֹל (ילי) אֲשֶׁר־לְךָ בָּעִיר (סוזפך, סנדלפון, ערי) הוֹצֵא
מִן־הַמָּקוֹם׃ (יג) כִּי־מַשְׁחִתִים אֲנַחְנוּ אֶת־הַמָּקוֹם הַזֶּה (והו)
כִּי־גָדְלָה צַעֲקָתָם אֶת־פְּנֵי (חכמה, בינה) יְהֹוָהאדנייאהדונהי וַיְשַׁלְּחֵנוּ
יְהֹוָהאדנייאהדונהי לְשַׁחֲתָהּ׃ (יד) וַיֵּצֵא לוֹט וַיְדַבֵּר (ראה) | אֶל־
חֲתָנָיו | לֹקְחֵי בְנֹתָיו וַיֹּאמֶר קוּמוּ צְּאוּ מִן־הַמָּקוֹם הַזֶּה
(והו) כִּי־מַשְׁחִית יְהֹוָהאדנייאהדונהי אֶת־הָעִיר (סוזפך, סנדלפון, ערי) וַיְהִי
כִמְצַחֵק בְּעֵינֵי (מ"ה בריבוע) חֲתָנָיו׃ (טו) **וּכְמוֹ** הַשַּׁחַר עָלָה

וּכְמוֹ - Letting go. The Angels instruct Lot to round up his family and leave Sodom at once before they unleash a torrent of destruction upon the city. But Lot hesitates. A part of him (the ego, which is the Satan within) still feels a dark attraction to the city and its nefarious inhabitants.

To save himself, Lot still needed to exert a spiritual effort to willingly break all ties to the place and to overcome the unclean yearnings that he still harbored. He needed to let go and break free of the dark, seductive energy that constantly pulled at him from Sodom.

Lot's sons-in-law think he is a fool and choose to remain behind. The angels are then forced to seize Lot by the hand and lead him, his wife, and his daughters out of the city.

The angels warn them not to look back as they leave, lest they be destroyed. Nevertheless, Lot's wife looks back and is destroyed, turned into a pillar of salt.

"Not looking back" is a metaphor for the concept of letting go.

וַיָּאִיצוּ הַמַּלְאָכִים בְּלוֹט לֵאמֹר קוּם קַח אֶת־אִשְׁתְּךָ וְאֶת־
שְׁתֵּי בְנֹתֶיךָ הַנִּמְצָאֹת פֶּן־תִּסָּפֶה בַּעֲוֺן הָעִיר (סוזחר, סנדלפון, ערי):
(טז) וַיִּתְמַהְמָהּ | וַיַּחֲזִקוּ הָאֲנָשִׁים בְּיָדוֹ וּבְיַד־אִשְׁתּוֹ וּבְיַד
שְׁתֵּי בְנֹתָיו בְּחֶמְלַת יְהֹוָאדניאהדונהי עָלָיו וַיֹּצִאֻהוּ וַיַּנִּחֻהוּ
מִחוּץ לָעִיר (סוזחר, סנדלפון, ערי): (יז) וַיְהִי כְהוֹצִיאָם אֹתָם הַחוּצָה

To grow spiritually, we must:

- Let go of the past and relinquish reckless traits.

- Commit ourselves to the spiritual path and to each new level that we attain, while resisting the desire to "look back" at our previous materialistic lifestyles.

- Resist the longing for the energy that once gratified our ego when we were in a lower, primal state of being.

Just as a recovering alcoholic must always resist a drink, we ought to view ourselves as recovering egoholics who must unceasingly defy the temptations and trappings of our illusionary material world, lest we fall and revert to our old ways.

This is not an easy task, as negative energy and the materialistic path is enticing and bewitching with an enigmatic and powerful pull upon us.

This passage is a gift to us, allowing us to draw upon the merit of Abraham and the influence of the angels to sever our ties to the sinful, self-indulgent elements of our former, selfish days. We grasp the hands of the angels and are lifted out of the mire of this earthly existence.

We forever recognize the senselessness of trading away eternal spiritual assets for the artificial, fleeting pleasures we derive by catering to our untamed impulses.

וַיֹּאמֶר הִמָּלֵט עַל־נַפְשֶׁךָ אַל־תַּבִּיט אַחֲרֶיךָ וְאַל־תַּעֲמֹד
בְּכָל (לכב)־ הַכִּכָּר הָהָרָה הִמָּלֵט פֶּן־תִּסָּפֶה׃ (יח) וַיֹּאמֶר
לוֹט אֲלֵהֶם אַל־נָא אֲדֹנָי׃ (יט) הִנֵּה־נָא מָצָא עַבְדְּךָ (פוי)
חֵן (מוחי) בְּעֵינֶיךָ (ע"ה קס"א) וַתַּגְדֵּל חַסְדְּךָ אֲשֶׁר עָשִׂיתָ עִמָּדִי
לְהַחֲיוֹת אֶת־נַפְשִׁי וְאָנֹכִי (אי"ע) לֹא אוּכַל לְהִמָּלֵט הָהָרָה
פֶּן־תִּדְבָּקַנִי הָרָעָה (רה"ע) וָמַתִּי׃ (כ) הִנֵּה־נָא הָעִיר (סוזוך, סנדלפון,
ער"י) הַזֹּאת קְרֹבָה לָנוּס שָׁמָּה וְהִוא מִצְעָר אִמָּלְטָה נָּא
שָׁמָּה הֲלֹא מִצְעָר הִוא וּתְחִי נַפְשִׁי׃

Fourth Reading - Moses - Netzach

(כא) וַיֹּאמֶר אֵלָיו הִנֵּה נָשָׂאתִי פָנֶיךָ (סמ"ב) גַּם לַדָּבָר (ראה) הַזֶּה
(והו) לְבִלְתִּי הָפְכִּי אֶת־הָעִיר (סוזוך, סנדלפון, ער"י) אֲשֶׁר דִּבַּרְתָּ
(ראה)׃ (כב) מַהֵר הִמָּלֵט שָׁמָּה כִּי לֹא אוּכַל לַעֲשׂוֹת דָּבָר
(ראה) עַד־בֹּאֲךָ שָׁמָּה עַל־כֵּן קָרָא שֵׁם־הָעִיר (סוזוך, סנדלפון, ער"י)
צוֹעַר׃ (כג) הַשֶּׁמֶשׁ יָצָא עַל־הָאָרֶץ (מילוי אלהים ע"ה) וְלוֹט בָּא
צֹעֲרָה׃ (כד) וַיהֹוָ֨אדני֨אהדונהי הִמְטִיר עַל־סְדֹם וְעַל־עֲמֹרָה
גָּפְרִית וָאֵשׁ מֵאֵת יְהֹוָ֨אדני֨אהדונהי מִן־הַשָּׁמָיִם (י"פ טל)׃ (כה)
וַיַּהֲפֹךְ אֶת־הֶעָרִים הָאֵל (לאה) וְאֵת כָּל (ילי)־הַכִּכָּר וְאֵת כָּל
(ילי)־יֹשְׁבֵי הֶעָרִים וְצֶמַח (ב"פ יהוה, אהיה, אדני) הָאֲדָמָה׃ (כו) וַתַּבֵּט
אִשְׁתּוֹ מֵאַחֲרָיו וַתְּהִי נְצִיב מֶלַח׃ (כז) וַיַּשְׁכֵּם אַבְרָהָם (רמ"ח)

בַּבֹּקֶר אֶל־הַמָּקוֹם אֲשֶׁר־עָמַד שָׁם אֶת־פְּנֵי (חכמה, בינה)
יְהֹוָהאדניאהדונהי: (כח) וַיַּשְׁקֵף עַל־פְּנֵי (חכמה, בינה) סְדֹם וַעֲמֹרָה
וְעַל־כָּל (ילי) (עמם)־פְּנֵי (חכמה, בינה) אֶרֶץ הַכִּכָּר וַיַּרְא וְהִנֵּה עָלָה
קִיטֹר הָאָרֶץ (מילוי אלהים ע״ה) כְּקִיטֹר הַכִּבְשָׁן: (כט) וַיְהִי בְּשַׁחֵת
אֱלֹהִים (ילה) אֶת־עָרֵי הַכִּכָּר וַיִּזְכֹּר (יהי אור ע״ה) אֱלֹהִים (ילה)
אֶת־ אַבְרָהָם (רמ״ח) וַיְשַׁלַּח אֶת־לוֹט מִתּוֹךְ הַהֲפֵכָה בַּהֲפֹךְ
אֶת־הֶעָרִים אֲשֶׁר־יָשַׁב בָּהֵן לוֹט: (ל) וַיַּעַל לוֹט מִצּוֹעַר

וַיַּעַל - Forgetfulness. The Torah says Lot and his two daughters sought refuge in a place called Tzoar after leaving Sodom. They soon left Tzoar, which Lot feared, and took residence up in the mountain where an incestuous relationship took place.

The Zohar says the Hebrew word Tzoar צוער is connected to the Hebrew word tza'ar צער, which means "agony." This is the agony of Hell - referring both to Hell after death and hell on earth - the pain and torment we suffer in this world as a result of our intolerant deeds and desires for materialism.

Lot entered Hell because of the sins of idol-worshipping in Sodom. Then he experienced the agony of Hell, and this is why he "feared" Tzoar.

However, up in the mountains, Lot's two daughters seduced him, without him even realizing it. Though Lot feared the repercussions associated with sinful behavior, he was unaware of what his daughters had done to him, as stated by the verse: "…and he perceived not when she lay down, nor when she arose." (Genesis 19:33)

Once again, we have a marvelous metaphor that speaks volumes about human nature. The daughters of Lot represent our Evil Inclination and the egocentric behavior it incites. Lot's fear is our fear, namely, our recognition and admission of our negative traits during the times when we're

וַיֵּשֶׁב בָּהָר וּשְׁתֵּי בְנֹתָיו עִמּוֹ כִּי יָרֵא לָשֶׁבֶת בְּצוֹעַר וַיֵּשֶׁב
בַּמְּעָרָה הוּא וּשְׁתֵּי בְנֹתָיו׃ (לא) **וַתֹּאמֶר** הַבְּכִירָה אֶל־

experiencing anguish. When we are distressed, we promise to change. We vow to alter our lifestyle and amend our conduct when the consequences of our misdeeds stand before us. But as soon as our suffering ceases and good times return, we forget those moments of clarity, those moments of truth. We are again seduced - unknowingly - by the trappings of a material world, caught up in the illusionary aspects of physicality. This truth can be found in the following verses of Zohar:

Rabbi Yitzchak said: If [Lot] was afraid, why then does the Evil Inclination come to misguide people? But this is indeed the way of the wicked. When he sees evil, his fear lasts only a moment. He then immediately returns to his wicked ways and fears nothing. Similarly, when the Evil Inclination sees the wicked being punished, it is afraid. But as soon as it leaves, it fears nothing.
- Zohar, Volume III, 23:322

The Torah verses relating to these Kabbalistic truths liberate us from the seductive charms of our Evil Inclination. Memory is restored. Clarity returns so that we forever remain true to our promise to transform and spiritually elevate our souls.

וַתֹּאמֶר - While Lot and his two daughters seek refuge in Tzoar, the cities of Sodom and Gomorrah are annihilated by fire and brimstone. Lot then leaves Tzoar, which he feared, to dwell up in a mountain cave.

While in the cave, Lot's two daughters fear the end of civilization after witnessing the massive destruction of Sodom and Gomorrah. The oldest daughter suggests they intoxicate their father with wine and sleep with him so that they may bear children and continue the human race.

Lot's two daughters then have sexual relations with their father while he is inebriated and virtually unconscious.

Both daughters eventually give birth to two male children, the older daughter to a boy named Moab, the younger to a son called Ben-Ammi.

The Zohar reveals that the child born to the older daughter is the seed and forefather of King David and the Messiah. Further confusing this Kabbalistic interpretation is the fact that there is a dot over the letter Vav in the word Uv'khumah וּבקומה that appears in a verse (Genesis 19:33) that describes how the daughter arose after having sex with her father.

In an attempt to unravel the mystery of a Messiah emerging from an incestuous relationship, the Zohar offers the following insight:

The potter and the importance of darkness. The Zohar tells us that the world and a man's soul are like a potter's slab of clay spinning on a stone wheel. While the wheel is in motion, the craftsman is able to remodel the shape of the clay any way he chooses. As long as the wheel revolves, the potter can create a vessel, a pot of clay, in any shape or form. Though the various shapes of the clay pot are many - some of them completely opposite in form to others - the potter is still working with a single slab of clay.

Following this profound metaphor, we are the potter. And our body and soul are the clay. We begin life as a clay pot molded into the shape of evil.

Our world constantly revolves so that our souls may evolve on the wheel of life as we shape and refashion our lives in an attempt to transform our nature completely from the extreme negative side (darkness) to the supreme positive side (Light).

The spinning of our world and the revolution of our souls over many lifetimes occur so that we become the craftsmen of Creation. This is how we become co-Creators of the Light in our lives - the cause of our own fulfillment - instead of having paradise handed to us freely like charity from the true supernal Creator.[18]
Moreover, the most negative situations invariably hold the greatest promise for positivity, for ours is a world of exquisite balance. Therefore, the ultimate darkness is inherently transformable into the brightest of Lights.

The Messiah is destined to generate the greatest possible spiritual Light in this world. Therefore, the Messiah must emerge from the lowest, darkest

הַצְּעִירָה אָבִינוּ זָקֵן וְאִישׁ אֵין בָּאָרֶץ לָבוֹא עָלֵינוּ כְּדֶרֶךְ
(ב"פ יב"ק) כָּל (ילי)־הָאָרֶץ (מילוי אלהים ע"ה)׃ (לב) לְכָה נַשְׁקֶה אֶת־
אָבִינוּ יַיִן (מיכ, י"פ האא) וְנִשְׁכְּבָה עִמּוֹ וּנְחַיֶּה מֵאָבִינוּ זָרַע׃ (לג)
וַתַּשְׁקֶיןָ אֶת־אֲבִיהֶן יַיִן (מיכ, י"פ האא) בַּלַּיְלָה (מלה) הוּא וַתָּבֹא
הַבְּכִירָה וַתִּשְׁכַּב אֶת־אָבִיהָ וְלֹא־יָדַע בְּשִׁכְבָהּ וּבְקוּמָהּ׃

realm - an incestuous relationship.

Each of us is born with the power to transform our nature completely and to achieve a personal state of Messiah within. Instead of experiencing guilt or shame - or even worse, apathy - as a consequence of our negative actions, we should be inspired by the opportunity to reshape our souls into the greatest of Lights. Today, in this portion, we are the potters.

[19] The dot. The Zohar's preceding explanation sheds light on the significance of the dot appearing over the letter Vav in the word Uv'khumah.

The word Uv'khumah, which means "when she arose," describes how both of Lot's daughters arose after having sexual relations with their father, unbeknownst to him. However, the word is spelled differently when it applies to the oldest daughter (Genesis 19:33).

The word is written with a vav and a dot above it. About the dot, the Zohar states:

This indicates that there was help from above in performing that action, which was to ultimately result in the birth of Mashiach [the Messiah]...
- Zohar, Volume III, 23:310

It was Divine assistance that ensured that the Messiah would emerge from the child of the eldest daughter.

וּבְקוּמָהּ - Meditating upon the dot. As we meditate upon this dot at the

(לד) וַיְהִי מִמָּחֳרָת וַתֹּאמֶר הַבְּכִירָה אֶל־הַצְּעִירָה הֵן־
שָׁכַבְתִּי אֶמֶשׁ אֶת־אָבִי נַשְׁקֶנּוּ יַיִן (מ״כ, י״פ האא) גַּם־הַלַּיְלָה
(מלה) וּבֹאִי שִׁכְבִי עִמּוֹ וּנְחַיֶּה מֵאָבִינוּ זָרַע׃ (לה) וַתַּשְׁקֶיןָ גַּם
בַּלַּיְלָה (מלה) הַהוּא אֶת־אֲבִיהֶן יָיִן (מ״כ, י״פ האא) וַתָּקָם הַצְּעִירָה
וַתִּשְׁכַּב עִמּוֹ וְלֹא־יָדַע בְּשִׁכְבָהּ וּבְקֻמָהּ׃ (לו) וַתַּהֲרֶיןָ שְׁתֵּי

appropriate moment in the reading, we personally enlist help from Above to ensure that our most negative traits are immediately transformed into positive attributes.

What's more, we can meditate to impart this sacred energy to the world, transforming the darkest elements of human civilization into luminous Light.

Finally, the dot connects us to the Upper World where we use the effulgent Light to commence the arrival of the Messiah, both our personal Messiah within and the global Messiah.

וַתַּהֲרֶיןָ - Deconstructing incest. According to the Zohar, the incestuous relationship between Lot and his daughters is also a metaphor for the machinations of our own Evil Inclination and the wickedness that men do. According to the Zohar, during sleep, the lowest level of our soul ignites evil desires and negative thoughts. These profane thoughts then conceive and are born into a man's heart. This process is the secret meaning behind Lot's daughters sleeping with their father, referring specifically the actual moment of conception.

The definition of sleep, according to Kabbalah, includes people who are unenlightened (that is, asleep in life) as well as people who live a shallow existence, lacking any awareness of spirituality. They live robotically, routinely, governed by ego, and controlled solely by their materialistic desires. This manner of existence is fertile ground for the seeds of evil thoughts.

בְּנוֹת־לוֹט מֵאֲבִיהֶן׃ (לז) וַתֵּלֶד הַבְּכִירָה בֵּן וַתִּקְרָא שְׁמוֹ

(מהש ע"ה) מוֹאָב הוּא אֲבִי־מוֹאָב עַד־הַיּוֹם (נגד, זן)׃ (לח)

וְהַצְּעִירָה גַם־הִוא יָלְדָה בֵּן וַתִּקְרָא שְׁמוֹ (מהש ע"ה) בֶּן־עַמִּי

הוּא אֲבִי בְנֵי־עַמּוֹן עַד־הַיּוֹם (נגד, זן)׃ ס כ (א) וַיִּסַּע מִשָּׁם

אַבְרָהָם (רמ"ח) אַרְצָה הַנֶּגֶב וַיֵּשֶׁב בֵּין־קָדֵשׁ וּבֵין שׁוּר (אבג

יתץ, ושר, אהבת חנם) וַיָּגָר בִּגְרָר׃ (ב) וַיֹּאמֶר אַבְרָהָם (רמ"ח) אֶל־

Next, the lowest level of our soul arouses and stimulates the power of the body until the evil thought in our heart becomes attached to it entirely. This is the hidden secret behind the physical birth of Lot's daughters' children as stated by the following Torah verse: "Thus were both the daughters of Lot with child by their father" (Genesis 19:36).

This story of incest, in truth, is a description of how evil takes hold in the human heart, seizes control of the body, and then impels us to behave with insensitivity, intolerance, and cruelty in varied measures, large and small. The power of this passage uproots the evil desires that lurk within the heart of mankind. The lowest level our soul is herewith subdued, and all mankind is awakened, elevated, and imbued with a higher level of soul.

Evil is not defined solely as wicked behavior in the form of murder, torture, or other bloodthirsty acts. Evil includes intolerance between two friends. Evil encompasses the envy that we feel over another person's possessions. Murder also includes character assassination by the words of gossip that we speak. Make no mistake: Insensitive acts, large and small, take their toll on humanity.

בִּגְרָר - Sarah and Abraham travel to the city of Gerar, where Abraham, to protect himself from being killed, tells everyone that Sarah is his sister. Sister is a code word that refers to the female Divine Presence known as the Shechinah. The city of Gerar is a code for negativity and darkness.

שָׂרָה אִשְׁתּוֹ אֲחֹתִי הִוא וַיִּשְׁלַח אֲבִימֶלֶךְ מֶלֶךְ גְּרָר וַיִּקַּח
(וזעם) אֶת־שָׂרָה׃ (ג) וַיָּבֹא אֱלֹהִים (ילה) אֶל־אֲבִימֶלֶךְ בַּחֲלוֹם
הַלָּיְלָה (מלה) וַיֹּאמֶר לוֹ הִנְּךָ מֵת עַל־הָאִשָּׁה אֲשֶׁר־לָקַחְתָּ
וְהִוא בְּעֻלַת בָּעַל׃ (ד) וַאֲבִימֶלֶךְ לֹא קָרַב אֵלֶיהָ וַיֹּאמַר
אֲדֹנָי הֲגוֹי גַּם־צַדִּיק תַּהֲרֹג׃ (ה) הֲלֹא הוּא אָמַר־לִי אֲחֹתִי
הִוא וְהִיא־גַם־הוּא אָמְרָה אָחִי הוּא בְּתָם־לְבָבִי וּבְנִקְיֹן
כַּפַּי עָשִׂיתִי זֹאת׃ (ו) וַיֹּאמֶר אֵלָיו הָאֱלֹהִים (ילה) בַּחֲלֹם גַּם
אָנֹכִי (איע) יָדַעְתִּי כִּי בְתָם־לְבָבְךָ עָשִׂיתָ זֹּאת וָאֶחְשֹׂךְ גַּם־
אָנֹכִי (איע) אוֹתְךָ מֵחֲטוֹ־לִי עַל־כֵּן לֹא־נְתַתִּיךָ לִנְגֹּעַ אֵלֶיהָ׃

In essence, before Abraham goes down to the darkness and negativity, he first attaches himself to the Creator via the Shechinah. The spiritual principle concealed in this story can be revealed by an analogy. If a person lowers himself into a deep, dark pit filled with deadly snakes to retrieve a great treasure, he first secures himself to a strong rope to ensure a safe retreat. The rope becomes his lifeline as he enters the dangerous environment. Likewise, Abraham attaches himself to the force called Shechinah before he enters the pit of negativity (the city of Gerar) so that he can maintain a lifeline to the Creator.

There are moments in life when we're lured into negative situations and seduced. Without supernal assistance, we fall prey to the traps and temptations set up by the forces of negativity. In addition, we are influenced by the negative influences of the stars and planets.

Here, we are building for ourselves a secure lifeline to the Creator for those challenging moments in life when we stumble and fall into negativity. We rise above all negative cosmic forces and become directors of our own destiny.

(ז) וְעַתָּה הָשֵׁב אֵשֶׁת־הָאִישׁ כִּי־נָבִיא הוּא וְיִתְפַּלֵּל בַּעַדְךָ
וֶחְיֵה וְאִם (יוהך)־אֵינְךָ מֵשִׁיב דַּע כִּי־מוֹת תָּמוּת אַתָּה וְכָל
(ילי)־אֲשֶׁר־לָךְ׃ (ח) וַיַּשְׁכֵּם אֲבִימֶלֶךְ בַּבֹּקֶר וַיִּקְרָא לְכָל (יה
אדני)־עֲבָדָיו וַיְדַבֵּר (ראה) אֶת־כָּל (ילי)־הַדְּבָרִים (ראה) הָאֵלֶּה
בְּאָזְנֵיהֶם (יוד הי ואו הה) וַיִּירְאוּ הָאֲנָשִׁים מְאֹד׃ (ט) וַיִּקְרָא
אֲבִימֶלֶךְ לְאַבְרָהָם (רמ"ח) וַיֹּאמֶר לוֹ מֶה (מ"ה)־עָשִׂיתָ לָּנוּ (מום)
וּמֶה (מ"ה)־חָטָאתִי לָךְ כִּי־הֵבֵאתָ עָלַי וְעַל־מַמְלַכְתִּי חֲטָאָה
גְדֹלָה מַעֲשִׂים אֲשֶׁר לֹא־יֵעָשׂוּ עָשִׂיתָ עִמָּדִי׃ (י) וַיֹּאמֶר
אֲבִימֶלֶךְ אֶל־אַבְרָהָם (רמ"ח) מָה (מ"ה) רָאִיתָ כִּי עָשִׂיתָ אֶת־
הַדָּבָר (ראה) הַזֶּה (והו)׃ (יא) וַיֹּאמֶר אַבְרָהָם (רמ"ח) כִּי אָמַרְתִּי רַק
אֵין־יִרְאַת אֱלֹהִים (ילה) בַּמָּקוֹם הַזֶּה (והו) וַהֲרָגוּנִי עַל־דְּבַר
(ראה) אִשְׁתִּי׃ (יב) וְגַם־אָמְנָה אֲחֹתִי בַת־אָבִי הִוא אַךְ (אהיה)
לֹא בַת־אִמִּי וַתְּהִי־לִי לְאִשָּׁה׃ (יג) וַיְהִי כַּאֲשֶׁר הִתְעוּ אֹתִי
אֱלֹהִים (ילה) מִבֵּית (ב"פ ראה) אָבִי וָאֹמַר לָהּ זֶה חַסְדֵּךְ אֲשֶׁר
תַּעֲשִׂי עִמָּדִי אֶל כָּל (ילי)־הַמָּקוֹם אֲשֶׁר נָבוֹא שָׁמָּה אִמְרִי־
לִי אָחִי הוּא׃ (יד) וַיִּקַּח (וזעם) אֲבִימֶלֶךְ צֹאן וּבָקָר וַעֲבָדִים
וּשְׁפָחֹת וַיִּתֵּן לְאַבְרָהָם (רמ"ח) וַיָּשֶׁב לוֹ אֵת שָׂרָה אִשְׁתּוֹ׃ (טו)
וַיֹּאמֶר אֲבִימֶלֶךְ הִנֵּה אַרְצִי לְפָנֶיךָ (סמ"ב) בַּטּוֹב (והו) בְּעֵינֶיךָ
(ע"ה קס"א) שֵׁב׃ (טז) וּלְשָׂרָה אָמַר הִנֵּה נָתַתִּי אֶלֶף כֶּסֶף לְאָחִיךְ

הִנֵּה הוּא־לָךְ כְּסוּת עֵינַיִם (מ"ה בריבוע) לְכֹל (יה אדני) אֲשֶׁר אִתָּךְ
וְאֵת כֹּל (ילי) וְנֹכָחַת׃ (יז) וַיִּתְפַּלֵּל אַבְרָהָם (רמ"ח) אֶל־הָאֱלֹהִים
(ילה) וַיִּרְפָּא אֱלֹהִים (ילה) אֶת־אֲבִימֶלֶךְ וְאֶת־אִשְׁתּוֹ וְאַמְהֹתָיו
וַיֵּלֵדוּ׃ (יח) כִּי־עָצֹר עָצַר יְהֹוָהאדניאהדונהי בְּעַד כָּל (ילי)־רֶחֶם
(אברהם) לְבֵית (ב"פ ראה) אֲבִימֶלֶךְ עַל־דְּבַר (ראה) שָׂרָה אֵשֶׁת
אַבְרָהָם (רמ"ח)׃ ס כא (א) וַיהֹוָהאדניאהדונהי פָּקַד אֶת־שָׂרָה

פָּקַד - The word Sarah represents human beings in a state of righteousness, when the ego is dead and the body rests within the grave. The Creator visiting Sarah refers to the Light of the Creator arriving in this world at the End of Days (our present day) to commence the Resurrection of the Dead and the Dawn of Immortality.

The Zohar then quotes the words of the Creator:

"I will open your graves, and cause you to come up out of your graves, and bring you into the land of Israel" (Yechezkel 37:12), which is followed by: "And I shall put my spirit in you, and you shall live...."
- Zohar, Volume III, 29:391

The Zohar explains that the Creator will then make the body of man as beautiful as Adam's was when he entered the Garden of Eden:

Then all creatures shall know of the soul that entered them - that it is the soul of Life, the soul of Delight, which has received all pleasures and delights for the body from above.
- Zohar Volume III, 29:393

The End of Days will see the dawning of an abundance of spiritual energy, unprecedented in human history. Who will safely harness this energy and generate a radiance of Light and who will short-circuit and suffer from the burning rays will be determined by one factor: Did we treat our fellow man

כַּאֲשֶׁר אָמָר וַיַּעַשׂ יְהֹוָהאדניאהדונהי לְשָׂרָה כַּאֲשֶׁר דִּבֵּר (ראה):
(ב) וַתַּהַר וַתֵּלֶד שָׂרָה לְאַבְרָהָם (רמ"ח) בֵּן לִזְקֻנָיו לַמּוֹעֵד

with human dignity?

Whereas in the past, the consequences of our intolerant behavior were delayed for years or even lifetimes, the End of Days will see the distance between cause and effect contract; the repercussions of our actions, either positive or negative, will be felt immediately. Judgment and mercy will co-exist side-by-side.

This single verse of Torah (Genesis 21:1) initiates the Resurrection of the Dead now, with an overflow of soft-heartedness and leniency. Moreover, by slaying our ego using a sword of Light drawn from this passage, we can be spiritually resurrected and will avoid the experience of physical death and interment.

וַתֵּלֶד - Fertility. The words that speak of the birth of Isaac radiate a force of fertility that helps all those who are unable to conceive children. We, through our caring and meditation, can transfer this energy to people in need, helping them remedy the root source of their infertility.

Laughter. The name Isaac refers to the concept and emotion of laughter.

We all in one degree or another need to express our true emotions in life - to laugh, to cry, to vent frustration. Oftentimes, we allow our emotions (such as anger, resentment, and grief) to build up inside. This prevents us from living joyfully, proactively, and peacefully.

Isaac's presence in this portion releases our pent-up emotions in a proactive fashion so that we can live fully, with feeling and honesty.

The death of death. On a deeper level of understanding, the Zohar explains that the name Sarah is a code for a person who has attained a state of righteousness and spiritual completeness, his or her Evil Inclination slain. This state of existence is achieved prior to the Resurrection of the Dead and

אֲשֶׁר־דִּבֶּר (ראה) אֹתוֹ אֱלֹהִים (ילה): (ג) וַיִּקְרָא אַבְרָהָם (רמ"ח)
אֶת־שֶׁם־ בְּנוֹ הַנּוֹלַד־לוֹ אֲשֶׁר־יָלְדָה־לּוֹ שָׂרָה יִצְחָק (ד"פ
ב"ן): (ד) וַיָּמָל אַבְרָהָם (רמ"ח) אֶת־יִצְחָק (ד"פ ב"ן) בְּנוֹ בֶּן־שְׁמֹנַת
יָמִים (נלך) כַּאֲשֶׁר צִוָּה אֹתוֹ אֱלֹהִים (ילה):

Fifth Reading - Aaron - Hod

(ה) וְאַבְרָהָם (רמ"ח) בֶּן־ מְאַת שָׁנָה בְּהִוָּלֶד לוֹ אֵת יִצְחָק (ד"פ ב"ן)
בְּנוֹ: (ו) וַתֹּאמֶר שָׂרָה צְחֹק עָשָׂה לִי אֱלֹהִים (כוק) (ילה) כָּל (ילי)־

the Dawn of Immortality.

The name Isaac is a metaphor for man immortalized, following the Resurrection after God has banished death forever. In this ultimate, eternal phase of existence, all of us will dwell in pure joy and will be unified with the Light of the Creator.

This secret is revealed by the following verse of the Zohar:

"He will swallow up death forever; and Hashem Elohim will wipe away tears from off all faces" (Yeshayah 25:8). Then it [the immortal body, named Sarah] shall be called Isaac (lit. "[to] be [laughter]"), because of the laughter and happiness of the righteous in the future.
- Zohar, Volume III, 29:401

The verses that tell of Isaac's birth cause the demise of the Angel of Death as we listen to this reading. The pleasure of endless laughter echoes throughout eternity.

The Angel of Death's influence extends beyond the destruction of the physical body. He is also responsible for the demise of our happiness, the dissolution of a marriage, the ruin of a person's livelihood. Thus, any area of our life that is in danger of coming to an end will be resurrected through this reading.

הֲשַׁמַּע יִצְחָק (ד"פ ב"ן)־לִי׃ (ז) וַתֹּאמֶר מִי (ילי) מִלֵּל לְאַבְרָהָם
(רמ"ח) הֵינִיקָה בָנִים שָׂרָה כִּי־יָלַדְתִּי בֵן לִזְקֻנָיו׃ (וז) וַיִּגְדַּל (יזל)
הַיֶּלֶד וַיִּגָּמַל וַיַּעַשׂ אַבְרָהָם (רמ"ח) מִשְׁתֶּה גָדוֹל (להח, מבה עד"א)
בְּיוֹם (נגד, זן) הִגָּמֵל אֶת־יִצְחָק (ד"פ ב"ן)׃ (ט) וַתֵּרֶא שָׂרָה אֶת־
בֶּן־הָגָר הַמִּצְרִית (מצר) אֲשֶׁר־יָלְדָה לְאַבְרָהָם (רמ"ח) מְצַחֵק׃
(י) וַתֹּאמֶר לְאַבְרָהָם (רמ"ח) גָּרֵשׁ הָאָמָה הַזֹּאת וְאֶת־בְּנָהּ

וַתֵּרֶא - Traits of evil. The characters Hagar and Ishmael are metaphors for our own immoral attributes. The banishment of Hagar and Ishmael corresponds to the expulsion of our own selfish desires from our inner most being.

The first step in transformation involves recognizing and admitting to our self-indulgent impulses. This self-acknowledgment, according to the sage Rav Yehuda Ashlag, is 90 per cent of the battle. The Light of the Creator that shines in this week's reading is then free to enter and eradicate the darkest recesses of our soul. Towards that end, this passage arouses self-awareness, thus banishing our own Evil Inclination along with the negative attributes from our character.

וַתֹּאמֶר - Abraham fathered two sons - Ishmael, who was conceived by an Egyptian woman named Hagar - and Isaac, whose mother is Sarah. Sarah was, of course, Abraham's wife while Hagar was one of Abraham's concubines.

Ishmael is the seed and progenitor of Islam and the entire Arab world. Isaac is the seed from which emerged the children of Israel.

The Torah tells us that Sarah instructs Abraham to banish Hagar and Ishmael from their home. One might ask how Abraham and Sarah, the personification of mercy and kindness, could behave with such cruelty? Moreover, this story has been the cause of endless conflict between Jews and Arabs.

כִּי לֹא יִירַשׁ בֶּן־הָאָמָה הַזֹּאת עִם־בְּנִי עִם־יִצְחָק (ד"פ ב"ן):
(יא) וַיֵּרַע הַדָּבָר (ראה) מְאֹד בְּעֵינֵי (מ"ה בריבוע) אַבְרָהָם (רמ"ח) עַל
אוֹדֹת בְּנוֹ: (יב) וַיֹּאמֶר אֱלֹהִים (ילה) אֶל־אַבְרָהָם (רמ"ח) אַל־
יֵרַע בְּעֵינֶיךָ (ע"ה קס"א) עַל־הַנַּעַר וְעַל־אֲמָתֶךָ כֹּל (ילי) אֲשֶׁר
תֹּאמַר אֵלֶיךָ שָׂרָה שְׁמַע בְּקֹלָהּ כִּי בְיִצְחָק (ד"פ ב"ן) יִקָּרֵא
לְךָ זָרַע: (יג) וְגַם אֶת־בֶּן־הָאָמָה לְגוֹי אֲשִׂימֶנּוּ כִּי זַרְעֲךָ
הוּא: (יד) וַיַּשְׁכֵּם אַבְרָהָם (רמ"ח) | בַּבֹּקֶר וַיִּקַּח (חעם)־לֶחֶם

וַיַּשְׁכֵּם - The separation of Isaac and Ishmael. Isaac is a code that corresponds to the Left Column force known as desire to receive for the self alone. This is the negative pole (–) of energy found in electricity. In human terms, this is our ego.

Ishmael is a formula describing the Right Column force known as sharing, which is a positive pole (+) of energy. This alludes to the material pleasures of life that indulge our ego.

In a battery, if the positive and negative poles connect directly via a wire, the battery short-circuits. It is drained of all its power.

Through Sarah's action of banishing Hagar and Ishmael, she separated Isaac and Ishmael. This indicates that we must separate ourselves from the pleasures that gratify our ego. Rather, we must lead by the will of our soul and its desires for spiritual fulfillment.

The Torah is telling us that if we, the children of Israel, do not separate ourselves from short-term selfish pleasures of life, then there will be continued separation between Jews and Arabs. We must live our lives according to the will of our soul as opposed to the influence of our ego.

When we do create this separation, we create energy for the world. Then the world will embrace us with love and Light.

(ג' הויות) וְחֵמַת מַיִם וַיִּתֵּן אֶל-הָגָר שָׂם עַל-שִׁכְמָהּ וְאֶת-
הַיֶּלֶד וַיְשַׁלְּחֶהָ וַתֵּלֶךְ וַתֵּתַע בְּמִדְבַּר בְּאֵר (קנ"א ב"ן) שָׁבַע׃
(טו) וַיִּכְלוּ (ע"ב) הַמַּיִם מִן-הַחֵמֶת וַתַּשְׁלֵךְ אֶת-הַיֶּלֶד תַּחַת
אַחַד (אהבה) הַשִּׂיחִם׃ (טז) וַתֵּלֶךְ וַתֵּשֶׁב לָהּ מִנֶּגֶד (זן, מזבח)

When Sarah separated Isaac and Ishmael, she was actually separating these two energy forces and desires. This is the deeper spiritual significance behind this story.

Regarding the name of Ishmael, the Zohar states:
"...Because his name should not be mentioned in the presence of Isaac.."
- Zohar Volume III, 33:463

The point here is profoundly simple. The Light of our soul cannot exist with our ego. The ego must be separated and removed to allow our soul to shine and thus guide us in life.

Put simply, if we activate only our desire to receive for the self alone, then this will cause a dangerous separation between Arabs and Jews. We must activate our desire to receive for the sake of sharing. This is our responsibility.

The desire to receive for the self alone, which is also known as reactive behavior, is the root cause behind all personal and collective chaos.

Ishmael is Right Column, which is positive charge of energy. Isaac is Left Column, which is a negative charge of energy. In a battery, if the positive and negative poles connect directly via a wire, the battery short-circuits and is drained of all its power.

The positive and negative poles must be separated. This is the inner meaning behind the banishment of Hagar. The two columns (positive right and negative left), moreover, must remain apart to prevent a short-circuit.

וַתֵּלֶךְ - Abraham sends Hagar and Ishmael away into the desert, giving

הַרְחֵק כִּמְטַחֲוֵי קֶשֶׁת כִּי אָמְרָה אַל־אֶרְאֶה בְּמוֹת הַיָּלֶד
וַתֵּשֶׁב מִנֶּגֶד (זן, מזבח) וַתִּשָּׂא אֶת־קֹלָהּ וַתֵּבְךְּ׃ (יז) וַיִּשְׁמַע
אֱלֹהִים (ילה) אֶת־קוֹל הַנַּעַר וַיִּקְרָא מַלְאַךְ אֱלֹהִים (ילה) |
אֶל־הָגָר מִן־הַשָּׁמַיִם (י״פ טל) וַיֹּאמֶר לָהּ מַה (מ״ה)־לָּךְ הָגָר
אַל־תִּירְאִי כִּי־שָׁמַע אֱלֹהִים (ילה) אֶל־קוֹל הַנַּעַר בַּאֲשֶׁר
הוּא־שָׁם׃ (יח) קוּמִי שְׂאִי אֶת־הַנַּעַר וְהַחֲזִיקִי אֶת־יָדֵךְ בּוֹ
כִּי־לְגוֹי גָּדוֹל (להח, מבה עד״א) אֲשִׂימֶנּוּ׃ (יט) וַיִּפְקַח אֱלֹהִים (ילה)
אֶת־עֵינֶיהָ (מ״ה בריבוע) וַתֵּרֶא בְּאֵר (קנ״א ב״ן) מָיִם וַתֵּלֶךְ וַתְּמַלֵּא
אֶת־הַחֵמֶת מַיִם וַתַּשְׁקְ אֶת־הַנָּעַר׃ (כ) וַיְהִי אֱלֹהִים (ילה)
אֶת־הַנַּעַר וַיִּגְדָּל (יזל) וַיֵּשֶׁב בַּמִּדְבָּר וַיְהִי רֹבֶה קַשָּׁת׃ (כא)
וַיֵּשֶׁב בְּמִדְבַּר פָּארָן וַתִּקַּח־לוֹ אִמּוֹ אִשָּׁה מֵאֶרֶץ מִצְרָיִם
(מצר)׃ פ

them some fruit and water for their journey. Hagar leaves the child, so she will not have to see him die. However, God calls out to Hagar and tells her not to worry, that Ishmael would survive and be the seed of a great nation. God then opens her eyes, revealing to her a well of water (in this case, not a miracle).

Sometimes, we have what we need right before our eyes, but we do not see it - this is the point of this verse. We have to understand the limitations of our five senses and stop ourselves from judging things based on what we see and feel.

Sixth Reading - Joseph - Yesod

(כב) וַיְהִי בָּעֵת הַהִוא וַיֹּאמֶר אֲבִימֶלֶךְ וּפִיכֹל שַׂר־
צְבָאוֹ אֶל־אַבְרָהָם (רמ"ח) לֵאמֹר אֱלֹהִים (ילה) עִמְּךָ בְּכֹל
(לכב) אֲשֶׁר־אַתָּה עֹשֶׂה׃ (כג) וְעַתָּה הִשָּׁבְעָה לִּי בֵאלֹהִים
(ילה) הֵנָּה אִם (יוהך)־תִּשְׁקֹר לִי וּלְנִינִי וּלְנֶכְדִּי כַּחֶסֶד (ע"ב)
אֲשֶׁר־עָשִׂיתִי עִמְּךָ תַּעֲשֶׂה עִמָּדִי וְעִם־הָאָרֶץ (מילוי אלהים ע"ה)
אֲשֶׁר־גַּרְתָּה בָּהּ׃ וַיֹּאמֶר אַבְרָהָם (רמ"ח) אָנֹכִי (אי"ע) אִשָּׁבֵעַ׃
(כד) וְהוֹכִחַ אַבְרָהָם (רמ"ח) אֶת־אֲבִימֶלֶךְ (כה) עַל־אֹדוֹת

וַיְהִי - The treaty between Abraham and Abimelech is the first peace treaty to appear in Torah, and as such, it is the seed and source of all peace treaties between nations. Conflict and war among nations begin with friction and disunity among individuals. A nation at war is merely the ultimate consequence of the spiritual darkness born of strife and intolerance among the individuals who comprise a nation. When two brothers find reason to disrespect one another, or when two friends find ways to fault each other, then two nations will devise reasons to engage in bloody battle.

Peace begins with the individual in the mirror. Peace is kept when that individual extends tolerance to his neighbor.

Spiritual influences arising herein can help prevent wars between nations by helping to end conflicts between individuals. Tolerance and compassion for others are summoned forth. When two people make the effort to find the good in one another, to overlook their differences for the simple sake of peace, then nations shall surely discover ways to achieve a lasting peace.

וְהוֹכִחַ - Abraham and Abimelech have a disagreement over a well that Abimelech's servant has stolen from Abraham. The significance of this

בְּאֵ֣ר (קנ"א ב"ן) הַמַּ֔יִם אֲשֶׁ֥ר גָּזְל֖וּ עַבְדֵ֥י אֲבִימֶֽלֶךְ׃ (כו) וַיֹּ֣אמֶר
אֲבִימֶ֔לֶךְ לֹ֣א יָדַ֔עְתִּי מִ֥י (ילי) עָשָׂ֖ה אֶת־הַדָּבָ֣ר (ראה) הַזֶּ֑ה (והו)
וְגַם־אַתָּ֞ה לֹא־הִגַּ֣דְתָּ לִּ֗י וְגַ֧ם אָנֹכִ֛י (איע) לֹ֥א שָׁמַ֖עְתִּי בִּלְתִּ֥י
הַיּֽוֹם (נגד, זן)׃ (כז) וַיִּקַּ֤ח (וזעם) אַבְרָהָם֙ (רמ"ח) צֹ֣אן וּבָקָ֔ר וַיִּתֵּ֖ן
לַאֲבִימֶ֑לֶךְ וַיִּכְרְת֥וּ שְׁנֵיהֶ֖ם בְּרִֽית׃ (כח) וַיַּצֵּ֣ב אַבְרָהָ֗ם (רמ"ח)
אֶת־שֶׁ֛בַע כִּבְשֹׂ֥ת הַצֹּ֖אן לְבַדְּהֶֽן׃ (כט) וַיֹּ֥אמֶר אֲבִימֶ֖לֶךְ
אֶל־אַבְרָהָ֑ם (רמ"ח) מָ֣ה (מ"ה) הֵ֗נָּה שֶׁ֤בַע כְּבָשֹׂת֙ הָאֵ֔לֶּה אֲשֶׁ֥ר
הִצַּ֖בְתָּ לְבַדָּֽנָה׃ (ל) וַיֹּ֕אמֶר כִּ֚י אֶת־שֶׁ֣בַע כְּבָשֹׂ֔ת תִּקַּ֖ח מִיָּדִ֑י
בַּעֲבוּר֙ תִּֽהְיֶה־לִּ֣י לְעֵדָ֔ה (סיט) כִּ֥י חָפַ֖רְתִּי אֶת־הַבְּאֵ֥ר (קנ"א ב"ן)
הַזֹּֽאת׃ (לא) עַל־כֵּ֗ן קָרָ֛א לַמָּק֥וֹם הַה֖וּא בְּאֵ֣ר (קנ"א ב"ן) שָׁ֑בַע
כִּ֛י שָׁ֥ם נִשְׁבְּע֖וּ שְׁנֵיהֶֽם׃ (לב) וַיִּכְרְת֥וּ בְרִ֖ית בִּבְאֵ֣ר (קנ"א ב"ן)
שָׁ֑בַע וַיָּ֣קָם אֲבִימֶ֗לֶךְ וּפִיכֹל֙ שַׂר־צְבָא֔וֹ וַיָּשֻׁ֖בוּ אֶל־אֶ֥רֶץ
פְּלִשְׁתִּֽים׃ (לג) וַיִּטַּ֥ע אֶ֖שֶׁל בִּבְאֵ֣ר (קנ"א ב"ן) שָׁ֑בַע וַיִּ֨קְרָא־שָׁ֔ם
בְּשֵׁ֖ם יְהֹוָ֥ה (יהוהאדניאהדונהי) אֵ֥ל עוֹלָֽם׃ (לד) וַיָּ֧גָר אַבְרָהָ֛ם (רמ"ח)
בְּאֶ֥רֶץ פְּלִשְׁתִּ֖ים יָמִ֥ים (נלך) רַבִּֽים׃ פ

disagreement is the effort made by Abraham to inject spiritual forces of healing into the water. Here, Abimelech symbolizes the contamination of the Earth's water, while Abraham symbolizes the rehabilitation of our oceans, lakes, rivers, and groundwater.

In our present day, we see this struggle to defend the sanctity of our environment, for example, in the struggle to protect water from nuclear

Seventh Reading - David - Malchut

כב (א) וַיְהִי אַחַר הַדְּבָרִים (ראה) הָאֵלֶּה וְהָאֱלֹהִים (ילה) נִסָּה
אֶת־אַבְרָהָם (רמ"ח) וַיֹּאמֶר אֵלָיו אַבְרָהָם (רמ"ח) וַיֹּאמֶר הִנֵּנִי:
(ב) וַיֹּאמֶר קַח־נָא אֶת־בִּנְךָ אֶת־יְחִידְךָ אֲשֶׁר־אָהַבְתָּ אֶת־
יִצְחָק (ד"פ ב"ן) וְלֶךְ־לְךָ אֶל־אֶרֶץ הַמֹּרִיָּה וְהַעֲלֵהוּ שָׁם לְעֹלָה
עַל אַחַד הֶהָרִים (אהבה) אֲשֶׁר אֹמַר אֵלֶיךָ:
(ג) וַיַּשְׁכֵּם אַבְרָהָם (רמ"ח) בַּבֹּקֶר וַיַּחֲבֹשׁ אֶת־חֲמֹרוֹ וַיִּקַּח

contamination. The verses of Scripture that relate this story will purify the waters of our planet.

וַיְהִי - Abraham undergoes ten tests in his lifetime to allow him to evolve and strengthen himself spiritually. The tenth test occurs when God instructs him to sacrifice his son, Isaac, upon an altar.

The magnitude of this test is exceptional. Abraham has waited until the age of 100 to finally have a child with Sarah. And now, the Creator has just asked him to sacrifice his only son, his only child.

How much are we willing to sacrifice for our connection to the Light of the Creator?

Not so paradoxically, the more we resist sacrifice and avoid the tests of life, the more we will lose in the long run. But the more willingly we give and embrace life's tests with certainty, the more we stand to gain.

The Light cast through the letters of this portion ignites conviction in our hearts and certainty in our consciousness so that the truth of the Creator may be everlastingly revealed to the world.

וַיַּשְׁכֵּם - Abraham, we're told, rose in the early morning on the day

(וזעם) אֶת־שְׁנֵי נְעָרָיו אִתּוֹ וְאֵת יִצְחָק (ד"פ ב"ן) בְּנוֹ וַיְבַקַּע עֲצֵי
עֹלָה וַיָּקָם וַיֵּלֶךְ (כלי) אֶל־הַמָּקוֹם אֲשֶׁר־אָמַר־לוֹ הָאֱלֹהִים
(ילה): (ד) בַּיּוֹם (נגד, זן) הַשְּׁלִישִׁי וַיִּשָּׂא אַבְרָהָם (רמ"ח) אֶת־עֵינָיו
(מ"ה בריבוע) וַיַּרְא אֶת־הַמָּקוֹם מֵרָחֹק (שדי): (ה) וַיֹּאמֶר אַבְרָהָם
(רמ"ח) אֶל־נְעָרָיו שְׁבוּ־לָכֶם פֹּה (ע"ה מום) עִם־הַחֲמוֹר (פירוש פה ג'ימ'
מילה, ועוד ע"ה ג'ימ' אלהים שהוא עולה למנין אהיה + אדני, להכניע הקליפות בסוד החמור וז"ס פה
עם החמור) וַאֲנִי (אני) וְהַנַּעַר נֵלְכָה עַד־כֹּה (היי) וְנִשְׁתַּחֲוֶה וְנָשׁוּבָה
אֲלֵיכֶם: (ו) וַיִּקַּח (וזעם) אַבְרָהָם (רמ"ח) אֶת־עֲצֵי הָעֹלָה וַיָּשֶׂם
עַל־יִצְחָק (ד"פ ב"ן) בְּנוֹ וַיִּקַּח (וזעם) בְּיָדוֹ אֶת־הָאֵשׁ (שאה) וְאֶת־
הַמַּאֲכֶלֶת וַיֵּלְכוּ שְׁנֵיהֶם יַחְדָּו: (ז) וַיֹּאמֶר יִצְחָק (ד"פ ב"ן) אֶל־
אַבְרָהָם (רמ"ח) אָבִיו וַיֹּאמֶר אָבִי וַיֹּאמֶר הִנֶּנִּי בְנִי וַיֹּאמֶר

of Isaac's sacrifice. Though an unimaginably painful test awaited him, Abraham proactively embraced the challenge.

Often, we are slow to action. We procrastinate, avoiding the difficult spiritual tasks that we must perform to transform. In truth, such delays provide a tiny measure of comfort and relief in the immediate moment, but over the long term, we bear increased pain.

Conversely, our nature is to engage eagerly in negative practices that gratify the narcissistic elements of our personality.

This final test of Abraham can be construed [interpreted] as our final test by virtue of the power of the Zohar. Abraham's success is bestowed upon us along with his fearlessness and unwavering trust in the Creator.

הִנֵּה הָאֵשׁ (שאה) וְהָעֵצִים וְאַיֵּה הַשֶּׂה לְעֹלָה׃ (ח) וַיֹּאמֶר
אַבְרָהָם (רמ"ח) אֱלֹהִים (ילה) יִרְאֶה (רי"ו) (ראה)־לּוֹ הַשֶּׂה לְעֹלָה
בְּנִי וַיֵּלְכוּ שְׁנֵיהֶם יַחְדָּו׃ (ט) וַיָּבֹאוּ אֶל־הַמָּקוֹם אֲשֶׁר
אָמַר־לוֹ הָאֱלֹהִים (ילה) וַיִּבֶן שָׁם אַבְרָהָם (רמ"ח) אֶת־הַמִּזְבֵּחַ
(ין) וַיַּעֲרֹךְ אֶת־הָעֵצִים וַיַּעֲקֹד אֶת־יִצְחָק (ד"פ ב"ן) בְּנוֹ (ויכוין כשם)

וַיַּעֲקֹד - Abraham takes his son Isaac up to the mountains. The Patriarch then constructs an altar and binds Isaac to it. Abraham raises his arm and is about to lower the knife when suddenly, an angel arrives to stop him. The angel tells Abraham that this was just a test of faith.

Immediately, Abraham finds a ram whose horns are caught in a thicket and sacrifices the animal in place of Isaac.

The Zohar offers penetrating insights into this story:

Sweetening judgment with mercy. The Zohar explains that Abraham represents the concept of mercy, whereas Isaac signifies the force of judgment. In our lives, we need to sweeten and temper our judgmental behavior with kindhearted mercy. Herein lies the inner significance of this passage. Striking a delicate balance between these two attributes can be lifelong spiritual work. Thankfully, the act of listening to this reading imbues our souls with mercy so that we are transformed into balanced and loving people.

Without Abraham's Light or these insights from the Zohar, this objective would be unattainable.

Sacrificing ego. Repeatedly, something in our nature provokes us to indulge in negative behavior, even though it goes against our very will. Likewise, we are compelled to forsake positive actions despite our best intentions to follow through. This uniquely human idiosyncrasy demonstrates the ongoing conflict between the body's desire to receive and the soul's desire to share. Our Evil Inclination is the culprit behind our choice to succumb to

שאברהם אע"ה בעל החסד עקד את יצחק בנו שהוא גבורה, כך הקב"ה עקד ויעקד למעלה כל שונאינו ואויבינו מעלינו ומעל כל ישראל, אמן וכן יהי רצון.

וַיָּשֶׂם אֹתוֹ עַל־הַמִּזְבֵּחַ (זן) מִמַּעַל (עלם) לָעֵצִים׃ (י)

וַיִּשְׁלַח אַבְרָהָם (רמ"ח) אֶת־יָדוֹ וַיִּקַּח (וזעם) אֶת־הַמַּאֲכֶלֶת

the whims of the body.

Isaac is a code referring to Left Column energy - our reactive, self-centered desire to receive, and our physical body. Abraham corresponds to the Right Column - our positive, sharing attributes, and our soul. This story is a metaphor for man's spiritual work, which is to bind (restrict) his selfish, reactive desires and unleash the power of his soul.

The ram caught in the thicket and sacrificed is a code for the actual eradication of our wicked and prideful traits - the sacrificing of our Evil Inclination. Thus, we learn that a man must constantly utilize the power of his soul (Abraham) to bind his own ego (the binding of Isaac onto the altar) and then eliminate all his selfish, self-destructive traits from his nature (the slaughtering of the ram). This entails giving up (sacrificing) short-term material pleasures for eternal spiritual joy.

Once again, through Abraham's Light, which serves as a timeless repository of energy for us to draw upon, we empower our souls and completely subjugate our selfish impulses. As our wicked traits are slaughtered through our meditation during the reading of this portion, wickedness in the world is slain in equal measure, for each of us is a microcosm of the world. All the sinful acts of behavior and wicked deeds depicted throughout this portion are herewith bound and sacrificed forevermore.

וַיִּשְׁלַח - To ignite the Light of the Creator in our lives and to pass the tests and challenges that come our way, we must be prepared to take physical action, indicated by the raising of Abraham's arm. Good intentions are never enough. We must follow through on our commitments to share more with others and complete our spiritual mission.

Abraham's body was so in tune with the Light of the Creator that he knew

לִשְׁחֹט אֶת־בְּנוֹ׃ (יא) וַיִּקְרָא אֵלָיו מַלְאַךְ יְהֹוָהאדני יאהדונהי
מִן־הַשָּׁמַיִם (י"פ טל) וַיֹּאמֶר אַבְרָהָם (רמ"ח) | אַבְרָהָם (רמ"ח)
וַיֹּאמֶר הִנֵּנִי׃ (יב) וַיֹּאמֶר אַל־תִּשְׁלַח יָדְךָ אֶל־הַנַּעַר וְאַל־
תַּעַשׂ לוֹ מְאוּמָה כִּי | עַתָּה יָדַעְתִּי כִּי־יְרֵא אֱלֹהִים (ילה)
אַתָּה וְלֹא חָשַׂכְתָּ אֶת־בִּנְךָ אֶת־יְחִידְךָ מִמֶּנִּי׃ (יג) וַיִּשָּׂא
אַבְרָהָם (רמ"ח) אֶת־עֵינָיו (מ"ה בריבוע) וַיַּרְא וְהִנֵּה־אַיִל אַחַר
נֶאֱחַז בַּסְּבַךְ בְּקַרְנָיו (כשאומר נאחז בסבך בקרניו יכוין לתיבות שאחר סבך הם
עגל, והשטן בעבור קיטרוג העגל היה מרחיק האיל, כדי שישחט יצחק, ומיכאל (גימ' ננא מעב"ש)
גימ' הנה איל נאחז בקרניו דהוא גימ' שס"ח סממני הקטורת הכניע את השטן) (כף החיים י"ב ג')
וַיֵּלֶךְ (כלי) אַבְרָהָם (רמ"ח) וַיִּקַּח (חעם) אֶת־הָאַיִל וַיַּעֲלֵהוּ לְעֹלָה
תַּחַת בְּנוֹ׃ (יד) וַיִּקְרָא אַבְרָהָם (רמ"ח) שֵׁם־הַמָּקוֹם הַהוּא
יְהֹוָהאדני יאהדונהי | יִרְאֶה (רי"ו) (ראה) אֲשֶׁר יֵאָמֵר הַיּוֹם (נגד, זן) בְּהַר
יְהֹוָהאדני יאהדונהי יֵרָאֶה (רי"ו) (ראה)׃ (טו) וַיִּקְרָא מַלְאַךְ יְהֹוָהאדני יאהדונהי
אֶל־אַבְרָהָם (רמ"ח) שֵׁנִית מִן־הַשָּׁמָיִם (י"פ טל)׃ (טז) וַיֹּאמֶר בִּי
נִשְׁבַּעְתִּי נְאֻם־יְהֹוָהאדני יאהדונהי כִּי יַעַן אֲשֶׁר עָשִׂיתָ אֶת־הַדָּבָר
הַזֶּה (והו) וְלֹא חָשַׂכְתָּ אֶת־בִּנְךָ אֶת־יְחִידֶךָ׃ (יז) כִּי־בָרֵךְ
אֲבָרֶכְךָ וְהַרְבָּה אַרְבֶּה (יצחק) אֶת־זַרְעֲךָ כְּכוֹכְבֵי הַשָּׁמַיִם

deep in his heart that God would not let him slaughter his son - yet he was fully prepared to make the sacrifice. When we are prepared to go all the way, we, too, resonate with the Light; thus, we are certain and confident in each action that we take, knowing with deep down that a positive outcome is the only outcome.

(י"פ טל) וְכַחוֹל אֲשֶׁר עַל־שְׂפַת הַיָּם (ילי) וְיִרַשׁ זַרְעֲךָ אֵת שַׁעַר
אֹיְבָיו: (יח) וְהִתְבָּרְכוּ (יהוה ריבוע יהוה ריבוע מ"ה) בְזַרְעֲךָ כֹּל (ילי) גּוֹיֵי
הָאָרֶץ (מילוי אלהים ע"ה) עֵקֶב (כ"פ מום) אֲשֶׁר שָׁמַעְתָּ בְּקֹלִי: (יט)
וַיָּשָׁב אַבְרָהָם (רמ"ח) אֶל־נְעָרָיו וַיָּקֻמוּ וַיֵּלְכוּ יַחְדָּו אֶל־בְּאֵר
(קנ"א ב"ן) שָׁבַע וַיֵּשֶׁב אַבְרָהָם (רמ"ח) בִּבְאֵר (קנ"א ב"ן) שָׁבַע: פ

Maftir

(כ) וַיְהִי אַחֲרֵי הַדְּבָרִים (ראה) הָאֵלֶּה וַיֻּגַּד לְאַבְרָהָם (רמ"ח)
לֵאמֹר הִנֵּה יָלְדָה מִלְכָּה גַם־הִוא בָּנִים לְנָחוֹר אָחִיךָ: (כא)
אֶת־עוּץ בְּכֹרוֹ וְאֶת־בּוּז אָחִיו וְאֶת־קְמוּאֵל אֲבִי אֲרָם:
(כב) וְאֶת־כֶּשֶׂד וְאֶת־חֲזוֹ וְאֶת־פִּלְדָּשׁ וְאֶת־יִדְלָף וְאֵת
בְּתוּאֵל: (כג) וּבְתוּאֵל יָלַד אֶת־רִבְקָה שְׁמֹנָה אֵלֶּה יָלְדָה
מִלְכָּה לְנָחוֹר אֲחִי אַבְרָהָם (רמ"ח): (כד) וּפִילַגְשׁוֹ וּשְׁמָהּ
רְאוּמָה וַתֵּלֶד גַּם־הִוא אֶת־טֶבַח וְאֶת־גַּחַם וְאֶת־תַּחַשׁ
וְאֶת־מַעֲכָה: פפפ

רִבְקָה - When Abraham returns after the binding of Isaac, Sarah has passed on. However, there must always be a beacon of Light in our world. Therefore, after Sarah leaves this world, Rebecca is born to Bethuel. This turn of events holds spiritual significance for our own life: When we do not seize the opportunity to share and perform positive actions, someone else will take our place. Accordingly, we [must] become enlightened and aware of opportunities for good deeds and actions, which bring about spiritual growth.

The Haftarah of Vayera

This is the story of Elisha. Just as Abraham was promised that his son would be born after a year had passed, Elisha also promised someone a son. But after a year passes and the birth takes place, the baby dies—and Elisha resurrects him. Through this event and through the birth of Isaac to Sarah and Abraham, we have the powers of resurrection and of mind over matter.

מלכים ב פרק ד

(א) וְאִשָּׁה אַחַת מִנְּשֵׁי בְנֵי־הַנְּבִיאִים צָעֲקָה אֶל־אֱלִישָׁע
לֵאמֹר עַבְדְּךָ (פוי) אִישִׁי מֵת וְאַתָּה יָדַעְתָּ כִּי עַבְדְּךָ (פוי) הָיָה
(יהה) יָרֵא אֶת־יְהוָה וְהַנֹּשֶׁה בָּא לָקַחַת אֶת־שְׁנֵי יְלָדַי לוֹ
לַעֲבָדִים: (ב) וַיֹּאמֶר אֵלֶיהָ אֱלִישָׁע מָה (יוד הא ואו הא) אֶעֱשֶׂה־
לָּךְ הַגִּידִי לִי מַה (יוד הא ואו הא) יֶּשׁ־לָךְ (כתיב: לכי) בַּבָּיִת (ב״פ ראה)
וַתֹּאמֶר אֵין לְשִׁפְחָתְךָ כֹל (ילי) בַּבַּיִת (ב״פ ראה) כִּי אִם (יוהך)
־אָסוּךְ שָׁמֶן: (ג) וַיֹּאמֶר לְכִי שַׁאֲלִי־לָךְ כֵּלִים מִן־הַחוּץ
מֵאֵת כָּל־שְׁכֵנָיִךְ (כתיב: שכנכי) כֵּלִים רֵקִים אַל־תַּמְעִיטִי: (ד)
וּבָאת וְסָגַרְתְּ הַדֶּלֶת בַּעֲדֵךְ וּבְעַד־בָּנַיִךְ וְיָצַקְתְּ עַל כָּל (ילי,
עמם) ־הַכֵּלִים הָאֵלֶּה וְהַמָּלֵא תַּסִּיעִי: (ה) וַתֵּלֶךְ מֵאִתּוֹ וַתִּסְגֹּר
הַדֶּלֶת בַּעֲדָהּ וּבְעַד בָּנֶיהָ הֵם מַגִּשִׁים אֵלֶיהָ וְהִיא (כתיב:
מיצקת) (מוֹצָקֶת): (ו) וַיְהִי | כִּמְלֹאת הַכֵּלִים וַתֹּאמֶר אֶל־בְּנָהּ
הַגִּישָׁה אֵלַי עוֹד כֶּלִי וַיֹּאמֶר אֵלֶיהָ אֵין עוֹד כֶּלִי וַיַּעֲמֹד
הַשָּׁמֶן: (ז) וַתָּבֹא וַתַּגֵּד לְאִישׁ הָאֱלֹהִים (דמב, ילה) וַיֹּאמֶר לְכִי

מִכְרִי אֶת־הַשֶּׁמֶן וְשַׁלְּמִי אֶת־נִשְׁיֵךְ (כתיב: נשיכי) וְאַתְּ וּבָנַיִךְ (כתיב:
בניכי) תִּחְיִי בַּנּוֹתָר: {פ}

(ח) וַיְהִי הַיּוֹם (נגד, מזבח, זן) וַיַּעֲבֹר (רפ"וז) אֱלִישָׁע אֶל־שׁוּנֵם וְשָׁם
אִשָּׁה גְדוֹלָה (להוו, מבה) וַתַּחֲזֶק־בּוֹ לֶאֱכָל־לָוחֶם וַיְהִי מִדֵּי
עָבְרוֹ יָסֻר שָׁמָּה לֶאֱכָל־לָוחֶם: (ט) וַתֹּאמֶר אֶל־אִישָׁהּ הִנֵּה־
נָא יָדַעְתִּי כִּי אִישׁ אֱלֹהִים (דמב, ילה) קָדוֹשׁ הוּא עֹבֵר עָלֵינוּ
תָּמִיד (נתה): (י) נַעֲשֶׂה־נָּא עֲלִיַּת־קִיר קְטַנָּה וְנָשִׂים לוֹ שָׁם
מִטָּה וְשֻׁלְחָן וְכִסֵּא וּמְנוֹרָה וְהָיָה (ייהה) בְּבֹאוֹ אֵלֵינוּ יָסוּר
שָׁמָּה: (יא) וַיְהִי הַיּוֹם (נגד, מזבח, זן) וַיָּבֹא שָׁמָּה וַיָּסַר אֶל־הָעֲלִיָּה
(פהל) וַיִּשְׁכַּב־שָׁמָּה: (יב) וַיֹּאמֶר אֶל־גֵּיחֲזִי נַעֲרוֹ קְרָא לַשּׁוּנַמִּית
הַזֹּאת וַיִּקְרָא־לָהּ וַתַּעֲמֹד לְפָנָיו: (יג) וַיֹּאמֶר לוֹ אֱמָר־נָא
אֵלֶיהָ הִנֵּה חָרַדְתְּ | אֵלֵינוּ אֶת־כָּל־הַחֲרָדָה הַזֹּאת מֶה (יוד
הא ואו הא) לַעֲשׂוֹת לָךְ הֲיֵשׁ לְדַבֶּר (ראה) ־לָךְ אֶל־הַמֶּלֶךְ אוֹ אֶל־
שַׂר הַצָּבָא וַתֹּאמֶר בְּתוֹךְ עַמִּי אָנֹכִי (איע) יֹשָׁבֶת: (יד) וַיֹּאמֶר
וּמֶה (יוד הא ואו הא) לַעֲשׂוֹת לָהּ וַיֹּאמֶר גֵּיחֲזִי אֲבָל בֵּן אֵין־לָהּ
וְאִישָׁהּ זָקֵן: (טו) וַיֹּאמֶר קְרָא־לָהּ וַיִּקְרָא־לָהּ וַתַּעֲמֹד
בַּפָּתַח: (טז) וַיֹּאמֶר לַמּוֹעֵד הַזֶּה (והו) כָּעֵת חַיָּה אַתְּ (כתיב: אתי)
חֹבֶקֶת בֵּן וַתֹּאמֶר אַל־אֲדֹנִי אִישׁ הָאֱלֹהִים (דמב, ילה) אַל־
תְּכַזֵּב בְּשִׁפְחָתֶךָ: (יז) וַתַּהַר הָאִשָּׁה (שאה) וַתֵּלֶד בֵּן לַמּוֹעֵד

הַזֶּה (והו) כָּעֵת חַיָּה אֲשֶׁר־דִּבֶּר (ראה) אֵלֶיהָ אֱלִישָׁע׃ (יח) וַיִּגְדַּל
(יזל) הַיֶּלֶד וַיְהִי הַיּוֹם (נגד, מזבוח, זן) וַיֵּצֵא אֶל־אָבִיו אֶל־הַקֹּצְרִים׃
(יט) וַיֹּאמֶר אֶל־אָבִיו רֹאשִׁי ׀ רֹאשִׁי וַיֹּאמֶר אֶל־הַנַּעַר שָׂאֵהוּ
אֶל־אִמּוֹ׃ (כ) וַיִּשָּׂאֵהוּ וַיְבִיאֵהוּ אֶל־אִמּוֹ וַיֵּשֶׁב עַל־בִּרְכֶּיהָ
עַד־הַצָּהֳרַיִם וַיָּמֹת׃ (כא) וַתַּעַל וַתַּשְׁכִּבֵהוּ עַל־מִטַּת אִישׁ
הָאֱלֹהִים (דמב, ילה) וַתִּסְגֹּר בַּעֲדוֹ וַתֵּצֵא׃ (כב) וַתִּקְרָא אֶל־
אִישָׁהּ וַתֹּאמֶר שִׁלְחָה נָא לִי אֶחָד (אהבה, דאגה) מִן־הַנְּעָרִים
וְאַחַת הָאֲתֹנוֹת וְאָרוּצָה עַד־אִישׁ הָאֱלֹהִים (דמב, ילה) וְאָשׁוּבָה
(הוש) ׃ (כג) וַיֹּאמֶר מַדּוּעַ אַתְּ (כתיב: אתי) הֹלֶכֶת (כתיב: הלכתי) אֵלָיו
הַיּוֹם (נגד, מזבוח, זן) לֹא־חֹדֶשׁ וְלֹא שַׁבָּת וַתֹּאמֶר שָׁלוֹם׃

Lesson of Chayei Sarah

In this portion, we have the small letter Caf in chapter 23:2

There are three sizes of letters in the Torah. In the introduction of the Zohar, the Sulam commentary, it is written: "And God made large letters that hint to Binah and smaller letters that hint to Malchut." Elsewhere, the Zohar explains that the normally sized letters come from the spiritual dimension of Zeir Anpin. So we see that there is a meaning to the different letters we have in the Torah. But our question this week is what does the small Caf teach us?

It is said that when Sarah died, Abraham wept only a little, and this was because Sarah was old. But why should this keep him from weeping? He loved Sarah more then anyone else in the world could love a wife. Abraham and Sarah were soul mates, they were chariots, they were prophets, and it is even written that Sarah was a better prophet than Abraham. What's more, Isaac was not at Sarah's funeral, and the explanation is that he was studying Torah. But is this really an explanation? Should studying Torah be used as an excuse for being absent at your mother's funeral?

How does this relate to the presence of the small letter Caf? What power can we receive from this letter? There is a very important teaching here, and it is related to the act of weeping.

From the story of Rabbi Shimon bar Yochai leaving this world, we can understand something of this. In the Zohar, in the portion Ha'azinu in the Idra Zutra (based on the Sulam commentary), it is written: "All the same day [that Rabbi Shimon passed away], the fire did not stop burning in the house, and no one could reach him because of the light and the fire that was around him. All that day, I [Rabbi Abba] fell on the earth. After the fire disappeared, I saw the holy light, the holy of holies that had left this world, who was wrapped up and lying on his right side and his face was laughing."

Rabbi Elazar, Rabbi Shimon's son, took Rabbi Shimon's hands and kissed them. Rabbi Elazar said, "Father, Father, there were three and now again there is only one." This means there had been three great men in the land–Rabbi Elazar; his father, Rabbi Shimon; and his Elder, Rabbi Pinchas ben Yair. And now Rabbi Elazar is the only one left in the world. This is a very powerful, very emotional statement. But it's important to realize that Rabbi Elazar did not weep.

When Rabbi Shimon left this world, his son, Rabbi Elazar, was of course in pain over the loss of his father. But it was more important to him that the

world would be without the Light that Rabbi Shimon had revealed. Rabbi Shimon's students also did not weep because of any physical connection with their Rabbi, but because of the Light that they would now lose. Another transition also caused them tremendous pain. In the time of Rabbi Shimon, "the sign of the rainbow was not seen, because he was the sign of the world." (This is in the song that the Ben Ish Chai wrote about Rabbi Shimon). All the world had been full of the Light of the Creator, and now this would be lacking.

Why do we weep when something happens that hurts us? In particular, why do we cry at the death of a person who was close to us? Is it because of the physical absence we experience? Kabbalah teaches that the physical transition is not what's important. In fact, we must remember that nothing physical really makes a difference in this world because truth comes only from the spiritual realm. The small Caf teaches us that we shouldn't cry about unimportant matters–about something we've lost, for example, whether it's a physical object like money or a quality like celebrity status or fame. My mother, my teacher, always says that whoever cries without a reason will, God forbid, have to cry with a reason. The strength we receive from the Caf is the ability to separate what's important from what is not. When we do weep, then, it will not be because someone who was close to us has left the world physically. We will weep for the Light that we had when that person was here–and that we no longer have now that the person is gone.

When Rabbi Brandwein, my father's teacher and master, left this world, my father wept for a long time and felt the absence of the Light of the Creator in his life. After some time, however, my father understood that now Rabbi Brandwein was helping him from the world of truth more than he could ever have helped in this world. We must remember that everything is from the Light; therefore, we should never become too involved with what takes place in the physical realm. If we let ourselves become too involved, it's as if we're saying that we don't agree with what happens, meaning that we don't agree with the Light!

My brother, Michael, tells a story about the difference between spirituality and physicality. A rabbi once held a beautiful wedding for his daughter in an expensive hotel. After the wedding, he went to the hotel owner and asked him how much this would cost.

The owner said, "I can't take money from you. You're my rabbi."

"No, I insist on paying. Just tell me how much."

"No, I can't take your money..."

They went on and on like this, until finally the rabbi said, "No, I'm paying you! Because in this world, we always have to pay, and money is the cheapest payment there is!"

When we cry over our payments, or over things that other people did to us, or if we say, "Why is the Light doing this to me?" we will cause this same payment to become due again. The only type of crying that is justified in this world should be because not enough Light is being revealed. Aside from this, we should not cry. Although it is written that except for the gate of tears, all the gates to the upper world have been locked since the destruction of the Temple, it is referring to tears that are shed as a result of the Light of the Creator not being revealed. There is no other reason to cry. The strength of the Caf is to give us the power to understand exactly why we are facing what we are facing and to receive everything with Light.

Obviously, the death of Sarah caused Abraham pain, but he did not give into it because he knew it was for the best. In the same way, when it is written that Isaac was studying Torah, this is to say that Isaac was working on revealing the Light of the Creator that would no longer be revealed into the world because of his mother's death.

Thus, though the death of Sarah certainly caused him pain, Abraham did not weep because he knew it was for the best. Let us learn from his example and live what we have learned.

Synopsis for Chayei Sarah

Why is this portion called "the Life of Sarah"? Why do we turn our attention to Sarah's life only after she has already passed on? We must understand that death and life can exist on many levels. Someone may be physically alive but impart no energy to us. In that sense, it's as if they were dead. In the same way, a person who has left this world can be very much alive in our hearts and minds. When we remember someone who has passed away, we keep that person alive; if we forget them, they are dead. The meaning of life and death should not be limited to the physical dimension.

First Reading - Abraham - Chesed

כג (א) וַיִּהְיוּ וַחַיֵּי שָׂרָה מֵאָה שָׁנָה וְעֶשְׂרִים שָׁנָה וְשֶׁבַע
שָׁנִים שְׁנֵי חַיֵּי שָׂרָה: (ב) וַתָּמָת שָׂרָה בְּקִרְיַת אַרְבַּע הִוא
חֶבְרוֹן בְּאֶרֶץ כְּנָעַן וַיָּבֹא אַבְרָהָם (רמ"ח) לִסְפֹּד לְשָׂרָה
וְלִבְכֹּתָהּ: (ג) וַיָּקָם אַבְרָהָם (רמ"ח) מֵעַל (עלם) פְּנֵי (חכמה, בינה)
מֵתוֹ וַיְדַבֵּר (ראה) אֶל-בְּנֵי-חֵת לֵאמֹר: (ד) גֵּר-וְתוֹשָׁב אָנֹכִי
(איע) עִמָּכֶם תְּנוּ לִי אֲחֻזַּת-קֶבֶר עִמָּכֶם וְאֶקְבְּרָה מֵתִי
מִלְּפָנָי: (ה) וַיַּעֲנוּ בְנֵי-חֵת אֶת-אַבְרָהָם (רמ"ח) לֵאמֹר לוֹ: (ו)
שְׁמָעֵנוּ | אֲדֹנִי נְשִׂיא אֱלֹהִים (ילה) אַתָּה בְּתוֹכֵנוּ בְּמִבְחַר
קְבָרֵינוּ קְבֹר אֶת-מֵתֶךָ אִישׁ מִמֶּנּוּ אֶת-קִבְרוֹ לֹא-יִכְלֶה
מִמְּךָ מִקְּבֹר מֵתֶךָ: (ז) וַיָּקָם אַבְרָהָם (רמ"ח) וַיִּשְׁתַּחוּ לְעַם

וַחַיֵּי שָׂרָה - Sarah lived 127 years, reincarnating as Queen Esther. Every year of Sarah's life was filled with Light, which gave her the merit in her incarnation as Esther to rule over 127 nations. Once again, we are shown how our actions in past lives can influence the present and future.

וְלִבְכֹּתָהּ - The small Chf. The letter Chf is in Velivkotach which means to cry over her. When we mourn a loss, often we feel pain and sorrow over the physical manifestation of the loss, rather than what has happened on the spiritual level. The small letters in the Torah represent Malchut, the level of our physical existence; these letters give us the power to transcend our present physical reality.

(עלם)-הָאָרֶץ (מילוי אלהים ע"ה) לִבְנֵי־חֵת׃ (ח) וַיְדַבֵּר (ראה) אִתָּם
לֵאמֹר אִם (יוהך)-יֵשׁ אֶת־נַפְשְׁכֶם לִקְבֹּר אֶת־מֵתִי מִלְּפָנַי
שְׁמָעוּנִי וּפִגְעוּ־לִי בְּעֶפְרוֹן בֶּן־צֹחַר׃ (ט) וְיִתֶּן־לִי אֶת־מְעָרַת
הַמַּכְפֵּלָה אֲשֶׁר־לוֹ אֲשֶׁר בִּקְצֵה שָׂדֵהוּ בְּכֶסֶף מָלֵא יִתְּנֶנָּה
לִּי בְּתוֹכְכֶם לַאֲחֻזַּת־קָבֶר׃ (י) וְעֶפְרוֹן יֹשֵׁב בְּתוֹךְ בְּנֵי־חֵת
וַיַּעַן עֶפְרוֹן הַחִתִּי אֶת־אַבְרָהָם (רמ"ח) בְּאָזְנֵי (יוד הי ואו הה) בְנֵי־
חֵת לְכֹל (יה אדני) בָּאֵי שַׁעַר־עִירוֹ (סוזהך, סנדלפון, ערי) לֵאמֹר׃ (יא)
לֹא־אֲדֹנִי שְׁמָעֵנִי הַשָּׂדֶה נָתַתִּי לָךְ וְהַמְּעָרָה אֲשֶׁר־בּוֹ לְךָ
נְתַתִּיהָ לְעֵינֵי (מ"ה בריבוע) בְנֵי־עַמִּי נְתַתִּיהָ לָּךְ קְבֹר מֵתֶךָ׃
(יב) וַיִּשְׁתַּחוּ אַבְרָהָם (רמ"ח) לִפְנֵי עַם הָאָרֶץ (מילוי אלהים ע"ה)׃ (יג)
וַיְדַבֵּר (ראה) אֶל־עֶפְרוֹן בְּאָזְנֵי (יוד הי ואו הה) עַם־הָאָרֶץ (מילוי אלהים
ע"ה) לֵאמֹר אַךְ (אהיה) אִם (יוהך)-אַתָּה לוּ שְׁמָעֵנִי נָתַתִּי כֶּסֶף
הַשָּׂדֶה קַח מִמֶּנִּי וְאֶקְבְּרָה אֶת־מֵתִי שָׁמָּה׃ (יד) וַיַּעַן עֶפְרוֹן
אֶת־אַבְרָהָם (רמ"ח) לֵאמֹר לוֹ׃ (טו) אֲדֹנִי שְׁמָעֵנִי אֶרֶץ אַרְבַּע
מֵאֹת שֶׁקֶל־כֶּסֶף בֵּינִי וּבֵינְךָ מַה (מ"ה)-הִוא וְאֶת־מֵתְךָ קְבֹר׃

וַיְדַבֵּר - Abraham is looking for a place to bury Sarah. He sees a small animal in the field and follows it into a cave where he sees Adam. Adam reveals to Abraham that this is where he and Eve are buried, and where Abraham and Sarah should be buried, too. In our own lives, we do not have the aid of Adam, but we should strive to see that the places where we live— and where we are buried— are positive places that bring us blessings.

(טז) וַיִּשְׁמַע אַבְרָהָם (רמ"ח) אֶל־עֶפְרוֹן וַיִּשְׁקֹל אַבְרָהָם (רמ"ח)
לְעֶפְרֹן אֶת־הַכֶּסֶף אֲשֶׁר דִּבֶּר (ראה) בְּאָזְנֵי (יוד הי ואו הה) בְנֵי־חֵת
אַרְבַּע מֵאוֹת שֶׁקֶל כֶּסֶף עֹבֵר לַסֹּחֵר׃

Second Reading - Issac - Gvurah

(יז) וַיָּקָם ׀ שְׂדֵה עֶפְרוֹן אֲשֶׁר בַּמַּכְפֵּלָה אֲשֶׁר לִפְנֵי מַמְרֵא
הַשָּׂדֶה וְהַמְּעָרָה אֲשֶׁר־בּוֹ וְכָל (ילי) הָעֵץ אֲשֶׁר בַּשָּׂדֶה
אֲשֶׁר בְּכָל (לכב) גְּבֻלוֹ סָבִיב׃ (יח) לְאַבְרָהָם (רמ"ח) לְמִקְנָה
לְעֵינֵי (מ"ה בריבוע) בְנֵי־חֵת בְּכֹל (לכב) בָּאֵי שַׁעַר־עִירוֹ (סנדלפון,
סנדלפון, ערי)׃ (יט) וְאַחֲרֵי־כֵן קָבַר אַבְרָהָם (רמ"ח) אֶת־שָׂרָה
אִשְׁתּוֹ אֶל־מְעָרַת שְׂדֵה הַמַּכְפֵּלָה עַל־פְּנֵי (חכמה, בינה) מַמְרֵא
הִוא חֶבְרוֹן בְּאֶרֶץ כְּנָעַן׃ (כ) וַיָּקָם הַשָּׂדֶה וְהַמְּעָרָה אֲשֶׁר־
בּוֹ לְאַבְרָהָם (רמ"ח) לַאֲחֻזַּת־קָבֶר מֵאֵת בְּנֵי־חֵת׃ ס כד (א)
וְאַבְרָהָם (רמ"ח) זָקֵן בָּא בַּיָּמִים (נלך) וַיהֹוָה אדני אהדונהי בֵּרַךְ אֶת־
אַבְרָהָם (רמ"ח) בַּכֹּל (לכב)׃ (ב) וַיֹּאמֶר אַבְרָהָם (רמ"ח) אֶל־עַבְדּוֹ
זְקַן בֵּיתוֹ (ב"פ ראה) הַמֹּשֵׁל בְּכָל (לכב) אֲשֶׁר־לוֹ שִׂים־נָא יָדְךָ
תַּחַת יְרֵכִי׃ (ג) וְאַשְׁבִּיעֲךָ בַּיהֹוָה אדני אהדונהי אֱלֹהֵי (דמב) הַשָּׁמַיִם

וְאַבְרָהָם - Every day of Abraham's life was important, because every day, Abraham was a channel for the Light. We are lucky if we occasionally have one such moment, so when we have that opportunity, we should take advantage of it!

(י"פ טל) וֵאלֹהֵי (לכב) הָאָרֶץ (מילוי אלהים ע"ה) אֲשֶׁר לֹא־תִקַּח אִשָּׁה
לִבְנִי מִבְּנוֹת הַכְּנַעֲנִי אֲשֶׁר אָנֹכִי (איע) יוֹשֵׁב בְּקִרְבּוֹ׃ (ד)
כִּי אֶל־אַרְצִי וְאֶל־מוֹלַדְתִּי תֵּלֵךְ **וְלָקַחְתָּ** אִשָּׁה לִבְנִי
לְיִצְחָק (ד"פ ב"ן)׃ (ה) וַיֹּאמֶר אֵלָיו הָעֶבֶד אוּלַי (אום) לֹא־תֹאבֶה
הָאִשָּׁה לָלֶכֶת אַחֲרַי אֶל־הָאָרֶץ (מילוי אלהים ע"ה) הַזֹּאת הֶהָשֵׁב
אָשִׁיב אֶת־בִּנְךָ אֶל־הָאָרֶץ (מילוי אלהים ע"ה) אֲשֶׁר־יָצָאתָ מִשָּׁם׃
(ו) וַיֹּאמֶר אֵלָיו אַבְרָהָם (רמ"ח) הִשָּׁמֶר לְךָ פֶּן־תָּשִׁיב אֶת־
בְּנִי שָׁמָּה׃ (ז) יְהֹוָהאדניאהדונהי | אֱלֹהֵי (דמב) הַשָּׁמַיִם (י"פ טל) אֲשֶׁר
לְקָחַנִי מִבֵּית (ב"פ ראה) אָבִי וּמֵאֶרֶץ מוֹלַדְתִּי וַאֲשֶׁר דִּבֶּר
(ראה)־לִי וַאֲשֶׁר נִשְׁבַּע־לִי לֵאמֹר לְזַרְעֲךָ אֶתֵּן אֶת־הָאָרֶץ
(מילוי אלהים ע"ה) הַזֹּאת הוּא יִשְׁלַח מַלְאָכוֹ לְפָנֶיךָ (סמ"ב) וְלָקַחְתָּ
אִשָּׁה לִבְנִי מִשָּׁם׃ (ח) וְאִם (יוהך)־ לֹא תֹאבֶה הָאִשָּׁה לָלֶכֶת
אַחֲרֶיךָ וְנִקִּיתָ מִשְּׁבֻעָתִי זֹאת רַק אֶת־בְּנִי לֹא תָשֵׁב שָׁמָּה׃

וְלָקַחְתָּ - Abraham instructs his servant to travel to Abraham's family and to return with Isaac's soul-mate, whom Abraham has foreseen will be Rebecca.

The servant chosen by Abraham had intended that his own daughter marry Isaac. When he was chosen for this mission, he could have taken the opportunity to sabotage the trip. But he puts aside his personal agenda and accomplishes his task successfully. When our actions are for ourselves alone, nothing can go right for us. It is only when we let go of our negative personal plans that we find fulfillment in what we do.

(ט) וַיָּשֶׂם הָעֶבֶד אֶת־יָדוֹ תַּחַת יֶרֶךְ אַבְרָהָם (רמ"ח) אֲדֹנָיו
וַיִּשָּׁבַע לוֹ עַל־הַדָּבָר (ראה) הַזֶּה (והו):

Third Reading - Jacob - Tiferet

(י) וַיִּקַּח (וזעם) הָעֶבֶד עֲשָׂרָה גְמַלִּים מִגְּמַלֵּי אֲדֹנָיו וַיֵּלֶךְ (כלי)
וְכָל (ילי)־טוּב (והו) אֲדֹנָיו בְּיָדוֹ וַיָּקָם וַיֵּלֶךְ (כלי) אֶל־אֲרַם נַהֲרַיִם
אֶל־עִיר (סנזחך, סנדלפון, ערי) נָחוֹר: (יא) וַיַּבְרֵךְ (עסמ"ב) הַגְּמַלִּים מִחוּץ
לָעִיר (סנזחך, סנדלפון, ערי) אֶל־בְּאֵר (קנ"א ב"ן) הַמָּיִם לְעֵת עֶרֶב לְעֵת
צֵאת הַשֹּׁאֲבֹת: (יב) וַיֹּאמַר | יְהֹוָאדנׄיאהדונהי אֱלֹהֵי (דמב) אֲדֹנִי
אַבְרָהָם (רמ"ח) הַקְרֵה־נָא לְפָנַי הַיּוֹם (נגד, זן) וַעֲשֵׂה־חֶסֶד (ע"ב)
עִם אֲדֹנִי אַבְרָהָם (רמ"ח): (יג) הִנֵּה אָנֹכִי (איע) נִצָּב עַל־עֵין (מ"ה
בריבוע) הַמָּיִם וּבְנוֹת אַנְשֵׁי הָעִיר (סנזחך, סנדלפון, ערי) יֹצְאֹת לִשְׁאֹב
מָיִם: (יד) וְהָיָה (יהה) (יהוה) הַנַּעֲרָ אֲשֶׁר אֹמַר אֵלֶיהָ הַטִּי־נָא
כַדֵּךְ וְאֶשְׁתֶּה וְאָמְרָה שְׁתֵה וְגַם־גְּמַלֶּיךָ אַשְׁקֶה אֹתָהּ
הֹכַחְתָּ לְעַבְדְּךָ (פוי) לְיִצְחָק (ד"פ ב"ן) וּבָהּ אֵדַע כִּי־עָשִׂיתָ

וַיֹּאמַר - Arriving in Abraham's home-town, the servant prays to God for success in his mission and for a sign by which to recognize Isaac's soul-mate. He meets with Rebecca near a well, which shows us how water has power not only to heal, but also to help us in our relationships and even to unite us with our soul-mate. We should note that Jacob's first meeting with Rachel was also by a well, as was Moses's meeting with Tzipporah.

וָחֶסֶד (ע"ב) עִם־אֲדֹנִי: (טו) וַיְהִי־הוּא טֶרֶם כִּלָּה לְדַבֵּר (ראה)
וְהִנֵּה רִבְקָה יֹצֵאת אֲשֶׁר יֻלְּדָה לִבְתוּאֵל בֶּן־מִלְכָּה אֵשֶׁת
נָחוֹר אֲחִי אַבְרָהָם (רמ"ח) וְכַדָּהּ עַל־שִׁכְמָהּ: (טז) וְהַנַּעֲרָ
טֹבַת מַרְאֶה מְאֹד בְּתוּלָה וְאִישׁ לֹא יְדָעָהּ וַתֵּרֶד הָעַיְנָה
וַתְּמַלֵּא כַדָּהּ וַתָּעַל: (יז) וַיָּרָץ הָעֶבֶד לִקְרָאתָהּ וַיֹּאמֶר
הַגְמִיאִינִי נָא מְעַט־מַיִם מִכַּדֵּךְ: (יח) וַתֹּאמֶר שְׁתֵה אֲדֹנִי
וַתְּמַהֵר וַתֹּרֶד כַּדָּהּ עַל־יָדָהּ וַתַּשְׁקֵהוּ: (יט) וַתְּכַל לְהַשְׁקֹתוֹ
וַתֹּאמֶר גַּם לִגְמַלֶּיךָ אֶשְׁאָב עַד אִם (יוהך)־כִּלּוּ לִשְׁתֹּת: (כ)
וַתְּמַהֵר וַתְּעַר כַּדָּהּ אֶל־הַשֹּׁקֶת וַתָּרָץ עוֹד אֶל־הַבְּאֵר
(קנ"א ב"ן) לִשְׁאֹב וַתִּשְׁאַב לְכָל (יה אדני)־גְּמַלָּיו: (כא) וְהָאִישׁ
מִשְׁתָּאֵה לָהּ מַחֲרִישׁ לָדַעַת הַהִצְלִיחַ יְהֹוָהאדניאהדונהי דַּרְכּוֹ
אִם (יוהך)־לֹא: (כב) וַיְהִי כַּאֲשֶׁר כִּלּוּ הַגְּמַלִּים לִשְׁתּוֹת וַיִּקַּח
(וזעם) הָאִישׁ נֶזֶם זָהָב בֶּקַע מִשְׁקָלוֹ וּשְׁנֵי צְמִידִים עַל־יָדֶיהָ
עֲשָׂרָה זָהָב מִשְׁקָלָם: (כג) וַיֹּאמֶר בַּת־מִי (ילי) אַתְּ הַגִּידִי נָא

וַיְהִי - The servant finds Rebecca, without even knowing her name or that she is from Abraham's family. He is able to do this through the power of his certainty that God would reveal Isaac's soul-mate at the right moment. Because of this certainty, the sign appears and he finds Rebecca. Only later does he learn that she has met Abraham's requirement that she be of his family. When we have certainty and make an effort for the sake of sharing and revealing light—that is, when we do our part —the Light will support us and help us complete our task.

לִי הֲיֵשׁ בֵּית (ב"פ ראה) ־אָבִיךָ מָקוֹם לָנוּ (מום) לָלִין: (כד) וַתֹּאמֶר
אֵלָיו בַּת־בְּתוּאֵל אָנֹכִי (אני) בֶּן־מִלְכָּה אֲשֶׁר יָלְדָה לְנָחוֹר:
(כה) וַתֹּאמֶר אֵלָיו גַּם־תֶּבֶן גַּם־מִסְפּוֹא רַב עִמָּנוּ (מילוי דמ"ה)
גַּם־מָקוֹם לָלוּן: (כו) וַיִּקֹּד הָאִישׁ וַיִּשְׁתַּחוּ לַיהֹוָהאדניאהדונהי:

Fourth Reading - Moses - Netzach

(כז) וַיֹּאמֶר בָּרוּךְ יְהֹוָהאדניאהדונהי אֱלֹהֵי (דמב) אֲדֹנִי אַבְרָהָם
(רמ"ח) אֲשֶׁר לֹא־עָזַב חַסְדּוֹ (ג' הויות) וַאֲמִתּוֹ מֵעִם אֲדֹנִי אָנֹכִי
(אני) בַּדֶּרֶךְ (ב"פ יב"ק) נָחַנִי יְהֹוָהאדניאהדונהי בֵּית (ב"פ ראה) אֲחֵי אֲדֹנִי:
(כח) וַתָּרָץ הַנַּעֲרָ וַתַּגֵּד לְבֵית (ב"פ ראה) אִמָּהּ כַּדְּבָרִים (ראה)
הָאֵלֶּה: (כט) וּלְרִבְקָה אָח וּשְׁמוֹ (מהש ע"ה) לָבָן וַיָּרָץ לָבָן
אֶל־הָאִישׁ הַחוּצָה אֶל־הָעָיִן (מ"ה בריבוע): (ל) וַיְהִי | כִּרְאֹת
אֶת־הַנֶּזֶם וְאֶת־הַצְּמִדִים עַל־יְדֵי אֲחֹתוֹ וּכְשָׁמְעוֹ אֶת־
דִּבְרֵי (ראה) רִבְקָה אֲחֹתוֹ לֵאמֹר כֹּה (הי) ־דִבֶּר (ראה) אֵלַי
הָאִישׁ וַיָּבֹא אֶל־הָאִישׁ וְהִנֵּה עֹמֵד עַל־הַגְּמַלִּים עַל־הָעָיִן
(מ"ה בריבוע): (לא) וַיֹּאמֶר בּוֹא בְּרוּךְ יְהֹוָהאדניאהדונהי לָמָּה תַעֲמֹד

לָבָן - Laban was a very negative force. He wanted to prevent Rebecca from going to marry Isaac. Laban, therefore, represents the dark forces that must be overcome before soul-mates can be joined. Though his name means "white," Laban was very dark in appearance. Here, Laban's presence teaches us that when the start of a relationship is simple and easy, there is less likelihood of revealing Light. However, when there are obstacles at the beginning of a relationship, the potential to reveal Light is great.

בַּחוּץ וְאָנֹכִי (איע) פִּנִּיתִי הַבַּיִת (ב"פ ראה) וּמָקוֹם לַגְּמַלִּים׃ (לב)
וַיָּבֹא הָאִישׁ הַבַּיְתָה (ב"פ ראה) וַיְפַתַּח הַגְּמַלִּים וַיִּתֵּן תֶּבֶן
וּמִסְפּוֹא לַגְּמַלִּים וּמַיִם לִרְחֹץ רַגְלָיו וְרַגְלֵי הָאֲנָשִׁים אֲשֶׁר
אִתּוֹ׃ (לג) וַיּוּשַׂם (ויישם כתיב) לְפָנָיו לֶאֱכֹל וַיֹּאמֶר לֹא אֹכַל
עַד אִם (יוהך)־דִּבַּרְתִּי (ראה) דְּבָרָי (ראה) וַיֹּאמֶר דַּבֵּר (ראה)׃ (לד)
וַיֹּאמַר **עֶבֶד** אַבְרָהָם (רמ"ח) אָנֹכִי (איע)׃ (לה) וַיהֹוָהאדניאהדונהי
בֵּרַךְ אֶת־אֲדֹנִי מְאֹד וַיִּגְדָּל (יזל) וַיִּתֶּן־לוֹ צֹאן וּבָקָר וְכֶסֶף
וְזָהָב וַעֲבָדִם וּשְׁפָחֹת וּגְמַלִּים וַחֲמֹרִים׃ (לו) וַתֵּלֶד שָׂרָה
אֵשֶׁת אֲדֹנִי בֵן לַאדֹנִי אַחֲרֵי זִקְנָתָהּ וַיִּתֶּן־לוֹ אֶת־כָּל (ילי)־
אֲשֶׁר־לוֹ׃ (לז) וַיַּשְׁבִּעֵנִי אֲדֹנִי לֵאמֹר לֹא־תִקַּח אִשָּׁה לִבְנִי
מִבְּנוֹת הַכְּנַעֲנִי אֲשֶׁר אָנֹכִי (איע) יֹשֵׁב בְּאַרְצוֹ׃ (לח) אִם
(יוהך)־ לֹא אֶל־בֵּית (ב"פ ראה)־אָבִי תֵּלֵךְ וְאֶל־מִשְׁפַּחְתִּי וְלָקַחְתָּ
אִשָּׁה לִבְנִי׃ (לט) וָאֹמַר אֶל־אֲדֹנִי אֻלַי לֹא־תֵלֵךְ הָאִשָּׁה

עֶבֶד - When the servant speaks to Rebecca's family, he does not reveal how he found her. Instead, he focuses on the details of her name and on the fact that Abraham had told him to go to his, Abraham's, family. The servant knew the importance of speaking to Rebecca's family at a level that was appropriate to them and that they could understand. We can receive only those messages that we are open to receiving and that correspond to our current state of spiritual development. We should continually push ourselves to grow spiritually, to accept the messages that come to us, and to take the action they require.

אַחֲרָי׃ (מ) וַיֹּאמֶר אֵלָי יְהֹוָה אדני אהדונהי אֲשֶׁר־הִתְהַלַּכְתִּי
לְפָנָיו יִשְׁלַח מַלְאָכוֹ אִתָּךְ וְהִצְלִיחַ דַּרְכֶּךָ וְלָקַחְתָּ אִשָּׁה
לִבְנִי מִמִּשְׁפַּחְתִּי וּמִבֵּית (ב״פ ראה) אָבִי׃ (מא) אָז תִּנָּקֶה מֵאָלָתִי
כִּי תָבוֹא אֶל־מִשְׁפַּחְתִּי וְאִם (יוהך)־לֹא יִתְּנוּ לָךְ וְהָיִיתָ נָקִי (ע״ה
קס״א) מֵאָלָתִי׃ (מב) וָאָבֹא הַיּוֹם (נגד, זן) אֶל־הָעָיִן (מ״ה בריבוע) וָאֹמַר
יְהֹוָה אדני אהדונהי אֱלֹהֵי (דמב) אֲדֹנִי אַבְרָהָם (רמ״ח) אִם (יוהך)־יֶשְׁךָ־
נָּא מַצְלִיחַ דַּרְכִּי אֲשֶׁר אָנֹכִי (איע) הֹלֵךְ (מיה) עָלֶיהָ (פהל)׃ (מג)
הִנֵּה אָנֹכִי (איע) נִצָּב עַל־עֵין (מ״ה בריבוע) הַמָּיִם וְהָיָה (יהה) (יהוה)
הָעַלְמָה הַיֹּצֵאת לִשְׁאֹב וְאָמַרְתִּי אֵלֶיהָ הַשְׁקִינִי־נָא מְעַט־
מַיִם מִכַּדֵּךְ׃ (מד) וְאָמְרָה אֵלַי גַּם־אַתָּה שְׁתֵה וְגַם לִגְמַלֶּיךָ
אֶשְׁאָב הִוא הָאִשָּׁה אֲשֶׁר־הֹכִיחַ יְהֹוָה אדני אהדונהי לְבֶן־אֲדֹנִי׃
(מה) אֲנִי (אני) טֶרֶם אֲכַלֶּה לְדַבֵּר (ראה) אֶל־לִבִּי וְהִנֵּה רִבְקָה
יֹצֵאת וְכַדָּהּ עַל־שִׁכְמָהּ וַתֵּרֶד הָעַיְנָה וַתִּשְׁאָב וָאֹמַר
אֵלֶיהָ הַשְׁקִינִי נָא׃ (מו) וַתְּמַהֵר וַתּוֹרֶד כַּדָּהּ מֵעָלֶיהָ (פהל)
וַתֹּאמֶר שְׁתֵה וְגַם־גְּמַלֶּיךָ אַשְׁקֶה וָאֵשְׁתְּ וְגַם הַגְּמַלִּים
הִשְׁקָתָה׃ (מז) וָאֶשְׁאַל אֹתָהּ וָאֹמַר בַּת־מִי (ילי) אַתְּ וַתֹּאמֶר
בַּת־בְּתוּאֵל בֶּן־נָחוֹר אֲשֶׁר יָלְדָה־לּוֹ מִלְכָּה וָאָשִׂם הַנֶּזֶם
עַל־אַפָּהּ וְהַצְּמִידִים עַל־יָדֶיהָ׃ (מח) וָאֶקֹּד וָאֶשְׁתַּחֲוֶה (י״פ ע״ב)
לַיהֹוָה אדני אהדונהי וָאֲבָרֵךְ אֶת־יְהֹוָה אדני אהדונהי אֱלֹהֵי (דמב) אֲדֹנִי

אַבְרָהָם (רמ"ח) אֲשֶׁר הִנְחַנִי בְּדֶרֶךְ (ב"פ יב"ק) אֱמֶת (אהיה פ' אהיה)
לָקַחַת אֶת־בַּת־אֲחִי אֲדֹנִי לִבְנוֹ׃ (מט) וְעַתָּה אִם (יוהך)־יֶשְׁכֶם
עֹשִׂים חֶסֶד (ע"ב) וֶאֱמֶת (אהיה פ' אהיה) אֶת־אֲדֹנִי הַגִּידוּ לִי וְאִם
(יוהך)־לֹא הַגִּידוּ לִי וְאֶפְנֶה עַל־יָמִין אוֹ עַל־שְׂמֹאל׃ (נ) וַיַּעַן
לָבָן וּבְתוּאֵל וַיֹּאמְרוּ מֵיְהֹוָה אדני אהדונהי יָצָא הַדָּבָר (ראה) לֹא
נוּכַל דַּבֵּר (ראה) אֵלֶיךָ רַע אוֹ־טוֹב (והו)׃ (נא) הִנֵּה־רִבְקָה
לְפָנֶיךָ (סמ"ב) קַח וָלֵךְ וּתְהִי אִשָּׁה לְבֶן־אֲדֹנֶיךָ כַּאֲשֶׁר דִּבֶּר
(ראה) יְהֹוָה אדני אהדונהי׃ (נב) וַיְהִי כַּאֲשֶׁר שָׁמַע עֶבֶד אַבְרָהָם (רמ"ח)
אֶת־דִּבְרֵיהֶם (ראה) וַיִּשְׁתַּחוּ אַרְצָה לַיהֹוָה אדני אהדונהי׃

Fifth Reading - Aaron - Hod

(נג) וַיּוֹצֵא הָעֶבֶד כְּלֵי־כֶסֶף וּכְלֵי זָהָב וּבְגָדִים וַיִּתֵּן
לְרִבְקָה וּמִגְדָּנֹת נָתַן לְאָחִיהָ וּלְאִמָּהּ׃ (נד) וַיֹּאכְלוּ וַיִּשְׁתּוּ
הוּא וְהָאֲנָשִׁים אֲשֶׁר־עִמּוֹ **וַיָּלִינוּ** וַיָּקוּמוּ בַבֹּקֶר וַיֹּאמֶר
שַׁלְּחֻנִי לַאדֹנִי׃ (נה) וַיֹּאמֶר אָחִיהָ וְאִמָּהּ תֵּשֵׁב הַנַּעֲרָ אִתָּנוּ

וַיָּלִינוּ - The servant spends the night at the home of Rebecca. Rebecca's father schemes to poison him to prevent him from taking Rebecca. But an angel switches the food, and it is Rebecca's father who is poisoned. All our actions have repercussions. In this case, the negative act of Rebecca's father elicited an immediate reaction. Often, there is a separation in time or location between an action and its consequences, but we should always be aware that sooner or later every cause has an effect.

יָמִים (נלך) אוֹ עָשׂוֹר אַחַ֤ר תֵּלֵֽךְ׃ (נו) וַיֹּ֨אמֶר אֲלֵהֶם֙ אַל־

תְּאַחֲר֣וּ אֹתִ֔י וַיהֹ֖וָֽאדנׇיאהדונהי הִצְלִ֣יחַ דַּרְכִּ֑י שַׁלְּח֕וּנִי וְאֵלְכָ֖ה

לַֽאדֹנִֽי׃ (נז) וַיֹּֽאמְר֖וּ נִקְרָ֣א לַֽנַּעֲרָ֑ וְנִשְׁאֲלָ֖ה אֶת־פִּֽיהָ׃ (נח)

וַיִּקְרְא֤וּ לְרִבְקָה֙ וַיֹּֽאמְר֣וּ אֵלֶ֔יהָ הֲתֵֽלְכִ֖י עִם־הָאִ֣ישׁ הַזֶּ֑ה

(והן) וַתֹּ֖אמֶר אֵלֵֽךְ׃ (נט) וַֽיְשַׁלְּח֛וּ אֶת־רִבְקָ֥ה אֲחֹתָ֖ם וְאֶת־

מֵנִקְתָּ֑הּ וְאֶת־עֶ֥בֶד אַבְרָהָ֖ם (רמ"ז) וְאֶת־אֲנָשָֽׁיו׃ (ס) וַיְבָֽרְכ֤וּ

(יהוה ריבוע יהוה ריבוע מ"ה) אֶת־רִבְקָה֙ וַיֹּ֣אמְרוּ לָ֔הּ אֲחֹתֵ֕נוּ אַ֥תְּ הֲיִ֖י

לְאַלְפֵ֣י רְבָבָ֑ה וְיִירַ֣שׁ זַרְעֵ֔ךְ אֵ֖ת שַׁ֥עַר שֹֽׂנְאָֽיו׃ (סא) וַתָּ֨קׇם

רִבְקָ֜ה וְנַֽעֲרֹתֶ֗יהָ וַתִּרְכַּ֨בְנָה֙ עַל־הַגְּמַלִּ֔ים וַתֵּלַ֖כְנָה אַֽחֲרֵ֣י

הָאִ֑ישׁ וַיִּקַּ֥ח (ועם) הָעֶ֛בֶד אֶת־רִבְקָ֖ה וַיֵּלַֽךְ׃ (כלי) (סב) וְיִצְחָק֙

(ד"פ ב"ן) בָּ֣א מִבּ֔וֹא בְּאֵ֥ר (קנ"א ב"ן) לַחַ֖י רֹאִ֑י וְה֥וּא יוֹשֵׁ֖ב בְּאֶ֥רֶץ

הַנֶּֽגֶב׃ (סג) וַיֵּצֵ֥א יִצְחָ֛ק (ד"פ ב"ן) לָשׂ֥וּחַ בַּשָּׂדֶ֖ה לִפְנ֣וֹת עָ֑רֶב

וַיִּשָּׂ֤א עֵינָיו֙ (מ"ה בריבוע) וַיַּ֔רְא וְהִנֵּ֥ה גְמַלִּ֖ים בָּאִֽים׃ (סד) וַתִּשָּׂ֤א

וַתֹּאמֶר - Rebecca's family asks her if she wants to stay or go with Abraham's servant. Knowing that she is in a negative environment, Rebecca says that she wants to go.

וַיֵּצֵא - Immediately before sunset is the most negative time of the day when there are more negative forces in power and more negative angels giving assistance to anyone with destructive intentions. We should use the Ana B'koach to help us through this transitional time when the light is disappearing.

רִבְקָה֙ אֶת־עֵינֶ֔יהָ (מ"ה ברבוע) וַתֵּ֖רֶא אֶת־יִצְחָ֑ק (ד"פ ב"ן) וַתִּפֹּ֖ל

מֵעַ֥ל (עלם) הַגָּמָֽל: (סה) וַתֹּ֣אמֶר אֶל־הָעֶ֗בֶד מִֽי־ (ילי) הָאִ֤ישׁ

הַלָּזֶה֙ הַהֹלֵ֤ךְ (מ"ה) בַּשָּׂדֶה֙ לִקְרָאתֵ֔נוּ וַיֹּ֥אמֶר הָעֶ֖בֶד ה֣וּא

אֲדֹנִ֑י וַתִּקַּ֥ח הַצָּעִ֖יף וַתִּתְכָּֽס: (סו) וַיְסַפֵּ֥ר הָעֶ֖בֶד לְיִצְחָ֑ק (ד"פ

ב"ן) אֵ֥ת כָּל־ (ילי) הַדְּבָרִ֖ים (ראה) אֲשֶׁ֥ר עָשָֽׂה: (סז) וַיְבִאֶ֣הָ יִצְחָ֗ק

(ד"פ ב"ן) הָאֹ֙הֱלָה֙ שָׂרָ֣ה אִמּ֔וֹ וַיִּקַּ֧ח (וזעם) אֶת־רִבְקָ֛ה וַתְּהִי־ל֥וֹ

לְאִשָּׁ֖ה וַיֶּאֱהָבֶ֑הָ וַיִּנָּחֵ֥ם יִצְחָ֖ק (ד"פ ב"ן) אַחֲרֵ֥י אִמּֽוֹ: פ

Sixth Reading - Joseph - Yesod

כה (א) וַיֹּ֧סֶף (ציון) אַבְרָהָ֛ם (רמ"ח) וַיִּקַּ֥ח (וזעם) אִשָּׁ֖ה וּשְׁמָ֥הּ

קְטוּרָֽה: (ב) וַתֵּ֣לֶד ל֗וֹ אֶת־זִמְרָן֙ וְאֶת־יָקְשָׁ֔ן וְאֶת־מְדָ֖ן וְאֶת־

מִדְיָ֑ן וְאֶת־יִשְׁבָּ֖ק וְאֶת־שֽׁוּחַ: (ג) וְיָקְשָׁ֣ן יָלַ֔ד אֶת־שְׁבָ֖א וְאֶת־

דְּדָ֑ן וּבְנֵ֣י דְדָ֗ן הָי֤וּ אַשּׁוּרִם֙ וּלְטוּשִׁ֖ים וּלְאֻמִּֽים: (ד) וּבְנֵ֣י

וַיְבִאֶהָ - Isaac brings Rebecca into his tent. At the moment Rebecca enters, the tent is filled with Light. When Sarah died, the Light in the tent went out, but when Rebecca is joined with Isaac, the Light could reappear. This demonstrates to Isaac that his union with Rebecca will be a channel of Light for the whole world.

וַיֹּסֶף - Abraham marries K'utarah and has children by her. K'utarah is actually Hagar, who has changed her name. The children of this union will travel to the East to spread the teachings of Kabbalah. Abraham's intention is to share the Light with all the nations of the world and to bring them assistance through knowledge of Kabbalah.

מִדְיָן עֵיפָה וָעֵפֶר וַחֲנֹךְ וַאֲבִידָע וְאֶלְדָּעָה כָּל (ילי) אֵלֶּה
בְּנֵי קְטוּרָה: (ה) וַיִּתֵּן אַבְרָהָם (רמ"ח) אֶת־כָּל (ילי) אֲשֶׁר־לוֹ
לְיִצְחָק (ד"פ ב"ן): (ו) וְלִבְנֵי הַפִּילַגְשִׁים אֲשֶׁר לְאַבְרָהָם (רמ"ח)
נָתַן אַבְרָהָם (רמ"ח) מַתָּנֹת וַיְשַׁלְּחֵם מֵעַל (עלם) יִצְחָק (ד"פ ב"ן)
בְּנוֹ בְּעוֹדֶנּוּ חַי קֵדְמָה אֶל־אֶרֶץ קֶדֶם: (ז) **וְאֵלֶּה** יְמֵי
שְׁנֵי־חַיֵּי אַבְרָהָם (רמ"ח) אֲשֶׁר־חָי מְאַת שָׁנָה וְשִׁבְעִים שָׁנָה
וְחָמֵשׁ שָׁנִים: (ח) וַיִּגְוַע וַיָּמָת אַבְרָהָם (רמ"ח) בְּשֵׂיבָה טוֹבָה
(אכא) זָקֵן וְשָׂבֵעַ וַיֵּאָסֶף אֶל־עַמָּיו: (ט) וַיִּקְבְּרוּ אֹתוֹ יִצְחָק
(ד"פ ב"ן) וְיִשְׁמָעֵאל בָּנָיו אֶל־מְעָרַת הַמַּכְפֵּלָה אֶל־שְׂדֵה
עֶפְרֹן בֶּן־צֹחַר הַחִתִּי אֲשֶׁר עַל־פְּנֵי (חכמה, בינה) מַמְרֵא: (י)
הַשָּׂדֶה אֲשֶׁר־קָנָה אַבְרָהָם (רמ"ח) מֵאֵת בְּנֵי־חֵת שָׁמָּה קֻבַּר
אַבְרָהָם (רמ"ח) וְשָׂרָה אִשְׁתּוֹ: (יא) וַיְהִי אַחֲרֵי מוֹת אַבְרָהָם
(רמ"ח) וַיְבָרֶךְ (עסמ"ב) אֱלֹהִים (ילה) אֶת־יִצְחָק (ד"פ ב"ן) בְּנוֹ וַיֵּשֶׁב
יִצְחָק (ד"פ ב"ן) עִם־בְּאֵר (קנ"א ב"ן) לַחַי רֹאִי: ס

וְאֵלֶּה - Abraham died at a good age because he had accomplished tremendous spiritual work. The Rav notes that we often express greater sorrow at the passing of a young person than at the passing of someone older. But we should feel sadness when anyone dies, regardless of his or her age. Just as important, we should hope that this individual has accomplished much, spiritually and otherwise, in the time that was granted to him or her. And every day, we ourselves should diligently perform our spiritual work.

Seventh Reading - David - Malchut

(יב) וְאֵלֶּה תֹּלְדֹת יִשְׁמָעֵאל בֶּן־אַבְרָהָם (רמ״ח) אֲשֶׁר יָלְדָה
הָגָר הַמִּצְרִית (מצר) שִׁפְחַת שָׂרָה לְאַבְרָהָם (רמ״ח): (יג) וְאֵלֶּה
שְׁמוֹת בְּנֵי יִשְׁמָעֵאל בִּשְׁמֹתָם לְתוֹלְדֹתָם בְּכֹר יִשְׁמָעֵאל
נְבָיֹת וְקֵדָר וְאַדְבְּאֵל וּמִבְשָׂם: (יד) וּמִשְׁמָע וְדוּמָה וּמַשָּׂא:
(טו) חֲדַד וְתֵימָא יְטוּר נָפִישׁ וָקֵדְמָה:

Maftir

(טז) אֵלֶּה הֵם בְּנֵי יִשְׁמָעֵאל וְאֵלֶּה שְׁמֹתָם בְּחַצְרֵיהֶם
וּבְטִירֹתָם שְׁנֵים־עָשָׂר נְשִׂיאִם לְאֻמֹּתָם: (יז) וְאֵלֶּה שְׁנֵי
חַיֵּי יִשְׁמָעֵאל מְאַת שָׁנָה וּשְׁלֹשִׁים שָׁנָה וְשֶׁבַע שָׁנִים וַיִּגְוַע
וַיָּמָת וַיֵּאָסֶף אֶל־עַמָּיו: (יח) וַיִּשְׁכְּנוּ מֵחֲוִילָה עַד־שׁוּר (אבג
יתץ, ושר, אהבת חנם) אֲשֶׁר עַל־פְּנֵי (חכמה, בינה) מִצְרַיִם (מצר) בֹּאֲכָה
אַשּׁוּרָה עַל־פְּנֵי (חכמה, בינה) כָל (ילי)־אֶחָיו נָפָל: פפפ

וְאֵלֶּה - The twelve sons of Jacob help us to rise above the influences of the planets and other astrological forces. In contrast, the 12 sons of Ishmael represent our being controlled by the forces of the zodiac. In our spiritual work, we strive to overcome the 12 sons of Ishmael and the forces they represent.

וְאֵלֶּה - Although he had been very negative all his life, Ishmael repents before his death and becomes a righteous person. No matter how negative some people are, no matter how much everyone believes they are lost, no matter how much they believe it themselves, Ishmael shows us that change is possible, even at the very last moment.

The Haftarah of Chayei Sarah

The portion deals with Abraham's last days, and the Haftarah concerns the last days of King David. For most people, reaching a certain age means they are simply waiting to die. But even on the last day of their lives, Abraham and King David asked themselves, "What Light can I reveal today?" They were never merely waiting to take their rest. They were always seeking higher spirituality and more opportunities for sharing.

מלכים א פרק א

(א) וְהַמֶּלֶךְ דָּוִד זָקֵן בָּא בַּיָּמִים (נלך) וַיְכַסֻּהוּ בַּבְּגָדִים וְלֹא
יִחַם לוֹ׃ (ב) וַיֹּאמְרוּ לוֹ עֲבָדָיו יְבַקְשׁוּ לַאדֹנִי הַמֶּלֶךְ נַעֲרָה
בְתוּלָה וְעָמְדָה לִפְנֵי הַמֶּלֶךְ וּתְהִי־לוֹ סֹכֶנֶת וְשָׁכְבָה
בְחֵיקֶךָ וְחַם לַאדֹנִי הַמֶּלֶךְ׃ (ג) וַיְבַקְשׁוּ נַעֲרָה יָפָה בְּכֹל
(לכב) גְּבוּל יִשְׂרָאֵל וַיִּמְצְאוּ אֶת־אֲבִישַׁג הַשּׁוּנַמִּית וַיָּבִאוּ
אֹתָהּ לַמֶּלֶךְ׃ (ד) וְהַנַּעֲרָה יָפָה עַד־מְאֹד וַתְּהִי לַמֶּלֶךְ סֹכֶנֶת
וַתְּשָׁרְתֵהוּ וְהַמֶּלֶךְ לֹא יְדָעָהּ׃ (ה) וַאֲדֹנִיָּה בֶן־חַגִּית מִתְנַשֵּׂא
לֵאמֹר אֲנִי (אני) אֶמְלֹךְ וַיַּעַשׂ לוֹ רֶכֶב וּפָרָשִׁים וַחֲמִשִּׁים אִישׁ
רָצִים לְפָנָיו׃ (ו) וְלֹא־עֲצָבוֹ אָבִיו מִיָּמָיו לֵאמֹר מַדּוּעַ כָּכָה
עָשִׂיתָ וְגַם־הוּא טוֹב (והו) ־תֹאַר מְאֹד וְאֹתוֹ יָלְדָה אַחֲרֵי
אַבְשָׁלוֹם׃ (ז) וַיִּהְיוּ דְבָרָיו עִם יוֹאָב בֶּן־צְרוּיָה וְעִם אֶבְיָתָר
הַכֹּהֵן (מלה) וַיַּעְזְרוּ אַחֲרֵי אֲדֹנִיָּה׃ (וז) וְצָדוֹק הַכֹּהֵן (מלה) וּבְנָיָהוּ
בֶּן־יְהוֹיָדָע וְנָתָן הַנָּבִיא וְשִׁמְעִי וְרֵעִי וְהַגִּבּוֹרִים אֲשֶׁר לְדָוִד

לֹא הָיוּ עִם־אֲדֹנִיָּהוּ: (ט) וַיִּזְבַּח אֲדֹנִיָּהוּ צֹאן וּבָקָר וּמְרִיא

עִם אֶבֶן הַזֹּחֶלֶת אֲשֶׁר־אֵצֶל עֵין רֹגֵל וַיִּקְרָא אֶת־כָּל־אֶחָיו

בְּנֵי הַמֶּלֶךְ וּלְכָל־אַנְשֵׁי יְהוּדָה עַבְדֵי הַמֶּלֶךְ: (י) וְאֶת־נָתָן

הַנָּבִיא וּבְנָיָהוּ וְאֶת־הַגִּבּוֹרִים וְאֶת־שְׁלֹמֹה אָחִיו לֹא קָרָא:

(יא) וַיֹּאמֶר נָתָן אֶל־בַּת־שֶׁבַע אֵם־שְׁלֹמֹה לֵאמֹר הֲלוֹא

שָׁמַעַתְּ כִּי מָלַךְ אֲדֹנִיָּהוּ בֶן־חַגִּית וַאֲדֹנֵינוּ דָוִד לֹא יָדָע:

(יב) וְעַתָּה לְכִי אִיעָצֵךְ נָא עֵצָה וּמַלְּטִי אֶת־נַפְשֵׁךְ וְאֶת־

נֶפֶשׁ בְּנֵךְ שְׁלֹמֹה: (יג) לְכִי וּבֹאִי | אֶל־הַמֶּלֶךְ דָּוִד וְאָמַרְתְּ

אֵלָיו הֲלֹא־אַתָּה אֲדֹנִי הַמֶּלֶךְ נִשְׁבַּעְתָּ לַאֲמָתְךָ לֵאמֹר כִּי־

שְׁלֹמֹה בְנֵךְ יִמְלֹךְ אַחֲרַי וְהוּא (מ"ם) יֵשֵׁב עַל־כִּסְאִי וּמַדּוּעַ

מָלַךְ אֲדֹנִיָּהוּ: (יד) הִנֵּה עוֹדָךְ מְדַבֶּרֶת שָׁם עִם־הַמֶּלֶךְ וַאֲנִי

(אני) אָבוֹא אַחֲרַיִךְ וּמִלֵּאתִי אֶת־דְּבָרָיִךְ: (טו) וַתָּבֹא בַת־שֶׁבַע

אֶל־הַמֶּלֶךְ הַחַדְרָה וְהַמֶּלֶךְ זָקֵן מְאֹד וַאֲבִישַׁג הַשּׁוּנַמִּית (ילי)

מְשָׁרַת אֶת־הַמֶּלֶךְ: (טז) וַתִּקֹּד בַּת־שֶׁבַע וַתִּשְׁתַּחוּ לַמֶּלֶךְ

וַיֹּאמֶר הַמֶּלֶךְ מַה־לָּךְ: (יז) וַתֹּאמֶר לוֹ אֲדֹנִי אַתָּה נִשְׁבַּעְתָּ

בַּיהוָה אֱלֹהֶיךָ (דמב, ילה) לַאֲמָתֶךָ כִּי־שְׁלֹמֹה בְנֵךְ יִמְלֹךְ אַחֲרָי

וְהוּא (מ"ם) יֵשֵׁב עַל־כִּסְאִי: (יח) וְעַתָּה הִנֵּה אֲדֹנִיָּה מָלָךְ וְעַתָּה

אֲדֹנִי הַמֶּלֶךְ לֹא יָדָעְתָּ: (יט) וַיִּזְבַּח שׁוֹר (ישׂר, אבג יתן, אהבת וזנם)

וּמְרִיא־וְצֹאן לָרֹב {פ} וַיִּקְרָא לְכָל־בְּנֵי הַמֶּלֶךְ וּלְאֶבְיָתָר

הַכֹּהֵן (מלה) וּלְיֹאָב שַׂר הַצָּבָא וְלִשְׁלֹמֹה עַבְדְּךָ (פוי) לֹא קָרָא׃
(כ) וְאַתָּה אֲדֹנִי הַמֶּלֶךְ עֵינֵי כָל־יִשְׂרָאֵל עָלֶיךָ לְהַגִּיד לָהֶם
מִי (ילי) יֵשֵׁב עַל־כִּסֵּא אֲדֹנִי־הַמֶּלֶךְ אַחֲרָיו׃ (כא) וְהָיָה (יהה)
כִּשְׁכַב אֲדֹנִי־הַמֶּלֶךְ עִם־אֲבֹתָיו וְהָיִיתִי אֲנִי (אני) וּבְנִי שְׁלֹמֹה
חַטָּאִים׃ (כב) וְהִנֵּה עוֹדֶנָּה מְדַבֶּרֶת עִם־הַמֶּלֶךְ וְנָתָן הַנָּבִיא
בָּא׃ (כג) וַיַּגִּידוּ לַמֶּלֶךְ לֵאמֹר הִנֵּה נָתָן הַנָּבִיא וַיָּבֹא לִפְנֵי
הַמֶּלֶךְ וַיִּשְׁתַּחוּ לַמֶּלֶךְ עַל־אַפָּיו אָרְצָה׃ (כד) וַיֹּאמֶר נָתָן
אֲדֹנִי הַמֶּלֶךְ אַתָּה אָמַרְתָּ אֲדֹנִיָּהוּ יִמְלֹךְ אַחֲרָי וְהוּא יֵשֵׁב
עַל־כִּסְאִי׃ (כה) כִּי ׀ יָרַד הַיּוֹם (נגד, מזבח, זן) וַיִּזְבַּח שׁוֹר (ושר,
אבג יתץ, אהבת חנם) וּמְרִיא־וְצֹאן לָרֹב וַיִּקְרָא לְכָל־בְּנֵי הַמֶּלֶךְ
וּלְשָׂרֵי הַצָּבָא וּלְאֶבְיָתָר הַכֹּהֵן (מלה) וְהִנָּם אֹכְלִים וְשֹׁתִים
לְפָנָיו וַיֹּאמְרוּ יְחִי הַמֶּלֶךְ אֲדֹנִיָּהוּ׃ (כו) וְלִי אֲנִי (אני)־עַבְדֶּךָ (פוי)
וּלְצָדֹק הַכֹּהֵן (מלה) וְלִבְנָיָהוּ בֶן־יְהוֹיָדָע וְלִשְׁלֹמֹה עַבְדְּךָ (פוי)
לֹא קָרָא׃ (כז) אִם (יוהך) מֵאֵת אֲדֹנִי הַמֶּלֶךְ נִהְיָה הַדָּבָר (ראה)
הַזֶּה (והו) וְלֹא הוֹדַעְתָּ אֶת־עַבְדְּךָ (כתיב עבדיך) מִי (ילי) יֵשֵׁב עַל־
כִּסֵּא אֲדֹנִי־הַמֶּלֶךְ אַחֲרָיו׃ {ס} (כח) וַיַּעַן הַמֶּלֶךְ דָּוִד וַיֹּאמֶר
קִרְאוּ־לִי לְבַת־שָׁבַע וַתָּבֹא לִפְנֵי הַמֶּלֶךְ וַתַּעֲמֹד לִפְנֵי
הַמֶּלֶךְ׃ (כט) וַיִּשָּׁבַע הַמֶּלֶךְ וַיֹּאמַר חַי־יְהוָה אֲשֶׁר־פָּדָה
אֶת־נַפְשִׁי מִכָּל־צָרָה׃ (ל) כִּי כַּאֲשֶׁר נִשְׁבַּעְתִּי לְךָ בַּיהוָה

אֱלֹהֵי (דמב,ילה) יִשְׂרָאֵל לֵאמֹר כִּי־שְׁלֹמֹה בְנֵךְ יִמְלֹךְ אַחֲרַי
וְהוּא יֵשֵׁב עַל־כִּסְאִי תַּחְתָּי כִּי כֵּן אֶעֱשֶׂה הַיּוֹם (נגד, מזבח, זן)
הַזֶּה (והו)׃ (לא) וַתִּקֹּד בַּת־שֶׁבַע אַפַּיִם אֶרֶץ וַתִּשְׁתַּחוּ לַמֶּלֶךְ
וַתֹּאמֶר יְחִי אֲדֹנִי הַמֶּלֶךְ דָּוִד לְעֹלָם׃ {פ}

Lesson of Toldot

The book of Beresheet includes the stories of the Creation, the Flood, the Separation, the lives of the Patriarchs and Matriarchs, and the selling of Joseph, until the time that the people of Israel go down to Egypt. Every story in the Torah is a lesson on how to worship the Creator. It is written in the Zohar that if anyone thinks that these are mere stories, it would be better if he were never born.

Rashi wrote: "The Torah should not have started from 'In the beginning God created' but rather from 'This month is for you' [a verse said in the book of Shemot, in the portion of "Bo," which is the first Mitzvah that the people of Israel received]." Rashi continued: "And why does it start from Beresheet? Because if the nations of the world turn to Israel and say you are thieves that conquered our lands..."

I believe that the true wisdom of the book of Beresheet is not concerned with specific Mitzvah, such as what to do and what not to do, or what to eat and what not to eat. Rather, the book of Beresheet teaches us how to live in the deepest sense, which is the basis for all the mitzvot and lessons that we find in the rest of the Torah. From Abraham the Patriarch, we learn how to behave with the people around us and how to make them feel welcome and safe. From Isaac the Patriarch, we learn how to use discernment and judgment as a tool for light. And from Jacob, we learn the power of truth, as it is written: "Give truth to Jacob and mercy to Abraham."

Every event in the Torah brings us a lesson we can learn and use in our daily lives. Whether we learn from the actions of our forefathers or from any other people that the Torah describes, all of us can find things in our lives similar to the events described in the Torah. And when we look deeply into the meaning of the Torah stories, not just seeing them as physical events that happened more than 3000 years ago, we will be able to live our lives as the Holy Torah teaches us.

The matter of Esau and Jacob

Jacob and Esau were born to the same mother at the same time. Even so, they were fundamentally different people from the moment of birth. Jacob was drawn to spirituality and Torah study, as it is written: "And Jacob was a simple man who sat in his tent." Esau was drawn by his desires, as we read: "And Esau was a man who knew how to hunt and was a man of the field." Here the word "field" hints at the level of Malchut, which is our physical world.

Every person has elements of both Jacob and Esau. Inside each of us is a never-ending battle between these two personalities. The Midrash says that when Rebecca was pregnant, she would pass the entrance to the place of learning, and Jacob would push within her womb. All through the nine months, there was an ongoing battle between the two: Who would be stronger and rule the world? Would it be Jacob and the powers of holiness or Esau and the powers of impurity?

This battle still continues, and we are all taking part in it. The first requirement for winning is the recognition that this is, in fact, a battle. Without that understanding, we have no chance for survival. And we must always remember that the opponent, the negative side, never rests. We must always be alert and ready for an attack. Regarding this, there is a story about a rabbi who one day was awakened for prayers by his students. Since he was very tired, he told them, "I won't go today." But after a second, he reconsidered. "No, I will go! I am tired and want to sleep, but other side never sleeps. If I sleep, I will have no chance against the Satan."

This portion gives us the strength and Light to connect to the side of Jacob and to win the battle against the negative side. The way to do this is to follow the example of Rachel, as it is written: "And she went to demand of God." When we come up against any problem in our spiritual work, we should go and "demand of God." We should ask help from the Creator or from people who are closer to Him.

This is why many people go to the Rav or to the graves of righteous people to receive suggestions and guidance. It's the only way to be safe, to be certain we are doing the right thing. An average person does not have the ability to see things as they really are. Only a righteous who is close to the Creator can see in this way. Until we achieve a higher level of spiritual being, there are veils that keep us separated from the Light. By helping us to see, a righteous or great teacher literally helps us to live.

From Jacob and Esau, we can also learn to use both the positive and negative sides to do the Creator's work. As it is written: "And you will love Adonai your God with all your heart." The sages explain that this means, "With both your desires."

How is it possible to worship the Creator even with traits such as pride and laziness? Aren't these from the negative powers? This is true, but everything has two sides. Ego, for example, may seem a very negative thing, but a person without self-esteem has no desire for achievement and will never put any effort into spiritual work.

Ego is negative when it makes us feel pride over others or it when it causes us to act only so others will appreciate us. But within ourselves, we must appreciate our strength and know that we can do great and amazing things. And by far, the most important of these is revealing the Light of the Creator.

In the verse "And Rebbeca said to Isaac... (28:46)" the letter Kof is a small letter. Kof is the only letter that extends below the baseline, symbolizing the effect of the Light given to the negative side. The presence of free will makes negativity inevitable in the world. The effects of this negativity come from the letter Kof because without energy from the Creator, nothing can exist.

Our negative traits give energy to the negative side. But as explained earlier, when we use these traits to serve the Creator, we are stopping the opponent from getting even more strength. We get this strength from the small letter Kof. This is the strength of Messiah: the power that no more Light of the Creator will go to the opponent, but only to the positive side.

Regarding the subject of ego, it is written in the book Avnei Zikaron: "Once the Seer of Lublin said, with happiness, that he sees with the divine spirit that redemption is very near. 'There has been an awakening because this is the time from above'. A short time after this, the Rabbi of Lublin cried and said that he saw with the divine spirit that a voice came out of the sky and called everybody back. The time of redemption has been pushed away, because the people of our generation are fighting about who will rule over each other."

And it is also written in the name of the Seer of Lublin: "He was once very anxious for the redemption to come that year, and it didn't happen. And he said that the everyday people had done total repentance and if it were up to them, the redemption would have come. But it did not come because of people whose position and pride prevented them from humbling themselves. They could not really repent."

From this, we learn the importance of working on our ego, although once again, we should not totally erase it. We should simply be aware that despite any power we have in the material world, the power of the Creator is always infinitely greater. We should use our awareness of our physical strength to humble ourselves in the spiritual realm.

Regarding the prayer of Isaac

It is written: "And Isaac prayed in front of his wife." As we know, Rebecca

did not have a womb and was unable to bear children, but because of Isaac's prayers, Jacob and Esau were born. Therefore, in the morning prayers of Shabbat, we say, "By the mouths of the upright, You shall be exalted. And by the lips of the righteous, You shall be blessed. And by the tongues of the pious, You shall be sanctified. And among the holy ones, You shall be lauded." In Hebrew, taking the first letter of each of these words spells out the names of Isaac and Rebecca. So here we can pray for others, just as Isaac prayed for Rebecca.

And it is written: "The Creator answered him, and his wife Rebecca became pregnant." Why were the prayers of Isaac answered, rather than those of Rebecca? The Creator is teaching us that we should pray not only for our own needs, but also for the needs of others. If not, there is a judgment on us, and our desires will be checked even if our actions are worthy. But when we pray for others as well as for ourselves, the Creator gives us what we ask even if we are unworthy of it.

Synopsis of Toldot

In this portion, the ultimate struggle between good and evil in the physical world is depicted for the first time. Jacob represents the forces of good, and Esau, the forces of evil. This portion enables us to connect with the forces represented by Jacob.

First Reading - Abraham - Chesed

(יט) וְאֵלֶּה תּוֹלְדֹת יִצְחָק (ד"פ ב"ן) בֶּן־אַבְרָהָם (רמ"ח) אַבְרָהָם (רמ"ח)
הוֹלִיד אֶת־יִצְחָק (ד"פ ב"ן): (כ) וַיְהִי יִצְחָק (ד"פ ב"ן) בֶּן־אַרְבָּעִים
שָׁנָה בְּקַחְתּוֹ אֶת־רִבְקָה בַּת־בְּתוּאֵל הָאֲרַמִּי מִפַּדַּן אֲרָם
אֲחוֹת לָבָן הָאֲרַמִּי לוֹ לְאִשָּׁה: (כא) וַיֶּעְתַּר יִצְחָק (ד"פ ב"ן)
לַיהֹוָהאדניאהדונהי לְנֹכַח אִשְׁתּוֹ כִּי עֲקָרָה הִוא וַיֵּעָתֶר לוֹ
יְהֹוָהאדניאהדונהי וַתַּהַר רִבְקָה אִשְׁתּוֹ: (כב) וַיִּתְרֹצְצוּ הַבָּנִים
בְּקִרְבָּהּ וַתֹּאמֶר אִם (יוהך)־כֵּן לָמָּה זֶּה אָנֹכִי (אי"ע) וַתֵּלֶךְ לִדְרֹשׁ
אֶת־יְהֹוָהאדניאהדונהי: (כג) וַיֹּאמֶר יְהֹוָהאדניאהדונהי לָהּ שְׁנֵי גוֹיִם
(גּיים כתיב) בְּבִטְנֵךְ וּשְׁנֵי לְאֻמִּים מִמֵּעַיִךְ יִפָּרֵדוּ וּלְאֹם מִלְאֹם

וַיֶּעְתַּר - Rebecca is born without a uterus, so she is unable to have children. Isaac prays that she will be able to conceive. It is important to note that Isaac can have children with someone else. From his act of sharing - that is, his prayers for Rebecca - we see the power of praying for others. Through prayer, we can even create miracles on their behalf.

וַיֹּאמֶר - Rebecca conceives twins: Jacob, who is completely positive, and Esau, who is thoroughly negative. During her pregnancy, Jacob would kick when Rebecca walked past a positive place where there was light being revealed through acts of sharing and Esau would kick near negative locations where acts of negativity were being manifested. This was very confusing to Rebecca and made her think she was carrying only one child, who seemed unable to distinguish between positive and negative energies. When people lack spiritual direction, they are never completely committed to growing one way or the other. In a way, this is the worst possible state of being. If a person is completely negative, at least the situation is clear, and there is potential for change.

יְאֱמָץ וְרַב יַעֲבֹד צָעִיר: (כד) וַיִּמְלְאוּ יָמֶיהָ לָלֶדֶת וְהִנֵּה
תוֹמִם בְּבִטְנָהּ: (כה) וַיֵּצֵא הָרִאשׁוֹן אַדְמוֹנִי כֻּלּוֹ כְּאַדֶּרֶת
שֵׂעָר וַיִּקְרְאוּ שְׁמוֹ (מהש ע"ה) עֵשָׂו: (כו) וְאַחֲרֵי־כֵן יָצָא אָחִיו
וְיָדוֹ אֹחֶזֶת בַּעֲקֵב (ב"פ מום) עֵשָׂו וַיִּקְרָא שְׁמוֹ (מהש ע"ה) יַעֲקֹב
(יאהדונהי אידהנויה) וְיִצְחָק (ד"פ ב"ן) בֶּן־שִׁשִּׁים שָׁנָה בְּלֶדֶת אֹתָם: (כז)
וַיִּגְדְּלוּ הַנְּעָרִים וַיְהִי עֵשָׂו אִישׁ יֹדֵעַ צַיִד אִישׁ שָׂדֶה וְיַעֲקֹב
(יאהדונהי אידהנויה) אִישׁ תָּם יֹשֵׁב אֹהָלִים: (כח) וַיֶּאֱהַב יִצְחָק (ד"פ ב"ן)
אֶת־עֵשָׂו כִּי־צַיִד בְּפִיו (פוי) וְרִבְקָה אֹהֶבֶת אֶת־יַעֲקֹב (יאהדונהי
אידהנויה): (כט) וַיָּזֶד יַעֲקֹב (יאהדונהי אידהנויה) נָזִיד וַיָּבֹא עֵשָׂו מִן־
הַשָּׂדֶה וְהוּא עָיֵף: (ל) וַיֹּאמֶר עֵשָׂו אֶל־יַעֲקֹב (יאהדונהי אידהנויה)
הַלְעִיטֵנִי נָא מִן־הָאָדֹם הָאָדֹם הַזֶּה (והו) כִּי עָיֵף אָנֹכִי (איע)
עַל־כֵּן קָרָא־שְׁמוֹ (מהש ע"ה) אֱדוֹם: (לא) וַיֹּאמֶר יַעֲקֹב (יאהדונהי
אידהנויה) מִכְרָה כַיּוֹם (נגד, זן) אֶת־בְּכֹרָתְךָ לִי: (לב) וַיֹּאמֶר עֵשָׂו
הִנֵּה אָנֹכִי (איע) הוֹלֵךְ לָמוּת וְלָמָּה־זֶּה לִי בְּכֹרָה: (לג) וַיֹּאמֶר
יַעֲקֹב (יאהדונהי אידהנויה) הִשָּׁבְעָה לִּי כַּיּוֹם (נגד, זן) וַיִּשָּׁבַע לוֹ וַיִּמְכֹּר

הַלְעִיטֵנִי - Esau comes home and finds that Jacob is making lentil soup in mourning of his grandfather, Abraham. Jacob is tired from making the lentil soup. Esau is tired because he has just killed Nimrod. Esau asks Jacob for lentil soup, and Jacob replies that he wants Esau's right of the first-born in exchange. Esau agrees, and Jacob gives him the soup. All of us make trade-offs in life, but we must take care lest we give up something very big to get something very small.

אֶת־בְּכֹרָתוֹ לְיַעֲקֹב (יאהדונהי אידהנויה)׃ (לד) וְיַעֲקֹב (יאהדונהי אידהנויה)
נָתַן לְעֵשָׂו לֶחֶם (ג' הויות) וּנְזִיד עֲדָשִׁים וַיֹּאכַל וַיֵּשְׁתְּ וַיָּקָם
וַיֵּלַךְ (כלי) וַיִּבֶז עֵשָׂו אֶת־הַבְּכֹרָה׃ פ כו (א) וַיְהִי רָעָב בָּאָרֶץ
מִלְּבַד הָרָעָב הָרִאשׁוֹן אֲשֶׁר הָיָה (יהה) בִּימֵי אַבְרָהָם (רמ"ח)
וַיֵּלֶךְ (כלי) יִצְחָק (ד"פ ב"ן) אֶל־אֲבִימֶלֶךְ מֶלֶךְ־פְּלִשְׁתִּים גְּרָרָה׃
(ב) **וַיֵּרָא** אֵלָיו יְהֹוָה (אדני אהדונהי) וַיֹּאמֶר אַל־תֵּרֵד מִצְרָיְמָה
(מצר) שְׁכֹן בָּאָרֶץ אֲשֶׁר אֹמַר אֵלֶיךָ׃ (ג) גּוּר בָּאָרֶץ הַזֹּאת
וְאֶהְיֶה עִמְּךָ וַאֲבָרְכֶךָּ כִּי־לְךָ וּלְזַרְעֲךָ אֶתֵּן אֶת־כָּל (ילי)־
הָאֲרָצֹת הָאֵל (לאה) וַהֲקִמֹתִי אֶת־הַשְּׁבֻעָה אֲשֶׁר נִשְׁבַּעְתִּי
לְאַבְרָהָם (רמ"ח) אָבִיךָ׃ (ד) וְהִרְבֵּיתִי אֶת־זַרְעֲךָ כְּכוֹכְבֵי
הַשָּׁמַיִם (י"פ טל) וְנָתַתִּי לְזַרְעֲךָ אֵת כָּל (ילי)־הָאֲרָצֹת הָאֵל (לאה)
וְהִתְבָּרְכוּ בְזַרְעֲךָ (יהוה ריבוע יהוה ריבוע מ"ה) כֹּל (ילי) גּוֹיֵי הָאָרֶץ (מילוי
אלהים ע"ה)׃ (ה) עֵקֶב (ב"פ מום) אֲשֶׁר־שָׁמַע אַבְרָהָם (רמ"ח) בְּקֹלִי
וַיִּשְׁמֹר מִשְׁמַרְתִּי מִצְוֹתַי חֻקּוֹתַי וְתוֹרֹתָי׃

וַיֵּרָא - Even though Abraham and Jacob could go to Egypt, Isaac was instructed not to go. Isaac could not leave Israel because as he represents the force judgment, if he left Israel judgment would be unleashed to reign free in the universe. To contain the strength and intensity of the power of this judgment, Isaac stayed in Israel. We, too, must be aware of the need to limit judgment. When we encounter people who hurt or anger us, we must use the tools of Kabbalah to compose ourselves so that our emotions are not allowed to run out of control.

Second Reading - Issac - Gvurah

(ו) וַיֵּשֶׁב יִצְחָק (ד"פ ב"ן) בִּגְרָר׃ (ז) וַיִּשְׁאֲלוּ אַנְשֵׁי הַמָּקוֹם
לְאִשְׁתּוֹ וַיֹּאמֶר אֲחֹתִי הִוא כִּי יָרֵא לֵאמֹר אִשְׁתִּי פֶּן־
יַהַרְגֻנִי אַנְשֵׁי הַמָּקוֹם עַל־רִבְקָה כִּי־טוֹבַת מַרְאֶה הִוא׃
(ח) וַיְהִי כִּי־אָרְכוּ־לוֹ שָׁם הַיָּמִים (נלך) וַיַּשְׁקֵף אֲבִימֶלֶךְ
מֶלֶךְ פְּלִשְׁתִּים בְּעַד הַחַלּוֹן (מנד) וַיַּרְא וְהִנֵּה יִצְחָק (ד"פ ב"ן)
מְצַחֵק אֵת רִבְקָה אִשְׁתּוֹ׃ (ט) וַיִּקְרָא אֲבִימֶלֶךְ לְיִצְחָק (ד"פ
ב"ן) וַיֹּאמֶר אַךְ הִנֵּה (אהיה) אִשְׁתְּךָ הִוא וְאֵיךְ אָמַרְתָּ אֲחֹתִי
הִוא וַיֹּאמֶר אֵלָיו יִצְחָק (ד"פ ב"ן) כִּי אָמַרְתִּי פֶּן־אָמוּת עָלֶיהָ
(פהל)׃ (י) וַיֹּאמֶר אֲבִימֶלֶךְ מַה (מ"ה)־זֹּאת עָשִׂיתָ לָּנוּ (מום) כִּמְעַט
שָׁכַב אַחַד (אהבה) הָעָם אֶת־אִשְׁתֶּךָ וְהֵבֵאתָ עָלֵינוּ אָשָׁם׃
(יא) וַיְצַו אֲבִימֶלֶךְ אֶת־כָּל (ילי)־הָעָם לֵאמֹר הַנֹּגֵעַ בָּאִישׁ
הַזֶּה (והו) וּבְאִשְׁתּוֹ מוֹת יוּמָת׃ (יב) וַיִּזְרַע יִצְחָק (ד"פ ב"ן) בָּאָרֶץ
הַהִוא וַיִּמְצָא בַּשָּׁנָה הַהִוא מֵאָה שְׁעָרִים (כתר) וַיְבָרְכֵהוּ
יְהֹוָהאדניאהדונהי׃

אֲחֹתִי - Isaac is afraid he will be killed for his wife, so he tells the townspeople that Rebecca is his sister. Abimelech, the Philistine king, becomes very angry with Isaac for lying to him, but like his father, Abraham, before him, Isaac is not lying. Rebecca is his soul-mate. Therefore, she embodies the Shechinah, which Kabbalah describes as our "sister."

Third Reading - Jacob - Tiferet

(יג) וַיִּגְדַּל (יזל) הָאִישׁ וַיֵּלֶךְ (כלי) הָלוֹךְ וְגָדֵל עַד כִּי־גָדַל מְאֹד׃
(יד) וַיְהִי־לוֹ מִקְנֵה־צֹאן וּמִקְנֵה בָקָר וַעֲבֻדָּה רַבָּה וַיְקַנְאוּ
אֹתוֹ פְּלִשְׁתִּים׃ (טו) וְכָל (ילי)־ **הַבְּאֵרֹת** אֲשֶׁר חָפְרוּ עַבְדֵי
אָבִיו בִּימֵי אַבְרָהָם (רמ"ח) אָבִיו סִתְּמוּם פְּלִשְׁתִּים וַיְמַלְאוּם
עָפָר׃ (טז) וַיֹּאמֶר אֲבִימֶלֶךְ אֶל־יִצְחָק (ד"פ ב"ן) לֵךְ מֵעִמָּנוּ (מילוי
דמ"ה) כִּי־עָצַמְתָּ מִמֶּנּוּ מְאֹד׃ (יז) וַיֵּלֶךְ (כלי) מִשָּׁם יִצְחָק (ד"פ ב"ן)
וַיִּחַן בְּנַחַל־גְּרָר וַיֵּשֶׁב שָׁם׃ (יח) וַיָּשָׁב יִצְחָק (ד"פ ב"ן) וַיַּחְפֹּר |
אֶת־בְּאֵרֹת הַמַּיִם אֲשֶׁר חָפְרוּ בִּימֵי אַבְרָהָם (רמ"ח) אָבִיו
וַיְסַתְּמוּם פְּלִשְׁתִּים אַחֲרֵי מוֹת אַבְרָהָם (רמ"ח) וַיִּקְרָא לָהֶן
שֵׁמוֹת כַּשֵּׁמֹת אֲשֶׁר־קָרָא לָהֶן אָבִיו׃ (יט) וַיַּחְפְּרוּ עַבְדֵי־
יִצְחָק (ד"פ ב"ן) בַּנָּחַל וַיִּמְצְאוּ־שָׁם בְּאֵר (קנ"א ב"ן) מַיִם חַיִּים (בינה
ע"ה)׃ (כ) וַיָּרִיבוּ רֹעֵי גְרָר עִם־רֹעֵי יִצְחָק (ד"פ ב"ן) לֵאמֹר לָנוּ
(מום) הַמָּיִם וַיִּקְרָא שֵׁם־הַבְּאֵר (קנ"א ב"ן) עֵשֶׂק כִּי הִתְעַשְּׂקוּ

הַבְּאֵרֹת - Isaac attempts to restore the power of water that was present before the Sin of Adam and the Flood. The negative side tries to take that power away. God appears to Isaac in a dream, assuring Isaac that he is protected, and in the next section Abimelech comes to him, seeking peace. No matter how many obstacles stand against us, no matter how vulnerable we feel, we will be protected and will succeed if we are connected to the Light of the Creator.

עִמּֽוֹ׃ (כא) וַֽיַּחְפְּרוּ֙ בְּאֵ֣ר (קנ"א ב"ן) אַחֶ֔רֶת וַיָּרִ֖יבוּ גַּם־עָלֶ֑יהָ (פהל)
וַיִּקְרָ֥א שְׁמָ֖הּ שִׂטְנָֽה׃ (כב) וַיַּעְתֵּ֣ק מִשָּׁ֗ם וַֽיַּחְפֹּר֙ בְּאֵ֣ר (קנ"א
ב"ן) אַחֶ֔רֶת וְלֹ֥א רָב֖וּ עָלֶ֑יהָ (פהל) וַיִּקְרָ֤א שְׁמָהּ֙ רְחֹב֔וֹת וַיֹּ֕אמֶר
כִּֽי־עַתָּ֞ה הִרְחִ֧יב יְהֹוָ֛ה אדני אהדונהי לָ֖נוּ (מום) וּפָרִ֥ינוּ בָאָֽרֶץ׃

Fourth Reading - Moses - Netzach

(כג) וַיַּ֥עַל מִשָּׁ֖ם בְּאֵ֥ר (קנ"א ב"ן) שָֽׁבַע׃ (כד) וַיֵּרָ֨א אֵלָ֤יו
יְהֹוָה֙ אדני אהדונהי בַּלַּ֣יְלָה (מלה) הַה֔וּא וַיֹּ֕אמֶר אָנֹכִ֕י (איע) אֱלֹהֵ֖י
(דמב) אַבְרָהָ֣ם (רמ"ח) אָבִ֑יךָ אַל־תִּירָא֙ כִּֽי־אִתְּךָ֣ אָנֹ֔כִי (איע)
וּבֵֽרַכְתִּ֙יךָ֙ וְהִרְבֵּיתִ֣י אֶֽת־זַרְעֲךָ֔ בַּעֲב֖וּר אַבְרָהָ֥ם (רמ"ח)
עַבְדִּֽי׃ (כה) וַיִּ֧בֶן שָׁ֣ם מִזְבֵּ֗חַ (זן) וַיִּקְרָא֙ בְּשֵׁ֣ם יְהֹוָ֔ה אדני אהדונהי
וַיֶּט־שָׁ֖ם אָהֳל֑וֹ וַיִּכְרוּ־שָׁ֥ם עַבְדֵֽי־יִצְחָ֖ק (ד"פ ב"ן) בְּאֵֽר (קנ"א ב"ן)׃
(כו) וַאֲבִימֶ֕לֶךְ הָלַ֥ךְ אֵלָ֖יו (מיה) מִגְּרָ֑ר וַאֲחֻזַּת֙ מֵֽרֵעֵ֔הוּ וּפִיכֹ֖ל
שַׂר־צְבָאֽוֹ׃ (כז) וַיֹּ֤אמֶר אֲלֵהֶם֙ יִצְחָ֔ק (ד"פ ב"ן) מַדּ֖וּעַ בָּאתֶ֣ם
אֵלָ֑י וְאַתֶּם֙ שְׂנֵאתֶ֣ם אֹתִ֔י וַתְּשַׁלְּח֖וּנִי מֵאִתְּכֶֽם׃ (כח) וַיֹּאמְר֗וּ
רָא֣וֹ רָאִינוּ֮ כִּֽי־הָיָ֣ה (יהה) יְהֹוָ֣ה אדני אהדונהי ׀ עִמָּךְ֒ וַנֹּ֗אמֶר תְּהִ֨י
נָ֥א אָלָ֛ה בֵּינוֹתֵ֖ינוּ בֵּינֵ֣ינוּ וּבֵינֶ֑ךָ וְנִכְרְתָ֥ה בְרִ֖ית עִמָּֽךְ׃ (כט)

וַיַּעְתֵּק - Now that Isaac and Abimelech have made peace, Isaac's servants come to tell him they have found water. Isaac is now able to restore the power of water that was present before the Sin of Adam and before the Flood.

אִם (יוהך)־תַּעֲשֵׂה עִמָּנוּ (מילוי דמ"ה) רָעָה (רהע) כַּאֲשֶׁר לֹא נְגַעֲנוּךָ
וְכַאֲשֶׁר עָשִׂינוּ עִמְּךָ רַק־טוֹב (והו) וַנְּשַׁלֵּחֲךָ בְּשָׁלוֹם אַתָּה
עַתָּה בְּרוּךְ יְהֹוָאדהנויה:

Fifth Reading - Aaron - Hod

(ל) וַיַּעַשׂ לָהֶם מִשְׁתֶּה וַיֹּאכְלוּ וַיִּשְׁתּוּ: (לא) וַיַּשְׁכִּימוּ בַבֹּקֶר
וַיִּשָּׁבְעוּ אִישׁ לְאָחִיו וַיְשַׁלְּחֵם יִצְחָק (ד"פ ב"ן) וַיֵּלְכוּ מֵאִתּוֹ
בְּשָׁלוֹם: (לב) וַיְהִי | בַּיּוֹם (נגד, זן) הַהוּא וַיָּבֹאוּ עַבְדֵי יִצְחָק (ד"פ
ב"ן) וַיַּגִּדוּ לוֹ עַל־אֹדוֹת הַבְּאֵר (קנ"א ב"ן) אֲשֶׁר חָפָרוּ וַיֹּאמְרוּ
לוֹ מָצָאנוּ מָיִם: (לג) וַיִּקְרָא אֹתָהּ שִׁבְעָה עַל־כֵּן שֵׁם־
הָעִיר (סנדלפון, ערי) בְּאֵר (קנ"א ב"ן) שֶׁבַע עַד הַיּוֹם (נגד, זן) הַזֶּה
(והו): ס (לד) וַיְהִי עֵשָׂו בֶּן־אַרְבָּעִים שָׁנָה וַיִּקַּח (ודעם) אִשָּׁה
אֶת־יְהוּדִית בַּת־בְּאֵרִי (אלד) הַחִתִּי וְאֶת־בָּשְׂמַת בַּת־אֵילֹן
הַחִתִּי: (לה) וַתִּהְיֶיןָ מֹרַת רוּחַ לְיִצְחָק (ד"פ ב"ן) וּלְרִבְקָה: ס כז
(א) וַיְהִי כִּי־זָקֵן יִצְחָק (ד"פ ב"ן) וַתִּכְהֶיןָ עֵינָיו (מ"ה בריבוע) מֵרְאֹת

בֶּן־אַרְבָּעִים - Esau copies his father by marrying at age forty (and indeed Esau copied Isaac in many respects). But Esau merely mimicked Isaac, without achieving the same consciousness. When we truly want to grow, we must go beyond external elements. We have to do the inner spiritual work to reach the next level.

זָקֵן יִצְחָק - Isaac has a blessing to give to one of his sons, and he chooses to give it to Esau. Isaac, who embodies the energy of judgment, recognizes

וַיִּקְרָא אֶת־עֵשָׂו | בְּנוֹ הַגָּדֹל (להח, מבה עד"א) וַיֹּאמֶר אֵלָיו בְּנִי
וַיֹּאמֶר אֵלָיו הִנֵּנִי׃ (ב) וַיֹּאמֶר הִנֵּה־נָא זָקַנְתִּי לֹא יָדַעְתִּי
יוֹם (נגד, זן) מוֹתִי׃ (ג) וְעַתָּה שָׂא־נָא כֵלֶיךָ תֶּלְיְךָ וְקַשְׁתֶּךָ וְצֵא
הַשָּׂדֶה וְצוּדָה לִּי צָיִד (צֵידה כתיב)׃ (ד) וַעֲשֵׂה־לִי מַטְעַמִּים
כַּאֲשֶׁר אָהַבְתִּי וְהָבִיאָה לִּי וְאֹכֵלָה בַּעֲבוּר תְּבָרֶכְךָ נַפְשִׁי
בְּטֶרֶם אָמוּת׃ (ה) וְרִבְקָה שֹׁמַעַת בְּדַבֵּר (ראה) יִצְחָק (ד"פ ב"ן)
אֶל־עֵשָׂו בְּנוֹ וַיֵּלֶךְ (כלי) עֵשָׂו הַשָּׂדֶה לָצוּד צַיִד לְהָבִיא׃ (ו)
וְרִבְקָה אָמְרָה אֶל־יַעֲקֹב בְּנָהּ (יאהדונהי אידהנויה) לֵאמֹר הִנֵּה
שָׁמַעְתִּי אֶת־אָבִיךָ מְדַבֵּר (ראה) אֶל־עֵשָׂו אָחִיךָ לֵאמֹר׃ (ז)
הָבִיאָה לִּי צַיִד וַעֲשֵׂה־לִי מַטְעַמִּים וְאֹכֵלָה וַאֲבָרֶכְכָה
לִפְנֵי יְהֹוָ֥אדנילאהדונהי לִפְנֵי מוֹתִי׃ (ח) וְעַתָּה בְנִי שְׁמַע בְּקֹלִי

the same energy in Esau. We should not judge Isaac's action, however. When we share, we often share with those whose nature seems most like our own.

וְרִבְקָה שֹׁמַעַת - When Rebecca hears of Isaac's intention, she instructs Jacob to bring her meat so that she can prepare a meal for Isaac. Isaac will then give the blessing to Jacob rather than Esau. But Jacob fears that he will be cursed rather than blessed if his father discovers the trick. Rebecca reassures Jacob by saying, "The curse will be unto me." The meaning of this stems from the fact that Rebecca is the reincarnation of Eve. As Eve, her actions brought a curse onto Adam and onto all mankind, and now as Rebecca, she is able to complete the Tikun ("correction") of Eve by helping Jacob to receive the blessing and restore the Light that she had taken from the world.

לַאֲשֶׁר אֲנִי (אני) מְצַוָּה אֹתָךְ: (ט) לֶךְ־נָא אֶל־הַצֹּאן וְקַח־לִי
מִשָּׁם שְׁנֵי גְּדָיֵי (והו) עִזִּים טֹבִים וְאֶעֱשֶׂה אֹתָם מַטְעַמִּים
לְאָבִיךָ כַּאֲשֶׁר אָהֵב: (י) וְהֵבֵאתָ לְאָבִיךָ וְאָכָל בַּעֲבֻר
אֲשֶׁר יְבָרֶכְךָ לִפְנֵי מוֹתוֹ: (יא) וַיֹּאמֶר יַעֲקֹב (יאהדונהי אידהנויה)
אֶל־רִבְקָה אִמּוֹ הֵן עֵשָׂו אָחִי אִישׁ שָׂעִר וְאָנֹכִי (איע) אִישׁ
חָלָק: (יב) אוּלַי (אום) יְמֻשֵּׁנִי אָבִי וְהָיִיתִי בְעֵינָיו (מ"ה בריבוע)
כִּמְתַעְתֵּעַ וְהֵבֵאתִי עָלַי קְלָלָה וְלֹא בְרָכָה: (יג) וַתֹּאמֶר לוֹ
אִמּוֹ עָלַי קִלְלָתְךָ בְּנִי אַךְ (אהיה) שְׁמַע בְּקֹלִי וְלֵךְ קַח־לִי:
(יד) וַיֵּלֶךְ (כלי) וַיִּקַּח (ועם) וַיָּבֵא לְאִמּוֹ וַתַּעַשׂ אִמּוֹ מַטְעַמִּים
כַּאֲשֶׁר אָהֵב אָבִיו: (טו) וַתִּקַּח רִבְקָה אֶת־בִּגְדֵי עֵשָׂו
בְּנָהּ הַגָּדֹל (להח, מבה עד"א) הַחֲמֻדֹת אֲשֶׁר אִתָּהּ בַּבָּיִת (ב"פ ראה)
וַתַּלְבֵּשׁ אֶת־יַעֲקֹב (יאהדונהי אידהנויה) בְּנָהּ הַקָּטָן: (טז) וְאֵת עֹרֹת
גְּדָיֵי (והו) הָעִזִּים הִלְבִּישָׁה עַל־יָדָיו וְעַל חֶלְקַת צַוָּארָיו:
(יז) וַתִּתֵּן (ב"פ כהת) אֶת־הַמַּטְעַמִּים וְאֶת־הַלֶּחֶם (ג' הויות) אֲשֶׁר

וַתִּקַּח - Rebecca dresses Jacob in the clothing of Esau, which was also the clothing of Adam. On the same day that Esau asked Jacob for the lentil soup, Esau had killed Nimrod earlier to obtain this clothing, which had the power to make animals bow down to whomever wore it. This is why hunting was so easy for Adam. Today, although we don't have the clothing that Adam wore to hunt, we do have spiritual clothing that can bring us protection and success.

עָשָׂתָה בְּיַד יַעֲקֹב (יאהדונהי אידהנויה) בְּנָהּ׃ (יח) וַיָּבֹא אֶל־אָבִיו
וַיֹּאמֶר אָבִי וַיֹּאמֶר הִנֶּנִּי מִי (ילי) אַתָּה בְּנִי׃ (יט) וַיֹּאמֶר יַעֲקֹב
(יאהדונהי אידהנויה) אֶל־אָבִיו אָנֹכִי (איע) עֵשָׂו בְּכֹרֶךָ עָשִׂיתִי כַּאֲשֶׁר
דִּבַּרְתָּ (ראה) אֵלָי קוּם־נָא שְׁבָה וְאָכְלָה מִצֵּידִי בַּעֲבוּר
תְּבָרְכַנִּי נַפְשֶׁךָ׃ (כ) וַיֹּאמֶר יִצְחָק (ד"פ ב"ן) אֶל־בְּנוֹ מַה (מ"ה)־זֶּה
מִהַרְתָּ לִמְצֹא בְּנִי וַיֹּאמֶר כִּי הִקְרָה יְהֹוָה (יאהדונהי) אֱלֹהֶיךָ
לְפָנָי׃ (ילה) (כא) וַיֹּאמֶר יִצְחָק (ד"פ ב"ן) אֶל־יַעֲקֹב (יאהדונהי אידהנויה)
גְּשָׁה־נָּא וַאֲמֻשְׁךָ בְּנִי הַאַתָּה זֶה בְּנִי עֵשָׂו אִם (יוהך)־לֹא׃
(כב) וַיִּגַּשׁ יַעֲקֹב (יאהדונהי אידהנויה) אֶל־יִצְחָק (ד"פ ב"ן) אָבִיו וַיְמֻשֵּׁהוּ
וַיֹּאמֶר **הַקֹּל קוֹל יַעֲקֹב** (יאהדונהי אידהנויה) וְהַיָּדַיִם יְדֵי עֵשָׂו׃ (כג)
וְלֹא הִכִּירוֹ כִּי־הָיוּ יָדָיו כִּידֵי עֵשָׂו אָחִיו שְׂעִרֹת וַיְבָרְכֵהוּ׃
(כד) וַיֹּאמֶר אַתָּה זֶה בְּנִי עֵשָׂו וַיֹּאמֶר אָנִי (אני)׃ (כה) וַיֹּאמֶר
הַגִּשָׁה לִּי וְאֹכְלָה מִצֵּיד בְּנִי לְמַעַן תְּבָרֶכְךָ נַפְשִׁי וַיַּגֶּשׁ־לוֹ
וַיֹּאכַל וַיָּבֵא לוֹ יַיִן (מיכ, י"פ האא) וַיֵּשְׁתְּ׃ (כו) וַיֹּאמֶר אֵלָיו יִצְחָק

הַקֹּל קוֹל יַעֲקֹב - Isaac, who is now blind, touches Jacob and says, "The hands are the hands of Esau, but the voice is the voice of Jacob." At the same moment, Isaac catches the scent of the Garden of Eden on Jacob's clothes; when Jacob entered Isaac's tent, the scent of the Garden of Eden entered with him because Jacob was the reincarnation of Adam. Isaac then blesses Jacob. We can connect with this blessing only when we are spiritually transformed. We cannot receive the blessing until this transformation takes place because we cannot appreciate what we have not earned.

(ד"פ ב"ן) אָבִיו גְּשָׁה־נָּא וּשְׁקָה־לִּי בְּנִי׃ (כז) וַיִּגַּשׁ וַיִּשַּׁק־לוֹ וַיָּרַח
אֶת־רֵיחַ בְּגָדָיו וַיְבָרְכֵהוּ וַיֹּאמֶר רְאֵה (ראה) רֵיחַ בְּנִי כְּרֵיחַ
שָׂדֶה אֲשֶׁר בֵּרֲכוֹ (יהוה ריבוע יהוה ריבוע מ"ה) יְהֹוָהאדניאהדונהי׃

Sixth Reading - Joseph - Yesod

(כח) וְיִתֶּן־לְךָ הָאֱלֹהִים (ילה) מִטַּל (כוזו) הַשָּׁמַיִם (י"פ טל) וּמִשְׁמַנֵּי
הָאָרֶץ (מילוי אלהים ע"ה) וְרֹב דָּגָן וְתִירֹשׁ׃ (כט) יַעַבְדוּךָ עַמִּים
וְיִשְׁתַּחֲוֻ לְךָ לְאֻמִּים הֱוֵה גְבִיר לְאַחֶיךָ וְיִשְׁתַּחֲוּוּ לְךָ בְּנֵי
אִמֶּךָ אֹרְרֶיךָ אָרוּר וּמְבָרְכֶיךָ בָּרוּךְ׃ (ל) וַיְהִי כַּאֲשֶׁר כִּלָּה
יִצְחָק (ד"פ ב"ן) לְבָרֵךְ אֶת־יַעֲקֹב (יאהדונהי אידהנויה) וַיְהִי אַךְ (אהיה)
יָצֹא יָצָא יַעֲקֹב (יאהדונהי אידהנויה) מֵאֵת פְּנֵי (חכמה, בינה) יִצְחָק (ד"פ ב"ן)
אָבִיו וְעֵשָׂו אָחִיו בָּא מִצֵּידוֹ׃ (לא) וַיַּעַשׂ גַּם־הוּא מַטְעַמִּים
וַיָּבֵא לְאָבִיו וַיֹּאמֶר לְאָבִיו יָקֻם אָבִי וְיֹאכַל מִצֵּיד בְּנוֹ
בַּעֲבֻר תְּבָרְכַנִּי נַפְשֶׁךָ׃ (לב) וַיֹּאמֶר לוֹ יִצְחָק (ד"פ ב"ן) אָבִיו מִי
(ילי)־אָתָּה וַיֹּאמֶר אֲנִי (אני) בִּנְךָ בְכֹרְךָ עֵשָׂו׃ (לג) וַיֶּחֱרַד יִצְחָק

וַיְהִי - After Jacob departs, Esau goes in to see Isaac. Isaac trembles when Esau enters because Esau, wearing the clothing of Adam, carries with him the scent of Hell. A situation can be heaven for one person, but hell for another. Everything depends on our consciousness, which is more powerful than any external circumstance.

וַיֶּחֱרַד - Esau has the energy of Hell. He pleads with his father to give him some blessing. The true blessing was given to Jacob, but Isaac gives Esau a

(ד"פ ב"ן) חֲרָדָה גְּדֹלָה עַד־מְאֹד וַיֹּאמֶר מִי (ילי)־אֵפוֹא הוּא
הַצָּד־צַיִד וַיָּבֵא לִי וָאֹכַל מִכֹּל (ילי) בְּטֶרֶם תָּבוֹא וָאֲבָרְכֵהוּ
גַּם־בָּרוּךְ יִהְיֶה (ייי): (לד) כִּשְׁמֹעַ עֵשָׂו אֶת־דִּבְרֵי (ראה) אָבִיו
וַיִּצְעַק צְעָקָה גְּדֹלָה וּמָרָה עַד־מְאֹד וַיֹּאמֶר לְאָבִיו בָּרְכֵנִי
גַם־אָנִי (אני) אָבִי: (לה) וַיֹּאמֶר בָּא אָחִיךָ בְּמִרְמָה וַיִּקַּח (וזעם)
בִּרְכָתֶךָ: (לו) וַיֹּאמֶר הֲכִי קָרָא שְׁמוֹ (מהש ע"ה) יַעֲקֹב (יאהדונהי
אידהנויה) וַיַּעְקְבֵנִי זֶה פַעֲמַיִם אֶת־בְּכֹרָתִי לָקָח וְהִנֵּה עַתָּה
לָקַח בִּרְכָתִי וַיֹּאמַר הֲלֹא־אָצַלְתָּ לִּי בְּרָכָה: (לז) וַיַּעַן יִצְחָק
(ד"פ ב"ן) וַיֹּאמֶר לְעֵשָׂו הֵן גְּבִיר שַׂמְתִּיו לָךְ וְאֶת־כָּל (ילי)־אֶחָיו
נָתַתִּי לוֹ לַעֲבָדִים וְדָגָן וְתִירֹשׁ סְמַכְתִּיו וּלְכָה אֵפוֹא מָה
(מ"ה) אֶעֱשֶׂה בְּנִי: (לח) וַיֹּאמֶר עֵשָׂו אֶל־אָבִיו הַבְרָכָה אַחַת
הִוא־לְךָ אָבִי בָּרְכֵנִי גַם־אָנִי (אני) אָבִי וַיִּשָּׂא עֵשָׂו קֹלוֹ וַיֵּבְךְּ:
(לט) וַיַּעַן יִצְחָק (ד"פ ב"ן) אָבִיו וַיֹּאמֶר אֵלָיו הִנֵּה מִשְׁמַנֵּי הָאָרֶץ
(מילוי אלהים ע"ה) יִהְיֶה (ייי) מוֹשָׁבֶךָ וּמִטַּל (כוזו) הַשָּׁמַיִם (י"פ טל) מֵעָל
(עלם): (מ) וְעַל־חַרְבְּךָ תִחְיֶה וְאֶת־אָחִיךָ תַּעֲבֹד וְהָיָה (יהה) (יהוה)
כַּאֲשֶׁר תָּרִיד וּפָרַקְתָּ עֻלּוֹ מֵעַל (עלם) צַוָּארֶךָ: (מא) וַיִּשְׂטֹם
עֵשָׂו אֶת־יַעֲקֹב (יאהדונהי אידהנויה) עַל־הַבְּרָכָה אֲשֶׁר בֵּרְכוֹ (יהוה

lesser form. This incident teaches us the danger of being content with less. In our spiritual work, we need to always push ourselves to the maximum.

(ריבוע יהוה ריבוע מ״ה) אָבִיו וַיֹּאמֶר עֵשָׂו בְּלִבּוֹ יִקְרְבוּ יְמֵי אֵבֶל אָבִי
וְאַהַרְגָה אֶת־יַעֲקֹב (יאהדונהי אידהנויה) אָחִי: (מב) וַיֻּגַּד לְרִבְקָה
אֶת־דִּבְרֵי (ראה) עֵשָׂו בְּנָהּ הַגָּדֹל (להח, מבה עד״א) וַתִּשְׁלַח וַתִּקְרָא
לְיַעֲקֹב (יאהדונהי אידהנויה) בְּנָהּ הַקָּטָן וַתֹּאמֶר אֵלָיו הִנֵּה עֵשָׂו
אָחִיךָ מִתְנַחֵם לְךָ לְהָרְגֶךָ: (מג) וְעַתָּה בְנִי שְׁמַע בְּקֹלִי וְקוּם
בְּרַח־לְךָ אֶל־לָבָן אָחִי חָרָנָה: (מד) וְיָשַׁבְתָּ עִמּוֹ יָמִים (נלך)
אֲחָדִים עַד אֲשֶׁר־תָּשׁוּב חֲמַת אָחִיךָ: (מה) עַד־שׁוּב אַף־
אָחִיךָ מִמְּךָ וְשָׁכַח אֵת אֲשֶׁר־עָשִׂיתָ לּוֹ וְשָׁלַחְתִּי וּלְקַחְתִּיךָ
מִשָּׁם לָמָה אֶשְׁכַּל גַּם־שְׁנֵיכֶם יוֹם (נגד, זן) אֶחָד (אהבה): (מו)
וַתֹּאמֶר רִבְקָה אֶל־יִצְחָק (ד״פ ב״ן) קַצְתִּי בְחַיַּי מִפְּנֵי בְּנוֹת
חֵת אִם (יוהך)־לֹקֵחַ יַעֲקֹב (יאהדונהי אידהנויה) אִשָּׁה מִבְּנוֹת־חֵת
כָּאֵלֶּה מִבְּנוֹת הָאָרֶץ (מילוי אלהים ע״ה) לָמָּה לִּי חַיִּים (בינה ע״ה):
כח (א) וַיִּקְרָא יִצְחָק (ד״פ ב״ן) אֶל־יַעֲקֹב (יאהדונהי אידהנויה) וַיְבָרֶךְ

וְאַהַרְגָה אֶת־יַעֲקֹב - Esau wants to kill Jacob because Jacob stole his blessing. So Rebecca instructs Jacob to run away to her family. This is not a coincidence. Jacob must go to through a cleansing process, a Tikun, to merit his eventual bringing of the Twelve Tribes into existence. The actions he now takes will affect the future of all humanity forever.

קַצְתִּי - The only Hebrew letter that goes below the baseline is the Kof. In this case, however, because the letter is small, it doesn't go below the line. The regular Kof gives a little taste of energy to the Satan, but the small Kof denies that taste.

(עסמ"ב) אֹתוֹ וַיְצַוֵּהוּ וַיֹּאמֶר לוֹ לֹא־תִקַּח אִשָּׁה מִבְּנוֹת כְּנָעַן׃
(ב) קוּם לֵךְ פַּדֶּנָה אֲרָם (כ"פ ראה) בֵּיתָה בְתוּאֵל אֲבִי אִמֶּךָ
וְקַח־לְךָ מִשָּׁם אִשָּׁה מִבְּנוֹת לָבָן אֲחִי אִמֶּךָ׃ (ג) וְאֵל שַׁדַּי
(מהש) יְבָרֵךְ (עסמ"ב) אֹתְךָ וְיַפְרְךָ וְיַרְבֶּךָ וְהָיִיתָ לִקְהַל עַמִּים׃
(ד) וְיִתֶּן־לְךָ אֶת־בִּרְכַּת אַבְרָהָם (רמ"ח) לְךָ וּלְזַרְעֲךָ אִתָּךְ
לְרִשְׁתְּךָ אֶת־אֶרֶץ מְגֻרֶיךָ אֲשֶׁר־נָתַן אֱלֹהִים (ילה) לְאַבְרָהָם
(רמ"ח)׃

Seventh Reading - David - Malchut

(ה) וַיִּשְׁלַח יִצְחָק (ד"פ ב"ן) אֶת־יַעֲקֹב (יאהדונהי אידהנויה) וַיֵּלֶךְ (כלי)
פַּדֶּנָה אֲרָם אֶל־לָבָן בֶּן־בְּתוּאֵל הָאֲרַמִּי אֲחִי רִבְקָה אֵם
(יוהך) יַעֲקֹב (יאהדונהי אידהנויה) וְעֵשָׂו׃ (ו) וַיַּרְא עֵשָׂו כִּי־בֵרַךְ יִצְחָק
(ד"פ ב"ן) אֶת־יַעֲקֹב (יאהדונהי אידהנויה) וְשִׁלַּח אֹתוֹ פַּדֶּנָה אֲרָם
לָקַחַת־לוֹ מִשָּׁם אִשָּׁה בְּבָרְכוֹ (יהוה ריבוע יהוה ריבוע מ"ה) אֹתוֹ וַיְצַו
עָלָיו לֵאמֹר לֹא־תִקַּח אִשָּׁה מִבְּנוֹת כְּנָעַן׃

וַיִּשְׁלַח - Isaac instructs Jacob to marry only someone from his own family, just as Isaac himself had once been instructed to marry a woman from his father, Abraham's, family. When Esau sees this, he goes to marry the daughter of Ishmael, his uncle. This action, however, represents only the surface of spiritual growth. Esau is not willing to do the real work behind the action. We must know that life is not about just doing things. True spirituality is about transformation.

Maftir

(ז) וַיִּשְׁמַ֣ע יַעֲקֹ֔ב (יאהדונהי אידהנויה) אֶל־אָבִ֖יו וְאֶל־אִמּ֑וֹ וַיֵּ֖לֶךְ (כלי)
פַּדֶּ֥נָֽה אֲרָֽם׃ (ח) וַיַּ֣רְא עֵשָׂ֔ו כִּ֥י רָע֖וֹת בְּנ֣וֹת כְּנָ֑עַן בְּעֵינֵ֖י (מ"ה
בריבוע) יִצְחָ֥ק (ד"פ ב"ן) אָבִֽיו׃ (ט) וַיֵּ֥לֶךְ (כלי) עֵשָׂ֖ו אֶל־יִשְׁמָעֵ֑אל
וַיִּקַּ֡ח (וזעם) אֶֽת־מָחֲלַ֣ת ׀ בַּת־יִשְׁמָעֵ֨אל בֶּן־אַבְרָהָ֜ם (רמ"ח)
אֲח֧וֹת נְבָי֛וֹת עַל־נָשָׁ֖יו ל֥וֹ לְאִשָּֽׁה׃ ססס

The Haftarah of Toldot

The prophet discusses Esau and Jacob and the differences between them. We must be able to see both the positive and the negative in ourselves. We must understand that this dichotomy exists in each of us, and we must work spiritually to reveal the positive in ourselves and minimize the negative.

מלאכי פרק א

א מַשָּׂא דְבַר־יְהוָה אֶל־יִשְׂרָאֵל בְּיַד מַלְאָכִי׃ ב אָהַבְתִּי
אֶתְכֶם אָמַר יְהוָה וַאֲמַרְתֶּם בַּמָּה אֲהַבְתָּנוּ הֲלוֹא־אָח
עֵשָׂו לְיַעֲקֹב (יאהדונהי אידהנויה) נְאֻם־יְהוָה וָאֹהַב אֶת־יַעֲקֹב (יאהדונהי
אידהנויה)׃ ג וְאֶת־עֵשָׂו שָׂנֵאתִי וָאָשִׂים אֶת־הָרָיו שְׁמָמָה וְאֶת־
נַחֲלָתוֹ לְתַנּוֹת מִדְבָּר׃ ד כִּי־תֹאמַר אֱדוֹם רֻשַּׁשְׁנוּ וְנָשׁוּב
וְנִבְנֶה חֳרָבוֹת כֹּה (הי) אָמַר יְהוָה צְבָאוֹת (פני שכינה) הֵמָּה יִבְנוּ
וַאֲנִי (אני) אֶהֱרוֹס וְקָרְאוּ לָהֶם גְּבוּל רִשְׁעָה וְהָעָם אֲשֶׁר־זָעַם
יְהוָה עַד־עוֹלָם׃ ה וְעֵינֵיכֶם תִּרְאֶינָה וְאַתֶּם תֹּאמְרוּ יִגְדַּל
(יזל) יְהוָה מֵעַל (עלם) לִגְבוּל יִשְׂרָאֵל׃ ו בֵּן יְכַבֵּד אָב וְעֶבֶד
אֲדֹנָיו וְאִם־אָב אָנִי (אני) אַיֵּה (ההה) כְבוֹדִי וְאִם־אֲדוֹנִים אָנִי
(אני) אַיֵּה מוֹרָאִי אָמַר ׀ יְהוָה צְבָאוֹת (פני שכינה) לָכֶם הַכֹּהֲנִים
(מלה) בּוֹזֵי שְׁמִי וַאֲמַרְתֶּם בַּמֶּה בָזִינוּ אֶת־שְׁמֶךָ׃ ז מַגִּישִׁים
עַל־מִזְבְּחִי (זן, נגד, מזבח) לֶחֶם מְגֹאָל וַאֲמַרְתֶּם בַּמֶּה גֵאַלְנוּךָ
בֶּאֱמָרְכֶם שֻׁלְחַן יְהוָה נִבְזֶה הוּא׃ ח וְכִי־תַגִּשׁוּן עִוֵּר לִזְבֹּחַ
אֵין רָע וְכִי תַגִּישׁוּ פִּסֵּחַ וְחֹלֶה (להח) אֵין רָע הַקְרִיבֵהוּ נָא

לְפֶחָתֶךָ הֲיִרְצְךָ אוֹ הֲיִשָּׂא פָנֶיךָ אָמַר יְהוָה צְבָאוֹת (פני שכינה):
ט וְעַתָּה חַלּוּ־נָא פְנֵי־אֵל וִיחָנֵנוּ מִיֶּדְכֶם הָיְתָה זֹּאת הֲיִשָּׂא
מִכֶּם פָּנִים אָמַר יְהוָה צְבָאוֹת (פני שכינה): י מִי (ילי) גַם־בָּכֶם
וְיִסְגֹּר דְּלָתַיִם וְלֹא־תָאִירוּ מִזְבְּחִי (זן, נגד, מזבח) חִנָּם אֵין־לִי חֵפֶץ
בָּכֶם אָמַר יְהוָה צְבָאוֹת (פני שכינה) וּמִנְחָה לֹא־אֶרְצֶה מִיֶּדְכֶם:
יא כִּי מִמִּזְרַח־שֶׁמֶשׁ וְעַד־מְבוֹאוֹ גָּדוֹל (להח, מבה) שְׁמִי בַּגּוֹיִם
וּבְכָל (לכב) ־מָקוֹם מֻקְטָר מֻגָּשׁ לִשְׁמִי וּמִנְחָה טְהוֹרָה (י"פ אכא)
כִּי־גָדוֹל (להח, מבה) שְׁמִי בַּגּוֹיִם אָמַר יְהוָה צְבָאוֹת (פני שכינה): יב
וְאַתֶּם מְחַלְּלִים אוֹתוֹ בֶּאֱמָרְכֶם שֻׁלְחַן אֲדֹנָי מְגֹאָל הוּא
וְנִיבוֹ נִבְזֶה אָכְלוֹ: יג וַאֲמַרְתֶּם הִנֵּה מַתְּלָאָה וְהִפַּחְתֶּם אוֹתוֹ
אָמַר יְהוָה צְבָאוֹת (פני שכינה) וַהֲבֵאתֶם גָּזוּל וְאֶת־הַפִּסֵּחַ וְאֶת־
הַחוֹלֶה וַהֲבֵאתֶם אֶת־הַמִּנְחָה הַאֶרְצֶה אוֹתָהּ מִיֶּדְכֶם
אָמַר יְהוָה: {ס} יד וְאָרוּר נוֹכֵל וְיֵשׁ בְּעֶדְרוֹ זָכָר וְנֹדֵר
וְזֹבֵחַ מָשְׁחָת לַאדֹנָי כִּי מֶלֶךְ גָּדוֹל (להח, מבה) אָנִי (אני) אָמַר
יְהוָה צְבָאוֹת (פני שכינה) וּשְׁמִי נוֹרָא בַגּוֹיִם: א וְעַתָּה אֲלֵיכֶם
הַמִּצְוָה הַזֹּאת הַכֹּהֲנִים (מלה): ב אִם־לֹא תִשְׁמְעוּ וְאִם־לֹא
תָשִׂימוּ עַל־לֵב לָתֵת כָּבוֹד לִשְׁמִי אָמַר יְהוָה צְבָאוֹת (פני
שכינה) וְשִׁלַּחְתִּי בָכֶם אֶת־הַמְּאֵרָה וְאָרוֹתִי אֶת־בִּרְכוֹתֵיכֶם
וְגַם אָרוֹתִיהָ כִּי אֵינְכֶם שָׂמִים (כוו, י"פ טל) עַל־לֵב: ג הִנְנִי גֹעֵר

לָכֶם֙ אֶת־הַזֶּ֔רַע וְזֵרִ֤יתִי פֶ֙רֶשׁ֙ עַל־פְּנֵיכֶ֔ם פֶּ֖רֶשׁ חַגֵּיכֶ֑ם וְנָשָׂ֥א
אֶתְכֶ֖ם אֵלָֽיו׃ ד וִֽידַעְתֶּ֕ם כִּ֚י שִׁלַּ֣חְתִּי אֲלֵיכֶ֔ם אֵ֖ת הַמִּצְוָ֣ה
הַזֹּ֑את לִֽהְי֤וֹת בְּרִיתִי֙ אֶת־לֵוִ֔י אָמַ֖ר יְהֹוָ֥ה צְבָאֽוֹת (פני שכינה)׃ ה
בְּרִיתִ֣י ׀ הָיְתָ֣ה אִתּ֗וֹ הַֽחַיִּים֙ (בינה) וְהַשָּׁל֔וֹם וָאֶתְּנֵֽם־ל֥וֹ מוֹרָ֖א
וַיִּֽירָאֵ֑נִי וּמִפְּנֵ֥י שְׁמִ֖י נִחַ֥ת הֽוּא׃ ו תּוֹרַ֤ת אֱמֶת֙ (ז"פ ס"ג) הָיְתָ֣ה
בְּפִ֔יהוּ וְעַוְלָ֖ה לֹא־נִמְצָ֣א בִשְׂפָתָ֑יו בְּשָׁל֤וֹם וּבְמִישׁוֹר֙ הָלַ֣ךְ
(מ"ה) אִתִּ֔י וְרַבִּ֖ים הֵשִׁ֥יב מֵעָוֺֽן׃ ז כִּֽי־שִׂפְתֵ֤י כֹהֵן֙ (מלכה) יִשְׁמְרוּ־
דַ֔עַת וְתוֹרָ֖ה יְבַקְשׁ֣וּ מִפִּ֑יהוּ כִּ֛י מַלְאַ֥ךְ יְהֹוָֽה־צְבָא֖וֹת (פני שכינה)
הֽוּא׃

Lesson of Vayetze

"And Jacob went out"

In this week's portion, Jacob leaves the land of Israel and goes to Charan at the suggestion of his parents. Rebecca sent him because the spirit of God told her that Esau wanted to kill Jacob. Isaac sent him because he was worried about the nationality of the woman whom Jacob would marry. Yet neither of these is the real reason that Jacob had to go.

The truth is that Jacob had to leave for his own sake. He had to go for himself and not because of his father or his mother or his brother. In the portion, it is simply written: "And Jacob left." No reason involving another person is given. Jacob had to go both because of his work in this world and because of the spiritual level that he embodied. We must understand that there are things in our lives that that we have to do–not that we want to do, but that we must do. When we see that this is true in a specific situation, that we really have no choice except to take a certain action, we can be sure this way to go is from the Creator. So we must act right away.

But even when we see that Jacob had to leave Israel as a result of the Creator's will, we can still ask why the Creator willed this? In Israel, there is holiness. It is written in the Zohar that the female aspect of God does not exist outside of Israel. The rest of the world is on a lower spiritual level than Israel, so why should Jacob have to leave? (In connection with this, the Rav, my father and my teacher, is sometimes asked why he doesn't live in Israel.)

Although it is true that leaving Israel is considered "going down" in a spiritual sense, this is not the case when it pertains to a righteous person like Jacob our Patriarch. He, after all, was a chariot for the level of Tiferet. He was the father of the tribes. The whole concept of the people of Israel comes from him because he was Israel. When Jacob left Beer Sheva, the holiness of Israel went with him, which is why it is not written that he "went down." Even though Jacob was physically outside of Israel, he was still there spiritually.

For us, too, being outside Israel is no real problem as long as we have the holiness of Israel within us. This is the channel that Jacob opened for us: that people who need to be away from Israel for any reason can take Israel with them.

Why was Jacob was chosen to be the channel for this–to bring the energy of Israel outside Israel? Jacob, of course, was an incarnation of Adam, the first human being. In fact, we are all part of Adam, and we were separated only after Adam sinned. Only Jacob could be a channel for the whole nation of

Israel to bring the light of Israel outside its physical borders. Only he could connect right and left, uniting elements that by nature are opposite to each other. Judgment and Mercy–that is, Abraham and Isaac–cannot be unified; we are in judgment or we are in mercy, but not both together. Only Jacob, the middle chariot, can resolve this difference. Jacob is the filament in the light bulb, the conduit between the positive and the negative energies.

But for us to connect to Jacob, we ourselves must be a central column like him. We must be channels for the same energy as Jacob was, regardless of where we live or where we are. Both people who live in Israel and people who live outside of Israel need the portion of Vayetze Ya'acov to connect to this power.

Rachel and Leah

When the Rav, my father and teacher, used to read the portion about Rachel and Leah, he always wept, even as a small child. Jacob loved Rachel, but the Creator gave Leah the merit to marry Jacob first. Later, Leah bore children when Rachel could not. Reading this story, one might wonder what kind of a Creator could do such a thing?

Even in death, Leah is buried with Jacob, while Rachel (who died giving birth to Benjamin) is buried alone on the road to Bet Lechem. But there is a reason for everything that happens. How we see things is not always how they really are. Jacob, Rachel, and Leah–their lives were not like other people's lives. Because they were all chariots, everything that happened to them would affect every single person who ever existed or would ever exist in the world.

Rachel symbolizes the way we think; Leah the way we should see our life. Rachel represents Malchut, the physical world; Leah represents Binah, the spiritual world. The problem is that we love Rachel, and we want so much for everything to be good for her. Leah, however, is the real life we don't even know we want. We must learn to live the life of Leah, which is the level of Binah, as if it were the life of Rachel, which is Malchut. We must love Leah as if she were Rachel–and love the spiritual as if it were the physical.

How many people in the world really care that there is no Temple? Who weeps over its destruction? But if, God forbid, we lose money on a business transaction, we will cry over the loss until we can't cry any more. We love Rachel so much that nothing happens spiritually. When we love Leah like Rachel, then we will really be able reveal the Light of the Creator in this world.

Synopsis of Vayetze

Vayetze means to go out. The message for humanity is that when we go out of ourselves, our comfort, our nature, our selfish desires - we begin our true spiritual journey. In this portion Jacob had to "go out" in order to begin his path towards becoming Israel - the chariot for the nation of Israel.

By connecting to this portion, we can get the power to go out of our nature and dramatically change our life and create a new destiny.

First Reading - Abraham - Chesed

(י) וַיֵּצֵא יַעֲקֹב (יאהדונהי אידהנויה) מִבְּאֵר (קנ"א ב"ן) שָׁבַע וַיֵּלֶךְ (כלי)
חָרָנָה: (יא) וַיִּפְגַּע בַּמָּקוֹם וַיָּלֶן שָׁם כִּי־בָא הַשֶּׁמֶשׁ וַיִּקַּח
(וזעם) מֵאַבְנֵי הַמָּקוֹם וַיָּשֶׂם מְרַאֲשֹׁתָיו וַיִּשְׁכַּב בַּמָּקוֹם
הַהוּא: (יב) וַיַּחֲלֹם וְהִנֵּה סֻלָּם מֻצָּב אַרְצָה וְרֹאשׁוֹ מַגִּיעַ
הַשָּׁמָיְמָה וְהִנֵּה מַלְאֲכֵי אֱלֹהִים (ילה) עֹלִים וְיֹרְדִים בּוֹ: (יג)
וְהִנֵּה יְהֹוָהאדני יאהדונהי נִצָּב עָלָיו וַיֹּאמַר אֲנִי (אני) יְהֹוָהאדני יאהדונהי
אֱלֹהֵי (דמב) אַבְרָהָם (רמ"ח) אָבִיךָ וֵאלֹהֵי (לכב) יִצְחָק (ד"פ ב"ן)
הָאָרֶץ (מילוי אלהים ע"ה) אֲשֶׁר אַתָּה שֹׁכֵב עָלֶיהָ (פהל) לְךָ אֶתְּנֶנָּה
וּלְזַרְעֶךָ: (יד) וְהָיָה (יהה) (יהוה) זַרְעֲךָ כַּעֲפַר הָאָרֶץ (מילוי אלהים ע"ה)
וּפָרַצְתָּ יָמָּה וָקֵדְמָה וְצָפֹנָה (ע"ה עסמ"ב) וָנֶגְבָּה וְנִבְרְכוּ (יהוה ריבוע
יהוה ריבוע מ"ה) בְךָ כָּל (ילי) ־מִשְׁפְּחֹת הָאֲדָמָה וּבְזַרְעֶךָ: (טו) וְהִנֵּה

וַיַּחֲלֹם - During his journey, Jacob has a dream in which he sees angels ascending and descending a ladder to Heaven. Throughout the dream, Jacob's current angels are being exchanged for others. When he was in Israel, Jacob needed angels to support him spiritually, but once he left his countr, he needed angels for both physical and spiritual support. In our own lives, we must learn to use the tools that are appropriate to our situation. We use Monday angels on Monday, Tuesday angels on Tuesday, and so on. We call upon the angels that are appropriate to a specific time and place.

The dream takes place on what is now the Temple Mount in Jerusalem. Jacob makes an agreement with God: If God gives him protection and blessings, Jacob will tithe. This is the beginning of tithing. By using spiritual tool of tithing, we form a partnership with God.

אָנֹכִי֮ (איע) עִמָּךְ֒ וּשְׁמַרְתִּ֙יךָ֙ בְּכֹ֣ל (לכב) אֲשֶׁר־תֵּלֵ֔ךְ וַהֲשִׁ֣בֹתִ֔יךָ
אֶל־הָאֲדָמָ֖ה הַזֹּ֑את כִּ֚י לֹ֣א אֶֽעֱזָבְךָ֔ עַ֚ד אֲשֶׁ֣ר אִם (יוהך)־
עָשִׂ֔יתִי אֵ֥ת אֲשֶׁר־דִּבַּ֖רְתִּי (ראה) לָֽךְ׃ (טז) וַיִּיקַ֣ץ יַעֲקֹב֮ (יאהדונהי
אידהנויה) מִשְּׁנָתוֹ֒ וַיֹּ֕אמֶר אָכֵן֙ יֵ֣שׁ יְהֹוָ֔ה (יאהדונהי) בַּמָּק֖וֹם הַזֶּ֑ה
(והו) וְאָנֹכִ֖י (איע) לֹ֥א יָדָֽעְתִּי׃ (יז) וַיִּירָא֙ וַיֹּאמַ֔ר מַה (מ"ה)־נּוֹרָ֖א
הַמָּק֣וֹם הַזֶּ֑ה (והו) אֵ֣ין זֶ֗ה כִּ֚י אִם (יוהך)־בֵּ֣ית (ב"פ ראה) אֱלֹהִ֔ים
(ילה) וְזֶ֖ה שַׁ֥עַר הַשָּׁמָֽיִם (י"פ טל)׃ (יוז) וַיַּשְׁכֵּ֨ם יַעֲקֹ֜ב (יאהדונהי אידהנויה)
בַּבֹּ֗קֶר וַיִּקַּ֤ח (וזעם) אֶת־הָאֶ֙בֶן֙ אֲשֶׁר־שָׂ֣ם מְרַֽאֲשֹׁתָ֔יו וַיָּ֥שֶׂם
אֹתָ֖הּ מַצֵּבָ֑ה וַיִּצֹ֥ק שֶׁ֖מֶן עַל־רֹאשָֽׁהּ׃ (יט) וַיִּקְרָ֛א אֶת־שֵֽׁם־
הַמָּק֥וֹם הַה֖וּא בֵּֽית (ב"פ ראה)־אֵ֑ל וְאוּלָ֛ם ל֥וּז שֵׁם־הָעִ֖יר (סוזוף,
סנדלפון, ערי) לָרִאשֹׁנָֽה׃ (כ) וַיִּדַּ֥ר יַעֲקֹ֖ב (יאהדונהי אידהנויה) נֶ֣דֶר לֵאמֹ֑ר
אִם (יוהך)־ יִהְיֶ֨ה (ייי) אֱלֹהִ֜ים (ילה) עִמָּדִ֗י וּשְׁמָרַ֙נִי֙ בַּדֶּ֤רֶךְ (ב"פ
יב"ק) הַזֶּה֙ (והו) אֲשֶׁ֣ר אָנֹכִ֣י (איע) הוֹלֵ֔ךְ וְנָֽתַן (אבג יתץ, ושר, אהבת חנם)־לִ֥י
לֶ֛חֶם (ג' הויות) לֶאֱכֹ֖ל וּבֶ֥גֶד לִלְבֹּֽשׁ׃ (כא) וְשַׁבְתִּ֥י בְשָׁל֖וֹם אֶל־
בֵּ֣ית (ב"פ ראה) אָבִ֑י וְהָיָ֧ה (יהה) (יהוה) יְהֹוָ֛ה (יאהדונהי) לִ֖י לֵאלֹהִֽים
(ילה)׃ (כב) וְהָאֶ֣בֶן הַזֹּ֗את אֲשֶׁר־שַׂ֙מְתִּי֙ מַצֵּבָ֔ה יִהְיֶ֖ה (ייי) בֵּ֣ית (ב"פ
ראה) אֱלֹהִ֑ים (ילה) וְכֹל֙ (ילי) אֲשֶׁ֣ר תִּתֶּן (ב"פ כהת)־לִ֔י עַשֵּׂ֖ר אֲעַשְּׂרֶ֥נּוּ
לָֽךְ׃

Second Reading - Issac - Gvurah

(א) וַיִּשָּׂא יַעֲקֹב (יאהדונהי אידהנויה) רַגְלָיו וַיֵּלֶךְ (כלי) אַרְצָה בְנֵי־
קֶדֶם׃ (ב) וַיַּרְא וְהִנֵּה בְאֵר (קנ״א ב״ן) בַּשָּׂדֶה וְהִנֵּה־שָׁם שְׁלֹשָׁה
עֶדְרֵי־צֹאן רֹבְצִים עָלֶיהָ (פהל) כִּי מִן־הַבְּאֵר (קנ״א ב״ן) הַהִוא
יַשְׁקוּ הָעֲדָרִים וְהָאֶבֶן גְּדֹלָה עַל־פִּי הַבְּאֵר (קנ״א ב״ן)׃ (ג)
וְנֶאֶסְפוּ־שָׁמָּה כָל (ילי)־הָעֲדָרִים וְגָלְלוּ אֶת־הָאֶבֶן מֵעַל
(עלם) פִּי הַבְּאֵר (קנ״א ב״ן) וְהִשְׁקוּ אֶת־הַצֹּאן וְהֵשִׁיבוּ אֶת־הָאֶבֶן
עַל־פִּי הַבְּאֵר (קנ״א ב״ן) לִמְקֹמָהּ׃ (ד) וַיֹּאמֶר לָהֶם יַעֲקֹב (יאהדונהי
אידהנויה) אַחַי מֵאַיִן אַתֶּם וַיֹּאמְרוּ מֵחָרָן אֲנָחְנוּ׃ (ה) וַיֹּאמֶר לָהֶם
הַיְדַעְתֶּם אֶת־לָבָן בֶּן־נָחוֹר וַיֹּאמְרוּ יָדָעְנוּ׃ (ו) וַיֹּאמֶר לָהֶם
הֲשָׁלוֹם לוֹ וַיֹּאמְרוּ שָׁלוֹם וְהִנֵּה רָחֵל בִּתּוֹ בָּאָה עִם־
הַצֹּאן׃ (ז) וַיֹּאמֶר הֵן עוֹד הַיּוֹם (נגד, זן) גָּדוֹל (להח, מבה עד״א) לֹא־
עֵת הֵאָסֵף הַמִּקְנֶה הַשְׁקוּ הַצֹּאן וּלְכוּ רְעוּ׃ (ח) וַיֹּאמְרוּ לֹא
נוּכַל עַד אֲשֶׁר יֵאָסְפוּ כָּל (ילי)־הָעֲדָרִים וְגָלְלוּ אֶת־הָאֶבֶן
מֵעַל (עלם) פִּי הַבְּאֵר (קנ״א ב״ן) וְהִשְׁקִינוּ הַצֹּאן׃ (ט) עוֹדֶנּוּ מְדַבֵּר
עִמָּם (ראה) וְרָחֵל ׀ בָּאָה עִם־הַצֹּאן אֲשֶׁר לְאָבִיהָ כִּי רֹעָה

רָחֵל - When he reaches Charan, Jacob meets Rachel at the well. Again, we see the power of water. Jacob kisses Rachel. and then begins to weep. He is seeing his future with Rachel: that their relationship will be a bittersweet one, that she will die in childbirth, and that they will not be buried together.

הוּא: (י) וַיְהִי כַּאֲשֶׁר רָאָה (ראה) יַעֲקֹב (יאהדונהי אידהנויה) אֶת־רָחֵל
בַּת־לָבָן אֲחִי אִמּוֹ וְאֶת־צֹאן לָבָן אֲחִי אִמּוֹ וַיִּגַּשׁ יַעֲקֹב
(יאהדונהי אידהנויה) וַיָּגֶל (להוו) אֶת־הָאֶבֶן מֵעַל (עלם) פִּי הַבְּאֵר (קנ״א ב״ן)
וַיַּשְׁקְ אֶת־צֹאן לָבָן אֲחִי אִמּוֹ: (יא) וַיִּשַּׁק יַעֲקֹב (יאהדונהי אידהנויה)
לְרָחֵל וַיִּשָּׂא אֶת־קֹלוֹ וַיֵּבְךְּ: (יב) וַיַּגֵּד יַעֲקֹב (יאהדונהי אידהנויה)
לְרָחֵל כִּי אֲחִי אָבִיהָ הוּא וְכִי בֶן־רִבְקָה הוּא וַתָּרָץ וַתַּגֵּד
לְאָבִיהָ: (יג) וַיְהִי כִשְׁמֹעַ לָבָן אֶת־שֵׁמַע | יַעֲקֹב (יאהדונהי אידה-
נויה) בֶּן־אֲחֹתוֹ וַיָּרָץ לִקְרָאתוֹ וַיְחַבֶּק־לוֹ וַיְנַשֶּׁק־לוֹ וַיְבִיאֵהוּ
אֶל־בֵּיתוֹ (ב״פ ראה) וַיְסַפֵּר לְלָבָן אֵת כָּל (ילי) ־הַדְּבָרִים (ראה)
הָאֵלֶּה: (יד) וַיֹּאמֶר לוֹ לָבָן אַךְ (אהיה) עַצְמִי וּבְשָׂרִי אָתָּה
וַיֵּשֶׁב עִמּוֹ חֹדֶשׁ (י״ב הויות) יָמִים (נלך): (טו) וַיֹּאמֶר לָבָן לְיַעֲקֹב

וַתָּרָץ - Rachel goes home and tells Laban, her father, that Jacob has arrived. Although Laban runs to Jacob and kisses and embraces him, he is trying to find out how much money Jacob has brought with him. When the servant of Abraham came for Rebecca, he brought with him a great herd of animals and many gifts. But Laban finds that Jacob has no money.

וַיֹּאמֶר - Laban demands a deal with Jacob: He will give Jacob his daughter Rachel if Jacob is willing to work for him for seven years. But seven years later, Laban tricks Jacob and gives him Leah to marry. Laban is trying to prevent the union of Rachel with Jacob, and thereby the creation of the Twelve Tribes of Israel. Laban in essence is trying to prevent the Light from being revealed through Jacob, Rachel, Leah and the Twelve Tribes. Jacob, however, eventually overcomes Laban's efforts. No matter how defeated we feel, we can still overcome the Satan.

(יאהדונהי אידהנויה) הֲכִי־אָחִי אַתָּה וַעֲבַדְתַּנִי חִנָּם הַגִּידָה לִּי מַה
(מ"ה)־מַּשְׂכֻּרְתֶּךָ׃ (טז) וּלְלָבָן שְׁתֵּי בָנוֹת שֵׁם הַגְּדֹלָה לֵאָה
וְשֵׁם הַקְּטַנָּה רָחֵל׃ (יז) וְעֵינֵי (מ"ה בריבוע) לֵאָה רַכּוֹת וְרָחֵל
הָיְתָה יְפַת־תֹּאַר וִיפַת מַרְאֶה׃

Third Reading - Jacob - Tiferet

(יח) וַיֶּאֱהַב יַעֲקֹב (יאהדונהי אידהנויה) אֶת־רָחֵל וַיֹּאמֶר אֶעֱבָדְךָ
שֶׁבַע שָׁנִים בְּרָחֵל בִּתְּךָ הַקְּטַנָּה׃ (יט) וַיֹּאמֶר לָבָן טוֹב (והו)
תִּתִּי אֹתָהּ לָךְ מִתִּתִּי אֹתָהּ לְאִישׁ אַחֵר שְׁבָה עִמָּדִי׃ (כ)
וַיַּעֲבֹד יַעֲקֹב (יאהדונהי אידהנויה) בְּרָחֵל שֶׁבַע שָׁנִים וַיִּהְיוּ בְעֵינָיו
(מ"ה בריבוע) כְּיָמִים (נלך) אֲחָדִים בְּאַהֲבָתוֹ אֹתָהּ׃ (כא) וַיֹּאמֶר
יַעֲקֹב (יאהדונהי אידהנויה) אֶל־לָבָן הָבָה אֶת־אִשְׁתִּי כִּי מָלְאוּ יָמָי

וַיֶּאֱהַב - Although it might seem odd for him to have had so many children with Leah, whom he loves less than Rachel, we should be cautious not to use our physical limited logic to understand a spiritual matter -- we will surely be misled.

תִּתִּי - Lavan demands a deal with Jacob . Lavan will give Jacob his daughter Rachel if Jacob is willing to work for him for seven years. But seven years later, Lavan tricks Jacob and gives him Leah to marry. Lavan is trying to prevent the union of Rachel with Jacob , and thereby the creation of the twelve tribes of Israel. Lavan is trying to prevent the Light from being revealed through Jacob , Rachel, Leah and the twelve tribes. Jacob , however, eventually overcomes Lavan's efforts. No matter how defeated we feel, we can overcome the Satan.

וְאָבוֹאָה אֵלֶיהָ׃ (כב) וַיֶּאֱסֹף לָבָן אֶת־כָּל (ילי) ־אַנְשֵׁי הַמָּקוֹם
וַיַּעַשׂ מִשְׁתֶּה׃ (כג) וַיְהִי בָעֶרֶב וַיִּקַּח (וזעם) אֶת־לֵאָה בִתּוֹ
וַיָּבֵא אֹתָהּ אֵלָיו וַיָּבֹא אֵלֶיהָ׃ (כד) וַיִּתֵּן לָבָן לָהּ אֶת־זִלְפָּה
שִׁפְחָתוֹ לְלֵאָה בִתּוֹ שִׁפְחָה׃ (כה) וַיְהִי בַבֹּקֶר וְהִנֵּה־הִוא
לֵאָה וַיֹּאמֶר אֶל־לָבָן מַה (מ״ה) ־זֹּאת עָשִׂיתָ לִּי הֲלֹא בְרָחֵל
עָבַדְתִּי עִמָּךְ וְלָמָּה רִמִּיתָנִי׃ (כו) וַיֹּאמֶר לָבָן לֹא־יֵעָשֶׂה כֵן
בִּמְקוֹמֵנוּ לָתֵת הַצְּעִירָה לִפְנֵי הַבְּכִירָה׃ (כז) מַלֵּא שְׁבֻעַ
זֹאת וְנִתְּנָה לְךָ גַּם־אֶת־זֹאת בַּעֲבֹדָה אֲשֶׁר תַּעֲבֹד עִמָּדִי
עוֹד שֶׁבַע־שָׁנִים אֲחֵרוֹת׃ (כח) וַיַּעַשׂ יַעֲקֹב (יאהדונהי אידהנויה) כֵּן
וַיְמַלֵּא שְׁבֻעַ זֹאת וַיִּתֶּן־לוֹ אֶת־רָחֵל בִּתּוֹ לוֹ לְאִשָּׁה׃ (כט)
וַיִּתֵּן לָבָן לְרָחֵל בִּתּוֹ אֶת־בִּלְהָה שִׁפְחָתוֹ לָהּ לְשִׁפְחָה׃ (ל)
וַיָּבֹא גַּם אֶל־רָחֵל וַיֶּאֱהַב גַּם־אֶת־רָחֵל מִלֵּאָה וַיַּעֲבֹד עִמּוֹ
עוֹד שֶׁבַע־שָׁנִים אֲחֵרוֹת׃ (לא) וַיַּרְא יְהֹוָה אדני יאהדונהי כִּי־שְׂנוּאָה
לֵאָה וַיִּפְתַּח אֶת־רַחְמָהּ וְרָחֵל עֲקָרָה׃ (לב) וַתַּהַר לֵאָה
וַתֵּלֶד בֵּן וַתִּקְרָא שְׁמוֹ (מהש ע״ה) רְאוּבֵן כִּי אָמְרָה כִּי־רָאָה

(ד״ה) – רְאוּבֵן - Reuben controls the month of Aries with the letters Dalet and Hei. When Jacob has intercourse with Leah, he thinks she is Rachel. Reuben is not truly conceived from the first drop of semen, and therefore, he is not actually the first-born. The first drop was kept by the Creator so that when Rachel conceives Joseph, he will be the real firstborn son.

(ראה) יְהֹוָ֨אדניאהדונהי בְּעָנְיִ֔י (מ"ה בריבוע) כִּ֥י עַתָּ֖ה יֶאֱהָבַ֥נִי אִישִֽׁי׃
(לג) וַתַּ֣הַר עוֹד֮ וַתֵּ֣לֶד בֵּן֒ וַתֹּ֗אמֶר כִּֽי־שָׁמַ֤ע יְהֹוָה֙אדניאהדונהי
כִּֽי־שְׂנוּאָ֣ה אָנֹ֔כִי (איע) וַיִּתֶּן־לִ֖י גַּם־אֶת־זֶ֑ה וַתִּקְרָ֥א שְׁמ֖וֹ (מהש
ע"ה) שִׁמְעֽוֹן׃ (לד) וַתַּ֣הַר עוֹד֮ וַתֵּ֣לֶד בֵּן֒ וַתֹּ֗אמֶר עַתָּ֤ה הַפַּ֙עַם֙
(מנק) יִלָּוֶ֤ה אִישִׁי֙ אֵלַ֔י כִּֽי־יָלַ֥דְתִּי ל֖וֹ שְׁלֹשָׁ֣ה בָנִ֑ים עַל־כֵּ֥ן
קָרָֽא־שְׁמ֖וֹ (מהש ע"ה) לֵוִֽי׃ (לה) וַתַּ֨הַר ע֜וֹד וַתֵּ֣לֶד בֵּ֗ן וַתֹּ֙אמֶר֙
הַפַּ֙עַם֙ (מנק) אוֹדֶ֣ה אֶת־יְהֹוָ֔האדניאהדונהי עַל־כֵּ֛ן קָרְאָ֥ה שְׁמ֖וֹ (מהש
ע"ה) יְהוּדָ֑ה וַֽתַּעֲמֹ֖ד מִלֶּֽדֶת׃ ל (א) וַתֵּ֣רֶא רָחֵ֗ל כִּ֣י לֹ֤א יָֽלְדָה֙
לְיַעֲקֹ֔ב (יאהדונהי אידהנויה) וַתְּקַנֵּ֥א רָחֵ֖ל בַּאֲחֹתָ֑הּ וַתֹּ֥אמֶר אֶל־

שִׁמְעוֹן – (פו) - Simon controls the month of Taurus with the letters Pe and Vav. Simon has the harsh judgment. He is the strongest of the brothers and the leader of the army.

לֵוִי – (רז) - Levi controls the month of Gemini with the letters Resh and Zayin. From Levi came Moses, Aaron, the Levites, and the Kohanim.

יְהוּדָה – (חת) - Judah controls the month of Cancer with the letters Chet and Tav. Judah controls the disease of cancer, but this does not refer only to the physical illness. Cancer can be present spiritually or in a human relationship as well as in the physical body.

וַתְּקַנֵּא - becomes jealous of Leah. She was angry that Jacob married Leah and not her. Without judging Rachel, we need to remember two things: first, that we must not be jealous of others based solely on what we see in the present moment, and second, that we cannot see the whole picture. Today's events may be the result of something that happened long ago, perhaps even in a previous lifetime.

יַעֲקֹב (יאהדונהי אידהנויה) הָבָה־לִּי בָנִים וְאִם (יוהך)־אַיִן מֵתָה אָנֹכִי
(איע): (ב) וַיִּחַר־אַף יַעֲקֹב (יאהדונהי אידהנויה) בְּרָחֵל וַיֹּאמֶר הֲתַחַת
אֱלֹהִים (ילה) אָנֹכִי (איע) אֲשֶׁר־מָנַע מִמֵּךְ פְּרִי־בָטֶן: (ג) וַתֹּאמֶר
הִנֵּה אֲמָתִי בִלְהָה בֹּא אֵלֶיהָ וְתֵלֵד עַל־בִּרְכַּי וְאִבָּנֶה גַם־
אָנֹכִי (איע) מִמֶּנָּה: (ד) וַתִּתֶּן (ב"פ כהת)־לוֹ אֶת־בִּלְהָה שִׁפְחָתָהּ
לְאִשָּׁה וַיָּבֹא אֵלֶיהָ יַעֲקֹב (יאהדונהי אידהנויה): (ה) וַתַּהַר בִּלְהָה
וַתֵּלֶד לְיַעֲקֹב (יאהדונהי אידהנויה) בֵּן: (ו) וַתֹּאמֶר רָחֵל דָּנַנִּי אֱלֹהִים
(ילה) וְגַם שָׁמַע בְּקֹלִי וַיִּתֶּן־לִי בֵּן עַל־כֵּן קָרְאָה שְׁמוֹ (מהש
ע"ה) דָּן: (ז) וַתַּהַר עוֹד וַתֵּלֶד בִּלְהָה שִׁפְחַת רָחֵל בֵּן שֵׁנִי
לְיַעֲקֹב (יאהדונהי אידהנויה): (ח) וַתֹּאמֶר רָחֵל נַפְתּוּלֵי אֱלֹהִים (ילה) |
נִפְתַּלְתִּי עִם־אֲחֹתִי גַּם־יָכֹלְתִּי וַתִּקְרָא שְׁמוֹ (מהש ע"ה) נַפְתָּלִי:
(ט) וַתֵּרֶא לֵאָה כִּי עָמְדָה מִלֶּדֶת וַתִּקַּח אֶת־זִלְפָּה שִׁפְחָתָהּ
וַתִּתֵּן (ב"פ כהת) אֹתָהּ לְיַעֲקֹב (יאהדונהי אידהנויה) לְאִשָּׁה: (י) וַתֵּלֶד

בִּלְהָה - Rachel gives her handmaiden, Bilhah, to Jacob so that he can father children with her.

דָּן – (דנ) - Dan controls the month of Scorpio (Mar-Cheshvan) with the letters Dalet and Nun.

נַפְתָּלִי – (סג) - Naftali controls the month of Sagittarius (Kislev) with the letters Samech and Gimel. This is the month of miracles.

זִלְפָּה שִׁפְחַת לֵאָה לְיַעֲקֹב (יאהדונהי אידהנויה) בֵּן׃ (יא) וַתֹּאמֶר
לֵאָה בָּא גָד (בְּגָד כתיב) וַתִּקְרָא אֶת־שְׁמוֹ (מהש ע״ה) גָּד׃ (יב)
וַתֵּלֶד זִלְפָּה שִׁפְחַת לֵאָה בֵּן שֵׁנִי לְיַעֲקֹב (יאהדונהי אידהנויה)׃ (יג)
וַתֹּאמֶר לֵאָה בְּאָשְׁרִי כִּי אִשְּׁרוּנִי בָּנוֹת וַתִּקְרָא אֶת־שְׁמוֹ
(מהש ע״ה) אָשֵׁר׃

Fourth Reading - Moses - Netzach

(יד) וַיֵּלֶךְ (כלי) רְאוּבֵן בִּימֵי קְצִיר־חִטִּים וַיִּמְצָא
דוּדָאִים בַּשָּׂדֶה וַיָּבֵא אֹתָם אֶל־לֵאָה אִמּוֹ וַתֹּאמֶר רָחֵל
אֶל־לֵאָה תְּנִי־נָא לִי מִדּוּדָאֵי בְּנֵךְ׃ (טו) וַתֹּאמֶר לָהּ הַמְעַט
קַחְתֵּךְ אֶת־אִישִׁי וְלָקַחַת גַּם אֶת־דּוּדָאֵי בְּנִי וַתֹּאמֶר רָחֵל

גָּד – (עב) - Gad controls the month of Capricorn (Tevet) with the letters Ayin and Bet. These two letters represent the 72 Names of God.

אָשֵׁר – (צב) - Asher controls the month of Aquarius (Shevat) with the letters Tzadi and Bet.

דּוּדָאִים - Mandrake roots were thought to cure infertility. When neither Rachel nor Leah can give birth, Reuben brings mandrake root for Leah, his mother. Rachel becomes jealous and demands that Leah give her the mandrake.

Leah tells Rachel, "You have taken everything from me: first, my husband, and now my ability to have children." But Leah restricts by giving Rachel the mandrake, and so Leah becomes pregnant with Yisaschar. By sharing, Leah enables both herself and Rachel to bear children.

לָכֵן יִשְׁכַּב עִמָּךְ הַלַּיְלָה (מלה) תַּחַת דּוּדָאֵי בְנֵךְ: (טז) וַיָּבֹא
יַעֲקֹב (יאהדונהי אידהנויה) מִן־הַשָּׂדֶה בָּעֶרֶב וַתֵּצֵא לֵאָה לִקְרָאתוֹ
וַתֹּאמֶר אֵלַי תָּבוֹא כִּי שָׂכֹר (י"פ ב"ן) שְׂכַרְתִּיךָ בְּדוּדָאֵי בְּנִי
וַיִּשְׁכַּב עִמָּהּ בַּלַּיְלָה (מלה) הוּא: (יז) וַיִּשְׁמַע אֱלֹהִים (ילה)
אֶל־לֵאָה וַתַּהַר וַתֵּלֶד לְיַעֲקֹב (יאהדונהי אידהנויה) בֵּן חֲמִישִׁי: (יח)
וַתֹּאמֶר לֵאָה נָתַן אֱלֹהִים (ילה) שְׂכָרִי אֲשֶׁר־נָתַתִּי שִׁפְחָתִי
לְאִישִׁי וַתִּקְרָא שְׁמוֹ (מהש ע"ה) יִשָּׂשכָר: (יט) וַתַּהַר עוֹד לֵאָה
וַתֵּלֶד בֵּן־שִׁשִּׁי לְיַעֲקֹב (יאהדונהי אידהנויה): (כ) וַתֹּאמֶר לֵאָה זְבָדַנִי
אֱלֹהִים (ילה) | אֹתִי זֵבֶד טוֹב (והו) הַפַּעַם (מנק) יִזְבְּלֵנִי אִישִׁי כִּי־
יָלַדְתִּי לוֹ שִׁשָּׁה בָנִים וַתִּקְרָא אֶת־שְׁמוֹ (מהש ע"ה) זְבֻלוּן: (כא)
וְאַחַר יָלְדָה בַּת וַתִּקְרָא אֶת־שְׁמָהּ דִּינָה: (כב) וַיִּזְכֹּר (יהי אור)

(כט) – יִשָּׂשכָר - Yisachar controls the month of Leo (Av) with the letters Caf and Tet.

(רי) – זְבֻלוּן - Zebulun controls the month of Virgo (Elul) with the letters Resh and Yud.
Yisaschar and Zebulon reached an agreement which divided the physical and the spiritual realms. Yisaschar studied all day, while Zebulon was responsible for business. Zebulon supported Yisaschar financially, and Yisaschar gave half of all his spiritual Light to Zebulon.

דִּינָה - Leah has a daughter, Dinah. Originally, the child was to be a boy, but Leah prayed for a girl so that Rachel could be the foundation of at least two tribes.

(ע"ה) אֱלֹהִים (ילה) אֶת־רָחֵל וַיִּשְׁמַע אֵלֶיהָ אֱלֹהִים (ילה) וַיִּפְתַּח
אֶת־רַחְמָהּ׃ (כג) וַתַּהַר וַתֵּלֶד בֵּן וַתֹּאמֶר אָסַף אֱלֹהִים (ילה)
אֶת־חֶרְפָּתִי׃ (כד) וַתִּקְרָא אֶת־ שְׁמוֹ (מהש ע"ה) יוֹסֵף (ציון) לֵאמֹר
יֹסֵף (ציון) יְהֹוָהאדניאהדונהי לִי בֵּן אַחֵר׃ (כה) וַיְהִי כַּאֲשֶׁר יָלְדָה
רָחֵל אֶת־יוֹסֵף (ציון) וַיֹּאמֶר יַעֲקֹב (יאהדונהי אידהנויה) אֶל־לָבָן
שַׁלְּחֵנִי וְאֵלְכָה אֶל־מְקוֹמִי וּלְאַרְצִי׃ (כו) תְּנָה (נתה) אֶת־
נָשַׁי וְאֶת־יְלָדַי אֲשֶׁר עָבַדְתִּי אֹתְךָ בָּהֵן וְאֵלֵכָה כִּי אַתָּה
יָדַעְתָּ אֶת־עֲבֹדָתִי אֲשֶׁר עֲבַדְתִּיךָ׃ (כז) וַיֹּאמֶר אֵלָיו לָבָן
אִם (יוהך)־נָא מָצָאתִי חֵן (מוזי) בְּעֵינֶיךָ (ע"ה קס"א) נִחַשְׁתִּי וַיְבָרְכֵנִי
יְהֹוָהאדניאהדונהי בִּגְלָלֶךָ׃

Fifth Reading - Aaron - Hod

(כח) וַיֹּאמַר נָקְבָה שְׂכָרְךָ עָלַי וְאֶתֵּנָה׃ (כט) וַיֹּאמֶר אֵלָיו אַתָּה
יָדַעְתָּ אֵת אֲשֶׁר עֲבַדְתִּיךָ וְאֵת אֲשֶׁר־הָיָה (יהה) מִקְנְךָ אִתִּי׃
(ל) כִּי מְעַט אֲשֶׁר־הָיָה (יהה) לְךָ לְפָנַי וַיִּפְרֹץ לָרֹב וַיְבָרֶךְ (עס־
מ"ב) יְהֹוָהאדניאהדונהי אֹתְךָ לְרַגְלִי וְעַתָּה מָתַי אֶעֱשֶׂה גַם־אָנֹכִי
(איע) לְבֵיתִי (ב"פ ראה)׃ (לא) וַיֹּאמֶר מָה (מ"ה) אֶתֶּן־לָךְ וַיֹּאמֶר יַעֲקֹב

יוֹסֵף – (קנ"ג) - At last, Rachel gives birth to Joseph. He was conceived from the first semen of Jacob, which God had intended for this purpose.

(יאהדונהי אידהנויה) לֹא־תִתֶּן (ב"פ כהת) ־לִי מְאוּמָה אִם (יוהך) ־תַּעֲשֶׂה־
לִי הַדָּבָר (ראה) הַזֶּה (והו) אָשׁוּבָה אֶרְעֶה צֹאנְךָ אֶשְׁמֹר׃ (לב)
אֶעֱבֹר בְּכָל (לכב) ־צֹאנְךָ הַיּוֹם (נגד, זן) הָסֵר מִשָּׁם כָּל (ילי) ־שֶׂה |
נָקֹד וְטָלוּא וְכָל (ילי) ־שֶׂה־חוּם בַּכְּשָׂבִים וְטָלוּא וְנָקֹד בָּעִזִּים
וְהָיָה (יהה) (יהוה) שְׂכָרִי׃ (לג) וְעָנְתָה־בִּי צִדְקָתִי בְּיוֹם (נגד, זן) מָחָר
כִּי־תָבוֹא עַל־שְׂכָרִי לְפָנֶיךָ (סמ"ב) כֹּל (ילי) אֲשֶׁר־אֵינֶנּוּ נָקֹד
וְטָלוּא בָּעִזִּים וְחוּם בַּכְּשָׂבִים גָּנוּב הוּא אִתִּי׃ (לד) וַיֹּאמֶר
לָבָן הֵן לוּ יְהִי כִדְבָרֶךָ (ראה)׃ (לה) וַיָּסַר בַּיּוֹם (נגד, זן) הַהוּא אֶת־
הַתְּיָשִׁים הָעֲקֻדִּים וְהַטְּלֻאִים וְאֵת כָּל (ילי) ־הָעִזִּים הַנְּקֻדּוֹת
וְהַטְּלֻאֹת כֹּל (ילי) אֲשֶׁר־לָבָן בּוֹ וְכָל (ילי) ־חוּם בַּכְּשָׂבִים
וַיִּתֵּן בְּיַד־בָּנָיו׃ (לו) וַיָּשֶׂם דֶּרֶךְ (ב"פ יב"ק) שְׁלֹשֶׁת יָמִים (נלך)
בֵּינוֹ וּבֵין יַעֲקֹב (יאהדונהי אידהנויה) וְיַעֲקֹב (יאהדונהי אידהנויה) רֹעֶה (רהע)
אֶת־צֹאן לָבָן הַנּוֹתָרֹת׃ (לז) וַיִּקַּח (זעם) ־לוֹ יַעֲקֹב (יאהדונהי אידה־
נויה) מַקַּל לִבְנֶה לַח וְלוּז וְעַרְמוֹן וַיְפַצֵּל בָּהֵן פְּצָלוֹת לְבָנוֹת

שְׂכָרִי - Now Jacob begins to work for physical sustenance. According to the agreement he made with Laban, Laban is allowed to keep all the spotted goats and sheep from the herd. Jacob can keep the solid-colored animals as well as any speckled animals born from those of solid color. The Light makes it so that all the newborns are born speckled so that everything will go to Jacob. In this way, God ensures Jacob's sustenance. When we follow a spiritual path, when we are entirely with the Light, our material needs are provided for.

מַחְשֹׂף הַלָּבָן אֲשֶׁר עַל־הַמַּקְלוֹת׃ (לח) וַיַּצֵּג אֶת־הַמַּקְלוֹת
אֲשֶׁר פִּצֵּל בָּרְהָטִים בְּשִׁקֲתוֹת הַמָּיִם אֲשֶׁר תָּבֹאןָ הַצֹּאן
לִשְׁתּוֹת לְנֹכַח (ג' הויות) הַצֹּאן וַיֵּחַמְנָה בְּבֹאָן לִשְׁתּוֹת׃ (לט)
וַיֶּחֱמוּ הַצֹּאן אֶל־הַמַּקְלוֹת וַתֵּלַדְןָ הַצֹּאן עֲקֻדִּים נְקֻדִּים
וּטְלֻאִים׃ (מ) וְהַכְּשָׂבִים הִפְרִיד יַעֲקֹב (יאהדונהי אידהנויה) וַיִּתֵּן פְּנֵי
(חכמה, בינה) הַצֹּאן אֶל־עָקֹד וְכָל (ילי) ־חוּם בְּצֹאן לָבָן וַיָּשֶׁת לוֹ
עֲדָרִים לְבַדּוֹ (מ"ב) וְלֹא שָׁתָם עַל־צֹאן לָבָן׃ (מא) וְהָיָה (יהה)
(יהוה) בְּכָל (לכב) ־יַחֵם הַצֹּאן הַמְקֻשָּׁרוֹת וְשָׂם יַעֲקֹב (יאהדונהי איד-
הנויה) אֶת־הַמַּקְלוֹת לְעֵינֵי (מ"ה בריבוע) הַצֹּאן בָּרְהָטִים לְיַחְמֵנָּה
בַּמַּקְלוֹת׃ (מב) וּבְהַעֲטִיף הַצֹּאן לֹא יָשִׂים וְהָיָה (יהה) (יהוה)
הָעֲטֻפִים לְלָבָן וְהַקְּשֻׁרִים לְיַעֲקֹב (יאהדונהי אידהנויה)׃ (מג) וַיִּפְרֹץ
הָאִישׁ מְאֹד מְאֹד וַיְהִי־לוֹ צֹאן רַבּוֹת וּשְׁפָחוֹת וַעֲבָדִים
וּגְמַלִּים וַחֲמֹרִים׃ לא (א) וַיִּשְׁמַע אֶת־דִּבְרֵי (ראה) בְנֵי־לָבָן
לֵאמֹר לָקַח יַעֲקֹב (יאהדונהי אידהנויה) אֵת כָּל (ילי) ־אֲשֶׁר לְאָבִינוּ
וּמֵאֲשֶׁר לְאָבִינוּ עָשָׂה אֵת כָּל (ילי) ־הַכָּבֹד הַזֶּה (והו)׃ (ב) וַיַּרְא

וַיִּשְׁמַע - Jacob hears Laban's son say that Jacob had stolen from him and from Laban. God now tells Jacob that his work in Laban's household is finished and it is now time to move on. Jacob had worked fourteen years for his two wives plus six more years for the sustenance provided from the sheep. But when he hears the accusation that he is a thief, he is open to God's message that he should depart.

יַעֲקֹב (יאהדונהי אידהנויה) אֶת־פְּנֵי (חכמה, בינה) לָבָן וְהִנֵּה אֵינֶנּוּ עִמּוֹ
כִּתְמוֹל שִׁלְשׁוֹם׃ (ג) וַיֹּאמֶר יְהֹוָהאדניאהדונהי אֶל־יַעֲקֹב (יאהדונהי
אידהנויה) שׁוּב אֶל־אֶרֶץ אֲבוֹתֶיךָ וּלְמוֹלַדְתֶּךָ וְאֶהְיֶה עִמָּךְ׃ (ד)
וַיִּשְׁלַח יַעֲקֹב (יאהדונהי אידהנויה) וַיִּקְרָא לְרָחֵל וּלְלֵאָה הַשָּׂדֶה
אֶל־צֹאנוֹ׃ (ה) וַיֹּאמֶר לָהֶן רֹאֶה (ראה) אָנֹכִי (איע) אֶת־פְּנֵי (חכמה,
בינה) אֲבִיכֶן כִּי־אֵינֶנּוּ אֵלַי כִּתְמֹל שִׁלְשֹׁם וֵאלֹהֵי (לכב) אָבִי
הָיָה (יהה) עִמָּדִי׃ (ו) וְאַתֵּנָה יְדַעְתֶּן כִּי בְּכָל (לכב)־כֹּחִי עָבַדְתִּי
אֶת־אֲבִיכֶן׃ (ז) וַאֲבִיכֶן הֵתֶל בִּי וְהֶחֱלִף אֶת־מַשְׂכֻּרְתִּי
עֲשֶׂרֶת מֹנִים וְלֹא־נְתָנוֹ אֱלֹהִים (ילה) לְהָרַע עִמָּדִי׃ (ח)
אִם (יוהך)־כֹּה (היי) יֹאמַר נְקֻדִּים יִהְיֶה (ייי) שְׂכָרֶךָ וְיָלְדוּ כָל
(ילי)־הַצֹּאן נְקֻדִּים וְאִם (יוהך)־כֹּה (היי) יֹאמַר עֲקֻדִּים יִהְיֶה
(ייי) שְׂכָרֶךָ וְיָלְדוּ כָל (ילי)־הַצֹּאן עֲקֻדִּים׃ (ט) וַיַּצֵּל אֱלֹהִים
(ילה) אֶת־מִקְנֵה אֲבִיכֶם וַיִּתֶּן־לִי׃ (י) וַיְהִי בְּעֵת יַחֵם הַצֹּאן
וָאֶשָּׂא עֵינַי (מ"ה בריבוע) וָאֵרֶא בַּחֲלוֹם וְהִנֵּה הָעַתֻּדִים הָעֹלִים
עַל־הַצֹּאן עֲקֻדִּים נְקֻדִּים וּבְרֻדִּים׃ (יא) וַיֹּאמֶר אֵלַי מַלְאַךְ

וַיֹּאמֶר - Jacob explains to Rachel and Leah how he acquired all his money. He had a dream in which animals were ringed, spotted, and flecked. The Ari has written that the dream refers to the dimensions of the Upper Worlds. Because Jacob came from the Upper Worlds, he held domain even in the Lower Realms.

הָאֱלֹהִים (ילה) בַּחֲלוֹם יַעֲקֹב (יאהדונהי אידהנויה) וָאֹמַר הִנֵּנִי׃ (יב)
וַיֹּאמֶר שָׂא־נָא עֵינֶיךָ (ע"ה קס"א) וּרְאֵה (ראה) כָּל (ילי)־הָעַתֻּדִים
הָעֹלִים עַל־הַצֹּאן עֲקֻדִּים נְקֻדִּים וּבְרֻדִּים כִּי רָאִיתִי אֵת
כָּל (ילי)־אֲשֶׁר לָבָן עֹשֶׂה לָּךְ׃ (יג) אָנֹכִי (איע) הָאֵל (לאה) בֵּית (ב"פ
ראה)־אֵל אֲשֶׁר מָשַׁחְתָּ שָּׁם מַצֵּבָה אֲשֶׁר נָדַרְתָּ לִּי שָׁם נֶדֶר
עַתָּה קוּם צֵא מִן־הָאָרֶץ (מילוי אלהים ע"ה) הַזֹּאת וְשׁוּב אֶל־אֶרֶץ
מוֹלַדְתֶּךָ׃ (יד) וַתַּעַן רָחֵל וְלֵאָה וַתֹּאמַרְנָה לוֹ הַעוֹד לָנוּ
(מום) חֵלֶק וְנַחֲלָה בְּבֵית (ב"פ ראה) אָבִינוּ׃ (טו) הֲלוֹא נָכְרִיּוֹת
נֶחְשַׁבְנוּ לוֹ כִּי מְכָרָנוּ וַיֹּאכַל גַּם־אָכוֹל אֶת־כַּסְפֵּנוּ׃ (טז) כִּי
כָל (ילי)־הָעֹשֶׁר אֲשֶׁר הִצִּיל אֱלֹהִים (ילה) מֵאָבִינוּ לָנוּ (מום)
הוּא וּלְבָנֵינוּ וְעַתָּה כֹּל (ילי) אֲשֶׁר אָמַר אֱלֹהִים (ילה) אֵלֶיךָ
עֲשֵׂה׃

Sixth Reading - Joseph - Yesod

(יז) וַיָּקָם יַעֲקֹב (יאהדונהי אידהנויה) וַיִּשָּׂא אֶת־בָּנָיו וְאֶת־נָשָׁיו עַל־
הַגְּמַלִּים׃ (יח) וַיִּנְהַג אֶת־כָּל (ילי)־מִקְנֵהוּ וְאֶת־כָּל (ילי)־רְכֻשׁוֹ
אֲשֶׁר רָכָשׁ מִקְנֵה קִנְיָנוֹ אֲשֶׁר רָכַשׁ בְּפַדַּן אֲרָם לָבוֹא

וַתַּעַן - Rachel and Leah answer that even they feel like strangers in their father's house because all money went to Laban. Their father shared nothing. So the whole family decides to run away, and Rachel takes her father's idols. These have the power of magic and prophecy, but from the Negative Side.

אֶל־יִצְחָק (ד"פ ב"ן) אָבִיו אַרְצָה כְּנָעַן: (יט) וְלָבָן הָלַךְ (מ"ה) לִגְזֹז
אֶת־צֹאנוֹ וַתִּגְנֹב רָחֵל אֶת־הַתְּרָפִים אֲשֶׁר לְאָבִיהָ: (כ) וַיִּגְנֹב
יַעֲקֹב (יאהדונהי אידהנויה) אֶת־לֵב לָבָן הָאֲרַמִּי עַל־בְּלִי הִגִּיד לוֹ
כִּי בֹרֵחַ הוּא: (כא) וַיִּבְרַח הוּא וְכָל (ילי)־אֲשֶׁר־לוֹ וַיָּקָם
וַיַּעֲבֹר (רפ"ח) אֶת־הַנָּהָר וַיָּשֶׂם אֶת־פָּנָיו הַר הַגִּלְעָד: (כב) וַיֻּגַּד
לְלָבָן בַּיּוֹם (נגד, זן) הַשְּׁלִישִׁי כִּי בָרַח יַעֲקֹב (יאהדונהי אידהנויה): (כג)
וַיִּקַּח (וזעם) אֶת־אֶחָיו עִמּוֹ וַיִּרְדֹּף אַחֲרָיו דֶּרֶךְ (ב"פ יב"ק) שִׁבְעַת
יָמִים (נלך) וַיַּדְבֵּק אֹתוֹ בְּהַר הַגִּלְעָד: (כד) וַיָּבֹא אֱלֹהִים (ילה)
אֶל־לָבָן הָאֲרַמִּי בַּחֲלֹם הַלָּיְלָה (מלה) וַיֹּאמֶר לוֹ הִשָּׁמֶר לְךָ
פֶּן־תְּדַבֵּר (ראה) עִם־יַעֲקֹב (יאהדונהי אידהנויה) מִטּוֹב (והו) עַד־רָע:
(כה) וַיַּשֵּׂג לָבָן אֶת־ יַעֲקֹב (יאהדונהי אידהנויה) וְיַעֲקֹב (יאהדונהי אידהנויה)
תָּקַע (ב"פ סוזך) אֶת־אָהֳלוֹ בָּהָר וְלָבָן תָּקַע (ב"פ סוזך) אֶת־אֶחָיו
בְּהַר הַגִּלְעָד: (כו) וַיֹּאמֶר לָבָן לְיַעֲקֹב (יאהדונהי אידהנויה) מֶה (מ"ה)
עָשִׂיתָ וַתִּגְנֹב אֶת־לְבָבִי וַתְּנַהֵג אֶת־בְּנֹתַי כִּשְׁבֻיוֹת חָרֶב: (כז)
לָמָּה נַחְבֵּאתָ לִבְרֹחַ וַתִּגְנֹב אֹתִי וְלֹא־הִגַּדְתָּ לִּי וָאֲשַׁלֵּחֲךָ

וַיֻּגַּד - When Laban discovers what has happened, he sets off in pursuit. God tells Laban not to give Jacob anything because Laban was so negative that everything he touched became corrupt, even things that would ordinarily be positive. In our own lives, we should be careful about receiving things from negative people, even if we are attracted to what they offer.

בְּשִׂמְחָה וּבְשִׁרִים בְּתֹף וּבְכִנּוֹר׃ (כח) וְלֹא נְטַשְׁתַּנִי לְנַשֵּׁק
לְבָנַי וְלִבְנֹתָי עַתָּה הִסְכַּלְתָּ עֲשׂוֹ׃ (כט) יֶשׁ־לְאֵל יָדִי לַעֲשׂוֹת
עִמָּכֶם רָע וֵאלֹהֵי (לכב) אֲבִיכֶם אֶמֶשׁ | אָמַר אֵלַי לֵאמֹר
הִשָּׁמֶר לְךָ מִדַּבֵּר (ראה) עִם־יַעֲקֹב (יאהדונהי אידהנויה) מִטּוֹב (והו)
עַד־רָע׃ (ל) וְעַתָּה הָלֹךְ (מיה) הָלַכְתָּ כִּי־נִכְסֹף נִכְסַפְתָּה
לְבֵית (ב"פ ראה) אָבִיךָ **לָמָּה** גָנַבְתָּ אֶת־אֱלֹהָי (דמב)׃ (לא) וַיַּעַן
יַעֲקֹב (יאהדונהי אידהנויה) וַיֹּאמֶר לְלָבָן כִּי יָרֵאתִי כִּי אָמַרְתִּי פֶּן
תִּגְזֹל אֶת־בְּנוֹתֶיךָ מֵעִמִּי׃ (לב) עִם אֲשֶׁר תִּמְצָא אֶת־אֱלֹהֶיךָ
(ילה) **לֹא יִחְיֶה** נֶגֶד (זן, מזבח) אַחֵינוּ הַכֶּר־לְךָ מָה (מ"ה) עִמָּדִי
וְקַח־לָךְ וְלֹא־יָדַע יַעֲקֹב (יאהדונהי אידהנויה) כִּי רָחֵל גְּנָבָתַם׃
(לג) וַיָּבֹא לָבָן בְּאֹהֶל־יַעֲקֹב (יאהדונהי אידהנויה) | וּבְאֹהֶל לֵאָה
וּבְאֹהֶל שְׁתֵּי הָאֲמָהֹת וְלֹא מָצָא וַיֵּצֵא מֵאֹהֶל לֵאָה וַיָּבֹא

לָמָּה - Laban declares that he has nothing to say to Jacob. But he does ask, "Who took my idols?" Jacob replies, "Who would do such a thing! Whoever stole your idols shall not live!" Jacob, however, does not know that it was Rachel who took the idols.

לֹא יִחְיֶה - The power of evil speech…
As a result of what Jacob said, Rachel had to die, and she died in childbirth. There is an overwhelmingly important lesson here: We must be very careful of what we say, evil speech (Heb. l'shon hara), especially when we are depressed or angry. The negative angels will hold our words against us. If a woman, God forbid, says in anger, "I'll never have children!" she will prevent herself from becoming pregnant even when she wants to conceive.

בְּאֹהֶל רָחֵל׃ (לד) וְרָחֵל לָקְחָה אֶת־הַתְּרָפִים וַתְּשִׂמֵם בְּכַר
הַגָּמָל וַתֵּשֶׁב עֲלֵיהֶם וַיְמַשֵּׁשׁ לָבָן אֶת־כָּל (ילי)־הָאֹהֶל וְלֹא
מָצָא׃ (לה) וַתֹּאמֶר אֶל־אָבִיהָ אַל־יִחַר בְּעֵינֵי (מ״ה בריבוע) אֲדֹנִי
כִּי לוֹא אוּכַל לָקוּם מִפָּנֶיךָ (סמ״ב) כִּי־דֶרֶךְ (ב״פ יב״ק) נָשִׁים לִי
וַיְחַפֵּשׂ וְלֹא מָצָא אֶת־הַתְּרָפִים׃ (לו) וַיִּחַר לְיַעֲקֹב (יאהדונהי אי־
דהנויה) וַיָּרֶב בְּלָבָן וַיַּעַן יַעֲקֹב (יאהדונהי אידהנויה) וַיֹּאמֶר לְלָבָן מַה
(מ״ה)־פִּשְׁעִי מַה (מ״ה) חַטָּאתִי כִּי דָלַקְתָּ אַחֲרָי׃ (לז) כִּי־מִשַּׁשְׁתָּ
אֶת־כָּל (ילי)־כֵּלַי מַה (מ״ה)־מָּצָאתָ מִכֹּל (ילי) כְּלֵי־בֵיתֶךָ (ב״פ ראה)
שִׂים כֹּה (היי) נֶגֶד (זן, מזבח) אַחַי וְאַחֶיךָ וְיוֹכִיחוּ בֵּין שְׁנֵינוּ׃ (לח)
זֶה עֶשְׂרִים שָׁנָה אָנֹכִי (איע) עִמָּךְ רְחֵלֶיךָ וְעִזֶּיךָ לֹא שִׁכֵּלוּ
וְאֵילֵי צֹאנְךָ לֹא אָכָלְתִּי׃ (לט) טְרֵפָה לֹא־הֵבֵאתִי אֵלֶיךָ
אָנֹכִי (איע) אֲחַטֶּנָּה מִיָּדִי תְּבַקְשֶׁנָּה גְּנֻבְתִי יוֹם (נגד, זן) וּגְנֻבְתִי
לָיְלָה (מלה)׃ (מ) הָיִיתִי בַיּוֹם (נגד, זן) אֲכָלַנִי חֹרֶב וְקֶרַח בַּלָּיְלָה
(מלה) וַתִּדַּד שְׁנָתִי מֵעֵינָי (מ״ה בריבוע)׃ (מא) זֶה־לִּי עֶשְׂרִים שָׁנָה
בְּבֵיתֶךָ (ב״פ ראה) עֲבַדְתִּיךָ אַרְבַּע־עֶשְׂרֵה שָׁנָה בִּשְׁתֵּי בְנֹתֶיךָ
וְשֵׁשׁ שָׁנִים בְּצֹאנֶךָ וַתַּחֲלֵף אֶת־מַשְׂכֻּרְתִּי עֲשֶׂרֶת מֹנִים׃ (מב)
לוּלֵי אֱלֹהֵי (דמב) אָבִי אֱלֹהֵי (דמב) אַבְרָהָם (רמ״ח) וּפַחַד יִצְחָק
(ד״פ ב״ן) הָיָה (יהה) לִי כִּי עַתָּה רֵיקָם שִׁלַּחְתָּנִי אֶת־עָנְיִי (מ״ה בריבוע)
וְאֶת־יְגִיעַ כַּפַּי רָאָה (ראה) אֱלֹהִים (ילה) וַיּוֹכַח אָמֶשׁ׃

Seventh Reading - David - Malchut

(מג) וַיַּעַן לָבָן וַיֹּאמֶר אֶל־יַעֲקֹב (יאהדונהי אידהנויה) הַבָּנוֹת בְּנֹתַי וְהַבָּנִים בָּנַי וְהַצֹּאן צֹאנִי וְכֹל (ילי) אֲשֶׁר־אַתָּה רֹאֶה לִי־הוּא וְלִבְנֹתַי מָה־(מ"ה) אֶעֱשֶׂה לָאֵלֶּה הַיּוֹם (נגד, זן) אוֹ לִבְנֵיהֶן אֲשֶׁר יָלָדוּ: (מד) וְעַתָּה לְכָה נִכְרְתָה בְרִית אֲנִי (אני) וְאַתָּה וְהָיָה (יהוה) לְעֵד בֵּינִי וּבֵינֶךָ: (מה) וַיִּקַּח (וזעם) יַעֲקֹב (יאהדונהי אידהנויה) אֶבֶן וַיְרִימֶהָ מַצֵּבָה: (מו) וַיֹּאמֶר יַעֲקֹב (יאהדונהי אידהנויה) לְאֶחָיו לִקְטוּ אֲבָנִים וַיִּקְחוּ אֲבָנִים וַיַּעֲשׂוּ־גָל וַיֹּאכְלוּ שָׁם עַל־הַגָּל: (מז) וַיִּקְרָא־לוֹ לָבָן יְגַר שָׂהֲדוּתָא וְיַעֲקֹב (יאהדונהי) קָרָא לוֹ גַּלְעֵד: (מח) וַיֹּאמֶר לָבָן הַגַּל הַזֶּה (והו) עֵד בֵּינִי וּבֵינְךָ הַיּוֹם (נגד, זן) עַל־כֵּן קָרָא־שְׁמוֹ (מהש ע"ה) גַּלְעֵד: (מט) וְהַמִּצְפָּה אֲשֶׁר אָמַר יִצֶף יְהֹוָה (יאהדונהי) בֵּינִי וּבֵינֶךָ כִּי נִסָּתֵר (כ"פ מצר) אִישׁ מֵרֵעֵהוּ: (נ) אִם (יוהך) תְּעַנֶּה אֶת־בְּנֹתַי וְאִם (יוהך) תִּקַּח נָשִׁים עַל־בְּנֹתַי אֵין אִישׁ עִמָּנוּ (מילוי דמ"ה) רְאֵה (ראה) אֱלֹהִים (ילה) עֵד בֵּינִי וּבֵינֶךָ: (נא) וַיֹּאמֶר לָבָן לְיַעֲקֹב (יאהדונהי)

בְּרִית - Now Jacob makes a pact of separation with Laban: Neither of them will pass into the other's territory. This represents the total separation of good and evil. Good and evil are clearly defined, yet we often cannot tell one from the other. This section give us the ability to clearly recognize positive and negative - and to make the right choice between them.

(אידהנויה) הִנֵּה | הַגַּל הַזֶּה (והו) וְהִנֵּה הַמַּצֵּבָה אֲשֶׁר יָרִיתִי בֵּינִי
וּבֵינֶךָ׃ (נב) עֵד הַגַּל הַזֶּה (והו) וְעֵדָה (סיט) הַמַּצֵּבָה אִם (יוהך)־אָנִי
(אני) לֹא־אֶעֱבֹר אֵלֶיךָ אֶת־הַגַּל הַזֶּה (והו) וְאִם (יוהך)־אַתָּה לֹא־
תַעֲבֹר אֵלַי אֶת־הַגַּל הַזֶּה (והו) וְאֶת־הַמַּצֵּבָה הַזֹּאת לְרָעָה
(רהע)׃ (נג) אֱלֹהֵי (דמב) אַבְרָהָם (רמ"ח) וֵאלֹהֵי (לכב) נָחוֹר יִשְׁפְּטוּ
בֵינֵינוּ אֱלֹהֵי (דמב) אֲבִיהֶם וַיִּשָּׁבַע יַעֲקֹב (יאהדונהי אידהנויה) בְּפַחַד
אָבִיו יִצְחָק (ד"פ ב"ן)׃ (נד) וַיִּזְבַּח יַעֲקֹב (יאהדונהי אידהנויה) זֶבַח בָּהָר
וַיִּקְרָא לְאֶחָיו לֶאֱכָל־לָחֶם (ג' הויות) וַיֹּאכְלוּ לֶחֶם וַיָּלִינוּ
בָּהָר׃

Maftir

לב (א) וַיַּשְׁכֵּם לָבָן בַּבֹּקֶר וַיְנַשֵּׁק לְבָנָיו וְלִבְנוֹתָיו
וַיְבָרֶךְ (עסמ"ב) אֶתְהֶם וַיֵּלֶךְ (כלי) וַיָּשָׁב לָבָן
לִמְקֹמוֹ׃ (ב) וְיַעֲקֹב (יאהדונהי אידהנויה) הָלַךְ (מיה) לְדַרְכּוֹ
וַיִּפְגְּעוּ־בוֹ מַלְאֲכֵי אֱלֹהִים (ילה)׃ (ג) וַיֹּאמֶר יַעֲקֹב (יאהדונהי
אידהנויה) כַּאֲשֶׁר רָאָם מַחֲנֵה אֱלֹהִים (ילה) זֶה וַיִּקְרָא שֵׁם־
הַמָּקוֹם הַהוּא מַחֲנָיִם׃ פפפ

וַיִּפְגְּעוּ־בוֹ - Jacob goes on his way. Although the angels meet him again, he no longer needs their spiritual protection, nor does he need their help in the cleansing process.

The Haftarah of Vayetze

The Haftarah discusses Jacob's running away. But it is the message against idol-worship that is the important lesson here. Ego, power, money, and a hundred other forces can be our idols in the material world. Anything is an idol if we are enslaved to it and if that slavery prevents us from connecting to the Light.

הוֹשֵׁעַ פֶּרֶק יא

ז וְעַמִּי תְלוּאִים לִמְשׁוּבָתִי וְאֶל־עַל יִקְרָאֻהוּ יַחַד לֹא
יְרוֹמֵם: ח אֵיךְ אֶתֶּנְךָ אֶפְרַיִם אֲמַגֶּנְךָ יִשְׂרָאֵל אֵיךְ אֶתֶּנְךָ
כְאַדְמָה אֲשִׂימְךָ (ילי) כִּצְבֹאיִם נֶהְפַּךְ עָלַי לִבִּי יַחַד נִכְמְרוּ
נִחוּמָי: ט לֹא אֶעֱשֶׂה חֲרוֹן אַפִּי לֹא אָשׁוּב לְשַׁחֵת אֶפְרָיִם
כִּי אֵל אָנֹכִי (אי"ע) וְלֹא־אִישׁ בְּקִרְבְּךָ קָדוֹשׁ וְלֹא אָבוֹא בְּעִיר
(ערי, מוזהך, סנדלפון): י אַחֲרֵי יְהֹוָה יֵלְכוּ כְּאַרְיֵה יִשְׁאָג כִּי־הוּא
יִשְׁאַג וְיֶחֶרְדוּ בָנִים מִיָּם (ילי): יא יֶחֶרְדוּ כְצִפּוֹר מִמִּצְרַיִם (מצר)
וּכְיוֹנָה מֵאֶרֶץ אַשּׁוּר וְהוֹשַׁבְתִּים עַל־בָּתֵּיהֶם נְאֻם־יְהֹוָה:
{ס} א סְבָבֻנִי בְכַחַשׁ אֶפְרַיִם וּבְמִרְמָה בֵּית (ב"פ ראה) יִשְׂרָאֵל
וִיהוּדָה עֹד רָד עִם־אֵל וְעִם־קְדוֹשִׁים נֶאֱמָן: ב אֶפְרַיִם רֹעֶה
(רהע) רוּחַ וְרֹדֵף קָדִים כָּל (ילי) ־הַיּוֹם (נגד, מזבח, זן) כָּזָב וָשֹׁד יַרְבֶּה
וּבְרִית עִם־אַשּׁוּר יִכְרֹתוּ וְשֶׁמֶן לְמִצְרַיִם (מצר) יוּבָל: ג וְרִיב
לַיהֹוָה עִם־יְהוּדָה וְלִפְקֹד עַל־יַעֲקֹב (יאהדונהי אידהנויה) כִּדְרָכָיו
כְּמַעֲלָלָיו יָשִׁיב לוֹ: ד בַּבֶּטֶן עָקַב (ב"פ יב"ק) (מום-מום) אֶת־אָחִיו

וּבְאוֹנוֹ שָׂרָה אֶת־אֱלֹהִים (דמב, ילה): ה וַיָּשַׂר אֶל־מַלְאָךְ וַיֻּכָל
בָּכָה וַיִּתְחַנֶּן־לוֹ (מוזי) בֵּית (ב"פ ראה) ־אֵל יִמְצָאֶנּוּ וְשָׁם יְדַבֵּר (ראה)
עִמָּנוּ: ו וַיהוָה אֱלֹהֵי (דמב, ילה) הַצְּבָאוֹת יְהוָה זִכְרוֹ: ז וְאַתָּה
בֵּאלֹהֶיךָ (דמב, ילה) תָשׁוּב חֶסֶד (ע"ב) וּמִשְׁפָּט שְׁמֹר וְקַוֵּה
אֶל־אֱלֹהֶיךָ (דמב, ילה) תָּמִיד (נתה): ח כְּנַעַן בְּיָדוֹ מֹאזְנֵי מִרְמָה
לַעֲשֹׁק אָהֵב: ט וַיֹּאמֶר אֶפְרַיִם אַךְ (אהיה) עָשַׁרְתִּי מָצָאתִי
אוֹן לִי כָּל־יְגִיעַי לֹא יִמְצְאוּ־לִי עָוֹן אֲשֶׁר־חֵטְא: י וְאָנֹכִי
(איע) יְהוָה אֱלֹהֶיךָ (דמב, ילה) מֵאֶרֶץ מִצְרָיִם (מצר) עֹד אוֹשִׁיבְךָ
בָאֳהָלִים כִּימֵי מוֹעֵד: יא וְדִבַּרְתִּי עַל־הַנְּבִיאִים וְאָנֹכִי (איע)
חָזוֹן הִרְבֵּיתִי וּבְיַד הַנְּבִיאִים אֲדַמֶּה: יב אִם־גִּלְעָד אָוֶן
אַךְ־שָׁוְא הָיוּ בַּגִּלְגָּל שְׁוָרִים זִבֵּחוּ גַּם מִזְבְּחוֹתָם (זן, (נגד, מזבח)
נגד) כְּגַלִּים עַל תַּלְמֵי שָׂדָי:

Lesson of Vayishlach

Rashi wrote concerning this verse: "Rabbi Shimon Bar Yochai said that Esau hated Jacob, but his mercy overcame him at that minute and he kissed him with all his heart." Very simply, this portion concerns hatred - and in the world, hatred seems to be everywhere. Many of us complain that we are hated by others, but Kabbalah teaches that hatred is no one's fault but our own. How can this be explained?

In thinking about this portion, if we focus only on Esau's hatred of Jacob, hatred is exactly what we will find. But when we focus on the other words - "...his mercy overcame him and he kissed him with all his heart" - we connect with a very different energy. It all depends on us, and only on us. If we can only see one side, it is our nature to receive for our self alone. This is the law of "Esau hates Jacob."

But we can also rise above our nature. We can rise above judgment, because if judgment comes onto us, God forbid, it is only because we bring judgment on others. If we don't bring judgment on other people, no one, not even the Satan himself, can condemn us. And the whole world will love us.

It is written: "If we do not see why suffering is coming to us, we should examine our actions, and if we don't find a reason, we should learn Torah." The question is why, if we don't find a reason, we should study? How can Torah study help us find what we did wrong? The answer is this: only by studying Torah will our eyes open a little to the truth. That's why it is written: "Go study Torah."

This week especially, where there is a unique energy to help us see the truth, we must commit to ourselves to study more than usual - at least one more hour a week. By doing this, we will merit seeing not just more happiness, but also miracles with our own eyes.

Synopsis of Vayishlach

Vayishlach means "to send away". It encompasses the energy and consciousness required to let go. Often, we have difficulty detaching ourselves from negative people and situations, and these readings give us the power to overcome such obstacles.

First Reading - Abraham - Chesed

(ד) וַיִּשְׁלַח יַעֲקֹב (יאהדונהי אידהנויה) מַלְאָכִים לְפָנָיו אֶל־עֵשָׂו
אָחִיו אַרְצָה שֵׂעִיר שְׂדֵה אֱדוֹם׃ (ה) וַיְצַו אֹתָם לֵאמֹר כֹּה
(הי) תֹאמְרוּן לַאדֹנִי לְעֵשָׂו כֹּה (הי) אָמַר עַבְדְּךָ (פוי) יַעֲקֹב
(יאהדונהי אידהנויה) עִם־לָבָן גַּרְתִּי וָאֵחַר עַד־עָתָּה׃ (ו) וַיְהִי־לִי שׁוֹר
(אבג יתץ, ושר, אהבת חנם) וַחֲמוֹר צֹאן וְעֶבֶד וְשִׁפְחָה וָאֶשְׁלְחָה לְהַגִּיד
לַאדֹנִי לִמְצֹא־חֵן (מוזי) בְּעֵינֶיךָ (ע"ה קס"א)׃ (ז) וַיָּשֻׁבוּ הַמַּלְאָכִים
אֶל־יַעֲקֹב (יאהדונהי אידהנויה) לֵאמֹר בָּאנוּ אֶל־אָחִיךָ אֶל־עֵשָׂו
וְגַם הֹלֵךְ (מיה) לִקְרָאתְךָ וְאַרְבַּע־מֵאוֹת אִישׁ עִמּוֹ׃ (ח) וַיִּירָא
יַעֲקֹב (יאהדונהי אידהנויה) מְאֹד וַיֵּצֶר לוֹ וַיַּחַץ אֶת־הָעָם אֲשֶׁר־
אִתּוֹ וְאֶת־הַצֹּאן וְאֶת־הַבָּקָר וְהַגְּמַלִּים לִשְׁנֵי מַחֲנוֹת׃ (ט)
וַיֹּאמֶר אִם (יוהך)־יָבוֹא עֵשָׂו אֶל־הַמַּחֲנֶה הָאַחַת וְהִכָּהוּ
וְהָיָה (יהה) (יהוה) הַמַּחֲנֶה הַנִּשְׁאָר לִפְלֵיטָה׃ (י) וַיֹּאמֶר יַעֲקֹב

וַיִּשְׁלַח - Jacob sends angels to his brother, Esau. The angels return to tell Jacob that Esau has 400 of the evil angels with him. Preparation is underway for the battle of good against evil.

וַיַּחַץ - Jacob splits the camp into two. By splitting the camp, Jacob hopes that one half will survive even if the other does not. Though Jacob knew that he might well be defeated, he makes sure that he is prepared. Although our first priority must always be the spiritual dimension, we must also take care of the physical realm.

וַיֹּאמַר - Jacob prays. When something potentially negative is coming our way, we can transform it through the power of prayer.

(יאהדונהי אידהנויה) אֱלֹהֵי (דמב) אָבִי אַבְרָהָם (רמ"ח) וֵאלֹהֵי (לכב)
אָבִי יִצְחָק (ד"פ ב"ן) יְהֹוָהאדנייאהדונהי הָאֹמֵר אֵלַי שׁוּב לְאַרְצְךָ
וּלְמוֹלַדְתְּךָ וְאֵיטִיבָה עִמָּךְ: (יא) קָטֹנְתִּי מִכֹּל (ילי) הַחֲסָדִים
וּמִכָּל (ילי)־הָאֱמֶת (אהיה פ' אהיה) אֲשֶׁר עָשִׂיתָ אֶת־עַבְדֶּךָ (פוי) כִּי
בְמַקְלִי עָבַרְתִּי אֶת־הַיַּרְדֵּן (י' הויות וד' אותיות) הַזֶּה (והו) וְעַתָּה
הָיִיתִי לִשְׁנֵי מַחֲנוֹת: (יב) הַצִּילֵנִי נָא מִיַּד אָחִי מִיַּד עֵשָׂו כִּי־
יָרֵא אָנֹכִי (איע) אֹתוֹ פֶּן־יָבוֹא וְהִכַּנִי אֵם (יוהך) עַל־בָּנִים: (יג)
וְאַתָּה אָמַרְתָּ הֵיטֵב אֵיטִיב עִמָּךְ וְשַׂמְתִּי אֶת־זַרְעֲךָ כְּחוֹל
הַיָּם (ילי) אֲשֶׁר לֹא־יִסָּפֵר מֵרֹב:

Second Reading - Issac - Gvurah

(יד) וַיָּלֶן שָׁם בַּלַּיְלָה (מלה) הַהוּא וַיִּקַּח (וזעם) מִן־הַבָּא בְיָדוֹ
מִנְחָה (ע"ה ב"פ ב"ן) לְעֵשָׂו אָחִיו: (טו) עִזִּים מָאתַיִם וּתְיָשִׁים
עֶשְׂרִים רְחֵלִים מָאתַיִם וְאֵילִים עֶשְׂרִים: (טז) גְּמַלִּים
מֵינִיקוֹת וּבְנֵיהֶם שְׁלֹשִׁים פָּרוֹת אַרְבָּעִים וּפָרִים עֲשָׂרָה
אֲתֹנֹת עֶשְׂרִים וַעְיָרִם עֲשָׂרָה: (יז) וַיִּתֵּן בְּיַד־עֲבָדָיו עֵדֶר

מִנְחָה - Jacob offers a sacrifice to Esau. This reminds us that we should always give something to the Negative Side, just as we give a small piece of challah on Shabbat. By distracting the Satan in this way, we can gain control over him and the negative energy he commands.

עֵדֶר לְבַדּוֹ (מ"ב) וַיֹּאמֶר אֶל־עֲבָדָיו עִבְרוּ לְפָנַי וְרֶוַח תָּשִׂימוּ
בֵּין עֵדֶר וּבֵין עֵדֶר׃ (יח) וַיְצַו אֶת־הָרִאשׁוֹן לֵאמֹר כִּי יִפְגָּשְׁךָ
עֵשָׂו אָחִי וּשְׁאֵלְךָ לֵאמֹר לְמִי (ילי)־אַתָּה וְאָנָה תֵלֵךְ וּלְמִי
(ילי) אֵלֶּה לְפָנֶיךָ (סמ"ב)׃ (יט) וְאָמַרְתָּ לְעַבְדְּךָ (פוי) לְיַעֲקֹב (יאהדונהי
אידהנויה) מִנְחָה (ע"ה ב"פ ב"ן) הִוא שְׁלוּחָה (מהש) לַאדֹנִי לְעֵשָׂו וְהִנֵּה
גַם־הוּא אַחֲרֵינוּ׃ (כ) וַיְצַו גַּם אֶת־הַשֵּׁנִי גַּם אֶת־הַשְּׁלִישִׁי גַּם
אֶת־כָּל (ילי)־הַהֹלְכִים אַחֲרֵי הָעֲדָרִים לֵאמֹר כַּדָּבָר (ראה)
הַזֶּה (והו) תְּדַבְּרוּן (ראה) אֶל־עֵשָׂו בְּמֹצַאֲכֶם אֹתוֹ׃ (כא) וַאֲמַרְתֶּם
גַּם הִנֵּה עַבְדְּךָ (פוי) יַעֲקֹב (יאהדונהי אידהנויה) אַחֲרֵינוּ כִּי־אָמַר
אֲכַפְּרָה פָנָיו בַּמִּנְחָה (ע"ה ב"פ ב"ן) הַהֹלֶכֶת לְפָנָי וְאַחֲרֵי־כֵן
אֶרְאֶה פָנָיו אוּלַי (אום) יִשָּׂא פָנָי (חכמה, בינה)׃ (כב) וַתַּעֲבֹר הַמִּנְחָה
(ע"ה ב"פ ב"ן) עַל־פָּנָיו וְהוּא לָן בַּלַּיְלָה (מלה)־הַהוּא בַּמַּחֲנֶה׃ (כג)
וַיָּקָם | בַּלַּיְלָה (מלה) הוּא וַיִּקַּח (וזעם) אֶת־שְׁתֵּי נָשָׁיו וְאֶת־שְׁתֵּי
שִׁפְחֹתָיו וְאֶת־אַחַד (אהבה) עָשָׂר יְלָדָיו וַיַּעֲבֹר (רפ"ח) אֵת מַעֲבַר
יַבֹּק׃ (כד) וַיִּקָּחֵם וַיַּעֲבִרֵם אֶת־הַנָּחַל וַיַּעֲבֵר אֶת־אֲשֶׁר־לוֹ׃
(כה) וַיִּוָּתֵר יַעֲקֹב (יאהדונהי אידהנויה) לְבַדּוֹ (מ"ב) וַיֵּאָבֵק אִישׁ עִמּוֹ

וַיֵּאָבֵק - Jacob fights with the angel of Esau. This is the battle between good and evil. What happens on the physical level is a manifestation of what happens "here" on the spiritual level: as above, so below.

עַד עֲלוֹת הַשָּׁחַר׃ (כו) וַיַּרְא כִּי לֹא יָכֹל לוֹ וַיִּגַּע בְּכַף־יְרֵכוֹ
וַתֵּקַע (כ"פ סוזפר) כַּף־יֶרֶךְ יַעֲקֹב (יאהדונהי אידהנויה) בְּהֵאָבְקוֹ עִמּוֹ׃
(כז) וַיֹּאמֶר שַׁלְּחֵנִי כִּי עָלָה הַשָּׁחַר וַיֹּאמֶר לֹא אֲשַׁלֵּחֲךָ כִּי
אִם (יוהך)־ בֵּרַכְתָּנִי׃ (כח) וַיֹּאמֶר אֵלָיו מַה (מ"ה)־שְּׁמֶךָ וַיֹּאמֶר
יַעֲקֹב (יאהדונהי אידהנויה)׃ (כט) וַיֹּאמֶר לֹא יַעֲקֹב (יאהדונהי אידהנויה) יֵאָמֵר
עוֹד שִׁמְךָ כִּי אִם (יוהך)־ יִשְׂרָאֵל כִּי־שָׂרִיתָ עִם־אֱלֹהִים (ילה)
וְעִם־אֲנָשִׁים וַתּוּכָל׃ (ל) וַיִּשְׁאַל יַעֲקֹב (יאהדונהי אידהנויה) וַיֹּאמֶר
הַגִּידָה־נָּא שְׁמֶךָ וַיֹּאמֶר לָמָּה זֶּה תִּשְׁאַל לִשְׁמִי וַיְבָרֶךְ
(עסמ"ב) אֹתוֹ שָׁם׃

Third Reading - Jacob - Tiferet

(לא) וַיִּקְרָא יַעֲקֹב (יאהדונהי אידהנויה) שֵׁם הַמָּקוֹם פְּנִיאֵל כִּי־רָאִיתִי
אֱלֹהִים (ילה) פָּנִים אֶל־פָּנִים וַתִּנָּצֵל נַפְשִׁי׃ (לב) וַיִּזְרַח־לוֹ

בֵּרַכְתָּנִי - When Jacob wins the battle with the angel, he asks the angel for a blessing. This is Esau's angel, and the lesson here pertains to Esau's letting go. When Esau asked Isaac for his blessing, he felt that Jacob had stolen it from him and that he still deserved it. Now, through the angel, we see that Esau is letting go of his desire for the blessing. Because Jacob wins, the Esau's angel gives up his claim to blessing, because he lost.

יִשְׂרָאֵל - The angel then changes Jacob's name to Israel , signifying Jacob's ascent to a higher spiritual level.

הַשֶּׁמֶשׁ כַּאֲשֶׁר עָבַר אֶת־פְּנוּאֵל וְהוּא צֹלֵעַ עַל־יְרֵכוֹ׃ (לג)
עַל־כֵּן לֹא־יֹאכְלוּ בְנֵי־יִשְׂרָאֵל אֶת־גִּיד הַנָּשֶׁה אֲשֶׁר עַל־
כַּף הַיָּרֵךְ עַד הַיּוֹם (נגד, זך) הַזֶּה (והו) כִּי נָגַע בְּכַף־יֶרֶךְ יַעֲקֹב
(יאהדונהי אידהנויה) בְּגִיד הַנָּשֶׁה׃ לג (א) וַיִּשָּׂא יַעֲקֹב (יאהדונהי אידהנויה)
עֵינָיו (מ"ה בריבוע) וַיַּרְא וְהִנֵּה עֵשָׂו בָּא וְעִמּוֹ אַרְבַּע מֵאוֹת אִישׁ
וַיַּחַץ אֶת־הַיְלָדִים עַל־לֵאָה וְעַל־רָחֵל וְעַל שְׁתֵּי הַשְּׁפָחוֹת׃
(ב) וַיָּשֶׂם אֶת־הַשְּׁפָחוֹת וְאֶת־יַלְדֵיהֶן רִאשֹׁנָה וְאֶת־לֵאָה
וִילָדֶיהָ אַחֲרֹנִים וְאֶת־רָחֵל וְאֶת־יוֹסֵף (ציון) אַחֲרֹנִים׃ (ג) וְהוּא
עָבַר לִפְנֵיהֶם וַיִּשְׁתַּחוּ אַרְצָה שֶׁבַע פְּעָמִים עַד־גִּשְׁתּוֹ
עַד־אָחִיו׃ (ד) וַיָּרָץ עֵשָׂו לִקְרָאתוֹ וַיְחַבְּקֵהוּ וַיִּפֹּל עַל־צַוָּארָו
וַיִּשָּׁקֵהוּ וַיִּבְכּוּ׃ (ה) וַיִּשָּׂא אֶת־עֵינָיו (מ"ה בריבוע) וַיַּרְא אֶת־

צֹלֵעַ - Jacob is limping from sciatica. During the struggle, the angel hit Jacob on the sciatic nerve. Of the 365 sinews of the body, it is only here in the sciatic nerve that the Satan has complete control. This was the only place on Jacob's body that the negative angel could penetrate.

וַיִּשָּׁקֵהוּ - Dots over Vayishakehu (Eng. 'he kissed him') - Esau runs to Jacob and kisses him. Rabbi Shimon Bar bar Yochai tells us that Esau hated Jacob, but at that moment he ran to kiss him, he loved him. People can be so different - Esau was totally negative, and Jacob was completely positive - but love and human dignity are always possible. If these positive feelings could exist between Jacob and Esau, how much more should we feel them for those around us! The dots over the Vayishakehu give us energy to do this.

הַנָּשִׁים וְאֶת־הַיְלָדִים וַיֹּאמֶר מִי (ילי)־אֵלֶּה לָּךְ וַיֹּאמַר
הַיְלָדִים אֲשֶׁר־חָנַן אֱלֹהִים (ילה) אֶת־עַבְדֶּךָ (פוי):

Fourth Reading - Moses - Netzach

(ו) וַתִּגַּשְׁןָ הַשְּׁפָחוֹת הֵנָּה וְיַלְדֵיהֶן וַתִּשְׁתַּחֲוֶיןָ: (ז) וַתִּגַּשׁ גַּם־
לֵאָה וִילָדֶיהָ וַיִּשְׁתַּחֲווּ וְאַחַר נִגַּשׁ יוֹסֵף (ציון) וְרָחֵל וַיִּשְׁתַּחֲווּ:
(ח) וַיֹּאמֶר מִי (ילי) לְךָ כָּל (ילי)־הַמַּחֲנֶה הַזֶּה (והו) אֲשֶׁר פָּגָשְׁתִּי
וַיֹּאמֶר לִמְצֹא־חֵן (מוזי) בְּעֵינֵי (מ"ה בריבוע) אֲדֹנִי: (ט) וַיֹּאמֶר עֵשָׂו
יֶשׁ־לִי רָב אָחִי יְהִי לְךָ אֲשֶׁר־לָךְ: (י) וַיֹּאמֶר יַעֲקֹב (יאהדונהי)
(אידהנויה) אַל־נָא אִם (יוהך)־נָא מָצָאתִי חֵן (מוזי) בְּעֵינֶיךָ (ע"ה קס"א)
וְלָקַחְתָּ מִנְחָתִי מִיָּדִי כִּי עַל־כֵּן רָאִיתִי פָנֶיךָ (סמ"ב) כִּרְאֹת
פְּנֵי (חכמה, בינה) אֱלֹהִים (ילה) וַתִּרְצֵנִי: (יא) קַח־נָא אֶת־בִּרְכָתִי
אֲשֶׁר הֻבָאת לָךְ כִּי־חַנַּנִי אֱלֹהִים (ילה) וְכִי יֶשׁ־לִי־כֹל (ילי)
וַיִּפְצַר־בּוֹ וַיִּקָּח (ועם): (יב) וַיֹּאמֶר נִסְעָה וְנֵלֵכָה וְאֵלְכָה
לְנֶגְדֶּךָ (זן, מזבח): (יג) וַיֹּאמֶר אֵלָיו אֲדֹנִי יֹדֵעַ כִּי־הַיְלָדִים רַכִּים
וְהַצֹּאן וְהַבָּקָר עָלוֹת עָלָי וּדְפָקוּם יוֹם (נגד, זן) אֶחָד (אהבה)

וְלָקַחְתָּ - Jacob wants to give Esau everything. Jacob wants to give Esau everything, but Esau doesn't want to accept. Jacob knows that the Satan has to get something, and by giving to Esau, Jacob will be able to control how much the Satan gets. Remember, the Satan will take some part of what we do. When something negative happens, we must resign ourselves to giving the Satan his due. If we resist this process, we make it possible for the Satan to take even more - and perhaps even everything.

וּמֵתוּ כָּל (ילי) ־הַצֹּאן׃ (יד) יַעֲבָר־נָא אֲדֹנִי לִפְנֵי עַבְדּוֹ וַאֲנִי
(אני) אֶתְנָהֲלָה לְאִטִּי לְרֶגֶל הַמְּלָאכָה אֲשֶׁר־לְפָנַי וּלְרֶגֶל
הַיְלָדִים עַד אֲשֶׁר־אָבֹא אֶל־אֲדֹנִי שֵׂעִירָה׃ (טו) וַיֹּאמֶר
עֵשָׂו אַצִּיגָה־נָּא עִמְּךָ מִן־הָעָם אֲשֶׁר אִתִּי וַיֹּאמֶר לָמָּה
זֶּה אֶמְצָא־חֵן (מוזי) בְּעֵינֵי (מ"ה בריבוע) אֲדֹנִי׃ (טז) וַיָּשָׁב בַּיּוֹם (נגד,
זן) הַהוּא עֵשָׂו לְדַרְכּוֹ שֵׂעִירָה׃ (יז) וְיַעֲקֹב (יאהדונהי אידהנויה) נָסַע
סֻכֹּתָה וַיִּבֶן לוֹ בָּיִת (ב"פ ראה) וּלְמִקְנֵהוּ עָשָׂה סֻכֹּת עַל־כֵּן
קָרָא שֵׁם־הַמָּקוֹם סֻכּוֹת׃ ס (יח) וַיָּבֹא יַעֲקֹב (יאהדונהי אידהנויה)
שָׁלֵם עִיר (סן זהר, סנדלפון, ערי) שְׁכֶם אֲשֶׁר בְּאֶרֶץ כְּנַעַן בְּבֹאוֹ
מִפַּדַּן אֲרָם וַיִּחַן אֶת־פְּנֵי (חכמה, בינה) הָעִיר (סן זהר, סנדלפון, ערי)׃ (יט)
וַיִּקֶן אֶת־חֶלְקַת הַשָּׂדֶה אֲשֶׁר נָטָה־שָׁם אָהֳלוֹ מִיַּד בְּנֵי־
חֲמוֹר אֲבִי שְׁכֶם בְּמֵאָה קְשִׂיטָה׃ (כ) וַיַּצֶּב־שָׁם מִזְבֵּחַ (זן)
וַיִּקְרָא־לוֹ אֵל אֱלֹהֵי (דמב) יִשְׂרָאֵל׃ ס

Fifth Reading - Aaron - Hod

לד (א) וַתֵּצֵא דִינָה בַּת־לֵאָה אֲשֶׁר יָלְדָה לְיַעֲקֹב (יאהדונהי איד־

שְׁכֶם - Jacob comes to the city of Sh'chem (Eng. 'Nablus'), Jacob buys a piece of land that will eventually be the burial place of Joseph. The spot is a place of high energy, but it is not Joseph being buried there that makes the place holy. The physical can never be a cause of the spiritual; the spiritual is always the cause, the seed level. Joseph will be buried in this spot because it is a place of high energy.

הנויה) לִרְאוֹת בִּבְנוֹת הָאָרֶץ (מילוי אלהים ע"ה): (ב) וַיַּרְא אֹתָהּ שְׁכֶם
בֶּן־חֲמוֹר הַחִוִּי נְשִׂיא הָאָרֶץ (מילוי אלהים ע"ה) וַיִּקַּח (וזעם) אֹתָהּ
וַיִּשְׁכַּב אֹתָהּ וַיְעַנֶּהָ: (ג) וַתִּדְבַּק נַפְשׁוֹ בְּדִינָה בַּת־יַעֲקֹב (יא־
הדונהי אידהנויה) וַיֶּאֱהַב אֶת־הַנַּעֲרָ וַיְדַבֵּר (ראה) עַל־לֵב הַנַּעֲרָ: (ד)
וַיֹּאמֶר שְׁכֶם אֶל־חֲמוֹר אָבִיו לֵאמֹר קַח־לִי אֶת־הַיַּלְדָּה
הַזֹּאת לְאִשָּׁה: (ה) וְיַעֲקֹב (יאהדונהי אידהנויה) שָׁמַע כִּי טִמֵּא אֶת־
דִּינָה בִתּוֹ וּבָנָיו הָיוּ אֶת־מִקְנֵהוּ בַּשָּׂדֶה וְהֶחֱרִשׁ יַעֲקֹב (יא־
הדונהי אידהנויה) עַד־בֹּאָם: (ו) וַיֵּצֵא חֲמוֹר אֲבִי־שְׁכֶם אֶל־יַעֲקֹב
(יאהדונהי אידהנויה) לְדַבֵּר (ראה) אִתּוֹ: (ז) וּבְנֵי יַעֲקֹב (יאהדונהי אידהנויה)
בָּאוּ מִן־הַשָּׂדֶה כְּשָׁמְעָם וַיִּתְעַצְּבוּ הָאֲנָשִׁים וַיִּחַר לָהֶם
מְאֹד כִּי־נְבָלָה עָשָׂה בְיִשְׂרָאֵל לִשְׁכַּב אֶת־בַּת־יַעֲקֹב (יאה־
דונהי אידהנויה) וְכֵן לֹא יֵעָשֶׂה: (ח) וַיְדַבֵּר (ראה) חֲמוֹר אִתָּם לֵאמֹר
שְׁכֶם בְּנִי חָשְׁקָה נַפְשׁוֹ בְּבִתְּכֶם תְּנוּ נָא אֹתָהּ לוֹ לְאִשָּׁה:
(ט) וְהִתְחַתְּנוּ אֹתָנוּ בְּנֹתֵיכֶם תִּתְּנוּ־לָנוּ (מום) וְאֶת־בְּנֹתֵינוּ תִּקְחוּ
לָכֶם: (י) וְאִתָּנוּ תֵּשֵׁבוּ וְהָאָרֶץ (מילוי אלהים ע"ה) תִּהְיֶה לִפְנֵיכֶם
שְׁבוּ וּסְחָרוּהָ וְהֵאָחֲזוּ בָּהּ: (יא) וַיֹּאמֶר שְׁכֶם אֶל־אָבִיהָ וְאֶל־
אַחֶיהָ אֶמְצָא־חֵן (מוזי) בְּעֵינֵיכֶם (מ"ה בריבוע) וַאֲשֶׁר תֹּאמְרוּ אֵלַי
אֶתֵּן: (יב) הַרְבּוּ עָלַי מְאֹד מֹהַר וּמַתָּן וְאֶתְּנָה כַּאֲשֶׁר תֹּאמְרוּ

אֵלָ֑י וּתְנוּ־לִ֥י אֶת־הַֽנַּעֲרָ֖ לְאִשָּֽׁה׃ (יג) וַיַּעֲנ֨וּ בְנֵֽי־יַעֲקֹ֜ב (יא־
הדונהי אידהנויה) אֶת־שְׁכֶ֨ם וְאֶת־חֲמ֥וֹר אָבִ֛יו בְּמִרְמָ֖ה וַיְדַבֵּ֑רוּ
(ראה) אֲשֶׁ֣ר טִמֵּ֔א אֵ֖ת דִּינָ֥ה אֲחֹתָֽם׃ (יד) וַיֹּאמְר֣וּ אֲלֵיהֶ֗ם לֹ֤א
נוּכַל֙ לַעֲשׂוֹת֙ הַדָּבָ֣ר (ראה) הַזֶּ֔ה (והו) לָתֵת֙ אֶת־אֲחֹתֵ֔נוּ לְאִ֖ישׁ
אֲשֶׁר־ל֣וֹ עָרְלָ֑ה כִּֽי־חֶרְפָּ֥ה הִ֖וא לָֽנוּ (מום)׃ (טו) אַ֥ךְ (אהיה)־בְּזֹ֖את
נֵא֣וֹת לָכֶ֑ם אִ֚ם תִּהְי֣וּ (יוהך) כָמֹ֔נוּ לְהִמֹּ֥ל לָכֶ֖ם כָּל (ילי)־זָכָֽר׃
(טז) וְנָתַ֤נּוּ אֶת־בְּנֹתֵ֙ינוּ֙ לָכֶ֔ם וְאֶת־בְּנֹתֵיכֶ֖ם נִֽקַּֽח־לָ֑נוּ (מום)
וְיָשַׁ֣בְנוּ אִתְּכֶ֔ם וְהָיִ֖ינוּ לְעַ֥ם (עלם) אֶחָֽד (אהבה)׃ (יז) וְאִם (יוהך)־לֹ֧א
תִשְׁמְע֛וּ אֵלֵ֖ינוּ לְהִמּ֑וֹל וְלָקַ֥חְנוּ אֶת־בִּתֵּ֖נוּ וְהָלָֽכְנוּ׃ (יח) וַיִּיטְב֥וּ
דִבְרֵיהֶ֖ם (ראה) בְּעֵינֵ֣י (מ"ה בריבוע) חֲמ֑וֹר וּבְעֵינֵ֖י (מ"ה בריבוע) שְׁכֶ֥ם
בֶּן־חֲמֽוֹר׃ (יט) וְלֹֽא־אֵחַ֤ר הַנַּ֙עַר֙ לַעֲשׂ֣וֹת הַדָּבָ֔ר (ראה) כִּ֥י חָפֵ֖ץ
בְּבַֽת־יַעֲקֹ֑ב (יאהדונהי אידהנויה) וְה֛וּא נִכְבָּ֔ד מִכֹּ֖ל (ילי) בֵּ֥ית (ב"פ ראה)
אָבִֽיו׃ (כ) וַיָּבֹ֥א חֲמ֛וֹר וּשְׁכֶ֥ם בְּנ֖וֹ אֶל־שַׁ֣עַר עִירָ֑ם (סוזוהך, סנדלפון,
ערי) וַיְדַבְּר֛וּ (ראה) אֶל־אַנְשֵׁ֥י עִירָ֖ם (סוזוהך, סנדלפון, ערי) לֵאמֹֽר׃ (כא)
הָאֲנָשִׁ֨ים הָאֵ֜לֶּה שְׁלֵמִ֧ים הֵ֣ם אִתָּ֗נוּ וְיֵשְׁב֤וּ בָאָ֙רֶץ֙ וְיִסְחֲר֣וּ
אֹתָ֔הּ וְהָאָ֛רֶץ הִנֵּ֥ה (מילוי אלהים ע"ה) רַחֲבַת־יָדַ֖יִם לִפְנֵיהֶ֑ם אֶת־

וּתְנוּ־לִי - Sh'chem wants to marry Dina, the daughter of Jacob and Leah Sh'chem states his wishes and is told that he can marry Dina if he circumcises all the men of his town.

בְּנֹתָם נִקַּח־לָנוּ (מום) לְנָשִׁים וְאֶת־בְּנֹתֵינוּ נִתֵּן לָהֶם: (כב) אַךְ
(אהיה) ־בְּזֹאת יֵאֹתוּ לָנוּ (מום) הָאֲנָשִׁים לָשֶׁבֶת אִתָּנוּ לִהְיוֹת
לְעַם (עלם) אֶחָד (אהבה) בְּהִמּוֹל לָנוּ (מום) כָּל (ילי) ־זָכָר כַּאֲשֶׁר
הֵם נִמֹּלִים: (כג) מִקְנֵהֶם וְקִנְיָנָם וְכָל (ילי) ־בְּהֶמְתָּם הֲלוֹא לָנוּ
(מום) הֵם אַךְ (אהיה) נֵאוֹתָה לָהֶם וְיֵשְׁבוּ אִתָּנוּ: (כד) וַיִּשְׁמְעוּ אֶל־
חֲמוֹר וְאֶל־שְׁכֶם בְּנוֹ כָּל (ילי) ־יֹצְאֵי שַׁעַר עִירוֹ (בן־זהר, סנדלפון, ערי)
וַיִּמֹּלוּ כָּל (ילי) ־זָכָר כָּל (ילי) ־ יֹצְאֵי שַׁעַר עִירוֹ (בן־זהר, סנדלפון, ערי):
(כה) וַיְהִי בַיּוֹם (נגד, זן) הַשְּׁלִישִׁי בִּהְיוֹתָם כֹּאֲבִים וַיִּקְחוּ שְׁנֵי־
בְנֵי־יַעֲקֹב (יאהדונהי אידהנויה) שִׁמְעוֹן וְלֵוִי אֲחֵי דִינָה אִישׁ חַרְבּוֹ
(רי״ו) וַיָּבֹאוּ עַל־הָעִיר (בן־זהר, סנדלפון, ערי) בֶּטַח וַיַּהַרְגוּ כָּל (ילי) ־
זָכָר: (כו) וְאֶת־חֲמוֹר וְאֶת־שְׁכֶם בְּנוֹ הָרְגוּ לְפִי־חָרֶב וַיִּקְחוּ
אֶת־דִּינָה מִבֵּית (ב״פ ראה) שְׁכֶם וַיֵּצֵאוּ: (כז) בְּנֵי יַעֲקֹב (יאהדונהי
אידהנויה) בָּאוּ עַל־הַחֲלָלִים וַיָּבֹזּוּ הָעִיר (בן־זהר, סנדלפון, ערי) אֲשֶׁר

וַיְהִי - On the third day, when the pain is at its worst, Shimon and Levy, Dina's brothers, slaughter all the newly circumcised men.

The city of Sh'chem was known as a place of negative energy and negative people. The deaths that occurred in this incident were a cleansing of the judgment that was in Sh'chem. There are some people who are completely negative. None of us can really determine who these people are, but Jacob and his sons were able to make this judgment. They knew exactly who needed to be eliminated for a cleansing to take place, and they carried out the task.

טִמְּאוּ אֲחוֹתָם׃ (כח) אֶת־צֹאנָם וְאֶת־בְּקָרָם וְאֶת־חֲמֹרֵיהֶם
וְאֵת אֲשֶׁר־בָּעִיר (סוזרך, סנדלפון, ערי) וְאֶת־אֲשֶׁר בַּשָּׂדֶה לָקָחוּ׃
(כט) וְאֶת־כָּל (ילי)־חֵילָם וְאֶת־כָּל (ילי)־טַפָּם וְאֶת־נְשֵׁיהֶם שָׁבוּ
וַיָּבֹזּוּ וְאֵת כָּל (ילי)־אֲשֶׁר בַּבָּיִת (ב"פ ראה)׃ (ל) וַיֹּאמֶר יַעֲקֹב (יא-
הדונהי אידהנויה) אֶל־שִׁמְעוֹן וְאֶל־לֵוִי עֲכַרְתֶּם אֹתִי לְהַבְאִישֵׁנִי
בְּיֹשֵׁב הָאָרֶץ (מילוי אלהים ע"ה) בַּכְּנַעֲנִי וּבַפְּרִזִּי וַאֲנִי (אני) מְתֵי
מִסְפָּר וְנֶאֶסְפוּ עָלַי וְהִכּוּנִי וְנִשְׁמַדְתִּי אֲנִי (אני) וּבֵיתִי (ב"פ ראה)׃
(לא) וַיֹּאמְרוּ הַכְזוֹנָה יַעֲשֶׂה אֶת־אֲחוֹתֵנוּ׃ פ לה (א) וַיֹּאמֶר
אֱלֹהִים (ילה) אֶל־יַעֲקֹב (יאהדונהי אידהנויה) קוּם עֲלֵה בֵית (ב"פ ראה)־
אֵל וְשֶׁב־שָׁם וַעֲשֵׂה־שָׁם מִזְבֵּחַ (זן) לָאֵל הַנִּרְאֶה אֵלֶיךָ
בְּבָרְחֲךָ מִפְּנֵי עֵשָׂו אָחִיךָ׃ (ב) וַיֹּאמֶר יַעֲקֹב (יאהדונהי אידהנויה)
אֶל־בֵּיתוֹ (ב"פ ראה) וְאֶל כָּל (ילי)־אֲשֶׁר עִמּוֹ הָסִרוּ אֶת־אֱלֹהֵי
(רמב) הַנֵּכָר אֲשֶׁר בְּתֹכְכֶם וְהִטַּהֲרוּ וְהַחֲלִיפוּ שִׂמְלֹתֵיכֶם׃ (ג)
וְנָקוּמָה וְנַעֲלֶה בֵּית (ב"פ ראה)־אֵל וְאֶעֱשֶׂה־שָּׁם מִזְבֵּחַ (זן) לָאֵל
הָעֹנֶה אֹתִי בְּיוֹם (נגד, זן) צָרָתִי וַיְהִי עִמָּדִי בַּדֶּרֶךְ (ב"פ יב"ק) אֲשֶׁר
הָלָכְתִּי׃ (ד) וַיִּתְּנוּ אֶל־יַעֲקֹב (יאהדונהי אידהנויה) אֵת כָּל (ילי)־אֱלֹהֵי

עֲלֵה - Going back into the land of Israel. God tells Jacob to return to the place where he dreamed of the angels and the ladder. This is the spot where the Temple will eventually be built. But first, there are idols and idol-worship that must be dealt with.

(דמב) הַנֵּכָר אֲשֶׁר בְּיָדָם וְאֶת־הַנְּזָמִים אֲשֶׁר בְּאָזְנֵיהֶם (יוד
הי ואו הה) וַיִּטְמֹן אֹתָם יַעֲקֹב (יאהדונהי אידהנויה) תַּחַת הָאֵלָה אֲשֶׁר
עִם־שְׁכֶם׃ (ה) וַיִּסָּעוּ וַיְהִי ׀ חִתַּת אֱלֹהִים (ילה) עַל־הֶעָרִים
אֲשֶׁר סְבִיבֹתֵיהֶם וְלֹא רָדְפוּ אַחֲרֵי בְּנֵי יַעֲקֹב (יאהדונהי אידהנויה)׃
(ו) וַיָּבֹא יַעֲקֹב (יאהדונהי אידהנויה) לוּזָה אֲשֶׁר בְּאֶרֶץ כְּנַעַן הִוא
בֵּית (ב"פ ראה) ־אֵל הוּא וְכָל (ילי) ־הָעָם אֲשֶׁר־עִמּוֹ׃ (ז) וַיִּבֶן שָׁם
מִזְבֵּחַ (זן) וַיִּקְרָא לַמָּקוֹם אֵל בֵּית (ב"פ ראה) ־אֵל כִּי שָׁם נִגְלוּ
אֵלָיו הָאֱלֹהִים (ילה) בְּבָרְחוֹ מִפְּנֵי אָחִיו׃ (ח) וַתָּמָת דְּבֹרָה
מֵינֶקֶת רִבְקָה וַתִּקָּבֵר מִתַּחַת לְבֵית (ב"פ ראה) ־אֵל תַּחַת

וַיִּטְמֹן - The meaning of idol-worship is often oversimplified. The concept is broader than the worship of trees or statues. The more prevalent and negative forms of idol-worship include devotion to such things as ego, power, control, and wealth. When there is something in our life that is more important to us than our devotion to the Light of the Creator, we are engaging in idol- worship.

וַתָּמָת - Rebecca's nurse, Deborah, dies. Quite abruptly, the Torah states that Rebecca's nurse has died. However, our sages explain that it is really Rebecca who died, but Jacob was not present to honor her at the time of her death. Why wasn't Jacob there, and why doesn't the Torah explicitly mention this? In fact, Jacob was allowed to be absent because he was engaged in the important spiritual work of struggling with the angel of Esau.

There are times when we cannot fulfill certain obligations because we have other, more pressing ones. Sometimes, a higher spiritual purpose takes us away from our everyday responsibilities. And sometimes, the Satan causes us to miss an obligation, and once he's accomplished this, he goes on to make us feel guilty about it!

הָאַלּוֹן וַיִּקְרָא שְׁמוֹ (מהש ע"ה) אַלּוֹן בָּכוּת: פ (ט) וַיֵּרָא אֱלֹהִים
(ילה) אֶל־יַעֲקֹב (יאהדונהי אידהנויה) עוֹד בְּבֹאוֹ מִפַּדַּן אֲרָם וַיְבָרֶךְ
אֹתוֹ: (עסמ"ב) (י) וַיֹּאמֶר־לוֹ אֱלֹהִים (ילה) שִׁמְךָ יַעֲקֹב (יאהדונהי
אידהנויה) לֹא־יִקָּרֵא שִׁמְךָ עוֹד יַעֲקֹב (יאהדונהי אידהנויה) כִּי אִם (יוהך)־
יִשְׂרָאֵל יִהְיֶה (ייי) שְׁמֶךָ וַיִּקְרָא אֶת־שְׁמוֹ (מהש ע"ה) יִשְׂרָאֵל: (יא)
וַיֹּאמֶר לוֹ אֱלֹהִים (ילה) אֲנִי (אני) אֵל שַׁדַּי (מהש) פְּרֵה וּרְבֵה גּוֹי
וּקְהַל גּוֹיִם יִהְיֶה (ייי) מִמֶּךָּ וּמְלָכִים מֵחֲלָצֶיךָ יֵצֵאוּ:

Sixth Reading - Joseph - Yesod

(יב) וְאֶת־הָאָרֶץ (מילוי אלהים ע"ה) אֲשֶׁר נָתַתִּי לְאַבְרָהָם (רמ"ח)
וּלְיִצְחָק (ד"פ ב"ן) לְךָ אֶתְּנֶנָּה וּלְזַרְעֲךָ אַחֲרֶיךָ אֶתֵּן אֶת־הָאָרֶץ
(מילוי אלהים ע"ה): (יג) וַיַּעַל מֵעָלָיו אֱלֹהִים (ילה) בַּמָּקוֹם אֲשֶׁר־
דִּבֶּר (ראה) אִתּוֹ: (יד) וַיַּצֵּב יַעֲקֹב (יאהדונהי אידהנויה) מַצֵּבָה בַּמָּקוֹם
אֲשֶׁר־דִּבֶּר (ראה) אִתּוֹ מַצֶּבֶת אָבֶן וַיַּסֵּךְ עָלֶיהָ (פהל) נֶסֶךְ וַיִּצֹק
עָלֶיהָ (פהל) שָׁמֶן: (טו) וַיִּקְרָא יַעֲקֹב (יאהדונהי אידהנויה) אֶת־שֵׁם
הַמָּקוֹם אֲשֶׁר דִּבֶּר (ראה) אִתּוֹ שָׁם אֱלֹהִים (ילה) בֵּית (ב"פ ראה)־

יִשְׂרָאֵל - God changes Jacob's name to Israel. The name Yisrael ("Israel") is truly all-inclusive. The Yud stands for "Jacob" and "Isaac" (Ya'akov and Yitzchak in Hebrew). Shin stands for "Sarah," the resh Resh for "Rachel" and "Rebecca," the Aleph for "Abraham," and the Lamed for "Leah". The name also represents the Twelve Tribes of Israel. Through this one name, we can connect with the power of all Twelve Tribes.

אֵל׃ (טז) וַיִּסְעוּ מִבֵּית (ב"פ ראה) אֵל וַיְהִי־עוֹד כִּבְרַת־הָאָרֶץ
(מילוי אלהים ע"ה) לָבוֹא אֶפְרָתָה וַתֵּלֶד רָחֵל וַתְּקַשׁ בְּלִדְתָּהּ׃
(יז) וַיְהִי בְהַקְשֹׁתָהּ בְּלִדְתָּהּ וַתֹּאמֶר לָהּ הַמְיַלֶּדֶת אַל־
תִּירְאִי כִּי־גַם־זֶה לָךְ בֵּן׃ (יח) וַיְהִי בְּצֵאת נַפְשָׁהּ כִּי מֵתָה
וַתִּקְרָא שְׁמוֹ (מהש ע"ה) בֶּן־אוֹנִי וְאָבִיו קָרָא־לוֹ בִנְיָמִין׃ (יט)
וַתָּמָת רָחֵל וַתִּקָּבֵר בְּדֶרֶךְ (ב"פ יב"ק) אֶפְרָתָה הִוא בֵּית (ב"פ
ראה) לָחֶם (ג' הויות)׃ (כ) וַיַּצֵּב יַעֲקֹב (יאהדונהי אידהנויה) מַצֵּבָה עַל־
קְבֻרָתָהּ הִוא מַצֶּבֶת קְבֻרַת־רָחֵל עַד־הַיּוֹם (נגד, זן)׃ (כא) וַיִּסַּע
יִשְׂרָאֵל וַיֵּט אָהֳלֹה מֵהָלְאָה לְמִגְדַּל־עֵדֶר׃ (כב) וַיְהִי בִּשְׁכֹּן
יִשְׂרָאֵל בָּאָרֶץ הַהִוא וַיֵּלֶךְ (כלי) רְאוּבֵן וַיִּשְׁכַּב אֶת־בִּלְהָה

(פל) – בִּנְיָמִין - Benjamin controls the month of Libra, symbolized by the letters Peh and Lamed. He is the twelfth son.

וַתָּמָת - Rachel dies. On superficial observation, it may seem that Rachel had a miserable life. She waited seven years to marry Jacob, who then married her sister, Leah. When she was finally allowed to marry Jacob, she was not able to bear children. When she was finally able to bear children, she died in childbirth. Her apparent misfortune continued even after her passing when she was not buried with her husband. All this teaches us that Rachel is our spiritual mother. By suffering these terrible trials, Rachel bears our pain.

וַיִּשְׁכַּב - Reuben, the son of Jacob, sleeps with Bilhah, his father's wife; A break in the verse indicates that something important is taking place. Reuben, the son of Jacob, sleeps with Bilhah, his father's wife. Although the commentaries teach that Reuben did not actually have intercourse with

פִּילֶגֶשׁ אָבִיו וַיִּשְׁמַע יִשְׂרָאֵל פ וַיִּהְיוּ בְנֵי־יַעֲקֹב (יאהדונהי אי־
דהנויה) שְׁנֵים עָשָׂר׃ (כג) בְּנֵי לֵאָה בְּכוֹר יַעֲקֹב (יאהדונהי אידהנויה)
רְאוּבֵן וְשִׁמְעוֹן וְלֵוִי וִיהוּדָה וְיִשָּׂשכָר וּזְבֻלוּן׃ (כד) בְּנֵי רָחֵל
יוֹסֵף (ציון) וּבִנְיָמִן׃ (כה) וּבְנֵי בִלְהָה שִׁפְחַת רָחֵל דָּן וְנַפְתָּלִי׃ (כו)
וּבְנֵי זִלְפָּה שִׁפְחַת לֵאָה גָּד וְאָשֵׁר אֵלֶּה בְּנֵי יַעֲקֹב (יאהדונהי אי־
דהנויה) אֲשֶׁר יֻלַּד־לוֹ בְּפַדַּן אֲרָם׃ (כז) וַיָּבֹא יַעֲקֹב (יאהדונהי אידהנויה)
אֶל־יִצְחָק (ד"פ ב"ן) אָבִיו מַמְרֵא קִרְיַת הָאַרְבַּע הִוא חֶבְרוֹן
אֲשֶׁר־גָּר־שָׁם אַבְרָהָם (רמ"ח) וְיִצְחָק (ד"פ ב"ן)׃ (כח) וַיִּהְיוּ יְמֵי
יִצְחָק (ד"פ ב"ן) מְאַת שָׁנָה וּשְׁמֹנִים שָׁנָה׃ (כט) וַיִּגְוַע יִצְחָק (ד"פ ב"ן)
וַיָּמָת וַיֵּאָסֶף אֶל־עַמָּיו זָקֵן וּשְׂבַע יָמִים (נלך) וַיִּקְבְּרוּ אֹתוֹ

Bilhah, some transgression did occur because he lost his birthright as a result.

When Rachel died, Reuben wanted Jacob, his father, to reside in the tent of Leah, Reuben's mother. But Jacob had already moved his bed into the tent of Bilhah, Leah's maidservant. Reuben then showed disrespect for his father by physically moving Jacob 's bed into Leah's tent. When Reuben went to move the bed, Bilhah was lying in it, and the moment Reuben saw her, he desired her. Our consciousness truly determines the nature of our actions. Because Reuben's consciousness included lust for Bilhah, it was as if he had already slept with her, regardless of what took actually place on the physical level.

וַיָּמָת - Isaac dies. At the precise moment we leave this world, our soul is in transition. We are still here physically, but we are also connected to the Upper Worlds. In the case of highly spiritual people, their righteousness and their consciousness is at the highest level precisely at the moment of their

עֵשָׂו וְיַעֲקֹב (יאהדונהי אידהנויה) בָּנָיו: פ לו (א) וְאֵלֶּה תֹּלְדוֹת עֵשָׂו
הוּא אֱדוֹם: (ב) עֵשָׂו לָקַח אֶת־נָשָׁיו מִבְּנוֹת כְּנָעַן אֶת־עָדָה
(סיט) בַּת־אֵילוֹן הַחִתִּי וְאֶת־ אָהֳלִיבָמָה בַּת־עֲנָה בַּת־צִבְעוֹן
הַחִוִּי: (ג) וְאֶת־בָּשְׂמַת בַּת־יִשְׁמָעֵאל אֲחוֹת נְבָיוֹת: (ד) וַתֵּלֶד
עָדָה (סיט) לְעֵשָׂו אֶת־אֱלִיפָז וּבָשְׂמַת יָלְדָה אֶת־רְעוּאֵל: (ה)
וְאָהֳלִיבָמָה יָלְדָה אֶת־יְעוּשׁ (יְעִישׁ כתיב) וְאֶת־יַעְלָם וְאֶת־קֹרַח
אֵלֶּה בְּנֵי עֵשָׂו אֲשֶׁר יֻלְּדוּ־לוֹ בְּאֶרֶץ כְּנָעַן: (ו) וַיִּקַּח (וזעם) עֵשָׂו
אֶת־נָשָׁיו וְאֶת־בָּנָיו וְאֶת־בְּנֹתָיו וְאֶת־ כָּל (ילי)־נַפְשׁוֹת בֵּיתוֹ
(ב"פ ראה) וְאֶת־מִקְנֵהוּ וְאֶת־כָּל (ילי)־בְּהֶמְתּוֹ וְאֵת כָּל (ילי)־קִנְיָנוֹ
אֲשֶׁר רָכַשׁ בְּאֶרֶץ כְּנָעַן וַיֵּלֶךְ (כלי) אֶל־אֶרֶץ מִפְּנֵי יַעֲקֹב
(יאהדונהי אידהנויה) אָחִיו: (ז) כִּי־הָיָה (יהה) רְכוּשָׁם רָב מִשֶּׁבֶת יַחְדָּו
וְלֹא יָכְלָה אֶרֶץ מְגוּרֵיהֶם לָשֵׂאת אֹתָם מִפְּנֵי מִקְנֵיהֶם: (וז)

passing. That is why we connect with our sages on their anniversaries of their deaths when their great spiritual energy is most present.

תֹּלְדוֹת - The descendants of Esau. The names of Esau's descendents represent categories of different types of negativity. This list provides a tool for us to overcome negativity in our own lives. Very often, we know that we have a problem in a general area, but we do not know the exact thing that we need to let go of. The key is to learn specifically what is causing the problem and precisely how the negativity is manifesting itself. The naming of the descendents of Esau in the Torah allows us to do this.

וַיֵּשֶׁב עֵשָׂו בְּהַר שֵׂעִיר עֵשָׂו הוּא אֱדוֹם׃ (ט) וְאֵלֶּה תֹּלְדוֹת
עֵשָׂו אֲבִי אֱדוֹם בְּהַר שֵׂעִיר׃ (י) אֵלֶּה שְׁמוֹת בְּנֵי־עֵשָׂו
אֱלִיפַז בֶּן־עָדָה (סיט) אֵשֶׁת עֵשָׂו רְעוּאֵל בֶּן־בָּשְׂמַת אֵשֶׁת
עֵשָׂו׃ (יא) וַיִּהְיוּ בְּנֵי אֱלִיפָז תֵּימָן אוֹמָר צְפוֹ וְגַעְתָּם וּקְנַז׃
(יב) וְתִמְנַע | הָיְתָה פִילֶגֶשׁ לֶאֱלִיפַז בֶּן־עֵשָׂו וַתֵּלֶד לֶאֱלִיפַז
אֶת־עֲמָלֵק אֵלֶּה בְּנֵי עָדָה (סיט) אֵשֶׁת עֵשָׂו׃ (יג) וְאֵלֶּה בְּנֵי
רְעוּאֵל נַחַת וָזֶרַח שַׁמָּה וּמִזָּה אֵלֶּה הָיוּ בְּנֵי בָשְׂמַת אֵשֶׁת
עֵשָׂו׃ (יד) וְאֵלֶּה הָיוּ בְּנֵי אָהֳלִיבָמָה בַת־עֲנָה בַּת־צִבְעוֹן
אֵשֶׁת עֵשָׂו וַתֵּלֶד לְעֵשָׂו אֶת־יְעוּשׁ (יְעִישׁ כתיב) וְאֶת־ יַעְלָם
וְאֶת־קֹרַח׃ (טו) אֵלֶּה אַלּוּפֵי בְנֵי־עֵשָׂו בְּנֵי אֱלִיפַז בְּכוֹר עֵשָׂו
אַלּוּף תֵּימָן אַלּוּף אוֹמָר אַלּוּף צְפוֹ אַלּוּף קְנַז׃ (טז) אַלּוּף־
קֹרַח אַלּוּף גַּעְתָּם אַלּוּף עֲמָלֵק אֵלֶּה אַלּוּפֵי אֱלִיפַז בְּאֶרֶץ
אֱדוֹם אֵלֶּה בְּנֵי עָדָה (סיט)׃ (יז) וְאֵלֶּה בְּנֵי רְעוּאֵל בֶּן־עֵשָׂו
אַלּוּף נַחַת אַלּוּף זֶרַח אַלּוּף שַׁמָּה אַלּוּף מִזָּה אֵלֶּה אַלּוּפֵי
רְעוּאֵל בְּאֶרֶץ אֱדוֹם אֵלֶּה בְּנֵי בָשְׂמַת אֵשֶׁת עֵשָׂו׃ (יח)
וְאֵלֶּה בְּנֵי אָהֳלִיבָמָה אֵשֶׁת עֵשָׂו אַלּוּף יְעוּשׁ אַלּוּף יַעְלָם
אַלּוּף קֹרַח אֵלֶּה אַלּוּפֵי אָהֳלִיבָמָה בַּת־עֲנָה אֵשֶׁת עֵשָׂו׃
(יט) אֵלֶּה בְנֵי־עֵשָׂו וְאֵלֶּה אַלּוּפֵיהֶם הוּא אֱדוֹם׃ ס

Seventh Reading - David - Malchut

(כ) אֵלֶּה בְנֵי־שֵׂעִיר הַחֹרִי יֹשְׁבֵי הָאָרֶץ (מילוי אלהים ע"ה) לוֹטָן
וְשׁוֹבָל וְצִבְעוֹן וַעֲנָה׃ (כא) וְדִשׁוֹן וְאֵצֶר וְדִישָׁן אֵלֶּה אַלּוּפֵי
הַחֹרִי בְּנֵי שֵׂעִיר בְּאֶרֶץ אֱדוֹם׃ (כב) וַיִּהְיוּ בְנֵי־לוֹטָן חֹרִי
וְהֵימָם וַאֲחוֹת לוֹטָן תִּמְנָע׃ (כג) וְאֵלֶּה בְּנֵי שׁוֹבָל עַלְוָן
וּמָנַחַת וְעֵיבָל שְׁפוֹ וְאוֹנָם׃ (כד) וְאֵלֶּה בְנֵי־צִבְעוֹן וְאַיָּה
וַעֲנָה הוּא עֲנָה אֲשֶׁר מָצָא אֶת־הַיֵּמִם בַּמִּדְבָּר בִּרְעֹתוֹ
אֶת־הַחֲמֹרִים לְצִבְעוֹן אָבִיו׃ (כה) וְאֵלֶּה בְנֵי־עֲנָה דִּשֹׁן
וְאָהֳלִיבָמָה בַּת־עֲנָה׃ (כו) וְאֵלֶּה בְּנֵי דִישָׁן חֶמְדָּן וְאֶשְׁבָּן
וְיִתְרָן וּכְרָן׃ (כז) אֵלֶּה בְּנֵי־אֵצֶר בִּלְהָן וְזַעֲוָן וַעֲקָן׃ (כח) אֵלֶּה
בְנֵי־דִישָׁן עוּץ וַאֲרָן׃ (כט) אֵלֶּה אַלּוּפֵי הַחֹרִי אַלּוּף לוֹטָן
אַלּוּף שׁוֹבָל אַלּוּף צִבְעוֹן אַלּוּף עֲנָה׃ (ל) אַלּוּף דִּשֹׁן אַלּוּף
אֵצֶר אַלּוּף דִּישָׁן אֵלֶּה אַלּוּפֵי הַחֹרִי לְאַלֻּפֵיהֶם בְּאֶרֶץ
שֵׂעִיר׃ פ (לא) וְאֵלֶּה הַמְּלָכִים אֲשֶׁר מָלְכוּ (פוי) בְּאֶרֶץ אֱדוֹם
לִפְנֵי מְלָךְ־מֶלֶךְ לִבְנֵי יִשְׂרָאֵל׃ (לב) וַיִּמְלֹךְ בֶּאֱדוֹם בֶּלַע

הַמְּלָכִים - The eight kings - The Ari writes that the story of the eight kings is actually concerns the giving of the Sefirot to the physical dimension in which we live. This section shows very clearly the importance of remembering that the Torah is a coded text that should not be understood literally. Rabbi Shimon Bar bar Yochai stated that it would be better for a person to never have been born than to take the Torah at face value, without penetrating the deeper codes.

בֶּן־בְּע֔וֹר וְשֵׁ֥ם עִיר֖וֹ ‹סוֹזֹהֵר, סנדלפון, עֵרֵי› דִּנְהָֽבָה: ‹לג› וַיָּ֖מָת בָּ֑לַע

וַיִּמְלֹ֣ךְ תַּחְתָּ֗יו יוֹבָ֛ב בֶּן־זֶ֖רַח מִבָּצְרָֽה: ‹לד› וַיָּ֖מָת יוֹבָ֑ב וַיִּמְלֹ֣ךְ

תַּחְתָּ֔יו חֻשָׁ֖ם מֵאֶ֥רֶץ הַתֵּֽימָנִֽי: ‹לה› וַיָּ֣מָת חֻשָׁ֔ם וַיִּמְלֹ֣ךְ תַּחְתָּ֗יו

הֲדַ֤ד בֶּן־בְּדַד֙ הַמַּכֶּ֤ה אֶת־מִדְיָן֙ בִּשְׂדֵ֣ה מוֹאָ֔ב וְשֵׁ֥ם עִיר֖וֹ

‹סוֹזֹהֵר, סנדלפון, עֵרֵי› עֲוִֽית: ‹לו› וַיָּ֖מָת הֲדָ֑ד וַיִּמְלֹ֣ךְ תַּחְתָּ֔יו שַׂמְלָ֖ה

מִמַּשְׂרֵקָֽה: ‹לז› וַיָּ֖מָת שַׂמְלָ֑ה וַיִּמְלֹ֣ךְ תַּחְתָּ֔יו שָׁא֖וּל מֵרְחֹב֥וֹת

הַנָּהָֽר: ‹לח› וַיָּ֖מָת שָׁא֑וּל וַיִּמְלֹ֣ךְ תַּחְתָּ֔יו בַּ֥עַל חָנָ֖ן בֶּן־עַכְבּֽוֹר:

‹לט› וַיָּ֗מָת בַּ֚עַל חָנָ֣ן בֶּן־עַכְבּ֔וֹר וַיִּמְלֹ֤ךְ תַּחְתָּיו֙ הֲדַ֔ר וְשֵׁ֥ם

עִיר֖וֹ ‹סוֹזֹהֵר, סנדלפון, עֵרֵי› פָּ֑עוּ וְשֵׁ֨ם אִשְׁתּ֤וֹ מְהֵֽיטַבְאֵל֙ בַּת־מַטְרֵ֔ד

בַּ֖ת מֵ֥י ‹יֵלֵי› זָהָֽב:

Maftir

‹מ› וְ֠אֵ֠לֶּה שְׁמ֞וֹת [אַלּוּפֵ֤י עֵשָׂו֙] לְמִשְׁפְּחֹתָ֔ם לִמְקֹֽמֹתָ֖ם

בִּשְׁמֹתָ֑ם אַלּ֥וּף תִּמְנָ֖ע אַלּ֣וּף עַֽלְוָ֑ה אַלּ֖וּף יְתֵֽת: ‹מא› אַלּ֧וּף

אָֽהֳלִֽיבָמָ֛ה אַלּ֥וּף אֵלָ֖ה אַלּ֥וּף פִּינֹֽן: ‹מב› אַלּ֥וּף קְנַ֛ז אַלּ֥וּף

תֵּימָ֖ן אַלּ֥וּף מִבְצָֽר: ‹מג› אַלּ֥וּף מַגְדִּיאֵ֖ל אַלּ֣וּף עִירָ֑ם ‹סוֹזֹהֵר,

סנדלפון, עֵרֵי› אֵ֣לֶּה | אַלּוּפֵ֣י אֱד֗וֹם לְמֹֽשְׁבֹתָם֙ בְּאֶ֣רֶץ אֲחֻזָּתָ֔ם

ה֥וּא עֵשָׂ֖ו אֲבִ֥י אֱדֽוֹם: פפפ

אַלּוּפֵ֤י עֵשָׂו - The generals of Esau - each of the generals represents a
different negative force.

The Haftarah of Vayishlach

The prophet discusses the demise of Edom. The Second Temple was destroyed by the Romans, who were Edom (that is, Esau). The end of our current exile will be the Final Redemption with its removal of all chaos and negativity.

The Haftarah concerns how supremely important things have been sold for financial gain, as when Joseph was sold by his brothers. When we commit such an act, we forfeit our ultimate fulfillment merely for the sake of immediate gratification.

עוֹבַדְיָה פֶּרֶק א

א חֲזוֹן עֹבַדְיָה כֹּה (הי״) אָמַר אֲדֹנָי יְהֹוִה לֶאֱדוֹם שְׁמוּעָה
שָׁמַעְנוּ מֵאֵת יְהֹוָה וְצִיר בַּגּוֹיִם שֻׁלָּח קוּמוּ וְנָקוּמָה עָלֶיהָ
לַמִּלְחָמָה׃ ב הִנֵּה קָטֹן נְתַתִּיךָ בַּגּוֹיִם בָּזוּי אַתָּה מְאֹד׃ (פהל)
ג זְדוֹן לִבְּךָ הִשִּׁיאֶךָ שֹׁכְנִי בְחַגְוֵי־סֶלַע מְרוֹם שִׁבְתּוֹ אֹמֵר
בְּלִבּוֹ מִי (ילי) יוֹרִדֵנִי אָרֶץ׃ ד אִם (יוהך) ־תַּגְבִּיהַּ כַּנֶּשֶׁר וְאִם (יוהך) ־
בֵּין כּוֹכָבִים שִׂים קִנֶּךָ מִשָּׁם אוֹרִידְךָ נְאֻם־יְהֹוָה׃ ה אִם (יוהך)
־גַּנָּבִים בָּאוּ־לְךָ אִם (יוהך) ־שׁוֹדְדֵי לַיְלָה (מלה) אֵיךְ נִדְמֵיתָה
הֲלוֹא יִגְנְבוּ דַּיָּם אִם (יוהך) ־בֹּצְרִים בָּאוּ לָךְ הֲלוֹא יַשְׁאִירוּ
עֹלֵלוֹת׃ ו אֵיךְ נֶחְפְּשׂוּ עֵשָׂו נִבְעוּ מַצְפֻּנָיו׃ ז עַד־הַגְּבוּל
שִׁלְּחוּךָ כֹּל (ילי) אַנְשֵׁי בְרִיתֶךָ הִשִּׁיאוּךָ יָכְלוּ לְךָ אַנְשֵׁי
שְׁלֹמֶךָ לַחְמְךָ יָשִׂימוּ מָזוֹר תַּחְתֶּיךָ אֵין תְּבוּנָה בּוֹ׃ ח הֲלוֹא
בַּיּוֹם (נגד, מזבח, זן) הַהוּא נְאֻם־יְהֹוָה וְהַאֲבַדְתִּי חֲכָמִים מֵאֱדוֹם
וּתְבוּנָה מֵהַר עֵשָׂו׃ ט וְחַתּוּ גִבּוֹרֶיךָ תֵּימָן לְמַעַן יִכָּרֶת־אִישׁ

מִהַר עֵשָׂו מִקָּטֶל׃ י מֵחֲמַס אָחִיךָ יַעֲקֹב (יאהדונהי אידהנויה) תְּכַסְּךָ
בוּשָׁה וְנִכְרַתָּ לְעוֹלָם׃ יא בְּיוֹם (נגד, מזבח, זן) עֲמָדְךָ מִנֶּגֶד (זן, נגד,
מזבח) בְּיוֹם (נגד, מזבח, זן) שְׁבוֹת זָרִים חֵילוֹ (ומב) וְנָכְרִים בָּאוּ שְׁעָרָו
וְעַל־יְרוּשָׁלִַם יַדּוּ גוֹרָל גַּם־אַתָּה כְּאַחַד (אהבה, דאגה) מֵהֶם׃ יב
וְאַל־תֵּרֶא בְיוֹם (נגד, מזבח, זן) ־אָחִיךָ בְּיוֹם (נגד, מזבח, זן) נָכְרוֹ וְאַל־
תִּשְׂמַח לִבְנֵי־יְהוּדָה בְּיוֹם (נגד, מזבח, זן) אָבְדָם וְאַל־תַּגְדֵּל פִּיךָ
בְּיוֹם (נגד, מזבח, זן) צָרָה׃ יג אַל־תָּבוֹא בְשַׁעַר־עַמִּי בְּיוֹם (נגד, מזבח,
זן) אֵידָם אַל־תֵּרֶא גַם־אַתָּה בְּרָעָתוֹ בְּיוֹם (נגד, מזבח, זן) אֵידוֹ
וְאַל־תִּשְׁלַחְנָה בְחֵילוֹ בְּיוֹם (נגד, מזבח, זן) אֵידוֹ׃ יד וְאַל־תַּעֲמֹד
עַל־הַפֶּרֶק לְהַכְרִית אֶת־פְּלִיטָיו וְאַל־תַּסְגֵּר שְׂרִידָיו בְּיוֹם
(נגד, מזבח, זן) צָרָה׃ טו כִּי־קָרוֹב יוֹם (נגד, מזבח, זן) ־יְהוָה עַל־כָּל (ילי)
־הַגּוֹיִם כַּאֲשֶׁר עָשִׂיתָ יֵעָשֶׂה לָּךְ גְּמֻלְךָ יָשׁוּב בְּרֹאשֶׁךָ׃ טז
כִּי כַּאֲשֶׁר שְׁתִיתֶם עַל־הַר קָדְשִׁי יִשְׁתּוּ כָל (ילי) ־הַגּוֹיִם
תָּמִיד (נתה) וְשָׁתוּ וְלָעוּ וְהָיוּ כְּלוֹא הָיוּ׃ יז וּבְהַר צִיּוֹן (יוסף) תִּהְיֶה
פְלֵיטָה וְהָיָה (יהה) קֹדֶשׁ וְיָרְשׁוּ בֵּית (ב״פ ראה) יַעֲקֹב (יאהדונהי אידהנויה)
אֵת מוֹרָשֵׁיהֶם׃ יח וְהָיָה (יהה) בֵית (ב״פ ראה) ־יַעֲקֹב (יאהדונהי אידהנויה)
אֵשׁ וּבֵית (ב״פ ראה) יוֹסֵף (ציון) לֶהָבָה וּבֵית (ב״פ ראה) עֵשָׂו לְקַשׁ
וְדָלְקוּ בָהֶם וַאֲכָלוּם וְלֹא־יִהְיֶה (ייי) שָׂרִיד לְבֵית (ב״פ ראה) עֵשָׂו
כִּי יְהוָה דִּבֵּר (ראה)׃ יט וְיָרְשׁוּ הַנֶּגֶב אֶת־הַר עֵשָׂו וְהַשְּׁפֵלָה

אֶת־פְּלִשְׁתִּ֔ים וְיָרְשׁוּ֙ אֶת־שְׂדֵ֣ה אֶפְרַ֔יִם וְאֵ֖ת שְׂדֵ֣ה שֹׁמְר֑וֹן
וּבִנְיָמִ֖ן אֶת־הַגִּלְעָֽד׃ כ וְגָלֻ֣ת הַֽחֵל־הַ֠זֶּה (והו) לִבְנֵ֨י יִשְׂרָאֵ֤ל
אֲשֶׁר־כְּנַעֲנִים֙ עַד־צָ֣רְפַ֔ת וְגָלֻ֥ת יְרוּשָׁלִַ֖ם אֲשֶׁ֣ר בִּסְפָרַ֑ד
יִֽרְשׁ֕וּ אֵ֖ת עָרֵ֥י הַנֶּֽגֶב׃ כא וְעָל֤וּ מֽוֹשִׁעִים֙ בְּהַ֣ר צִיּ֔וֹן (יוסף)
לִשְׁפֹּ֖ט אֶת־הַ֣ר עֵשָׂ֑ו וְהָיְתָ֥ה לַיהוָ֖ה הַמְּלוּכָֽה׃ {ש}

Lesson of Vayeshev

"The Light was there when they decided to sell Joseph"

In this week's portion, we encounter something that happens only ten times in the whole Torah. Only ten times do we have the merit of two dots over the word. This week we have dots over the word Et (Eng. 'the').
Before we can answer the question of why the dots are present, we need to address another question about this verse. The Zohar says that the word Et is extraneous; we can understand the verse even without it. In fact, there isn't even a translation for Et in English or in any other language.

All this is very confusing. The passage reads: "...the light was there when they decided to sell Joseph." But why is there a dot over the letter Aleph and Tav? Elsewhere in the Torah, there are no dots when the Light is present. The Light was with Abraham and the other righteous people, but there was no dot.

Furthermore, are we to understand that the Light desired Joseph to be sold to Egypt? Ten people were reincarnated and killed because of the sin of selling Joseph. If the Light intended Joseph's brothers to undertake this action, why was there punishment afterward?

One thing is clear: Joseph had to arrive in Egypt. This was necessary so that the cleansing of the people could take place that would allow them to receive the Torah. In this sense, Joseph's going to Egypt was essential not just for his own Tikkun (Eng. 'correction'), but for the Tikkun of the whole world. This, in fact, is the lesson and power in the two dots–that the Light of the Creator is with us not just in the good things, but also in the things that seem negative to us at the moment.

Suppose a man misses his airplane flight. He's furious. He has so many things to do at his destination. If he only knew that there was a bomb on the plane, he would kiss the ground under him! Most of us miss the second part of the picture. But people who really connected to the Light see and appreciate at every moment what the Light does for them.

The Gemara tells of a man called Nachum. No matter what happened, he would say, "This is also for the best." Once the people of Israel wanted to send a present to the king. They asked Nachum to take the present because he was learned in the way of miracles. They sent him with a box full of precious stones.

He traveled and at night slept at an inn. The owners of the inn opened the box, stole the precious stones, and filled the box with ashes. When Nachum

arrived at the king's palace, the box was opened and the ashes found.

The king thundered, "Are the Jews laughing at me?" He ordered Nachum killed, but still Nachum said, "This also for the best!" At that moment, his purity and certainty were such that he merited the presence of the prophet Elijah, who approached the king disguised as one of his most trusted courtiers. Elijah said, "Sire, these ashes are from their patriarch Abraham. When Abraham used to throw these ashes, they would turn into swords. With the swords, he could vanquish any enemy."

Astonished by the news of his good fortune, the king filled the box with precious stones and sent Nachum home with great respect and gratitude. On the way back, Nachum again slept in the inn, where the innkeeper was surprised to see him still alive.

The innkeeper asked, "What did you bring to the king?

Nachum answered, "Just what I took from the inn."

So the innkeeper took all the ashes from his house and brought them to the king. But Elijah, still disguised as the trusted courtier, told the king that they had no magical power. The king was furious and ordered the innkeeper killed.

In everything that happens from day to day, it's as if the Light comes to us and says, "This will help you in your life." Most of the time, we don't listen–and this is a huge mistake. The Light intends only what is best for us. By understanding the dots in this portion and by connecting with their power, we will all merit to see the good in everything that happens.

"And Reuben heard and saved him from their hands."

There are teachings in the Torah that are hugely important, but we miss their importance because they are mentioned in just a few words. Examples of this are the events in Abraham's life from his childhood until he was 74 and in Moses's life from the age of thirteen to eighty. After all, these are not just ordinary people: They are Chariots of the spiritual system. Every moment of their lives was crucial and affects every moment of ours.

In a similar way, our own actions reverberate throughout the world. Often we fail to see the importance of what we do. Each of us has a unique Light that only we can reveal.

When Reuben came to save Joseph, he understood that he was doing the right thing to save his brother, but he did not know how much of an effect his action would have on generations to come. If Reuben had known how much the Light took his act into account, he certainly would have attached greater significance to what he did. This teaches us that our every deed should be considered as if it were building a whole world for all time. Every one of us must do more in every moment to reveal the Light. We can never know if "just one more thing" will change not just our own lives, but will transform the whole world.

Synopsis of Vayeshev

Jacob becomes complacent. After all his trials and tests, he feels that he has accomplished everything. It is at this point that his son Joseph is taken from him. From this, we learn that we should never rest on our laurels, spiritually speaking. We should always be ready to grow and to don the spiritual work that growth includes.

First Reading - Abraham - Chesed

לז (א) וַיֵּשֶׁב יַעֲקֹב (יאהדונהי אידהנויה) בְּאֶרֶץ מְגוּרֵי אָבִיו בְּאֶרֶץ
כְּנָעַן׃ (ב) אֵלֶּה | תֹּלְדוֹת יַעֲקֹב (יאהדונהי אידהנויה) יוֹסֵף (ציון) בֶּן־
שְׁבַע־עֶשְׂרֵה שָׁנָה הָיָה (יהה) רֹעֶה אֶת־אֶחָיו בַּצֹּאן וְהוּא
נַעַר אֶת־בְּנֵי בִלְהָה וְאֶת־בְּנֵי זִלְפָּה נְשֵׁי אָבִיו וַיָּבֵא יוֹסֵף
(ציון) אֶת־דִּבָּתָם רָעָה (רהע) אֶל־אֲבִיהֶם׃ (ג) וְיִשְׂרָאֵל אָהַב
אֶת־יוֹסֵף (ציון) מִכָּל (ילי)־בָּנָיו כִּי־בֶן־זְקֻנִים הוּא לוֹ וְעָשָׂה
לוֹ כְּתֹנֶת פַּסִּים׃ (ד) וַיִּרְאוּ אֶחָיו כִּי־אֹתוֹ אָהַב אֲבִיהֶם
מִכָּל (ילי)־אֶחָיו וַיִּשְׂנְאוּ אֹתוֹ וְלֹא יָכְלוּ דַּבְּרוֹ (ראה) לְשָׁלֹם׃
(ה) וַיַּחֲלֹם יוֹסֵף (ציון) חֲלוֹם וַיַּגֵּד לְאֶחָיו וַיּוֹסִפוּ עוֹד שְׂנֹא

כְּתֹנֶת פַּסִּים - Jacob makes a coat of many colors for Joseph. The Hebrew word for the coat is kutonet passim, an acronym for the four special angels who would protect him all the time. Although we don't have the physical code today, we have both the spiritual code and the angels who protect us.

וַיִּשְׂנְאוּ - The brothers are jealous of Joseph's relationship with Jacob. Jacob was partly responsible for this because he appeared to favor Joseph. As parents, we must make an extra effort to treat our children evenhandedly. Although we may feel a greater affinity for one child or another, we should make an effort to keep this from influencing our actions. If we do not make this effort, we are partly responsible for any jealousy that may result.

וַיַּחֲלֹם - Joseph has two dreams that reveal the ways in which his life will differ from his brothers'. This portion shows us the power of dreams. Dreams tell the future, but there are some principles we must respect so that we can understand and use our dreams correctly. Not everything in a dream

אֹתוֹ: (ו) וַיֹּאמֶר אֲלֵיהֶם שִׁמְעוּ־נָא הַחֲלוֹם הַזֶּה (והו) אֲשֶׁר
חָלָמְתִּי: (ז) וְהִנֵּה אֲנַחְנוּ מְאַלְּמִים אֲלֻמִּים בְּתוֹךְ הַשָּׂדֶה
וְהִנֵּה קָמָה אֲלֻמָּתִי וְגַם־נִצָּבָה וְהִנֵּה תְסֻבֶּינָה אֲלֻמֹּתֵיכֶם
וַתִּשְׁתַּחֲוֶיןָ לַאֲלֻמָּתִי: (ח) וַיֹּאמְרוּ לוֹ אֶחָיו הֲמָלֹךְ תִּמְלֹךְ
עָלֵינוּ אִם (ייהך)־מָשׁוֹל תִּמְשֹׁל בָּנוּ וַיּוֹסִפוּ עוֹד שְׂנֹא אֹתוֹ
עַל־חֲלֹמֹתָיו וְעַל־דְּבָרָיו (ראה): (ט) וַיַּחֲלֹם עוֹד חֲלוֹם אַחֵר
וַיְסַפֵּר אֹתוֹ לְאֶחָיו וַיֹּאמֶר הִנֵּה חָלַמְתִּי חֲלוֹם עוֹד וְהִנֵּה
הַשֶּׁמֶשׁ וְהַיָּרֵחַ וְאַחַד (אהבה) עָשָׂר כּוֹכָבִים מִשְׁתַּחֲוִים לִי: (י)
וַיְסַפֵּר אֶל־אָבִיו וְאֶל־אֶחָיו וַיִּגְעַר־בּוֹ אָבִיו וַיֹּאמֶר לוֹ מָה
(מ"ה) הַחֲלוֹם הַזֶּה (והו) אֲשֶׁר חָלָמְתָּ הֲבוֹא נָבוֹא אֲנִי (אני) וְאִמְּךָ
וְאַחֶיךָ לְהִשְׁתַּחֲוֺת לְךָ אָרְצָה: (יא) וַיְקַנְאוּ־בוֹ אֶחָיו וְאָבִיו
שָׁמַר אֶת־הַדָּבָר (ראה):

Second Reading - Issac - Gvurah

(יב) וַיֵּלְכוּ אֶחָיו לִרְעוֹת אֶת־צֹאן אֲבִיהֶם בִּשְׁכֶם: (יג) וַיֹּאמֶר

will necessarily take place in our waking lives, nor is everything important. Because of this, we should carefully select those people with whom we choose to discuss our dreams. Their interpretation will have an impact on the dream's meaning for us and on the parts of the dream that seem important. We should tell our dreams to someone who cares for us, who loves us, and whom we love in return.

אֶת - Dots over the word 'Et' (Eng. 'the')

יִשְׂרָאֵל אֶל־יוֹסֵף (צ״ון) הֲלוֹא אַחֶיךָ רֹעִים בִּשְׁכֶם לְכָה
וְאֶשְׁלָחֲךָ אֲלֵיהֶם וַיֹּאמֶר לוֹ הִנֵּנִי׃ (יד) וַיֹּאמֶר לוֹ לֶךְ־נָא
רְאֵה (ראה) אֶת־שְׁלוֹם אַחֶיךָ וְאֶת־שְׁלוֹם הַצֹּאן וַהֲשִׁבֵנִי
דָּבָר (ראה) וַיִּשְׁלָחֵהוּ מֵעֵמֶק חֶבְרוֹן וַיָּבֹא שְׁכֶמָה׃ (טו) וַיִּמְצָאֵהוּ
אִישׁ וְהִנֵּה תֹעֶה בַּשָּׂדֶה וַיִּשְׁאָלֵהוּ הָאִישׁ לֵאמֹר מַה
(מ״ה)־תְּבַקֵּשׁ׃ (טז) וַיֹּאמֶר אֶת־אַחַי אָנֹכִי (א״ע) מְבַקֵּשׁ הַגִּידָה־
נָּא לִי אֵיפֹה הֵם רֹעִים׃ (יז) וַיֹּאמֶר הָאִישׁ נָסְעוּ מִזֶּה כִּי
שָׁמַעְתִּי אֹמְרִים נֵלְכָה דֹּתָיְנָה וַיֵּלֶךְ (כל״י) יוֹסֵף (צ״ון) אַחַר
אֶחָיו וַיִּמְצָאֵם בְּדֹתָן׃ (יח) וַיִּרְאוּ אֹתוֹ מֵרָחֹק (שד״י) וּבְטֶרֶם
יִקְרַב אֲלֵיהֶם **וַיִּתְנַכְּלוּ** אֹתוֹ לַהֲמִיתוֹ׃ (יט) וַיֹּאמְרוּ אִישׁ

In the entire Torah, there are only ten instances of dots appearing over words, and this is one of them. Joseph goes to Egypt, and the Zohar reveals that God was involved in this event. Although the brothers were wrong to sell Joseph, the Light was always in control. When painful things happen to us, we should always remember to connect to the fact that the Light is still present. We are never alone.

אִישׁ - Joseph is looking for his brothers, but he has no idea where they are. He asks someone for help, and this man, whose name is not given, tells Joseph where his brothers can be found. The word used for this man is ish. It is important to note that the word ish is also used with reference to the angel of Esau. We know that this man is positive and the angel of Esau was negative, yet they are both referred to by the same word. From this, we learn that actions express our spiritual nature. Actions are the evidence of our consciousness. Ish shows that we can be both positive and negative.

וַיִּתְנַכְּלוּ - When Joseph meets his brothers, they want to kill him. Instead,

אֶל־אָחִיו הִנֵּה בַּעַל הַחֲלֹמוֹת הַלָּזֶה בָּא׃ (כ) וְעַתָּה ׀ לְכוּ
וְנַהַרְגֵהוּ וְנַשְׁלִכֵהוּ בְּאַחַד (אהבה) הַבֹּרוֹת וְאָמַרְנוּ חַיָּה רָעָה
(רהע) אֲכָלָתְהוּ וְנִרְאֶה מַה (מ"ה) יִּהְיוּ חֲלֹמֹתָיו׃ (כא) וַיִּשְׁמַע
רְאוּבֵן וַיַּצִּלֵהוּ מִיָּדָם וַיֹּאמֶר לֹא נַכֶּנּוּ נָפֶשׁ׃ (כב) וַיֹּאמֶר
אֲלֵהֶם ׀ רְאוּבֵן אַל־תִּשְׁפְּכוּ־דָם הַשְׁלִיכוּ אֹתוֹ אֶל־הַבּוֹר
הַזֶּה (והו) אֲשֶׁר בַּמִּדְבָּר וְיָד אַל־תִּשְׁלְחוּ־בוֹ לְמַעַן הַצִּיל
אֹתוֹ מִיָּדָם לַהֲשִׁיבוֹ אֶל־אָבִיו׃

Third Reading - Jacob - Tiferet

(כג) וַיְהִי כַּאֲשֶׁר־בָּא יוֹסֵף (ציון) אֶל־אֶחָיו וַיַּפְשִׁיטוּ אֶת־יוֹסֵף
(ציון) אֶת־כֻּתָּנְתּוֹ אֶת־כְּתֹנֶת הַפַּסִּים אֲשֶׁר עָלָיו׃ (כד) וַיִּקָּחֻהוּ
וַיַּשְׁלִכוּ אֹתוֹ הַבֹּרָה וְהַבּוֹר רֵק אֵין בּוֹ מָיִם׃ (כה) וַיֵּשְׁבוּ
לֶאֱכָל־לֶחֶם (ג' הויות) וַיִּשְׂאוּ עֵינֵיהֶם (מ"ה בריבוע) וַיִּרְאוּ וְהִנֵּה

Reuben convinces them to throw Joseph into a pit. Eventually, the brothers sell Joseph into slavery and he is brought down to Egypt.

How could the brothers do this Joseph? The Zohar explains that the brothers knew some Kabbalah. With the little knowledge that they had, they concluded that it was not necessary for Joseph to live. The brothers knew just enough to be dangerous.

This is an excellent example of the principle that a little knowledge is a dangerous thing. We must never be complacent or arrogant about our knowledge. We must always be proactive about learning more, about asking questions of our teachers, about striving for greater understanding.

אֹרְחַת יִשְׁמְעֵאלִים בָּאָה מִגִּלְעָד וּגְמַלֵּיהֶם נֹשְׂאִים נְכֹאת
וּצְרִי וָלֹט הוֹלְכִים לְהוֹרִיד מִצְרָיְמָה (מצר)׃ (כו) וַיֹּאמֶר יְהוּדָה
אֶל־אֶחָיו מַה (מ"ה)־בֶּצַע כִּי נַהֲרֹג אֶת־אָחִינוּ וְכִסִּינוּ אֶת־דָּמוֹ׃
(כז) לְכוּ וְנִמְכְּרֶנּוּ לַיִּשְׁמְעֵאלִים וְיָדֵנוּ אַל־תְּהִי־בוֹ כִּי־אָחִינוּ
בְשָׂרֵנוּ הוּא וַיִּשְׁמְעוּ אֶחָיו׃ (כח) וַיַּעַבְרוּ אֲנָשִׁים מִדְיָנִים
סֹחֲרִים וַיִּמְשְׁכוּ וַיַּעֲלוּ אֶת־יוֹסֵף (ציון) מִן־הַבּוֹר וַיִּמְכְּרוּ
אֶת־יוֹסֵף (ציון) לַיִּשְׁמְעֵאלִים בְּעֶשְׂרִים כָּסֶף וַיָּבִיאוּ אֶת־
יוֹסֵף (ציון) מִצְרָיְמָה (מצר)׃ (כט) וַיָּשָׁב רְאוּבֵן אֶל־הַבּוֹר וְהִנֵּה
אֵין־יוֹסֵף (ציון) בַּבּוֹר וַיִּקְרַע אֶת־בְּגָדָיו׃ (ל) וַיָּשָׁב אֶל־אֶחָיו
וַיֹּאמַר הַיֶּלֶד אֵינֶנּוּ וַאֲנִי (אני) אָנָה אֲנִי (אני)־בָא׃ (לא) וַיִּקְחוּ אֶת־

בְּעֶשְׂרִים כָּסֶף - The amount of money for which Joseph is sold is related to the redemption of the first-born. When the firstborn is redeemed in the Pidyon haben, the money offered up is to complete some of the Tikkun that the brothers acquired for the sin of selling Joseph.

וַיָּשָׁב - Reuben believed that the brothers had only thrown Joseph into a pit. But he returns to find that they have sold Joseph into slavery. Each day, one of the brothers was entrusted with the responsibility for everything that took place during that day. Reuben was responsible for the day that Joseph was thrown in the pit. He did make sure that Joseph was safe in the pit and that nothing happened to him while he was there. However, he did not make the additional effort of getting Joseph out of the pit or of helping him to escape. He did only the minimum. When we undertake a spiritual action, we should not be satisfied with doing the minimum. We must always motivate ourselves to be proactive, to seek the opportunity to build our Vessel.

כְּתֹנֶת יוֹסֵף (צִיּוֹן) וַיִּשְׁחֲטוּ שְׂעִיר עִזִּים וַיִּטְבְּלוּ אֶת־הַכֻּתֹּנֶת
בַּדָּם׃ (לב) וַיְשַׁלְּחוּ אֶת־כְּתֹנֶת הַפַּסִּים וַיָּבִיאוּ אֶל־אֲבִיהֶם
וַיֹּאמְרוּ זֹאת מָצָאנוּ הַכֶּר־נָא הַכְּתֹנֶת בִּנְךָ הִוא אִם (יוהך)־
לֹא׃ (לג) וַיַּכִּירָהּ וַיֹּאמֶר כְּתֹנֶת בְּנִי חַיָּה רָעָה (רהע) אֲכָלָתְהוּ
טָרֹף טֹרַף יוֹסֵף (צִיּוֹן)׃ (לד) וַיִּקְרַע יַעֲקֹב (יאהדונהי אידהנויה) שִׂמְלֹתָיו
וַיָּשֶׂם שַׂק בְּמָתְנָיו וַיִּתְאַבֵּל עַל־בְּנוֹ יָמִים (נלך) רַבִּים׃ (לה)
וַיָּקֻמוּ כָל (ילי)־בָּנָיו וְכָל (ילי)־בְּנֹתָיו לְנַחֲמוֹ וַיְמָאֵן לְהִתְנַחֵם
וַיֹּאמֶר כִּי־אֵרֵד אֶל־בְּנִי אָבֵל שְׁאֹלָה וַיֵּבְךְּ אֹתוֹ אָבִיו׃
(לו) וְהַמְּדָנִים מָכְרוּ אֹתוֹ אֶל־מִצְרָיִם (מצר) לְפוֹטִיפַר סְרִיס
פַּרְעֹה שַׂר הַטַּבָּחִים׃ פ

וַיָּבִיאוּ - The brothers reveal the coat of Joseph to Jacob

The brothers do not know how to tell their father what they have done to Joseph. Rather than tell the truth or even speak a lie, they merely take the multi-colored coat of Joseph, dip it in goat's blood, and show it to Jacob. They do not actually lie, but their actions cause Jacob to believe something that is not true.

Jacob, of course, did something very similar to his own father. He deceived Isaac by presenting himself in Esau's clothing. Without actually lying, he caused Isaac to draw an untrue conclusion.

There are many ways to lie. All of them, however, eventually require us to pay a price, and sometimes the price is that we ourselves will be lied to.

Fourth Reading - Moses - Netzach

לח (א) וַיְהִי בָּעֵת הַהִוא **וַיֵּרֶד** (רי"י) יְהוּדָה מֵאֵת אֶחָיו וַיֵּט
עַד־אִישׁ עֲדֻלָּמִי וּשְׁמוֹ (מהש ע"ה) חִירָה: (ב) וַיַּרְא־שָׁם יְהוּדָה
בַּת־אִישׁ כְּנַעֲנִי וּשְׁמוֹ (מהש ע"ה) שׁוּעַ וַיִּקָּחֶהָ וַיָּבֹא אֵלֶיהָ: (ג)
וַתַּהַר וַתֵּלֶד בֵּן וַיִּקְרָא אֶת־שְׁמוֹ (מהש ע"ה) עֵר: (ד) וַתַּהַר עוֹד
וַתֵּלֶד בֵּן וַתִּקְרָא אֶת־שְׁמוֹ (מהש ע"ה) אוֹנָן: (ה) וַתֹּסֶף עוֹד וַתֵּלֶד
בֵּן וַתִּקְרָא אֶת־שְׁמוֹ (מהש ע"ה) שֵׁלָה וְהָיָה (יהה) (יהוה) בִכְזִיב
בְּלִדְתָּהּ אֹתוֹ: (ו) וַיִּקַּח (וזעם) יְהוּדָה אִשָּׁה לְעֵר בְּכוֹרוֹ
וּשְׁמָהּ תָּמָר: (ז) וַיְהִי עֵר בְּכוֹר יְהוּדָה רַע בְּעֵינֵי (מ"ה בריבוע)
יְהֹוָה אדני אהדונהי וַיְמִתֵהוּ יְהֹוָה אדני אהדונהי: (ח) וַיֹּאמֶר יְהוּדָה לְאוֹנָן
בֹּא אֶל־אֵשֶׁת אָחִיךָ וְיַבֵּם אֹתָהּ וְהָקֵם זֶרַע לְאָחִיךָ: (ט)
וַיֵּדַע אוֹנָן כִּי לֹּא לוֹ יִהְיֶה (ייי) הַזָּרַע וְהָיָה (יהה) (יהוה) אִם (יוהך)־
בָּא אֶל־אֵשֶׁת אָחִיו וְשִׁחֵת אַרְצָה לְבִלְתִּי נְתָן־זֶרַע לְאָחִיו:
(י) וַיֵּרַע בְּעֵינֵי (מ"ה בריבוע) יְהֹוָה אדני אהדונהי אֲשֶׁר עָשָׂה וַיָּמֶת גַּם־

וַיֵּרֶד - Yehuda is the brother who suggested that they sell Joseph
Judah made the suggestion to sell Joseph. Now he is overcome with guilt, and he leaves the family. He marries and has three children. Eventually, his oldest child takes a wife whose name is Tamar. When this oldest son dies without children, his brother is supposed to marry the widow, so the line can be continued. But this brother also dies. Both perished for their negativity.

אֹתוֹ׃ (יא) **וַיֹּאמֶר** יְהוּדָה לְתָמָר כַּלָּתוֹ שְׁבִי אַלְמָנָה בֵית־
(כ"פ ראה) אָבִיךְ עַד־יִגְדַּל (יזל) שֵׁלָה בְנִי כִּי אָמַר פֶּן־יָמוּת
גַּם־הוּא כְּאֶחָיו וַתֵּלֶךְ תָּמָר וַתֵּשֶׁב בֵּית (כ"פ ראה) אָבִיהָ׃
(יב) וַיִּרְבּוּ הַיָּמִים (נלך) וַתָּמָת בַּת־שׁוּעַ אֵשֶׁת־יְהוּדָה וַיִּנָּחֶם
יְהוּדָה וַיַּעַל עַל־גֹּזְזֵי צֹאנוֹ הוּא וְחִירָה רֵעֵהוּ הָעֲדֻלָּמִי
תִּמְנָתָה׃ (יג) וַיֻּגַּד לְתָמָר לֵאמֹר הִנֵּה חָמִיךְ עֹלֶה תִמְנָתָה
לָגֹז צֹאנוֹ׃ (יד) וַתָּסַר בִּגְדֵי אַלְמְנוּתָהּ מֵעָלֶיהָ (פהל) וַתְּכַס
בַּצָּעִיף וַתִּתְעַלָּף וַתֵּשֶׁב בְּפֶתַח עֵינַיִם (מ"ה בריבוע) אֲשֶׁר עַל־
דֶּרֶךְ (כ"פ יב"ק) תִּמְנָתָה כִּי רָאֲתָה כִּי־גָדַל שֵׁלָה וְהִוא לֹא־
נִתְּנָה לוֹ לְאִשָּׁה׃ (טו) וַיִּרְאֶהָ (רי"ו) (ראה) יְהוּדָה וַיַּחְשְׁבֶהָ לְזוֹנָה
כִּי כִסְּתָה פָּנֶיהָ׃ (טז) וַיֵּט אֵלֶיהָ אֶל־הַדֶּרֶךְ (כ"פ יב"ק) וַיֹּאמֶר

וַיֹּאמֶר - Rather than having Tamar marry his third son (and perhaps causing his death), Judah sends Tamar away. After Judah's wife dies, he decides to visit a prostitute. Tamar dresses as a prostitute, and Judah ends up having sexual relations with his daughter-in-law. King David comes from this line. What can all this possibly mean?

The Zohar tells us that when a righteous soul is about to come to this world, the Satan tries to put obstacles in the way of this happening. In this case, David comes from ancestors who existed in very negative situations. When circumstances seem sufficiently negative, the Satan does not feel that it is necessary to intervene. But the Light overcame the negativity, and King David came into this world. This is also the line from which the Messiah will come.

הָבָה־נָּא֙ אָב֣וֹא אֵלַ֔יִךְ כִּ֚י לֹ֣א יָדַ֔ע כִּ֥י כַלָּת֖וֹ הִ֑וא וַתֹּ֙אמֶר֙
מַה (מ"ה)־תִּתֶּן (כ"פ כהת)־ לִּ֔י כִּ֥י תָב֖וֹא אֵלָֽי׃ (יז) וַיֹּ֗אמֶר אָנֹכִ֛י (א"ע)
אֲשַׁלַּ֥ח גְּדִֽי (והו)־עִזִּ֖ים מִן־הַצֹּ֑אן וַתֹּ֕אמֶר אִם (יוהך)־תִּתֵּ֥ן (כ"פ כהת)
עֵרָב֖וֹן עַ֥ד שָׁלְחֶֽךָ׃ (יח) וַיֹּ֗אמֶר מָ֣ה (מ"ה) הָעֵרָבוֹן֮ אֲשֶׁ֣ר אֶתֶּן־
לָּךְ֒ וַתֹּ֗אמֶר חֹתָֽמְךָ֙ וּפְתִילֶ֔ךָ (י"פ ב"ן) וּמַטְּךָ֖ אֲשֶׁ֣ר בְּיָדֶ֑ךָ וַיִּתֶּן־
לָ֛הּ וַיָּבֹ֥א אֵלֶ֖יהָ וַתַּ֥הַר לֽוֹ׃ (יט) וַתָּ֣קָם וַתֵּ֔לֶךְ וַתָּ֥סַר צְעִיפָ֖הּ
מֵעָלֶ֑יהָ (פהל) וַתִּלְבַּ֖שׁ בִּגְדֵ֥י אַלְמְנוּתָֽהּ׃ (כ) וַיִּשְׁלַ֨ח יְהוּדָ֜ה
אֶת־גְּדִ֣י (והו) הָֽעִזִּ֗ים בְּיַד֙ רֵעֵ֣הוּ הָעֲדֻלָּמִ֔י לָקַ֥חַת הָעֵרָב֖וֹן
מִיַּ֣ד הָאִשָּׁ֑ה וְלֹ֖א מְצָאָֽהּ׃ (כא) וַיִּשְׁאַ֞ל אֶת־אַנְשֵׁ֤י מְקֹמָהּ֙
לֵאמֹ֔ר אַיֵּ֧ה הַקְּדֵשָׁ֛ה הִ֥וא בָעֵינַ֖יִם (מ"ה בריבוע) עַל־הַדָּ֑רֶךְ (כ"פ
יב"ק) וַיֹּ֣אמְר֔וּ לֹא־הָיְתָ֥ה בָזֶ֖ה קְדֵשָֽׁה׃ (כב) וַיָּ֙שָׁב֙ אֶל־יְהוּדָ֔ה
וַיֹּ֖אמֶר לֹ֣א מְצָאתִ֑יהָ וְגַ֨ם אַנְשֵׁ֤י הַמָּקוֹם֙ אָֽמְר֔וּ לֹא־הָיְתָ֥ה
בָזֶ֖ה קְדֵשָֽׁה׃ (כג) וַיֹּ֤אמֶר יְהוּדָה֙ תִּֽקַּֽח־לָ֔הּ פֶּ֖ן נִהְיֶ֣ה לָב֑וּז
הִנֵּ֤ה שָׁלַ֙חְתִּי֙ הַגְּדִ֣י (והו) הַזֶּ֔ה (והו) וְאַתָּ֖ה לֹ֥א מְצָאתָֽהּ׃ (כד) וַיְהִ֣י
׀ כְּמִשְׁלֹ֣שׁ חֳדָשִׁ֗ים וַיֻּגַּ֨ד לִֽיהוּדָ֤ה לֵאמֹר֙ זָֽנְתָה֙ תָּמָ֣ר כַּלָּתֶ֔ךָ
וְגַ֛ם הִנֵּ֥ה הָרָ֖ה לִזְנוּנִ֑ים וַיֹּ֣אמֶר יְהוּדָ֔ה הוֹצִיא֖וּהָ וְתִשָּׂרֵֽף׃
(כה) הִ֣וא מוּצֵ֗את וְהִ֨יא שָׁלְחָ֤ה אֶל־חָמִ֙יהָ֙ לֵאמֹ֔ר לְאִ֙ישׁ֙
אֲשֶׁר־אֵ֣לֶּה לּ֔וֹ אָנֹכִ֖י (א"ע) הָרָ֑ה וַתֹּ֙אמֶר֙ הַכֶּר־נָ֔א לְמִ֞י (ילי)
הַחֹתֶ֧מֶת וְהַפְּתִילִ֛ים (י"פ ב"ן) וְהַמַּטֶּ֖ה הָאֵֽלֶּה׃ (כו) וַיַּכֵּ֣ר יְהוּדָ֗ה

וַיֹּאמֶר צָדְקָה (ע"ה אלהים בריבוע) מִמֶּנִּי כִּי־עַל־כֵּן לֹא־נְתַתִּיהָ
לְשֵׁלָה בְנִי וְלֹא־יָסַף עוֹד לְדַעְתָּהּ׃ (כז) וַיְהִי בְּעֵת לִדְתָּהּ
וְהִנֵּה תְאוֹמִים בְּבִטְנָהּ׃ (כח) וַיְהִי בְלִדְתָּהּ וַיִּתֶּן־יָד וַתִּקַּח
הַמְיַלֶּדֶת וַתִּקְשֹׁר עַל־יָדוֹ שָׁנִי לֵאמֹר זֶה יָצָא רִאשֹׁנָה׃ (כט)
וַיְהִי ׀ כְּמֵשִׁיב יָדוֹ וְהִנֵּה יָצָא אָחִיו וַתֹּאמֶר מַה (מ"ה) ־פָּרַצְתָּ
עָלֶיךָ פָּרֶץ וַיִּקְרָא שְׁמוֹ (מהש ע"ה) פָּרֶץ׃ (ל) וְאַחַר יָצָא אָחִיו
אֲשֶׁר עַל־יָדוֹ הַשָּׁנִי וַיִּקְרָא שְׁמוֹ (מהש ע"ה) זָרַח׃ ס

Fifth Reading - Aaron - Hod

לט (א) וְיוֹסֵף (ציון) הוּרַד מִצְרָיְמָה (מצר) וַיִּקְנֵהוּ פּוֹטִיפַר סְרִיס
פַּרְעֹה שַׂר הַטַּבָּחִים אִישׁ מִצְרִי (מצר) מִיַּד הַיִּשְׁמְעֵאלִים
אֲשֶׁר הוֹרִדֻהוּ שָׁמָּה׃ (ב) וַיְהִי יְהֹוָהאדניאהדונהי אֶת־יוֹסֵף (ציון)
וַיְהִי אִישׁ מַצְלִיחַ וַיְהִי בְּבֵית (ב"פ ראה) אֲדֹנָיו הַמִּצְרִי (מצר)׃ (ג)
וַיַּרְא אֲדֹנָיו כִּי יְהֹוָהאדניאהדונהי אִתּוֹ וְכֹל (ילי) אֲשֶׁר־הוּא עֹשֶׂה
יְהֹוָהאדניאהדונהי מַצְלִיחַ בְּיָדוֹ׃ (ד) וַיִּמְצָא יוֹסֵף (ציון) חֵן (מוזי) בְּעֵינָיו
(מ"ה בריבוע) וַיְשָׁרֶת אֹתוֹ וַיַּפְקִדֵהוּ עַל־בֵּיתוֹ (ב"פ ראה) וְכָל (ילי) ־יֶשׁ־

הוּרַד - Joseph is taken to Egypt as a slave, but he never has to live his life in bondage. Wherever he is, he becomes the master. Why is this so? It is because Joseph never pities himself or sees himself as a victim. Because he always maintains an elevated consciousness and does not take on the consciousness of a slave, he always becomes a master.

לוֹ נָתַן בְּיָדוֹ: (ה) וַיְהִי מֵאָז (ומב) הִפְקִיד אֹתוֹ בְּבֵיתוֹ (ב"פ ראה) וְעַל
כָּל (ילי) (עמם)-אֲשֶׁר יֶשׁ-לוֹ וַיְבָרֶךְ (עסמ"ב) יְהֹוָהאדניאהדונהי אֶת-בֵּית
(ב"פ ראה) הַמִּצְרִי (מצר) בִּגְלַל יוֹסֵף (ציון) וַיְהִי בִּרְכַּת יְהֹוָהאדניאהדונהי
בְּכָל (לכב)-אֲשֶׁר יֶשׁ-לוֹ בַּבַּיִת (ב"פ ראה) וּבַשָּׂדֶה: (ו) וַיַּעֲזֹב כָּל
(ילי)-אֲשֶׁר-לוֹ בְּיַד-יוֹסֵף (ציון) וְלֹא-יָדַע אִתּוֹ מְאוּמָה כִּי אִם
(יוהך)-הַלֶּחֶם (ג' הויות) אֲשֶׁר-הוּא אוֹכֵל וַיְהִי יוֹסֵף (ציון) יְפֵה-תֹאַר
וִיפֵה מַרְאֶה:

Sixth Reading - Joseph - Yesod

(ז) וַיְהִי אַחַר הַדְּבָרִים (ראה) הָאֵלֶּה וַתִּשָּׂא אֵשֶׁת-אֲדֹנָיו
אֶת-עֵינֶיהָ (מ"ה בריבוע) אֶל-יוֹסֵף (ציון) וַתֹּאמֶר שִׁכְבָה עִמִּי: (ח)
וַיְמָאֵן | וַיֹּאמֶר אֶל-אֵשֶׁת אֲדֹנָיו הֵן אֲדֹנִי לֹא-יָדַע אִתִּי
מַה (מ"ה)-בַּבָּיִת (ב"פ ראה) וְכֹל (ילי) אֲשֶׁר-יֶשׁ-לוֹ נָתַן בְּיָדִי: (ט)
אֵינֶנּוּ גָדוֹל (להח, מבה עד"א) בַּבַּיִת (ב"פ ראה) הַזֶּה (והו) מִמֶּנִּי וְלֹא-
חָשַׂךְ מִמֶּנִּי מְאוּמָה כִּי אִם (יוהך)-אוֹתָךְ בַּאֲשֶׁר אַתְּ-אִשְׁתּוֹ
וְאֵיךְ אֶעֱשֶׂה הָרָעָה (רהע) הַגְּדֹלָה הַזֹּאת וְחָטָאתִי לֵאלֹהִים
(ילה): (י) וַיְהִי כְּדַבְּרָהּ (ראה) אֶל-יוֹסֵף (ציון) יוֹם (נגד, זן) | יוֹם (נגד,

וַתֹּאמֶר - The wife of Joseph's master tries to seduce him. Joseph refuses to be seduced by the wife of Potiphar, his master. She grabs at his clothing, but he escapes. Out of spite, she accuses Joseph of raping her, and he is thrown in jail.

(זן) וְלֹא־שָׁמַע אֵלֶיהָ לִשְׁכַּב אֶצְלָהּ לִהְיוֹת עִמָּהּ׃ (יא) וַיְהִי
כְּהַיּוֹם (נגד, זן) הַזֶּה (והו) וַיָּבֹא הַבַּיְתָה (כ"פ ראה) לַעֲשׂוֹת מְלַאכְתּוֹ
וְאֵין אִישׁ מֵאַנְשֵׁי הַבַּיִת (כ"פ ראה) שָׁם בַּבָּיִת (כ"פ ראה)׃ (יב)
וַתִּתְפְּשֵׂהוּ בְּבִגְדוֹ לֵאמֹר שִׁכְבָה עִמִּי וַיַּעֲזֹב בִּגְדוֹ בְּיָדָהּ
וַיָּנָס וַיֵּצֵא הַחוּצָה׃ (יג) וַיְהִי כִּרְאוֹתָהּ כִּי־עָזַב בִּגְדוֹ בְּיָדָהּ
וַיָּנָס הַחוּצָה׃ (יד) וַתִּקְרָא לְאַנְשֵׁי בֵיתָהּ (כ"פ ראה) וַתֹּאמֶר
לָהֶם לֵאמֹר רְאוּ הֵבִיא לָנוּ (מום) אִישׁ עִבְרִי לְצַחֶק בָּנוּ
בָּא אֵלַי לִשְׁכַּב עִמִּי וָאֶקְרָא בְּקוֹל גָּדוֹל (להוו, מבה ע"ד"א)׃
(טו) וַיְהִי כְשָׁמְעוֹ כִּי־הֲרִימֹתִי קוֹלִי וָאֶקְרָא וַיַּעֲזֹב בִּגְדוֹ
אֶצְלִי וַיָּנָס וַיֵּצֵא הַחוּצָה׃ (טז) וַתַּנַּח בִּגְדוֹ אֶצְלָהּ עַד־בּוֹא
אֲדֹנָיו אֶל־בֵּיתוֹ (כ"פ ראה)׃ (יז) וַתְּדַבֵּר (ראה) אֵלָיו כַּדְּבָרִים (ראה)
הָאֵלֶּה לֵאמֹר בָּא־אֵלַי הָעֶבֶד הָעִבְרִי אֲשֶׁר־הֵבֵאתָ לָּנוּ

וַיָּנָס - At the time of Joseph 's restriction, he achieves the level of Yesod, which he is expected to reach in his lifetime. We learn from Joseph that two conditions must be met for us to reach our expected spiritual level. First, we must to undergo an intense restriction, and second, we must go through a process of cleansing.

When Potiphar's wife tries to seduce Joseph, he desires her, but he restricts. After this act of restriction, Joseph is condemned to prison, and this is his cleansing. By enacting restriction and by being willing to undergo a cleansing, we can connect with our higher spiritual level and complete our Tikkun. Joseph's example gives us the opportunity and the spiritual energy to do this.

לְצַחֶק בִּי׃ (יח) וַיְהִי כַּהֲרִימִי קוֹלִי וָאֶקְרָא וַיַּעֲזֹב בִּגְדוֹ (מום)
אֶצְלִי וַיָּנָס הַחוּצָה׃ (יט) וַיְהִי כִשְׁמֹעַ אֲדֹנָיו אֶת־דִּבְרֵי (ראה)
אִשְׁתּוֹ אֲשֶׁר דִּבְּרָה (ראה) אֵלָיו לֵאמֹר כַּדְּבָרִים (ראה) הָאֵלֶּה
עָשָׂה לִי עַבְדֶּךָ (פוי) וַיִּחַר אַפּוֹ׃ (כ) וַיִּקַּח (ווזעם) אֲדֹנֵי יוֹסֵף (ציון)
אֹתוֹ וַיִּתְּנֵהוּ אֶל־בֵּית (ב"פ ראה) הַסֹּהַר מְקוֹם אֲשֶׁר־אֲסִירֵי
(אֲסוּרֵי כתיב) הַמֶּלֶךְ אֲסוּרִים וַיְהִי־שָׁם בְּבֵית (ב"פ ראה) הַסֹּהַר׃ (כא)
וַיְהִי יְהֹוָה (יאהדונהי) אֶת־יוֹסֵף (ציון) וַיֵּט אֵלָיו חָסֶד (ע"ב) וַיִּתֵּן חִנּוֹ
בְּעֵינֵי (מ"ה בריבוע) שַׂר בֵּית (ב"פ ראה)־הַסֹּהַר׃ (כב) וַיִּתֵּן שַׂר בֵּית (ב"פ
ראה)־הַסֹּהַר בְּיַד־יוֹסֵף (ציון) אֵת כָּל (ילי)־הָאֲסִירִם אֲשֶׁר בְּבֵית
(ב"פ ראה) הַסֹּהַר וְאֵת כָּל (ילי)־אֲשֶׁר עֹשִׂים שָׁם הוּא הָיָה (יהה)
עֹשֶׂה׃ (כג) אֵין | שַׂר בֵּית (ב"פ ראה)־ הַסֹּהַר רֹאֶה (ראה) אֶת־כָּל
(ילי)־מְאוּמָה בְּיָדוֹ בַּאֲשֶׁר יְהֹוָה (יאהדונהי) אִתּוֹ וַאֲשֶׁר־הוּא
עֹשֶׂה יְהֹוָה (יאהדונהי) מַצְלִיחַ׃ פ

Seventh Reading - David - Malchut

מ (א) וַיְהִי אַחַר הַדְּבָרִים (ראה) הָאֵלֶּה חָטְאוּ מַשְׁקֵה מֶלֶךְ־

הַסֹּהַר - Joseph is in jail, but he is loved by the master of the jail. Again, Joseph has a high spiritual consciousness. He does not see himself as a victim, and as a result, he becomes the master of the jail. How we experience life is not determined by our physical circumstances. Our spiritual level is the most important factor.

מִצְרָ֑יִם (מצר) וְהָ֣אֹפֶ֔ה לַאֲדֹנֵיהֶ֖ם לְמֶ֥לֶךְ מִצְרָֽיִם (מצר)׃ (ב)
וַיִּקְצֹ֣ף פַּרְעֹ֔ה עַ֖ל שְׁנֵ֣י סָרִיסָ֑יו עַ֚ל שַׂ֣ר הַמַּשְׁקִ֔ים וְעַ֖ל שַׂ֥ר
הָאוֹפִֽים׃ (ג) וַיִּתֵּ֨ן אֹתָ֜ם בְּמִשְׁמַ֗ר בֵּ֛ית (כ"פ ראה) שַׂ֥ר הַטַּבָּחִ֖ים
אֶל־בֵּ֣ית (כ"פ ראה) הַסֹּ֑הַר מְק֕וֹם אֲשֶׁ֥ר יוֹסֵ֖ף (ציון) אָס֥וּר שָֽׁם׃
(ד) וַ֠יִּפְקֹד (מנק) שַׂ֣ר הַטַּבָּחִ֧ים אֶת־יוֹסֵ֛ף (ציון) אִתָּ֖ם וַיְשָׁ֣רֶת
אֹתָ֑ם וַיִּהְי֥וּ יָמִ֖ים (נלך) בְּמִשְׁמָֽר׃ (ה) וַיַּֽחַלְמוּ֩ חֲל֨וֹם שְׁנֵיהֶ֜ם
אִ֤ישׁ חֲלֹמוֹ֙ בְּלַ֣יְלָה (מלה) אֶחָ֔ד (אהבה) אִ֖ישׁ כְּפִתְר֣וֹן חֲלֹמ֑וֹ
הַמַּשְׁקֶ֣ה וְהָאֹפֶ֗ה אֲשֶׁר֙ לְמֶ֣לֶךְ מִצְרַ֔יִם (מצר) אֲשֶׁ֥ר אֲסוּרִ֖ים

וַיִּתֵּן - The wine steward and the chief baker are sent to the jail.
Our dreams are expressions of our consciousness, and our consciousness determines what happens to us in the world. The wine steward and the chief baker are imprisoned with Joseph, and both have dreams that fill them with concern. Joseph interprets their dreams and determines that one of the two men, the wine steward, will live. But the chief baker must die.

The Zohar asks: “Why did Joseph make this interpretation? What are the differences between the dreams?” The wine steward dreamed about grapes, and grapes relate to the building of the Temple. Grapes (and wine) have the power to elevate the spirit. This was a positive dream about creating something. But the baker had a dream about baskets of bread, which Joseph understood to be a vision of the destruction of the Temple. Based on the positive and negative content of the two men’s dreams, Joseph immediately knew their destiny.

In the men’s dreams, there were three baskets of bread and three vines of grapes. Joseph interprets this as a reference to Pharaoh’s birthday, which is to occur in three days. When the three days have passed, both the wine steward and the baker are released from prison, but the wine steward is reinstated to his former position, while the baker is killed.

בְּבֵית (כ״פ ראה) הַסֹּהַר׃ (ו) וַיָּבֹא אֲלֵיהֶם יוֹסֵף (ציון) בַּבֹּקֶר וַיַּרְא
אֹתָם וְהִנָּם זֹעֲפִים׃ (ז) וַיִּשְׁאַל אֶת־סְרִיסֵי פַרְעֹה אֲשֶׁר
אִתּוֹ בְמִשְׁמַר בֵּית (כ״פ ראה) אֲדֹנָיו לֵאמֹר מַדּוּעַ פְּנֵיכֶם
רָעִים הַיּוֹם (נגד, זן)׃ (ח) וַיֹּאמְרוּ אֵלָיו חֲלוֹם חָלַמְנוּ וּפֹתֵר אֵין
אֹתוֹ וַיֹּאמֶר אֲלֵהֶם יוֹסֵף (ציון) הֲלוֹא לֵאלֹהִים (ילה) פִּתְרֹנִים
סַפְּרוּ־נָא לִי׃ (ט) וַיְסַפֵּר שַׂר־הַמַּשְׁקִים אֶת־חֲלֹמוֹ לְיוֹסֵף (ציון)
וַיֹּאמֶר לוֹ בַּחֲלוֹמִי וְהִנֵּה־גֶפֶן לְפָנָי׃ (י) וּבַגֶּפֶן שְׁלֹשָׁה שָׂרִיגִם
וְהִוא כְפֹרַחַת עָלְתָה נִצָּהּ הִבְשִׁילוּ אַשְׁכְּלֹתֶיהָ עֲנָבִים׃ (יא)
וְכוֹס (מום) פַּרְעֹה בְּיָדִי וָאֶקַּח אֶת־הָעֲנָבִים וָאֶשְׂחַט אֹתָם
אֶל־כּוֹס (מום) פַּרְעֹה וָאֶתֵּן אֶת־הַכּוֹס (מום) עַל־כַּף פַּרְעֹה׃
(יב) וַיֹּאמֶר לוֹ יוֹסֵף (ציון) זֶה פִּתְרֹנוֹ שְׁלֹשֶׁת הַשָּׂרִגִים שְׁלֹשֶׁת
יָמִים (נלך) הֵם׃ (יג) בְּעוֹד | שְׁלֹשֶׁת יָמִים (נלך) יִשָּׂא פַרְעֹה
אֶת־רֹאשֶׁךָ וַהֲשִׁיבְךָ עַל־כַּנֶּךָ וְנָתַתָּ כוֹס (מום)־פַּרְעֹה בְּיָדוֹ
כַּמִּשְׁפָּט (ע״ה ה״פ אלהים) הָרִאשׁוֹן אֲשֶׁר הָיִיתָ מַשְׁקֵהוּ׃ (יד) כִּי
אִם (יוהך)־זְכַרְתַּנִי אִתְּךָ כַּאֲשֶׁר יִיטַב לָךְ וְעָשִׂיתָ־נָּא עִמָּדִי
חָסֶד (ע״ב) וְהִזְכַּרְתַּנִי אֶל־פַּרְעֹה וְהוֹצֵאתַנִי מִן־הַבַּיִת (כ״פ

וְהִזְכַּרְתַּנִי - Joseph asks the wine steward to plead on his behalf to Pharaoh, but the Torah says that the wine steward forgets Joseph. The Zohar explains that Joseph, by asking this favor of the wine steward, has put his

(ראה) הַזֶּה (והו)׃ (טו) כִּי־גֻנֹּב גֻּנַּבְתִּי מֵאֶרֶץ הָעִבְרִים וְגַם־פֹּה
(ע"ה מום) לֹא־עָשִׂיתִי מְאוּמָה כִּי־שָׂמוּ (מהש ע"ה) אֹתִי בַּבּוֹר׃ (טז)
וַיַּרְא שַׂר־הָאֹפִים כִּי טוֹב (והו) (אום) פָּתָר וַיֹּאמֶר אֶל־יוֹסֵף (ציון)
אַף־אֲנִי (אני) בַּחֲלוֹמִי וְהִנֵּה שְׁלֹשָׁה סַלֵּי חֹרִי עַל־רֹאשִׁי׃ (יז)
וּבַסַּל הָעֶלְיוֹן מִכֹּל (ילי) מַאֲכַל פַּרְעֹה מַעֲשֵׂה אֹפֶה וְהָעוֹף
אֹכֵל אֹתָם מִן־הַסַּל מֵעַל (עלם) רֹאשִׁי׃ (יח) וַיַּעַן יוֹסֵף (ציון)
וַיֹּאמֶר זֶה פִּתְרֹנוֹ שְׁלֹשֶׁת הַסַּלִּים שְׁלֹשֶׁת יָמִים (נלך) הֵם׃ (יט)
בְּעוֹד | שְׁלֹשֶׁת יָמִים (נלך) יִשָּׂא פַרְעֹה אֶת־רֹאשְׁךָ מֵעָלֶיךָ
וְתָלָה אוֹתְךָ עַל־עֵץ וְאָכַל הָעוֹף אֶת־בְּשָׂרְךָ מֵעָלֶיךָ׃
(כ) וַיְהִי | בַּיּוֹם (נגד, זן) הַשְּׁלִישִׁי יוֹם (נגד, זן) הֻלֶּדֶת אֶת־פַּרְעֹה
וַיַּעַשׂ מִשְׁתֶּה לְכָל (יה אדני)־עֲבָדָיו וַיִּשָּׂא אֶת־רֹאשׁ | שַׂר
הַמַּשְׁקִים וְאֶת־רֹאשׁ שַׂר הָאֹפִים בְּתוֹךְ עֲבָדָיו׃ (כא) וַיָּשֶׁב
אֶת־שַׂר הַמַּשְׁקִים עַל־מַשְׁקֵהוּ וַיִּתֵּן הַכּוֹס (מום) עַל־כַּף
פַּרְעֹה׃ (כב) וְאֵת שַׂר הָאֹפִים תָּלָה כַּאֲשֶׁר פָּתַר לָהֶם יוֹסֵף
(ציון)׃ (כג) וְלֹא־זָכַר שַׂר־הַמַּשְׁקִים אֶת־יוֹסֵף (ציון) וַיִּשְׁכָּחֵהוּ׃

פפפ

hope in a human being rather than simply trusting the Light. By doing so, Joseph actually lengthened the cleansing process of his imprisonment by two years.

The Haftarah of Vayeshev

This Haftarah portion clearly shares with us that often in life we give away a lot for very little in return – we sell ourselves short. We tend to settle for the immediate gratification because we don't have the trust or the patience that the fulfillment will come.

There is a story about a poor, lonely man who prayed to the Creator to send him someone to share the Shabbat with. The Creator had such compassion for the poor man that He decided to send Elijah the prophet to him, which would have helped the man reach great spiritual heights. As Elijah was preparing for his journey, the man became desperate and impatient. He decided to begin the Shabbat, by going into his barn and making a blessing on the wine and the bread, only with his donkey to accompany him. The Creator saw this and decided that the man did not need Elijah the prophet after all. The man spent the rest of Shabbat alone with his mule.

This reading of this portion will assist us in building our trust in the Light and fortify us for the times when our patience wears thin.

עָמוֹס פרק ב

א כֹּה (הי״) אָמַר יְהוָה עַל־שְׁלֹשָׁה פִּשְׁעֵי מוֹאָב וְעַל־
אַרְבָּעָה לֹא אֲשִׁיבֶנּוּ עַל־שָׂרְפוֹ עַצְמוֹת מֶלֶךְ־אֱדוֹם
לַשִּׂיד׃ ב וְשִׁלַּחְתִּי־אֵשׁ בְּמוֹאָב וְאָכְלָה אַרְמְנוֹת הַקְּרִיּוֹת
וּמֵת בְּשָׁאוֹן מוֹאָב בִּתְרוּעָה בְּקוֹל שׁוֹפָר׃ ג וְהִכְרַתִּי שׁוֹפֵט
מִקִּרְבָּהּ וְכָל־שָׂרֶיהָ אֶהֱרוֹג עִמּוֹ אָמַר יְהוָה׃ {פ} ד כֹּה
(הי״) אָמַר יְהוָה עַל־שְׁלֹשָׁה פִּשְׁעֵי יְהוּדָה וְעַל־אַרְבָּעָה
לֹא אֲשִׁיבֶנּוּ עַל־מָאֳסָם אֶת־תּוֹרַת יְהוָה וְחֻקָּיו לֹא שָׁמָרוּ
וַיַּתְעוּם כִּזְבֵיהֶם אֲשֶׁר־הָלְכוּ (מ״ה) אֲבוֹתָם אַחֲרֵיהֶם׃ ה
וְשִׁלַּחְתִּי אֵשׁ בִּיהוּדָה וְאָכְלָה אַרְמְנוֹת יְרוּשָׁלִָם׃ {פ} ו כֹּה

(הי״) אָמַר יְהוָה עַל־שְׁלֹשָׁה פִּשְׁעֵי יִשְׂרָאֵל וְעַל־אַרְבָּעָה לֹא
אֲשִׁיבֶנּוּ עַל־מִכְרָם בַּכֶּסֶף צַדִּיק וְאֶבְיוֹן בַּעֲבוּר נַעֲלָיִם׃ ז
הַשֹּׁאֲפִים עַל־עֲפַר־אֶרֶץ בְּרֹאשׁ דַּלִּים וְדֶרֶךְ (כ״פ יב״ק) עֲנָוִים
(ענו) יַטּוּ וְאִישׁ וְאָבִיו יֵלְכוּ אֶל־הַנַּעֲרָה לְמַעַן חַלֵּל אֶת־שֵׁם
קָדְשִׁי׃ ח וְעַל־בְּגָדִים חֲבֻלִים יַטּוּ אֵצֶל כָּל־מִזְבֵּחַ (זן, נגד)
וְיֵין (מ״כ, י״פ האא) עֲנוּשִׁים יִשְׁתּוּ (כ״פ ראה) בֵּית אֱלֹהֵיהֶם (דמב, ילה)׃
ט וְאָנֹכִי (אי״ע) הִשְׁמַדְתִּי אֶת־הָאֱמֹרִי מִפְּנֵיהֶם אֲשֶׁר כְּגֹבַהּ
אֲרָזִים גָּבְהוֹ וְחָסֹן הוּא כָּאַלּוֹנִים וָאַשְׁמִיד פִּרְיוֹ מִמַּעַל (עלם)
וְשָׁרָשָׁיו מִתָּחַת׃ י וְאָנֹכִי (אי״ע) הֶעֱלֵיתִי אֶתְכֶם מֵאֶרֶץ מִצְרָיִם
(מצר) וָאוֹלֵךְ אֶתְכֶם בַּמִּדְבָּר אַרְבָּעִים שָׁנָה לָרֶשֶׁת אֶת־
אֶרֶץ הָאֱמֹרִי׃ יא וָאָקִים מִבְּנֵיכֶם לִנְבִיאִים וּמִבַּחוּרֵיכֶם
לִנְזִרִים הַאַף אֵין־זֹאת בְּנֵי יִשְׂרָאֵל נְאֻם־יְהוָה׃ יב וַתַּשְׁקוּ
אֶת־הַנְּזִרִים יָיִן (מ״כ, י״פ האא) וְעַל־הַנְּבִיאִים צִוִּיתֶם (פוי) לֵאמֹר
לֹא תִנָּבְאוּ׃ יג הִנֵּה אָנֹכִי (אי״ע) מֵעִיק תַּחְתֵּיכֶם כַּאֲשֶׁר תָּעִיק
הָעֲגָלָה הַמְלֵאָה לָהּ עָמִיר׃ יד וְאָבַד מָנוֹס מִקָּל (נמם) וְחָזָק
(פהל) לֹא־יְאַמֵּץ כֹּחוֹ וְגִבּוֹר לֹא־יְמַלֵּט נַפְשׁוֹ׃ טו וְתֹפֵשׂ
הַקֶּשֶׁת לֹא יַעֲמֹד וְקַל (נמם) בְּרַגְלָיו לֹא יְמַלֵּט וְרֹכֵב הַסּוּס
(כוק) לֹא יְמַלֵּט נַפְשׁוֹ׃ טז וְאַמִּיץ לִבּוֹ בַּגִּבּוֹרִים עָרוֹם יָנוּס
בַּיּוֹם (נגד, מזבח, זן) ־הַהוּא נְאֻם־יְהוָה׃ {פ} א שִׁמְעוּ אֶת־הַדָּבָר

(ראה) הַזֶּה (והו) אֲשֶׁר דִּבֶּר (ראה) יְהֹוָה עֲלֵיכֶם בְּנֵי יִשְׂרָאֵל עַל
כָּל־הַמִּשְׁפָּחָה אֲשֶׁר הֶעֱלֵיתִי מֵאֶרֶץ מִצְרַיִם (מצר) לֵאמֹר:
ב רַק אֶתְכֶם יָדַעְתִּי מִכֹּל מִשְׁפְּחוֹת הָאֲדָמָה עַל־כֵּן
אֶפְקֹד עֲלֵיכֶם אֵת כָּל־עֲוֺנֹתֵיכֶם: ג הֲיֵלְכוּ שְׁנַיִם יַחְדָּו
בִּלְתִּי אִם־נוֹעָדוּ: ד הֲיִשְׁאַג אַרְיֵה בַּיַּעַר (ערי, סןזחך, סנדלפון)
וְטֶרֶף אֵין לוֹ הֲיִתֵּן כְּפִיר קוֹלוֹ מִמְּעֹנָתוֹ בִּלְתִּי אִם־לָכָד:
(יוהך) ה הֲתִפֹּל צִפּוֹר עַל־פַּח הָאָרֶץ וּמוֹקֵשׁ אֵין לָהּ הֲיַעֲלֶה־
פַּח מִן־הָאֲדָמָה וְלָכוֹד לֹא יִלְכּוֹד: ו אִם (יוהך) ־יִתָּקַע שׁוֹפָר
בְּעִיר (ערי, סןזחך, סנדלפון) וְעָם לֹא יֶחֱרָדוּ אִם (יוהך) ־תִּהְיֶה רָעָה (רהע)
בְּעִיר (ערי, סןזחך, סנדלפון) וַיהֹוָה לֹא עָשָׂה: ז כִּי לֹא יַעֲשֶׂה אֲדֹנָי
יְהֹוִה דָּבָר (ראה) כִּי אִם (יוהך) ־גָּלָה סוֹדוֹ (מיכ, י״פ האא) אֶל־עֲבָדָיו
הַנְּבִיאִים: (ילי) ח אַרְיֵה שָׁאָג מִי (ילי) לֹא יִירָא אֲדֹנָי יְהֹוִה דִּבֶּר
(ראה) מִי (ילי) לֹא יִנָּבֵא:

Lesson of Miketz

"It was at the end of two years...."

This portion begins: "It was at the end of two years and Pharaoh dreamed...." His dream concerned the lean cattle and the fattened cattle. But the real purpose of the dream was not only that it should be explained, but that it should be explained by Joseph, so that he could be appointed second to the king. Actually, the dream was supposed to have occurred two years earlier, but because Joseph had two years added onto his prison sentence, the dream was delayed for that length of time. This is clear in the way the verse is written: "...at the end of two years and Pharaoh dreamed..."

The lesson here concerns the way we try to make things happen as quickly as possible–or at least things that we want to happen. We should remember that everything has already been prepared for us. Our efforts and our desires are important and can have an effect. When our efforts are on behalf of ourselves, however, our power is drastically limited

The secret is knowing what kind of effort is important and how much of an effort is enough. Many people come to the Kabbalah Centre to pray in the morning, and sometimes the prayers end very late. People ask themselves if it pays to come early in the morning to pray if it makes them late for work. The answer is, of course it pays, but there also has to be an understanding and a willingness to make the extra effort

The truth is, having our heart and consciousness in the right place would allow us to have everything we need in just one second. So it is never right to say, "He should have been at work earlier because he needs the money." It's very nice to have money, of course, but the effort to raise spiritual consciousness that we're talking about brings not just money but literally complete joy and fulfillment in all things.

Imagine two stores. In one, the employees work all day and succeed in making a certain amount of money. In the other store, the staff sees no action all day, but just before closing a customer appears and spends thousands of dollars. You don't have to be running yourself ragged at every moment to get what you want and need. It is possible to gain more in a second than you have gained in a year. And this doesn't apply only to money.

The result in our lives of all of this, lies not in the physical effort we make but in the real effort between man and himself, -- in how much he really believes that blessings come not as a result of his own actions, but that blessings come from the Creator.

A person who believes only in himself might make some money, but in the end, he will not be happy. We are not, God forbid, judging Joseph on what he did or did not do, but we are coming to learn from him for our lives.

There is a story about the head of a Yeshivah who asked the Chafetz Chaim, a great scholar and spiritual leader, to recommend a supervisor for his Yeshivah. The Chafetz Chaim suggested a certain young man who had a big heart and could make a difference in the spiritual level of the Yeshivah, and of course, the head of the yeshivah took his advice.

After a short time, the Chafetz Chaim reconsidered his recommendation. When the head of the Yeshivah asked the reason, the Chafetz Chaim answered that he did not, God forbid, see anything wrong in the young supervisor, but that several days earlier, the young man had been complaining about his life and about not having any money. The Chafetz Chaim said that because of this, he took back his recommendation since a person who complained about the physical conditions of his life could not be a spiritual influence in a Yeshivah.

If Joseph had agreed with and accepted the judgment that was upon him, he could have avoided the two additional years in prison. If he had been patient for just a few more days, his problem would have been solved. But because he lost his patience and complained, he had an additional judgment placed upon him.

It has been said that people get sick according to their judgment and regain their health through their desire for God. Even if they are working hard towards healing themselves, it is God who makes that healing possible. Thus, it is written in the Gemara: "...a doctor will heal." This means that permission is given to doctors for healing–permission from the Creator. It does not necessarily mean that the sick had permission to be healed, but rather that the doctors were allowed to heal them.

It is written that a man who is truly in awe of God will be released from the constraints of natural law. This is because nature was created for those people who did not make an effort in their lives to discover the truth of the Creator. Nature takes its course with those people. But when a person is above this and knows that he can trust in God alone all his life, God will be his security. Any and all circumstances in our lives are a direct effect of the desire of the Creator.

So when we feel pressure and stress, we need to stop reacting! By not reacting, we make room for the Light to reveal Itself within us. Ultimately, that is the only way we can really eliminate chaos from our lives.

Synopsis of Miketz

This portion is almost always read on the Shabbat of Chanukah, the holiday of miracles. Most holidays possess a lower level of spiritual energy than Shabbat. The energy of holidays is spread over an entire year, while the energy of Shabbat is more potent because it controls a shorter period of time. So when a holiday occurs on Shabbat, the holiday's spiritual level is affected.

When Joseph put his faith in the wine steward instead of in the Light, two years were added to his time in prison. This portion begins at the conclusion of those two years.

First Reading - Abraham - Chesed

מא (א) וַיְהִי מִקֵּץ (מנק) שְׁנָתַיִם יָמִים (נלך) וּפַרְעֹה **חֹלֵם** וְהִנֵּה
עֹמֵד עַל־הַיְאֹר: (כף ויו זין ויו) (ב) וְהִנֵּה מִן־הַיְאֹר (כף ויו זין ויו)
עֹלֹת (אבג יתץ, ושר, אהבת חנם) שֶׁבַע פָּרוֹת יְפוֹת מַרְאֶה וּבְרִיאֹת
בָּשָׂר וַתִּרְעֶינָה בָּאָחוּ: (ג) וְהִנֵּה שֶׁבַע פָּרוֹת אֲחֵרוֹת עֹלוֹת
אַחֲרֵיהֶן מִן־הַיְאֹר (כף ויו זין ויו) רָעוֹת מַרְאֶה וְדַקּוֹת בָּשָׂר
וַתַּעֲמֹדְנָה אֵצֶל הַפָּרוֹת עַל־שְׂפַת הַיְאֹר: (כף ויו זין ויו) (ד)
וַתֹּאכַלְנָה הַפָּרוֹת רָעוֹת הַמַּרְאֶה וְדַקֹּת הַבָּשָׂר אֵת שֶׁבַע
הַפָּרוֹת יְפֹת הַמַּרְאֶה וְהַבְּרִיאֹת וַיִּיקַץ פַּרְעֹה: (ה) וַיִּישָׁן
וַיַּחֲלֹם שֵׁנִית וְהִנֵּה | שֶׁבַע שִׁבֳּלִים עֹלוֹת בְּקָנֶה אֶחָד (אהבה)
בְּרִיאוֹת וְטֹבוֹת: (ו) וְהִנֵּה שֶׁבַע שִׁבֳּלִים דַּקּוֹת וּשְׁדוּפֹת
קָדִים צֹמְחוֹת אַחֲרֵיהֶן: (ז) וַתִּבְלַעְנָה הַשִּׁבֳּלִים הַדַּקּוֹת אֵת
שֶׁבַע הַשִּׁבֳּלִים הַבְּרִיאוֹת וְהַמְּלֵאוֹת וַיִּיקַץ פַּרְעֹה וְהִנֵּה
חֲלוֹם: (ח) וַיְהִי בַבֹּקֶר וַתִּפָּעֶם רוּחוֹ וַיִּשְׁלַח וַיִּקְרָא אֶת־כָּל
(ילי)־חַרְטֻמֵּי מִצְרַיִם (מצר) וְאֶת־כָּל (ילי)־חֲכָמֶיהָ וַיְסַפֵּר פַּרְעֹה

חֹלֵם - Pharaoh has two dreams - Pharaoh's dreams show him the future of Egypt. Because he is responsible for the country, Pharaoh is allowed to receive these messages despite his not being at a very high spiritual level. The same principle applies in our own lives. We are granted dreams pertaining to areas over which we have domain, about the people and things we are close to, even though we may not be on a very high spiritual level. Parents, for example, often receive dreams about their families.

לָהֶם אֶת־חֲלֹמוֹ וְאֵין־פּוֹתֵר אוֹתָם לְפַרְעֹה׃ (ט) וַיְדַבֵּר
(ראה) שַׂר הַמַּשְׁקִים אֶת־פַּרְעֹה לֵאמֹר אֶת־חֲטָאַי אֲנִי (אני)
מַזְכִּיר הַיּוֹם (נגד, זן)׃ (י) פַּרְעֹה קָצַף עַל־עֲבָדָיו וַיִּתֵּן אֹתִי
בְּמִשְׁמַר בֵּית (כ״פ ראה) שַׂר הַטַּבָּחִים אֹתִי וְאֵת שַׂר הָאֹפִים׃
(יא) וַנַּחַלְמָה חֲלוֹם בְּלַיְלָה (מלה) אֶחָד (אהבה) אֲנִי (אני) וָהוּא אִישׁ
כְּפִתְרוֹן חֲלֹמוֹ חָלָמְנוּ׃ (יב) וְשָׁם אִתָּנוּ נַעַר עִבְרִי עֶבֶד לְשַׂר
הַטַּבָּחִים וַנְּסַפֶּר־לוֹ וַיִּפְתָּר־לָנוּ (מום) אֶת־חֲלֹמֹתֵינוּ אִישׁ
כַּחֲלֹמוֹ פָּתָר׃ (יג) וַיְהִי כַּאֲשֶׁר פָּתַר־לָנוּ (מום) כֵּן הָיָה (יהה) אֹתִי
הֵשִׁיב עַל־כַּנִּי וְאֹתוֹ תָלָה׃ (יד) וַיִּשְׁלַח פַּרְעֹה **וַיִּקְרָא** אֶת־
יוֹסֵף (ציון) וַיְרִיצֻהוּ מִן־הַבּוֹר וַיְגַלַּח וַיְחַלֵּף שִׂמְלֹתָיו וַיָּבֹא
אֶל־פַּרְעֹה׃

מַזְכִּיר - The wine steward remembers Joseph

Although Joseph's interpretation of the dream saved the wine steward's life, he forgets Joseph once he is out of the prison. Then after two years, the wine steward remembers. We often behave in the same way, forgetting what someone has done for us in the past, with a consciousness of "What have you done for me lately?"

וַיִּקְרָא - Joseph is summoned to Pharaoh.

To speak to Pharaoh, one had to be able to climb seventy steps, with each step requiring knowledge of a different language. The night before Joseph was to appear before Pharaoh, an angel visited him in prison and taught him the 70 languages. Joseph also gained protection from the negative forces and the black magic that surrounded Pharaoh. Whenever we have to be on the defensive or appear before people who may in some way be our adversaries,

Second Reading - Issac - Gvurah

(טו) וַיֹּאמֶר פַּרְעֹה אֶל-יוֹסֵף (ציון) חֲלוֹם חָלַמְתִּי וּפֹתֵר אֵין אֹתוֹ
וַאֲנִי (אני) שָׁמַעְתִּי עָלֶיךָ לֵאמֹר תִּשְׁמַע חֲלוֹם לִפְתֹּר אֹתוֹ׃
(טז) וַיַּעַן יוֹסֵף (ציון) אֶת-פַּרְעֹה לֵאמֹר בִּלְעָדָי אֱלֹהִים (ילה)
יַעֲנֶה אֶת-שְׁלוֹם פַּרְעֹה׃ (יז) וַיְדַבֵּר (ראה) פַּרְעֹה אֶל-יוֹסֵף (ציון)
בַּחֲלֹמִי הִנְנִי עֹמֵד עַל-שְׂפַת הַיְאֹר׃ (כף ויו זין ויו) (יח) וְהִנֵּה מִן-
הַיְאֹר׃ (כף ויו זין ויו) עֹלֹת (אבג יתץ, ושר, אהבת חנם) שֶׁבַע פָּרוֹת בְּרִיאוֹת
בָּשָׂר וִיפֹת תֹּאַר וַתִּרְעֶינָה בָּאָחוּ׃ (יט) וְהִנֵּה שֶׁבַע פָּרוֹת
אֲחֵרוֹת עֹלוֹת אַחֲרֵיהֶן דַּלּוֹת וְרָעוֹת תֹּאַר מְאֹד וְרַקּוֹת
בָּשָׂר לֹא-רָאִיתִי כָהֵנָּה בְּכָל (לכב)-אֶרֶץ מִצְרַיִם (מצר) לָרֹעַ׃
(כ) וַתֹּאכַלְנָה הַפָּרוֹת הָרַקּוֹת וְהָרָעוֹת אֵת שֶׁבַע הַפָּרוֹת
הָרִאשֹׁנוֹת הַבְּרִיאֹת׃ (כא) וַתָּבֹאנָה אֶל-קִרְבֶּנָה וְלֹא נוֹדַע
כִּי-בָאוּ אֶל-קִרְבֶּנָה וּמַרְאֵיהֶן רַע כַּאֲשֶׁר בַּתְּחִלָּה וָאִיקָץ׃

we must acquire the appropriate protection. In addition, we must ask the Light to speak through us. This is the “right language” we need to call upon in uncertain situations.

בַּחֲלֹמִי - Pharaoh tells the two dreams to Joseph
When Pharaoh recounts his dreams to Joseph, he changes some details to test Joseph’s understanding. Joseph not only tells Pharaoh the meaning of the dreams, he is also able to correct Pharaoh’s recounting of them. Joseph was in tune not only with the inner meaning of the dreams, but also with the signs that appeared in them.

(כב) וָאֵרֶא בַּחֲלֹמִי וְהִנֵּה | שֶׁבַע שִׁבֳּלִים עֹלֹת (אבג יתץ, ושר, אהבת
חנם) בְּקָנֶה אֶחָד (אהבה) מְלֵאֹת וְטֹבוֹת׃ (כג) וְהִנֵּה שֶׁבַע שִׁבֳּלִים
צְנֻמוֹת דַּקּוֹת שְׁדֻפוֹת קָדִים צֹמְחוֹת אַחֲרֵיהֶם׃ (כד) וַתִּבְלַעְןָ
הַשִּׁבֳּלִים הַדַּקֹּת אֵת שֶׁבַע הַשִּׁבֳּלִים הַטֹּבוֹת וָאֹמַר אֶל־
הַחַרְטֻמִּים וְאֵין מַגִּיד לִי׃ (כה) וַיֹּאמֶר יוֹסֵף (ציון) אֶל־פַּרְעֹה
חֲלוֹם פַּרְעֹה אֶחָד (אהבה) הוּא אֵת אֲשֶׁר הָאֱלֹהִים (ילה) עֹשֶׂה
הִגִּיד לְפַרְעֹה׃ (כו) שֶׁבַע פָּרֹת הַטֹּבֹת שֶׁבַע שָׁנִים הֵנָּה
וְשֶׁבַע הַשִּׁבֳּלִים הַטֹּבֹת שֶׁבַע שָׁנִים הֵנָּה חֲלוֹם אֶחָד (אהבה)
הוּא׃ (כז) וְשֶׁבַע הַפָּרוֹת הָרַקּוֹת וְהָרָעֹת הָעֹלֹת (אבג יתץ, ושר,
אהבת חנם) אַחֲרֵיהֶן שֶׁבַע שָׁנִים הֵנָּה וְשֶׁבַע הַשִּׁבֳּלִים הָרֵקוֹת
שְׁדֻפוֹת הַקָּדִים יִהְיוּ שֶׁבַע שְׁנֵי רָעָב׃ (כח) הוּא הַדָּבָר (ראה)
אֲשֶׁר דִּבַּרְתִּי (ראה) אֶל־פַּרְעֹה אֲשֶׁר הָאֱלֹהִים (ילה) עֹשֶׂה
הֶרְאָה אֶת־פַּרְעֹה׃ (כט) הִנֵּה שֶׁבַע שָׁנִים בָּאוֹת שָׂבָע גָּדוֹל
(להח, מבה עד"א) בְּכָל (לכב)־אֶרֶץ מִצְרָיִם (מצר)׃ (ל) וְקָמוּ שֶׁבַע שְׁנֵי
רָעָב אַחֲרֵיהֶן וְנִשְׁכַּח כָּל (ילי)־הַשָּׂבָע בְּאֶרֶץ מִצְרָיִם (מצר)
וְכִלָּה הָרָעָב אֶת־הָאָרֶץ (מילוי אלהים ע"ה)׃ (לא) וְלֹא־יִוָּדַע הַשָּׂבָע

וַיֹּאמֶר - Joseph interprets the dream

Joseph foresees seven plentiful years and seven years of famine. In our own lives, we can always choose between feast and famine. We need only use the tools of Kabbalah to connect with abundance and prosperity.

בָּאָרֶץ מִפְּנֵי הָרָעָב הַהוּא אַחֲרֵי־כֵן כִּי־כָבֵד הוּא מְאֹד׃ (לב)
וְעַל הִשָּׁנוֹת הַחֲלוֹם אֶל־פַּרְעֹה פַּעֲמָיִם כִּי־נָכוֹן הַדָּבָר (ראה)
מֵעִם הָאֱלֹהִים (ילה) וּמְמַהֵר הָאֱלֹהִים (ילה) לַעֲשֹׂתוֹ׃ (לג) וְעַתָּה
יֵרֶא פַרְעֹה אִישׁ נָבוֹן וְחָכָם וִישִׁיתֵהוּ עַל־אֶרֶץ מִצְרָיִם
(מצר)׃ (לד) יַעֲשֶׂה פַרְעֹה וְיַפְקֵד פְּקִדִים עַל־הָאָרֶץ (מילוי אלהים
ע"ה) וְחִמֵּשׁ אֶת־אֶרֶץ מִצְרַיִם (מצר) בְּשֶׁבַע שְׁנֵי הַשָּׂבָע׃ (לה)
וְיִקְבְּצוּ אֶת־כָּל (ילי)־אֹכֶל הַשָּׁנִים הַטֹּבֹת הַבָּאֹת הָאֵלֶּה
וְיִצְבְּרוּ־בָר תַּחַת יַד־פַּרְעֹה אֹכֶל בֶּעָרִים וְשָׁמָרוּ׃ (לו) וְהָיָה
(יהה) (יהוה) הָאֹכֶל לְפִקָּדוֹן לָאָרֶץ לְשֶׁבַע שְׁנֵי הָרָעָב אֲשֶׁר
תִּהְיֶיןָ בְּאֶרֶץ מִצְרָיִם (מצר) וְלֹא־תִכָּרֵת הָאָרֶץ (מילוי אלהים ע"ה)
בָּרָעָב׃ (לז) וַיִּיטַב הַדָּבָר (ראה) בְּעֵינֵי (מ"ה בריבוע) פַרְעֹה וּבְעֵינֵי
(מ"ה בריבוע) כָּל (ילי)־עֲבָדָיו׃ (לח) וַיֹּאמֶר פַּרְעֹה אֶל־עֲבָדָיו

וִישִׁיתֵהוּ - Joseph becomes Pharaoh's closest advisor, second in rank to the ruler himself. This is the person who was sold into slavery and who spent years in prison. Now he is second only to the king of Egypt. This teaches us that if we keep the right consciousness, everything will turn out well for us. If our consciousness is incorrect, on the other hand, the present may look fine, but eventually things will fall apart.

לְפִקָּדוֹן - Joseph had a plan to save Egypt in the years of famine Joseph had control over all the food in Egypt. For us today, there are two people with whom we must connect to ensure sustenance. One is Joseph and the other is Rabbi Shimon bar Yochai. The importance of Rabbi Shimon in this area was revealed to Rav Berg by his teacher, Rabbi Brandwein.

הֲנִמְצָא כָזֶה אִישׁ אֲשֶׁר רוּחַ אֱלֹהִים (ילה) בּוֹ׃

Third Reading - Jacob - Tiferet

(לט) וַיֹּאמֶר פַּרְעֹה אֶל־יוֹסֵף (ציון) אַחֲרֵי הוֹדִיעַ אֱלֹהִים (ילה)
אוֹתְךָ אֶת־כָּל (ילי)־זֹאת אֵין־נָבוֹן וְחָכָם כָּמוֹךָ׃ (מ) אַתָּה
תִּהְיֶה עַל־בֵּיתִי (ב"פ ראה) וְעַל־פִּיךָ יִשַּׁק כָּל (ילי)־עַמִּי רַק
הַכִּסֵּא אֶגְדַּל מִמֶּךָּ׃ (מא) וַיֹּאמֶר פַּרְעֹה אֶל־יוֹסֵף (ציון) רְאֵה
(ראה) נָתַתִּי אֹתְךָ עַל כָּל (ילי) (עממ)־אֶרֶץ מִצְרָיִם (מצר)׃ (מב) וַיָּסַר
פַּרְעֹה אֶת־טַבַּעְתּוֹ מֵעַל (עלם) יָדוֹ וַיִּתֵּן אֹתָהּ עַל־יַד יוֹסֵף (ציון)
וַיַּלְבֵּשׁ אֹתוֹ בִּגְדֵי־שֵׁשׁ וַיָּשֶׂם רְבִד הַזָּהָב (והו) עַל־צַוָּארוֹ׃
(מג) וַיַּרְכֵּב אֹתוֹ בְּמִרְכֶּבֶת הַמִּשְׁנֶה אֲשֶׁר־לוֹ וַיִּקְרְאוּ לְפָנָיו
אַבְרֵךְ וְנָתוֹן אֹתוֹ עַל כָּל (ילי) (עממ)־אֶרֶץ מִצְרָיִם (מצר)׃ (מד)
וַיֹּאמֶר פַּרְעֹה אֶל־יוֹסֵף (ציון) אֲנִי (אני) פַּרְעֹה וּבִלְעָדֶיךָ לֹא־
יָרִים אִישׁ אֶת־יָדוֹ וְאֶת־רַגְלוֹ בְּכָל (לכב)־אֶרֶץ מִצְרָיִם (מצר)׃
(מה) וַיִּקְרָא פַרְעֹה שֵׁם־יוֹסֵף (ציון) צָפְנַת פַּעְנֵחַ וַיִּתֶּן־לוֹ אֶת־
אָסְנַת בַּת־פּוֹטִי פֶרַע כֹּהֵן (מלה) אֹן לְאִשָּׁה וַיֵּצֵא יוֹסֵף

אָסְנַת - Joseph marries the daughter of his former master's wife, the woman who had tried to seduce him. When people come into our lives, we must recognize that we have a Tikkun with them. We don't always know how long it will take to complete our Tikkun—it could be a minute, a few weeks, or a lifetime —so it is important to neither underestimate nor overestimate the importance to our lives of the people we meet.

(ציון) עַל־אֶרֶץ מִצְרָיִם (מצר): (מו) וְיוֹסֵף (ציון) בֶּן־שְׁלֹשִׁים שָׁנָה

בְּעָמְדוֹ לִפְנֵי פַּרְעֹה מֶלֶךְ־מִצְרָיִם (מצר) וַיֵּצֵא יוֹסֵף (ציון) מִלִּפְנֵי

פַרְעֹה וַיַּעֲבֹר (רפ"ח) בְּכָל (לכב)־אֶרֶץ מִצְרָיִם (מצר): (מז) וַתַּעַשׂ

הָאָרֶץ (מילוי אלהים ע"ה) בְּשֶׁבַע שְׁנֵי הַשָּׂבָע לִקְמָצִים: (מח) וַיִּקְבֹּץ

אֶת־כָּל (ילי)־ אֹכֶל | שֶׁבַע שָׁנִים אֲשֶׁר הָיוּ בְּאֶרֶץ מִצְרַיִם

(מצר) וַיִּתֶּן־אֹכֶל בֶּעָרִים אֹכֶל שְׂדֵה־ הָעִיר (סןזופר, סנדלפון, ערי)

אֲשֶׁר סְבִיבֹתֶיהָ נָתַן בְּתוֹכָהּ: (מט) וַיִּצְבֹּר יוֹסֵף (ציון) בָּר כְּחוֹל

הַיָּם (ילי) הַרְבֵּה מְאֹד עַד כִּי־חָדַל לִסְפֹּר כִּי־אֵין מִסְפָּר: (נ)

וּלְיוֹסֵף (ציון) יֻלַּד שְׁנֵי בָנִים בְּטֶרֶם תָּבוֹא שְׁנַת הָרָעָב אֲשֶׁר

יָלְדָה־לּוֹ אָסְנַת בַּת־פּוֹטִי פֶרַע כֹּהֵן (מלה) אוֹן: (נא) וַיִּקְרָא

יוֹסֵף (ציון) אֶת־שֵׁם הַבְּכוֹר מְנַשֶּׁה כִּי־נַשַּׁנִי אֱלֹהִים (ילה) אֶת־

כָּל (ילי)־ עֲמָלִי וְאֵת כָּל (ילי)־בֵּית (כ"פ ראה) אָבִי: (נב) וְאֵת שֵׁם

הַשֵּׁנִי קָרָא אֶפְרָיִם כִּי־הִפְרַנִי אֱלֹהִים (ילה) בְּאֶרֶץ עָנְיִי (מ"ה

בריבוע):

Fourth Reading - Moses - Netzach

(נג) וַתִּכְלֶינָה שֶׁבַע שְׁנֵי הַשָּׂבָע אֲשֶׁר הָיָה (יהה) בְּאֶרֶץ
מִצְרָיִם (מצר)׃ (נד) וַתְּחִלֶּינָה שֶׁבַע שְׁנֵי הָרָעָב לָבוֹא כַּאֲשֶׁר
אָמַר יוֹסֵף (ציון) וַיְהִי רָעָב בְּכָל (לכב)־הָאֲרָצוֹת וּבְכָל (לכב)־
אֶרֶץ מִצְרַיִם (מצר) הָיָה (יהה) לָחֶם (ג' הויות)׃ (נה) וַתִּרְעַב כָּל
(ילי)־ אֶרֶץ מִצְרַיִם (מצר) וַיִּצְעַק הָעָם אֶל־פַּרְעֹה לַלָּחֶם (ג'
הויות) וַיֹּאמֶר פַּרְעֹה לְכָל (יה אדני)־מִצְרַיִם (מצר) לְכוּ אֶל־יוֹסֵף
(ציון) אֲשֶׁר־יֹאמַר לָכֶם תַּעֲשׂוּ׃ (נו) וְהָרָעָב הָיָה (יהה) עַל כָּל
(ילי) (עמם)־פְּנֵי (חכמה, בינה) הָאָרֶץ (מילוי אלהים ע״ה) וַיִּפְתַּח יוֹסֵף (ציון)
אֶת־כָּל (ילי)־אֲשֶׁר בָּהֶם וַיִּשְׁבֹּר לְמִצְרַיִם (מצר) וַיֶּחֱזַק הָרָעָב
בְּאֶרֶץ מִצְרָיִם (מצר)׃ (נז) וְכָל (ילי)־הָאָרֶץ (מילוי אלהים ע״ה) בָּאוּ
מִצְרַיְמָה (מצר) לִשְׁבֹּר אֶל־יוֹסֵף (ציון) כִּי־חָזַק (פהל) הָרָעָב
בְּכָל (לכב)־הָאָרֶץ (מילוי אלהים ע״ה)׃ מב (א) וַיַּרְא יַעֲקֹב (יאהדונהי
אידהנויה) כִּי יֶשׁ־שֶׁבֶר בְּמִצְרָיִם (מצר) וַיֹּאמֶר יַעֲקֹב (יאהדונהי אידהנויה)
לְבָנָיו לָמָּה תִּתְרָאוּ׃ (ב) וַיֹּאמֶר הִנֵּה שָׁמַעְתִּי כִּי יֶשׁ־שֶׁבֶר

רָעָב - The famine devastates Egypt
From this, we learn that certain times of the year have extra energy, which may be either positive or negative. By connecting with the periods of positive energy, we gain strength for difficult times. The energy of Shabbat, for example, can sustain us for the entire week.

בְּמִצְרָיִם (מצר) רְדוּ־שָׁמָּה וְשִׁבְרוּ־לָנוּ (מום) מִשָּׁם וְנִחְיֶה וְלֹא
נָמוּת׃ (ג) וַיֵּרְדוּ אֲחֵי־יוֹסֵף (ציון) עֲשָׂרָה לִשְׁבֹּר בָּר מִמִּצְרָיִם
(מצר)׃ (ד) וְאֶת־בִּנְיָמִין אֲחִי יוֹסֵף (ציון) לֹא־שָׁלַח יַעֲקֹב (יאהדונהי
אידהנויה) אֶת־אֶחָיו כִּי אָמַר פֶּן־יִקְרָאֶנּוּ אָסוֹן׃ (ה) וַיָּבֹאוּ בְּנֵי
יִשְׂרָאֵל לִשְׁבֹּר בְּתוֹךְ הַבָּאִים כִּי־הָיָה (יהה) הָרָעָב בְּאֶרֶץ
כְּנָעַן׃ (ו) וְיוֹסֵף (ציון) הוּא הַשַּׁלִּיט עַל־הָאָרֶץ (מילוי אלהים ע"ה)
הוּא הַמַּשְׁבִּיר לְכָל (יה אדני)־עַם הָאָרֶץ (מילוי אלהים ע"ה) וַיָּבֹאוּ
אֲחֵי יוֹסֵף (ציון) וַיִּשְׁתַּחֲווּ־לוֹ אַפַּיִם אָרְצָה׃ (ז) וַיַּרְא יוֹסֵף
(ציון) אֶת־אֶחָיו וַיַּכִּרֵם וַיִּתְנַכֵּר אֲלֵיהֶם וַיְדַבֵּר (ראה) אִתָּם
קָשׁוֹת וַיֹּאמֶר אֲלֵהֶם מֵאַיִן בָּאתֶם וַיֹּאמְרוּ מֵאֶרֶץ כְּנַעַן

רְדוּ - Jacob sends his sons to Egypt to get food, When the brothers enter Egypt, this is the true start of our exile in that country. Because this is the seed level of the exile, we have the power through this portion to gain freedom from any spiritual "Egypt" or enslavement that we have in our life.

וַיַּרְא - When Joseph sees his brothers coming to ask for food, he is very cruel to them and accuses them of being spies. He does this because he knows that they need to be cleansed for what they did. Joseph wants to be part of the cleansing, which he can administer in a merciful way, rather than leave their cleansing to the Satan.

If there is a cleansing that needs to take place in our lives, it is first undertaken with mercy by the Light. If we resist, the Satan takes over, and the cleansing becomes more painful.

לִשְׁבָּר־אֹכֶל׃ (ח) וַיַּכֵּר יוֹסֵף (ציון) אֶת־אֶחָיו וְהֵם לֹא הִכִּרֻהוּ׃
(ט) וַיִּזְכֹּר (יהי אור ע"ה) יוֹסֵף (ציון) אֵת הַחֲלֹמוֹת אֲשֶׁר חָלַם לָהֶם
וַיֹּאמֶר אֲלֵהֶם מְרַגְּלִים אַתֶּם לִרְאוֹת אֶת־עֶרְוַת הָאָרֶץ
(מילוי אלהים ע"ה) בָּאתֶם׃ (י) וַיֹּאמְרוּ אֵלָיו לֹא אֲדֹנִי וַעֲבָדֶיךָ בָּאוּ
לִשְׁבָּר־אֹכֶל׃ (יא) כֻּלָּנוּ בְּנֵי אִישׁ־אֶחָד (אהבה) נָחְנוּ כֵּנִים
אֲנַחְנוּ לֹא־הָיוּ עֲבָדֶיךָ מְרַגְּלִים׃ (יב) וַיֹּאמֶר אֲלֵהֶם לֹא כִּי־
עֶרְוַת הָאָרֶץ (מילוי אלהים ע"ה) בָּאתֶם לִרְאוֹת׃ (יג) וַיֹּאמְרוּ שְׁנֵים
עָשָׂר עֲבָדֶיךָ אַחִים | אֲנַחְנוּ בְּנֵי אִישׁ־אֶחָד (אהבה) בְּאֶרֶץ
כְּנָעַן וְהִנֵּה הַקָּטֹן אֶת־אָבִינוּ הַיּוֹם (נגד, זן) וְהָאֶחָד (אהבה) אֵינֶנּוּ׃
(יד) וַיֹּאמֶר אֲלֵהֶם יוֹסֵף (ציון) הוּא אֲשֶׁר דִּבַּרְתִּי (ראה) אֲלֵכֶם
לֵאמֹר מְרַגְּלִים אַתֶּם׃ (טו) בְּזֹאת תִּבָּחֵנוּ חֵי פַרְעֹה אִם
(יוהך)־תֵּצְאוּ מִזֶּה כִּי אִם (יוהך)־ בְּבוֹא אֲחִיכֶם הַקָּטֹן הֵנָּה׃
(טז) שִׁלְחוּ מִכֶּם אֶחָד (אהבה) וְיִקַּח (וזעם) אֶת־אֲחִיכֶם וְאַתֶּם
הֵאָסְרוּ וְיִבָּחֲנוּ דִּבְרֵיכֶם (ראה) הַאֱמֶת (אהיה פ' אהיה) אִתְּכֶם
וְאִם (יוהך)־לֹא חֵי פַרְעֹה כִּי מְרַגְּלִים אַתֶּם׃ (יז) וַיֶּאֱסֹף אֹתָם
אֶל־מִשְׁמָר שְׁלֹשֶׁת יָמִים (נלך)׃ (יח) וַיֹּאמֶר אֲלֵהֶם יוֹסֵף (ציון)
בַּיּוֹם (נגד, זן) הַשְּׁלִישִׁי זֹאת עֲשׂוּ וִחְיוּ אֶת־הָאֱלֹהִים (ילה) אֲנִי
(אני) יָרֵא׃

Fifth Reading - Aaron - Hod

(יט) אִם (יוהך)-כֵּנִים אַתֶּם אֲחִיכֶם אֶחָד (אהבה) יֵאָסֵר בְּבֵית (ב"פ
ראה) מִשְׁמַרְכֶם וְאַתֶּם לְכוּ הָבִיאוּ שֶׁבֶר רַעֲבוֹן בָּתֵּיכֶם:
(כ) וְאֶת-אֲחִיכֶם הַקָּטֹן תָּבִיאוּ אֵלַי וְיֵאָמְנוּ דִבְרֵיכֶם (ראה)
וְלֹא תָמוּתוּ וַיַּעֲשׂוּ-כֵן: (כא) וַיֹּאמְרוּ אִישׁ אֶל-אָחִיו אֲבָל
אֲשֵׁמִים | אֲנַחְנוּ עַל-אָחִינוּ אֲשֶׁר רָאִינוּ צָרַת נַפְשׁוֹ
בְּהִתְחַנְנוֹ אֵלֵינוּ וְלֹא שָׁמָעְנוּ עַל-כֵּן בָּאָה אֵלֵינוּ הַצָּרָה
(מילוי אלהים) הַזֹּאת: (כב) וַיַּעַן רְאוּבֵן אֹתָם לֵאמֹר הֲלוֹא אָמַרְתִּי
אֲלֵיכֶם | לֵאמֹר אַל-תֶּחֶטְאוּ בַיֶּלֶד וְלֹא שְׁמַעְתֶּם וְגַם-
דָּמוֹ הִנֵּה נִדְרָשׁ: (כג) וְהֵם לֹא יָדְעוּ כִּי שֹׁמֵעַ יוֹסֵף (ציון) כִּי
הַמֵּלִיץ בֵּינֹתָם: (כד) וַיִּסֹּב מֵעֲלֵיהֶם וַיֵּבְךְּ וַיָּשָׁב אֲלֵהֶם
וַיְדַבֵּר (ראה) אֲלֵהֶם וַיִּקַּח (ווֹעם) מֵאִתָּם אֶת-שִׁמְעוֹן וַיֶּאֱסֹר
אֹתוֹ לְעֵינֵיהֶם (מ"ה בריבוע): (כה) וַיְצַו יוֹסֵף (ציון) וַיְמַלְאוּ אֶת-

אֲשֵׁמִים - Out of nowhere, one of the brothers remarks, "Maybe this is happening because we sold our brother..." We should note here that the brothers had gone through many years of spiritual exercises—each night, they examined their shortcomings, and they searched their souls on Yom Kippur—but they had never before remembered the wrong they had done to Joseph. It was only when they experienced physical cleansing that they became aware of their true misdeeds. Sometimes, we, too, must wait for the Satan to cleanse us. We need a physical manifestation of our transgressions before we finally recognize them.

וַיְצַו - Joseph sends the brothers back with some food, but with one condition:

כְּלֵיהֶם בָּר וּלְהָשִׁיב כַּסְפֵּיהֶם אִישׁ אֶל־שַׂקּוֹ וְלָתֵת לָהֶם
צֵדָה לַדָּרֶךְ (ב״פ יב״ק) וַיַּעַשׂ לָהֶם כֵּן: (כו) וַיִּשְׂאוּ אֶת־שִׁבְרָם
עַל־חֲמֹרֵיהֶם וַיֵּלְכוּ מִשָּׁם: (כז) וַיִּפְתַּח הָאֶחָד (אהבה) אֶת־שַׂקּוֹ
לָתֵת מִסְפּוֹא לַחֲמֹרוֹ בַּמָּלוֹן וַיַּרְא אֶת־כַּסְפּוֹ וְהִנֵּה־הוּא
בְּפִי אַמְתַּחְתּוֹ: (כח) וַיֹּאמֶר אֶל־אֶחָיו הוּשַׁב כַּסְפִּי וְגַם הִנֵּה
בְאַמְתַּחְתִּי וַיֵּצֵא לִבָּם וַיֶּחֶרְדוּ אִישׁ אֶל־אָחִיו לֵאמֹר מַה
(מ״ה)־זֹּאת עָשָׂה אֱלֹהִים (ילה) לָנוּ (מום): (כט) וַיָּבֹאוּ אֶל־יַעֲקֹב
(יאהדונהי אידהנויה) אֲבִיהֶם אַרְצָה כְּנָעַן וַיַּגִּידוּ לוֹ אֵת כָּל (ילי)־
הַקֹּרֹת אֹתָם לֵאמֹר: (ל) דִּבֶּר (ראה) הָאִישׁ אֲדֹנֵי הָאָרֶץ (מילוי
אלהים ע״ה) אִתָּנוּ קָשׁוֹת וַיִּתֵּן אֹתָנוּ כִּמְרַגְּלִים אֶת־הָאָרֶץ (מילוי
אלהים ע״ה): (לא) וַנֹּאמֶר אֵלָיו כֵּנִים אֲנָחְנוּ לֹא הָיִינוּ מְרַגְּלִים:
(לב) שְׁנֵים־עָשָׂר אֲנַחְנוּ אַחִים בְּנֵי אָבִינוּ הָאֶחָד (אהבה) אֵינֶנּוּ
וְהַקָּטֹן הַיּוֹם (נגד, זן) אֶת־אָבִינוּ בְּאֶרֶץ כְּנָעַן: (לג) וַיֹּאמֶר אֵלֵינוּ

They must send back their youngest brother, Benjamin. As collateral, Joseph takes Simon as a hostage, because he knew what had happened in Nablus, the city of Sh'chem. He knew that if Simon and Levi were together, they could defeat anyone.

וַיָּבֹאוּ - Returning home, the brothers tell Jacob what happened in Egypt. Reuben tells the brothers to send Benjamin with him, and he swears on the heads of his two sons that he will bring back Benjamin. Jacob refuses the offer because he no longer trusts Reuben. He remembers that Reuben was in charge the day that Joseph disappeared.

הָאִישׁ אֲדֹנֵי הָאָרֶץ (מילוי אלהים ע"ה) בְּזֹאת אֵדַע כִּי כֵנִים אַתֶּם
אֲחִיכֶם הָאֶחָד (אהבה) הַנִּיחוּ אִתִּי וְאֶת־רַעֲבוֹן בָּתֵּיכֶם קְחוּ
וָלֵכוּ׃ (לד) וְהָבִיאוּ אֶת־אֲחִיכֶם הַקָּטֹן אֵלַי וְאֵדְעָה כִּי לֹא
מְרַגְּלִים אַתֶּם כִּי כֵנִים אַתֶּם אֶת־אֲחִיכֶם אֶתֵּן לָכֶם וְאֶת־
הָאָרֶץ (מילוי אלהים ע"ה) תִּסְחָרוּ׃ (לה) וַיְהִי הֵם מְרִיקִים שַׂקֵּיהֶם
וְהִנֵּה־אִישׁ צְרוֹר־כַּסְפּוֹ בְּשַׂקּוֹ וַיִּרְאוּ אֶת־צְרֹרוֹת כַּסְפֵּיהֶם
הֵמָּה וַאֲבִיהֶם וַיִּירָאוּ׃ (לו) וַיֹּאמֶר אֲלֵהֶם יַעֲקֹב (יאהדונהי אידהנויה)
אֲבִיהֶם אֹתִי שִׁכַּלְתֶּם יוֹסֵף (ציון) אֵינֶנּוּ וְשִׁמְעוֹן אֵינֶנּוּ וְאֶת־
בִּנְיָמִן תִּקָּחוּ עָלַי הָיוּ כֻלָּנָה׃ (לז) וַיֹּאמֶר רְאוּבֵן אֶל־אָבִיו
לֵאמֹר אֶת־שְׁנֵי בָנַי תָּמִית אִם (יוהך)־לֹא אֲבִיאֶנּוּ אֵלֶיךָ תְּנָה
(נתה) אֹתוֹ עַל־יָדִי וַאֲנִי (אני) אֲשִׁיבֶנּוּ אֵלֶיךָ׃ (לח) וַיֹּאמֶר לֹא־יֵרֵד
בְּנִי עִמָּכֶם כִּי־אָחִיו מֵת וְהוּא לְבַדּוֹ (מ"ב) נִשְׁאָר וּקְרָאָהוּ
אָסוֹן בַּדֶּרֶךְ (ב"פ יב"ק) אֲשֶׁר תֵּלְכוּ־בָהּ וְהוֹרַדְתֶּם אֶת־שֵׂיבָתִי
בְּיָגוֹן שְׁאוֹלָה׃ מג (א) וְהָרָעָב כָּבֵד בָּאָרֶץ׃ (ב) וַיְהִי כַּאֲשֶׁר
כִּלּוּ לֶאֱכֹל אֶת־הַשֶּׁבֶר אֲשֶׁר הֵבִיאוּ מִמִּצְרָיִם (מצר) וַיֹּאמֶר
אֲלֵיהֶם אֲבִיהֶם **שֻׁבוּ** שִׁבְרוּ־לָנוּ (מום) מְעַט־אֹכֶל׃ (ג)

שֻׁבוּ - The famine persists. As food runs out, Jacob tells the sons to go to Egypt for more food. The sons protest that they will not be able to get more food without taking Benjamin.

וַיֹּאמֶר אֵלָיו יְהוּדָה לֵאמֹר הָעֵד הֵעִד בָּנוּ הָאִישׁ לֵאמֹר
לֹא־תִרְאוּ פָנַי (חכמה, בינה) בִּלְתִּי אֲחִיכֶם אִתְּכֶם׃ (ד) אִם (יוהך)־
יֶשְׁךָ מְשַׁלֵּחַ אֶת־אָחִינוּ אִתָּנוּ נֵרְדָה וְנִשְׁבְּרָה לְךָ אֹכֶל׃
(ה) וְאִם (יוהך)־אֵינְךָ מְשַׁלֵּחַ לֹא נֵרֵד כִּי־הָאִישׁ אָמַר אֵלֵינוּ
לֹא־תִרְאוּ פָנַי (חכמה, בינה) בִּלְתִּי אֲחִיכֶם אִתְּכֶם׃ (ו) וַיֹּאמֶר
יִשְׂרָאֵל לָמָה הֲרֵעֹתֶם לִי לְהַגִּיד לָאִישׁ הַעוֹד לָכֶם אָח׃
(ז) וַיֹּאמְרוּ שָׁאוֹל שָׁאַל־הָאִישׁ לָנוּ (מום) וּלְמוֹלַדְתֵּנוּ לֵאמֹר
הַעוֹד אֲבִיכֶם חַי הֲיֵשׁ לָכֶם אָח וַנַּגֶּד (זן, מזבח)־לוֹ עַל־פִּי
הַדְּבָרִים (ראה) הָאֵלֶּה הֲיָדוֹעַ נֵדַע כִּי יֹאמַר הוֹרִידוּ אֶת־
אֲחִיכֶם׃ (ח) וַיֹּאמֶר יְהוּדָה אֶל־יִשְׂרָאֵל אָבִיו שִׁלְחָה הַנַּעַר
אִתִּי וְנָקוּמָה וְנֵלֵכָה וְנִחְיֶה וְלֹא נָמוּת גַּם־אֲנַחְנוּ גַם־אַתָּה
גַּם־טַפֵּנוּ׃ (ט) אָנֹכִי (איע) אֶעֶרְבֶנּוּ מִיָּדִי תְּבַקְשֶׁנּוּ אִם (יוהך)־לֹא
הֲבִיאֹתִיו אֵלֶיךָ וְהִצַּגְתִּיו לְפָנֶיךָ (סמ"ב) וְחָטָאתִי לְךָ כָּל (ילי)־

וְחָטָאתִי - Yehuda now begins his Tikkun ("correction process"). Because it was he who actually sold Joseph into slavery, he is now willing to undergo the necessary cleansing. It is this willingness that makes it possible for the brothers and Joseph to be reunited physically, emotionally, and spiritually. Connecting to Yehuda helps us to initiate the correction process in our own lives. Whenever we take an action, the energy of that action comes back to us. Yehuda initiated the brothers' selling of Joseph, so he in turn becomes the vehicle of their cleansing. If we show love and care for others, that love and care will come back to us. If we show jealousy or anger towards others, that negativity will eventually reappear.

הַיָּמִים (נלך): (י) כִּי לוּלֵא (בינה, ע"ה וזיים) הִתְמַהְמָהְנוּ כִּי־עַתָּה
שַׁבְנוּ זֶה פַעֲמָיִם: (יא) וַיֹּאמֶר אֲלֵהֶם יִשְׂרָאֵל אֲבִיהֶם אִם
(יוהך)־כֵּן | אֵפוֹא זֹאת עֲשׂוּ קְחוּ מִזִּמְרַת הָאָרֶץ (מילוי אלהים ע"ה)
בִּכְלֵיכֶם וְהוֹרִידוּ לָאִישׁ מִנְחָה (ע"ה ב"פ ב"ן) מְעַט צֳרִי (מצפצ)
וּמְעַט דְּבַשׁ נְכֹאת וָלֹט בָּטְנִים וּשְׁקֵדִים: (יב) וְכֶסֶף מִשְׁנֶה
קְחוּ בְיֶדְכֶם וְאֶת־הַכֶּסֶף הַמּוּשָׁב בְּפִי אַמְתְּחֹתֵיכֶם תָּשִׁיבוּ
בְיֶדְכֶם אוּלַי (אום) מִשְׁגֶּה הוּא: (יג) וְאֶת־אֲחִיכֶם קָחוּ וְקוּמוּ
שׁוּבוּ אֶל־הָאִישׁ: (יד) וְאֵל שַׁדַּי (מהש) יִתֵּן לָכֶם רַחֲמִים לִפְנֵי
הָאִישׁ וְשִׁלַּח לָכֶם אֶת־אֲחִיכֶם אַחֵר וְאֶת־בִּנְיָמִין וַאֲנִי (אני)
כַּאֲשֶׁר שָׁכֹלְתִּי שָׁכָלְתִּי: (טו) וַיִּקְחוּ הָאֲנָשִׁים אֶת־הַמִּנְחָה
(ע"ה ב"פ ב"ן) הַזֹּאת וּמִשְׁנֶה־כֶּסֶף לָקְחוּ בְיָדָם וְאֶת־בִּנְיָמִן וַיָּקֻמוּ
וַיֵּרְדוּ מִצְרַיִם (מצר) וַיַּעַמְדוּ לִפְנֵי יוֹסֵף (ציון):

Sixth Reading - Joseph - Yesod

(טז) וַיַּרְא יוֹסֵף (ציון) אִתָּם אֶת־בִּנְיָמִין וַיֹּאמֶר לַאֲשֶׁר עַל־בֵּיתוֹ
(ב"פ ראה) הָבֵא אֶת־הָאֲנָשִׁים הַבָּיְתָה (ב"פ ראה) וּטְבֹחַ טֶבַח וְהָכֵן
כִּי אִתִּי יֹאכְלוּ הָאֲנָשִׁים בַּצָּהֳרָיִם: (יז) וַיַּעַשׂ הָאִישׁ כַּאֲשֶׁר
אָמַר יוֹסֵף (ציון) וַיָּבֵא הָאִישׁ אֶת־הָאֲנָשִׁים בֵּיתָה (ב"פ ראה) יוֹסֵף
(ציון): (יח) וַיִּירְאוּ הָאֲנָשִׁים כִּי הוּבְאוּ בֵּית (ב"פ ראה) יוֹסֵף (ציון)

וַיֹּאמְרוּ עַל־דְּבַר (ראה) הַכֶּסֶף הַשָּׁב בְּאַמְתְּחֹתֵינוּ בַּתְּחִלָּה
אֲנַחְנוּ מוּבָאִים לְהִתְגֹּלֵל עָלֵינוּ וּלְהִתְנַפֵּל עָלֵינוּ וְלָקַחַת
אֹתָנוּ לַעֲבָדִים וְאֶת־חֲמֹרֵינוּ: (יט) וַיִּגְּשׁוּ אֶל־הָאִישׁ אֲשֶׁר
עַל־בֵּית (ב"פ ראה) יוֹסֵף (ציון) וַיְדַבְּרוּ (ראה) אֵלָיו פֶּתַח הַבָּיִת (ב"פ
ראה): (כ) וַיֹּאמְרוּ בִּי אֲדֹנִי יָרֹד יָרַדְנוּ בַּתְּחִלָּה לִשְׁבָּר־אֹכֶל:
(כא) וַיְהִי כִּי־בָאנוּ אֶל־הַמָּלוֹן וַנִּפְתְּחָה אֶת־אַמְתְּחֹתֵינוּ
וְהִנֵּה כֶסֶף־אִישׁ בְּפִי אַמְתַּחְתּוֹ כַּסְפֵּנוּ בְּמִשְׁקָלוֹ וַנָּשֶׁב
אֹתוֹ בְּיָדֵנוּ: (כב) וְכֶסֶף אַחֵר הוֹרַדְנוּ בְיָדֵנוּ לִשְׁבָּר־אֹכֶל
לֹא יָדַעְנוּ מִי (ילי)־שָׂם כַּסְפֵּנוּ בְּאַמְתְּחֹתֵינוּ: (כג) וַיֹּאמֶר
שָׁלוֹם לָכֶם אַל־תִּירָאוּ אֱלֹהֵיכֶם (ילה) וֵאלֹהֵי (לכב) אֲבִיכֶם
נָתַן לָכֶם מַטְמוֹן בְּאַמְתְּחֹתֵיכֶם כַּסְפְּכֶם בָּא אֵלָי וַיּוֹצֵא
אֲלֵהֶם אֶת־שִׁמְעוֹן: (כד) וַיָּבֵא הָאִישׁ אֶת־הָאֲנָשִׁים בֵּיתָה
(ב"פ ראה) יוֹסֵף (ציון) וַיִּתֶּן־מַיִם וַיִּרְחֲצוּ רַגְלֵיהֶם וַיִּתֵּן מִסְפּוֹא
לַחֲמֹרֵיהֶם: (כה) וַיָּכִינוּ אֶת־הַמִּנְחָה (ע"ה ב"פ ב"ן) עַד־בּוֹא יוֹסֵף
(ציון) בַּצָּהֳרָיִם כִּי שָׁמְעוּ כִּי־שָׁם יֹאכְלוּ לָחֶם (ג' הויות): (כו) וַיָּבֹא
יוֹסֵף (ציון) הַבַּיְתָה (ב"פ ראה) וַיָּבִיאוּ לוֹ אֶת־הַמִּנְחָה (ע"ה ב"פ ב"ן)
אֲשֶׁר־בְּיָדָם הַבָּיְתָה (ב"פ ראה) וַיִּשְׁתַּחֲווּ־לוֹ אָרְצָה: (כז) וַיִּשְׁאַל
לָהֶם לְשָׁלוֹם וַיֹּאמֶר הֲשָׁלוֹם אֲבִיכֶם הַזָּקֵן אֲשֶׁר אֲמַרְתֶּם
הַעוֹדֶנּוּ חָי: (כח) וַיֹּאמְרוּ שָׁלוֹם לְעַבְדְּךָ (פוי) לְאָבִינוּ עוֹדֶנּוּ

וַיִּקְּדוּ וַיִּשְׁתַּחֲוֻּ׃ (כט) וַיִּשָּׂא עֵינָיו (מ"ה בריבוע) וַיַּרְא אֶת־בִּנְיָמִין
אָחִיו בֶּן־אִמּוֹ וַיֹּאמֶר הֲזֶה (והו) אֲחִיכֶם הַקָּטֹן אֲשֶׁר אֲמַרְתֶּם
אֵלָי וַיֹּאמַר אֱלֹהִים (ילה) יָחְנְךָ בְּנִי׃

Seventh Reading - David - Malchut

(ל) וַיְמַהֵר יוֹסֵף (ציון) כִּי־נִכְמְרוּ רַחֲמָיו אֶל־אָחִיו וַיְבַקֵּשׁ
לִבְכּוֹת וַיָּבֹא הַחַדְרָה וַיֵּבְךְּ שָׁמָּה׃ (לא) וַיִּרְחַץ פָּנָיו וַיֵּצֵא
וַיִּתְאַפַּק וַיֹּאמֶר שִׂימוּ לָחֶם (ג' הויות)׃ (לב) וַיָּשִׂימוּ לוֹ לְבַדּוֹ
(מ"ב) וְלָהֶם לְבַדָּם וְלַמִּצְרִים (מצר) הָאֹכְלִים אִתּוֹ לְבַדָּם כִּי
לֹא יוּכְלוּן הַמִּצְרִים (מצר) לֶאֱכֹל אֶת־הָעִבְרִים לֶחֶם (ג'
הויות) כִּי־תוֹעֵבָה הִוא לְמִצְרָיִם (מצר)׃ (לג) וַיֵּשְׁבוּ לְפָנָיו הַבְּכֹר
כִּבְכֹרָתוֹ וְהַצָּעִיר כִּצְעִרָתוֹ וַיִּתְמְהוּ הָאֲנָשִׁים אִישׁ אֶל־
רֵעֵהוּ׃ (לד) וַיִּשָּׂא מַשְׂאֹת מֵאֵת פָּנָיו אֲלֵהֶם וַתֵּרֶב מַשְׂאַת
בִּנְיָמִן מִמַּשְׂאֹת כֻּלָּם חָמֵשׁ יָדוֹת וַיִּשְׁתּוּ וַיִּשְׁכְּרוּ עִמּוֹ׃
מד (א) וַיְצַו אֶת־אֲשֶׁר עַל־בֵּיתוֹ (ב"פ ראה) לֵאמֹר מַלֵּא אֶת־
אַמְתְּחֹת הָאֲנָשִׁים אֹכֶל כַּאֲשֶׁר יוּכְלוּן שְׂאֵת וְשִׂים כֶּסֶף־
אִישׁ בְּפִי אַמְתַּחְתּוֹ׃ (ב) וְאֶת־גְּבִיעִי גְּבִיעַ הַכֶּסֶף תָּשִׂים בְּפִי
אַמְתַּחַת הַקָּטֹן וְאֵת כֶּסֶף שִׁבְרוֹ וַיַּעַשׂ כִּדְבַר (ראה) יוֹסֵף
(ציון) אֲשֶׁר דִּבֵּר (ראה)׃ (ג) הַבֹּקֶר אוֹר (רז) וְהָאֲנָשִׁים שֻׁלְּחוּ
הֵמָּה וַחֲמֹרֵיהֶם׃ (ד) הֵם יָצְאוּ אֶת־הָעִיר (מזחך, סנדלפון, ערי) לֹא

הִרְחִיקוּ וְיוֹסֵף (ציון) אָמַר לַאֲשֶׁר עַל־בֵּיתוֹ (כ"פ ראה) קוּם רְדֹף
אַחֲרֵי הָאֲנָשִׁים וְהִשַּׂגְתָּם וְאָמַרְתָּ אֲלֵהֶם לָמָּה שִׁלַּמְתֶּם
רָעָה (רהע) תַּחַת טוֹבָה (אכא): (ה) הֲלוֹא זֶה אֲשֶׁר יִשְׁתֶּה אֲדֹנִי
בּוֹ וְהוּא נַחֵשׁ יְנַחֵשׁ בּוֹ הֲרֵעֹתֶם אֲשֶׁר עֲשִׂיתֶם: (ו) וַיַּשִּׂגֵם
וַיְדַבֵּר (ראה) אֲלֵהֶם אֶת־הַדְּבָרִים (ראה) הָאֵלֶּה: (ז) וַיֹּאמְרוּ
אֵלָיו לָמָּה יְדַבֵּר (ראה) אֲדֹנִי כַּדְּבָרִים (ראה) הָאֵלֶּה חָלִילָה
לַעֲבָדֶיךָ מֵעֲשׂוֹת כַּדָּבָר (ראה) הַזֶּה (והו): (ח) הֵן כֶּסֶף אֲשֶׁר
מָצָאנוּ בְּפִי אַמְתְּחֹתֵינוּ הֱשִׁיבֹנוּ אֵלֶיךָ מֵאֶרֶץ כְּנָעַן וְאֵיךְ
נִגְנֹב מִבֵּית (כ"פ ראה) אֲדֹנֶיךָ כֶּסֶף אוֹ זָהָב: (ט) אֲשֶׁר יִמָּצֵא אִתּוֹ
מֵעֲבָדֶיךָ וָמֵת וְגַם־אֲנַחְנוּ נִהְיֶה לַאדֹנִי לַעֲבָדִים: (י) וַיֹּאמֶר
גַּם־עַתָּה כְדִבְרֵיכֶם (ראה) כֶּן־הוּא אֲשֶׁר יִמָּצֵא אִתּוֹ יִהְיֶה
(ייי)־לִּי עָבֶד וְאַתֶּם תִּהְיוּ נְקִיִּם: (יא) וַיְמַהֲרוּ וַיּוֹרִדוּ אִישׁ אֶת־
אַמְתַּחְתּוֹ אָרְצָה וַיִּפְתְּחוּ אִישׁ אַמְתַּחְתּוֹ: (יב) וַיְחַפֵּשׂ בַּגָּדוֹל
(להח, מבה עד"א) הֵחֵל וּבַקָּטֹן כִּלָּה וַיִּמָּצֵא הַגָּבִיעַ בְּאַמְתַּחַת
בִּנְיָמִן: (יג) וַיִּקְרְעוּ שִׂמְלֹתָם וַיַּעֲמֹס אִישׁ עַל־חֲמֹרוֹ וַיָּשֻׁבוּ

בִּנְיָמִן - The final test of the brothers - When the brothers return to Egypt, Benjamin is accused of thievery. Again and again, as the brothers feel that things can't get any worse, they do. The brothers had been comfortable with their own negativity, so as a result, their situation continues to deteriorate until they are called upon to leave Benjamin in Egypt as a thief. We should never be complacent about our lives, assuming that that things won't get any worse; with that attitude, they most certainly will.

הָעִֽירָה (סוֹף פָּסוּק, סנדלפון, ערי)׃

Maftir

(יד) וַיָּבֹ֨א יְהוּדָ֤ה וְאֶחָיו֙ בֵּ֣יתָה (ב"פ ראה) יוֹסֵ֔ף (ציון) וְה֖וּא עוֹדֶ֣נּוּ
שָׁ֑ם וַיִּפְּל֥וּ לְפָנָ֖יו אָֽרְצָה׃ (טו) וַיֹּ֤אמֶר לָהֶם֙ יוֹסֵ֔ף (ציון) מָֽה (מ"ה)־
הַמַּעֲשֶׂ֥ה הַזֶּ֖ה (והו) אֲשֶׁ֣ר עֲשִׂיתֶ֑ם הֲל֣וֹא יְדַעְתֶּ֔ם כִּֽי־ נַחֵ֧שׁ
יְנַחֵ֛שׁ אִ֖ישׁ אֲשֶׁ֥ר כָּמֹֽנִי׃ (טז) וַיֹּ֣אמֶר יְהוּדָ֗ה מַה (מ"ה)־נֹּאמַר֙
לַֽאדֹנִ֔י מַה (מ"ה)־נְּדַבֵּ֖ר (ראה) וּמַה (מ"ה)־נִּצְטַדָּ֑ק הָאֱלֹהִ֗ים (ילה)
מָצָא֙ אֶת־עֲוֺ֣ן עֲבָדֶ֔יךָ הִנֶּ֤נּוּ עֲבָדִים֙ לַֽאדֹנִ֔י גַּם־אֲנַ֕חְנוּ גַּ֛ם
אֲשֶׁר־נִמְצָ֥א הַגָּבִ֖יעַ בְּיָדֽוֹ׃ (יז) וַיֹּ֕אמֶר חָלִ֣ילָה לִּ֔י מֵעֲשׂ֖וֹת
זֹ֑את הָאִ֡ישׁ אֲשֶׁר֩ נִמְצָ֨א הַגָּבִ֜יעַ בְּיָד֗וֹ ה֚וּא יִהְיֶה (ייי)־לִּ֣י
עָ֔בֶד וְאַתֶּ֕ם עֲל֥וּ לְשָׁל֖וֹם אֶל־אֲבִיכֶֽם׃ פפפ

The Haftarah of Miketz

The Haftarah speaks of the famous tale of the judgment of Solomon, in which the king mediated between two women who claimed motherhood of a single baby.

The wonder of this tale is that a person existed who would rather have a baby sliced in half than surrender the child to the other woman. Too many people can feel justified even in taking someone's life in order to gratify their own selfish desires.

מלכים א פרק ג

טו ויקץ שלמה (יוד הא ואו הא) והנה חלום ויבוא ירושלם ויעמד
| לפני | ארון ברית־אדני ויעל עלות ויעש שלמים ויעש
משתה לכל־עבדיו: {פ} טז אז תבאנה שתים נשים זנות
אל־המלך ותעמדנה לפניו: יז ותאמר (יהך) האשה (שאה)
האחת בי אדני אני (אני) והאשה (שאה) הזאת ישבת בבית
(ב"פ ראה) אחד (אהבה, דאגה) ואלד (אלד) עמה בבית (ב"פ ראה): יח ויהי
ביום (נגד, מזבח, זן) השלישי ללדתי ותלד גם־האשה (שאה)
הזאת ואנחנו יחדו אין־זר אתנו בבית (ב"פ ראה) זולתי שתים־
אנחנו בבית (ב"פ ראה): יט וימת בן־האשה (שאה) הזאת לילה
(מלה) אשר שכבה עליו: כ ותקם בתוך הלילה (מלה) ותקח
את־בני מאצלי ואמתך ישנה ותשכיבהו בחיקה ואת־
בנה המת השכיבה בחיקי: כא ואקם בבקר להיניק
את־בני והנה־מת ואתבונן אליו בבקר והנה לא־היה (יהה)

בְּנִ֖י אֲשֶׁ֥ר יָלָֽדְתִּי׃ כב וַתֹּ֩אמֶר֩ הָֽאִשָּׁ֨ה (שׂאה) הָאַחֶ֜רֶת לֹ֣א כִ֗י
בְּנִ֤י הַחַי֙ וּבְנֵ֣ךְ הַמֵּ֔ת וְזֹ֤את אֹמֶ֙רֶת֙ לֹ֣א כִ֔י בְּנֵ֥ךְ הַמֵּ֖ת וּבְנִ֣י
הֶחָ֑י וַתְּדַבֵּ֖רְנָה לִפְנֵ֥י הַמֶּֽלֶךְ׃ כג וַיֹּ֣אמֶר הַמֶּ֗לֶךְ זֹ֣את אֹמֶ֔רֶת
זֶה־בְּנִ֥י הַחַ֖י וּבְנֵ֣ךְ הַמֵּ֑ת וְזֹ֤את אֹמֶ֙רֶת֙ לֹ֣א כִ֔י בְּנֵ֥ךְ הַמֵּ֖ת וּבְנִ֥י
הֶחָֽי׃ {פ} כד וַיֹּ֥אמֶר הַמֶּ֖לֶךְ קְח֣וּ לִי־חָ֑רֶב וַיָּבִ֥אוּ הַחֶ֖רֶב לִפְנֵ֥י
הַמֶּֽלֶךְ׃ כה וַיֹּ֣אמֶר הַמֶּ֔לֶךְ גִּזְר֛וּ אֶת־הַיֶּ֥לֶד הַחַ֖י לִשְׁנָ֑יִם וּתְנ֤וּ
אֶת־הַחֲצִי֙ לְאַחַ֔ת וְאֶת־הַחֲצִ֖י לְאֶחָֽת׃ כו וַתֹּ֣אמֶר הָאִשָּׁ֡ה
(שׂאה) אֲשֶׁר־בְּנָ֨הּ הַחַ֜י אֶל־הַמֶּ֗לֶךְ כִּֽי־נִכְמְר֣וּ רַחֲמֶיהָ֮ (אברהם,
רמ"ח) עַל־בְּנָהּ֒ וַתֹּ֣אמֶר ׀ בִּ֣י אֲדֹנִ֗י תְּנוּ־לָהּ֙ אֶת־הַיָּל֣וּד הַחַ֔י
וְהָמֵ֖ת אַל־תְּמִיתֻ֑הוּ וְזֹ֣את אֹמֶ֗רֶת גַּם־לִ֛י גַּם־לָ֖ךְ לֹ֥א יִהְיֶ֖ה (ייי)
גְּזֹֽרוּ׃ כז וַיַּ֨עַן הַמֶּ֜לֶךְ וַיֹּ֗אמֶר תְּנוּ־לָהּ֙ אֶת־הַיָּל֣וּד הַחַ֔י וְהָמֵ֖ת
לֹ֣א תְמִיתֻ֑הוּ הִ֖יא אִמּֽוֹ׃ {ס} כח וַיִּשְׁמְע֣וּ כָל־יִשְׂרָאֵ֗ל אֶת־
הַמִּשְׁפָּט֙ אֲשֶׁ֣ר שָׁפַ֣ט הַמֶּ֔לֶךְ וַיִּרְא֖וּ מִפְּנֵ֣י הַמֶּ֑לֶךְ כִּ֣י רָא֔וּ
כִּֽי־חָכְמַ֧ת אֱלֹהִ֛ים (דמב, ילה) בְּקִרְבּ֖וֹ לַעֲשׂ֥וֹת מִשְׁפָּֽט׃ {ס} א
וַיְהִי֙ הַמֶּ֣לֶךְ שְׁלֹמֹ֔ה (יוד הא ואו הא) מֶ֖לֶךְ עַל־כָּל־יִשְׂרָאֵֽל׃

Lesson of Vayigash

"And Joseph said to his brothers, 'I am Joseph.'"

In this week's portion, Joseph reveals himself to his brothers. When Joseph's brothers came to buy food in Egypt, Joseph treated them coldly from the very start. Questions arose in their minds. Why was this happening? They blamed each other and struggled to understand what the Creator had done to them. But this ended as soon as they heard the words, "I am Joseph." At that moment, all their questions were answered. They stopped blaming each other and they stopped doubting God.

Every day, every hour, every minute, we blame someone for what is happening to us–until the Creator says, "I am here," and we know that everything is for the best. But we have to take the first step. We have to stop our blame and anger so that we can see the big picture. The small picture is what's happening now. The big picture is "I am Joseph," or in our own lives: "I am God. I am the One Who did all of this for you." We must always remember this. We must reach a spiritual level in which we know at every minute that everything in our lives comes from the Creator.

"All the souls that came to Egypt are fulfilled"

When Jacob, his sons, and their families all went down to Egypt, it is written: "All the souls that came to Egypt are fulfilled." The phrase "all the souls" is written in the singular form even though the plural form is correct. So why in the same section is it written in the plural form: "Esau, Jacob's brother, took all his household"?

To answer this question, Rabbi Joseph Chaim, the Ben Ish Chai, offers a fable:

There once was a king who had two advisors: one, a righteous Jew; the other, an idol-worshipper. Each of the advisors had a newborn son.

One day, the king was angry at both his advisors. He did not punish them or kill them. Instead, he circumcised the non-Jewish infant so that no one could know the difference between the two boys. The sons both grew up in the king's house. They looked alike, acted alike, and wore the same clothes. Only the king knew which was the son of the righteous Jew and which the son of the idol-worshipper

When the children were six years old, the king brought them in front of his two advisors and told them to take their sons. And the righteous man began

to cry because he didn't know which boy was his. He wanted the child whose soul had been born from his, not the boy with the negativity of another man. But the second advisor didn't care. He didn't worry about which was which as long as he had a child.

Seeing that the first advisor was upset, the king said, "If you wish, you can make a test to determine which is your child." The righteous advisor thought for a moment and then asked for two bags filled with grapes. In one bag, the grapes were still attached to the vine, while in the other, they were separated.

The king was puzzled, but the righteous advisor told the children to examine the bags and choose the one they wanted. When one child picked the grapes that were still attached to the vine, the righteous advisor knew that this was his son. The king was surprised, and told the righteous advisor that he was correct. But how had he known the difference? The righteous advisor answered that even when we are all separated all over the world, our souls are always together like the attached grapes.

This answers the question of why Jacob and his family are referred to in the singular, while Esau and his family are in the plural. The righteous can be apart in many different places in the world, but they are always connected as one. When we say in our prayers, "One soul together," we are really together all over the world.

We speak about, "Love your neighbor as yourself." But we cannot get to this level if we think that "you are you and I am me." Only through unity consciousness can we love our neighbor as ourselves. If someone is in pain or difficulty, we should go to help, not because we are "good people," but because we feel the pain as our own. If there is a pain in your right hand, your left hand doesn't say, "Well, that's not my problem." Just as we each have one body, we must see our oneness with other people. When Jacob and his family went "as one," it was because Jacob knew that this was the only way they could leave Egypt. In every generation we have an Egypt, and the only way out of our Egypt is through unity. By understanding this, we will be able to do our spiritual work.

Benjamin's gifts

It is written this week that Joseph gave more to Benjamin than to his other brothers–and not just more, but five times as much. Why did Joseph act in a way that might awaken jealousy among the brothers, especially among the brothers who had sold Joseph because of jealousy in the first place?

To understand this, we must know that all the actions of our Patriarchs were not only for themselves or for their time, but for the whole world and for all generations. If Joseph had not given Benjamin the clothes that he gave him, Mordechai would not have had the strength to fight against the wicked Haman. Only through the merit of Joseph's strength as the leader of Egypt was Mordechai able to defeat Haman. Because he was aware of the long-term effects of his actions, Joseph took a risk and put his brothers to a test.

What should we learn from this? All the actions of all the previous generations have prepared our way. Everything is ready. God is not asking us to overcome the Satan by ourselves. We are not on the level of Rabbi Shimon or the Ari–but we don't need to be. They prepared everything for us. All we have to do is use the tools they left us, such as the Zohar and the writings of the Ari. All we have to do is read these teachings, and things will happen by themselves. It's just like using a telephone: To make a phone call, we don't need to know how to build a phone. All it takes is using what is already prepared.

"Little and bad were the days of my two lives."

The Midrash tells us that when Jacob said, "Little and bad," God said to him, "I saved you from Esau, I brought Dinah and Joseph back to you. Why are you complaining?" Because of this, 33 years were taken off Jacob's life.

We are not, God forbid, judging Jacob, but here we can learn a beautiful lesson. If Jacob, at his level of consciousness, would have accepted with love everything that happened to him, his physical appearance would have changed to that of somebody younger and happier. His hair would not have been white, and he would have looked younger than his age. We grow older because we don't appreciate what the Light does for us. When we are feeling good, we take things for granted. But when we are going through hard times, we cry out to the Creator, "What are You doing to us?"

But it's more than this. It's not enough that we appreciate or even know the Light. The Light has to become part of us. Our connection to the Light has to be with every muscle, every nerve, every hair, until there is no room left for grief, suffering, old age, or even death.

Synopsis of Vayigash

Vayigash means "to come close," to draw near to the light of the Creator. There are things we can do to help us move closer to the Light, while other things cause us to become more distant. Sharing brings us closer, for instance, while doubt and anger take us away. This portion gives us the power to come closer to the Light of the Creator.

First Reading - Abraham - Chesed

(יח) וַיִּגַּשׁ אֵלָיו יְהוּדָה וַיֹּאמֶר בִּי אֲדֹנִי יְדַבֶּר (ראה)־נָא עַבְדְּךָ
(פוי) דָבָר (ראה) בְּאָזְנֵי (יוד הי ואו הה) אֲדֹנִי וְאַל־יִחַר אַפְּךָ בְּעַבְדֶּךָ
(פוי) כִּי כָמוֹךָ כְּפַרְעֹה׃ (יט) אֲדֹנִי שָׁאַל אֶת־עֲבָדָיו לֵאמֹר
הֲיֵשׁ־לָכֶם אָב אוֹ־אָח׃ (כ) וַנֹּאמֶר אֶל־אֲדֹנִי יֶשׁ־לָנוּ (מום)
אָב זָקֵן וְיֶלֶד זְקֻנִים קָטָן וְאָחִיו מֵת וַיִּוָּתֵר הוּא לְבַדּוֹ (מ"ב)
לְאִמּוֹ וְאָבִיו אֲהֵבוֹ׃ (כא) וַתֹּאמֶר אֶל־עֲבָדֶיךָ הוֹרִדֻהוּ אֵלָי
וְאָשִׂימָה עֵינִי (מ"ה בריבוע) עָלָיו׃ (כב) וַנֹּאמֶר אֶל־אֲדֹנִי לֹא־יוּכַל
הַנַּעַר לַעֲזֹב אֶת־אָבִיו וְעָזַב אֶת־אָבִיו וָמֵת׃ (כג) וַתֹּאמֶר אֶל־
עֲבָדֶיךָ אִם (יוהך)־לֹא יֵרֵד אֲחִיכֶם הַקָּטֹן אִתְּכֶם לֹא תֹסִפוּן
לִרְאוֹת פָּנָי (חכמה, בינה)׃ (כד) וַיְהִי כִּי עָלִינוּ אֶל־עַבְדְּךָ (פוי) אָבִי
וַנַּגֶּד (זן, מזבח)־לוֹ אֵת דִּבְרֵי (ראה) אֲדֹנִי׃ (כה) וַיֹּאמֶר אָבִינוּ שֻׁבוּ
שִׁבְרוּ־לָנוּ (מום) מְעַט־אֹכֶל׃ (כו) וַנֹּאמֶר לֹא נוּכַל לָרֶדֶת אִם
(יוהך)־יֵשׁ אָחִינוּ הַקָּטֹן אִתָּנוּ וְיָרַדְנוּ כִּי־לֹא נוּכַל לִרְאוֹת פְּנֵי
(חכמה, בינה) הָאִישׁ וְאָחִינוּ הַקָּטֹן אֵינֶנּוּ אִתָּנוּ׃ (כז) וַיֹּאמֶר עַבְדְּךָ

וַיִּגַּשׁ - Yehuda comes to Joseph. Yehuda now completes his correction by saving Benjamin and by bringing Joseph back into the family. Because of the cause and effect process, long periods of time may intervene between the beginning and end of our correction. Cause is often separated from effect by the passage of time. By connecting with Yehuda, we can gain control of time. We can bring the cause and the effect of our actions closer together.

(פוי) אָבִי אֵלֵינוּ אַתֶּם יְדַעְתֶּם כִּי שְׁנַיִם יָלְדָה־לִּי אִשְׁתִּי׃
(כח) וַיֵּצֵא הָאֶחָד (אהבה) מֵאִתִּי וָאֹמַר אַךְ (אהיה) טָרֹף טֹרָף
וְלֹא רְאִיתִיו עַד־הֵנָּה׃ (כט) וּלְקַחְתֶּם גַּם־אֶת־זֶה מֵעִם פָּנַי
(וחכמה, בינה) וְקָרָהוּ אָסוֹן וְהוֹרַדְתֶּם אֶת־שֵׂיבָתִי בְּרָעָה (רהע)
שְׁאֹלָה׃ (ל) וְעַתָּה כְּבֹאִי אֶל־עַבְדְּךָ (פוי) אָבִי וְהַנַּעַר אֵינֶנּוּ
אִתָּנוּ וְנַפְשׁוֹ קְשׁוּרָה בְנַפְשׁוֹ׃

Second Reading - Issac - Gvurah

(לא) וְהָיָה (יהה) (יהוה) כִּרְאוֹתוֹ כִּי־אֵין הַנַּעַר וָמֵת וְהוֹרִידוּ
עֲבָדֶיךָ אֶת־שֵׂיבַת עַבְדְּךָ (פוי) אָבִינוּ בְּיָגוֹן שְׁאֹלָה׃ (לב)
כִּי עַבְדְּךָ (פוי) עָרַב אֶת־הַנַּעַר מֵעִם אָבִי לֵאמֹר אִם
(יוהך)־לֹא אֲבִיאֶנּוּ אֵלֶיךָ וְחָטָאתִי לְאָבִי כָּל (ילי)־הַיָּמִים
(נלך)׃ (לג) וְעַתָּה יֵשֶׁב־נָא עַבְדְּךָ (פוי) תַּחַת הַנַּעַר עֶבֶד
לַאדֹנִי וְהַנַּעַר יַעַל עִם־אֶחָיו׃ (לד) כִּי־אֵיךְ אֶעֱלֶה אֶל־אָבִי
וְהַנַּעַר אֵינֶנּוּ אִתִּי פֶּן אֶרְאֶה בָרָע אֲשֶׁר יִמְצָא אֶת־אָבִי׃
מה (א) וְלֹא־יָכֹל יוֹסֵף (ציון) לְהִתְאַפֵּק לְכֹל (יה אדני) הַנִּצָּבִים
עָלָיו וַיִּקְרָא הוֹצִיאוּ כָל (ילי)־אִישׁ מֵעָלָי וְלֹא־עָמַד אִישׁ
אִתּוֹ בְּהִתְוַדַּע יוֹסֵף (ציון) אֶל־אֶחָיו׃ (ב) וַיִּתֵּן אֶת־קֹלוֹ בִּבְכִי
וַיִּשְׁמְעוּ מִצְרַיִם (מצר) וַיִּשְׁמַע בֵּית (כ״פ ראה) פַּרְעֹה׃ (ג) וַיֹּאמֶר
יוֹסֵף (ציון) אֶל־אֶחָיו אֲנִי (אני) יוֹסֵף (ציון) הַעוֹד אָבִי חָי וְלֹא־

אֲנִי - Joseph identifies himself to his brothers
Yehuda makes his case to Joseph, saying that he must take Benjamin back

יָכְלוּ אֶחָיו לַעֲנוֹת אֹתוֹ כִּי נִבְהֲלוּ מִפָּנָיו: (ד) וַיֹּאמֶר יוֹסֵף
(ציון) אֶל־אֶחָיו גְּשׁוּ־נָא אֵלַי וַיִּגָּשׁוּ וַיֹּאמֶר אֲנִי (אני) יוֹסֵף (ציון)
אֲחִיכֶם אֲשֶׁר־מְכַרְתֶּם אֹתִי מִצְרָיְמָה (מצר): (ה) וְעַתָּה | אַל־
תֵּעָצְבוּ וְאַל־יִחַר בְּעֵינֵיכֶם (מ"ה בריבוע) כִּי־מְכַרְתֶּם אֹתִי הֵנָּה
כִּי לְמִחְיָה **שְׁלָחַנִי** אֱלֹהִים (ילה) לִפְנֵיכֶם: (ו) כִּי־זֶה שְׁנָתַיִם
הָרָעָב בְּקֶרֶב הָאָרֶץ (מילוי אלהים ע"ה) וְעוֹד חָמֵשׁ שָׁנִים אֲשֶׁר
אֵין־חָרִישׁ וְקָצִיר: (ז) וַיִּשְׁלָחֵנִי אֱלֹהִים (ילה) לִפְנֵיכֶם לָשׂוּם
לָכֶם שְׁאֵרִית בָּאָרֶץ וּלְהַחֲיוֹת לָכֶם לִפְלֵיטָה גְּדֹלָה:

to his father Jacob. Then Joseph says, "I am Joseph. Is my father alive?" But Yehuda has already said that Jacob is alive. Why does Joseph ask this question? It is because there is suddenly a tremendous amount of care directed toward Jacob. But when the brothers sold Joseph, they didn't care. Now that Yehuda is responsible for returning Benjamin, he has more invested. His own being is on the line. Things become personal, more effort is involved, and Yehuda puts more care into the process of saving Benjamin, because his own fate is in the balance.

We often behave in the same way. We are lax about spiritual work until we become personally involved, and until our personal agenda is at stake.

שְׁלָחַנִי - Joseph tells the brothers, "You didn't send me here; God sent me here." Joseph was trying to console his brothers by letting them know that the Light was always in control. No matter what situation we're in, we should remember that we must trust the Light. We should not be looking for either blame or credit—whether for ourselves or for anyone else—because everything comes from the Light.

Third Reading - Jacob - Tiferet

(ח) וְעַתָּה לֹא־אַתֶּם שְׁלַחְתֶּם אֹתִי הֵנָּה כִּי הָאֱלֹהִים (ילה)
וַיְשִׂימֵנִי לְאָב לְפַרְעֹה וּלְאָדוֹן (אני) לְכָל (יה אדני)־בֵּיתוֹ (ב"פ ראה)
וּמֹשֵׁל בְּכָל (לכב)־אֶרֶץ מִצְרָיִם (מצר): (ט) מַהֲרוּ וַעֲלוּ אֶל־
אָבִי וַאֲמַרְתֶּם אֵלָיו כֹּה (היי) אָמַר בִּנְךָ יוֹסֵף (ציון) שָׂמַנִי
אֱלֹהִים (ילה) לְאָדוֹן (אני) לְכָל (יה אדני)־מִצְרָיִם (מצר) רְדָה אֵלַי
אַל־תַּעֲמֹד: (י) וְיָשַׁבְתָּ בְאֶרֶץ־גֹּשֶׁן וְהָיִיתָ קָרוֹב אֵלַי אַתָּה
וּבָנֶיךָ וּבְנֵי בָנֶיךָ וְצֹאנְךָ וּבְקָרְךָ וְכָל (ילי)־אֲשֶׁר־לָךְ: (יא)
וְכִלְכַּלְתִּי אֹתְךָ שָׁם כִּי־עוֹד חָמֵשׁ שָׁנִים רָעָב פֶּן־תִּוָּרֵשׁ
אַתָּה וּבֵיתְךָ (ב"פ ראה) וְכָל (ילי)־אֲשֶׁר־לָךְ: (יב) וְהִנֵּה עֵינֵיכֶם (מ"ה
בריבוע) רֹאוֹת וְעֵינֵי (מ"ה בריבוע) אָחִי בִנְיָמִין כִּי־פִי הַמְדַבֵּר (ראה)
אֲלֵיכֶם: (יג) וְהִגַּדְתֶּם לְאָבִי אֶת־כָּל (ילי)־כְּבוֹדִי בְּמִצְרַיִם
(מצר) וְאֵת כָּל (ילי)־אֲשֶׁר רְאִיתֶם וּמִהַרְתֶּם וְהוֹרַדְתֶּם אֶת־
אָבִי הֵנָּה: (יד) וַיִּפֹּל עַל־צַוְּארֵי בִנְיָמִן־אָחִיו וַיֵּבְךְּ וּבִנְיָמִן
בָּכָה עַל־צַוָּארָיו: (טו) וַיְנַשֵּׁק לְכָל (יה אדני)־אֶחָיו וַיֵּבְךְּ עֲלֵיהֶם

וַעֲלוּ - Joseph tests his brothers by sending them back to Israel once again. He gives each of the brothers a certain amount of food, but he gives Benjamin five times what he gives to the others. Joseph does this to see if the brothers will be jealous of Benjamin, and if they'll harm them in any way. It is a test of their spiritual growth since they sold Joseph into slavery.

וְאַחֲרֵי כֵן דִּבְּרוּ (ראה) אֶחָיו אִתּוֹ׃ (טז) וְהַקֹּל נִשְׁמַע בֵּית (ב"פ
ראה) פַּרְעֹה לֵאמֹר בָּאוּ אֲחֵי יוֹסֵף (ציון) וַיִּיטַב בְּעֵינֵי (מ"ה בריבוע)
פַּרְעֹה וּבְעֵינֵי (מ"ה בריבוע) עֲבָדָיו׃ (יז) וַיֹּאמֶר פַּרְעֹה אֶל־יוֹסֵף
(ציון) אֱמֹר אֶל־אַחֶיךָ זֹאת עֲשׂוּ טַעֲנוּ אֶת־בְּעִירְכֶם (סוזדפר,
סנדלפון, ער"י) וּלְכוּ־בֹאוּ אַרְצָה כְּנָעַן׃ (יח) וּקְחוּ אֶת־אֲבִיכֶם
וְאֶת־בָּתֵּיכֶם וּבֹאוּ אֵלָי וְאֶתְּנָה לָכֶם אֶת־טוּב (והו) אֶרֶץ
מִצְרַיִם (מצר) וְאִכְלוּ אֶת־חֵלֶב הָאָרֶץ (מילוי אלהים ע"ה)׃

Fourth Reading - Moses - Netzach

(יט) וְאַתָּה צֻוֵּיתָה זֹאת עֲשׂוּ קְחוּ־לָכֶם מֵאֶרֶץ מִצְרַיִם (מצר)
עֲגָלוֹת לְטַפְּכֶם וְלִנְשֵׁיכֶם וּנְשָׂאתֶם אֶת־אֲבִיכֶם וּבָאתֶם׃
(כ) וְעֵינְכֶם (מ"ה בריבוע) אַל־תָּחֹס עַל־כְּלֵיכֶם כִּי־טוּב (והו) (אום)
כָּל (ילי)־אֶרֶץ מִצְרַיִם (מצר) לָכֶם הוּא׃ (כא) וַיַּעֲשׂוּ־כֵן בְּנֵי
יִשְׂרָאֵל וַיִּתֵּן לָהֶם יוֹסֵף (ציון) עֲגָלוֹת עַל־פִּי פַרְעֹה וַיִּתֵּן לָהֶם
צֵדָה לַדָּרֶךְ (ב"פ יב"ק)׃ (כב) לְכֻלָּם נָתַן לָאִישׁ חֲלִפוֹת שְׂמָלֹת
וּלְבִנְיָמִן נָתַן שְׁלֹשׁ מֵאוֹת כֶּסֶף וְחָמֵשׁ חֲלִפֹת שְׂמָלֹת׃ (כג)
וּלְאָבִיו שָׁלַח כְּזֹאת עֲשָׂרָה חֲמֹרִים נֹשְׂאִים מִטּוּב (והו)
מִצְרָיִם (מצר) וְעֶשֶׂר אֲתֹנֹת נֹשְׂאֹת בָּר וָלֶחֶם (ג' הויות) וּמָזוֹן
לְאָבִיו לַדָּרֶךְ (ב"פ יב"ק)׃ (כד) וַיְשַׁלַּח אֶת־אֶחָיו וַיֵּלֵכוּ וַיֹּאמֶר
אֲלֵהֶם אַל־תִּרְגְּזוּ בַּדָּרֶךְ (ב"פ יב"ק)׃ (כה) וַיַּעֲלוּ מִמִּצְרָיִם (מצר)

וַיָּבֹאוּ אֶרֶץ כְּנַעַן אֶל־יַעֲקֹב (יאהדונהי אידהנויה) אֲבִיהֶם׃ (כו) וַיַּגִּדוּ
לוֹ לֵאמֹר עוֹד יוֹסֵף (ציון) חַי וְכִי־הוּא מֹשֵׁל בְּכָל (לכב) ־אֶרֶץ
מִצְרָיִם (מצר) וַיָּפָג לִבּוֹ כִּי לֹא־הֶאֱמִין לָהֶם׃ (כז) וַיְדַבְּרוּ (ראה)
אֵלָיו אֵת כָּל (ילי) ־דִּבְרֵי (ראה) יוֹסֵף (ציון) אֲשֶׁר דִּבֶּר (ראה) אֲלֵהֶם
וַיַּרְא אֶת־הָעֲגָלוֹת אֲשֶׁר־שָׁלַח יוֹסֵף (ציון) לָשֵׂאת אֹתוֹ וַתְּחִי
רוּחַ יַעֲקֹב (יאהדונהי אידהנויה) אֲבִיהֶם׃

Fifth Reading - Aaron - Hod

(כח) וַיֹּאמֶר יִשְׂרָאֵל רַב עוֹד־יוֹסֵף (ציון) בְּנִי חָי אֵלְכָה וְאֶרְאֶנּוּ
בְּטֶרֶם אָמוּת׃ מו (א) וַיִּסַּע יִשְׂרָאֵל וְכָל (ילי) ־אֲשֶׁר־לוֹ וַיָּבֹא
בְּאֵרָה (קנ"א ב"ן) שָּׁבַע וַיִּזְבַּח זְבָחִים לֵאלֹהֵי (דמב) אָבִיו יִצְחָק
(ד"פ ב"ן)׃ (ב) וַיֹּאמֶר אֱלֹהִים (ילה) | לְיִשְׂרָאֵל בְּמַרְאֹת הַלַּיְלָה

וַיָּפָג - The brothers tell Jacob that Joseph is still alive. Jacob doesn't believe them, and since Jacob was such a high soul and a prophet, we must ask why he couldn't see that his son Joseph was still alive. Again, we are not judging Jacob, but at the moment Jacob saw Joseph's bloodied clothing, he became depressed. And the moment we become depressed, we lose the power of prophecy. We deny ourselves the opportunity to receive messages.

וַיִּסַּע - Jacob goes down into Egypt
God appears to Jacob and tells him not to fear, that he will be safe. Jacob then goes down into Egypt. In the same way, when each of us goes down into our own personal Egypt, we need to arm ourselves by scanning the Zohar, the Ana B'koach, or the 72 Names of God. We should do this whenever we face a difficult situation.

(מלה) וַיֹּאמֶר יַעֲקֹב (יאהדונהי אידהנויה) | יַעֲקֹב (יאהדונהי אידהנויה) וַיֹּאמֶר
הִנֵּנִי: (ג) וַיֹּאמֶר אָנֹכִי (איע) הָאֵל (לאה) אֱלֹהֵי (דמב) אָבִיךָ אַל-
תִּירָא מֵרְדָה מִצְרַיְמָה (מצר) כִּי-לְגוֹי גָּדוֹל (להוו, מבה עד"א)
אֲשִׂימְךָ שָׁם: (ד) אָנֹכִי (איע) אֵרֵד עִמְּךָ מִצְרַיְמָה (מצר) וְאָנֹכִי
(איע) אַעַלְךָ גַם-עָלֹה וְיוֹסֵף (ציון) יָשִׁית יָדוֹ עַל-עֵינֶיךָ (ע"ה
קס"א): (ה) וַיָּקָם יַעֲקֹב (יאהדונהי אידהנויה) מִבְּאֵר (קנ"א ב"ן) שָׁבַע וַיִּשְׂאוּ
בְנֵי-יִשְׂרָאֵל אֶת-יַעֲקֹב (יאהדונהי אידהנויה) אֲבִיהֶם וְאֶת-טַפָּם
וְאֶת-נְשֵׁיהֶם בָּעֲגָלוֹת אֲשֶׁר-שָׁלַח פַּרְעֹה לָשֵׂאת אֹתוֹ: (ו)
וַיִּקְחוּ אֶת-מִקְנֵיהֶם וְאֶת-רְכוּשָׁם אֲשֶׁר רָכְשׁוּ בְּאֶרֶץ כְּנַעַן
וַיָּבֹאוּ מִצְרָיְמָה (מצר) יַעֲקֹב (יאהדונהי אידהנויה) וְכָל (ילי)-זַרְעוֹ אִתּוֹ:
(ז) בָּנָיו וּבְנֵי בָנָיו אִתּוֹ בְּנֹתָיו וּבְנוֹת בָּנָיו וְכָל (ילי)-זַרְעוֹ הֵבִיא
אִתּוֹ מִצְרָיְמָה (מצר): ס (ח) וְאֵלֶּה שְׁמוֹת בְּנֵי-יִשְׂרָאֵל הַבָּאִים
מִצְרַיְמָה (מצר) יַעֲקֹב (יאהדונהי אידהנויה) וּבָנָיו בְּכֹר יַעֲקֹב (יאהדונהי
אידהנויה) רְאוּבֵן: (ט) וּבְנֵי רְאוּבֵן חֲנוֹךְ וּפַלּוּא וְחֶצְרֹן וְכַרְמִי:
(י) וּבְנֵי שִׁמְעוֹן יְמוּאֵל וְיָמִין וְאֹהַד וְיָכִין וְצֹחַר וְשָׁאוּל בֶּן-
הַכְּנַעֲנִית: (יא) וּבְנֵי לֵוִי גֵּרְשׁוֹן קְהָת וּמְרָרִי: (יב) וּבְנֵי יְהוּדָה
עֵר וְאוֹנָן וְשֵׁלָה וָפֶרֶץ וָזָרַח וַיָּמָת עֵר וְאוֹנָן בְּאֶרֶץ כְּנַעַן
וַיִּהְיוּ בְנֵי-פֶרֶץ חֶצְרֹן וְחָמוּל: (יג) וּבְנֵי יִשָּׂשכָר תּוֹלָע וּפֻוָּה
וְיוֹב וְשִׁמְרֹן: (יד) וּבְנֵי זְבֻלוּן סֶרֶד וְאֵלוֹן וְיַחְלְאֵל: (טו) אֵלֶּה

| בְּנֵי לֵאָה אֲשֶׁר יָלְדָה לְיַעֲקֹב (יאהדונהי אידהנויה) בְּפַדַּן אֲרָם
וְאֵת דִּינָה בִתּוֹ כָּל (ילי)־נֶפֶשׁ בָּנָיו וּבְנוֹתָיו שְׁלֹשִׁים וְשָׁלֹשׁ׃
(טז) וּבְנֵי גָד צִפְיוֹן וְחַגִּי שׁוּנִי וְאֶצְבֹּן עֵרִי וַאֲרוֹדִי וְאַרְאֵלִי׃ (יז)
וּבְנֵי אָשֵׁר יִמְנָה וְיִשְׁוָה וְיִשְׁוִי וּבְרִיעָה וְשֶׂרַח אֲחֹתָם וּבְנֵי
בְרִיעָה חֶבֶר וּמַלְכִּיאֵל׃ (יח) אֵלֶּה בְּנֵי זִלְפָּה אֲשֶׁר־נָתַן
לָבָן לְלֵאָה בִתּוֹ וַתֵּלֶד אֶת־אֵלֶּה לְיַעֲקֹב (יאהדונהי אידהנויה)
שֵׁשׁ עֶשְׂרֵה נָפֶשׁ׃ (יט) בְּנֵי רָחֵל אֵשֶׁת יַעֲקֹב (יאהדונהי אידהנויה)
יוֹסֵף (ציון) וּבִנְיָמִן׃ (כ) וַיִּוָּלֵד לְיוֹסֵף (ציון) בְּאֶרֶץ מִצְרַיִם (מצר)
אֲשֶׁר יָלְדָה־לּוֹ אָסְנַת בַּת־פּוֹטִי פֶרַע כֹּהֵן (מלה) אֹן אֶת־
מְנַשֶּׁה וְאֶת־אֶפְרָיִם׃ (כא) וּבְנֵי בִנְיָמִן בֶּלַע וָבֶכֶר וְאַשְׁבֵּל
גֵּרָא וְנַעֲמָן אֵחִי וָרֹאשׁ מֻפִּים וְחֻפִּים וָאָרְדְּ׃ (כב) אֵלֶּה בְּנֵי
רָחֵל אֲשֶׁר יֻלַּד לְיַעֲקֹב (יאהדונהי אידהנויה) כָּל (ילי)־נֶפֶשׁ אַרְבָּעָה
עָשָׂר׃ (כג) וּבְנֵי־דָן חֻשִׁים׃ (כד) וּבְנֵי נַפְתָּלִי יַחְצְאֵל וְגוּנִי וְיֵצֶר
וְשִׁלֵּם׃ (כה) אֵלֶּה בְּנֵי בִלְהָה אֲשֶׁר־נָתַן לָבָן לְרָחֵל בִּתּוֹ
וַתֵּלֶד אֶת־אֵלֶּה לְיַעֲקֹב (יאהדונהי אידהנויה) כָּל (ילי)־נֶפֶשׁ שִׁבְעָה׃
(כו) כָּל (ילי)־הַנֶּפֶשׁ הַבָּאָה לְיַעֲקֹב (יאהדונהי אידהנויה) מִצְרַיְמָה (מצר)
יֹצְאֵי יְרֵכוֹ מִלְּבַד נְשֵׁי בְנֵי־יַעֲקֹב (יאהדונהי אידהנויה) כָּל (ילי)־נֶפֶשׁ
שִׁשִּׁים וָשֵׁשׁ׃ (כז) וּבְנֵי יוֹסֵף (ציון) אֲשֶׁר־יֻלַּד־לוֹ בְמִצְרַיִם (מצר)
נֶפֶשׁ שְׁנָיִם כָּל (ילי)־הַנֶּפֶשׁ לְבֵית (ב"פ ראה)־יַעֲקֹב (יאהדונהי אידהנויה)

הַבָּאָה מִצְרַיְמָה (מצר) שִׁבְעִים׃ ס

Sixth Reading - Joseph - Yesod

(כח) וְאֶת־יְהוּדָה שָׁלַח לְפָנָיו אֶל־יוֹסֵף (ציון) לְהוֹרֹת לְפָנָיו
גֹּשְׁנָה וַיָּבֹאוּ אַרְצָה גֹּשֶׁן׃ (כט) וַיֶּאְסֹר יוֹסֵף (ציון) מֶרְכַּבְתּוֹ
וַיַּעַל לִקְרַאת־יִשְׂרָאֵל אָבִיו גֹּשְׁנָה וַיֵּרָא אֵלָיו וַיִּפֹּל עַל־
צַוָּארָיו וַיֵּבְךְּ עַל־צַוָּארָיו עוֹד׃ (ל) וַיֹּאמֶר יִשְׂרָאֵל אֶל־יוֹסֵף
(ציון) אָמוּתָה הַפָּעַם (מנק) אַחֲרֵי רְאוֹתִי אֶת־פָּנֶיךָ (סמ"ב) כִּי
עוֹדְךָ חָי׃ (לא) וַיֹּאמֶר יוֹסֵף (ציון) אֶל־אֶחָיו וְאֶל־בֵּית (כ"פ ראה)
אָבִיו אֶעֱלֶה וְאַגִּידָה לְפַרְעֹה וְאֹמְרָה אֵלָיו אַחַי וּבֵית (כ"פ
ראה)־אָבִי אֲשֶׁר בְּאֶרֶץ־כְּנַעַן בָּאוּ אֵלָי׃ (לב) וְהָאֲנָשִׁים רֹעֵי
צֹאן כִּי־אַנְשֵׁי מִקְנֶה הָיוּ וְצֹאנָם וּבְקָרָם וְכָל (יל"י)־ אֲשֶׁר
לָהֶם הֵבִיאוּ׃ (לג) וְהָיָה (יהה) (יהוה) כִּי־יִקְרָא לָכֶם פַּרְעֹה
וְאָמַר מַה (מ"ה)־מַּעֲשֵׂיכֶם׃ (לד) וַאֲמַרְתֶּם אַנְשֵׁי מִקְנֶה הָיוּ
עֲבָדֶיךָ מִנְּעוּרֵינוּ וְעַד־עַתָּה גַּם־אֲנַחְנוּ גַּם־אֲבֹתֵינוּ בַּעֲבוּר

שִׁבְעִים - Seventy people go into Egypt (Jacob 's family)
Each of the people going into Egypt represents a nation. Although there are more than 200 nations in the world, each of them originated from one of these seventy.
Each person going down to Egypt is given Light representing one of the nations. Whenever we are given Light, w must be aware that it is for others -- even for whole nations -- as well as for ourselves. We are responsible for sharing our Light with the entire world.

תֵּשְׁבוּ בְּאֶרֶץ גֹּשֶׁן כִּי־תוֹעֲבַת מִצְרַיִם (מצר) כָּל (ילי)־רֹעֵה
צֹאן׃ מז (א) וַיָּבֹא יוֹסֵף (ציון) וַיַּגֵּד לְפַרְעֹה וַיֹּאמֶר אָבִי וְאַחַי
וְצֹאנָם וּבְקָרָם וְכָל (ילי)־אֲשֶׁר לָהֶם בָּאוּ מֵאֶרֶץ כְּנָעַן וְהִנָּם
בְּאֶרֶץ גֹּשֶׁן׃ (ב) וּמִקְצֵה אֶחָיו לָקַח חֲמִשָּׁה אֲנָשִׁים וַיַּצִּגֵם
לִפְנֵי פַרְעֹה׃ (ג) וַיֹּאמֶר פַּרְעֹה אֶל־אֶחָיו מַה (מ"ה)־מַּעֲשֵׂיכֶם
וַיֹּאמְרוּ אֶל־פַּרְעֹה רֹעֵה צֹאן עֲבָדֶיךָ גַּם־אֲנַחְנוּ גַּם־
אֲבוֹתֵינוּ׃ (ד) וַיֹּאמְרוּ אֶל־פַּרְעֹה לָגוּר בָּאָרֶץ בָּאנוּ כִּי אֵין
מִרְעֶה לַצֹּאן אֲשֶׁר לַעֲבָדֶיךָ כִּי־כָבֵד הָרָעָב בְּאֶרֶץ כְּנָעַן
וְעַתָּה יֵשְׁבוּ נָא עֲבָדֶיךָ בְּאֶרֶץ גֹּשֶׁן׃ (ה) וַיֹּאמֶר פַּרְעֹה אֶל־
יוֹסֵף (ציון) לֵאמֹר אָבִיךָ וְאַחֶיךָ בָּאוּ אֵלֶיךָ׃ (ו) אֶרֶץ מִצְרַיִם
(מצר) לְפָנֶיךָ (סמ"ב) הִוא בְּמֵיטַב הָאָרֶץ (מילוי אלהים ע"ה) הוֹשֵׁב
אֶת־אָבִיךָ וְאֶת־אַחֶיךָ יֵשְׁבוּ בְּאֶרֶץ גֹּשֶׁן וְאִם (יוהך)־יָדַעְתָּ

תֵּשְׁבוּ - Jacob enters Egypt

Although the famine was supposed to last for seven years, it ended the moment Jacob entered Egypt. Why? Because righteous people have the power to connect with the power of mind over matter. In this way, they are able to change destinies and create miracles.

Instead of his family remaining in Egypt, Joseph ensures that they go to the land of Goshen

Joseph doesn't want his family to be surrounded by the negative forces embodied by the Egyptians.

וְיֶשׁ־בָּם (מ"ב) אַנְשֵׁי־חַיִל (ומב) וְשַׂמְתָּם שָׂרֵי מִקְנֶה עַל־אֲשֶׁר־
לִי׃ (ז) וַיָּבֵא יוֹסֵף (ציון) אֶת־יַעֲקֹב (יאהדונהי אידהנויה) אָבִיו וַיַּעֲמִדֵהוּ
לִפְנֵי פַרְעֹה וַיְבָרֶךְ (עסמ"ב) יַעֲקֹב (יאהדונהי אידהנויה) אֶת־פַּרְעֹה׃ (ח)
וַיֹּאמֶר פַּרְעֹה אֶל־יַעֲקֹב (יאהדונהי אידהנויה) כַּמָּה יְמֵי שְׁנֵי חַיֶּיךָ׃
(ט) וַיֹּאמֶר יַעֲקֹב (יאהדונהי אידהנויה) אֶל־פַּרְעֹה יְמֵי שְׁנֵי מְגוּרַי
שְׁלֹשִׁים וּמְאַת שָׁנָה מְעַט וְרָעִים הָיוּ יְמֵי שְׁנֵי חַיַּי וְלֹא
הִשִּׂיגוּ אֶת־יְמֵי שְׁנֵי חַיֵּי אֲבֹתַי בִּימֵי מְגוּרֵיהֶם׃ (י) וַיְבָרֶךְ
(עסמ"ב) יַעֲקֹב (יאהדונהי אידהנויה) אֶת־פַּרְעֹה וַיֵּצֵא מִלִּפְנֵי פַרְעֹה׃

Seventh Reading - David - Malchut

(יא) וַיּוֹשֵׁב יוֹסֵף (ציון) אֶת־אָבִיו וְאֶת־אֶחָיו וַיִּתֵּן לָהֶם אֲחֻזָּה
בְּאֶרֶץ מִצְרַיִם (מצר) בְּמֵיטַב הָאָרֶץ (מילוי אלהים ע"ה) בְּאֶרֶץ
רַעְמְסֵס כַּאֲשֶׁר צִוָּה פַרְעֹה׃ (יב) וַיְכַלְכֵּל יוֹסֵף (ציון) אֶת־
אָבִיו וְאֶת־אֶחָיו וְאֵת כָּל (ילי)־ בֵּית (ב"פ ראה) אָבִיו לֶחֶם (ג' הויות)

לִפְנֵי - Jacob and Pharaoh meet.
When Pharaoh asks Jacob his age, Jacob replies that he is 130 years old and that he has faced many difficulties in his life. Kabbalah teaches that the human aging process did not exist before Jacob. People simply died. Aging is actually a blessing, reminding us that time is passing and that our spiritual work needs to be done. Without wishing to judge Jacob, we can learn from him not to complain about our lives or about where we are on our spiritual path. Everything comes from the Light, and every obstacle is an opportunity to work on our selves.

לְפִי הַטָּף׃ (יג) וְלֶחֶם (ג' הויות) אֵין בְּכָל (לכב) ־הָאָרֶץ (מילוי אלהים)
(ע"ה) כִּי־כָבֵד הָרָעָב מְאֹד וַתֵּלַהּ אֶרֶץ מִצְרַיִם (מצר) וְאֶרֶץ
כְּנַעַן מִפְּנֵי הָרָעָב׃ (יד) וַיְלַקֵּט יוֹסֵף (ציון) אֶת־כָּל (ילי) ־הַכֶּסֶף
הַנִּמְצָא בְאֶרֶץ־מִצְרַיִם (מצר) וּבְאֶרֶץ כְּנַעַן בַּשֶּׁבֶר אֲשֶׁר־הֵם
שֹׁבְרִים וַיָּבֵא יוֹסֵף (ציון) אֶת־הַכֶּסֶף בֵּיתָה (ב"פ ראה) פַּרְעֹה׃ (טו)
וַיִּתֹּם הַכֶּסֶף מֵאֶרֶץ מִצְרַיִם (מצר) וּמֵאֶרֶץ כְּנַעַן וַיָּבֹאוּ כָל
(ילי) ־מִצְרַיִם (מצר) אֶל־יוֹסֵף (ציון) לֵאמֹר הָבָה־לָּנוּ (מום) לֶחֶם (ג'
הויות) וְלָמָּה נָמוּת נֶגְדֶּךָ (זן, מזבח) כִּי אָפֵס כָּסֶף׃ (טז) וַיֹּאמֶר יוֹסֵף
(ציון) הָבוּ (אחד, אהבה, דאגה) מִקְנֵיכֶם וְאֶתְּנָה לָכֶם בְּמִקְנֵיכֶם אִם
(יוהך) ־אָפֵס כָּסֶף׃ (יז) וַיָּבִיאוּ אֶת־מִקְנֵיהֶם אֶל־יוֹסֵף (ציון) וַיִּתֵּן
לָהֶם יוֹסֵף (ציון) לֶחֶם (ג' הויות) בַּסּוּסִים וּבְמִקְנֵה הַצֹּאן וּבְמִקְנֵה
הַבָּקָר וּבַחֲמֹרִים וַיְנַהֲלֵם בַּלֶּחֶם (ג' הויות) בְּכָל (לכב) ־מִקְנֵהֶם
בַּשָּׁנָה הַהִוא׃ (יח) וַתִּתֹּם הַשָּׁנָה הַהִוא וַיָּבֹאוּ אֵלָיו בַּשָּׁנָה
הַשֵּׁנִית וַיֹּאמְרוּ לוֹ לֹא־נְכַחֵד מֵאֲדֹנִי כִּי אִם (יוהך) ־תַּם הַכֶּסֶף

וַיְלַקֵּט - The money of Egypt flows through Joseph.

Joseph is the chariot, the channel for the Sfirat Yesod. To reach the level of Malchut, all Light must flow through Joseph. Because the Light flows through Joseph, all money flows through him, too. This is connected to the concept "as above, so below." If we pursue the Light with certainty, all else will come to us. Often, we pursue only the physical manifestation. But if we pursue the spiritual first, we will receive on the physical level as well.

וּמִקְנֵה הַבְּהֵמָה (לכב) אֶל־אֲדֹנִי לֹא נִשְׁאַר לִפְנֵי אֲדֹנִי בִּלְתִּי
אִם (יוהך)־גְּוִיָּתֵנוּ וְאַדְמָתֵנוּ׃ (יט) לָמָּה נָמוּת לְעֵינֶיךָ (ע"ה קס"א)
גַּם־אֲנַחְנוּ גַּם אַדְמָתֵנוּ קְנֵה־אֹתָנוּ וְאֶת־אַדְמָתֵנוּ בַּלָּחֶם (ג'
הויות) וְנִהְיֶה אֲנַחְנוּ וְאַדְמָתֵנוּ עֲבָדִים לְפַרְעֹה וְתֶן־זֶרַע וְנִחְיֶה
וְלֹא נָמוּת וְהָאֲדָמָה לֹא תֵשָׁם׃ (כ) וַיִּקֶן יוֹסֵף (ציון) אֶת־כָּל
(ילי)־אַדְמַת מִצְרַיִם (מצר) לְפַרְעֹה כִּי־מָכְרוּ מִצְרַיִם (מצר) אִישׁ
שָׂדֵהוּ כִּי־חָזַק (פהל) עֲלֵהֶם הָרָעָב וַתְּהִי הָאָרֶץ (מילוי אלהים ע"ה)
לְפַרְעֹה׃ (כא) וְאֶת־הָעָם הֶעֱבִיר אֹתוֹ לֶעָרִים מִקְצֵה גְבוּל־
מִצְרַיִם (מצר) וְעַד־קָצֵהוּ׃ (כב) רַק אַדְמַת הַכֹּהֲנִים לֹא קָנָה
כִּי חֹק לַכֹּהֲנִים מֵאֵת פַּרְעֹה וְאָכְלוּ אֶת־חֻקָּם אֲשֶׁר נָתַן
לָהֶם פַּרְעֹה עַל־כֵּן לֹא מָכְרוּ אֶת־אַדְמָתָם׃ (כג) וַיֹּאמֶר יוֹסֵף
(ציון) אֶל־הָעָם הֵן קָנִיתִי אֶתְכֶם הַיּוֹם (נגד, זן) וְאֶת־אַדְמַתְכֶם
לְפַרְעֹה הֵא־לָכֶם זֶרַע וּזְרַעְתֶּם אֶת־הָאֲדָמָה׃ (כד) וְהָיָה
(יהה) (יהוה) בַּתְּבוּאֹת וּנְתַתֶּם חֲמִישִׁית לְפַרְעֹה וְאַרְבַּע הַיָּדֹת
יִהְיֶה (ייי) לָכֶם לְזֶרַע הַשָּׂדֶה וּלְאָכְלְכֶם וְלַאֲשֶׁר בְּבָתֵּיכֶם
וְלֶאֱכֹל לְטַפְּכֶם׃

Maftir

(כה) וַיֹּאמְרוּ הֶחֱיִתָנוּ נִמְצָא־חֵן (מוזי) בְּעֵינֵי (מ"ה בריבוע) אֲדֹנִי וְהָיִינוּ
עֲבָדִים לְפַרְעֹה׃ (כו) וַיָּשֶׂם אֹתָהּ יוֹסֵף (ציון) לְחֹק עַד־הַיּוֹם

(נגד, זן) הַזֶּה (והו) עַל־אַדְמַת מִצְרַיִם (מצר) לְפַרְעֹה לַחֹמֶשׁ
רַק אַדְמַת הַכֹּהֲנִים לְבַדָּם לֹא הָיְתָה לְפַרְעֹה׃ (כז) וַיֵּשֶׁב
יִשְׂרָאֵל בְּאֶרֶץ מִצְרַיִם (מצר) בְּאֶרֶץ גֹּשֶׁן וַיֵּאָחֲזוּ בָהּ וַיִּפְרוּ
וַיִּרְבּוּ מְאֹד׃

The Haftarah of Vayigash

The Resurrection of the Dead is discussed through Ezekiel's prophecy of the dead bones. The Rav often gives the names "Joseph" and "Yehuda" because these two names are specifically mentioned in this prophecy. The prevalence of these names, when held by righteous people, hastens the Final Redemption, the Resurrection of the Dead, and the restoration of immortality.

יחזקאל פרק לז

טו וַיְהִי דְבַר (ראה) -יְהֹוָה אֵלַי לֵאמֹר: טז וְאַתָּה בֶן-אָדָם קַח-
לְךָ עֵץ אֶחָד (אהבה, דאגה) וּכְתֹב עָלָיו לִיהוּדָה וְלִבְנֵי יִשְׂרָאֵל
חֲבֵרָו וּלְקַח עֵץ אֶחָד (אהבה, דאגה) וּכְתוֹב עָלָיו לְיוֹסֵף (ציון) עֵץ
אֶפְרַיִם וְכָל (ילי) -בֵּית (ב"פ ראה) יִשְׂרָאֵל חֲבֵרָו: יז וְקָרַב אֹתָם
אֶחָד (אהבה, דאגה) אֶל-אֶחָד (אהבה, דאגה) לְךָ לְעֵץ אֶחָד (אהבה, דאגה)
וְהָיוּ לַאֲחָדִים (אהבה, דאגה) בְּיָדֶךָ: יח וְכַאֲשֶׁר יֹאמְרוּ אֵלֶיךָ בְּנֵי
עַמְּךָ לֵאמֹר הֲלוֹא-תַגִּיד לָנוּ (מום, אלהים, אהיה-אדני) מָה-אֵלֶּה
לָּךְ: יט דַּבֵּר (ראה) אֲלֵהֶם כֹּה (הי) -אָמַר אֲדֹנָי יְהֹוִה הִנֵּה
אֲנִי (אני) לֹקֵחַ אֶת-עֵץ יוֹסֵף (ציון) אֲשֶׁר בְּיַד-אֶפְרַיִם וְשִׁבְטֵי
יִשְׂרָאֵל חֲבֵרָו וְנָתַתִּי אוֹתָם עָלָיו אֶת-עֵץ יְהוּדָה וַעֲשִׂיתִם
לְעֵץ אֶחָד (אהבה, דאגה) וְהָיוּ אֶחָד (אהבה, דאגה) בְּיָדִי: כ וְהָיוּ
הָעֵצִים אֲשֶׁר-תִּכְתֹּב עֲלֵיהֶם בְּיָדְךָ לְעֵינֵיהֶם: כא וְדַבֵּר
(ראה) אֲלֵיהֶם כֹּה-אָמַר אֲדֹנָי יְהֹוִה הִנֵּה אֲנִי (אני) לֹקֵחַ אֶת-בְּנֵי
יִשְׂרָאֵל מִבֵּין הַגּוֹיִם אֲשֶׁר הָלְכוּ (מיה) -שָׁם וְקִבַּצְתִּי אֹתָם

מִסָּבִיב וְהֵבֵאתִי אוֹתָם אֶל־אַדְמָתָם: כב וְעָשִׂיתִי אֹתָם
לְגוֹי אֶחָד (אהבה, דאגה) בָּאָרֶץ בְּהָרֵי יִשְׂרָאֵל וּמֶלֶךְ אֶחָד (אהבה,
דאגה) יִהְיֶה (ייי) לְכֻלָּם לְמֶלֶךְ וְלֹא יִהְיוּ־ (כתיב: יהיה־) עוֹד לִשְׁנֵי
גוֹיִם וְלֹא יֵחָצוּ עוֹד לִשְׁתֵּי מַמְלָכוֹת עוֹד: כג וְלֹא יִטַּמְּאוּ
עוֹד בְּגִלּוּלֵיהֶם וּבְשִׁקּוּצֵיהֶם וּבְכֹל (לכב) פִּשְׁעֵיהֶם וְהוֹשַׁעְתִּי
אֹתָם מִכֹּל מוֹשְׁבֹתֵיהֶם אֲשֶׁר חָטְאוּ בָהֶם וְטִהַרְתִּי אוֹתָם
וְהָיוּ־לִי לְעָם (עלם) וַאֲנִי (אני) אֶהְיֶה (יהה) לָהֶם לֵאלֹהִים (דמב, ילה):
כד וְעַבְדִּי דָוִד מֶלֶךְ עֲלֵיהֶם וְרוֹעֶה אֶחָד (אהבה, דאגה) יִהְיֶה
(ייי) לְכֻלָּם וּבְמִשְׁפָּטַי יֵלֵכוּ (כלי) וְחֻקֹּתַי יִשְׁמְרוּ וְעָשׂוּ אוֹתָם:
כה וְיָשְׁבוּ עַל־הָאָרֶץ אֲשֶׁר נָתַתִּי לְעַבְדִּי לְיַעֲקֹב (יאהדונהי
אידהנויה) אֲשֶׁר יָשְׁבוּ־בָהּ אֲבוֹתֵיכֶם וְיָשְׁבוּ עָלֶיהָ (פהל) הֵמָּה
וּבְנֵיהֶם וּבְנֵי בְנֵיהֶם עַד־עוֹלָם וְדָוִד עַבְדִּי נָשִׂיא לָהֶם
לְעוֹלָם: כו וְכָרַתִּי לָהֶם בְּרִית שָׁלוֹם בְּרִית עוֹלָם יִהְיֶה (ייי)
אוֹתָם וּנְתַתִּים וְהִרְבֵּיתִי אוֹתָם וְנָתַתִּי אֶת־מִקְדָּשִׁי בְּתוֹכָם
לְעוֹלָם: כז וְהָיָה (יהה) מִשְׁכָּנִי עֲלֵיהֶם וְהָיִיתִי לָהֶם לֵאלֹהִים
(דמב, ילה) וְהֵמָּה יִהְיוּ־לִי לְעָם (עלם): כח וְיָדְעוּ הַגּוֹיִם כִּי אֲנִי (אני)
יְהוָה מְקַדֵּשׁ אֶת־יִשְׂרָאֵל בִּהְיוֹת מִקְדָּשִׁי בְּתוֹכָם לְעוֹלָם:

{פ}

Lesson of Vayechi

"And he said, 'Swear to me,' and he swore to him..."

As the Ramban explains, one of the reasons that Jacob made Joseph swear to bury him in Israel was to hurry him up. If Jacob hadn't forced Joseph to swear, there was a possibility that Joseph would not have made the extra effort and perhaps would not have buried his father in Israel.

Still, we know that Joseph's love for his father was something no words can to begin to describe. So what did Jacob want to teach us by making Joseph swear? We know that Joseph was in danger during Jacob's funeral. If Jacob had not made Joseph swear, Joseph might have been frightened and might have felt it was impossible to go through all the problems of bringing his father to Israel. When Jacob made him swear, Joseph received new strength, knowing he had the power to overcome any obstacles in his way.

If we tell ourselves that we cannot restrict our desires–that doing so seems impossible–we must awaken ourselves to how much we owe the Creator. He gives us air to breathe, food to eat, and a house to live in. More than that, He wants to help us. As the Talmud says: "More than the calf wants to eat, the cow wants to feed." More than we want to receive from the Creator, the Creator wants to give.

We must remember that there is no limit to how much Light we can receive if only we have the desire. Therefore, nothing is impossible. As the kabbalists say, "There is no such thing as can't. There is only won't."

"God Who is my shepherd"

In the writings of the Grandfather of Kelm, it is written: "Here I have never heard from a middle-class person or from the rich of the people who will say bless God that I had this year something to eat or that I wasn't sick." But sometimes a righteous person will bless God that everything is good, even if the situation is not so good. "God is my shepherd" means "God who sustains me."

We constantly think and feel that we deserve things! "Why don't I have this and why I don't have that?" But it is written in the Gemara: "A person can be poor only in consciousness." A poor person is a person who feels that he lacks something, even if he has everything. The truth is, we don't deserve anything. This world does not belong to us; we are just tools to reveal the

Light of the Creator. Even though it is written: "If you worked for it and you found it, believe it," it's not that we work and therefore deserve something for our work. Whatever we get is through the mercy and justice of the Creator. This is a very important lesson. Whoever feels that he deserves something will not have anything in the end. Whoever believes that he doesn't deserve anything, in the end will receive everything.

"He taught his hands."

The great Rabbi Eliezer said about himself, not from pride, God forbid, but to teach us to be like him: "My two arms are like two Torah scrolls."

A person who studies Torah becomes connected to the Torah. Whatever he does is with the Light. His hands become like the hands of the Creator. The Creator enters every single part of his body, so his hands automatically know to do the will of God. The body of Jacob our Patriarch was literally part of the Creator. We must reach the level where every part of us, including our physical body, is a channel for the Light so that we can ignite the Godly part from above in every atom of our body.

There is a story of a righteous man who wanted to see the Garden of Eden. He had a dream in which he was shown the way to the Garden. As he followed the directions, he was expecting to see beautiful lakes, waterfalls, trees, and all the other trappings of paradise. Suddenly, he came upon two people who were sitting at a broken table eating dry bread and drinking water from broken cups. They were studying Torah. "Where is the Garden of Eden?" he asked them. They answered that the Garden of Eden is not a place that you go to or are inside of. The Garden of Eden is part of you.

Spirituality is not something that is "done" or "gone to" for a few hours a day. It is something we become part of. It is there inside us, wherever we are.

The meaning of rest

To receive the Torah, we must achieve a great inner peace. But what is real peace? It is something much more than just physical rest and comfort. A person who desires to rest only in the physical sense is like a man who wants to put out a fire by pouring gas onto it. For an instant, it appears he has put out the fire, but then we see that he has only made it bigger.

The real rest that we need in order to receive the Torah will only happen by breaking our body's desire to avoid discomfort. Regarding this, Yisaschar was

given responsibility for the tribes who studied the Torah. He knew the level of rest that one needs to be connected to the Light. So he became accustomed to suffering, and because of this, attained real peace.

Once a man came to Rabbi Elimelech and asked, "How is it possible to work for God when there are so many problems"? Rabbi Elimelech told the man to go to Rabbi Elimelech's brother, the holy Rabbi Zushah because everyone knew that Rabbi Zusha was beset by all the problems that could exist in the world. But when the man asked Rabbi Zusha the same question, the rabbi answered, "I don't have any problems!" The only way to reach real peace is to seek out the uncomfortable–until such discomfort becomes restful in itself. This is the only way we can bring real peace and rest to the world.

Synopsis of Vayechi

Usually, there is some physical space between the Parashot in the Torah scroll. Sometimes, it is a whole line; sometimes it is nine characters. But here, we have only one letter's width of space. This is to remind us of how we create opportunities for the Satan. Even a little opening for jealousy, anger, or other forms of negativity allows the Satan to get his foot in the door.

First Reading - Abraham - Chesed

(כוז) ויחי יעקב (יאהדונהי אידהנויה) בארץ מצרים (מצר) שבע
עשרה שנה ויהי ימי־יעקב (יאהדונהי אידהנויה) שני חייו שבע
שנים וארבעים ומאת שנה: (כט) ויקרבו ימי־ישראל למות
ויקרא | לבנו ליוסף (ציון) ויאמר לו אם (ייהך)־נא מצאתי חן
(מוזי) בעיניך (ע"ה קס"א) שים־נא ידך תחת ירכי ועשית עמדי
חסד (ע"ב) ואמת (אהיה פ' אהיה) אל־נא תקברני במצרים (מצר):
(ל) ושכבתי עם־אבתי ונשאתני ממצרים (מצר) וקברתני
בקברתם ויאמר אנכי (איע) אעשה כדברך (ראה): (לא)
ויאמר השבעה לי וישבע לו וישתחו ישראל על־ראש
המטה: פ מוז (א) ויהי אחרי הדברים (ראה) האלה ויאמר

וַיְחִי - And Jacob lived. After all the suffering he had endured, Jacob receives seventeen years of happiness in his life. Vayechi means "to live." We sometimes fall into the trap of existing without really living. For example, a father who works twenty hours a day "for his children" cannot really be working for them. He's working and living for himself or even for the Satan. By the time he can appreciate his children, it is too late for him to even know them.

וַיֹּאמֶר - Jacob makes Joseph swear to bury him in Israel
Jacob fears that Pharaoh will not allow Joseph to do this. If Jacob didn't make Joseph swear to this—if he had simply requested it—Joseph might have given up if Pharaoh had created obstacles. By forcing Joseph to swear, Jacob reminds him that nothing is impossible.

לְיוֹסֵף (ציון) הִנֵּה אָבִיךָ חֹלֶה (להוו) וַיִּקַּח (ווּעם) אֶת־שְׁנֵי בָנָיו
עִמּוֹ אֶת־מְנַשֶּׁה וְאֶת־אֶפְרָיִם׃ (ב) וַיַּגֵּד לְיַעֲקֹב (יאהדונהי אידהנויה)
וַיֹּאמֶר הִנֵּה בִּנְךָ יוֹסֵף (ציון) בָּא אֵלֶיךָ וַיִּתְחַזֵּק יִשְׂרָאֵל וַיֵּשֶׁב
עַל־הַמִּטָּה׃ (ג) וַיֹּאמֶר יַעֲקֹב (יאהדונהי אידהנויה) אֶל־יוֹסֵף (ציון) אֵל
שַׁדַּי (מהש) נִרְאָה־אֵלַי בְּלוּז בְּאֶרֶץ כְּנָעַן וַיְבָרֶךְ (עסמ"ב) אֹתִי׃
(ד) וַיֹּאמֶר אֵלַי הִנְנִי מַפְרְךָ וְהִרְבִּיתִךָ וּנְתַתִּיךָ לִקְהַל עַמִּים
וְנָתַתִּי אֶת־הָאָרֶץ (מילוי אלהים ע"ה) הַזֹּאת לְזַרְעֲךָ אַחֲרֶיךָ אֲחֻזַּת
עוֹלָם׃ (ה) וְעַתָּה שְׁנֵי־בָנֶיךָ הַנּוֹלָדִים לְךָ בְּאֶרֶץ מִצְרַיִם
(מצר) עַד־בֹּאִי אֵלֶיךָ מִצְרַיְמָה (מצר) לִי־הֵם אֶפְרַיִם וּמְנַשֶּׁה
כִּרְאוּבֵן וְשִׁמְעוֹן יִהְיוּ־לִי׃ (ו) וּמוֹלַדְתְּךָ אֲשֶׁר־הוֹלַדְתָּ
אַחֲרֵיהֶם לְךָ יִהְיוּ עַל שֵׁם אֲחֵיהֶם יִקָּרְאוּ בְּנַחֲלָתָם׃ (ז) וַאֲנִי
(אני) | בְּבֹאִי מִפַּדָּן מֵתָה עָלַי רָחֵל בְּאֶרֶץ כְּנַעַן בַּדֶּרֶךְ (ב"פ
יב"ק) בְּעוֹד כִּבְרַת־אֶרֶץ לָבֹא אֶפְרָתָה וָאֶקְבְּרֶהָ שָּׁם בְּדֶרֶךְ
(ב"פ יב"ק) אֶפְרָת הִוא בֵּית (ב"פ ראה) לָחֶם (ג' הויות)׃ (ח) וַיַּרְא יִשְׂרָאֵל
אֶת־בְּנֵי יוֹסֵף (ציון) וַיֹּאמֶר מִי (ילי)־אֵלֶּה׃ (ט) וַיֹּאמֶר יוֹסֵף (ציון)
אֶל־אָבִיו בָּנַי הֵם אֲשֶׁר־נָתַן־לִי אֱלֹהִים (כוק) (ילה) בָּזֶה וַיֹּאמַר

חֹלֶה - Jacob's illness
Jacob is the first person ever to get sick. From this portion, we can receive the energy of protection from any illness as well as the power to heal.

קָחֶם־נָא אֵלַי וַאֲבָרְכֵם׃

Second Reading - Issac - Gvurah

(י) וְעֵינֵי (מ"ה בריבוע) יִשְׂרָאֵל כָּבְדוּ מִזֹּקֶן לֹא יוּכַל לִרְאוֹת וַיַּגֵּשׁ
אֹתָם אֵלָיו וַיִּשַּׁק לָהֶם וַיְחַבֵּק לָהֶם׃ (יא) וַיֹּאמֶר יִשְׂרָאֵל
אֶל־יוֹסֵף (ציון) רְאֹה (ראה) פָנֶיךָ (סמ"ב) לֹא פִלָּלְתִּי וְהִנֵּה הֶרְאָה
אֹתִי אֱלֹהִים (ילה) גַּם אֶת־זַרְעֶךָ׃ (יב) וַיּוֹצֵא יוֹסֵף (ציון) אֹתָם
מֵעִם בִּרְכָּיו וַיִּשְׁתַּחוּ לְאַפָּיו אָרְצָה׃ (יג) וַיִּקַּח (וזעם) יוֹסֵף (ציון)
אֶת־שְׁנֵיהֶם אֶת־אֶפְרַיִם בִּימִינוֹ מִשְּׂמֹאל יִשְׂרָאֵל וְאֶת־
מְנַשֶּׁה בִשְׂמֹאלוֹ מִימִין יִשְׂרָאֵל וַיַּגֵּשׁ אֵלָיו׃ (יד) וַיִּשְׁלַח
יִשְׂרָאֵל אֶת־יְמִינוֹ וַיָּשֶׁת עַל־רֹאשׁ אֶפְרַיִם וְהוּא הַצָּעִיר
וְאֶת־שְׂמֹאלוֹ עַל־רֹאשׁ מְנַשֶּׁה שִׂכֵּל אֶת־יָדָיו כִּי מְנַשֶּׁה
הַבְּכוֹר׃ (טו) וַיְבָרֶךְ (עסמ"ב) אֶת־יוֹסֵף (ציון) וַיֹּאמַר הָאֱלֹהִים (ילה)
אֲשֶׁר הִתְהַלְּכוּ אֲבֹתַי לְפָנָיו אַבְרָהָם (רמ"ח) וְיִצְחָק (ד"פ ב"ן)
הָאֱלֹהִים (ילה) הָרֹעֶה אֹתִי מֵעוֹדִי עַד־הַיּוֹם (נגד, זן) הַזֶּה (והו)׃
(טז) הַמַּלְאָךְ (פוי) הַגֹּאֵל (א"ת ב"ש כתר) אֹתִי מִכָּל (ילי)־רָע יְבָרֵךְ
(עסמ"ב) אֶת־הַנְּעָרִים וְיִקָּרֵא בָהֶם שְׁמִי וְשֵׁם אֲבֹתַי אַבְרָהָם
(רמ"ח) וְיִצְחָק (ד"פ ב"ן) וְיִדְגּוּ לָרֹב בְּקֶרֶב הָאָרֶץ (מילוי אלהים ע"ה)׃

Third Reading - Jacob - Tiferet

(יז) וַיַּרְא יוֹסֵף (ציון) כִּי־יָשִׁית אָבִיו יַד־יְמִינוֹ עַל־רֹאשׁ
אֶפְרַיִם וַיֵּרַע בְּעֵינָיו (מ"ה בריבוע) וַיִּתְמֹךְ יַד־אָבִיו לְהָסִיר אֹתָהּ
מֵעַל (עלם) רֹאשׁ־אֶפְרַיִם עַל־רֹאשׁ מְנַשֶּׁה: (יח) וַיֹּאמֶר יוֹסֵף
(ציון) אֶל־אָבִיו לֹא־כֵן אָבִי כִּי־זֶה הַבְּכֹר שִׂים יְמִינְךָ עַל־
רֹאשׁוֹ: (יט) וַיְמָאֵן אָבִיו וַיֹּאמֶר יָדַעְתִּי בְנִי יָדַעְתִּי גַּם־הוּא
יִהְיֶה (ייי)־לְּעָם (עלם) וְגַם־הוּא יִגְדָּל (יזל) וְאוּלָם אָחִיו הַקָּטֹן
יִגְדַּל (יזל) מִמֶּנּוּ וְזַרְעוֹ יִהְיֶה (ייי) מְלֹא־הַגּוֹיִם: (כ) וַיְבָרְכֵם בַּיּוֹם
(נגד, זן) הַהוּא לֵאמוֹר בְּךָ יְבָרֵךְ (עסמ"ב) יִשְׂרָאֵל לֵאמֹר יְשִׂמְךָ
אֱלֹהִים (ילה) כְּאֶפְרַיִם וְכִמְנַשֶּׁה וַיָּשֶׂם אֶת־אֶפְרַיִם לִפְנֵי
מְנַשֶּׁה: (כא) וַיֹּאמֶר יִשְׂרָאֵל אֶל־יוֹסֵף (ציון) הִנֵּה אָנֹכִי (איע) מֵת
וְהָיָה (יהה) (יהוה) אֱלֹהִים (ילה) עִמָּכֶם וְהֵשִׁיב אֶתְכֶם אֶל־אֶרֶץ

וַיַּרְא - Joseph's two sons
Instead of putting his right hand on the older son and his left hand on the younger, Jacob crosses his hands. When Joseph questions this, Jacob replies that the younger son has greater need for the blessing because the children that would come from the younger son would be on a higher spiritual level.

From this, we can draw two lessons. First, we should never judge events by appearances; things are almost never what they seem. Second, there is no such thing as protocol in spiritual matters. We must do what is necessary and whatever the situation demands. Spiritual work is not rote behavior. Our actions should be in accord with our circumstances.

אֲבֹתֵיכֶם: (כב) וַאֲנִ֞י (אני) נָתַ֧תִּי לְךָ֛ שְׁכֶ֥ם אַחַ֖ד (אהבה) עַל־אַחֶ֑יךָ

אֲשֶׁ֤ר לָקַ֙חְתִּי֙ מִיַּ֣ד הָֽאֱמֹרִ֔י בְּחַרְבִּ֖י (ריי) וּבְקַשְׁתִּֽי: פ

Fourth Reading - Moses - Netzach

מט (א) וַיִּקְרָ֥א יַעֲקֹ֖ב (יאהדונהי אידהנויה) אֶל־בָּנָ֑יו וַיֹּ֗אמֶר הֵאָֽסְפוּ֙

וְאַגִּ֣ידָה לָכֶ֔ם אֵ֛ת אֲשֶׁר־יִקְרָ֥א אֶתְכֶ֖ם בְּאַחֲרִ֥ית הַיָּמִֽים

(ילך): (ב) הִקָּבְצ֥וּ וְשִׁמְע֖וּ בְּנֵ֣י יַעֲקֹ֑ב (יאהדונהי אידהנויה) וְשִׁמְע֖וּ

אֶל־יִשְׂרָאֵ֖ל אֲבִיכֶֽם: (ג) רְאוּבֵן֙ בְּכֹ֣רִי אַ֔תָּה כֹּחִ֖י

וְרֵאשִׁ֣ית אוֹנִ֑י יֶ֥תֶר שְׂאֵ֖ת וְיֶ֥תֶר עָֽז: (ד) פַּ֤חַז כַּמַּ֙יִם֙ אַל־

תּוֹתַ֔ר כִּ֥י עָלִ֖יתָ מִשְׁכְּבֵ֣י אָבִ֑יךָ אָ֥ז חִלַּ֖לְתָּ יְצוּעִ֥י עָלָֽה: פ (ה)

שִׁמְע֥וֹן וְלֵוִ֖י אַחִ֑ים כְּלֵ֣י חָמָ֖ס מְכֵרֹתֵיהֶֽם: (ו) בְּסֹדָם֙ אַל־

וַיִּקְרָא - Jacob gathers his own sons to bless them before he dies
Jacob blesses his sons individually and as a group. To gain a blessing, we must have unity. A consciousness of "every man for himself" cancels the energy and the purpose of blessing.

רְאוּבֵן - Blessing of Reuben. The Zohar tells us that the first three sons didn't really receive the blessing. In Reuben's case, this was because of his failure to be proactive in moving his father's bed. Also, Reuben's place in the family was somewhat unclear. At the time of his conception, God withheld the first drop of Jacob's semen to save it for Joseph.

שִׁמְעוֹן וְלֵוִי - Blessing of Shimon and Levi
Because of their association with the energy of judgment, Simon and Levi also were denied a blessing. If Jacob had blessed them, the judgment in the world would have been overwhelming.

תָּבֹא נַפְשִׁי בִּקְהָלָם אַל־תֵּחַד כְּבֹדִי כִּי בְאַפָּם הָרְגוּ אִישׁ
וּבִרְצֹנָם עִקְּרוּ־שׁוֹר (אבג יתץ, ושר, אהבת חנם)׃ (ז) אָרוּר אַפָּם כִּי עָז
וְעֶבְרָתָם כִּי קָשָׁתָה אֲחַלְּקֵם בְּיַעֲקֹב (יאהדונהי אידהנויה) וַאֲפִיצֵם
בְּיִשְׂרָאֵל׃ ס (ח) יְהוּדָה אַתָּה יוֹדוּךָ אַחֶיךָ יָדְךָ בְּעֹרֶף
אֹיְבֶיךָ יִשְׁתַּחֲווּ לְךָ בְּנֵי אָבִיךָ׃ (ט) גּוּר אַרְיֵה יְהוּדָה מִטֶּרֶף
בְּנִי עָלִיתָ כָּרַע רָבַץ כְּאַרְיֵה וּכְלָבִיא מִי (ילי) יְקִימֶנּוּ׃ (י)
לֹא־יָסוּר שֵׁבֶט מִיהוּדָה וּמְחֹקֵק מִבֵּין רַגְלָיו עַד כִּי־יָבֹא
שִׁילֹה וְלוֹ יִקְּהַת עַמִּים׃ (יא) אֹסְרִי לַגֶּפֶן עִירֹה וְלַשֹּׂרֵקָה בְּנִי
אֲתֹנוֹ כִּבֵּס בַּיַּיִן (מיכ, י״פ האא) לְבֻשׁוֹ וּבְדַם־עֲנָבִים סוּתֹה׃ (יב)
חַכְלִילִי עֵינַיִם (מ״ה בריבוע) מִיָּיִן (מיכ, י״פ האא) וּלְבֶן־שִׁנַּיִם מֵחָלָב׃
פ (יג) זְבוּלֻן לְחוֹף יַמִּים (נלך) יִשְׁכֹּן וְהוּא לְחוֹף אֳנִיֹּת וְיַרְכָתוֹ

יְהוּדָה - Blessing of Yehuda

Through the blessing of Yehuda, we can connect to the coming of the Messianic era and gain a glimpse of what that era will be like. Chaos will be gone forever, and the Tree of Life reality will be restored.

זְבוּלֻן - Blessing of Zebulun. Zebulun is a business-oriented personality. Jacob gives Zebulun a blessing for physical sustenance because this is Zebulun's area of power and responsibility. Zebulun gets his blessing before Yisaschar, who is more of a spiritual person, demonstrating the importance of those individuals who do well in the material world. There are people who provide sustenance through their work or their financial contributions, thereby enabling others to study spirituality.

עַל־צִידֹן׃ ס (יד) יִשָּׂשכָר חֲמֹר גָּרֶם רֹבֵץ בֵּין הַמִּשְׁפְּתָיִם׃

(טו) וַיַּרְא מְנֻחָה (ע"ה ב"פ ב"ן) כִּי טוֹב (והו) (אום) וְאֶת־הָאָרֶץ (מילוי

אלהים ע"ה) כִּי נָעֵמָה וַיֵּט שִׁכְמוֹ לִסְבֹּל וַיְהִי לְמַס־עֹבֵד׃ ס (טז)

דָּן יָדִין עַמּוֹ כְּאַחַד (אהבה) שִׁבְטֵי יִשְׂרָאֵל׃ (יז) יְהִי־דָן נָחָשׁ

עֲלֵי־דֶרֶךְ (ב"פ יב"ק) שְׁפִיפֹן עֲלֵי־אֹרַח הַנֹּשֵׁךְ עִקְּבֵי־סוּס (כוק)

וַיִּפֹּל רֹכְבוֹ אָחוֹר׃ (ייז) לִישׁוּעָתְךָ קִוִּיתִי יְהוָה(יאהדונהי)׃ ס

Fifth Reading - Aaron - Hod

(יט) גָּד גְּדוּד יְגוּדֶנּוּ וְהוּא יָגֻד עָקֵב (ב"פ מום)׃ ס (כ) מֵאָשֵׁר שְׁמֵנָה

יִשָּׂשכָר - The Torah calls Issachar a donkey. This might seem to be an insult, especially since Yisaschar has spent his entire life studying the Torah's secrets. By referring to him as a donkey, however, the Torah is speaking of his power to bear weight and perform work without complaint. We need this quality to pursue our spiritual work.

דָּן - After blessing Dan, Jacob actually prays for the first and only time. He adds a special verse of prayer for Dan because Dan's purpose is judgment. In fact, the name "Dan" and the word "judgment" have the same root.
When judgment comes upon us, it is because we directed judgment toward others. Even if we deserve a certain judgment we will not receive it unless, we activated its manifestation by our own judgmental thoughts and feelings.

גָּד - There will be many blessings on the g'dud ("battalions") so that they may be powerful in war. Our battle with the Satan within us is like a war: If we let our guard down, he defeats us. This struggle requires at least as much preparation as a war in the physical world.

אָשֵׁר - Asher controls the month of Aquarius. The end of chaos on the

לַחְמוֹ וְהוּא יִתֵּן מַעֲדַנֵּי־מֶלֶךְ׃ ס (כא) נַפְתָּלִי אַיָּלָה שְׁלֻחָה
הַנֹּתֵן (אבג יתץ, ושר, אהבת חנם) אִמְרֵי־שָׁפֶר׃ ס (כב) בֵּן פֹּרָת יוֹסֵף
(ציון) בֵּן פֹּרָת עֲלֵי־עָיִן (מ"ה בריבוע) בָּנוֹת צָעֲדָה עֲלֵי־שׁוּר (אבג
יתץ, ושר, אהבת חנם)׃ (כג) וַיְמָרְרֻהוּ וָרֹבּוּ וַיִּשְׂטְמֻהוּ בַּעֲלֵי חִצִּים׃
(כד) וַתֵּשֶׁב בְּאֵיתָן קַשְׁתּוֹ וַיָּפֹזּוּ זְרֹעֵי יָדָיו מִידֵי אֲבִיר (הרוז)
יַעֲקֹב (יאהדונהי אידהנויה) מִשָּׁם רֹעֶה אֶבֶן יִשְׂרָאֵל׃ (כה) מֵאֵל
אָבִיךָ וְיַעְזְרֶךָּ וְאֵת שַׁדַּי וִיבָרְכֶךָּ בִּרְכֹת שָׁמַיִם (י"פ טל) מֵעָל
(עלם) בִּרְכֹת תְּהוֹם רֹבֶצֶת תָּחַת בִּרְכֹת שָׁדַיִם וָרָחַם (אברהם)׃

personal level comes through Asher, as does the Final Redemption when chaos will be banished forever from all Creation. In our relationships, our business, our health, and all other areas of life, Asher allows us to rise above negativity.

נַפְתָּלִי - Blessing of Naphtali

Naphtali physically was blessed with speed. Often, when there is something we should not do, we are quick to do it. However, when there is something that is spiritually worthwhile, we are often slow and lazy to begin. Naphtali gives us the potential to be slow in things that we should avoid and to move quickly in our spiritual tasks.

בֵּן פֹּרָת - The Blessing of Joseph-against evil eye

This is the verse that removes evil eye. Joseph controls the month of Pisces, whose symbol is the fish. Fish don't have evil eye because they are always surrounded by water, which embodies the power of mercy. We also can be protected against evil eye through the power of the Zohar and by doing acts of sharing. Even if someone deliberately intends to do us harm, the Zohar is a shield that evil eye cannot penetrate.

(כו) בִּרְכֹת אָבִיךָ גָּבְרוּ עַל־בִּרְכֹת הוֹרַי עַד־תַּאֲוַת גִּבְעֹת
עוֹלָם תִּהְיֶיןָ לְרֹאשׁ יוֹסֵף (ציון) וּלְקָדְקֹד נְזִיר אֶחָיו: פ

Sixth Reading - Joseph - Yesod

(כז) בִּנְיָמִין זְאֵב יִטְרָף בַּבֹּקֶר יֹאכַל עַד וְלָעֶרֶב יְחַלֵּק
שָׁלָל: (כח) כָּל (ילי)־אֵלֶּה שִׁבְטֵי יִשְׂרָאֵל שְׁנֵים עָשָׂר וְזֹאת
אֲשֶׁר־דִּבֶּר (ראה) לָהֶם אֲבִיהֶם וַיְבָרֶךְ (עסמ"ב) אוֹתָם אִישׁ
אֲשֶׁר כְּבִרְכָתוֹ בֵּרַךְ אֹתָם: (כט) וַיְצַו אוֹתָם וַיֹּאמֶר אֲלֵהֶם
אֲנִי (אני) נֶאֱסָף אֶל־עַמִּי קִבְרוּ אֹתִי אֶל־אֲבֹתָי אֶל־הַמְּעָרָה
אֲשֶׁר בִּשְׂדֵה עֶפְרוֹן הַחִתִּי: (ל) בַּמְּעָרָה אֲשֶׁר בִּשְׂדֵה
הַמַּכְפֵּלָה אֲשֶׁר עַל־פְּנֵי (חכמה, בינה)־מַמְרֵא בְּאֶרֶץ כְּנָעַן אֲשֶׁר
קָנָה אַבְרָהָם (רמ"ח) אֶת־הַשָּׂדֶה מֵאֵת עֶפְרֹן הַחִתִּי לַאֲחֻזַּת־
קָבֶר: (לא) שָׁמָּה קָבְרוּ אֶת־אַבְרָהָם (רמ"ח) וְאֵת שָׂרָה אִשְׁתּוֹ
שָׁמָּה קָבְרוּ אֶת־יִצְחָק (ד"פ ב"ן) וְאֵת רִבְקָה אִשְׁתּוֹ וְשָׁמָּה
קָבַרְתִּי אֶת־לֵאָה: (לב) מִקְנֵה הַשָּׂדֶה וְהַמְּעָרָה אֲשֶׁר־בּוֹ
מֵאֵת בְּנֵי־חֵת: (לג) וַיְכַל יַעֲקֹב (יאהדונהי אידהנויה) לְצַוֹּת אֶת־בָּנָיו

בִּנְיָמִין - Blessing of Benjamin
Although it seems that there were separate blessings for each tribe, we learn that Jacob blessed them together. Even though we all have different gifts and abilities, we must always remember that we are in this world together. Everything we do has an impact on the lives of other people. Therefore we cannot think of "me first." Through sharing, we will reveal our awareness that we are all blessed together.

וַיֶּאֱסֹף רַגְלָיו אֶל־הַמִּטָּה וַיִּגְוַע וַיֵּאָסֶף אֶל־עַמָּיו׃ נ (א) וַיִּפֹּל
יוֹסֵף (ציון) עַל־פְּנֵי (וחכמה, בינה) אָבִיו וַיֵּבְךְּ עָלָיו וַיִּשַּׁק־לוֹ׃ (ב) וַיְצַו
יוֹסֵף (ציון) אֶת־עֲבָדָיו אֶת־הָרֹפְאִים לַחֲנֹט אֶת־אָבִיו וַיַּחַנְטוּ
הָרֹפְאִים אֶת־יִשְׂרָאֵל׃ (ג) וַיִּמְלְאוּ־לוֹ אַרְבָּעִים יוֹם (נגד, זן) כִּי
כֵּן יִמְלְאוּ יְמֵי הַחֲנֻטִים וַיִּבְכּוּ אֹתוֹ מִצְרַיִם (מצר) שִׁבְעִים יוֹם
(נגד, זן)׃ (ד) וַיַּעַבְרוּ יְמֵי בְכִיתוֹ וַיְדַבֵּר (ראה) יוֹסֵף (ציון) אֶל־בֵּית
(ב״פ ראה) פַּרְעֹה לֵאמֹר אִם (יוהך)־נָא מָצָאתִי חֵן (מוחי) בְּעֵינֵיכֶם
(מ״ה בריבוע) דַּבְּרוּ (ראה)־נָא בְּאָזְנֵי (יוד הי ואו הה) פַרְעֹה לֵאמֹר׃ (ה)
אָבִי הִשְׁבִּיעַנִי לֵאמֹר הִנֵּה אָנֹכִי (איע) מֵת בְּקִבְרִי אֲשֶׁר
כָּרִיתִי לִי בְּאֶרֶץ כְּנַעַן שָׁמָּה תִּקְבְּרֵנִי וְעַתָּה אֶעֱלֶה־נָּא
וְאֶקְבְּרָה אֶת־אָבִי וְאָשׁוּבָה׃ (ו) וַיֹּאמֶר פַּרְעֹה עֲלֵה וּקְבֹר
אֶת־אָבִיךָ כַּאֲשֶׁר הִשְׁבִּיעֶךָ׃ (ז) וַיַּעַל יוֹסֵף (ציון) לִקְבֹּר
אֶת־אָבִיו וַיַּעֲלוּ אִתּוֹ כָּל (ילי)־עַבְדֵי פַרְעֹה זִקְנֵי בֵיתוֹ (ב״פ
ראה) וְכֹל (ילי) זִקְנֵי אֶרֶץ־מִצְרָיִם (מצר)׃ (ח) וְכֹל (ילי) בֵּית (ב״פ ראה)
יוֹסֵף (ציון) וְאֶחָיו וּבֵית (ב״פ ראה) אָבִיו רַק טַפָּם וְצֹאנָם וּבְקָרָם

וַיֵּאָסֶף - The Zohar and Talmud say that Jacob did not actually die, only that there is a grave for him and that someone is buried there. Death can be overcome, even physical death, but especially death in relationships, in our work, and in our consciousness at every moment of our lives.

עָזְבוּ בְּאֶרֶץ גֹּשֶׁן׃ (ט) וַיַּעַל עִמּוֹ גַּם־רֶכֶב גַּם־פָּרָשִׁים וַיְהִי
הַמַּחֲנֶה כָּבֵד מְאֹד׃ (י) וַיָּבֹאוּ עַד־גֹּרֶן הָאָטָד אֲשֶׁר בְּעֵבֶר
הַיַּרְדֵּן (י' הויות וד' אותיות) וַיִּסְפְּדוּ־שָׁם מִסְפֵּד (ע"ב בריבוע) גָּדוֹל (להח,
מבה עד"א) וְכָבֵד מְאֹד וַיַּעַשׂ לְאָבִיו אֵבֶל שִׁבְעַת יָמִים (נלך)׃
(יא) וַיַּרְא יוֹשֵׁב הָאָרֶץ (מילוי אלהים ע"ה) הַכְּנַעֲנִי אֶת־הָאֵבֶל בְּגֹרֶן
הָאָטָד וַיֹּאמְרוּ אֵבֶל־כָּבֵד זֶה לְמִצְרָיִם (מצר) עַל־כֵּן קָרָא
שְׁמָהּ אָבֵל מִצְרַיִם (מצר) אֲשֶׁר בְּעֵבֶר הַיַּרְדֵּן (י' הויות וד' אותיות)׃
(יב) וַיַּעֲשׂוּ בָנָיו לוֹ כֵּן כַּאֲשֶׁר צִוָּם׃ (יג) וַיִּשְׂאוּ אֹתוֹ בָנָיו אַרְצָה
כְּנַעַן **וַיִּקְבְּרוּ** אֹתוֹ בִּמְעָרַת שְׂדֵה הַמַּכְפֵּלָה אֲשֶׁר קָנָה
אַבְרָהָם (רמ"ח) אֶת־הַשָּׂדֶה לַאֲחֻזַּת־קֶבֶר מֵאֵת עֶפְרֹן הַחִתִּי
עַל־פְּנֵי (חכמה, בינה) מַמְרֵא׃ (יד) וַיָּשָׁב יוֹסֵף (ציון) מִצְרַיְמָה (מצר)
הוּא וְאֶחָיו וְכָל (ילי)־הָעֹלִים אִתּוֹ לִקְבֹּר אֶת־אָבִיו אַחֲרֵי
קָבְרוֹ אֶת־אָבִיו׃ (טו) וַיִּרְאוּ אֲחֵי־יוֹסֵף (ציון) כִּי־מֵת אֲבִיהֶם
וַיֹּאמְרוּ לוּ **יִשְׂטְמֵנוּ** יוֹסֵף (ציון) וְהָשֵׁב יָשִׁיב לָנוּ (מום) אֵת

וַיִּקְבְּרוּ - The Burying of Jacob

When we attend someone's funeral, we perform an action for which we expect nothing in return. There are many areas of our lives when we should have this same consciousness. This is true particularly in our relationships. We must try to detach ourselves from the compensations that we think we deserve.

יִשְׂטְמֵנוּ - After Jacob 's death, the brothers are fearful because of all they have done to Joseph, especially now that Joseph is their ruler. They make

כָּל (ילי)־הָרָעָה (רהע) אֲשֶׁר גָּמַלְנוּ אֹתוֹ׃ (טז) וַיְצַוּוּ אֶל־יוֹסֵף (ציון)
לֵאמֹר אָבִיךָ צִוָּה לִפְנֵי מוֹתוֹ לֵאמֹר׃ (יז) כֹּה (הי)־תֹאמְרוּ
לְיוֹסֵף (ציון) אָנָּא (לכב) שָׂא נָא פֶּשַׁע אַחֶיךָ וְחַטָּאתָם כִּי־רָעָה
(רהע) גְמָלוּךָ וְעַתָּה שָׂא נָא לְפֶשַׁע עַבְדֵי אֱלֹהֵי (דמב) אָבִיךָ
וַיֵּבְךְּ יוֹסֵף (ציון) בְּדַבְּרָם (ראה) אֵלָיו׃ (יח) וַיֵּלְכוּ גַּם־אֶחָיו וַיִּפְּלוּ
לְפָנָיו וַיֹּאמְרוּ הִנֶּנּוּ לְךָ לַעֲבָדִים׃ (יט) וַיֹּאמֶר אֲלֵהֶם יוֹסֵף
(ציון) אַל־תִּירָאוּ כִּי הֲתַחַת אֱלֹהִים (ילה) אָנִי (אני)׃ (כ) וְאַתֶּם
חֲשַׁבְתֶּם עָלַי רָעָה (רהע) אֱלֹהִים (ילה) חֲשָׁבָהּ לְטֹבָה לְמַעַן
עֲשֹׂה כַּיּוֹם (נגד, זן) הַזֶּה (והו) לְהַחֲיֹת עַם־רָב׃

Seventh Reading - David - Malchut

(כא) וְעַתָּה אַל־תִּירָאוּ אָנֹכִי (איע) אֲכַלְכֵּל אֶתְכֶם וְאֶת־
טַפְּכֶם וַיְנַחֵם אוֹתָם וַיְדַבֵּר (ראה) עַל־לִבָּם׃ (כב) וַיֵּשֶׁב יוֹסֵף
(ציון) בְּמִצְרַיִם (מצר) הוּא וּבֵית (ב"פ ראה) אָבִיו וַיְחִי יוֹסֵף (ציון) מֵאָה
וָעֶשֶׂר שָׁנִים׃

up a story: Jacob told them to tell Joseph not to harm or persecute them. However, Jacob did not say any such thing, nor did he ever think that Joseph would persecute his brothers.

A truly spiritual person does not constantly look for the negative in other people. For example, if a spiritual person is harmed in some way, he or she focuses less on the harm and more on what can be learned. A spiritual person understands that the person who caused the harm has a Tikkun process and that there is always something to be learned from every event, whether good or bad.

Maftir

(כג) וַיַּרְא יוֹסֵף (ציון) לְאֶפְרַיִם בְּנֵי שִׁלֵּשִׁים גַּם בְּנֵי מָכִיר בֶּן־
מְנַשֶּׁה יֻלְּדוּ עַל־בִּרְכֵּי יוֹסֵף (ציון)׃ (כד) וַיֹּאמֶר יוֹסֵף (ציון) אֶל־
אֶחָיו אָנֹכִי (איע) מֵת וֵאלֹהִים (ילה) פָּקֹד (מנק) יִפְקֹד (מנק) אֶתְכֶם
וְהֶעֱלָה אֶתְכֶם מִן־הָאָרֶץ (מילוי אלהים ע"ה) הַזֹּאת אֶל־הָאָרֶץ
(מילוי אלהים ע"ה) אֲשֶׁר נִשְׁבַּע לְאַבְרָהָם (רמ"ח) לְיִצְחָק (ד"פ ב"ן)
וּלְיַעֲקֹב (יאהדונהי אידהנויה)׃ (כה) וַיַּשְׁבַּע יוֹסֵף (ציון) אֶת־בְּנֵי יִשְׂרָאֵל
לֵאמֹר פָּקֹד (מנק) יִפְקֹד (מנק) אֱלֹהִים (ילה) אֶתְכֶם וְהַעֲלִתֶם
אֶת־עַצְמֹתַי מִזֶּה׃ (כו) וַיָּמָת יוֹסֵף (ציון) בֶּן־מֵאָה וָעֶשֶׂר שָׁנִים
וַיַּחַנְטוּ אֹתוֹ וַיִּישֶׂם בָּאָרוֹן בְּמִצְרָיִם (מצר)׃ חזק (סוף ספר בראשית)

וַיָּמָת - Joseph Dies. Joseph dies when he is 110 years old. The Zohar tells us that Joseph was supposed to live until 120 years of age, but he gave ten years of his life for King David. Many of King David's ancestors gave David years because he was actually destined to die at birth. David was aware of this fact and knew that each moment of his life was a gift. From David, we can learn that our own lives are borrowed time, so we must make the most of every moment through our spiritual work.

חזק - The End of the Book of Genesis. When we finish reading a book of the Torah, we repeat the word Cazzak three times. This word means "strength," and it has the same numerical value as Pe Hei Lamed and Mem Hei Shin, the codes of the 72 Names of God that connect us to strength and to healing.

The Haftarah of Vayechi

King's David's last days are discussed here. During the last moments of a person's life, the soul is partly in the Upper Worlds even though the body is still a physical object. For this reason, the Light of their whole life is manifested during these moments. Through our connection to King David in this Haftarah, we don't have to wait until our final moments to be a channel between the Upper and Lower Worlds; we can be a channel throughout our lives.

מלכים א פרק ב

א וַיִּקְרְב֥וּ יְמֵֽי־דָוִ֖ד לָמ֑וּת וַיְצַ֛ו אֶת־שְׁלֹמֹ֥ה (יוד הא ואו הא) בְנ֖וֹ
לֵאמֹֽר׃ ב אָנֹכִ֣י (איע) הֹלֵ֔ךְ (מיה) בְּדֶ֖רֶךְ (ב״פ יב״ק) כָּל־הָאָ֑רֶץ וְחָזַקְתָּ֖
וְהָיִ֥יתָ לְאִֽישׁ׃ ג וְשָׁמַרְתָּ֞ אֶת־מִשְׁמֶ֣רֶת ׀ יְהֹוָ֣ה אֱלֹהֶ֗יךָ
לָלֶ֣כֶת בִּדְרָכָ֗יו (ב״פ יב״ק) לִשְׁמֹ֨ר חֻקֹּתָ֤יו מִצְוֺתָיו֙ וּמִשְׁפָּטָ֣יו
וְעֵדְוֺתָ֔יו כַּכָּת֖וּב בְּתוֹרַ֣ת מֹשֶׁ֑ה (מהש) לְמַ֣עַן תַּשְׂכִּ֗יל אֵ֚ת
כָּל־אֲשֶׁ֣ר תַּעֲשֶׂ֔ה וְאֵ֛ת כָּל־אֲשֶׁ֥ר תִּפְנֶ֖ה שָֽׁם׃ ד לְמַעַן֩ יָקִ֨ים
יְהֹוָ֜ה אֶת־דְּבָר֗וֹ אֲשֶׁ֨ר דִּבֶּ֥ר (ראה) עָלַי֮ לֵאמֹר֒ אִם (יוהך) ־יִשְׁמְר֨וּ
בָנֶ֜יךָ אֶת־דַּרְכָּ֗ם לָלֶ֤כֶת לְפָנַי֙ בֶּאֱמֶ֔ת בְּכָל (לכב) ־לְבָבָ֖ם
וּבְכָל (לכב) ־נַפְשָׁ֑ם לֵאמֹ֕ר לֹֽא־יִכָּרֵ֤ת לְךָ֙ אִ֔ישׁ מֵעַ֖ל (עלם) כִּסֵּ֥א
יִשְׂרָאֵֽל׃ ה וְגַ֣ם אַתָּ֣ה יָדַ֡עְתָּ אֵת֩ אֲשֶׁר־עָ֨שָׂה לִ֜י יוֹאָ֣ב בֶּן־
צְרוּיָ֗ה אֲשֶׁ֣ר עָשָׂה֩ לִשְׁנֵֽי־שָׂרֵ֨י צִבְא֜וֹת יִשְׂרָאֵ֗ל לְאַבְנֵ֨ר בֶּן־
נֵ֜ר וְלַעֲמָשָׂ֤א בֶן־יֶ֙תֶר֙ וַיַּ֣הַרְגֵ֔ם וַיָּ֥שֶׂם דְּמֵי־מִלְחָמָ֖ה בְּשָׁלֹ֑ם
וַיִּתֵּ֞ן דְּמֵ֣י מִלְחָמָ֗ה בַּחֲגֹֽרָתוֹ֙ אֲשֶׁ֣ר בְּמָתְנָ֔יו וּבְנַעֲל֖וֹ אֲשֶׁ֥ר

בְּרַגְלָיו: ו וְעָשִׂיתָ כְּחָכְמָתֶךָ וְלֹא־תוֹרֵד שֵׂיבָתוֹ בְּשָׁלֹם
שְׁאֹל: ז וְלִבְנֵי בַרְזִלַּי הַגִּלְעָדִי (כ״פ ב״ן) תַּעֲשֶׂה־חֶסֶד (ע״ב) וְהָיוּ
בְּאֹכְלֵי שֻׁלְחָנֶךָ כִּי־כֵן קָרְבוּ אֵלַי בְּבָרְחִי מִפְּנֵי אַבְשָׁלוֹם
אָחִיךָ: ח וְהִנֵּה עִמְּךָ שִׁמְעִי בֶן־גֵּרָא בֶן־הַיְמִינִי מִבַּחֻרִים
וְהוּא קִלְלַנִי קְלָלָה נִמְרֶצֶת בְּיוֹם (נגד, מזבח, זן) לֶכְתִּי מַחֲנָיִם
וְהוּא־יָרַד לִקְרָאתִי הַיַּרְדֵּן וָאֶשָּׁבַע לוֹ בַיהוָה לֵאמֹר אִם
(יוהך) ־אֲמִיתְךָ בֶּחָרֶב: ט וְעַתָּה אַל־תְּנַקֵּהוּ כִּי אִישׁ חָכָם
אָתָּה וְיָדַעְתָּ אֵת אֲשֶׁר תַּעֲשֶׂה־לּוֹ וְהוֹרַדְתָּ אֶת־שֵׂיבָתוֹ
בְּדָם שְׁאוֹל: י וַיִּשְׁכַּב דָּוִד עִם־אֲבֹתָיו וַיִּקָּבֵר בְּעִיר (ערי,
סנדלפון) דָּוִד: {פ} יא וְהַיָּמִים (נלך) אֲשֶׁר מָלַךְ דָּוִד עַל־יִשְׂרָאֵל
אַרְבָּעִים שָׁנָה בְּחֶבְרוֹן מָלַךְ שֶׁבַע שָׁנִים וּבִירוּשָׁלַםִ מָלַךְ
שְׁלֹשִׁים וְשָׁלֹשׁ שָׁנִים: יב וּשְׁלֹמֹה יָשַׁב עַל־כִּסֵּא דָּוִד אָבִיו
וַתִּכֹּן מַלְכֻתוֹ מְאֹד: {ס}

Maftir of Shabbat Chanukkah

במדבר פרק ז

א וַיְהִי בְּיוֹם (נגד, מזבח, זן) כַּלּוֹת מֹשֶׁה (מהש) לְהָקִים אֶת־הַמִּשְׁכָּן
וַיִּמְשַׁח אֹתוֹ וַיְקַדֵּשׁ אֹתוֹ וְאֶת־כָּל־כֵּלָיו וְאֶת־הַמִּזְבֵּחַ (זן, נגד)
וְאֶת־כָּל־כֵּלָיו וַיִּמְשָׁחֵם וַיְקַדֵּשׁ אֹתָם׃ ב וַיַּקְרִיבוּ נְשִׂיאֵי
יִשְׂרָאֵל רָאשֵׁי בֵּית (כ"פ ראה) אֲבֹתָם הֵם נְשִׂיאֵי הַמַּטֹּת הֵם
הָעֹמְדִים עַל־הַפְּקֻדִים׃ (ילי) ג וַיָּבִיאוּ אֶת־קָרְבָּנָם לִפְנֵי יְהוָה
שֵׁשׁ־עֶגְלֹת צָב וּשְׁנֵי עָשָׂר בָּקָר עֲגָלָה עַל־שְׁנֵי הַנְּשִׂאִים
וְשׁוֹר (ושר, אבג יתץ, אהבת חנם) לְאֶחָד (אהבה, דאגה) וַיַּקְרִיבוּ אוֹתָם לִפְנֵי
הַמִּשְׁכָּן׃ ד וַיֹּאמֶר יְהוָה אֶל־מֹשֶׁה (מהש) לֵּאמֹר׃ ה קַח מֵאִתָּם
וְהָיוּ לַעֲבֹד אֶת־עֲבֹדַת אֹהֶל מוֹעֵד וְנָתַתָּה אוֹתָם אֶל־
הַלְוִיִּם אִישׁ כְּפִי עֲבֹדָתוֹ׃ ו וַיִּקַּח (וזעם) מֹשֶׁה (מהש) אֶת־הָעֲגָלֹת
וְאֶת־הַבָּקָר וַיִּתֵּן אוֹתָם אֶל־הַלְוִיִּם׃ ז אֵת | שְׁתֵּי הָעֲגָלוֹת
וְאֵת אַרְבַּעַת הַבָּקָר נָתַן לִבְנֵי גֵרְשׁוֹן כְּפִי עֲבֹדָתָם׃ ח וְאֵת
| אַרְבַּע הָעֲגָלֹת וְאֵת שְׁמֹנַת הַבָּקָר נָתַן לִבְנֵי מְרָרִי כְּפִי
עֲבֹדָתָם בְּיַד אִיתָמָר בֶּן־אַהֲרֹן הַכֹּהֵן (מלה)׃ ט וְלִבְנֵי קְהָת
לֹא נָתָן כִּי־עֲבֹדַת הַקֹּדֶשׁ עֲלֵהֶם בַּכָּתֵף יִשָּׂאוּ׃ י וַיַּקְרִיבוּ
הַנְּשִׂאִים אֵת חֲנֻכַּת הַמִּזְבֵּחַ (זן, נגד) בְּיוֹם (נגד, מזבח, זן) הִמָּשַׁח אֹתוֹ
וַיַּקְרִיבוּ הַנְּשִׂיאִם אֶת־קָרְבָּנָם לִפְנֵי הַמִּזְבֵּחַ (זן, נגד)׃ יא וַיֹּאמֶר

יְהוָה אֶל־מֹשֶׁה (מהש) נָשִׂיא אֶחָד (אהבה, דאגה) לַיּוֹם (נגד, מזבח, זן)
נָשִׂיא אֶחָד (אהבה, דאגה) לַיּוֹם (נגד, מזבח, זן) יַקְרִיבוּ אֶת־קָרְבָּנָם
לַחֲנֻכַּת הַמִּזְבֵּחַ: (זן, נגד) {ס}

Reading for the first day

Controlling the month of Nissan -

ד - Mars ה - Aries

יב וַיְהִי הַמַּקְרִיב בַּיּוֹם (נגד, מזבח, זן) הָרִאשׁוֹן אֶת־קָרְבָּנוֹ נַחְשׁוֹן
בֶּן־עַמִּינָדָב לְמַטֵּה יְהוּדָה: יג וְקָרְבָּנוֹ קַעֲרַת־כֶּסֶף אַחַת
שְׁלֹשִׁים וּמֵאָה מִשְׁקָלָהּ מִזְרָק אֶחָד (אהבה, דאגה) כֶּסֶף שִׁבְעִים
שֶׁקֶל בְּשֶׁקֶל הַקֹּדֶשׁ שְׁנֵיהֶם מְלֵאִים סֹלֶת בְּלוּלָה בַשֶּׁמֶן
לְמִנְחָה (ב"פ בין): יד כַּף אַחַת עֲשָׂרָה זָהָב מְלֵאָה קְטֹרֶת: טו
פַּר אֶחָד (אהבה, דאגה) בֶּן־בָּקָר אַיִל אֶחָד (אהבה, דאגה) כֶּבֶשׂ־אֶחָד
(אהבה, דאגה) בֶּן־שְׁנָתוֹ לְעֹלָה: טז שְׂעִיר־עִזִּים אֶחָד (אהבה, דאגה)
לְחַטָּאת: יז וּלְזֶבַח הַשְּׁלָמִים בָּקָר שְׁנַיִם אֵילִם חֲמִשָּׁה
עַתֻּדִים חֲמִשָּׁה כְּבָשִׂים בְּנֵי־שָׁנָה חֲמִשָּׁה זֶה קָרְבַּן נַחְשׁוֹן
בֶּן־עַמִּינָדָב: {פ}

Reading for the second day
Controlling the month of Iyar
פּ - *Venus* ו - *Taurus*

יח בַּיּוֹם (נגד, מזבח, זן) הַשֵּׁנִי הִקְרִיב נְתַנְאֵל בֶּן־צוּעָר נְשִׂיא
יִשָּׂשכָר: יט הִקְרִב אֶת־קָרְבָּנוֹ קַעֲרַת־כֶּסֶף אַחַת שְׁלֹשִׁים
וּמֵאָה מִשְׁקָלָהּ מִזְרָק אֶחָד (אהבה, דאגה) כֶּסֶף שִׁבְעִים שֶׁקֶל
בְּשֶׁקֶל הַקֹּדֶשׁ שְׁנֵיהֶם ׀ מְלֵאִים סֹלֶת בְּלוּלָה בַשֶּׁמֶן
לְמִנְחָה (ב"פ ב"ן): כ כַּף אַחַת עֲשָׂרָה זָהָב מְלֵאָה קְטֹרֶת: כא
פַּר אֶחָד (אהבה, דאגה) בֶּן־בָּקָר אַיִל אֶחָד (אהבה, דאגה) כֶּבֶשׂ־אֶחָד
(אהבה, דאגה) בֶּן־שְׁנָתוֹ לְעֹלָה: כב שְׂעִיר־עִזִּים אֶחָד (אהבה, דאגה)
לְחַטָּאת: כג וּלְזֶבַח הַשְּׁלָמִים בָּקָר שְׁנַיִם אֵילִם חֲמִשָּׁה
עַתֻּדִים חֲמִשָּׁה כְּבָשִׂים בְּנֵי־שָׁנָה חֲמִשָּׁה זֶה קָרְבַּן נְתַנְאֵל
בֶּן־צוּעָר: {פ}

Reading for the third day
Controlling the month of Sivan
ר - *Mercury* ז - *Gemini*

כד בַּיּוֹם (נגד, מזבח, זן) הַשְּׁלִישִׁי נָשִׂיא לִבְנֵי זְבוּלֻן אֱלִיאָב בֶּן־
חֵלֹן: כה קָרְבָּנוֹ קַעֲרַת־כֶּסֶף אַחַת שְׁלֹשִׁים וּמֵאָה מִשְׁקָלָהּ
מִזְרָק אֶחָד (אהבה, דאגה) כֶּסֶף שִׁבְעִים שֶׁקֶל בְּשֶׁקֶל הַקֹּדֶשׁ
שְׁנֵיהֶם | מְלֵאִים סֹלֶת בְּלוּלָה בַשֶּׁמֶן לְמִנְחָה (כ"פ ב"ן): כו
כַּף אַחַת עֲשָׂרָה זָהָב מְלֵאָה קְטֹרֶת: כז פַּר אֶחָד (אהבה,
דאגה) בֶּן־בָּקָר אַיִל אֶחָד (אהבה, דאגה) כֶּבֶשׂ־אֶחָד (אהבה, דאגה) בֶּן־
שְׁנָתוֹ לְעֹלָה: כח שְׂעִיר־עִזִּים אֶחָד (אהבה, דאגה) לְחַטָּאת: כט
וּלְזֶבַח הַשְּׁלָמִים בָּקָר שְׁנַיִם אֵילִם חֲמִשָּׁה עַתֻּדִים חֲמִשָּׁה
כְּבָשִׂים בְּנֵי־שָׁנָה חֲמִשָּׁה זֶה קָרְבַּן אֱלִיאָב בֶּן־חֵלֹן: {פ}

Reading for the fourth day
Controlling the month of Tammuz
ת - *Moon*   וֹז - *Cancer*

ל בַּיּוֹם (נגד, מזבח, זן) הָרְבִיעִי נָשִׂיא לִבְנֵי רְאוּבֵן אֱלִיצוּר בֶּן־
שְׁדֵיאוּר׃ לא קָרְבָּנוֹ קַעֲרַת־כֶּסֶף אַחַת שְׁלֹשִׁים וּמֵאָה
מִשְׁקָלָהּ מִזְרָק אֶחָד (אהבה, דאגה) כֶּסֶף שִׁבְעִים שֶׁקֶל בְּשֶׁקֶל
הַקֹּדֶשׁ שְׁנֵיהֶם ׀ מְלֵאִים סֹלֶת בְּלוּלָה בַשֶּׁמֶן לְמִנְחָה (כ"פ
ב"ן)׃ לב כַּף אַחַת עֲשָׂרָה זָהָב מְלֵאָה קְטֹרֶת׃ לג פַּר אֶחָד
(אהבה, דאגה) בֶּן־בָּקָר אַיִל אֶחָד (אהבה, דאגה) כֶּבֶשׂ־אֶחָד (אהבה, דאגה)
בֶּן־שְׁנָתוֹ לְעֹלָה׃ לד שְׂעִיר־עִזִּים אֶחָד (אהבה, דאגה) לְחַטָּאת׃
לה וּלְזֶבַח הַשְּׁלָמִים בָּקָר שְׁנַיִם אֵילִם חֲמִשָּׁה עַתֻּדִים
חֲמִשָּׁה כְּבָשִׂים בְּנֵי־שָׁנָה חֲמִשָּׁה זֶה קָרְבַּן אֱלִיצוּר בֶּן־
שְׁדֵיאוּר׃ {פ}

Reading for the fifth day
Controlling the month of Av
כ - *Sun* ט - *Leo*

לו בַּיּוֹם (נגד, מזבח, זן) הַחֲמִישִׁי נָשִׂיא לִבְנֵי שִׁמְעוֹן שְׁלֻמִיאֵל
בֶּן־צוּרִישַׁדָּי: לז קָרְבָּנוֹ קְעָרַת־כֶּסֶף אַחַת שְׁלֹשִׁים וּמֵאָה
מִשְׁקָלָהּ מִזְרָק אֶחָד (אהבה, דאגה) כֶּסֶף שִׁבְעִים שֶׁקֶל בְּשֶׁקֶל
הַקֹּדֶשׁ שְׁנֵיהֶם | מְלֵאִים סֹלֶת בְּלוּלָה בַשֶּׁמֶן לְמִנְחָה (כ"פ
בין): לח כַּף אַחַת עֲשָׂרָה זָהָב מְלֵאָה קְטֹרֶת: לט פַּר אֶחָד
(אהבה, דאגה) בֶּן־בָּקָר אַיִל אֶחָד (אהבה, דאגה) כֶּבֶשׂ־אֶחָד (אהבה, דאגה)
בֶּן־שְׁנָתוֹ לְעֹלָה: מ שְׂעִיר־עִזִּים אֶחָד (אהבה, דאגה) לְחַטָּאת:
מא וּלְזֶבַח הַשְּׁלָמִים בָּקָר שְׁנַיִם אֵילִם חֲמִשָּׁה עַתֻּדִים
חֲמִשָּׁה כְּבָשִׂים (ילי) בְּנֵי־שָׁנָה חֲמִשָּׁה זֶה קָרְבַּן שְׁלֻמִיאֵל
בֶּן־צוּרִישַׁדָּי: {פ}

Reading for the sixth day
Controlling the month of Elul
ר *- Mercury* י *- Virgo*

מב בַּיּוֹם (נגד, מזבח, זן) הַשִּׁשִּׁי נָשִׂיא לִבְנֵי גָד אֶלְיָסָף בֶּן־דְּעוּאֵל׃
מג קָרְבָּנוֹ קַעֲרַת־כֶּסֶף אַחַת שְׁלֹשִׁים וּמֵאָה מִשְׁקָלָהּ (נמם)
מִזְרָק אֶחָד (אהבה, דאגה) כֶּסֶף שִׁבְעִים שֶׁקֶל בְּשֶׁקֶל הַקֹּדֶשׁ
שְׁנֵיהֶם | מְלֵאִים סֹלֶת בְּלוּלָה בַשֶּׁמֶן לְמִנְחָה (כ״פ ב״ן)׃ מד
כַּף אַחַת עֲשָׂרָה זָהָב מְלֵאָה קְטֹרֶת׃ מה פַּר אֶחָד (אהבה,
דאגה) בֶּן־בָּקָר אַיִל אֶחָד (אהבה, דאגה) כֶּבֶשׂ־אֶחָד (אהבה, דאגה) בֶּן־
שְׁנָתוֹ לְעֹלָה׃ מו שְׂעִיר־עִזִּים אֶחָד (אהבה, דאגה) לְחַטָּאת׃ מז
וּלְזֶבַח הַשְּׁלָמִים בָּקָר שְׁנַיִם אֵילִם וַחֲמִשָּׁה עַתֻּדִים וַחֲמִשָּׁה
כְּבָשִׂים (ילי) בְּנֵי־שָׁנָה וַחֲמִשָּׁה זֶה קָרְבַּן אֶלְיָסָף בֶּן־דְּעוּאֵל׃

{פ}

Reading for the seventh day
Controlling the month of Tishrei
פּ *- Venus* ל *- Libra*

מח בַּיּוֹם֙ (נגד, מזבח, זן) הַשְּׁבִיעִ֔י נָשִׂ֖יא לִבְנֵ֣י אֶפְרָ֑יִם אֱלִישָׁמָ֖ע
בֶּן־עַמִּיהֽוּד׃ מט קָרְבָּנ֞וֹ קַֽעֲרַת־כֶּ֣סֶף אַחַ֗ת שְׁלֹשִׁ֣ים וּמֵאָה֮
מִשְׁקָלָהּ֒ מִזְרָ֣ק אֶחָד֙ (אהבה, דאגה) כֶּ֔סֶף שִׁבְעִ֥ים שֶׁ֖קֶל בְּשֶׁ֣קֶל
הַקֹּ֑דֶשׁ שְׁנֵיהֶ֣ם ׀ מְלֵאִ֗ים סֹ֛לֶת בְּלוּלָ֥ה בַשֶּׁ֖מֶן לְמִנְחָֽה (ב"פ
ב"ן)׃ נ כַּ֥ף אַחַ֛ת עֲשָׂרָ֥ה זָהָ֖ב מְלֵאָ֥ה קְטֹֽרֶת׃ נא פַּ֣ר אֶחָ֞ד
(אהבה, דאגה) בֶּן־בָּקָ֗ר אַ֧יִל אֶחָ֛ד (אהבה, דאגה) כֶּֽבֶשׂ־אֶחָ֥ד (אהבה, דאגה)
בֶּן־שְׁנָת֖וֹ לְעֹלָֽה׃ נב שְׂעִיר־עִזִּ֥ים אֶחָ֖ד (אהבה, דאגה) לְחַטָּֽאת׃ נג
וּלְזֶ֣בַח הַשְּׁלָמִים֮ בָּקָ֣ר שְׁנַ֒יִם֒ אֵילִ֤ם חֲמִשָּׁה֙ עַתֻּדִ֣ים חֲמִשָּׁ֔ה
כְּבָשִׂ֥ים בְּנֵי־שָׁנָ֖ה חֲמִשָּׁ֑ה זֶ֛ה קָרְבַּ֥ן אֱלִישָׁמָ֖ע בֶּן־עַמִּיהֽוּד׃

{פ}

Haftarah of Shabbat Chanukkah

This Haftarah speaks about the High Priest and of a vision of the prophet concerning the High Priest. In the vision, the Satan is standing to the right of the High Priest. The Satan is very cunning. He has 5700 years of experience, and he appears when we least expect him. Usually he comes from the left side, pushing us to do negative things. But occasionally, he comes from the right, pushing us to overload ourselves with positive tasks and responsibilities. We must always be aware that the Satan may confront us from any direction. Whatever seems extreme and overwhelming (even if it is positive) is definitely coming from the Satan.

זכריה פרק ב

יד רָנִּי וְשִׂמְחִי בַּת־צִיּוֹן (יוסף) כִּי הִנְנִי־בָא וְשָׁכַנְתִּי בְתוֹכֵךְ
נְאֻם־יְהוָה: טו וְנִלְווּ גוֹיִם רַבִּים אֶל־יְהוָה בַּיּוֹם (נגד, מזבח, זן)
הַהוּא וְהָיוּ לִי לְעָם (עלם) וְשָׁכַנְתִּי בְתוֹכֵךְ וְיָדַעַתְּ כִּי־יְהוָה
צְבָאוֹת (פני שכינה) שְׁלָחַנִי אֵלָיִךְ: טז וְנָחַל יְהוָה אֶת־יְהוּדָה חֶלְקוֹ
עַל אַדְמַת הַקֹּדֶשׁ וּבָחַר עוֹד בִּירוּשָׁלִָם: יז הַס כָּל־בָּשָׂר
מִפְּנֵי יְהוָה כִּי נֵעוֹר מִמְּעוֹן קָדְשׁוֹ: {ס} א וַיַּרְאֵנִי אֶת־יְהוֹשֻׁעַ
הַכֹּהֵן (מלה) הַגָּדוֹל (להח, מבה) עֹמֵד לִפְנֵי מַלְאַךְ יְהוָה וְהַשָּׂטָן
עֹמֵד עַל־יְמִינוֹ (ילי) לְשִׂטְנוֹ: ב וַיֹּאמֶר יְהוָה אֶל־הַשָּׂטָן יִגְעַר
יְהוָה בְּךָ הַשָּׂטָן וְיִגְעַר יְהוָה בְּךָ הַבֹּחֵר בִּירוּשָׁלִָם הֲלוֹא
זֶה אוּד מֻצָּל מֵאֵשׁ: ג וִיהוֹשֻׁעַ הָיָה (יהה) לָבֻשׁ בְּגָדִים צוֹאִים
וְעֹמֵד לִפְנֵי הַמַּלְאָךְ: ד וַיַּעַן וַיֹּאמֶר אֶל־הָעֹמְדִים לְפָנָיו
לֵאמֹר הָסִירוּ הַבְּגָדִים הַצֹּאִים מֵעָלָיו וַיֹּאמֶר אֵלָיו רְאֵה

(ראה) הֶעֱבַרְתִּי מֵעָלֶיךָ עֲוֺנֶךָ וְהַלְבֵּשׁ אֹתְךָ מַחֲלָצוֹת: ה וָאֹמַר
יָשִׂימוּ צָנִיף טָהוֹר (י"פ אכא) עַל־רֹאשׁוֹ וַיָּשִׂימוּ הַצָּנִיף הַטָּהוֹר (י"פ
אכא) עַל־רֹאשׁוֹ וַיַּלְבִּשֻׁהוּ בְּגָדִים וּמַלְאַךְ יְהוָה עֹמֵד: ו וַיָּעַד
מַלְאַךְ יְהוָה בִּיהוֹשֻׁעַ לֵאמֹר: ז כֹּה (הי) ־אָמַר יְהוָה צְבָאוֹת
(פני שכינה) אִם־בִּדְרָכַי (כ"פ יב"ק) תֵּלֵךְ וְאִם (יוהך) אֶת־מִשְׁמַרְתִּי
תִשְׁמֹר וְגַם־אַתָּה תָּדִין אֶת־בֵּיתִי (כ"פ ראה) וְגַם תִּשְׁמֹר
אֶת־חֲצֵרָי וְנָתַתִּי לְךָ מַהְלְכִים בֵּין הָעֹמְדִים הָאֵלֶּה (לאה):
ח שְׁמַע־נָא יְהוֹשֻׁעַ | הַכֹּהֵן (מלה) הַגָּדוֹל (להח, מבה) אַתָּה וְרֵעֶיךָ
הַיֹּשְׁבִים לְפָנֶיךָ כִּי־אַנְשֵׁי מוֹפֵת הֵמָּה כִּי־הִנְנִי מֵבִיא אֶת־
עַבְדִּי צֶמַח: ט כִּי | הִנֵּה הָאֶבֶן אֲשֶׁר נָתַתִּי לִפְנֵי יְהוֹשֻׁעַ
עַל־אֶבֶן אַחַת שִׁבְעָה עֵינָיִם הִנְנִי מְפַתֵּחַ פִּתֻּחָהּ נְאֻם יְהוָה
צְבָאוֹת (פני שכינה) וּמַשְׁתִּי אֶת־עֲוֺן הָאָרֶץ־הַהִיא בְּיוֹם (נגד, מזבח,
זן) אֶחָד: (אהבה, דאגה) י בַּיּוֹם (נגד, מזבח, זן) הַהוּא נְאֻם יְהוָה צְבָאוֹת
(פני שכינה) תִּקְרְאוּ אִישׁ לְרֵעֵהוּ (רהע) אֶל־תַּחַת גֶּפֶן וְאֶל־תַּחַת
תְּאֵנָה: א וַיָּשָׁב הַמַּלְאָךְ (פוי) הַדֹּבֵר (ראה) בִּי וַיְעִירֵנִי כְּאִישׁ
אֲשֶׁר־יֵעוֹר מִשְּׁנָתוֹ: ב וַיֹּאמֶר אֵלַי מָה אַתָּה רֹאֶה (ראה) וָאֹמַר
(כתיב: ויאמר) רָאִיתִי | וְהִנֵּה מְנוֹרַת זָהָב כֻּלָּהּ וְגֻלָּהּ עַל־רֹאשָׁהּ
וְשִׁבְעָה נֵרֹתֶיהָ עָלֶיהָ (פהל) שִׁבְעָה וְשִׁבְעָה מוּצָקוֹת לַנֵּרוֹת
אֲשֶׁר עַל־רֹאשָׁהּ: ג וּשְׁנַיִם זֵיתִים עָלֶיהָ (פהל) אֶחָד (אהבה, דאגה)

מִימִין הַגֻּלָּה וְאֶחָד (אהבה, דאגה) עַל־שְׂמֹאלָהּ׃ ד וָאַעַן וָאֹמַר
אֶל־הַמַּלְאָךְ (פוי) הַדֹּבֵר (ראה) בִּי לֵאמֹר מָה־אֵלֶּה אֲדֹנִי׃ ה
וַיַּעַן הַמַּלְאָךְ (פוי) הַדֹּבֵר (ראה) בִּי וַיֹּאמֶר אֵלַי הֲלוֹא יָדַעְתָּ
מָה־הֵמָּה אֵלֶּה וָאֹמַר לֹא אֲדֹנִי׃ ו וַיַּעַן וַיֹּאמֶר אֵלַי לֵאמֹר
זֶה דְּבַר (ראה) ־יְהוָה אֶל־זְרֻבָּבֶל לֵאמֹר לֹא בְחַיִל (ומב) וְלֹא
בְכֹחַ כִּי אִם (יוהך) ־בְּרוּחִי אָמַר יְהוָה צְבָאוֹת (פני שכינה)׃ ז מִי
(ילי) ־אַתָּה הַר־הַגָּדוֹל (להח, מבה) לִפְנֵי זְרֻבָּבֶל לְמִישֹׁר וְהוֹצִיא
אֶת־הָאֶבֶן הָרֹאשָׁה תְּשֻׁאוֹת חֵן (מוזי) חֵן (מוזי) לָהּ׃ {פ}

Maftir of Second Shabbat Chanukkah

במדבר פרק ז

Controlling the month of Cheshvan

ד - *Mars* נ - *Scorpio*

נד בַּיּוֹם֙ (נגד, מזבח, זן) הַשְּׁמִינִ֔י נָשִׂ֖יא לִבְנֵ֣י מְנַשֶּׁ֑ה גַּמְלִיאֵ֖ל בֶּן־
פְּדָהצֽוּר׃ נה קָרְבָּנ֞וֹ קַֽעֲרַת־כֶּ֣סֶף אַחַ֗ת שְׁלֹשִׁ֣ים וּמֵאָה֮
מִשְׁקָלָהּ֒ מִזְרָ֤ק אֶחָד֙ (אהבה, דאגה) כֶּ֔סֶף שִׁבְעִ֥ים שֶׁ֖קֶל בְּשֶׁ֣קֶל
הַקֹּ֑דֶשׁ שְׁנֵיהֶ֣ם ׀ מְלֵאִ֗ים סֹ֛לֶת בְּלוּלָ֥ה בַשֶּׁ֖מֶן לְמִנְחָֽה׃ (ב״פ
ב״ן) נו כַּ֥ף אַחַ֛ת עֲשָׂרָ֥ה זָהָ֖ב מְלֵאָ֥ה קְטֹֽרֶת׃ נז פַּ֣ר אֶחָ֡ד
(אהבה, דאגה) בֶּן־בָּקָ֜ר אַ֧יִל אֶחָ֛ד (אהבה, דאגה) כֶּֽבֶשׂ־אֶחָ֥ד (אהבה, דאגה)
בֶּן־שְׁנָת֖וֹ לְעֹלָֽה׃ נח שְׂעִיר־עִזִּ֥ים אֶחָ֖ד (אהבה, דאגה) לְחַטָּֽאת׃ נט
וּלְזֶ֣בַח הַשְּׁלָמִים֮ בָּקָ֣ר שְׁנַ֒יִם֒ אֵילִ֤ם חֲמִשָּׁה֙ עַתֻּדִ֣ים חֲמִשָּׁ֔ה
כְּבָשִׂ֥ים בְּנֵֽי־שָׁנָ֖ה חֲמִשָּׁ֑ה זֶ֛ה קָרְבַּ֥ן גַּמְלִיאֵ֖ל בֶּן־פְּדָהצֽוּר׃

{פ}

Controlling the month of Kislev

ג - *Jupiter* ס - *Sagittarius*

ס בַּיּוֹם (נגד, מזבח, זן) הַתְּשִׁיעִי נָשִׂיא לִבְנֵי בִנְיָמִן אֲבִידָן בֶּן־
גִּדְעֹנִי׃ סא קָרְבָּנוֹ קַעֲרַת־כֶּסֶף אַחַת שְׁלֹשִׁים וּמֵאָה
מִשְׁקָלָהּ מִזְרָק אֶחָד (אהבה, דאגה) כֶּסֶף שִׁבְעִים שֶׁקֶל בְּשֶׁקֶל
הַקֹּדֶשׁ שְׁנֵיהֶם | מְלֵאִים סֹלֶת בְּלוּלָה בַשֶּׁמֶן לְמִנְחָה (כ"פ
כ"ן)׃ סב כַּף אַחַת עֲשָׂרָה זָהָב מְלֵאָה קְטֹרֶת׃ סג פַּר אֶחָד
(אהבה, דאגה) בֶּן־בָּקָר אַיִל אֶחָד (אהבה, דאגה) כֶּבֶשׂ־אֶחָד (אהבה, דאגה)
בֶּן־שְׁנָתוֹ לְעֹלָה׃ סד שְׂעִיר־עִזִּים אֶחָד (אהבה, דאגה) לְחַטָּאת׃ סה
וּלְזֶבַח הַשְּׁלָמִים בָּקָר שְׁנַיִם אֵילִם חֲמִשָּׁה עַתֻּדִים חֲמִשָּׁה
כְּבָשִׂים בְּנֵי־שָׁנָה חֲמִשָּׁה זֶה קָרְבַּן אֲבִידָן בֶּן־גִּדְעֹנִי׃ {פ}

Controlling the month of Tevet

ב - *Saturn* ע - *Capricorn*

סו בַּיּוֹם (נגד, מזבח, זן) הָעֲשִׂירִי נָשִׂיא לִבְנֵי דָן אֲחִיעֶזֶר בֶּן־
עַמִּישַׁדָּי׃ סז קָרְבָּנוֹ קַעֲרַת־כֶּסֶף אַחַת שְׁלֹשִׁים וּמֵאָה
מִשְׁקָלָהּ מִזְרָק אֶחָד (אהבה, דאגה) כֶּסֶף שִׁבְעִים שֶׁקֶל בְּשֶׁקֶל
הַקֹּדֶשׁ שְׁנֵיהֶם | מְלֵאִים סֹלֶת בְּלוּלָה בַשֶּׁמֶן לְמִנְחָה (כ"פ
כ"ן)׃ סח כַּף אַחַת עֲשָׂרָה זָהָב מְלֵאָה קְטֹרֶת׃ סט פַּר אֶחָד
(אהבה, דאגה) בֶּן־בָּקָר אַיִל אֶחָד (אהבה, דאגה) כֶּבֶשׂ־אֶחָד (אהבה, דאגה)
בֶּן־שְׁנָתוֹ לְעֹלָה׃ ע שְׂעִיר־עִזִּים אֶחָד (אהבה, דאגה) לְחַטָּאת׃ עא
וּלְזֶבַח הַשְּׁלָמִים בָּקָר שְׁנַיִם אֵילִם חֲמִשָּׁה עַתֻּדִים חֲמִשָּׁה
כְּבָשִׂים בְּנֵי־שָׁנָה חֲמִשָּׁה זֶה קָרְבַּן אֲחִיעֶזֶר בֶּן־עַמִּישַׁדָּי׃

{פ}

Controlling the month of Shvat

ב - *Saturn* צ - *Aquarius*

עב בְּיוֹם (נגד, מזבח, זן) עַשְׁתֵּי עָשָׂר יוֹם (נגד, מזבח, זן) נָשִׂיא לִבְנֵי אָשֵׁר
פַּגְעִיאֵל בֶּן־עָכְרָן׃ עג קָרְבָּנוֹ קַעֲרַת־כֶּסֶף אַחַת שְׁלֹשִׁים
וּמֵאָה מִשְׁקָלָהּ מִזְרָק אֶחָד (אהבה, דאגה) כֶּסֶף שִׁבְעִים שֶׁקֶל
בְּשֶׁקֶל הַקֹּדֶשׁ שְׁנֵיהֶם ׀ מְלֵאִים סֹלֶת בְּלוּלָה בַשֶּׁמֶן
לְמִנְחָה (כ"פ ב"ן)׃ עד כַּף אַחַת עֲשָׂרָה זָהָב מְלֵאָה קְטֹרֶת׃ עה
פַּר אֶחָד (אהבה, דאגה) בֶּן־בָּקָר אַיִל אֶחָד (אהבה, דאגה) כֶּבֶשׂ־אֶחָד
(אהבה, דאגה) בֶּן־שְׁנָתוֹ לְעֹלָה׃ עו שְׂעִיר־עִזִּים אֶחָד (אהבה, דאגה)
לְחַטָּאת׃ עז וּלְזֶבַח הַשְּׁלָמִים בָּקָר שְׁנַיִם אֵילִם חֲמִשָּׁה
עַתֻּדִים חֲמִשָּׁה כְּבָשִׂים (ילי) בְּנֵי־שָׁנָה חֲמִשָּׁה זֶה קָרְבַּן
פַּגְעִיאֵל בֶּן־עָכְרָן׃ {פ}

Controlling the month of Adar

ג - *Jupiter* ק - *Pisces*

עח בְּיוֹם (נגד, מזבח, זן) שְׁנֵים עָשָׂר יוֹם (נגד, מזבח, זן) נָשִׂיא לִבְנֵי נַפְתָּלִי
אֲחִירַע בֶּן־עֵינָן׃ עט קָרְבָּנוֹ קַעֲרַת־כֶּסֶף אַחַת שְׁלֹשִׁים
וּמֵאָה מִשְׁקָלָהּ מִזְרָק אֶחָד (אהבה, דאגה) כֶּסֶף שִׁבְעִים שֶׁקֶל
בְּשֶׁקֶל הַקֹּדֶשׁ שְׁנֵיהֶם | מְלֵאִים (ילי) סֹלֶת בְּלוּלָה בַשֶּׁמֶן
לְמִנְחָה (כ״פ בין)׃ פ כַּף אַחַת עֲשָׂרָה זָהָב מְלֵאָה קְטֹרֶת׃ פא
פַּר אֶחָד (אהבה, דאגה) בֶּן־בָּקָר אַיִל אֶחָד (אהבה, דאגה) כֶּבֶשׂ־אֶחָד
(אהבה, דאגה) בֶּן־שְׁנָתוֹ לְעֹלָה׃ פב שְׂעִיר־עִזִּים אֶחָד (אהבה, דאגה)
לְחַטָּאת׃ פג וּלְזֶבַח הַשְּׁלָמִים בָּקָר שְׁנַיִם אֵילִם חֲמִשָּׁה
עַתֻּדִים חֲמִשָּׁה כְּבָשִׂים בְּנֵי־שָׁנָה חֲמִשָּׁה זֶה קָרְבַּן אֲחִירַע
בֶּן־עֵינָן׃ {פ}

פד זֹאת | חֲנֻכַּת הַמִּזְבֵּחַ (זן, נגד) בְּיוֹם (נגד, מזבח, זן) הִמָּשַׁח אֹתוֹ מֵאֵת
נְשִׂיאֵי יִשְׂרָאֵל קַעֲרֹת כֶּסֶף שְׁתֵּים עֶשְׂרֵה מִזְרְקֵי־כֶסֶף
שְׁנֵים עָשָׂר כַּפּוֹת זָהָב שְׁתֵּים עֶשְׂרֵה׃ פה שְׁלֹשִׁים וּמֵאָה
הַקְּעָרָה הָאַחַת כֶּסֶף וְשִׁבְעִים (יל״) הַמִּזְרָק הָאֶחָד (אהבה, דאגה)
כֹּל (יל״) כֶּסֶף הַכֵּלִים אַלְפַּיִם וְאַרְבַּע־מֵאוֹת בְּשֶׁקֶל הַקֹּדֶשׁ׃
פו כַּפּוֹת זָהָב שְׁתֵּים־עֶשְׂרֵה מְלֵאֹת קְטֹרֶת עֲשָׂרָה עֲשָׂרָה
הַכַּף בְּשֶׁקֶל הַקֹּדֶשׁ כָּל־זְהַב הַכַּפּוֹת עֶשְׂרִים וּמֵאָה׃ פז
כָּל (יל״) ־הַבָּקָר לָעֹלָה שְׁנֵים עָשָׂר פָּרִים אֵילִם שְׁנֵים־עָשָׂר
כְּבָשִׂים בְּנֵי־שָׁנָה שְׁנֵים עָשָׂר וּמִנְחָתָם וּשְׂעִירֵי עִזִּים שְׁנֵים
עָשָׂר לְחַטָּאת׃ פח וְכֹל בְּקַר | זֶבַח הַשְּׁלָמִים עֶשְׂרִים
וְאַרְבָּעָה פָּרִים אֵילִם שִׁשִּׁים עַתֻּדִים (יל״) שִׁשִּׁים כְּבָשִׂים
בְּנֵי־שָׁנָה שִׁשִּׁים זֹאת חֲנֻכַּת הַמִּזְבֵּחַ (זן, נגד) אַחֲרֵי הִמָּשַׁח
אֹתוֹ׃ פט וּבְבֹא מֹשֶׁה (מהש) אֶל־אֹהֶל מוֹעֵד לְדַבֵּר (ראה) אִתּוֹ
וַיִּשְׁמַע אֶת־הַקּוֹל מִדַּבֵּר (ראה) אֵלָיו מֵעַל (עלם) הַכַּפֹּרֶת אֲשֶׁר
עַל־אֲרֹן הָעֵדֻת מִבֵּין שְׁנֵי הַכְּרֻבִים וַיְדַבֵּר (ראה) אֵלָיו׃ {פ}
א וַיְדַבֵּר (ראה) יְהֹוָה אֶל־מֹשֶׁה (מהש) לֵּאמֹר׃ ב דַּבֵּר (ראה) אֶל־
אַהֲרֹן וְאָמַרְתָּ אֵלָיו בְּהַעֲלֹתְךָ אֶת־הַנֵּרֹת אֶל־מוּל פְּנֵי
הַמְּנוֹרָה יָאִירוּ שִׁבְעַת הַנֵּרוֹת׃ ג וַיַּעַשׂ כֵּן אַהֲרֹן אֶל־מוּל
פְּנֵי הַמְּנוֹרָה הֶעֱלָה נֵרֹתֶיהָ כַּאֲשֶׁר צִוָּה (פוי) יְהֹוָה אֶת־מֹשֶׁה׃

(מהש) ד וְזֶ֨ה מַעֲשֵׂ֤ה הַמְּנֹרָה֙ מִקְשָׁ֣ה זָהָ֔ב עַד־יְרֵכָ֥הּ עַד־
פִּרְחָ֖הּ מִקְשָׁ֣ה הִ֑וא כַּמַּרְאֶ֗ה (ראה) אֲשֶׁ֨ר הֶרְאָ֤ה (ראה) יְהוָה֙
אֶת־מֹשֶׁ֔ה (מהש) כֵּ֥ן עָשָׂ֖ה אֶת־הַמְּנֹרָֽה׃ {פ}

Haftarah for Second Shabbat of Chanukkah

Occasionally, we have a second Shabbat during Hanukkah. Here we learn about the men who helped Solomon build the First Temple, and we find a prophecy concerning the Temple. At present, we do not have a physical Temple, but the spiritual Temple exists within each of us. The energy of the Temple is always available. We just need to tap into it and prepare ourselves to receive its energy.

מלכים א פרק ז

מ וַיַּעַשׂ חִירוֹם אֶת־הַכִּיֹּרוֹת וְאֶת־הַיָּעִים וְאֶת־הַמִּזְרָקוֹת
וַיְכַל חִירָם לַעֲשׂוֹת אֶת־כָּל (ילי) ־הַמְּלָאכָה (פוי) אֲשֶׁר עָשָׂה
לַמֶּלֶךְ שְׁלֹמֹה בֵּית (ב"פ ראה) יְהוָה׃ מא עַמֻּדִים שְׁנַיִם וְגֻלֹּת
הַכֹּתָרֹת אֲשֶׁר־עַל־רֹאשׁ הָעַמֻּדִים שְׁתָּיִם וְהַשְּׂבָכוֹת
שְׁתַּיִם לְכַסּוֹת אֶת־שְׁתֵּי גֻּלּוֹת הַכֹּתָרֹת אֲשֶׁר עַל־רֹאשׁ
הָעַמּוּדִים׃ מב וְאֶת־הָרִמֹּנִים אַרְבַּע מֵאוֹת לִשְׁתֵּי הַשְּׂבָכוֹת
שְׁנֵי־טוּרִים רִמֹּנִים לַשְּׂבָכָה הָאֶחָת לְכַסּוֹת אֶת־שְׁתֵּי גֻּלֹּת
הַכֹּתָרֹת אֲשֶׁר עַל־פְּנֵי הָעַמּוּדִים׃ מג וְאֶת־הַמְּכֹנוֹת עֶשֶׂר
וְאֶת־הַכִּיֹּרֹת עֲשָׂרָה עַל־הַמְּכֹנוֹת׃ מד וְאֶת־הַיָּם (ילי) הָאֶחָד
(אהבה, דאגה) וְאֶת־הַבָּקָר שְׁנֵים־עָשָׂר תַּחַת הַיָּם (ילי)׃ מה וְאֶת־
הַסִּירוֹת וְאֶת־הַיָּעִים וְאֶת־הַמִּזְרָקוֹת וְאֵת כָּל (ילי) ־הַכֵּלִים
הָאֵלֶּה (כתיב: האהל) (לאה) אֲשֶׁר עָשָׂה חִירָם לַמֶּלֶךְ שְׁלֹמֹה בֵּית
(ב"פ ראה) יְהוָה נְחֹשֶׁת מְמֹרָט׃ מו בְּכִכַּר הַיַּרְדֵּן יְצָקָם הַמֶּלֶךְ
בְּמַעֲבֵה הָאֲדָמָה בֵּין סֻכּוֹת וּבֵין צָרְתָן׃ מז וַיַּנַּח שְׁלֹמֹה

אֶת־כָּל (ילי) ־הַכֵּלִים מֵרֹב מְאֹד מְאֹד לֹא נֶחְקַר מִשְׁקַל
הַנְּחֹשֶׁת׃ מח וַיַּעַשׂ שְׁלֹמֹה אֵת כָּל (ילי) ־הַכֵּלִים אֲשֶׁר בֵּית
(כ"פ ראה) יְהוָה אֵת מִזְבַּח (זן, נגד) הַזָּהָב (ווהו) וְאֶת־הַשֻּׁלְחָן אֲשֶׁר
עָלָיו לֶחֶם הַפָּנִים זָהָב׃ מט וְאֶת־הַמְּנֹרוֹת חָמֵשׁ מִיָּמִין
וְחָמֵשׁ מִשְּׂמֹאול לִפְנֵי הַדְּבִיר (רי"ו, גבורה) זָהָב סָגוּר וְהַפֶּרַח
וְהַנֵּרֹת וְהַמֶּלְקָחַיִם זָהָב׃ נ וְהַסִּפּוֹת וְהַמְזַמְּרוֹת וְהַמִּזְרָקוֹת
וְהַכַּפּוֹת וְהַמַּחְתּוֹת זָהָב סָגוּר וְהַפֹּתוֹת לְדַלְתוֹת הַבַּיִת (כ"פ
ראה) הַפְּנִימִי לְקֹדֶשׁ הַקֳּדָשִׁים לְדַלְתֵי הַבַּיִת (כ"פ ראה) לַהֵיכָל
(אדני) זָהָב׃ {פ}

Haftarah for the Eve of Rosh Chodesh

On one level, this Haftarah concerns the eve of Rosh Chodesh. In a deeper sense, this Haftarah speaks of the love between David and Jonathan. Although he himself was heir to the throne, Jonathan knew that David might become king. Yet Jonathan loved David and felt no jealously. To truly feel love for another person, we must give up our own selfish desires. To have a successful relationship of any kind, we must be willing to sacrifice.

שמואל א פרק כ

יח וַיֹּאמֶר־לוֹ יְהוֹנָתָן מָחָר חֹדֶשׁ וְנִפְקַדְתָּ כִּי יִפָּקֵד מוֹשָׁבֶךָ׃
יט וְשִׁלַּשְׁתָּ תֵּרֵד מְאֹד וּבָאתָ אֶל־הַמָּקוֹם אֲשֶׁר־נִסְתַּרְתָּ
שָּׁם בְּיוֹם (נגד, מזבח, זן) הַמַּעֲשֶׂה וְיָשַׁבְתָּ אֵצֶל הָאֶבֶן הָאָזֶל׃
כ וַאֲנִי (אני) שְׁלֹשֶׁת הַחִצִּים צִדָּה אוֹרֶה (רז,אין סוף) לְשַׁלַּח־לִי
לְמַטָּרָה׃ כא וְהִנֵּה אֶשְׁלַח אֶת־הַנַּעַר לֵךְ מְצָא אֶת־הַחִצִּים
אִם־אָמֹר אֹמַר לַנַּעַר הִנֵּה הַחִצִּים | מִמְּךָ וָהֵנָּה קָחֶנּוּ |
וָבֹאָה כִּי־שָׁלוֹם לְךָ וְאֵין דָּבָר (ראה) חַי־יְהוָה׃ כב וְאִם־כֹּה
(הי״) אֹמַר לָעֶלֶם הִנֵּה הַחִצִּים מִמְּךָ וָהָלְאָה לֵךְ כִּי שִׁלַּחֲךָ
יְהוָה׃ כג וְהַדָּבָר (ראה) אֲשֶׁר דִּבַּרְנוּ (ראה) אֲנִי (אני) וָאָתָּה הִנֵּה
יְהוָה בֵּינִי וּבֵינְךָ עַד־עוֹלָם׃ {ס} כד וַיִּסָּתֵר דָּוִד בַּשָּׂדֶה
וַיְהִי הַחֹדֶשׁ וַיֵּשֶׁב הַמֶּלֶךְ אֶל־ (כתיב: עַל־) הַלֶּחֶם לֶאֱכוֹל׃ כה
וַיֵּשֶׁב הַמֶּלֶךְ עַל־מוֹשָׁבוֹ כְּפַעַם (מנק) | בְּפַעַם (מנק) אֶל־מוֹשַׁב
הַקִּיר וַיָּקָם יְהוֹנָתָן וַיֵּשֶׁב אַבְנֵר מִצַּד שָׁאוּל וַיִּפָּקֵד מְקוֹם

דָּוִד׃ כו וְלֹא־דִבֶּר (ראה) שָׁאוּל מְאוּמָה בַּיּוֹם (נגד, מזבח, זן) הַהוּא
כִּי אָמַר מִקְרֶה הוּא בִּלְתִּי טָהוֹר (י"פ אכא) הוּא כִּי־לֹא טָהוֹר׃
(י"פ אכא) {ס} כז וַיְהִי מִמָּחֳרַת הַחֹדֶשׁ הַשֵּׁנִי וַיִּפָּקֵד מְקוֹם דָּוִד
{פ} וַיֹּאמֶר שָׁאוּל אֶל־יְהוֹנָתָן בְּנוֹ מַדּוּעַ לֹא־בָא בֶן־יִשַׁי
גַּם־תְּמוֹל גַּם־הַיּוֹם (נגד, מזבח, זן) אֶל־הַלָּחֶם׃ כח וַיַּעַן יְהוֹנָתָן
אֶת־שָׁאוּל נִשְׁאֹל נִשְׁאַל דָּוִד מֵעִמָּדִי עַד־בֵּית (כ"פ ראה)
לָחֶם׃ כט וַיֹּאמֶר שַׁלְּחֵנִי נָא כִּי זֶבַח מִשְׁפָּחָה לָנוּ (מום, אהיה-אדני)
בָּעִיר (ערי, סחצפך, סנדלפון) וְהוּא צִוָּה (פוי) ־לִי אָחִי וְעַתָּה אִם־מָצָאתִי
חֵן (מוזי) בְּעֵינֶיךָ אִמָּלְטָה נָּא וְאֶרְאֶה (ראה) אֶת־אֶחָי עַל־כֵּן
לֹא־בָא אֶל־שֻׁלְחַן הַמֶּלֶךְ׃ {ס} ל וַיִּחַר־אַף שָׁאוּל בִּיהוֹנָתָן
וַיֹּאמֶר לוֹ בֶּן־נַעֲוַת הַמַּרְדּוּת הֲלוֹא יָדַעְתִּי כִּי־בֹחֵר אַתָּה
לְבֶן־יִשַׁי לְבָשְׁתְּךָ וּלְבֹשֶׁת עֶרְוַת אִמֶּךָ׃ לא כִּי כָל (ילי)
־הַיָּמִים (נלך) אֲשֶׁר בֶּן־יִשַׁי חַי עַל־הָאֲדָמָה לֹא תִכּוֹן אַתָּה
וּמַלְכוּתֶךָ וְעַתָּה שְׁלַח וְקַח אֹתוֹ אֵלַי כִּי בֶן־מָוֶת הוּא׃ {ס}
לב וַיַּעַן יְהוֹנָתָן אֶת־שָׁאוּל אָבִיו וַיֹּאמֶר אֵלָיו לָמָּה יוּמַת
מֶה עָשָׂה׃ לג וַיָּטֶל שָׁאוּל אֶת־הַחֲנִית עָלָיו לְהַכֹּתוֹ וַיֵּדַע
יְהוֹנָתָן כִּי־כָלָה הִיא מֵעִם אָבִיו לְהָמִית אֶת־דָּוִד׃ {ס} לד
וַיָּקָם יְהוֹנָתָן מֵעִם הַשֻּׁלְחָן בָּחֳרִי־אָף וְלֹא־אָכַל בְּיוֹם (נגד,
מזבח, זן) ־הַחֹדֶשׁ הַשֵּׁנִי לֶחֶם כִּי נֶעְצַב אֶל־דָּוִד כִּי הִכְלִמוֹ

אָבִיו׃ {ס} לה וַיְהִי בַבֹּקֶר וַיֵּצֵא יְהוֹנָתָן הַשָּׂדֶה לְמוֹעֵד דָּוִד
וְנַעַר קָטֹן עִמּוֹ׃ לו וַיֹּאמֶר לְנַעֲרוֹ רֻץ מְצָא נָא אֶת־הַחִצִּים
אֲשֶׁר אָנֹכִי (א״ע) מוֹרֶה הַנַּעַר רָץ וְהוּא־יָרָה הַחֵצִי לְהַעֲבִרוֹ׃
לז וַיָּבֹא הַנַּעַר עַד־מְקוֹם הַחֵצִי אֲשֶׁר יָרָה יְהוֹנָתָן וַיִּקְרָא
יְהוֹנָתָן אַחֲרֵי הַנַּעַר וַיֹּאמֶר הֲלוֹא הַחֵצִי מִמְּךָ וָהָלְאָה׃
לח וַיִּקְרָא יְהוֹנָתָן אַחֲרֵי הַנַּעַר מְהֵרָה חוּשָׁה אַל־תַּעֲמֹד
וַיְלַקֵּט נַעַר יְהוֹנָתָן אֶת־הַחִצִּים (כתיב: ־החצי) וַיָּבֹא אֶל־אֲדֹנָיו׃
לט וְהַנַּעַר לֹא־יָדַע מְאוּמָה אַךְ (אהיה) יְהוֹנָתָן וְדָוִד יָדְעוּ אֶת־
הַדָּבָר (ראה)׃ {ס} מ וַיִּתֵּן יְהוֹנָתָן אֶת־כֵּלָיו אֶל־הַנַּעַר אֲשֶׁר־לוֹ
וַיֹּאמֶר לוֹ לֵךְ הָבֵיא הָעִיר (ערי, סנזדך, סנדלפון)׃ מא הַנַּעַר בָּא וְדָוִד
קָם מֵאֵצֶל הַנֶּגֶב וַיִּפֹּל לְאַפָּיו אַרְצָה וַיִּשְׁתַּחוּ שָׁלֹשׁ פְּעָמִים
(מנק) וַיִּשְּׁקוּ ׀ אִישׁ אֶת־רֵעֵהוּ (רהע) וַיִּבְכּוּ אִישׁ אֶת־רֵעֵהוּ (רהע)
עַד־דָּוִד הִגְדִּיל׃ מב וַיֹּאמֶר יְהוֹנָתָן לְדָוִד לֵךְ לְשָׁלוֹם אֲשֶׁר
נִשְׁבַּעְנוּ שְׁנֵינוּ אֲנַחְנוּ בְּשֵׁם יְהוָה לֵאמֹר יְהוָה יִהְיֶה (ייי) ׀ בֵּינִי
וּבֵינֶךָ וּבֵין זַרְעִי וּבֵין זַרְעֲךָ עַד־עוֹלָם׃ {פ}

Maftir of Shabbat Rosh Chodesh

במדבר פרק כח

ט וּבְיוֹם (נגד, מזבח, זן) הַשַּׁבָּת שְׁנֵי־כְבָשִׂים בְּנֵי־שָׁנָה תְּמִימִם
וּשְׁנֵי עֶשְׂרֹנִים סֹלֶת מִנְחָה (כ"פ בן) בְּלוּלָה בַשֶּׁמֶן וְנִסְכּוֹ׃
י עֹלַת שַׁבַּת בְּשַׁבַּתּוֹ עַל־עֹלַת הַתָּמִיד (נתה) וְנִסְכָּהּ׃ {פ}
יא וּבְרָאשֵׁי חָדְשֵׁיכֶם תַּקְרִיבוּ עֹלָה לַיהוָה פָּרִים בְּנֵי־
בָקָר שְׁנַיִם וְאַיִל אֶחָד (אהבה, דאגה) כְּבָשִׂים בְּנֵי־שָׁנָה שִׁבְעָה
תְּמִימִם׃ יב וּשְׁלֹשָׁה עֶשְׂרֹנִים סֹלֶת מִנְחָה (כ"פ בן) בְּלוּלָה
בַשֶּׁמֶן לַפָּר הָאֶחָד (אהבה, דאגה) וּשְׁנֵי עֶשְׂרֹנִים סֹלֶת מִנְחָה (כ"פ
בן) בְּלוּלָה בַשֶּׁמֶן לָאַיִל הָאֶחָד׃ (אהבה, דאגה) יג וְעִשָּׂרֹן עִשָּׂרוֹן
סֹלֶת מִנְחָה (כ"פ בן) בְּלוּלָה בַשֶּׁמֶן לַכֶּבֶשׂ הָאֶחָד (אהבה, דאגה)
עֹלָה רֵיחַ נִיחֹחַ אִשֶּׁה לַיהוָה׃ יד וְנִסְכֵּיהֶם חֲצִי הַהִין יִהְיֶה
(ייי) לַפָּר וּשְׁלִישִׁת הַהִין לָאַיִל וּרְבִיעִת הַהִין לַכֶּבֶשׂ יָיִן (מ"כ,
י"פ האא) זֹאת עֹלַת חֹדֶשׁ בְּחָדְשׁוֹ לְחָדְשֵׁי הַשָּׁנָה׃ טו וּשְׂעִיר
עִזִּים אֶחָד (אהבה, דאגה) לְחַטָּאת לַיהוָה עַל־עֹלַת הַתָּמִיד (נתה)
יֵעָשֶׂה וְנִסְכּוֹ׃ {ס}

Haftarah of Rosh Chodesh

We often underestimate the power of Rosh Chodesh. Just as the fires of Hell are cooled on Shabbat, these very same fires are shut down on Rosh Chodesh as well. Through Rosh Chodesh, therefore, we can gain the power to deflect and avoid judgment.

ישעיהו פרק סו

א כֹּה (היי) אָמַר יְהוָה הַשָּׁמַיִם (כוזו, י"פ טל) כִּסְאִי וְהָאָרֶץ הֲדֹם
רַגְלָי אֵי־זֶה בַיִת (כ"פ ראה) אֲשֶׁר תִּבְנוּ־לִי וְאֵי־זֶה מָקוֹם
מְנוּחָתִי׃ ב וְאֶת־כָּל־אֵלֶּה יָדִי עָשָׂתָה וַיִּהְיוּ כָל (ילי) ־אֵלֶּה
נְאֻם־יְהוָה (ייא"י מילוי דס"ג) וְאֶל־זֶה אַבִּיט אֶל־עָנִי וּנְכֵה־רוּחַ
וְחָרֵד עַל־דְּבָרִי׃ ג שׁוֹחֵט הַשּׁוֹר (ושר, אבג יתץ, אהבת חנם) מַכֵּה־
אִישׁ זוֹבֵחַ הַשֶּׂה עֹרֵף כֶּלֶב מַעֲלֵה (עלם) מִנְחָה (כ"פ ב"ן) דַּם־
חֲזִיר מַזְכִּיר לְבֹנָה מְבָרֵךְ אָוֶן גַּם־הֵמָּה בָּחֲרוּ בְּדַרְכֵיהֶם
(כ"פ יב"ק) וּבְשִׁקּוּצֵיהֶם נַפְשָׁם חָפֵצָה׃ ד גַּם־אֲנִי (אני) אֶבְחַר
בְּתַעֲלֻלֵיהֶם וּמְגוּרֹתָם אָבִיא לָהֶם יַעַן קָרָאתִי וְאֵין עוֹנֶה
דִּבַּרְתִּי (ראה) וְלֹא שָׁמֵעוּ וַיַּעֲשׂוּ הָרַע בְּעֵינַי וּבַאֲשֶׁר לֹא־
חָפַצְתִּי בָּחָרוּ׃ {ס} ה שִׁמְעוּ דְּבַר (ראה) ־יְהוָה הַחֲרֵדִים
אֶל־דְּבָרוֹ (ראה) אָמְרוּ אֲחֵיכֶם שֹׂנְאֵיכֶם מְנַדֵּיכֶם לְמַעַן
שְׁמִי יִכְבַּד יְהוָה וְנִרְאֶה בְשִׂמְחַתְכֶם וְהֵם יֵבֹשׁוּ׃ ו קוֹל
שָׁאוֹן מֵעִיר (ערי, סוזחך, סנדלפון) קוֹל מֵהֵיכָל (אדני) קוֹל יְהוָה מְשַׁלֵּם

גְּמוּל לְאֹיְבָיו׃ ז בְּטֶרֶם תָּחִיל יָלָדָה בְּטֶרֶם יָבוֹא חֵבֶל לָהּ
וְהִמְלִיטָה זָכָר׃ ח מִי (ילי) ־שָׁמַע כָּזֹאת מִי (ילי) רָאָה (ראה) כָּאֵלֶּה
הֲיוּחַל אֶרֶץ בְּיוֹם (נגד, מזבח, זן) אֶחָד (אהבה, דאגה) אִם (יוהך) ־יִוָּלֵד גּוֹי
פַּעַם (מנק) אֶחָת כִּי־חָלָה (להח) גַּם־יָלְדָה צִיּוֹן (יוסף) אֶת־בָּנֶיהָ׃ ט
הַאֲנִי (אני) אַשְׁבִּיר וְלֹא אוֹלִיד יֹאמַר יְהוָה אִם (יוהך) ־אֲנִי (אני)
הַמּוֹלִיד וְעָצַרְתִּי אָמַר אֱלֹהָיִךְ (דמב, ילה)׃ {ס} י שִׂמְחוּ אֶת־
יְרוּשָׁלַ͏ִם וְגִילוּ בָהּ כָּל (ילי) ־אֹהֲבֶיהָ שִׂישׂוּ אִתָּהּ מָשׂוֹשׂ
כָּל (ילי) ־הַמִּתְאַבְּלִים עָלֶיהָ (פהל)׃ יא לְמַעַן תִּינְקוּ וּשְׂבַעְתֶּם
מִשֹּׁד תַּנְחֻמֶיהָ לְמַעַן תָּמֹצּוּ וְהִתְעַנַּגְתֶּם מִזִּיז כְּבוֹדָהּ׃ {ס}
יב כִּי־כֹה (היי) | אָמַר יְהוָה הִנְנִי נֹטֶה־אֵלֶיהָ כְּנָהָר שָׁלוֹם
וּכְנַחַל שׁוֹטֵף כְּבוֹד גּוֹיִם וִינַקְתֶּם עַל־צַד תִּנָּשֵׂאוּ וְעַל־
בִּרְכַּיִם תְּשָׁעֳשָׁעוּ׃ יג כְּאִישׁ אֲשֶׁר אִמּוֹ תְּנַחֲמֶנּוּ כֵּן אָנֹכִי
(איע) אֲנַחֶמְכֶם וּבִירוּשָׁלַ͏ִם תְּנֻחָמוּ׃ יד וּרְאִיתֶם וְשָׂשׂ לִבְּכֶם
וְעַצְמוֹתֵיכֶם כַּדֶּשֶׁא תִפְרַחְנָה וְנוֹדְעָה יַד־יְהוָה אֶת־עֲבָדָיו
וְזָעַם אֶת־אֹיְבָיו׃ {ס} טו כִּי־הִנֵּה יְהוָה בָּאֵשׁ יָבוֹא וְכַסּוּפָה
מַרְכְּבֹתָיו לְהָשִׁיב בְּחֵמָה אַפּוֹ וְגַעֲרָתוֹ בְּלַהֲבֵי־אֵשׁ׃ טז כִּי
בָאֵשׁ יְהוָה נִשְׁפָּט וּבְחַרְבּוֹ (רי״ו, גבורה) אֶת־כָּל (ילי) ־בָּשָׂר וְרַבּוּ
חַלְלֵי יְהוָה׃ יז הַמִּתְקַדְּשִׁים וְהַמִּטַּהֲרִים אֶל־הַגַּנּוֹת אַחַר
אחד (אהבה, דאגה) (אַחַת) בַּתָּוֶךְ אֹכְלֵי בְּשַׂר הַחֲזִיר וְהַשֶּׁקֶץ

וְהָעַכְבָּר יַחְדָּו יָסֻפוּ נְאֻם־יְהוָה׃ יח וְאָנֹכִי (אי"ע) מַעֲשֵׂיהֶם
וּמַחְשְׁבֹתֵיהֶם בָּאָה לְקַבֵּץ אֶת־כָּל־הַגּוֹיִם (ילי) וְהַלְּשֹׁנוֹת
וּבָאוּ וְרָאוּ אֶת־כְּבוֹדִי׃ יט וְשַׂמְתִּי בָהֶם אוֹת וְשִׁלַּחְתִּי מֵהֶם
| פְּלֵיטִים אֶל־הַגּוֹיִם תַּרְשִׁישׁ פּוּל וְלוּד מֹשְׁכֵי קֶשֶׁת תֻּבַל
(כ"פ רי"ו, ב"פ גבורה) וְיָוָן הָאִיִּים הָרְחֹקִים אֲשֶׁר לֹא־שָׁמְעוּ אֶת־
שִׁמְעִי וְלֹא־רָאוּ אֶת־כְּבוֹדִי וְהִגִּידוּ אֶת־כְּבוֹדִי בַּגּוֹיִם׃ כ
וְהֵבִיאוּ אֶת־כָּל־אֲחֵיכֶם מִכָּל־הַגּוֹיִם | מִנְחָה (כ"פ ב"ן) | לַיהוָה
בַּסּוּסִים (כוק) וּבָרֶכֶב וּבַצַּבִּים וּבַפְּרָדִים וּבַכִּרְכָּרוֹת עַל הַר
קָדְשִׁי יְרוּשָׁלִַם אָמַר יְהוָה כַּאֲשֶׁר יָבִיאוּ בְנֵי יִשְׂרָאֵל אֶת־
הַמִּנְחָה (כ"פ ב"ן) בִּכְלִי טָהוֹר (י"פ אכא) בֵּית (כ"פ ראה) יְהוָה׃ כא וְגַם־
מֵהֶם אֶקַּח לַכֹּהֲנִים (מלה) לַלְוִיִּם אָמַר יְהוָה׃ כב כִּי כַאֲשֶׁר
הַשָּׁמַיִם (כוזו, י"פ טל) הַחֲדָשִׁים וְהָאָרֶץ הַחֲדָשָׁה אֲשֶׁר אֲנִי (אני)
עֹשֶׂה עֹמְדִים לְפָנַי נְאֻם־יְהוָה כֵּן יַעֲמֹד זַרְעֲכֶם וְשִׁמְכֶם׃
כג וְהָיָה (יהה) מִדֵּי־חֹדֶשׁ בְּחָדְשׁוֹ וּמִדֵּי שַׁבָּת בְּשַׁבַּתּוֹ יָבוֹא
כָל־בָּשָׂר לְהִשְׁתַּחֲוֺת לְפָנַי אָמַר יְהוָה׃

English Portion of Beresheet

1,1 In the beginning God created the heaven and the earth. 1,2 Now the earth was unformed and void, and darkness was upon the face of the deep; and the spirit of God hovered over the face of the waters. 1,3 And God said: 'Let there be light.' And there was light. 1,4 And God saw the light, that it was good; and God divided the light from the darkness. 1,5 And God called the light Day, and the darkness He called Night. And there was evening and there was morning, one day. {P}

1,6 And God said: 'Let there be a firmament in the midst of the waters, and let it divide the waters from the waters.' 1,7 And God made the firmament, and divided the waters which were under the firmament from the waters which were above the firmament; and it was so. 1,8 And God called the firmament Heaven. And there was evening and there was morning, a second day. {P}

1,9 And God said: 'Let the waters under the heaven be gathered together unto one place, and let the dry land appear.' And it was so. 1,10 And God called the dry land Earth, and the gathering together of the waters called He Seas; and God saw that it was good. 1,11 And God said: 'Let the earth put forth grass, herb yielding seed, and fruit-tree bearing fruit after its kind, wherein is the seed thereof, upon the earth.' And it was so. 1,12 And the earth brought forth grass, herb yielding seed after its kind, and tree bearing fruit, wherein is the seed thereof, after its kind; and God saw that it was good. 1,13 And there was evening and there was morning, a third day. {P}

1,14 And God said: 'Let there be lights in the firmament of the heaven to divide the day from the night; and let them be for signs, and for seasons, and for days and years; 1,15 and let them be for lights in the firmament of the heaven to give light upon the earth.' And it was so. 1,16 And God made the two great lights: the greater light to rule the day, and the lesser light to rule the night; and the stars. 1,17 And God set them in the firmament of the heaven to give light upon the earth, 1,18 and to rule over the day and over the night, and to divide the light from the darkness; and God saw that it was good. 1,19 And there was evening and there was morning, a fourth day. {P}

1,20 And God said: 'Let the waters swarm with swarms of living creatures, and let fowl fly above the earth in the open firmament of heaven.' 1,21 And God created the great sea-monsters, and every living creature that creepeth, wherewith the waters swarmed, after its kind, and every winged fowl after its kind; and God saw that it was good. 1,22 And God blessed them, saying: 'Be fruitful, and multiply, and fill the waters in the seas, and let fowl multiply in the earth.' 1,23 And there was evening and there was morning, a fifth day. {P}

1,24 And God said: 'Let the earth bring forth the living creature after its kind, cattle, and creeping thing, and beast of the earth after its kind.' And it was so. 1,25 And God made the beast of the earth after its kind, and the cattle after their kind, and every thing that creepeth upon the ground after its kind; and God saw that it was good. 1,26 And God said: 'Let us make man in our image, after our likeness; and let them have dominion over the fish of the sea, and over the fowl of the air, and over the cattle, and over all the earth, and over every creeping thing that creepeth upon the earth.' 1,27 And God created man in His own image, in the image of God created He him; male and female created He them. 1,28 And God blessed them; and God said unto them: 'Be fruitful, and multiply, and replenish the earth, and subdue it; and have dominion over the fish of the sea, and over the fowl of the air, and over every living thing that creepeth upon the earth.' 1,29 And God said: 'Behold, I have given you every herb yielding seed, which is upon the face of all the earth, and every tree, in which is the fruit of a tree yielding seed--to you it shall be for food; 1,30 and to every beast of the earth, and to every fowl of the air, and to every thing that creepeth upon the earth, wherein there is a living soul, [I have given] every green herb for food.' And it was so. 1,31 And God saw every thing that He had made, and, behold, it was very good. And there was evening and there was morning, the sixth day. {P}

2,1 And the heaven and the earth were finished, and all the host of them. 2,2 And on the seventh day God finished His work which He had made; and He rested on the seventh day from all His work which He had made. 2,3 And God blessed the seventh day, and hallowed it; because that in it He rested from all His work which God in creating had made. {P}

2,4 These are the generations of the heaven and of the earth when they were created, in the day that God God made earth and heaven. 2,5 No shrub of the field was yet in the earth, and no herb of the field had yet sprung up; for God God had not caused it to rain upon the earth, and there was not a man to till the ground; 2,6 but there went up a mist from the earth, and watered the whole face of the ground. 2,7 Then God God formed man of the dust of the ground, and breathed into his nostrils the breath of life; and man became a living soul. 2,8 And God God planted a garden eastward, in Eden; and there He put the man whom He had formed. 2,9 And out of the ground made God God to grow every tree that is pleasant to the sight, and good for food; the tree of life also in the midst of the garden, and the tree of the knowledge of good and evil. 2,10 And a river went out of Eden to water the garden; and from thence it was parted, and became four heads. 2,11 The name of the first is Pishon; that is it which compasseth the whole land of Havilah, where there is gold; 2,12 and the gold of that land is good; there is bdellium and the onyx stone. 2,13 And the name of the second river is Gihon; the same is it that compasseth the whole land of Cush. 2,14 And the name of the third river is Tigris; that is it which goeth toward the east of Asshur. And the fourth river is the Euphrates. 2,15 And God God took the man, and put him

into the garden of Eden to dress it and to keep it. 2,16 And God God commanded the man, saying: 'Of every tree of the garden thou mayest freely eat; 2,17 but of the tree of the knowledge of good and evil, thou shalt not eat of it; for in the day that thou eatest thereof thou shalt surely die.' 2,18 And God God said: 'It is not good that the man should be alone; I will make him a help meet for him.' 2,19 And out of the ground God God formed every beast of the field, and every fowl of the air; and brought them unto the man to see what he would call them; and whatsoever the man would call every living creature, that was to be the name thereof. 2,20 And the man gave names to all cattle, and to the fowl of the air, and to every beast of the field; but for Adam there was not found a help meet for him. 2,21 And God God caused a deep sleep to fall upon the man, and he slept; and He took one of his ribs, and closed up the place with flesh instead thereof. 2,22 And the rib, which God God had taken from the man, made He a woman, and brought her unto the man. 2,23 And the man said: 'This is now bone of my bones, and flesh of my flesh; she shall be called Woman, because she was taken out of Man.' 2,24 Therefore shall a man leave his father and his mother, and shall cleave unto his wife, and they shall be one flesh. 2,25 And they were both naked, the man and his wife, and were not ashamed. 3,1 Now the serpent was more subtle than any beast of the field which God God had made. And he said unto the woman: 'Yea, hath God said: Ye shall not eat of any tree of the garden?' 3,2 And the woman said unto the serpent: 'Of the fruit of the trees of the garden we may eat; 3,3 but of the fruit of the tree which is in the midst of the garden, God hath said: Ye shall not eat of it, neither shall ye touch it, lest ye die.' 3,4 And the serpent said unto the woman: 'Ye shall not surely die; 3,5 for God doth know that in the day ye eat thereof, then your eyes shall be opened, and ye shall be as God, knowing good and evil.' 3,6 And when the woman saw that the tree was good for food, and that it was a delight to the eyes, and that the tree was to be desired to make one wise, she took of the fruit thereof, and did eat; and she gave also unto her husband with her, and he did eat. 3,7 And the eyes of them both were opened, and they knew that they were naked; and they sewed fig-leaves together, and made themselves girdles. 3,8 And they heard the voice of God God walking in the garden toward the cool of the day; and the man and his wife hid themselves from the presence of God God amongst the trees of the garden. 3,9 And God God called unto the man, and said unto him: 'Where art thou?' 3,10 And he said: 'I heard Thy voice in the garden, and I was afraid, because I was naked; and I hid myself.' 3,11 And He said: 'Who told thee that thou wast naked? Hast thou eaten of the tree, whereof I commanded thee that thou shouldest not eat?' 3,12 And the man said: 'The woman whom Thou gavest to be with me, she gave me of the tree, and I did eat.' 3,13 And God God said unto the woman: 'What is this thou hast done?' And the woman said: 'The serpent beguiled me, and I did eat.' 3,14 And God God said unto the serpent: 'Because thou hast done this, cursed art thou from among all cattle, and from among all beasts of the field; upon thy belly shalt thou go, and dust shalt thou eat all the days of thy life. 3,15 And I will put enmity between thee and the woman, and between thy seed and her seed; they shall bruise thy head, and thou shalt bruise their heel.' {S} 3,16 Unto the woman He said: 'I will greatly multiply thy pain and thy travail; in pain thou shalt bring forth children; and thy desire shall be to thy husband, and he shall rule over thee.' {S} 3,17 And unto Adam He said: 'Because thou hast hearkened unto the voice of thy wife, and hast eaten of the tree, of which I commanded thee, saying: Thou shalt not eat of it; cursed is the ground for thy sake; in toil shalt thou eat of it all the days of thy life. 3,18 Thorns also and thistles shall it bring forth to thee; and thou shalt eat the herb of the field. 3,19 In the sweat of thy face shalt thou eat bread, till thou return unto the ground; for out of it wast thou taken; for dust thou art, and unto dust shalt thou return.' 3,20 And the man called his wife's name Eve; because she was the mother of all living. 3,21 And God God made for Adam and for his wife garments of skins, and clothed them. {P}

3,22 And God God said: 'Behold, the man is become as one of us, to know good and evil; and now, lest he put forth his hand, and take also of the tree of life, and eat, and live for ever.' 3,23 Therefore God God sent him forth from the garden of Eden, to till the ground from whence he was taken. 3,24 So He drove out the man; and He placed at the east of the garden of Eden the cherubim, and the flaming sword which turned every way, to keep the way to the tree of life. {S} 4,1 And the man knew Eve his wife; and she conceived and bore Cain, and said: 'I have gotten a man with the help of God.' 4,2 And again she bore his brother Abel. And Abel was a keeper of sheep, but Cain was a tiller of the ground. 4,3 And in process of time it came to pass, that Cain brought of the fruit of the ground an offering unto God. 4,4 And Abel, he also brought of the firstlings of his flock and of the fat thereof. And God had respect unto Abel and to his offering; 4,5 but unto Cain and to his offering He had not respect. And Cain was very wroth, and his countenance fell. 4,6 And God said unto Cain: 'Why art thou wroth? and why is thy countenance fallen? 4,7 If thou doest well, shall it not be lifted up? and if thou doest not well, sin coucheth at the door; and unto thee is its desire, but thou mayest rule over it.' 4,8 And Cain spoke unto Abel his brother. And it came to pass, when they were in the field, that Cain rose up against Abel his brother, and slew him. 4,9 And God said unto Cain: 'Where is Abel thy brother?' And he said: 'I know not; am I my brother's keeper?' 4,10 And He said: 'What hast thou done? the voice of thy brother's blood crieth unto Me from the ground. 4,11 And now cursed art thou from the ground, which hath opened her mouth to receive thy brother's blood from thy hand. 4,12 When thou tillest the ground, it shall not henceforth yield unto thee her strength; a fugitive and a wanderer shalt thou be in the earth.' 4,13 And Cain said unto God: 'My punishment is greater than I can bear. 4,14 Behold, Thou hast driven me out this day from the face of the land; and from Thy face shall I be hid; and I shall be a fugitive and a wanderer in the earth; and it will come to pass, that whosoever findeth me will slay me.' 4,15 And God said unto him: 'Therefore whosoever slayeth Cain, vengeance shall be

taken on him sevenfold.' And God set a sign for Cain, lest any finding him should smite him. 4,16 And Cain went out from the presence of God, and dwelt in the land of Nod, on the east of Eden. 4,17 And Cain knew his wife; and she conceived, and bore Enoch; and he builded a city, and called the name of the city after the name of his son Enoch. 4,18 And unto Enoch was born Irad; and Irad begot Mehujael; and Mehujael begot Methushael; and Methushael begot Lamech. 4,19 And Lamech took unto him two wives; the name of one was Adah, and the name of the other Zillah. 4,20 And Adah bore Jabal; he was the father of such as dwell in tents and have cattle. 4,21 And his brother's name was Jubal; he was the father of all such as handle the harp and pipe. 4,22 And Zillah, she also bore Tubal-cain, the forger of every cutting instrument of brass and iron; and the sister of Tubal-cain was Naamah. 4,23 And Lamech said unto his wives: Adah and Zillah, hear my voice; ye wives of Lamech, hearken unto my speech; for I have slain a man for wounding me, and a young man for bruising me; 4,24 If Cain shall be avenged sevenfold, truly Lamech seventy and sevenfold. 4,25 And Adam knew his wife again; and she bore a son, and called his name Seth: 'for God hath appointed me another seed instead of Abel; for Cain slew him.' 4,26 And to Seth, to him also there was born a son; and he called his name Enosh; then began men to call upon the name of God. {S} 5,1 This is the book of the generations of Adam. In the day that God created man, in the likeness of God made He him; 5,2 male and female created He them, and blessed them, and called their name Adam, in the day when they were created. 5,3 And Adam lived a hundred and thirty years, and begot a son in his own likeness, after his image; and called his name Seth. 5,4 And the days of Adam after he begot Seth were eight hundred years; and he begot sons and daughters. 5,5 And all the days that Adam lived were nine hundred and thirty years; and he died. {S} 5,6 And Seth lived a hundred and five years, and begot Enosh. 5,7 And Seth lived after he begot Enosh eight hundred and seven years, and begot sons and daughters. 5,8 And all the days of Seth were nine hundred and twelve years; and he died. {S} 5,9 And Enosh lived ninety years, and begot Kenan. 5,10 And Enosh lived after he begot Kenan eight hundred and fifteen years, and begot sons and daughters. 5,11 And all the days of Enosh were nine hundred and five years; and he died. {S} 5,12 And Kenan lived seventy years, and begot Mahalalel. 5,13 And Kenan lived after he begot Mahalalel eight hundred and forty years, and begot sons and daughters. 5,14 And all the days of Kenan were nine hundred and ten years; and he died. {S} 5,15 And Mahalalel lived sixty and five years, and begot Jared. 5,16 And Mahalalel lived after he begot Jared eight hundred and thirty years, and begot sons and daughters. 5,17 And all the days of Mahalalel were eight hundred ninety and five years; and he died. {S} 5,18 And Jared lived a hundred sixty and two years, and begot Enoch. 5,19 And Jared lived after he begot Enoch eight hundred years, and begot sons and daughters. 5,20 And all the days of Jared were nine hundred sixty and two years; and he died. {S} 5,21 And Enoch lived sixty and five years, and begot Methuselah. 5,22 And Enoch walked with God after he begot Methuselah three hundred years, and begot sons and daughters. 5,23 And all the days of Enoch were three hundred sixty and five years. 5,24 And Enoch walked with God, and he was not; for God took him. {S} 5,25 And Methuselah lived a hundred eighty and seven years, and begot Lamech. 5,26 And Methuselah lived after he begot Lamech seven hundred eighty and two years, and begot sons and daughters. 5,27 And all the days of Methuselah were nine hundred sixty and nine years; and he died. {S} 5,28 And Lamech lived a hundred eighty and two years, and begot a son. 5,29 And he called his name Noach, saying: 'This same shall comfort us in our work and in the toil of our hands, which cometh from the ground which God hath cursed.' 5,30 And Lamech lived after he begot Noach five hundred ninety and five years, and begot sons and daughters. 5,31 And all the days of Lamech were seven hundred seventy and seven years; and he died. {S} 5,32 And Noach was five hundred years old; and Noach begot Shem, Ham, and Japheth. 6,1 And it came to pass, when men began to multiply on the face of the earth, and daughters were born unto them, 6,2 that the sons of God saw the daughters of men that they were fair; and they took them wives, whomsoever they chose. 6,3 And God said: 'My spirit shall not abide in man for ever, for that he also is flesh; therefore shall his days be a hundred and twenty years.' 6,4 The Nephilim were in the earth in those days, and also after that, when the sons of God came in unto the daughters of men, and they bore children to them; the same were the mighty men that were of old, the men of renown. {P}

6,5 And God saw that the wickedness of man was great in the earth, and that every imagination of the thoughts of his heart was only evil continually. 6,6 And it repented God that He had made man on the earth, and it grieved Him at His heart. 6,7 And God said: 'I will blot out man whom I have created from the face of the earth; both man, and beast, and creeping thing, and fowl of the air; for it repenteth Me that I have made them.' 6,8 But Noach found grace in the eyes of God. {P}

English Haftara of Beresheet

Isaiah

42,5 Thus saith God God, He that created the heavens, and stretched them forth, He that spread forth the earth and that which cometh out of it, He that giveth breath unto the people upon it, and spirit to them that walk therein: 42,6 I God have called thee in righteousness, and have taken hold of thy hand, and kept thee, and set thee for a covenant of the people, for a light of the nations; 42,7 To open the blind eyes, to bring out the prisoners from the dungeon, and them that sit in darkness out of the prison-house. 42,8 I am God, that is

My name; and My glory will I not give to another, neither My praise to graven images. 42,9 Behold, the former things are come to pass, and new things do I declare; before they spring forth I tell you of them. {P}

42,10 Sing unto God a new song, and His praise from the end of the earth; ye that go down to the sea, and all that is therein, the isles, and the inhabitants thereof. 42,11 Let the wilderness and the cities thereof lift up their voice, the villages that Kedar doth inhabit; let the inhabitants of Sela exult, let them shout from the top of the mountains. 42,12 Let them give glory unto God, and declare His praise in the islands. 42,13 God will go forth as a mighty man, He will stir up jealousy like a man of war; He will cry, yea, He will shout aloud, He will prove Himself mighty against His enemies. {S} 42,14 I have long time held My peace, I have been still, and refrained Myself; now will I cry like a travailing woman, gasping and panting at once. 42,15 I will make waste mountains and hills, and dry up all their herbs; and I will make the rivers islands, and will dry up the pools. 42,16 And I will bring the blind by a way that they knew not, in paths that they knew not will I lead them; I will make darkness light before them, and rugged places plain. These things will I do, and I will not leave them undone. 42,17 They shall be turned back, greatly ashamed, that trust in graven images, that say unto molten images: 'Ye are our gods.' {P}

42,18 Hear, ye deaf, and look, ye blind, that ye may see. 42,19 Who is blind, but My servant? Or deaf, as My messenger that I send? Who is blind as he that is wholehearted, and blind as God'S servant? 42,20 Seeing many things, thou observest not; opening the ears, he heareth not. 42,21 God was pleased, for His righteousness' sake, to make the teaching great and glorious. 42,22 But this is a people robbed and spoiled, they are all of them snared in holes, and they are hid in prison-houses; they are for a prey, and none delivereth, for a spoil, and none saith: 'Restore.' 42,23 Who among you will give ear to this? Who will hearken and hear for the time to come? 42,24 Who gave Jacob for a spoil, and Israel to the robbers? Did not God? He against whom we have sinned, and in whose ways they would not walk, neither were they obedient unto His law. 42,25 Therefore He poured upon him the fury of His anger, and the strength of battle; and it set him on fire round about, yet he knew not, and it burned him, yet he laid it not to heart. 43,1 But now thus saith God that created thee, O Jacob, and He that formed thee, O Israel: Fear not, for I have redeemed thee, I have called thee by thy name, thou art Mine. 43,2 When thou passest through the waters, I will be with thee, and through the rivers, they shall not overflow thee; when thou walkest through the fire, thou shalt not be burned, neither shall the flame kindle upon thee. 43,3 For I am God thy God, The Holy One of Israel, thy Saviour; I have given Egypt as thy ransom, Ethiopia and Seba for thee. 43,4 Since thou art precious in My sight, and honourable, and I have loved thee; therefore will I give men for thee, and peoples for thy life. 43,5 Fear not, for I am with thee; I will bring thy seed from the east, and gather thee from the west; 43,6 I will say to the north: 'Give up,' and to the south: 'Keep not back, bring My sons from far, and My daughters from the end of the earth; 43,7 Every one that is called by My name, and whom I have created for My glory, I have formed him, yea, I have made him.' 43,8 The blind people that have eyes shall be brought forth, and the deaf that have ears. 43,9 All the nations are gathered together, and the peoples are assembled; who among them can declare this, and announce to us former things? Let them bring their witnesses, that they may be justified; and let them hear, and say: 'It is truth.' 43,10 Ye are My witnesses, saith God, and My servant whom I have chosen; that ye may know and believe Me, and understand that I am He; before Me there was no God formed, neither shall any be after Me. {S} 43,11 I, even I, am God; and beside Me there is no saviour. 43,12 I have declared, and I have saved, and I have announced, and there was no strange god among you; therefore ye are My witnesses, saith God, and I am God. 43,13 Yea, since the day was I am He, and there is none that can deliver out of My hand; I will work, and who can reverse it? {S} 43,14 Thus saith God, your Redeemer, The Holy One of Israel: For your sake I have sent to Babylon, and I will bring down all of them as fugitives, even the Chaldeans, in the ships of their shouting. 43,15 I am God, your Holy One, the Creator of Israel, your King. {S} 43,16 Thus saith God, who maketh a way in the sea, and a path in the mighty waters; 43,17 Who bringeth forth the chariot and horse, the army and the power--they lie down together, they shall not rise, they are extinct, they are quenched as a wick: 43,18 Remember ye not the former things, neither consider the things of old. 43,19 Behold, I will do a new thing; now shall it spring forth; shall ye not know it? I will even make a way in the wilderness, and rivers in the desert. 43,20 The beasts of the field shall honour Me, the jackals and the ostriches; because I give waters in the wilderness, and rivers in the desert, to give drink to My people, Mine elect; 43,21 The people which I formed for Myself, that they might tell of My praise. {S}

English Portion of Noach

6,9 These are the generations of Noach. Noach was in his generations a man righteous and whole-hearted; Noach walked with God. 6,10 And Noach begot three sons, Shem, Ham, and Japheth. 6,11 And the earth was corrupt before God, and the earth was filled with violence. 6,12 And God saw the earth, and, behold, it was corrupt; for all flesh had corrupted their way upon the earth. {S} 6,13 And God said unto Noach: 'The end of all flesh is come before Me; for the earth is filled with violence through them; and, behold, I will destroy them with the earth. 6,14 Make thee an ark of gopher wood; with rooms shalt thou make the ark, and shalt pitch it within

and without with pitch. 6,15 And this is how thou shalt make it: the length of the ark three hundred cubits, the breadth of it fifty cubits, and the height of it thirty cubits. 6,16 A light shalt thou make to the ark, and to a cubit shalt thou finish it upward; and the door of the ark shalt thou set in the side thereof; with lower, second, and third stories shalt thou make it. 6,17 And I, behold, I do bring the flood of waters upon the earth, to destroy all flesh, wherein is the breath of life, from under heaven; every thing that is in the earth shall perish. 6,18 But I will establish My covenant with thee; and thou shalt come into the ark, thou, and thy sons, and thy wife, and thy sons' wives with thee. 6,19 And of every living thing of all flesh, two of every sort shalt thou bring into the ark, to keep them alive with thee; they shall be male and female. 6,20 Of the fowl after their kind, and of the cattle after their kind, of every creeping thing of the ground after its kind, two of every sort shall come unto thee, to keep them alive. 6,21 And take thou unto thee of all food that is eaten, and gather it to thee; and it shall be for food for thee, and for them.' 6,22 Thus did Noach; according to all that God commanded him, so did he. 7,1 And God said unto Noach: 'Come thou and all thy house into the ark; for thee have I seen righteous before Me in this generation. 7,2 Of every clean beast thou shalt take to thee seven and seven, each with his mate; and of the beasts that are not clean two [and two], each with his mate; 7,3 of the fowl also of the air, seven and seven, male and female; to keep seed alive upon the face of all the earth. 7,4 For yet seven days, and I will cause it to rain upon the earth forty days and forty nights; and every living substance that I have made will I blot out from off the face of the earth.' 7,5 And Noach did according unto all that God commanded him. 7,6 And Noach was six hundred years old when the flood of waters was upon the earth. 7,7 And Noach went in, and his sons, and his wife, and his sons' wives with him, into the ark, because of the waters of the flood. 7,8 Of clean beasts, and of beasts that are not clean, and of fowls, and of every thing that creepeth upon the ground, 7,9 there went in two and two unto Noach into the ark, male and female, as God commanded Noach. 7,10 And it came to pass after the seven days, that the waters of the flood were upon the earth. 7,11 In the six hundredth year of Noach's life, in the second month, on the seventeenth day of the month, on the same day were all the fountains of the great deep broken up, and the windows of heaven were opened. 7,12 And the rain was upon the earth forty days and forty nights. 7,13 In the selfsame day entered Noach, and Shem, and Ham, and Japheth, the sons of Noach, and Noach's wife, and the three wives of his sons with them, into the ark; 7,14 they, and every beast after its kind, and all the cattle after their kind, and every creeping thing that creepeth upon the earth after its kind, and every fowl after its kind, every bird of every sort. 7,15 And they went in unto Noach into the ark, two and two of all flesh wherein is the breath of life. 7,16 And they that went in, went in male and female of all flesh, as God commanded him; and God shut him in. 7,17 And the flood was forty days upon the earth; and the waters increased, and bore up the ark, and it was lifted up above the earth. 7,18 And the waters prevailed, and increased greatly upon the earth; and the ark went upon the face of the waters. 7,19 And the waters prevailed exceedingly upon the earth; and all the high mountains that were under the whole heaven were covered. 7,20 Fifteen cubits upward did the waters prevail; and the mountains were covered. 7,21 And all flesh perished that moved upon the earth, both fowl, and cattle, and beast, and every swarming thing that swarmeth upon the earth, and every man; 7,22 all in whose nostrils was the breath of the spirit of life, whatsoever was in the dry land, died. 7,23 And He blotted out every living substance which was upon the face of the ground, both man, and cattle, and creeping thing, and fowl of the heaven; and they were blotted out from the earth; and Noach only was left, and they that were with him in the ark. 7,24 And the waters prevailed upon the earth a hundred and fifty days. 8,1 And God remembered Noach, and every living thing, and all the cattle that were with him in the ark; and God made a wind to pass over the earth, and the waters assuaged; 8,2 the fountains also of the deep and the windows of heaven were stopped, and the rain from heaven was restrained. 8,3 And the waters returned from off the earth continually; and after the end of a hundred and fifty days the waters decreased. 8,4 And the ark rested in the seventh month, on the seventeenth day of the month, upon the mountains of Ararat. 8,5 And the waters decreased continually until the tenth month; in the tenth month, on the first day of the month, were the tops of the mountains seen. 8,6 And it came to pass at the end of forty days, that Noach opened the window of the ark which he had made. 8,7 And he sent forth a raven, and it went forth to and fro, until the waters were dried up from off the earth. 8,8 And he sent forth a dove from him, to see if the waters were abated from off the face of the ground. 8,9 But the dove found no rest for the sole of her foot, and she returned unto him to the ark, for the waters were on the face of the whole earth; and he put forth his hand, and took her, and brought her in unto him into the ark. 8,10 And he stayed yet other seven days; and again he sent forth the dove out of the ark. 8,11 And the dove came in to him at eventide; and lo in her mouth an olive-leaf freshly plucked; so Noach knew that the waters were abated from off the earth. 8,12 And he stayed yet other seven days; and sent forth the dove; and she returned not again unto him any more. 8,13 And it came to pass in the six hundred and first year, in the first month, the first day of the month, the waters were dried up from off the earth; and Noach removed the covering of the ark, and looked, and behold, the face of the ground was dried. 8,14 And in the second month, on the seven and twentieth day of the month, was the earth dry. {S} 8,15 And God spoke unto Noach, saying: 8,16 'Go forth from the ark, thou, and thy wife, and thy sons, and thy sons' wives with thee. 8,17 Bring forth with thee every living thing that is with thee of all flesh, both fowl, and cattle, and every creeping thing that creepeth upon the earth; that they may swarm in the earth, and be fruitful, and multiply upon the earth.' 8,18 And Noach went forth, and his sons, and his wife, and his sons' wives with him; 8,19 every beast, every creeping thing, and every fowl, whatsoever moveth upon the earth, after their

families; went forth out of the ark. 8,20 And Noach builded an altar unto God; and took of every clean beast,
and of every clean fowl, and offered burnt-offerings on the altar. 8,21 And God smelled the sweet savour; and
God said in His heart: 'I will not again curse the ground any more for man's sake; for the imagination of man's
heart is evil from his youth; neither will I again smite any more every thing living, as I have done. 8,22 While the
earth remaineth, seedtime and harvest, and cold and heat, and summer and winter, and day and night shall
not cease.' 9,1 And God blessed Noach and his sons, and said unto them: 'Be fruitful and multiply, and
replenish the earth. 9,2 And the fear of you and the dread of you shall be upon every beast of the earth, and
upon every fowl of the air, and upon all wherewith the ground teemeth, and upon all the fishes of the sea: into
your hand are they delivered. 9,3 Every moving thing that liveth shall be for food for you; as the green herb have
I given you all. 9,4 Only flesh with the life thereof, which is the blood thereof, shall ye not eat. 9,5 And surely
your blood of your lives will I require; at the hand of every beast will I require it; and at the hand of man, even
at the hand of every man's brother, will I require the life of man. 9,6 Whoso sheddeth man's blood, by man shall
his blood be shed; for in the image of God made He man. 9,7 And you, be ye fruitful, and multiply; swarm in
the earth, and multiply therein.' {S} 9,8 And God spoke unto Noach, and to his sons with him, saying: 9,9 'As
for Me, behold, I establish My covenant with you, and with your seed after you; 9,10 and with every living
creature that is with you, the fowl, the cattle, and every beast of the earth with you; of all that go out of the ark,
even every beast of the earth. 9,11 And I will establish My covenant with you; neither shall all flesh be cut off
any more by the waters of the flood; neither shall there any more be a flood to destroy the earth.' 9,12 And God
said: 'This is the token of the covenant which I make between Me and you and every living creature that is with
you, for perpetual generations: 9,13 I have set My bow in the cloud, and it shall be for a token of a covenant
between Me and the earth. 9,14 And it shall come to pass, when I bring clouds over the earth, and the bow is
seen in the cloud, 9,15 that I will remember My covenant, which is between Me and you and every living
creature of all flesh; and the waters shall no more become a flood to destroy all flesh. 9,16 And the bow shall
be in the cloud; and I will look upon it, that I may remember the everlasting covenant between God and every
living creature of all flesh that is upon the earth.' 9,17 And God said unto Noach: 'This is the token of the
covenant which I have established between Me and all flesh that is upon the earth.' {P}

9,18 And the sons of Noach, that went forth from the ark, were Shem, and Ham, and Japheth; and Ham is
the father of Canaan. 9,19 These three were the sons of Noach, and of these was the whole earth overspread.
9,20 And Noach the husbandman began, and planted a vineyard. 9,21 And he drank of the wine, and was
drunken; and he was uncovered within his tent. 9,22 And Ham, the father of Canaan, saw the nakedness of
his father, and told his two brethren without. 9,23 And Shem and Japheth took a garment, and laid it upon
both their shoulders, and went backward, and covered the nakedness of their father; and their faces were
backward, and they saw not their father's nakedness. 9,24 And Noach awoke from his wine, and knew what
his youngest son had done unto him. 9,25 And he said: Cursed be Canaan; a servant of servants shall he be
unto his brethren. 9,26 And he said: Blessed be God, the God of Shem; and let Canaan be their servant. 9,27
God enlarge Japheth, and he shall dwell in the tents of Shem; and let Canaan be their servant. 9,28 And Noach
lived after the flood three hundred and fifty years. 9,29 And all the days of Noach were nine hundred and fifty
years; and he died. {P}

10,1 Now these are the generations of the sons of Noach: Shem, Ham, and Japheth; and unto them were sons
born after the flood. 10,2 The sons of Japheth: Gomer, and Magog, and Madai, and Javan, and Tubal, and
Meshech, and Tiras. 10,3 And the sons of Gomer: Ashkenaz, and Riphath, and Togarmah. 10,4 And the sons
of Javan: Elishah, and Tarshish, Kittim, and Dodanim. 10,5 Of these were the isles of the nations divided in
their lands, every one after his tongue, after their families, in their nations. 10,6 And the sons of Ham: Cush,
and Mizraim, and Put, and Canaan. 10,7 And the sons of Cush: Seba, and Havilah, and Sabtah, and Raamah,
and Sabteca; and the sons of Raamah: Sheba, and Dedan. 10,8 And Cush begot Nimrod; he began to be a
mighty one in the earth. 10,9 He was a mighty hunter before God; wherefore it is said: 'Like Nimrod a mighty
hunter before God.' 10,10 And the beginning of his kingdom was Babel, and Erech, and Accad, and Calneh,
in the land of Shinar. 10,11 Out of that land went forth Asshur, and builded Nineveh, and Rehoboth-ir, and
Calah, 10,12 and Resen between Nineveh and Calah--the same is the great city. 10,13 And Mizraim begot
Ludim, and Anamim, and Lehabim, and Naphtuhim, 10,14 and Pathrusim, and Casluhim--whence went forth
the Philistines--and Caphtorim. {S} 10,15 And Canaan begot Zidon his firstborn, and Heth; 10,16 and the
Jebusite, and the Amorite, and the Girgashite; 10,17 and the Hivite, and the Arkite, and the Sinite; 10,18 and
the Arvadite, and the Zemarite, and the Hamathite; and afterward were the families of the Canaanite spread
abroad. 10,19 And the border of the Canaanite was from Zidon, as thou goest toward Gerar, unto Gaza; as thou
goest toward Sodom and Gomorrah and Admah and Zeboiim, unto Lasha. 10,20 These are the sons of Ham,
after their families, after their tongues, in their lands, in their nations. {S} 10,21 And unto Shem, the father of
all the children of Eber, the elder brother of Japheth, to him also were children born. 10,22 The sons of Shem:
Elam, and Asshur, and Arpachshad, and Lud, and Aram. 10,23 And the sons of Aram: Uz, and Hul, and
Gether, and Mash. 10,24 And Arpachshad begot Shelah; and Shelah begot Eber. 10,25 And unto Eber were
born two sons; the name of the one was Peleg; for in his days was the earth divided; and his brother's name was
Joktan. 10,26 And Joktan begot Almodad, and Sheleph, and Hazarmaveth, and Jerah; 10,27 and Hadoram,
and Uzal, and Diklah; 10,28 and Obal, and Abimael, and Sheba; 10,29 and Ophir, and Havilah, and Jobab; all

these were the sons of Joktan. 10,30 And their dwelling was from Mesha, as thou goest toward Sephar, unto the mountain of the east. 10,31 These are the sons of Shem, after their families, after their tongues, in their lands, after their nations. 10,32 These are the families of the sons of Noach, after their generations, in their nations; and of these were the nations divided in the earth after the flood. {P}
11,1 And the whole earth was of one language and of one speech. 11,2 And it came to pass, as they journeyed east, that they found a plain in the land of Shinar; and they dwelt there. 11,3 And they said one to another: 'Come, let us make brick, and burn them thoroughly.' And they had brick for stone, and slime had they for mortar. 11,4 And they said: 'Come, let us build us a city, and a tower, with its top in heaven, and let us make us a name; lest we be scattered abroad upon the face of the whole earth.' 11,5 And God came down to see the city and the tower, which the children of men builded. 11,6 And God said: 'Behold, they are one people, and they have all one language; and this is what they begin to do; and now nothing will be withholden from them, which they purpose to do. 11,7 Come, let us go down, and there confound their language, that they may not understand one another's speech.' 11,8 So God scattered them abroad from thence upon the face of all the earth; and they left off to build the city. 11,9 Therefore was the name of it called Babel; because God did there confound the language of all the earth; and from thence did God scatter them abroad upon the face of all the earth. {P}
11,10 These are the generations of Shem. Shem was a hundred years old, and begot Arpachshad two years after the flood. 11,11 And Shem lived after he begot Arpachshad five hundred years, and begot sons and daughters. {S} 11,12 And Arpachshad lived five and thirty years, and begot Shelah. 11,13 And Arpachshad lived after he begot Shelah four hundred and three years, and begot sons and daughters. {S} 11,14 And Shelah lived thirty years, and begot Eber. 11,15 And Shelah lived after he begot Eber four hundred and three years, and begot sons and daughters. {S} 11,16 And Eber lived four and thirty years, and begot Peleg. 11,17 And Eber lived after he begot Peleg four hundred and thirty years, and begot sons and daughters. {S} 11,18 And Peleg lived thirty years, and begot Reu. 11,19 And Peleg lived after he begot Reu two hundred and nine years, and begot sons and daughters. {S} 11,20 And Reu lived two and thirty years, and begot Serug. 11,21 And Reu lived after he begot Serug two hundred and seven years, and begot sons and daughters. {S} 11,22 And Serug lived thirty years, and begot Nahor. 11,23 And Serug lived after he begot Nahor two hundred years, and begot sons and daughters. {S} 11,24 And Nahor lived nine and twenty years, and begot Terah. 11,25 And Nahor lived after he begot Terah a hundred and nineteen years, and begot sons and daughters. {S} 11,26 And Terah lived seventy years, and begot Abram, Nahor, and Haran. 11,27 Now these are the generations of Terah. Terah begot Abram, Nahor, and Haran; and Haran begot Lot. 11,28 And Haran died in the presence of his father Terah in the land of his nativity, in Ur of the Chaldees. 11,29 And Abram and Nahor took them wives: the name of Abram's wife was Sarai; and the name of Nahor's wife, Milcah, the daughter of Haran, the father of Milcah, and the father of Iscah. 11,30 And Sarai was barren; she had no child. 11,31 And Terah took Abram his son, and Lot the son of Haran, his son's son, and Sarai his daughter-in-law, his son Abram's wife; and they went forth with them from Ur of the Chaldees, to go into the land of Canaan; and they came unto Haran, and dwelt there. 11,32 And the days of Terah were two hundred and five years; and Terah died in Haran. {P}

English Haftara of Noach

Isaia

54,1 Sing, O barren, thou that didst not bear, break forth into singing, and cry aloud, thou that didst not travail; for more are the children of the desolate than the children of the married wife, saith God. 54,2 Enlarge the place of thy tent, and let them stretch forth the curtains of thy habitations, spare not; lengthen thy cords, and strengthen thy stakes. 54,3 For thou shalt spread abroad on the right hand and on the left; and thy seed shall possess the nations, and make the desolate cities to be inhabited. 54,4 Fear not, for thou shalt not be ashamed. Neither be thou confounded, for thou shalt not be put to shame; for thou shalt forget the shame of thy youth, and the reproach of thy widowhood shalt thou remember no more. 54,5 For thy Maker is thy husband, God of hosts is His name; and the Holy One of Israel is thy Redeemer, the God of the whole earth shall He be called. 54,6 For God hath called thee as a wife forsaken and grieved in spirit; and a wife of youth, can she be rejected? saith thy God. 54,7 For a small moment have I forsaken thee; but with great compassion will I gather thee. 54,8 In a little wrath I hid My face from thee for a moment; but with everlasting kindness will I have compassion on thee, saith God thy Redeemer. {S} 54,9 For this is as the waters of Noach unto Me; for as I have sworn that the waters of Noach should no more go over the earth, so have I sworn that I would not be wroth with thee, nor rebuke thee. 54,10 For the mountains may depart, and the hills be removed; but My kindness shall not depart from thee, neither shall My covenant of peace be removed, saith God that hath compassion on thee. {S}

English Portion of Lech Lecha

12,1 Now God said unto Abram: 'Get thee out of thy country, and from thy kindred, and from thy father's house,
unto the land that I will show thee. 12,2 And I will make of thee a great nation, and I will bless thee, and make
thy name great; and be thou a blessing. 12,3 And I will bless them that bless thee, and him that curseth thee
will I curse; and in thee shall all the families of the earth be blessed.' 12,4 So Abram went, as God had spoken
unto him; and Lot went with him; and Abram was seventy and five years old when he departed out of Haran.
12,5 And Abram took Sarai his wife, and Lot his brother's son, and all their substance that they had gathered,
and the souls that they had gotten in Haran; and they went forth to go into the land of Canaan; and into the
land of Canaan they came. 12,6 And Abram passed through the land unto the place of Shechem, unto the
terebinth of Moreh. And the Canaanite was then in the land. 12,7 And God appeared unto Abram, and said:
'Unto thy seed will I give this land'; and he builded there an altar unto God, who appeared unto him. 12,8 And
he removed from thence unto the mountain on the east of Beth-el, and pitched his tent, having Beth-el on the
west, and Ai on the east; and he builded there an altar unto God, and called upon the name of God. 12,9 And
Abram journeyed, going on still toward the South. {P}

12,10 And there was a famine in the land; and Abram went down into Egypt to sojourn there; for the famine was
sore in the land. 12,11 And it came to pass, when he was come near to enter into Egypt, that he said unto Sarai
his wife: 'Behold now, I know that thou art a fair woman to look upon. 12,12 And it will come to pass, when the
Egyptians shall see thee, that they will say: This is his wife; and they will kill me, but thee they will keep alive.
12,13 Say, I pray thee, thou art my sister; that it may be well with me for thy sake, and that my soul may live
because of thee.' 12,14 And it came to pass, that, when Abram was come into Egypt, the Egyptians beheld the
woman that she was very fair. 12,15 And the princes of Pharaoh saw her, and praised her to Pharaoh; and the
woman was taken into Pharaoh's house. 12,16 And he dealt well with Abram for her sake; and he had sheep,
and oxen, and he-asses, and men-servants, and maid-servants, and she-asses, and camels. 12,17 And God
plagued Pharaoh and his house with great plagues because of Sarai Abram's wife. 12,18 And Pharaoh called
Abram, and said: 'What is this that thou hast done unto me? why didst thou not tell me that she was thy wife?
12,19 Why saidst thou: She is my sister? so that I took her to be my wife; now therefore behold thy wife, take
her, and go thy way.' 12,20 And Pharaoh gave men charge concerning him; and they brought him on the way,
and his wife, and all that he had. 13,1 And Abram went up out of Egypt, he, and his wife, and all that he had,
and Lot with him, into the South. 13,2 And Abram was very rich in cattle, in silver, and in gold. 13,3 And he
went on his journeys from the South even to Beth-el, unto the place where his tent had been at the beginning,
between Beth-el and Ai; 13,4 unto the place of the altar, which he had made there at the first; and Abram called
there on the name of God. 13,5 And Lot also, who went with Abram, had flocks, and herds, and tents. 13,6 And
the land was not able to bear them, that they might dwell together; for their substance was great, so that they
could not dwell together. 13,7 And there was a strife between the herdmen of Abram's cattle and the herdmen
of Lot's cattle. And the Canaanite and the Perizzite dwelt then in the land. 13,8 And Abram said unto Lot: 'Let
there be no strife, I pray thee, between me and thee, and between my herdmen and thy herdmen; for we are
brethren. 13,9 Is not the whole land before thee? separate thyself, I pray thee, from me; if thou wilt take the
left hand, then I will go to the right; or if thou take the right hand, then I will go to the left.' 13,10 And Lot lifted
up his eyes, and beheld all the plain of the Jordan, that it was well watered every where, before God destroyed
Sodom and Gomorrah, like the garden of God, like the land of Egypt, as thou goest unto Zoar. 13,11 So Lot
chose him all the plain of the Jordan; and Lot journeyed east; and they separated themselves the one from the
other. 13,12 Abram dwelt in the land of Canaan, and Lot dwelt in the cities of the Plain, and moved his tent as
far as Sodom. 13,13 Now the men of Sodom were wicked and sinners against God exceedingly. 13,14 And God
said unto Abram, after that Lot was separated from him: 'Lift up now thine eyes, and look from the place where
thou art, northward and southward and eastward and westward; 13,15 for all the land which thou seest, to thee
will I give it, and to thy seed for ever. 13,16 And I will make thy seed as the dust of the earth; so that if a man
can number the dust of the earth, then shall thy seed also be numbered. 13,17 Arise, walk through the land in
the length of it and in the breadth of it; for unto thee will I give it.' 13,18 And Abram moved his tent, and came
and dwelt by the terebinths of Mamre, which are in Hebron, and built there an altar unto God. {P}

14,1 And it came to pass in the days of Amraphel king of Shinar, Arioch king of Ellasar, Chedorlaomer king of
Elam, and Tidal king of Goiim, 14,2 that they made war with Bera king of Sodom, and with Birsha king of
Gomorrah, Shinab king of Admah, and Shemeber king of Zeboiim, and the king of Bela--the same is Zoar. 14,3
All these came as allies unto the vale of Siddim--the same is the Salt Sea. 14,4 Twelve years they served
Chedorlaomer, and in the thirteenth year they rebelled. 14,5 And in the fourteenth year came Chedorlaomer
and the kings that were with him, and smote the Rephaim in Ashteroth-karnaim, and the Zuzim in Ham, and
the Emim in Shaveh-kiriathaim, 14,6 and the Horites in their mount Seir, unto El-paran, which is by the
wilderness. 14,7 And they turned back, and came to En-mishpat--the same is Kadesh--and smote all the
country of the Amalekites, and also the Amorites, that dwelt in Hazazon-tamar. 14,8 And there went out the
king of Sodom, and the king of Gomorrah, and the king of Admah, and the king of Zeboiim, and the king of
Bela--the same is Zoar; and they set the battle in array against them in the vale of Siddim; 14,9 against

Chedorlaomer king of Elam, and Tidal king of Goiim, and Amraphel king of Shinar, and Arioch king of Ellasar; four kings against the five. 14,10 Now the vale of Siddim was full of slime pits; and the kings of Sodom and Gomorrah fled, and they fell there, and they that remained fled to the mountain. 14,11 And they took all the goods of Sodom and Gomorrah, and all their victuals, and went their way. 14,12 And they took Lot, Abram's brother's son, who dwelt in Sodom, and his goods, and departed. 14,13 And there came one that had escaped, and told Abram the Hebrew--now he dwelt by the terebinths of Mamre the Amorite, brother of Eshcol, and brother of Aner; and these were confederate with Abram. 14,14 And when Abram heard that his brother was taken captive, he led forth his trained men, born in his house, three hundred and eighteen, and pursued as far as Dan. 14,15 And he divided himself against them by night, he and his servants, and smote them, and pursued them unto Hobah, which is on the left hand of Damascus. 14,16 And he brought back all the goods, and also brought back his brother Lot, and his goods, and the women also, and the people. 14,17 And the king of Sodom went out to meet him, after his return from the slaughter of Chedorlaomer and the kings that were with him, at the vale of Shaveh--the same is the King's Vale. 14,18 And Melchizedek king of Salem brought forth bread and wine; and he was priest of God the Most High. 14,19 And he blessed him, and said: 'Blessed be Abram of God Most High, Maker of heaven and earth; 14,20 and blessed be God the Most High, who hath delivered thine enemies into thy hand.' And he gave him a tenth of all. 14,21 And the king of Sodom said unto Abram: 'Give me the persons, and take the goods to thyself.' 14,22 And Abram said to the king of Sodom: 'I have lifted up my hand unto God, God Most High, Maker of heaven and earth, 14,23 that I will not take a thread nor a shoe-latchet nor aught that is thine, lest thou shouldest say: I have made Abram rich; 14,24 save only that which the young men have eaten, and the portion of the men which went with me, Aner, Eshcol, and Mamre, let them take their portion.' {S} 15,1 After these things the word of God came unto Abram in a vision, saying: 'Fear not, Abram, I am thy shield, thy reward shall be exceeding great.' 15,2 And Abram said: 'O Lord GOD, what wilt Thou give me, seeing I go hence childless, and he that shall be possessor of my house is Eliezer of Damascus?' 15,3 And Abram said: 'Behold, to me Thou hast given no seed, and, lo, one born in my house is to be mine heir.' 15,4 And, behold, the word of God came unto him, saying: 'This man shall not be thine heir; but he that shall come forth out of thine own bowels shall be thine heir.' 15,5 And He brought him forth abroad, and said: 'Look now toward heaven, and count the stars, if thou be able to count them'; and He said unto him: 'So shall thy seed be.' 15,6 And he believed in God; and He counted it to him for righteousness. 15,7 And He said unto him: 'I am God that brought thee out of Ur of the Chaldees, to give thee this land to inherit it.' 15,8 And he said: 'O Lord GOD, whereby shall I know that I shall inherit it?' 15,9 And He said unto him: 'Take Me a heifer of three years old, and a she-goat of three years old, and a ram of three years old, and a turtle-dove, and a young pigeon.' 15,10 And he took him all these, and divided them in the midst, and laid each half over against the other; but the birds divided he not. 15,11 And the birds of prey came down upon the carcasses, and Abram drove them away. 15,12 And it came to pass, that, when the sun was going down, a deep sleep fell upon Abram; and, lo, a dread, even a great darkness, fell upon him. 15,13 And He said unto Abram: 'Know of a surety that thy seed shall be a stranger in a land that is not theirs, and shall serve them; and they shall afflict them four hundred years; 15,14 and also that nation, whom they shall serve, will I judge; and afterward shall they come out with great substance. 15,15 But thou shalt go to thy fathers in peace; thou shalt be buried in a good old age. 15,16 And in the fourth generation they shall come back hither; for the iniquity of the Amorite is not yet full.' 15,17 And it came to pass, that, when the sun went down, and there was thick darkness, behold a smoking furnace, and a flaming torch that passed between these pieces. 15,18 In that day God made a covenant with Abram, saying: 'Unto thy seed have I given this land, from the river of Egypt unto the great river, the river Euphrates; 15,19 the Kenite, and the Kenizzite, and the Kadmonite, 15,20 and the Hittite, and the Perizzite, and the Rephaim, 15,21 and the Amorite, and the Canaanite, and the Girgashite, and the Jebusite.' {S} 16,1 Now Sarai Abram's wife bore him no children; and she had a handmaid, an Egyptian, whose name was Hagar. 16,2 And Sarai said unto Abram: 'Behold now, God hath restrained me from bearing; go in, I pray thee, unto my handmaid; it may be that I shall be builded up through her.' And Abram hearkened to the voice of Sarai. 16,3 And Sarai Abram's wife took Hagar the Egyptian, her handmaid, after Abram had dwelt ten years in the land of Canaan, and gave her to Abram her husband to be his wife. 16,4 And he went in unto Hagar, and she conceived; and when she saw that she had conceived, her mistress was despised in her eyes. 16,5 And Sarai said unto Abram: 'My wrong be upon thee: I gave my handmaid into thy bosom; and when she saw that she had conceived, I was despised in her eyes: God judge between me and thee.' 16,6 But Abram said unto Sarai: 'Behold, thy maid is in thy hand; do to her that which is good in thine eyes.' And Sarai dealt harshly with her, and she fled from her face. 16,7 And the angel of God found her by a fountain of water in the wilderness, by the fountain in the way to Shur. 16,8 And he said: 'Hagar, Sarai's handmaid, whence camest thou? and whither goest thou?' And she said: 'I flee from the face of my mistress Sarai.' 16,9 And the angel of God said unto her: 'Return to thy mistress, and submit thyself under her hands.' 16,10 And the angel of God said unto her: 'I will greatly multiply thy seed, that it shall not be numbered for multitude. 16,11 And the angel of God said unto her: 'Behold, thou art with child, and shalt bear a son; and thou shalt call his name Ishmael, because God hath heard thy affliction. 16,12 And he shall be a wild ass of a man: his hand shall be against every man, and every man's hand against him; and he shall dwell in the face of all his brethren.' 16,13 And she called the name of God that spoke unto her, Thou art a God of seeing; for she said: 'Have I even here seen Him that seeth

Me?' 16,14 Wherefore the well was called 'Beer-lahai-roi; behold, it is between Kadesh and Bered. 16,15 And Hagar bore Abram a son; and Abram called the name of his son, whom Hagar bore, Ishmael. 16,16 And Abram was fourscore and six years old, when Hagar bore Ishmael to Abram. {S} 17,1 And when Abram was ninety years old and nine, God appeared to Abram, and said unto him: 'I am God Almighty; walk before Me, and be thou wholehearted. 17,2 And I will make My covenant between Me and thee, and will multiply thee exceedingly.' 17,3 And Abram fell on his face; and God talked with him, saying: 17,4 'As for Me, behold, My covenant is with thee, and thou shalt be the father of a multitude of nations. 17,5 Neither shall thy name any more be called Abram, but thy name shall be Abraham; for the father of a multitude of nations have I made thee. 17,6 And I will make thee exceeding fruitful, and I will make nations of thee, and kings shall come out of thee. 17,7 And I will establish My covenant between Me and thee and thy seed after thee throughout their generations for an everlasting covenant, to be a God unto thee and to thy seed after thee. 17,8 And I will give unto thee, and to thy seed after thee, the land of thy sojournings, all the land of Canaan, for an everlasting possession; and I will be their God.' 17,9 And God said unto Abraham: 'And as for thee, thou shalt keep My covenant, thou, and thy seed after thee throughout their generations. 17,10 This is My covenant, which ye shall keep, between Me and you and thy seed after thee: every male among you shall be circumcised. 17,11 And ye shall be circumcised in the flesh of your foreskin; and it shall be a token of a covenant betwixt Me and you. 17,12 And he that is eight days old shall be circumcised among you, every male throughout your generations, he that is born in the house, or bought with money of any foreigner, that is not of thy seed. 17,13 He that is born in thy house, and he that is bought with thy money, must needs be circumcised; and My covenant shall be in your flesh for an everlasting covenant. 17,14 And the uncircumcised male who is not circumcised in the flesh of his foreskin, that soul shall be cut off from his people; he hath broken My covenant.' {S} 17,15 And God said unto Abraham: 'As for Sarai thy wife, thou shalt not call her name Sarai, but Sarah shall her name be. 17,16 And I will bless her, and moreover I will give thee a son of her; yea, I will bless her, and she shall be a mother of nations; kings of peoples shall be of her.' 17,17 Then Abraham fell upon his face, and laughed, and said in his heart: 'Shall a child be born unto him that is a hundred years old? and shall Sarah, that is ninety years old, bear?' 17,18 And Abraham said unto God: 'Oh that Ishmael might live before Thee!' 17,19 And God said: 'Nay, but Sarah thy wife shall bear thee a son; and thou shalt call his name Isaac; and I will establish My covenant with him for an everlasting covenant for his seed after him. 17,20 And as for Ishmael, I have heard thee; behold, I have blessed him, and will make him fruitful, and will multiply him exceedingly; twelve princes shall he beget, and I will make him a great nation. 17,21 But My covenant will I establish with Isaac, whom Sarah shall bear unto thee at this set time in the next year.' 17,22 And He left off talking with him, and God went up from Abraham. 17,23 And Abraham took Ishmael his son, and all that were born in his house, and all that were bought with his money, every male among the men of Abraham's house, and circumcised the flesh of their foreskin in the selfsame day, as God had said unto him. 17,24 And Abraham was ninety years old and nine, when he was circumcised in the flesh of his foreskin. 17,25 And Ishmael his son was thirteen years old, when he was circumcised in the flesh of his foreskin. 17,26 In the selfsame day was Abraham circumcised, and Ishmael his son. 17,27 And all the men of his house, those born in the house, and those bought with money of a foreigner, were circumcised with him. {P}

English Haftara of Lech Lecha

Isaiah

40,27 Why sayest thou, O Jacob, and speakest, O Israel: 'My way is hid from God, and my right is passed over from my God'? 40,28 Hast thou not known? hast thou not heard that the everlasting God, God, the Creator of the ends of the earth, fainteth not, neither is weary? His discernment is past searching out. 40,29 He giveth power to the faint; and to him that hath no might He increaseth strength. 40,30 Even the youths shall faint and be weary, and the young men shall utterly fall; 40,31 But they that wait for God shall renew their strength; they shall mount up with wings as eagles; they shall run, and not be weary; they shall walk, and not faint. {S} 41,1 Keep silence before Me, O islands, and let the peoples renew their strength; let them draw near, then let them speak; let us come near together to judgment. 41,2 Who hath raised up one from the east, at whose steps victory attendeth? He giveth nations before him, and maketh him rule over kings; his sword maketh them as the dust, his bow as the driven stubble. 41,3 He pursueth them, and passeth on safely; the way with his feet he treadeth not. 41,4 Who hath wrought and done it? He that called the generations from the beginning. I, God, who am the first, and with the last am the same. 41,5 The isles saw, and feared; the ends of the earth trembled; they drew near, and came. 41,6 They helped every one his neighbour; and every one said to his brother: 'Be of good courage.' 41,7 So the carpenter encouraged the goldsmith, and he that smootheth with the hammer him that smiteth the anvil, saying of the soldering: 'It is good'; and he fastened it with nails, that it should not be moved. {S} 41,8 But thou, Israel, My servant, Jacob whom I have chosen, the seed of Abraham My friend; 41,9 Thou whom I have taken hold of from the ends of the earth, and called thee from the uttermost parts thereof, and said unto thee: 'Thou art My servant, I have chosen thee and not cast thee away'; 41,10 Fear thou not, for I am with thee, be not dismayed, for I am thy God; I strengthen thee, yea, I help thee; yea,

I uphold thee with My victorious right hand. 41,11 Behold, all they that were incensed against thee shall be ashamed and confounded; they that strove with thee shall be as nothing, and shall perish. 41,12 Thou shalt seek them, and shalt not find them, even them that contended with thee; they that warred against thee shall be as nothing, and as a thing of nought. 41,13 For I God thy God hold thy right hand, who say unto thee: 'Fear not, I help thee.' {S} 41,14 Fear not, thou worm Jacob, and ye men of Israel; I help thee, saith God, and thy Redeemer, the Holy One of Israel. 41,15 Behold, I make thee a new threshing-sledge having sharp teeth; thou shalt thresh the mountains, and beat them small, and shalt make the hills as chaff. 41,16 Thou shalt fan them, and the wind shall carry them away, and the whirlwind shall scatter them; and thou shalt rejoice in God, thou shalt glory in the Holy One of Israel. {S}

English Portion of Vayera

18,1 And God appeared unto him by the terebinths of Mamre, as he sat in the tent door in the heat of the day; 18,2 and he lifted up his eyes and looked, and, lo, three men stood over against him; and when he saw them, he ran to meet them from the tent door, and bowed down to the earth, 18,3 and said: 'My lord, if now I have found favour in thy sight, pass not away, I pray thee, from thy servant. 18,4 Let now a little water be fetched, and wash your feet, and recline yourselves under the tree. 18,5 And I will fetch a morsel of bread, and stay ye your heart; after that ye shall pass on; forasmuch as ye are come to your servant.' And they said: 'So do, as thou hast said.' 18,6 And Abraham hastened into the tent unto Sarah, and said: 'Make ready quickly three measures of fine meal, knead it, and make cakes.' 18,7 And Abraham ran unto the herd, and fetched a calf tender and good, and gave it unto the servant; and he hastened to dress it. 18,8 And he took curd, and milk, and the calf which he had dressed, and set it before them; and he stood by them under the tree, and they did eat. 18,9 And they said unto him: 'Where is Sarah thy wife?' And he said: 'Behold, in the tent.' 18,10 And He said: 'I will certainly return unto thee when the season cometh round; and, lo, Sarah thy wife shall have a son.' And Sarah heard in the tent door, which was behind him.-- 18,11 Now Abraham and Sarah were old, and well stricken in age; it had ceased to be with Sarah after the manner of women.-- 18,12 And Sarah laughed within herself, saying: 'After I am waxed old shall I have pleasure, my lord being old also?' 18,13 And God said unto Abraham: 'Wherefore did Sarah laugh, saying: Shall I of a surety bear a child, who am old? 18,14 Is any thing too hard for God. At the set time I will return unto thee, when the season cometh round, and Sarah shall have a son.' 18,15 Then Sarah denied, saying: 'I laughed not'; for she was afraid. And He said: 'Nay; but thou didst laugh.' 18,16 And the men rose up from thence, and looked out toward Sodom; and Abraham went with them to bring them on the way. 18,17 And God said: 'Shall I hide from Abraham that which I am doing; 18,18 seeing that Abraham shall surely become a great and mighty nation, and all the nations of the earth shall be blessed in him? 18,19 For I have known him, to the end that he may command his children and his household after him, that they may keep the way of God, to do righteousness and justice; to the end that God may bring upon Abraham that which He hath spoken of him.' 18,20 And God said: 'Verily, the cry of Sodom and Gomorrah is great, and, verily, their sin is exceeding grievous. 18,21 I will go down now, and see whether they have done altogether according to the cry of it, which is come unto Me; and if not, I will know.' 18,22 And the men turned from thence, and went toward Sodom; but Abraham stood yet before God. 18,23 And Abraham drew near, and said: 'Wilt Thou indeed sweep away the righteous with the wicked? 18,24 Peradventure there are fifty righteous within the city; wilt Thou indeed sweep away and not forgive the place for the fifty righteous that are therein? 18,25 That be far from Thee to do after this manner, to slay the righteous with the wicked, that so the righteous should be as the wicked; that be far from Thee; shall not the Judge of all the earth do justly?' 18,26 And God said: 'If I find in Sodom fifty righteous within the city, then I will forgive all the place for their sake.' 18,27 And Abraham answered and said: 'Behold now, I have taken upon me to speak unto God, who am but dust and ashes. 18,28 Peradventure there shall lack five of the fifty righteous; wilt Thou destroy all the city for lack of five?' And He said: 'I will not destroy it, if I find there forty and five.' 18,29 And he spoke unto Him yet again, and said: 'Peradventure there shall be forty found there.' And He said: 'I will not do it for the forty's sake.' 18,30 And he said: 'Oh, let not God be angry, and I will speak. Peradventure there shall thirty be found there.' And He said: 'I will not do it, if I find thirty there.' 18,31 And he said: 'Behold now, I have taken upon me to speak unto God. Peradventure there shall be twenty found there.' And He said: 'I will not destroy it for the twenty's sake.' 18,32 And he said: 'Oh, let not God be angry, and I will speak yet but this once. Peradventure ten shall be found there.' And He said: 'I will not destroy it for the ten's sake.' 18,33 And God went His way, as soon as He had left off speaking to Abraham; and Abraham returned unto his place. 19,1 And the two angels came to Sodom at even; and Lot sat in the gate of Sodom; and Lot saw them, and rose up to meet them; and he fell down on his face to the earth; 19,2 and he said: 'Behold now, my lords, turn aside, I pray you, into your servant's house, and tarry all night, and wash your feet, and ye shall rise up early, and go on your way.' And they said: 'Nay; but we will abide in the broad place all night.' 19,3 And he urged them greatly; and they turned in unto him, and

entered into his house; and he made them a feast, and did bake unleavened bread, and they did eat. 19,4 But
before they lay down, the men of the city, even the men of Sodom, compassed the house round, both young
and old, all the people from every quarter. 19,5 And they called unto Lot, and said unto him: 'Where are the
men that came in to thee this night? bring them out unto us, that we may know them.' 19,6 And Lot went out
unto them to the door, and shut the door after him. 19,7 And he said: 'I pray you, my brethren, do not so
wickedly. 19,8 Behold now, I have two daughters that have not known man; let me, I pray you, bring them out
unto you, and do ye to them as is good in your eyes; only unto these men do nothing; forasmuch as they are
come under the shadow of my roof.' 19,9 And they said: 'Stand back.' And they said: 'This one fellow came in
to sojourn, and he will needs play the judge; now will we deal worse with thee, than with them.' And they
pressed sore upon the man, even Lot, and drew near to break the door. 19,10 But the men put forth their hand,
and brought Lot into the house to them, and the door they shut. 19,11 And they smote the men that were at
the door of the house with blindness, both small and great; so that they wearied themselves to find the door.
19,12 And the men said unto Lot: 'Hast thou here any besides? son-in-law, and thy sons, and thy daughters,
and whomsoever thou hast in the city; bring them out of the place; 19,13 for we will destroy this place, because
the cry of them is waxed great before God; and God hath sent us to destroy it.' 19,14 And Lot went out, and
spoke unto his sons-in-law, who married his daughters, and said: 'Up, get you out of this place; for God will
destroy the city.' But he seemed unto his sons-in-law as one that jested. 19,15 And when the morning arose,
then the angels hastened Lot, saying: 'Arise, take thy wife, and thy two daughters that are here; lest thou be
swept away in the iniquity of the city.' 19,16 But he lingered; and the men laid hold upon his hand, and upon
the hand of his wife, and upon the hand of his two daughters; God being merciful unto him. And they brought
him forth, and set him without the city. 19,17 And it came to pass, when they had brought them forth abroad,
that he said: 'Escape for thy life; look not behind thee, neither stay thou in all the Plain; escape to the mountain,
lest thou be swept away.' 19,18 And Lot said unto them: 'Oh, not so, my lord; 19,19 behold now, thy servant
hath found grace in thy sight, and thou hast magnified thy mercy, which thou hast shown unto me in saving my
life; and I cannot escape to the mountain, lest the evil overtake me, and I die. 19,20 Behold now, this city is
near to flee unto, and it is a little one; oh, let me escape thither--is it not a little one?--and my soul shall live.'
19,21 And he said unto him: 'See, I have accepted thee concerning this thing also, that I will not overthrow the
city of which thou hast spoken. 19,22 Hasten thou, escape thither; for I cannot do any thing till thou be come
thither.'--Therefore the name of the city was called Zoar.-- 19,23 The sun was risen upon the earth when Lot
came unto Zoar. 19,24 Then God caused to rain upon Sodom and upon Gomorrah brimstone and fire from God
out of heaven; 19,25 and He overthrow those cities, and all the Plain, and all the inhabitants of the cities, and
that which grew upon the ground. 19,26 But his wife looked back from behind him, and she became a pillar
of salt. 19,27 And Abraham got up early in the morning to the place where he had stood before God. 19,28 And
he looked out toward Sodom and Gomorrah, and toward all the land of the Plain, and beheld, and, lo, the
smoke of the land went up as the smoke of a furnace. 19,29 And it came to pass, when God destroyed the cities
of the Plain, that God remembered Abraham, and sent Lot out of the midst of the overthrow, when He overthrew
the cities in which Lot dwelt. 19,30 And Lot went up out of Zoar, and dwelt in the mountain, and his two
daughters with him; for he feared to dwell in Zoar; and he dwelt in a cave, he and his two daughters. 19,31 And
the first-born said unto the younger: 'Our father is old, and there is not a man in the earth to come in unto us
after the manner of all the earth. 19,32 Come, let us make our father drink wine, and we will lie with him, that
we may preserve seed of our father.' 19,33 And they made their father drink wine that night. And the first-born
went in, and lay with her father; and he knew not when she lay down, nor when she arose. 19,34 And it came
to pass on the morrow, that the first-born said unto the younger: 'Behold, I lay yesternight with my father. Let
us make him drink wine this night also; and go thou in, and lie with him, that we may preserve seed of our
father.' 19,35 And they made their father drink wine that night also. And the younger arose, and lay with him;
and he knew not when she lay down, nor when she arose. 19,36 Thus were both the daughters of Lot with child
by their father. 19,37 And the first-born bore a son, and called his name Moab--the same is the father of the
Moabites unto this day. 19,38 And the younger, she also bore a son, and called his name Ben-ammi--the same
is the father of the children of Ammon unto this day. {S} 20,1 And Abraham journeyed from thence toward the
land of the South, and dwelt between Kadesh and Shur; and he sojourned in Gerar. 20,2 And Abraham said of
Sarah his wife: 'She is my sister.' And Abimelech king of Gerar sent, and took Sarah. 20,3 But God came to
Abimelech in a dream of the night, and said to him: 'Behold, thou shalt die, because of the woman whom thou
hast taken; for she is a man's wife.' 20,4 Now Abimelech had not come near her; and he said: 'LORD, wilt Thou
slay even a righteous nation? 20,5 Said he not himself unto me: She is my sister? and she, even she herself
said: He is my brother. In the simplicity of my heart and the innocency of my hands have I done this.' 20,6 And
God said unto him in the dream: 'Yea, I know that in the simplicity of thy heart thou hast done this, and I also
withheld thee from sinning against Me. Therefore suffered I thee not to touch her. 20,7 Now therefore restore
the man's wife; for he is a prophet, and he shall pray for thee, and thou shalt live; and if thou restore her not,
know thou that thou shalt surely die, thou, and all that are thine.' 20,8 And Abimelech rose early in the morning,
and called all his servants, and told all these things in their ears; and the men were sore afraid. 20,9 Then
Abimelech called Abraham, and said unto him: 'What hast thou done unto us? and wherein have I sinned
against thee, that thou hast brought on me and on my kingdom a great sin? thou hast done deeds unto me that

ought not to be done.' 20,10 And Abimelech said unto Abraham: 'What sawest thou, that thou hast done this thing?' 20,11 And Abraham said: 'Because I thought: Surely the fear of God is not in this place; and they will slay me for my wife's sake. 20,12 And moreover she is indeed my sister, the daughter of my father, but not the daughter of my mother; and so she became my wife. 20,13 And it came to pass, when God caused me to wander from my father's house, that I said unto her: This is thy kindness which thou shalt show unto me; at every place whither we shall come, say of me: He is my brother.' 20,14 And Abimelech took sheep and oxen, and men-servants and women-servants, and gave them unto Abraham, and restored him Sarah his wife. 20,15 And Abimelech said: 'Behold, my land is before thee: dwell where it pleaseth thee.' 20,16 And unto Sarah he said: 'Behold, I have given thy brother a thousand pieces of silver; behold, it is for thee a covering of the eyes to all that are with thee; and before all men thou art righted.' 20,17 And Abraham prayed unto God; and God healed Abimelech, and his wife, and his maid-servants; and they bore children. 20,18 For God had fast closed up all the wombs of the house of Abimelech, because of Sarah Abraham's wife. {S} 21,1 And God remembered Sarah as He had said, and God did unto Sarah as He had spoken. 21,2 And Sarah conceived, and bore Abraham a son in his old age, at the set time of which God had spoken to him. 21,3 And Abraham called the name of his son that was born unto him, whom Sarah bore to him, Isaac. 21,4 And Abraham circumcised his son Isaac when he was eight days old, as God had commanded him. 21,5 And Abraham was a hundred years old, when his son Isaac was born unto him. 21,6 And Sarah said: 'God hath made laughter for me; every one that heareth will laugh on account of me.' 21,7 And she said: 'Who would have said unto Abraham, that Sarah should give children suck? for I have borne him a son in his old age.' 21,8 And the child grew, and was weaned. And Abraham made a great feast on the day that Isaac was weaned. 21,9 And Sarah saw the son of Hagar the Egyptian, whom she had borne unto Abraham, making sport. 21,10 Wherefore she said unto Abraham: 'Cast out this bondwoman and her son; for the son of this bondwoman shall not be heir with my son, even with Isaac.' 21,11 And the thing was very grievous in Abraham's sight on account of his son. 21,12 And God said unto Abraham: 'Let it not be grievous in thy sight because of the lad, and because of thy bondwoman; in all that Sarah saith unto thee, hearken unto her voice; for in Isaac shall seed be called to thee. 21,13 And also of the son of the bondwoman will I make a nation, because he is thy seed.' 21,14 And Abraham arose up early in the morning, and took bread and a bottle of water, and gave it unto Hagar, putting it on her shoulder, and the child, and sent her away; and she departed, and strayed in the wilderness of Beer-sheba. 21,15 And the water in the bottle was spent, and she cast the child under one of the shrubs. 21,16 And she went, and sat her down over against him a good way off, as it were a bow-shot; for she said: 'Let me not look upon the death of the child.' And she sat over against him, and lifted up her voice, and wept. 21,17 And God heard the voice of the lad; and the angel of God called to Hagar out of heaven, and said unto her: 'What aileth thee, Hagar? fear not; for God hath heard the voice of the lad where he is. 21,18 Arise, lift up the lad, and hold him fast by thy hand; for I will make him a great nation.' 21,19 And God opened her eyes, and she saw a well of water; and she went, and filled the bottle with water, and gave the lad drink. 21,20 And God was with the lad, and he grew; and he dwelt in the wilderness, and became an archer. 21,21 And he dwelt in the wilderness of Paran; and his mother took him a wife out of the land of Egypt. {P}

21,22 And it came to pass at that time, that Abimelech and Phicol the captain of his host spoke unto Abraham, saying: 'God is with thee in all that thou doest. 21,23 Now therefore swear unto me here by God that thou wilt not deal falsely with me, nor with my son, nor with my son's son; but according to the kindness that I have done unto thee, thou shalt do unto me, and to the land wherein thou hast sojourned.' 21,24 And Abraham said: 'I will swear.' 21,25 And Abraham reproved Abimelech because of the well of water, which Abimelech's servants had violently taken away. 21,26 And Abimelech said: 'I know not who hath done this thing; neither didst thou tell me, neither yet heard I of it, but to-day.' 21,27 And Abraham took sheep and oxen, and gave them unto Abimelech; and they two made a covenant. 21,28 And Abraham set seven ewe-lambs of the flock by themselves. 21,29 And Abimelech said unto Abraham: 'What mean these seven ewe-lambs which thou hast set by themselves?' 21,30 And he said: 'Verily, these seven ewe-lambs shalt thou take of my hand, that it may be a witness unto me, that I have digged this well.' 21,31 Wherefore that place was called Beer-sheba; because there they swore both of them. 21,32 So they made a covenant at Beer-sheba; and Abimelech rose up, and Phicol the captain of his host, and they returned into the land of the Philistines. 21,33 And Abraham planted a tamarisk-tree in Beer-sheba, and called there on the name of God, the Everlasting God. 21,34 And Abraham sojourned in the land of the Philistines many days. {P}

22,1 And it came to pass after these things, that God did prove Abraham, and said unto him: 'Abraham'; and he said: 'Here am I.' 22,2 And He said: 'Take now thy son, thine only son, whom thou lovest, even Isaac, and get thee into the land of Moriah; and offer him there for a burnt-offering upon one of the mountains which I will tell thee of.' 22,3 And Abraham rose early in the morning, and saddled his ass, and took two of his young men with him, and Isaac his son; and he cleaved the wood for the burnt-offering, and rose up, and went unto the place of which God had told him. 22,4 On the third day Abraham lifted up his eyes, and saw the place afar off. 22,5 And Abraham said unto his young men: 'Abide ye here with the ass, and I and the lad will go yonder; and we will worship, and come back to you.' 22,6 And Abraham took the wood of the burnt-offering, and laid it upon Isaac his son; and he took in his hand the fire and the knife; and they went both of them together. 22,7 And Isaac spoke unto Abraham his father, and said: 'My father.' And he said: 'Here am I, my son.' And he said: 'Behold

the fire and the wood; but where is the lamb for a burnt-offering?' 22,8 And Abraham said: 'God will provide Himself the lamb for a burnt-offering, my son.' So they went both of them together. 22,9 And they came to the place which God had told him of; and Abraham built the altar there, and laid the wood in order, and bound Isaac his son, and laid him on the altar, upon the wood. 22,10 And Abraham stretched forth his hand, and took the knife to slay his son. 22,11 And the angel of God called unto him out of heaven, and said: 'Abraham, Abraham.' And he said: 'Here am I.' 22,12 And he said: 'Lay not thy hand upon the lad, neither do thou any thing unto him; for now I know that thou art a God-fearing man, seeing thou hast not withheld thy son, thine only son, from Me.' 22,13 And Abraham lifted up his eyes, and looked, and behold behind him a ram caught in the thicket by his horns. And Abraham went and took the ram, and offered him up for a burnt-offering in the stead of his son. 22,14 And Abraham called the name of that place Adonai-jireh; as it is said to this day: 'In the mount where God is seen.' 22,15 And the angel of God called unto Abraham a second time out of heaven, 22,16 and said: 'By Myself have I sworn, saith God, because thou hast done this thing, and hast not withheld thy son, thine only son, 22,17 that in blessing I will bless thee, and in multiplying I will multiply thy seed as the stars of the heaven, and as the sand which is upon the seashore; and thy seed shall possess the gate of his enemies; 22,18 and in thy seed shall all the nations of the earth be blessed; because thou hast hearkened to My voice.' 22,19 So Abraham returned unto his young men, and they rose up and went together to Beer-sheba; and Abraham dwelt at Beer-sheba. {P}

22,20 And it came to pass after these things, that it was told Abraham, saying: 'Behold, Milcah, she also hath borne children unto thy brother Nahor: 22,21 Uz his first-born, and Buz his brother, and Kemuel the father of Aram; 22,22 and Chesed, and Hazo, and Pildash, and Jidlaph, and Bethuel.' 22,23 And Bethuel begot Rebekah; these eight did Milcah bear to Nahor, Abraham's brother. 22,24 And his concubine, whose name was Reumah, she also bore Tebah, and Gaham, and Tahash, and Maacah. {P}

English Haftara of Vayera

2 Kings

2 4,1 Now there cried a certain woman of the wives of the sons of the prophets unto Elisha, saying: 'Thy servant my husband is dead; and thou knowest that thy servant did fear God; and the creditor is come to take unto him my two children to be bondmen.' 2 4,2 And Elisha said unto her: 'What shall I do for thee? tell me; what hast thou in the house?' And she said: 'Thy handmaid hath not any thing in the house, save a pot of oil.' 2 4,3 Then he said: 'Go, borrow thee vessels abroad of all thy neighbours, even empty vessels; borrow not a few. 2 4,4 And thou shalt go in, and shut the door upon thee and upon thy sons, and pour out into all those vessels; and thou shalt set aside that which is full.' 2 4,5 So she went from him, and shut the door upon her and upon her sons; they brought the vessels to her, and she poured out. 2 4,6 And it came to pass, when the vessels were full, that she said unto her son: 'Bring me yet a vessel.' And he said unto her: 'There is not a vessel more.' And the oil stayed. 2 4,7 Then she came and told the man of God. And he said: 'Go, sell the oil, and pay thy debt, and live thou and thy sons of the rest.' {P}

2 4,8 And it fell on a day, that Elisha passed to Shunem, where was a great woman; and she constrained him to eat bread. And so it was, that as oft as he passed by, he turned in thither to eat bread. 2 4,9 And she said unto her husband: 'Behold now, I perceive that this is a holy man of God, that passeth by us continually. 2 4,10 Let us make, I pray thee, a little chamber on the roof; and let us set for him there a bed, and a table, and a stool, and a candlestick; and it shall be, when he cometh to us, that he shall turn in thither.' 2 4,11 And it fell on a day, that he came thither, and he turned into the upper chamber and lay there. 2 4,12 And he said to Gehazi his servant: 'Call this Shunammite.' And when he had called her, she stood before him. 2 4,13 And he said unto him: 'Say now unto her: Behold, thou hast been careful for us with all this care; what is to be done for thee? wouldest thou be spoken for to the king, or to the captain of the host?' And she answered: 'I dwell among mine own people.' 2 4,14 And he said: 'What then is to be done for her?' And Gehazi answered: 'Verily she hath no son, and her husband is old.' 2 4,15 And he said: 'Call her.' And when he had called her, she stood in the door. 2 4,16 And he said: 'At this season, when the time cometh round, thou shalt embrace a son.' And she said: 'Nay, my lord, thou man of God, do not lie unto thy handmaid.' 2 4,17 And the woman conceived, and bore a son at that season, when the time came round, as Elisha had said unto her. 2 4,18 And when the child was grown, it fell on a day, that he went out to his father to the reapers. 2 4,19 And he said unto his father: 'My head, my head.' And he said to his servant: 'Carry him to his mother.' 2 4,20 And when he had taken him, and brought him to his mother, he sat on her knees till noon, and then died. 2 4,21 And she went up, and laid him on the bed of the man of God, and shut the door upon him, and went out. 2 4,22 And she called unto her husband, and said: 'Send me, I pray thee, one of the servants, and one of the asses, that I may run to the man of God, and come back.' 2 4,23 And he said: Wherefore wilt thou go to him today? it is neither new moon nor sabbath.' And she said: 'It shall be well.' 2

English Portion of Chayei Sarah

23,1 And the life of Sarah was a hundred and seven and twenty years; these were the years of the life of Sarah.
23,2 And Sarah died in Kiriatharba--the same is Hebron--in the land of Canaan; and Abraham came to mourn
for Sarah, and to weep for her. 23,3 And Abraham rose up from before his dead, and spoke unto the children
of Heth, saying: 23,4 'I am a stranger and a sojourner with you: give me a possession of a burying-place with
you, that I may bury my dead out of my sight.' 23,5 And the children of Heth answered Abraham, saying unto
him: 23,6 'Hear us, my lord: thou art a mighty prince among us; in the choice of our sepulchres bury thy dead;
none of us shall withhold from thee his sepulchre, but that thou mayest bury thy dead.' 23,7 And Abraham rose
up, and bowed down to the people of the land, even to the children of Heth. 23,8 And he spoke with them,
saying: 'If it be your mind that I should bury my dead out of my sight, hear me, and entreat for me to Ephron
the son of Zohar, 23,9 that he may give me the cave of Machpelah, which he hath, which is in the end of his
field; for the full price let him give it to me in the midst of you for a possession of a burying-place.' 23,10 Now
Ephron was sitting in the midst of the children of Heth; and Ephron the Hittite answered Abraham in the hearing
of the children of Heth, even of all that went in at the gate of his city, saying: 23,11 'Nay, my lord, hear me: the
field give I thee, and the cave that is therein, I give it thee; in the presence of the sons of my people give I it
thee; bury thy dead.' 23,12 And Abraham bowed down before the people of the land. 23,13 And he spoke unto
Ephron in the hearing of the people of the land, saying: 'But if thou wilt, I pray thee, hear me: I will give the price
of the field; take it of me, and I will bury my dead there.' 23,14 And Ephron answered Abraham, saying unto
him: 23,15 'My lord, hearken unto me: a piece of land worth four hundred shekels of silver, what is that betwixt
me and thee? bury therefore thy dead.' 23,16 And Abraham hearkened unto Ephron; and Abraham weighed
to Ephron the silver, which he had named in the hearing of the children of Heth, four hundred shekels of silver,
current money with the merchant. 23,17 So the field of Ephron, which was in Machpelah, which was before
Mamre, the field, and the cave which was therein, and all the trees that were in the field, that were in all the
border thereof round about, were made sure 23,18 unto Abraham for a possession in the presence of the
children of Heth, before all that went in at the gate of his city. 23,19 And after this, Abraham buried Sarah his
wife in the cave of the field of Machpelah before Mamre--the same is Hebron--in the land of Canaan. 23,20
And the field, and the cave that is therein, were made sure unto Abraham for a possession of a burying-place
by the children of Heth. {S} 24,1 And Abraham was old, well stricken in age; and God had blessed Abraham in
all things. 24,2 And Abraham said unto his servant, the elder of his house, that ruled over all that he had: 'Put,
I pray thee, thy hand under my thigh. 24,3 And I will make thee swear by God, the God of heaven and the God
of the earth, that thou shalt not take a wife for my son of the daughters of the Canaanites, among whom I dwell.
24,4 But thou shalt go unto my country, and to my kindred, and take a wife for my son, even for Isaac.' 24,5
And the servant said unto him: 'Peradventure the woman will not be willing to follow me unto this land; must I
needs bring thy son back unto the land from whence thou camest?' 24,6 And Abraham said unto him: 'Beware
thou that thou bring not my son back thither. 24,7 God, the God of heaven, who took me from my father's
house, and from the land of my nativity, and who spoke unto me, and who swore unto me, saying: Unto thy
seed will I give this land; He will send His angel before thee, and thou shalt take a wife for my son from thence.
24,8 And if the woman be not willing to follow thee, then thou shalt be clear from this my oath; only thou shalt
not bring my son back thither.' 24,9 And the servant put his hand under the thigh of Abraham his master, and
swore to him concerning this matter. 24,10 And the servant took ten camels, of the camels of his master, and
departed; having all goodly things of his master's in his hand; and he arose, and went to Aram-naharaim, unto
the city of Nahor. 24,11 And he made the camels to kneel down without the city by the well of water at the time
of evening, the time that women go out to draw water. 24,12 And he said: 'O LORD, the God of my master
Abraham, send me, I pray Thee, good speed this day, and show kindness unto my master Abraham. 24,13
Behold, I stand by the fountain of water; and the daughters of the men of the city come out to draw water. 24,14
So let it come to pass, that the damsel to whom I shall say: Let down thy pitcher, I pray thee, that I may drink;
and she shall say: Drink, and I will give thy camels drink also; let the same be she that Thou hast appointed for
Thy servant, even for Isaac; and thereby shall I know that Thou hast shown kindness unto my master.' 24,15
And it came to pass, before he had done speaking, that, behold, Rebekah came out, who was born to Bethuel
the son of Milcah, the wife of Nahor, Abraham's brother, with her pitcher upon her shoulder. 24,16 And the
damsel was very fair to look upon, a virgin, neither had any man known her; and she went down to the fountain,
and filled her pitcher, and came up. 24,17 And the servant ran to meet her, and said: 'Give me to drink, I pray
thee, a little water of thy pitcher.' 24,18 And she said: 'Drink, my lord'; and she hastened, and let down her
pitcher upon her hand, and gave him drink. 24,19 And when she had done giving him drink, she said: 'I will
draw for thy camels also, until they have done drinking.' 24,20 And she hastened, and emptied her pitcher into
the trough, and ran again unto the well to draw, and drew for all his camels. 24,21 And the man looked
stedfastly on her; holding his peace, to know whether God had made his journey prosperous or not. 24,22 And
it came to pass, as the camels had done drinking, that the man took a golden ring of half a shekel weight, and
two bracelets for her hands of ten shekels weight of gold; 24,23 and said: 'Whose daughter art thou? tell me, I
pray thee. Is there room in thy father's house for us to lodge in?' 24,24 And she said unto him: 'I am the

daughter of Bethuel the son of Milcah, whom she bore unto Nahor.' 24,25 She said moreover unto him: 'We
have both straw and provender enough, and room to lodge in.' 24,26 And the man bowed his head, and
prostrated himself before God. 24,27 And he said: 'Blessed be God, the God of my master Abraham, who hath
not forsaken His mercy and His truth toward my master; as for me, God hath led me in the way to the house of
my master's brethren.' 24,28 And the damsel ran, and told her mother's house according to these words.
24,29 And Rebekah had a brother, and his name was Laban; and Laban ran out unto the man, unto the
fountain. 24,30 And it came to pass, when he saw the ring, and the bracelets upon his sister's hands, and when
he heard the words of Rebekah his sister, saying: 'Thus spoke the man unto me,' that he came unto the man;
and, behold, he stood by the camels at the fountain. 24,31 And he said: 'Come in, thou blessed of God;
wherefore standest thou without? for I have cleared the house, and made room for the camels.' 24,32 And the
man came into the house, and he ungirded the camels; and he gave straw and provender for the camels, and
water to wash his feet and the feet of the men that were with him. 24,33 And there was set food before him to
eat; but he said: 'I will not eat, until I have told mine errand.' And he said: 'Speak on.' 24,34 And he said: 'I am
Abraham's servant. 24,35 And God hath blessed my master greatly; and he is become great; and He hath given
him flocks and herds, and silver and gold, and men-servants and maid-servants, and camels and asses. 24,36
And Sarah my master's wife bore a son to my master when she was old; and unto him hath he given all that he
hath. 24,37 And my master made me swear, saying: Thou shalt not take a wife for my son of the daughters of
the Canaanites, in whose land I dwell. 24,38 But thou shalt go unto my father's house, and to my kindred, and
take a wife for my son. 24,39 And I said unto my master: Peradventure the woman will not follow me. 24,40
And he said unto me: God, before whom I walk, will send His angel with thee, and prosper thy way; and thou
shalt take a wife for my son of my kindred, and of my father's house; 24,41 then shalt thou be clear from my
oath, when thou comest to my kindred; and if they give her not to thee, thou shalt be clear from my oath. 24,42
And I came this day unto the fountain, and said: O LORD, the God of my master Abraham, if now Thou do
prosper my way which I go: 24,43 behold, I stand by the fountain of water; and let it come to pass, that the
maiden that cometh forth to draw, to whom I shall say: Give me, I pray thee, a little water from thy pitcher to
drink; 24,44 and she shall say to me: Both drink thou, and I will also draw for thy camels; let the same be the
woman whom God hath appointed for my master's son. 24,45 And before I had done speaking to my heart,
behold, Rebekah came forth with her pitcher on her shoulder; and she went down unto the fountain, and drew.
And I said unto her: Let me drink, I pray thee. 24,46 And she made haste, and let down her pitcher from her
shoulder, and said: Drink, and I will give thy camels drink also. So I drank, and she made the camels drink also.
24,47 And I asked her, and said: Whose daughter art thou? And she said: The daughter of Bethuel, Nahor's
son, whom Milcah bore unto him. And I put the ring upon her nose, and the bracelets upon her hands. 24,48
And I bowed my head, and prostrated myself before God, and blessed God, the God of my master Abraham,
who had led me in the right way to take my master's brother's daughter for his son. 24,49 And now if ye will
deal kindly and truly with my master, tell me; and if not, tell me; that I may turn to the right hand, or to the left.'
24,50 Then Laban and Bethuel answered and said: 'The thing proceedeth from God; we cannot speak unto
thee bad or good. 24,51 Behold, Rebekah is before thee, take her, and go, and let her be thy master's son's
wife, as God hath spoken.' 24,52 And it came to pass, that, when Abraham's servant heard their words, he
bowed himself down to the earth unto God. 24,53 And the servant brought forth jewels of silver, and jewels of
gold, and raiment, and gave them to Rebekah; he gave also to her brother and to her mother precious things.
24,54 And they did eat and drink, he and the men that were with him, and tarried all night; and they rose up
in the morning, and he said: 'Send me away unto my master.' 24,55 And her brother and her mother said: 'Let
the damsel abide with us a few days, at the least ten; after that she shall go.' 24,56 And he said unto them:
'Delay me not, seeing God hath prospered my way; send me away that I may go to my master.' 24,57 And they
said: 'We will call the damsel, and inquire at her mouth.' 24,58 And they called Rebekah, and said unto her:
'Wilt thou go with this man?' And she said: 'I will go.' 24,59 And they sent away Rebekah their sister, and her
nurse, and Abraham's servant, and his men. 24,60 And they blessed Rebekah, and said unto her: 'Our sister,
be thou the mother of thousands of ten thousands, and let thy seed possess the gate of those that hate them.'
24,61 And Rebekah arose, and her damsels, and they rode upon the camels, and followed the man. And the
servant took Rebekah, and went his way. 24,62 And Isaac came from the way of Beer-lahai-roi; for he dwelt in
the land of the South. 24,63 And Isaac went out to meditate in the field at the eventide; and he lifted up his
eyes, and saw, and, behold, there were camels coming. 24,64 And Rebekah lifted up her eyes, and when she
saw Isaac, she alighted from the camel. 24,65 And she said unto the servant: 'What man is this that walketh in
the field to meet us?' And the servant said: 'It is my master.' And she took her veil, and covered herself. 24,66
And the servant told Isaac all the things that he had done. 24,67 And Isaac brought her into his mother Sarah's
tent, and took Rebekah, and she became his wife; and he loved her. And Isaac was comforted for his mother.
{P}

25,1 And Abraham took another wife, and her name was Keturah. 25,2 And she bore him Zimran, and
Jokshan, and Medan, and Midian, and Ishbak, and Shuah. 25,3 And Jokshan begot Sheba, and Dedan. And
the sons of Dedan were Asshurim, and Letushim, and Leummim. 25,4 And the sons of Midian: Ephah, and
Epher, and Hanoch, and Abida, and Eldaah. All these were the children of Keturah. 25,5 And Abraham gave
all that he had unto Isaac. 25,6 But unto the sons of the concubines, that Abraham had, Abraham gave gifts;

and he sent them away from Isaac his son, while he yet lived, eastward, unto the east country. 25,7 And these are the days of the years of Abraham's life which he lived, a hundred threescore and fifteen years. 25,8 And Abraham expired, and died in a good old age, an old man, and full of years; and was gathered to his people. 25,9 And Isaac and Ishmael his sons buried him in the cave of Machpelah, in the field of Ephron the son of Zohar the Hittite, which is before Mamre; 25,10 the field which Abraham purchased of the children of Heth; there was Abraham buried, and Sarah his wife. 25,11 And it came to pass after the death of Abraham, that God blessed Isaac his son; and Isaac dwelt by Beer-lahai-roi. {P}
25,12 Now these are the generations of Ishmael, Abraham's son, whom Hagar the Egyptian, Sarah's handmaid, bore unto Abraham. 25,13 And these are the names of the sons of Ishmael, by their names, according to their generations: the first-born of Ishmael, Nebaioth; and Kedar, and Adbeel, and Mibsam, 25,14 and Mishma, and Dumah, and Massa; 25,15 Hadad, and Tema, Jetur, Naphish, and Kedem; 25,16 these are the sons of Ishmael, and these are their names, by their villages, and by their encampments; twelve princes according to their nations. 25,17 And these are the years of the life of Ishmael, a hundred and thirty and seven years; and he expired and died; and was gathered unto his people. 25,18 And they dwelt from Havilah unto Shur that is before Egypt, as thou goest toward Asshur: over against all his brethren he did settle. {P}

English Haftara of Chayei Sarah

1 Kings

1 1,1 Now king David was old and stricken in years; and they covered him with clothes, but he could get no heat. 1 1,2 Wherefore his servants said unto him: 'Let there be sought for my lord the king a young virgin; and let her stand before the king, and be a companion unto him; and let her lie in thy bosom, that my lord the king may get heat.' 1 1,3 So they sought for a fair damsel throughout all the borders of Israel, and found Abishag the Shunammite, and brought her to the king. 1 1,4 And the damsel was very fair; and she became a companion unto the king, and ministered to him; but the king knew her not. 1 1,5 Now Adonijah the son of Haggith exalted himself, saying: 'I will be king'; and he prepared him chariots and horsemen, and fifty men to run before him. 1 1,6 And his father had not grieved him all his life in saying: 'Why hast thou done so?' and he was also a very goodly man; and he was born after Absalom. 1 1,7 And he conferred with Joab the son of Zeruiah, and with Abiathar the priest; and they following Adonijah helped him. 1 1,8 But Zadok the priest, and Benaiah the son of Jehoiada, and Nathan the prophet, and Shimei, and Rei, and the mighty men that belonged to David, were not with Adonijah. 1 1,9 And Adonijah slew sheep and oxen and fatlings by the stone of Zoheleth, which is beside En-rogel; and he called all his brethren the king's sons, and all the men of Judah the king's servants; 1 1,10 but Nathan the prophet, and Benaiah, and the mighty men, and Solomon his brother, he called not. 1 1,11 Then Nathan spoke unto Bath-sheba the mother of Solomon, saying: 'Hast thou not heard that Adonijah the son of Haggith doth reign, and David our lord knoweth it not? 1 1,12 Now therefore come, let me, I pray thee, give thee counsel, that thou mayest save thine own life, and the life of thy son Solomon. 1 1,13 Go and get thee in unto king David, and say unto him: Didst not thou, my lord, O king, swear unto thy handmaid, saying: Assuredly Solomon thy son shall reign after me, and he shall sit upon my throne? why then doth Adonijah reign? 1 1,14 Behold, while thou yet talkest there with the king, I also will come in after thee, and confirm thy words.' 1 1,15 And Bath-sheba went in unto the king into the chamber.--Now the king was very old; and Abishag the Shunammite ministered unto the king.-- 1 1,16 And Bath-sheba bowed, and prostrated herself unto the king. And the king said: 'What wouldest thou?' 1 1,17 And she said unto him: 'My lord, thou didst swear by God thy God unto thy handmaid: Assuredly Solomon thy son shall reign after me, and he shall sit upon my throne. 1 1,18 And now, behold, Adonijah reigneth; and thou, my lord the king, knowest it not. 1 1,19 And he hath slain oxen and fatlings and sheep in abundance, {P}

and hath called all the sons of the king, and Abiathar, the priest, and Joab the captain of the host; but Solomon thy servant hath he not called. 1 1,20 And thou, my lord the king, the eyes of all Israel are upon thee, that thou shouldest tell them who shall sit on the throne of my lord the king after him. 1 1,21 Otherwise it will come to pass, when my lord the king shall sleep with his fathers, that I and my son Solomon shall be counted offenders.' 1 1,22 And, lo, while she yet talked with the king, Nathan the prophet came in. 1 1,23 And they told the king, saying: 'Behold Nathan the prophet.' And when he was come in before the king, he bowed down before the king with his face to the ground. 1 1,24 And Nathan said: 'My lord, O king, hast thou said: Adonijah shall reign after me, and he shall sit upon my throne? 1 1,25 For he is gone down this day, and hath slain oxen and fatlings and sheep in abundance, and hath called all the king's sons, and the captains of the host, and Abiathar the priest; and, behold, they eat and drink before him, and say: Long live king Adonijah. 1 1,26 But me, even me thy servant, and Zadok the priest, and Benaiah the son of Jehoiada, and thy servant Solomon hath he not called. 1 1,27 Is this thing done by my lord the king, and thou hast not declared unto thy servant who should sit on the throne of my lord the king after him?' {S} 1 1,28 Then king David answered and said: 'Call me Bath-sheba.' And she came into the king's presence, and stood before the king. 1 1,29 And the king swore and said: 'As God liveth, who hath redeemed my soul out of all adversity, 1 1,30 verily as I swore unto thee by God, the

God of Israel, saying: Assuredly Solomon thy son shall reign after me, and he shall sit upon my throne in my stead; verily so will I do this day.' 1 1,31 Then Bath-sheba bowed with her face to the earth, and prostrated herself to the king, and said: 'Let my lord king David live for ever.' {P}

English Portion of Toldot

25,19 And these are the generations of Isaac, Abraham's son: Abraham begot Isaac. 25,20 And Isaac was forty years old when he took Rebekah, the daughter of Bethuel the Aramean, of Paddan-aram, the sister of Laban the Aramean, to be his wife. 25,21 And Isaac entreated God for his wife, because she was barren; and God let Himself be entreated of him, and Rebekah his wife conceived. 25,22 And the children struggled together within her; and she said: 'If it be so, wherefore do I live?' And she went to inquire of God. 25,23 And God said unto her: Two nations are in thy womb, and two peoples shall be separated from thy bowels; and the one people shall be stronger than the other people; and the elder shall serve the younger. 25,24 And when her days to be delivered were fulfilled, behold, there were twins in her womb. 25,25 And the first came forth ruddy, all over like a hairy mantle; and they called his name Esau. 25,26 And after that came forth his brother, and his hand had hold on Esau's heel; and his name was called Jacob. And Isaac was threescore years old when she bore them. 25,27 And the boys grew; and Esau was a cunning hunter, a man of the field; and Jacob was a quiet man, dwelling in tents. 25,28 Now Isaac loved Esau, because he did eat of his venison; and Rebekah loved Jacob. 25,29 And Jacob sod pottage; and Esau came in from the field, and he was faint. 25,30 And Esau said to Jacob: 'Let me swallow, I pray thee, some of this red, red pottage; for I am faint.' Therefore was his name called Edom. 25,31 And Jacob said: 'Sell me first thy birthright.' 25,32 And Esau said: 'Behold, I am at the point to die; and what profit shall the birthright do to me?' 25,33 And Jacob said: 'Swear to me first'; and he swore unto him; and he sold his birthright unto Jacob. 25,34 And Jacob gave Esau bread and pottage of lentils; and he did eat and drink, and rose up, and went his way. So Esau despised his birthright. {P}

26,1 And there was a famine in the land, beside the first famine that was in the days of Abraham. And Isaac went unto Abimelech king of the Philistines unto Gerar. 26,2 And God appeared unto him, and said: 'Go not down unto Egypt; dwell in the land which I shall tell thee of. 26,3 Sojourn in this land, and I will be with thee, and will bless thee; for unto thee, and unto thy seed, I will give all these lands, and I will establish the oath which I swore unto Abraham thy father; 26,4 and I will multiply thy seed as the stars of heaven, and will give unto thy seed all these lands; and by thy seed shall all the nations of the earth bless themselves; 26,5 because that Abraham hearkened to My voice, and kept My charge, My commandments, My statutes, and My laws.' 26,6 And Isaac dwelt in Gerar. 26,7 And the men of the place asked him of his wife; and he said: 'She is my sister'; for he feared to say: 'My wife'; 'lest the men of the place should kill me for Rebekah, because she is fair to look upon.' 26,8 And it came to pass, when he had been there a long time, that Abimelech king of the Philistines looked out at a window, and saw, and, behold, Isaac was sporting with Rebekah his wife. 26,9 And Abimelech called Isaac, and said: 'Behold, of a surety she is thy wife; and how saidst thou: She is my sister?' And Isaac said unto him: 'Because I said: Lest I die because of her.' 26,10 And Abimelech said: 'What is this thou hast done unto us? one of the people might easily have lain with thy wife, and thou wouldest have brought guiltiness upon us.' 26,11 And Abimelech charged all the people, saying: 'He that toucheth this man or his wife shall surely be put to death.' 26,12 And Isaac sowed in that land, and found in the same year a hundredfold; and God blessed him. 26,13 And the man waxed great, and grew more and more until he became very great. 26,14 And he had possessions of flocks, and possessions of herds, and a great household; and the Philistines envied him. 26,15 Now all the wells which his father's servants had digged in the days of Abraham his father, the Philistines had stopped them, and filled them with earth. 26,16 And Abimelech said unto Isaac: 'Go from us; for thou art much mightier than we.' 26,17 And Isaac departed thence, and encamped in the valley of Gerar, and dwelt there. 26,18 And Isaac digged again the wells of water, which they had digged in the days of Abraham his father; for the Philistines had stopped them after the death of Abraham; and he called their names after the names by which his father had called them. 26,19 And Isaac's servants digged in the valley, and found there a well of living water. 26,20 And the herdmen of Gerar strove with Isaac's herdmen, saying: 'The water is ours.' And he called the name of the well Esek; because they contended with him. 26,21 And they digged another well, and they strove for that also. And he called the name of it Sitnah. 26,22 And he removed from thence, and digged another well; and for that they strove not. And he called the name of it Rehoboth; and he said: 'For now God hath made room for us, and we shall be fruitful in the land.' 26,23 And he went up from thence to Beer-sheba. 26,24 And God appeared unto him the same night, and said: 'I am the God of Abraham thy father. Fear not, for I am with thee, and will bless thee, and multiply thy seed for My servant Abraham's sake.' 26,25 And he builded an altar there, and called upon the name of God, and pitched his tent there; and there Isaac's servants digged a well. 26,26 Then Abimelech went to him from Gerar, and Ahuzzath his friend, and Phicol the captain of his host. 26,27 And Isaac said unto them: 'Wherefore are ye come unto me, seeing ye hate me, and have sent me away from you?' 26,28 And they said: 'We saw plainly that God was with thee; and we said: Let there now be an oath betwixt us, even betwixt us and thee, and let us make a covenant with thee; 26,29 that thou wilt do us no hurt, as we have not touched thee, and as we have done unto thee nothing

but good, and have sent thee away in peace; thou art now the blessed of God.' 26,30 And he made them a feast, and they did eat and drink. 26,31 And they rose up betimes in the morning, and swore one to another; and Isaac sent them away, and they departed from him in peace. 26,32 And it came to pass the same day, that Isaac's servants came, and told him concerning the well which they had digged, and said unto him: 'We have found water.' 26,33 And he called it Shibah. Therefore the name of the city is Beer-sheba unto this day. {S} 26,34 And when Esau was forty years old, he took to wife Judith the daughter of Beeri the Hittite, and Basemath the daughter of Elon the Hittite. 26,35 And they were a bitterness of spirit unto Isaac and to Rebekah. {S} 27,1 And it came to pass, that when Isaac was old, and his eyes were dim, so that he could not see, he called Esau his elder son, and said unto him: 'My son'; and he said unto him: 'Here am I.' 27,2 And he said: 'Behold now, I am old, I know not the day of my death. 27,3 Now therefore take, I pray thee, thy weapons, thy quiver and thy bow, and go out to the field, and take me venison; 27,4 and make me savoury food, such as I love, and bring it to me, that I may eat; that my soul may bless thee before I die.' 27,5 And Rebekah heard when Isaac spoke to Esau his son. And Esau went to the field to hunt for venison, and to bring it. 27,6 And Rebekah spoke unto Jacob her son, saying: 'Behold, I heard thy father speak unto Esau thy brother, saying: 27,7 Bring me venison, and make me savoury food, that I may eat, and bless thee before God before my death. 27,8 Now therefore, my son, hearken to my voice according to that which I command thee. 27,9 Go now to the flock, and fetch me from thence two good kids of the goats; and I will make them savoury food for thy father, such as he loveth; 27,10 and thou shalt bring it to thy father, that he may eat, so that he may bless thee before his death.' 27,11 And Jacob said to Rebekah his mother: 'Behold, Esau my brother is a hairy man, and I am a smooth man. 27,12 My father peradventure will feel me, and I shall seem to him as a mocker; and I shall bring a curse upon me, and not a blessing.' 27,13 And his mother said unto him: 'Upon me be thy curse, my son; only hearken to my voice, and go fetch me them.' 27,14 And he went, and fetched, and brought them to his mother; and his mother made savoury food, such as his father loved. 27,15 And Rebekah took the choicest garments of Esau her elder son, which were with her in the house, and put them upon Jacob her younger son. 27,16 And she put the skins of the kids of the goats upon his hands, and upon the smooth of his neck. 27,17 And she gave the savoury food and the bread, which she had prepared, into the hand of her son Jacob. 27,18 And he came unto his father, and said: 'My father'; and he said: 'Here am I; who art thou, my son?' 27,19 And Jacob said unto his father: 'I am Esau thy first-born; I have done according as thou badest me. Arise, I pray thee, sit and eat of my venison, that thy soul may bless me.' 27,20 And Isaac said unto his son: 'How is it that thou hast found it so quickly, my son?' And he said: 'Because God thy God sent me good speed.' 27,21 And Isaac said unto Jacob: 'Come near, I pray thee, that I may feel thee, my son, whether thou be my very son Esau or not.' 27,22 And Jacob went near unto Isaac his father; and he felt him, and said: 'The voice is the voice of Jacob, but the hands are the hands of Esau.' 27,23 And he discerned him not, because his hands were hairy, as his brother Esau's hands; so he blessed him. 27,24 And he said: 'Art thou my very son Esau?' And he said: 'I am.' 27,25 And he said: 'Bring it near to me, and I will eat of my son's venison, that my soul may bless thee.' And he brought it near to him, and he did eat; and he brought him wine, and he drank. 27,26 And his father Isaac said unto him: 'Come near now, and kiss me, my son.' 27,27 And he came near, and kissed him. And he smelled the smell of his raiment, and blessed him, and said: See, the smell of my son is as the smell of a field which God hath blessed. 27,28 So God give thee of the dew of heaven, and of the fat places of the earth, and plenty of corn and wine. 27,29 Let peoples serve thee, and nations bow down to thee. Be lord over thy brethren, and let thy mother's sons bow down to thee. Cursed be every one that curseth thee, and blessed be every one that blesseth thee. 27,30 And it came to pass, as soon as Isaac had made an end of blessing Jacob, and Jacob was yet scarce gone out from the presence of Isaac his father, that Esau his brother came in from his hunting. 27,31 And he also made savoury food, and brought it unto his father; and he said unto his father: 'Let my father arise, and eat of his son's venison, that thy soul may bless me.' 27,32 And Isaac his father said unto him: 'Who art thou?' And he said: 'I am thy son, thy first-born, Esau.' 27,33 And Isaac trembled very exceedingly, and said: 'Who then is he that hath taken venison, and brought it me, and I have eaten of all before thou camest, and have blessed him? yea, and he shall be blessed.' 27,34 When Esau heard the words of his father, he cried with an exceeding great and bitter cry, and said unto his father: 'Bless me, even me also, O my father.' 27,35 And he said: 'Thy brother came with guile, and hath taken away thy blessing.' 27,36 And he said: 'Is not he rightly named Jacob? for he hath supplanted me these two times: he took away my birthright; and, behold, now he hath taken away my blessing.' And he said: 'Hast thou not reserved a blessing for me?' 27,37 And Isaac answered and said unto Esau: 'Behold, I have made him thy lord, and all his brethren have I given to him for servants; and with corn and wine have I sustained him; and what then shall I do for thee, my son?' 27,38 And Esau said unto his father: 'Hast thou but one blessing, my father? bless me, even me also, O my father.' And Esau lifted up his voice, and wept. 27,39 And Isaac his father answered and said unto him: Behold, of the fat places of the earth shall be thy dwelling, and of the dew of heaven from above; 27,40 And by thy sword shalt thou live, and thou shalt serve thy brother; and it shall come to pass when thou shalt break loose, that thou shalt shake his yoke from off thy neck. 27,41 And Esau hated Jacob because of the blessing wherewith his father blessed him. And Esau said in his heart: 'Let the days of mourning for my father be at hand; then will I slay my brother Jacob.' 27,42 And the words of Esau her elder son were told to Rebekah; and she sent and called Jacob her younger son, and said unto him: 'Behold, thy brother Esau, as touching thee, doth comfort himself,

purposing to kill thee. 27,43 Now therefore, my son, hearken to my voice; and arise, flee thou to Laban my brother to Haran; 27,44 and tarry with him a few days, until thy brother's fury turn away; 27,45 until thy brother's anger turn away from thee, and he forget that which thou hast done to him; then I will send, and fetch thee from thence; why should I be bereaved of you both in one day?' 27,46 And Rebekah said to Isaac: 'I am weary of my life because of the daughters of Heth. If Jacob take a wife of the daughters of Heth, such as these, of the daughters of the land, what good shall my life do me?' 28,1 And Isaac called Jacob, and blessed him, and charged him, and said unto him: 'Thou shalt not take a wife of the daughters of Canaan. 28,2 Arise, go to Paddan-aram, to the house of Bethuel thy mother's father; and take thee a wife from thence of the daughters of Laban thy mother's brother. 28,3 And God Almighty bless thee, and make thee fruitful, and multiply thee, that thou mayest be a congregation of peoples; 28,4 and give thee the blessing of Abraham, to thee, and to thy seed with thee; that thou mayest inherit the land of thy sojournings, which God gave unto Abraham.' 28,5 And Isaac sent away Jacob; and he went to Paddan-aram unto Laban, son of Bethuel the Aramean, the brother of Rebekah, Jacob's and Esau's mother. 28,6 Now Esau saw that Isaac had blessed Jacob and sent him away to Paddan-aram, to take him a wife from thence; and that as he blessed him he gave him a charge, saying: 'Thou shalt not take a wife of the daughters of Canaan'; 28,7 and that Jacob hearkened to his father and his mother, and was gone to Paddan-aram; 28,8 and Esau saw that the daughters of Canaan pleased not Isaac his father; 28,9 so Esau went unto Ishmael, and took unto the wives that he had Mahalath the daughter of Ishmael Abraham's son, the sister of Nebaioth, to be his wife. {S}

English Haftara of Toldot

Malachi

1,1 The burden of the word of God to Israel by Malachi. 1,2 I have loved you, saith God. Yet ye say: 'Wherein hast Thou loved us?' Was not Esau Jacob's brother? saith God; yet I loved Jacob; 1,3 But Esau I hated, and made his mountains a desolation, and gave his heritage to the jackals of the wilderness. 1,4 Whereas Edom saith: 'We are beaten down, but we will return and build the waste places'; thus saith God of hosts: They shall build, but I will throw down; and they shall be called The border of wickedness, and The people whom God execrateth for ever. 1,5 And your eyes shall see, and ye shall say: 'God is great beyond the border of Israel.' 1,6 A son honoureth his father, and a servant his master; if then I be a father, where is My honour? and if I be a master, where is My fear? saith God of hosts unto you, O priests, that despise My name. And ye say: 'Wherein have we despised Thy name?' 1,7 Ye offer polluted bread upon Mine altar. And ye say: 'Wherein have we polluted thee?' In that ye say: 'The table of God is contemptible.' 1,8 And when ye offer the blind for sacrifice, is it no evil! And when ye offer the lame and sick, is it no evil! Present it now unto thy governor; will he be pleased with thee? or will he accept thy person? saith God of hosts. 1,9 And now, I pray you, entreat the favour of God that He may be gracious unto us!--this hath been of your doing.--will He accept any of your persons? saith God of hosts. 1,10 Oh that there were even one among you that would shut the doors, that ye might not kindle fire on Mine altar in vain! I have no pleasure in you, saith God of hosts, neither will I accept an offering at your hand. 1,11 For from the rising of the sun even unto the going down of the same My name is great among the nations; and in every place offerings are presented unto My name, even pure oblations; for My name is great among the nations, saith God of hosts. 1,12 But ye profane it, in that ye say: 'The table of God is polluted, and the fruit thereof, even the food thereof, is contemptible.' 1,13 Ye say also: 'Behold, what a weariness is it!' and ye have snuffed at it, saith God of hosts; and ye have brought that which was taken by violence, and the lame, and the sick; thus ye bring the offering; should I accept this of your hand? saith God. {S} 1,14 But cursed be he that dealeth craftily, whereas he hath in his flock a male, and voweth, and sacrificeth unto God a blemished thing; for I am a great King, saith God of hosts, and My name is feared among the nations. 2,1 And now, this commandment is for you, O ye priests. 2,2 If ye will not hearken, and if ye will not lay it to heart, to give glory unto My name, saith God of hosts, then will I send the curse upon you, and I will curse your blessings; yea, I curse them, because ye do not lay it to heart. 2,3 Behold, I will rebuke the seed for your hurt, and will spread dung upon your faces, even the dung of your sacrifices; and ye shall be taken away unto it. 2,4 Know then that I have sent this commandment unto you, that My covenant might be with Levi, saith God of hosts. 2,5 My covenant was with him of life and peace, and I gave them to him, and of fear, and he feared Me, and was afraid of My name. 2,6 The law of truth was in his mouth, and unrighteousness was not found in his lips; he walked with Me in peace and uprightness, and did turn many away from iniquity. 2,7 For the priest's lips should keep knowledge, and they should seek the law at his mouth; for he is the messenger of God of hosts. 2,8 But ye are turned aside out of the way; ye have caused many to stumble in the law; ye have corrupted the covenant of Levi, saith God of hosts. 2,9 Therefore have I also made you contemptible and base before all the people, according as ye have not kept My ways, but have had respect of persons in the law. {P}

2,10 Have we not all one father? Hath not one God created us? Why do we deal treacherously every man against his brother, profaning the covenant of our fathers? 2,11 Judah hath dealt treacherously, and an abomination is committed in Israel and in Jerusalem; for Judah hath profaned the holiness of God which He loveth, and hath married the daughter of a strange god. 2,12 May God cut off to the man that doeth this, him that calleth and

him that answereth out of the tents of Jacob, and him that offereth an offering unto God of hosts. {P}
2,13 And this further ye do: ye cover the altar of God with tears, with weeping, and with sighing, insomuch that He regardeth not the offering any more, neither receiveth it with good will at your hand. 2,14 Yet ye say: 'Wherefore?' Because God hath been witness between thee and the wife of thy youth, against whom thou hast dealt treacherously, though she is thy companion, and the wife of thy covenant. 2,15 And not one hath done so who had exuberance of spirit! For what seeketh the one? a seed given of God. Therefore take heed to your spirit, and let none deal treacherously against the wife of his youth. 2,16 For I hate putting away, saith God, the God of Israel, and him that covereth his garment with violence, saith God of hosts; therefore take heed to your spirit, that ye deal not treacherously. {P}
2,17 Ye have wearied God with your words. Yet ye say: 'Wherein have we wearied Him?' In that ye say: 'Every one that doeth evil is good in the sight of God, and He delighteth in them; or where is the God of justice?'

English Portion of Vayetze

28,10 And Jacob went out from Beer-sheba, and went toward Haran. 28,11 And he lighted upon the place, and tarried there all night, because the sun was set; and he took one of the stones of the place, and put it under his head, and lay down in that place to sleep. 28,12 And he dreamed, and behold a ladder set up on the earth, and the top of it reached to heaven; and behold the angels of God ascending and descending on it. 28,13 And, behold, God stood beside him, and said: 'I am God, the God of Abraham thy father, and the God of Isaac. The land whereon thou liest, to thee will I give it, and to thy seed. 28,14 And thy seed shall be as the dust of the earth, and thou shalt spread abroad to the west, and to the east, and to the north, and to the south. And in thee and in thy seed shall all the families of the earth be blessed. 28,15 And, behold, I am with thee, and will keep thee whithersoever thou goest, and will bring thee back into this land; for I will not leave thee, until I have done that which I have spoken to thee of.' 28,16 And Jacob awaked out of his sleep, and he said: 'Surely God is in this place; and I knew it not.' 28,17 And he was afraid, and said: 'How full of awe is this place! this is none other than the house of God, and this is the gate of heaven.' 28,18 And Jacob rose up early in the morning, and took the stone that he had put under his head, and set it up for a pillar, and poured oil upon the top of it. 28,19 And he called the name of that place Beth-el, but the name of the city was Luz at the first. 28,20 And Jacob vowed a vow, saying: 'If God will be with me, and will keep me in this way that I go, and will give me bread to eat, and raiment to put on, 28,21 so that I come back to my father's house in peace, then shall God be my God, 28,22 and this stone, which I have set up for a pillar, shall be God's house; and of all that Thou shalt give me I will surely give the tenth unto Thee.' 29,1 Then Jacob went on his journey, and came to the land of the children of the east. 29,2 And he looked, and behold a well in the field, and, lo, three flocks of sheep lying there by it.--For out of that well they watered the flocks. And the stone upon the well's mouth was great. 29,3 And thither were all the flocks gathered; and they rolled the stone from the well's mouth, and watered the sheep, and put the stone back upon the well's mouth in its place.-- 29,4 And Jacob said unto them: 'My brethren, whence are ye?' And they said: 'Of Haran are we.' 29,5 And he said unto them: 'Know ye Laban the son of Nahor?' And they said: 'We know him.' 29,6 And he said unto them: 'Is it well with him?' And they said: 'It is well; and, behold, Rachel his daughter cometh with the sheep.' 29,7 And he said: 'Lo, it is yet high day, neither is it time that the cattle should be gathered together; water ye the sheep, and go and feed them.' 29,8 And they said: 'We cannot, until all the flocks be gathered together, and they roll the stone from the well's mouth; then we water the sheep.' 29,9 While he was yet speaking with them, Rachel came with her father's sheep; for she tended them. 29,10 And it came to pass, when Jacob saw Rachel the daughter of Laban his mother's brother, and the sheep of Laban his mother's brother, that Jacob went near, and rolled the stone from the well's mouth, and watered the flock of Laban his mother's brother. 29,11 And Jacob kissed Rachel, and lifted up his voice, and wept. 29,12 And Jacob told Rachel that he was her father's brother, and that he was Rebekah's son; and she ran and told her father. 29,13 And it came to pass, when Laban heard the tidings of Jacob his sister's son, that he ran to meet him, and embraced him, and kissed him, and brought him to his house. And he told Laban all these things. 29,14 And Laban said to him: 'Surely thou art my bone and my flesh.' And he abode with him the space of a month. 29,15 And Laban said unto Jacob: 'Because thou art my brother, shouldest thou therefore serve me for nought? tell me, what shall thy wages be?' 29,16 Now Laban had two daughters: the name of the elder was Leah, and the name of the younger was Rachel. 29,17 And Leah's eyes were weak; but Rachel was of beautiful form and fair to look upon. 29,18 And Jacob loved Rachel; and he said: 'I will serve thee seven years for Rachel thy younger daughter.' 29,19 And Laban said: 'It is better that I give her to thee, than that I should give her to another man; abide with me.' 29,20 And Jacob served seven years for Rachel; and they seemed unto him but a few days, for the love he had to her. 29,21 And Jacob said unto Laban: 'Give me my wife, for my days are filled, that I may go in unto her.' 29,22 And Laban gathered together all the men of the place, and made a feast. 29,23 And it came to pass in the evening, that he took Leah his daughter, and brought her to him; and he went in unto her. 29,24 And Laban gave Zilpah his handmaid unto his daughter Leah for a handmaid. 29,25 And it came to pass in the morning that, behold, it was Leah; and he said to Laban: 'What is this thou hast done unto me? did not I serve with thee for Rachel? wherefore then hast thou beguiled me?'

29,26 And Laban said: 'It is not so done in our place, to give the younger before the first-born. 29,27 Fulfil the
week of this one, and we will give thee the other also for the service which thou shalt serve with me yet seven
other years.' 29,28 And Jacob did so, and fulfilled her week; and he gave him Rachel his daughter to wife.
29,29 And Laban gave to Rachel his daughter Bilhah his handmaid to be her handmaid. 29,30 And he went
in also unto Rachel, and he loved Rachel more than Leah, and served with him yet seven other years. 29,31
And God saw that Leah was hated, and he opened her womb; but Rachel was barren. 29,32 And Leah
conceived, and bore a son, and she called his name Reuben; for she said: 'Because God hath looked upon my
affliction; for now my husband will love me.' 29,33 And she conceived again, and bore a son; and said:
'Because God hath heard that I am hated, He hath therefore given me this son also.' And she called his name
Simeon. 29,34 And she conceived again, and bore a son; and said: 'Now this time will my husband be joined
unto me, because I have borne him three sons.' Therefore was his name called Levi. 29,35 And she conceived
again, and bore a son; and she said: 'This time will I praise God.' Therefore she called his name Judah; and
she left off bearing. 30,1 And when Rachel saw that she bore Jacob no children, Rachel envied her sister; and
she said unto Jacob: 'Give me children, or else I die.' 30,2 And Jacob's anger was kindled against Rachel; and
he said: 'Am I in God's stead, who hath withheld from thee the fruit of the womb?' 30,3 And she said: 'Behold
my maid Bilhah, go in unto her; that she may bear upon my knees, and I also may be builded up through her.'
30,4 And she gave him Bilhah her handmaid to wife; and Jacob went in unto her. 30,5 And Bilhah conceived,
and bore Jacob a son. 30,6 And Rachel said: 'God hath judged me, and hath also heard my voice, and hath
given me a son.' Therefore called she his name Dan. 30,7 And Bilhah Rachel's handmaid conceived again, and
bore Jacob a second son. 30,8 And Rachel said: 'With mighty wrestlings have I wrestled with my sister, and
have prevailed.' And she called his name Naphtali. 30,9 When Leah saw that she had left off bearing, she took
Zilpah her handmaid, and gave her to Jacob to wife. 30,10 And Zilpah Leah's handmaid bore Jacob a son.
30,11 And Leah said: 'Fortune is come!' And she called his name Gad. 30,12 And Zilpah Leah's handmaid
bore Jacob a second son. 30,13 And Leah said: 'Happy am I! for the daughters will call me happy.' And she
called his name Asher. 30,14 And Reuben went in the days of wheat harvest, and found mandrakes in the field,
and brought them unto his mother Leah. Then Rachel said to Leah: 'Give me, I pray thee, of thy son's
mandrakes.' 30,15 And she said unto her: 'Is it a small matter that thou hast taken away my husband? and
wouldest thou take away my son's mandrakes also?' And Rachel said: 'Therefore he shall lie with thee to-night
for thy son's mandrakes.' 30,16 And Jacob came from the field in the evening, and Leah went out to meet him,
and said: 'Thou must come in unto me; for I have surely hired thee with my son's mandrakes.' And he lay with
her that night. 30,17 And God hearkened unto Leah, and she conceived, and bore Jacob a fifth son. 30,18 And
Leah said: 'God hath given me my hire, because I gave my handmaid to my husband. And she called his name
Issachar. 30,19 And Leah conceived again, and bore a sixth son to Jacob. 30,20 And Leah said: 'God hath
endowed me with a good dowry; now will my husband dwell with me, because I have borne him six sons.' And
she called his name Zebulun. 30,21 And afterwards she bore a daughter, and called her name Dinah. 30,22
And God remembered Rachel, and God hearkened to her, and opened her womb. 30,23 And she conceived,
and bore a son, and said: 'God hath taken away my reproach.' 30,24 And she called his name Joseph, saying:
'God add to me another son.' 30,25 And it came to pass, when Rachel had borne Joseph, that Jacob said unto
Laban: 'Send me away, that I may go unto mine own place, and to my country. 30,26 Give me my wives and
my children for whom I have served thee, and let me go; for thou knowest my service wherewith I have served
thee.' 30,27 And Laban said unto him: 'If now I have found favour in thine eyes--I have observed the signs, and
God hath blessed me for thy sake.' 30,28 And he said: 'Appoint me thy wages, and I will give it.' 30,29 And he
said unto him: 'Thou knowest how I have served thee, and how thy cattle have fared with me. 30,30 For it was
little which thou hadst before I came, and it hath increased abundantly; and God hath blessed thee
whithersoever I turned. And now when shall I provide for mine own house also?' 30,31 And he said: 'What shall
I give thee?' And Jacob said: 'Thou shalt not give me aught; if thou wilt do this thing for me, I will again feed thy
flock and keep it. 30,32 I will pass through all thy flock to-day, removing from thence every speckled and
spotted one, and every dark one among the sheep, and the spotted and speckled among the goats; and of such
shall be my hire. 30,33 So shall my righteousness witness against me hereafter, when thou shalt come to look
over my hire that is before thee: every one that is not speckled and spotted among the goats, and dark among
the sheep, that if found with me shall be counted stolen.' 30,34 And Laban said: 'Behold, would it might be
according to thy word.' 30,35 And he removed that day the he-goats that were streaked and spotted, and all
the she-goats that were speckled and spotted, every one that had white in it, and all the dark ones among the
sheep, and gave them into the hand of his sons. 30,36 And he set three days' journey betwixt himself and
Jacob. And Jacob fed the rest of Laban's flocks. 30,37 And Jacob took him rods of fresh poplar, and of the
almond and of the plane-tree; and peeled white streaks in them, making the white appear which was in the
rods. 30,38 And he set the rods which he had peeled over against the flocks in the gutters in the watering-
troughs where the flocks came to drink; and they conceived when they came to drink. 30,39 And the flocks
conceived at the sight of the rods, and the flocks brought forth streaked, speckled, and spotted. 30,40 And
Jacob separated the lambs--he also set the faces of the flocks toward the streaked and all the dark in the flock
of Laban--and put his own droves apart, and put them not unto Laban's flock. 30,41 And it came to pass,
whensoever the stronger of the flock did conceive, that Jacob laid the rods before the eyes of the flock in the

gutters, that they might conceive among the rods; 30,42 but when the flock were feeble, he put them not in; so the feebler were Laban's, and the stronger Jacob's. 30,43 And the man increased exceedingly, and had large flocks, and maid-servants and men-servants, and camels and asses. 31,1 And he heard the words of Laban's sons, saying: 'Jacob hath taken away all that was our father's; and of that which was our father's hath he gotten all this wealth.' 31,2 And Jacob beheld the countenance of Laban, and, behold, it was not toward him as beforetime. 31,3 And God said unto Jacob: 'Return unto the land of thy fathers, and to thy kindred; and I will be with thee.' 31,4 And Jacob sent and called Rachel and Leah to the field unto his flock, 31,5 and said unto them: 'I see your father's countenance, that it is not toward me as beforetime; but the God of my father hath been with me. 31,6 And ye know that with all my power I have served your father. 31,7 And your father hath mocked me, and changed my wages ten times; but God suffered him not to hurt me. 31,8 If he said thus: The speckled shall be thy wages; then all the flock bore speckled; and if he said thus: The streaked shall be thy wages; then bore all the flock streaked. 31,9 Thus God hath taken away the cattle of your father, and given them to me. 31,10 And it came to pass at the time that the flock conceived, that I lifted up mine eyes, and saw in a dream, and, behold, the he-goats which leaped upon the flock were streaked, speckled, and grizzled. 31,11 And the angel of God said unto me in the dream: Jacob; and I said: Here am I. 31,12 And he said: Lift up now thine eyes, and see, all the he-goats which leap upon the flock are streaked, speckled, and grizzled; for I have seen all that Laban doeth unto thee. 31,13 I am the God of Beth-el, where thou didst anoint a pillar, where thou didst vow a vow unto Me. Now arise, get thee out from this land, and return unto the land of thy nativity.' 31,14 And Rachel and Leah answered and said unto him: 'Is there yet any portion or inheritance for us in our father's house? 31,15 Are we not accounted by him strangers? for he hath sold us, and hath also quite devoured our price. 31,16 For all the riches which God hath taken away from our father, that is ours and our children's. Now then, whatsoever God hath said unto thee, do.' 31,17 Then Jacob rose up, and set his sons and his wives upon the camels; 31,18 and he carried away all his cattle, and all his substance which he had gathered, the cattle of his getting, which he had gathered in Paddan-aram, to go to Isaac his father unto the land of Canaan. 31,19 Now Laban was gone to shear his sheep. And Rachel stole the teraphim that were her father's. 31,20 And Jacob outwitted Laban the Aramean, in that he told him not that he fled. 31,21 So he fled with all that he had; and he rose up, and passed over the River, and set his face toward the mountain of Gilead. 31,22 And it was told Laban on the third day that Jacob was fled. 31,23 And he took his brethren with him, and pursued after him seven days' journey; and he overtook him in the mountain of Gilead. 31,24 And God came to Laban the Aramean in a dream of the night, and said unto him: 'Take heed to thyself that thou speak not to Jacob either good or bad.' 31,25 And Laban came up with Jacob. Now Jacob had pitched his tent in the mountain; and Laban with his brethren pitched in the mountain of Gilead. 31,26 And Laban said to Jacob: 'What hast thou done, that thou hast outwitted me, and carried away my daughters as though captives of the sword? 31,27 Wherefore didst thou flee secretly, and outwit me; and didst not tell me, that I might have sent thee away with mirth and with songs, with tabret and with harp; 31,28 and didst not suffer me to kiss my sons and my daughters? now hast thou done foolishly. 31,29 It is in the power of my hand to do you hurt; but the God of your father spoke unto me yesternight, saying: Take heed to thyself that thou speak not to Jacob either good or bad. 31,30 And now that thou art surely gone, because thou sore longest after thy father's house, wherefore hast thou stolen my gods?' 31,31 And Jacob answered and said to Laban: 'Because I was afraid; for I said: Lest thou shouldest take thy daughters from me by force. 31,32 With whomsoever thou findest thy gods, he shall not live; before our brethren discern thou what is thine with me, and take it to thee.'--For Jacob knew not that Rachel had stolen them.-- 31,33 And Laban went into Jacob's tent, and into Leah's tent, and into the tent of the two maid-servants; but he found them not. And he went out of Leah's tent, and entered into Rachel's tent. 31,34 Now Rachel had taken the teraphim, and put them in the saddle of the camel, and sat upon them. And Laban felt about all the tent, but found them not. 31,35 And she said to her father: 'Let not my lord be angry that I cannot rise up before thee; for the manner of women is upon me.' And he searched, but found not the teraphim. 31,36 And Jacob was wroth, and strove with Laban. And Jacob answered and said to Laban: 'What is my trespass? what is my sin, that thou hast hotly pursued after me? 31,37 Whereas thou hast felt about all my stuff, what hast thou found of all thy household stuff? Set it here before my brethren and thy brethren, that they may judge betwixt us two. 31,38 These twenty years have I been with thee; thy ewes and thy she-goats have not cast their young, and the rams of thy flocks have I not eaten. 31,39 That which was torn of beasts I brought not unto thee; I bore the loss of it; of my hand didst thou require it, whether stolen by day or stolen by night. 31,40 Thus I was: in the day the drought consumed me, and the frost by night; and my sleep fled from mine eyes. 31,41 These twenty years have I been in thy house: I served thee fourteen years for thy two daughters, and six years for thy flock; and thou hast changed my wages ten times. 31,42 Except the God of my father, the God of Abraham, and the Fear of Isaac, had been on my side, surely now hadst thou sent me away empty. God hath seen mine affliction and the labour of my hands, and gave judgment yesternight.' 31,43 And Laban answered and said unto Jacob: 'The daughters are my daughters, and the children are my children, and the flocks are my flocks, and all that thou seest is mine; and what can I do this day for these my daughters, or for their children whom they have borne? 31,44 And now come, let us make a covenant, I and thou; and let it be for a witness between me and thee.' 31,45 And Jacob took a stone, and set it up for a pillar. 31,46 And Jacob said unto his brethren: 'Gather stones'; and they took stones, and made a heap. And they did eat there

by the heap. 31,47 And Laban called it Jegar-sahadutha; but Jacob called it Galeed. 31,48 And Laban said: 'This heap is witness between me and thee this day.' Therefore was the name of it called Galeed; 31,49 and Mizpah, for he said: 'God watch between me and thee, when we are absent one from another. 31,50 If thou shalt afflict my daughters, and if thou shalt take wives beside my daughters, no man being with us; see, God is witness betwixt me and thee.' 31,51 And Laban said to Jacob: 'Behold this heap, and behold the pillar, which I have set up betwixt me and thee. 31,52 This heap be witness, and the pillar be witness, that I will not pass over this heap to thee, and that thou shalt not pass over this heap and this pillar unto me, for harm. 31,53 The God of Abraham, and the God of Nahor, the God of their father, judge betwixt us.' And Jacob swore by the Fear of his father Isaac. 31,54 And Jacob offered a sacrifice in the mountain, and called his brethren to eat bread; and they did eat bread, and tarried all night in the mountain. 32,1 And early in the morning Laban rose up, and kissed his sons and his daughters, and blessed them. And Laban departed, and returned unto his place. 32,2 And Jacob went on his way, and the angels of God met him. 32,3 And Jacob said when he saw them: 'This is God's camp.' And he called the name of that place Mahanaim. {P}

English Haftara of Vayetze

Hosea

11,7 And My people are in suspense about returning to Me; and though they call them upwards, none at all will lift himself up. 11,8 How shall I give thee up, Ephraim? How shall I surrender thee, Israel? How shall I make thee as Admah? How shall I set thee as Zeboim? My heart is turned within Me, My compassions are kindled together. 11,9 I will not execute the fierceness of Mine anger, I will not return to destroy Ephraim; for I am God, and not man, the Holy One in the midst of thee; and I will not come in fury. 11,10 They shall walk after God, who shall roar like a lion; for He shall roar, and the children shall come trembling from the west. 11,11 They shall come trembling as a bird out of Egypt, and as a dove out of the land of Assyria; and I will make them to dwell in their houses, saith God. {S} 12,1 Ephraim compasseth Me about with lies, and the house of Israel with deceit; and Judah is yet wayward towards God, and towards the Holy One who is faithful. 12,2 Ephraim striveth after wind, and followeth after the east wind; all the day he multiplieth lies and desolation; and they make a covenant with Assyria, and oil is carried into Egypt. 12,3 God hath also a controversy with Judah, and will punish Jacob according to his ways, according to his doings will He recompense him. 12,4 In the womb he took his brother by the heel, and by his strength he strove with a godlike being; 12,5 So he strove with an angel, and prevailed; he wept, and made supplication unto him; at Beth-el he would find him, and there he would speak with us; 12,6 But God, the God of hosts, God is His name. 12,7 Therefore turn thou to thy God; keep mercy and justice, and wait for thy God continually. 12,8 As for the trafficker, the balances of deceit are in his hand. He loveth to oppress. 12,9 And Ephraim said: 'Surely I am become rich, I have found me wealth; in all my labours they shall find in me no iniquity that were sin.' 12,10 But I am God thy God from the land of Egypt; I will yet again make thee to dwell in tents, as in the days of the appointed season. 12,11 I have also spoken unto the prophets, and I have multiplied visions; and by the ministry of the prophets have I used similitudes. 12,12 If Gilead be given to iniquity becoming altogether vanity, in Gilgal they sacrifice unto bullocks; yea, their altars shall be as heaps in the furrows of the field.

English Portion of Vayishlach

32,4 And Jacob sent messengers before him to Esau his brother unto the land of Seir, the field of Edom. 32,5 And he commanded them, saying: 'Thus shall ye say unto my lord Esau: Thus saith thy servant Jacob: I have sojourned with Laban, and stayed until now. 32,6 And I have oxen, and asses and flocks, and men-servants and maid-servants; and I have sent to tell my lord, that I may find favour in thy sight.' 32,7 And the messengers returned to Jacob, saying: 'We came to thy brother Esau, and moreover he cometh to meet thee, and four hundred men with him.' 32,8 Then Jacob was greatly afraid and was distressed. And he divided the people that was with him, and the flocks, and the herds, and the camels, into two camps. 32,9 And he said: 'If Esau come to the one camp, and smite it, then the camp which is left shall escape.' 32,10 And Jacob said: 'O God of my father Abraham, and God of my father Isaac, O LORD, who saidst unto me: Return unto thy country, and to thy kindred, and I will do thee good; 32,11 I am not worthy of all the mercies, and of all the truth, which Thou hast shown unto Thy servant; for with my staff I passed over this Jordan; and now I am become two camps. 32,12 Deliver me, I pray Thee, from the hand of my brother, from the hand of Esau; for I fear him, lest he come and smite me, the mother with the children. 32,13 And Thou saidst: I will surely do thee good, and make thy seed as the sand of the sea, which cannot be numbered for multitude.' 32,14 And he lodged there that night; and took of that which he had with him a present for Esau his brother: 32,15 two hundred she-goats and twenty he-goats, two hundred ewes and twenty rams, 32,16 thirty milch camels and their colts, forty kine and ten bulls, twenty she-asses and ten foals. 32,17 And he delivered them into the hand of his servants, every drove by itself; and said unto his servants: 'Pass over before me, and put a space betwixt drove and drove.' 32,18 And

he commanded the foremost, saying: 'When Esau my brother meeteth thee, and asketh thee, saying: Whose art thou? and whither goest thou? and whose are these before thee? 32,19 then thou shalt say: They are thy servant Jacob's; it is a present sent unto my lord, even unto Esau; and, behold, he also is behind us.' 32,20 And he commanded also the second, and the third, and all that followed the droves, saying: 'In this manner shall ye speak unto Esau, when ye find him; 32,21 and ye shall say: Moreover, behold, thy servant Jacob is behind us.' For he said: 'I will appease him with the present that goeth before me, and afterward I will see his face; peradventure he will accept me.' 32,22 So the present passed over before him; and he himself lodged that night in the camp. 32,23 And he rose up that night, and took his two wives, and his two handmaids, and his eleven children, and passed over the ford of the Jabbok. 32,24 And he took them, and sent them over the stream, and sent over that which he had. 32,25 And Jacob was left alone; and there wrestled a man with him until the breaking of the day. 32,26 And when he saw that he prevailed not against him, he touched the hollow of his thigh; and the hollow of Jacob's thigh was strained, as he wrestled with him. 32,27 And he said: 'Let me go, for the day breaketh.' And he said: 'I will not let thee go, except thou bless me.' 32,28 And he said unto him: 'What is thy name?' And be said: 'Jacob.' 32,29 And he said: 'Thy name shall be called no more Jacob, but Israel; for thou hast striven with God and with men, and hast prevailed.' 32,30 And Jacob asked him, and said: 'Tell me, I pray thee, thy name.' And he said: 'Wherefore is it that thou dost ask after my name?' And he blessed him there. 32,31 And Jacob called the name of the place Peniel: 'for I have seen God face to face, and my life is preserved.' 32,32 And the sun rose upon him as he passed over Peniel, and he limped upon his thigh. 32,33 Therefore the children of Israel eat not the sinew of the thigh-vein which is upon the hollow of the thigh, unto this day; because he touched the hollow of Jacob's thigh, even in the sinew of the thigh-vein. 33,1 And Jacob lifted up his eyes and looked, and, behold, Esau came, and with him four hundred men. And he divided the children unto Leah, and unto Rachel, and unto the two handmaids. 33,2 And he put the handmaids and their children foremost, and Leah and her children after, and Rachel and Joseph hindermost. 33,3 And he himself passed over before them, and bowed himself to the ground seven times, until he came near to his brother. 33,4 And Esau ran to meet him, and embraced him, and fell on his neck, and kissed him; and they wept. 33,5 And he lifted up his eyes, and saw the women and the children; and said: 'Who are these with thee?' And he said: 'The children whom God hath graciously given thy servant.' 33,6 Then the handmaids came near, they and their children, and they bowed down. 33,7 And Leah also and her children came near, and bowed down; and after came Joseph near and Rachel, and they bowed down. 33,8 And he said: 'What meanest thou by all this camp which I met?' And he said: 'To find favour in the sight of my lord.' 33,9 And Esau said: 'I have enough; my brother, let that which thou hast be thine.' 33,10 And Jacob said: 'Nay, I pray thee, if now I have found favour in thy sight, then receive my present at my hand; forasmuch as I have seen thy face, as one seeth the face of God, and thou wast pleased with me. 33,11 Take, I pray thee, my gift that is brought to thee; because God hath dealt graciously with me, and because I have enough.' And he urged him, and he took it. 33,12 And he said: 'Let us take our journey, and let us go, and I will go before thee.' 33,13 And he said unto him: 'My lord knoweth that the children are tender, and that the flocks and herds giving suck are a care to me; and if they overdrive them one day, all the flocks will die. 33,14 Let my lord, I pray thee, pass over before his servant; and I will journey on gently, according to the pace of the cattle that are before me and according to the pace of the children, until I come unto my lord unto Seir.' 33,15 And Esau said: 'Let me now leave with thee some of the folk that are with me.' And he said: 'What needeth it? let me find favour in the sight of my lord.' 33,16 So Esau returned that day on his way unto Seir. 33,17 And Jacob journeyed to Succoth, and built him a house, and made booths for his cattle. Therefore the name of the place is called Succoth. {S} 33,18 And Jacob came in peace to the city of Shechem, which is in the land of Canaan, when he came from Paddan-aram; and encamped before the city. 33,19 And he bought the parcel of ground, where he had spread his tent, at the hand of the children of Hamor, Shechem's father, for a hundred pieces of money. 33,20 And he erected there an altar, and called it El-elohe-Israel. {S} 34,1 And Dinah the daughter of Leah, whom she had borne unto Jacob, went out to see the daughters of the land. 34,2 And Shechem the son of Hamor the Hivite, the prince of the land, saw her; and he took her, and lay with her, and humbled her. 34,3 And his soul did cleave unto Dinah the daughter of Jacob, and he loved the damsel, and spoke comfortingly unto the damsel. 34,4 And Shechem spoke unto his father Hamor, saying: 'Get me this damsel to wife.' 34,5 Now Jacob heard that he had defiled Dinah his daughter; and his sons were with his cattle in the field; and Jacob held his peace until they came. 34,6 And Hamor the father of Shechem went out unto Jacob to speak with him. 34,7 And the sons of Jacob came in from the field when they heard it; and the men were grieved, and they were very wroth, because he had wrought a vile deed in Israel in lying with Jacob's daughter; which thing ought not to be done. 34,8 And Hamor spoke with them, saying 'The soul of my son Shechem longeth for your daughter. I pray you give her unto him to wife. 34,9 And make ye marriages with us; give your daughters unto us, and take our daughters unto you. 34,10 And ye shall dwell with us; and the land shall be before you; dwell and trade ye therein, and get you possessions therein.' 34,11 And Shechem said unto her father and unto her brethren: 'Let me find favour in your eyes, and what ye shall say unto me I will give. 34,12 Ask me never so much dowry and gift, and I will give according as ye shall say unto me; but give me the damsel to wife.' 34,13 And the sons of Jacob answered Shechem and Hamor his father with guile, and spoke, because he had defiled Dinah their sister, 34,14 and said unto them: 'We cannot do this thing, to give our sister to one that is uncircumcised; for that were

a reproach unto us. 34,15 Only on this condition will we consent unto you: if ye will be as we are, that every male of you be circumcised; 34,16 then will we give our daughters unto you, and we will take your daughters to us, and we will dwell with you, and we will become one people. 34,17 But if ye will not hearken unto us, to be circumcised; then will we take our daughter, and we will be gone.' 34,18 And their words pleased Hamor, and Shechem Hamor's son. 34,19 And the young man deferred not to do the thing, because he had delight in Jacob's daughter. And he was honoured above all the house of his father. 34,20 And Hamor and Shechem his son came unto the gate of their city, and spoke with the men of their city, saying: 34,21 'These men are peaceable with us; therefore let them dwell in the land, and trade therein; for, behold, the land is large enough for them; let us take their daughters to us for wives, and let us give them our daughters. 34,22 Only on this condition will the men consent unto us to dwell with us, to become one people, if every male among us be circumcised, as they are circumcised. 34,23 Shall not their cattle and their substance and all their beasts be ours? only let us consent unto them, and they will dwell with us.' 34,24 And unto Hamor and unto Shechem his son hearkened all that went out of the gate of his city; and every male was circumcised, all that went out of the gate of his city. 34,25 And it came to pass on the third day, when they were in pain, that two of the sons of Jacob, Simeon and Levi, Dinah's brethren, took each man his sword, and came upon the city unawares, and slew all the males. 34,26 And they slew Hamor and Shechem his son with the edge of the sword, and took Dinah out of Shechem's house, and went forth. 34,27 The sons of Jacob came upon the slain, and spoiled the city, because they had defiled their sister. 34,28 They took their flocks and their herds and their asses, and that which was in the city and that which was in the field; 34,29 and all their wealth, and all their little ones and their wives, took they captive and spoiled, even all that was in the house. 34,30 And Jacob said to Simeon and Levi: 'Ye have troubled me, to make me odious unto the inhabitants of the land, even unto the Canaanites and the Perizzites; and, I being few in number, they will gather themselves together against me and smite me; and I shall be destroyed, I and my house.' 34,31 And they said: 'Should one deal with our sister as with a harlot?' {P}

35,1 And God said unto Jacob: 'Arise, go up to Beth-el, and dwell there; and make there an altar unto God, who appeared unto thee when thou didst flee from the face of Esau thy brother.' 35,2 Then Jacob said unto his household, and to all that were with him: 'Put away the strange gods that are among you, and purify yourselves, and change your garments; 35,3 and let us arise, and go up to Beth-el; and I will make there an altar unto God, who answered me in the day of my distress, and was with me in the way which I went.' 35,4 And they gave unto Jacob all the foreign gods which were in their hand, and the rings which were in their ears; and Jacob hid them under the terebinth which was by Shechem. 35,5 And they journeyed; and a terror of God was upon the cities that were round about them, and they did not pursue after the sons of Jacob. 35,6 So Jacob came to Luz, which is in the land of Canaan--the same is Beth-el--he and all the people that were with him. 35,7 And he built there an altar, and called the place El-beth-el, because there God was revealed unto him, when he fled from the face of his brother. 35,8 And Deborah Rebekah's nurse died, and she was buried below Beth-el under the oak; and the name of it was called Allon-bacuth. {P}

35,9 And God appeared unto Jacob again, when he came from Paddan-aram, and blessed him. 35,10 And God said unto him: 'Thy name is Jacob: thy name shall not be called any more Jacob, but Israel shall be thy name'; and He called his name Israel. 35,11 And God said unto him: 'I am God Almighty. Be fruitful and multiply; a nation and a company of nations shall be of thee, and kings shall come out of thy loins; 35,12 and the land which I gave unto Abraham and Isaac, to thee I will give it, and to thy seed after thee will I give the land.' 35,13 And God went up from him in the place where He spoke with him. 35,14 And Jacob set up a pillar in the place where He spoke with him, a pillar of stone, and he poured out a drink-offering thereon, and poured oil thereon. 35,15 And Jacob called the name of the place where God spoke with him, Beth-el. 35,16 And they journeyed from Beth-el; and there was still some way to come to Ephrath; and Rachel travailed, and she had hard labour. 35,17 And it came to pass, when she was in hard labour, that the mid-wife said unto her: 'Fear not; for this also is a son for thee.' 35,18 And it came to pass, as her soul was in departing--for she died--that she called his name Ben-oni; but his father called him Benjamin. 35,19 And Rachel died, and was buried in the way to Ephrath--the same is Beth-lehem. 35,20 And Jacob set up a pillar upon her grave; the same is the pillar of Rachel's grave unto this day. 35,21 And Israel journeyed, and spread his tent beyond Migdal-eder. 35,22 And it came to pass, while Israel dwelt in that land, that Reuben went and lay with Bilhah his father's concubine; and Israel heard of it. {P} Now the sons of Jacob were twelve: 35,23 the sons of Leah: Reuben, Jacob's first-born, and Simeon, and Levi, and Judah, and Issachar, and Zebulun; 35,24 the sons of Rachel: Joseph and Benjamin; 35,25 and the sons of Bilhah, Rachel's handmaid: Dan and Naphtali; 35,26 and the sons of Zilpah, Leah's handmaid: Gad and Asher. These are the sons of Jacob, that were born to him in Paddan-aram. 35,27 And Jacob came unto Isaac his father to Mamre, to Kiriatharba--the same is Hebron--where Abraham and Isaac sojourned. 35,28 And the days of Isaac were a hundred and fourscore years. 35,29 And Isaac expired, and died, and was gathered unto his people, old and full of days; and Esau and Jacob his sons buried him. {P}

36,1 Now these are the generations of Esau--the same is Edom. 36,2 Esau took his wives of the daughters of Canaan; Adah the daughter of Elon the Hittite, and Oholibamah the daughter of Anah, the daughter of Zibeon the Hivite, 36,3 and Basemath Ishmael's daughter, sister of Nebaioth. 36,4 And Adah bore to Esau Eliphaz;

and Basemath bore Reuel; 36,5 and Oholibamah bore Jeush, and Jalam, and Korah. These are the sons of Esau, that were born unto him in the land of Canaan. 36,6 And Esau took his wives, and his sons, and his daughters, and all the souls of his house, and his cattle, and all his beasts, and all his possessions, which he had gathered in the land of Canaan; and went into a land away from his brother Jacob. 36,7 For their substance was too great for them to dwell together; and the land of their sojournings could not bear them because of their cattle. 36,8 And Esau dwelt in the mountain-land of Seir--Esau is Edom. 36,9 And these are the generations of Esau the father of a the Edomites in the mountain-land of Seir. 36,10 These are the names of Esau's sons: Eliphaz the son of Adah the wife of Esau, Reuel the son of Basemath the wife of Esau. 36,11 And the sons of Eliphaz were Teman, Omar, Zepho, and Gatam, and Kenaz. 36,12 And Timna was concubine to Eliphaz Esau's son; and she bore to Eliphaz Amalek. These are the sons of Adah Esau's wife. 36,13 And these are the sons of Reuel: Nahath, and Zerah, Shammah, and Mizzah. These were the sons of Basemath Esau's wife. 36,14 And these were the sons of Oholibamah the daughter of Anah, the daughter of Zibeon, Esau's wife; and she bore to Esau Jeush, and Jalam, and Korah. 36,15 These are the chiefs of the sons of Esau: the sons of Eliphaz the first-born of Esau: the chief of Teman, the chief of Omar, the chief of Zepho, the chief of Kenaz, 36,16 the chief of Korah, the chief of Gatam, the chief of Amalek. These are the chiefs that came of Eliphaz in the land of Edom. These are the sons of Adah. 36,17 And these are the sons of Reuel Esau's son: the chief of Nahath, the chief of Zerah, the chief of Shammah, the chief of Mizzah. These are the chiefs that came of Reuel in the land of Edom. These are the sons of Basemath Esau's wife. 36,18 And these are the sons of Oholibamah Esau's wife: the chief of Jeush, the chief of Jalam, the chief of Korah. These are the chiefs that came of Oholibamah the daughter of Anah, Esau's wife. 36,19 These are the sons of Esau, and these are their chiefs; the same is Edom. {S} 36,20 These are the sons of Seir the Horite, the inhabitants of the land: Lotan and Shobal and Zibeon and Anah, 36,21 and Dishon and Ezer and Dishan. These are the chiefs that came of the Horites, the children of Seir in the land of Edom. 36,22 And the children of Lotan were Hori and Hemam; and Lotan's sister was Timna. 36,23 And these are the children of Shobal: Alvan and Manahath and Ebal, Shepho and Onam. 36,24 And these are the children of Zibeon: Aiah and Anah--this is Anah who found the hot springs in the wilderness, as he fed the asses of Zibeon his father. 36,25 And these are the children of Anah: Dishon and Oholibamah the daughter of Anah. 36,26 And these are the children of Dishon: Hemdan and Eshban and Ithran and Cheran. 36,27 These are the children of Ezer: Bilhan and Zaavan and Akan. 36,28 These are the children of Dishan: Uz and Aran. 36,29 These are the chiefs that came of the Horites: the chief of Lotan, the chief of Shobal, the chief of Zibeon, the chief of Anah, 36,30 the chief of Dishon, the chief of Ezer, the chief of Dishan. These are the chiefs that came of the Horites, according to their chiefs in the land of Seir. {P}

36,31 And these are the kings that reigned in the land of Edom, before there reigned any king over the children of Israel. 36,32 And Bela the son of Beor reigned in Edom; and the name of his city was Dinhabah. 36,33 And Bela died, and Jobab the son of Zerah of Bozrah reigned in his stead. 36,34 And Jobab died, and Husham of the land of the Temanites reigned in his stead. 36,35 And Husham died, and Hadad the son of Bedad, who smote Midian in the field of Moab, reigned in his stead; and the name of his city was Avith. 36,36 And Hadad died, and Samlah of Masrekah reigned in his stead. 36,37 And Samlah died, and Shaul of Rehoboth by the River reigned in his stead. 36,38 And Shaul died, and Baal-hanan the son of Achbor reigned in his stead. 36,39 And Baal-hanan the son of Achbor died, and Hadar reigned in his stead; and the name of the city was Pau; and his wife's name was Mehetabel, the daughter of Matred, the daughter of Me-zahab. 36,40 And these are the names of the chiefs that came of Esau, according to their families, after their places, by their names: the chief of Timna, the chief of Alvah, the chief of Jetheth; 36,41 the chief of Oholibamah, the chief of Elah, the chief of Pinon; 36,42 the chief of Kenaz, the chief of Teman, the chief of Mibzar; 36,43 the chief of Magdiel, the chief of Iram. These are the chiefs of Edom, according to their habitations in the land of their possession. This is Esau the father of the Edomites. {P}

English Haftara of Vayishlach

Obadiah

1,1 The vision of Obadiah. Thus saith God GOD concerning Edom: We have heard a message from God, and an ambassador is sent among the nations: 'Arise ye, and let us rise up against her in battle.' 1,2 Behold, I make thee small among the nations; thou art greatly despised. 1,3 The pride of thy heart hath beguiled thee, O thou that dwellest in the clefts of the rock, thy habitation on high; that sayest in thy heart: 'Who shall bring me down to the ground?' 1,4 Though thou make thy nest as high as the eagle, and though thou set it among the stars, I will bring thee down from thence, saith God. 1,5 If thieves came to thee, if robbers by night--how art thou cut off!--would they not steal till they had enough? If grape-gatherers came to thee, would they not leave some gleaning grapes? 1,6 How is Esau searched out! How are his hidden places sought out! 1,7 All the men of thy confederacy have conducted thee to the border; the men that were at peace with thee have beguiled thee, and prevailed against thee; they that eat thy bread lay a snare under thee, in whom there is no discernment. 1,8 Shall I not in that day, saith God, destroy the wise men out of Edom, and discernment out of the mount of Esau? 1,9 And thy mighty men, O Teman, shall be dismayed, to the end that every one may be cut off from the mount

of Esau by slaughter. 1,10 For the violence done to thy brother Jacob shame shall cover thee, and thou shalt be cut off for ever. 1,11 In the day that thou didst stand aloof, in the day that strangers carried away his substance, and foreigners entered into his gates, and cast lots upon Jerusalem, even thou wast as one of them. 1,12 But thou shouldest not have gazed on the day of thy brother in the day of his disaster, neither shouldest thou have rejoiced over the children of Judah in the day of their destruction; neither shouldest thou have spoken proudly in the day of distress. 1,13 Thou shouldest not have entered into the gate of My people in the day of their calamity; yea, thou shouldest not have gazed on their affliction in the day of their calamity, nor have laid hands on their substance in the day of their calamity. 1,14 Neither shouldest thou have stood in the crossway, to cut off those of his that escape; neither shouldest thou have delivered up those of his that did remain in the day of distress. 1,15 For the day of God is near upon all the nations; as thou hast done, it shall be done unto thee; thy dealing shall return upon thine own head. 1,16 For as ye have drunk upon My holy mountain, so shall all the nations drink continually, yea, they shall drink, and swallow down, and shall be as though they had not been. 1,17 But in mount Zion there shall be those that escape, and it shall be holy; and the house of Jacob shall possess their possessions. 1,18 And the house of Jacob shall be a fire, and the house of Joseph a flame, and the house of Esau for stubble, and they shall kindle in them, and devour them; and there shall not be any remaining of the house of Esau; for God hath spoken. 1,19 And they of the South shall possess the mount of Esau, and they of the Lowland the Philistines; and they shall possess the field of Ephraim, and the field of Samaria; and Benjamin shall possess Gilead. 1,20 And the captivity of this host of the children of Israel, that are among the Canaanites, even unto Zarephath, and the captivity of Jerusalem, that is in Sepharad, shall possess the cities of the South. 1,21 And saviours shall come up on mount Zion to judge the mount of Esau; and the kingdom shall be God'S. {P}

English Portion of Vayeshev

37,1 And Jacob dwelt in the land of his father's sojournings, in the land of Canaan. 37,2 These are the generations of Jacob. Joseph, being seventeen years old, was feeding the flock with his brethren, being still a lad even with the sons of Bilhah, and with the sons of Zilpah, his father's wives; and Joseph brought evil report of them unto their father. 37,3 Now Israel loved Joseph more than all his children, because he was the son of his old age; and he made him a coat of many colours. 37,4 And when his brethren saw that their father loved him more than all his brethren, they hated him, and could not speak peaceably unto him. 37,5 And Joseph dreamed a dream, and he told it to his brethren; and they hated him yet the more. 37,6 And he said unto them: 'Hear, I pray you, this dream which I have dreamed: 37,7 for, behold, we were binding sheaves in the field, and, lo, my sheaf arose, and also stood upright; and, behold, your sheaves came round about, and bowed down to my sheaf.' 37,8 And his brethren said to him: 'Shalt thou indeed reign over us? or shalt thou indeed have dominion over us?' And they hated him yet the more for his dreams, and for his words. 37,9 And he dreamed yet another dream, and told it to his brethren, and said: 'Behold, I have dreamed yet a dream: and, behold, the sun and the moon and eleven stars bowed down to me.' 37,10 And he told it to his father, and to his brethren; and his father rebuked him, and said unto him: 'What is this dream that thou hast dreamed? Shall I and thy mother and thy brethren indeed come to bow down to thee to the earth?' 37,11 And his brethren envied him; but his father kept the saying in mind. 37,12 And his brethren went to feed their father's flock in Shechem. 37,13 And Israel said unto Joseph: 'Do not thy brethren feed the flock in Shechem? come, and I will send thee unto them.' And he said to him: 'Here am I.' 37,14 And he said to him: 'Go now, see whether it is well with thy brethren, and well with the flock; and bring me back word.' So he sent him out of the vale of Hebron, and he came to Shechem. 37,15 And a certain man found him, and, behold, he was wandering in the field. And the man asked him, saying: 'What seekest thou?' 37,16 And he said: 'I seek my brethren. Tell me, I pray thee, where they are feeding the flock.' 37,17 And the man said: 'They are departed hence; for I heard them say: Let us go to Dothan.' And Joseph went after his brethren, and found them in Dothan. 37,18 And they saw him afar off, and before he came near unto them, they conspired against him to slay him. 37,19 And they said one to another: 'Behold, this dreamer cometh. 37,20 Come now therefore, and let us slay him, and cast him into one of the pits, and we will say: An evil beast hath devoured him; and we shall see what will become of his dreams.' 37,21 And Reuben heard it, and delivered him out of their hand; and said: 'Let us not take his life.' 37,22 And Reuben said unto them: 'Shed no blood; cast him into this pit that is in the wilderness, but lay no hand upon him'--that he might deliver him out of their hand, to restore him to his father. 37,23 And it came to pass, when Joseph was come unto his brethren, that they stripped Joseph of his coat, the coat of many colours that was on him; 37,24 and they took him, and cast him into the pit--and the pit was empty, there was no water in it. 37,25 And they sat down to eat bread; and they lifted up their eyes and looked, and, behold, a caravan of Ishmaelites came from Gilead, with their camels bearing spicery and balm and ladanum, going to carry it down to Egypt. 37,26 And Judah said unto his brethren: 'What profit is it if we slay our brother and conceal his blood? 37,27 Come, and let us sell him to the Ishmaelites, and let not our hand be upon him; for he is our brother, our flesh.' And his brethren hearkened unto him. 37,28 And there passed by Midianites, merchantmen; and they drew and lifted up Joseph out of the pit, and sold Joseph to the Ishmaelites for twenty shekels of silver. And they brought Joseph into Egypt. 37,29 And Reuben returned unto the pit; and, behold, Joseph was not in

the pit; and he rent his clothes. 37,30 And he returned unto his brethren, and said: 'The child is not; and as for me, whither shall I go?' 37,31 And they took Joseph's coat, and killed a he-goat, and dipped the coat in the blood; 37,32 and they sent the coat of many colours, and they brought it to their father; and said: 'This have we found. Know now whether it is thy son's coat or not.' 37,33 And he knew it, and said: 'It is my son's coat; an evil beast hath devoured him; Joseph is without doubt torn in pieces.' 37,34 And Jacob rent his garments, and put sackcloth upon his loins, and mourned for his son many days. 37,35 And all his sons and all his daughters rose up to comfort him; but he refused to be comforted; and he said: 'Nay, but I will go down to the grave to my son mourning.' And his father wept for him. 37,36 And the Midianites sold him into Egypt unto Potiphar, an officer of Pharaoh's, the captain of the guard. {P}

38,1 And it came to pass at that time, that Judah went down from his brethren, and turned in to a certain Adullamite, whose name was Hirah. 38,2 And Judah saw there a daughter of a certain Canaanite whose name was Shua; and he took her, and went in unto her. 38,3 And she conceived, and bore a son; and he called his name Er. 38,4 And she conceived again, and bore a son; and she called his name Onan. 38,5 And she yet again bore a son, and called his name Shelah; and he was at Chezib, when she bore him. 38,6 And Judah took a wife for Er his first-born, and her name was Tamar. 38,7 And Er, Judah's first-born, was wicked in the sight of God; and God slew him. 38,8 And Judah said unto Onan: 'Go in unto thy brother's wife, and perform the duty of a husband's brother unto her, and raise up seed to thy brother.' 38,9 And Onan knew that the seed would not be his; and it came to pass when he went in unto his brother's wife, that he spilled it on the ground, lest he should give seed to his brother. 38,10 And the thing which he did was evil in the sight of God; and He slew him also. 38,11 Then said Judah to Tamar his daughter-in-law: 'Remain a widow in thy father's house, till Shelah my son be grown up'; for he said: 'Lest he also die, like his brethren.' And Tamar went and dwelt in her father's house. 38,12 And in process of time Shua's daughter, the wife of Judah, died; and Judah was comforted, and went up unto his sheep-shearers to Timnah, he and his friend Hirah the Adullamite. 38,13 And it was told Tamar, saying: 'Behold, thy father-in-law goeth up to Timnah to shear his sheep.' 38,14 And she put off from her the garments of her widowhood, and covered herself with her veil, and wrapped herself, and sat in the entrance of Enaim, which is by the way to Timnah; for she saw that Shelah was grown up, and she was not given unto him to wife. 38,15 When Judah saw her, he thought her to be a harlot; for she had covered her face. 38,16 And he turned unto her by the way, and said: 'Come, I pray thee, let me come in unto thee'; for he knew not that she was his daughter-in-law. And she said: 'What wilt thou give me, that thou mayest come in unto me?' 38,17 And he said: 'I will send thee a kid of the goats from the flock.' And she said: 'Wilt thou give me a pledge, till thou send it?' 38,18 And he said: 'What pledge shall I give thee?' And she said: 'Thy signet and thy cord, and thy staff that is in thy hand.' And he gave them to her, and came in unto her, and she conceived by him. 38,19 And she arose, and went away, and put off her veil from her, and put on the garments of her widowhood. 38,20 And Judah sent the kid of the goats by the hand of his friend the Adullamite, to receive the pledge from the woman's hand; but he found her not. 38,21 Then he asked the men of her place, saying: 'Where is the harlot, that was at Enaim by the wayside?' And they said: 'There hath been no harlot here.' 38,22 And he returned to Judah, and said: 'I have not found her; and also the men of the place said: There hath been no harlot here.' 38,23 And Judah said: 'Let her take it, lest we be put to shame; behold, I sent this kid, and thou hast not found her.' 38,24 And it came to pass about three months after, that it was told Judah, saying: 'Tamar thy daughter-in-law hath played the harlot; and moreover, behold, she is with child by harlotry.' And Judah said: 'Bring her forth, and let her be burnt.' 38,25 When she was brought forth, she sent to her father-in-law, saying: 'By the man, whose these are, am I with child'; and she said: 'Discern, I pray thee, whose are these, the signet, and the cords, and the staff.' 38,26 And Judah acknowledged them, and said: 'She is more righteous than I; forasmuch as I gave her not to Shelah my son.' And he knew her again no more. 38,27 And it came to pass in the time of her travail, that, behold, twins were in her womb. 38,28 And it came to pass, when she travailed, that one put out a hand; and the midwife took and bound upon his hand a scarlet thread, saying: 'This came out first.' 38,29 And it came to pass, as he drew back his hand, that, behold his brother came out; and she said: 'Wherefore hast thou made a breach for thyself?' Therefore his name was called Perez. 38,30 And afterward came out his brother, that had the scarlet thread upon his hand; and his name was called Zerah. {S}

39,1 And Joseph was brought down to Egypt; and Potiphar, an officer of Pharaoh's, the captain of the guard, an Egyptian, bought him of the hand of the Ishmaelites, that had brought him down thither. 39,2 And God was with Joseph, and he was a prosperous man; and he was in the house of his master the Egyptian. 39,3 And his master saw that God was with him, and that God made all that he did to prosper in his hand. 39,4 And Joseph found favour in his sight, and he ministered unto him. And he appointed him overseer over his house, and all that he had he put into his hand. 39,5 And it came to pass from the time that he appointed him overseer in his house, and over all that he had, that God blessed the Egyptian's house for Joseph's sake; and the blessing of God was upon all that he had, in the house and in the field. 39,6 And he left all that he had in Joseph's hand; and, having him, he knew not aught save the bread which he did eat. And Joseph was of beautiful form, and fair to look upon. 39,7 And it came to pass after these things, that his master's wife cast her eyes upon Joseph; and she said: 'Lie with me.' 39,8 But he refused, and said unto his master's wife: 'Behold, my master, having me, knoweth not what is in the house, and he hath put all that he hath into my hand; 39,9 he is not greater in this house than I; neither hath he kept back any thing from me but thee, because thou art his wife. How then

can I do this great wickedness, and sin against God?' 39,10 And it came to pass, as she spoke to Joseph day by day, that he hearkened not unto her, to lie by her, or to be with her. 39,11 And it came to pass on a certain day, when he went into the house to do his work, and there was none of the men of the house there within, 39,12 that she caught him by his garment, saying: 'Lie with me.' And he left his garment in her hand, and fled, and got him out. 39,13 And it came to pass, when she saw that he had left his garment in her hand, and was fled forth, 39,14 that she called unto the men of her house, and spoke unto them, saying: 'See, he hath brought in a Hebrew unto us to mock us; he came in unto me to lie with me, and I cried with a loud voice. 39,15 And it came to pass, when he heard that I lifted up my voice and cried, that he left his garment by me, and fled, and got him out.' 39,16 And she laid up his garment by her, until his master came home. 39,17 And she spoke unto him according to these words, saying: 'The Hebrew servant, whom thou hast brought unto us, came in unto me to mock me. 39,18 And it came to pass, as I lifted up my voice and cried, that he left his garment by me, and fled out.' 39,19 And it came to pass, when his master heard the words of his wife, which she spoke unto him, saying: 'After this manner did thy servant to me'; that his wrath was kindled. 39,20 And Joseph's master took him, and put him into the prison, the place where the king's prisoners were bound; and he was there in the prison. 39,21 But God was with Joseph, and showed kindness unto him, and gave him favour in the sight of the keeper of the prison. 39,22 And the keeper of the prison committed to Joseph's hand all the prisoners that were in the prison; and whatsoever they did there, he was the doer of it. 39,23 The keeper of the prison looked not to any thing that was under his hand, because God was with him; and that which he did, God made it to prosper. {P}

40,1 And it came to pass after these things, that the butler of the king of Egypt and his baker offended their lord the king of Egypt. 40,2 And Pharaoh was wroth against his two officers, against the chief of the butlers, and against the chief of the bakers. 40,3 And he put them in ward in the house of the captain of the guard, into the prison, the place where Joseph was bound. 40,4 And the captain of the guard charged Joseph to be with them, and he ministered unto them; and they continued a season in ward. 40,5 And they dreamed a dream both of them, each man his dream, in one night, each man according to the interpretation of his dream, the butler and the baker of the king of Egypt, who were bound in the prison. 40,6 And Joseph came in unto them in the morning, and saw them, and, behold, they were sad. 40,7 And he asked Pharaoh's officers that were with him in the ward of his master's house, saying: 'Wherefore look ye so sad to-day?' 40,8 And they said unto him: 'We have dreamed a dream, and there is none that can interpret it.' And Joseph said unto them: 'Do not interpretations belong to God? tell it me, I pray you.' 40,9 And the chief butler told his dream to Joseph, and said to him: 'In my dream, behold, a vine was before me; 40,10 and in the vine were three branches; and as it was budding, its blossoms shot forth, and the clusters thereof brought forth ripe grapes, 40,11 and Pharaoh's cup was in my hand; and I took the grapes, and pressed them into Pharaoh's cup, and I gave the cup into Pharaoh's hand.' 40,12 And Joseph said unto him: 'This is the interpretation of it: the three branches are three days; 40,13 within yet three days shall Pharaoh lift up thy head, and restore thee unto thine office; and thou shalt give Pharaoh's cup into his hand, after the former manner when thou wast his butler. 40,14 But have me in thy remembrance when it shall be well with thee, and show kindness, I pray thee, unto me, and make mention of me unto Pharaoh, and bring me out of this house. 40,15 For indeed I was stolen away out of the land of the Hebrews; and here also have I done nothing that they should put me into the dungeon.' 40,16 When the chief baker saw that the interpretation was good, he said unto Joseph: 'I also saw in my dream, and, behold, three baskets of white bread were on my head; 40,17 and in the uppermost basket there was of all manner of baked food for Pharaoh; and the birds did eat them out of the basket upon my head.' 40,18 And Joseph answered and said: 'This is the interpretation thereof: the three baskets are three days; 40,19 within yet three days shall Pharaoh lift up thy head from off thee, and shall hang thee on a tree; and the birds shall eat thy flesh from off thee.' 40,20 And it came to pass the third day, which was Pharaoh's birthday, that he made a feast unto all his servants; and he lifted up the head of the chief butler and the head of the chief baker among his servants. 40,21 And he restored the chief butler back unto his butlership; and he gave the cup into Pharaoh's hand. 40,22 But he hanged the chief baker, as Joseph had interpreted to them. 40,23 Yet did not the chief butler remember Joseph, but forgot him. {P}

English Hafrara of Vayeshev

Amos

2,6 Thus saith God: For three transgressions of Israel, yea, for four, I will not reverse it: because they sell the righteous for silver, and the needy for a pair of shoes; 2,7 That pant after the dust of the earth on the head of the poor, and turn aside the way of the humble; and a man and his father go unto the same maid, to profane My holy name; 2,8 And they lay themselves down beside every altar upon clothes taken in pledge, and in the house of their God they drink the wine of them that have been fined. 2,9 Yet destroyed I the Amorite before them, whose height was like the height of the cedars, and he was strong as the oaks; yet I destroyed his fruit from above, and his roots from beneath. 2,10 Also I brought you up out of the land of Egypt, and led you forty years in the wilderness, to possess the land of the Amorites. 2,11 And I raised up of your sons for prophets,

and of your young men for Nazirites. Is it not even thus, O ye children of Israel? saith God. 2,12 But ye gave the
Nazirites wine to drink; and commanded the prophets, saying: 'Prophesy not.' 2,13 Behold, I will make it creak
under you, as a cart creaketh that is full of sheaves. 2,14 And flight shall fail the swift, and the strong shall not
exert his strength, neither shall the mighty deliver himself; 2,15 Neither shall he stand that handleth the bow;
and he that is swift of foot shall not deliver himself; neither shall he that rideth the horse deliver himself; 2,16
And he that is courageous among the mighty shall flee away naked in that day, saith God. {P}
3,1 Hear this word that God hath spoken against you, O children of Israel, against the whole family which I
brought up out of the land of Egypt, saying: 3,2 You only have I known of all the families of the earth; therefore I
will visit upon you all your iniquities. 3,3 Will two walk together, except they have agreed? 3,4 Will a lion roar in
the forest, when he hath no prey? Will a young lion give forth his voice out of his den, if he have taken nothing?
3,5 Will a bird fall in a snare upon the earth, where there is no lure for it? Will a snare spring up from the ground,
and have taken nothing at all? 3,6 Shall the horn be blown in a city, and the people not tremble? Shall evil befall a
city, and God hath not done it? 3,7 For God GOD will do nothing, but He revealeth His counsel unto His servants
the prophets. 3,8 The lion hath roared, who will not fear? God GOD hath spoken, who can but prophesy?

English Portion of Miketz

41,1 And it came to pass at the end of two full years, that Pharaoh dreamed: and, behold, he stood by the river.
41,2 And, behold, there came up out of the river seven kine, well-favoured and fat-fleshed; and they fed in the
reed-grass. 41,3 And, behold, seven other kine came up after them out of the river, ill favoured and lean-
fleshed; and stood by the other kine upon the brink of the river. 41,4 And the ill-favoured and lean-fleshed kine
did eat up the seven well-favoured and fat kine. So Pharaoh awoke. 41,5 And he slept and dreamed a second
time: and, behold, seven ears of corn came up upon one stalk, rank and good. 41,6 And, behold, seven ears,
thin and blasted with the east wind, sprung up after them. 41,7 And the thin ears swallowed up the seven rank
and full ears. And Pharaoh awoke, and, behold, it was a dream. 41,8 And it came to pass in the morning that
his spirit was troubled; and he sent and called for all the magicians of Egypt, and all the wise men thereof; and
Pharaoh told them his dream; but there was none that could interpret them unto Pharaoh. 41,9 Then spoke
the chief butler unto Pharaoh, saying: 'I make mention of my faults this day: 41,10 Pharaoh was wroth with his
servants, and put me in the ward of the house of the captain of the guard, me and the chief baker. 41,11 And
we dreamed a dream in one night, I and he; we dreamed each man according to the interpretation of his
dream. 41,12 And there was with us there a young man, a Hebrew, servant to the captain of the guard; and we
told him, and he interpreted to us our dreams; to each man according to his dream he did interpret. 41,13 And
it came to pass, as he interpreted to us, so it was: I was restored unto mine office, and he was hanged.' 41,14
Then Pharaoh sent and called Joseph, and they brought him hastily out of the dungeon. And he shaved
himself, and changed his raiment, and came in unto Pharaoh. 41,15 And Pharaoh said unto Joseph: 'I have
dreamed a dream, and there is none that can interpret it; and I have heard say of thee, that when thou hearest
a dream thou canst interpret it.' 41,16 And Joseph answered Pharaoh, saying: 'It is not in me; God will give
Pharaoh an answer of peace.' 41,17 And Pharaoh spoke unto Joseph: 'In my dream, behold, I stood upon the
brink of the river. 41,18 And, behold, there came up out of the river seven kine, fat-fleshed and well-favoured;
and they fed in the reed-grass. 41,19 And, behold, seven other kine came up after them, poor and very ill-
favoured and lean-fleshed, such as I never saw in all the land of Egypt for badness. 41,20 And the lean and
ill-favoured kine did eat up the first seven fat kine. 41,21 And when they had eaten them up, it could not be
known that they had eaten them; but they were still ill-favoured as at the beginning. So I awoke. 41,22 And I
saw in my dream, and, behold, seven ears came up upon one stalk, full and good. 41,23 And, behold, seven
ears, withered, thin, and blasted with the east wind, sprung up after them. 41,24 And the thin ears swallowed
up the seven good ears. And I told it unto the magicians; but there was none that could declare it to me.' 41,25
And Joseph said unto Pharaoh: 'The dream of Pharaoh is one; what God is about to do He hath declared unto
Pharaoh. 41,26 The seven good kine are seven years; and the seven good ears are seven years: the dream is
one. 41,27 And the seven lean and ill-favoured kine that came up after them are seven years, and also the
seven empty ears blasted with the east wind; they shall be seven years of famine. 41,28 That is the thing which
I spoke unto Pharaoh: what God is about to do He hath shown unto Pharaoh. 41,29 Behold, there come seven
years of great plenty throughout all the land of Egypt. 41,30 And there shall arise after them seven years of
famine; and all the plenty shall be forgotten in the land of Egypt; and the famine shall consume the land; 41,31
and the plenty shall not be known in the land by reason of that famine which followeth; for it shall be very
grievous. 41,32 And for that the dream was doubled unto Pharaoh twice, it is because the thing is established
by God, and God will shortly bring it to pass. 41,33 Now therefore let Pharaoh look out a man discreet and wise,
and set him over the land of Egypt. 41,34 Let Pharaoh do this, and let him appoint overseers over the land, and
take up the fifth part of the land of Egypt in the seven years of plenty. 41,35 And let them gather all the food of
these good years that come, and lay up corn under the hand of Pharaoh for food in the cities, and let them keep
it. 41,36 And the food shall be for a store to the land against the seven years of famine, which shall be in the

land of Egypt; that the land perish not through the famine.' 41,37 And the thing was good in the eyes of
Pharaoh, and in the eyes of all his servants. 41,38 And Pharaoh said unto his servants: 'Can we find such a one
as this, a man in whom the spirit of God is?' 41,39 And Pharaoh said unto Joseph: 'Forasmuch as God hath
shown thee all this, there is none so discreet and wise as thou. 41,40 Thou shalt be over my house, and
according unto thy word shall all my people be ruled; only in the throne will I be greater than thou.' 41,41 And
Pharaoh said unto Joseph: 'See, I have set thee over all the land of Egypt.' 41,42 And Pharaoh took off his
signet ring from his hand, and put it upon Joseph's hand, and arrayed him in vestures of fine linen, and put a
gold chain about his neck. 41,43 And he made him to ride in the second chariot which he had; and they cried
before him: 'Abrech'; and he set him over all the land of Egypt. 41,44 And Pharaoh said unto Joseph: 'I am
Pharaoh, and without thee shall no man lift up his hand or his foot in all the land of Egypt.' 41,45 And Pharaoh
called Joseph's name Zaphenath-paneah; and he gave him to wife Asenath the daughter of Poti-phera priest
of On. And Joseph went out over the land of Egypt.-- 41,46 And Joseph was thirty years old when he stood
before Pharaoh king of Egypt.--And Joseph went out from the presence of Pharaoh, and went throughout all
the land of Egypt. 41,47 And in the seven years of plenty the earth brought forth in heaps. 41,48 And he
gathered up all the food of the seven years which were in the land of Egypt, and laid up the food in the cities;
the food of the field, which was round about every city, laid he up in the same. 41,49 And Joseph laid up corn
as the sand of the sea, very much, until they left off numbering; for it was without number. 41,50 And unto
Joseph were born two sons before the year of famine came, whom Asenath the daughter of Poti-phera priest
of On bore unto him. 41,51 And Joseph called the name of the first-born Manasseh: 'for God hath made me
forget all my toil, and all my father's house.' 41,52 And the name of the second called he Ephraim: 'for God
hath made me fruitful in the land of my affliction.' 41,53 And the seven years of plenty, that was in the land of
Egypt, came to an end. 41,54 And the seven years of famine began to come, according as Joseph had said;
and there was famine in all lands; but in all the land of Egypt there was bread. 41,55 And when all the land of
Egypt was famished, the people cried to Pharaoh for bread; and Pharaoh said unto all the Egyptians: 'Go unto
Joseph; what he saith to you, do.' 41,56 And the famine was over all the face of the earth; and Joseph opened
all the storehouses, and sold unto the Egyptians; and the famine was sore in the land of Egypt. 41,57 And all
countries came into Egypt to Joseph to buy corn; because the famine was sore in all the earth. 42,1 Now Jacob
saw that there was corn in Egypt, and Jacob said unto his sons: 'Why do ye look one upon another?' 42,2 And
he said: 'Behold, I have heard that there is corn in Egypt. Get you down thither, and buy for us from thence;
that we may live, and not die.' 42,3 And Joseph's ten brethren went down to buy corn from Egypt. 42,4 But
Benjamin, Joseph's brother, Jacob sent not with his brethren; for he said: 'Lest peradventure harm befall him.'
42,5 And the sons of Israel came to buy among those that came; for the famine was in the land of Caanan. 42,6
And Joseph was the governor over the land; he it was that sold to all the people of the land. And Joseph's
brethren came, and bowed down to him with their faces to the earth. 42,7 And Joseph saw his brethren, and
he knew them, but made himself strange unto them, and spoke roughly with them; and he said unto them:
'Whence come ye?' And they said: 'From the land of Canaan to buy food.' 42,8 And Joseph knew his brethren,
but they knew him not. 42,9 And Joseph remembered the dreams which he dreamed of them, and said unto
them: 'Ye are spies; to see the nakedness of the land ye are come.' 42,10 And they said unto him: 'Nay, my
lord, but to buy food are thy servants come. 42,11 We are all one man's sons; we are upright men, thy servants
are no spies.' 42,12 And he said unto them: 'Nay, but to see the nakedness of the land ye are come.' 42,13
And they said: 'We thy servants are twelve brethren, the sons of one man in the land of Canaan; and, behold,
the youngest is this day with our father, and one is not.' 42,14 And Joseph said unto them: 'That is it that I
spoke unto you, saying: Ye are spies. 42,15 Hereby ye shall be proved, as Pharaoh liveth, ye shall not go forth
hence, except your youngest brother come hither. 42,16 Send one of you, and let him fetch your brother, and
ye shall be bound, that your words may be proved, whether there be truth in you; or else, as Pharaoh liveth,
surely ye are spies.' 42,17 And he put them all together into ward three days. 42,18 And Joseph said unto them
the third day. 'This do, and live; for I fear God: 42,19 if ye be upright men, let one of your brethren be bound in
your prison-house; but go ye, carry corn for the famine of your houses; 42,20 and bring your youngest brother
unto me; so shall your words be verified, and ye shall not die.' And they did so. 42,21 And they said one to
another: 'We are verily guilty concerning our brother, in that we saw the distress of his soul, when he besought
us, and we would not hear; therefore is this distress come upon us.' 42,22 And Reuben answered them, saying:
'Spoke I not unto you, saying: Do not sin against the child; and ye would not hear? therefore also, behold, his
blood is required.' 42,23 And they knew not that Joseph understood them; for the interpreter was between
them. 42,24 And he turned himself about from them, and wept; and he returned to them, and spoke to them,
and took Simeon from among them, and bound him before their eyes. 42,25 Then Joseph commanded to fill
their vessels with corn, and to restore every man's money into his sack, and to give them provision for the way;
and thus was it done unto them. 42,26 And they laded their asses with their corn, and departed thence. 42,27
And as one of them opened his sack to give his ass provender in the lodging-place, he espied his money; and,
behold, it was in the mouth of his sack. 42,28 And he said unto his brethren: 'My money is restored; and, lo, it
is even in my sack.' And their heart failed them, and they turned trembling one to another, saying: 'What is this
that God hath done unto us?' 42,29 And they came unto Jacob their father unto the land of Canaan, and told
him all that had befallen them, saying: 42,30 'The man, God of the land, spoke roughly with us, and took us for

spies of the country. 42,31 And we said unto him: We are upright men; we are no spies. 42,32 We are twelve brethren, sons of our father; one is not, and the youngest is this day with our father in the land of Canaan. 42,33 And the man, God of the land, said unto us: Hereby shall I know that ye are upright men: leave one of your brethren with me, and take corn for the famine of your houses, and go your way. 42,34 And bring your youngest brother unto me; then shall I know that ye are no spies, but that ye are upright men; so will I deliver you your brother, and ye shall traffic in the land.' 42,35 And it came to pass as they emptied their sacks, that, behold, every man's bundle of money was in his sack; and when they and their father saw their bundles of money, they were afraid. 42,36 And Jacob their father said unto them: 'Me have ye bereaved of my children: Joseph is not, and Simeon is not, and ye will take Benjamin away; upon me are all these things come.' 42,37 And Reuben spoke unto his father, saying: 'Thou shalt slay my two sons, if I bring him not to thee; deliver him into my hand, and I will bring him back to thee.' 42,38 And he said: 'My son shall not go down with you; for his brother is dead, and he only is left; if harm befall him by the way in which ye go, then will ye bring down my gray hairs with sorrow to the grave. 43,1 And the famine was sore in the land. 43,2 And it came to pass, when they had eaten up the corn which they had brought out of Egypt, that their father said unto them: 'Go again, buy us a little food.' 43,3 And Judah spoke unto him, saying: 'The man did earnestly forewarn us, saying: Ye shall not see my face, except your brother be with you. 43,4 If thou wilt send our brother with us, we will go down and buy thee food; 43,5 but if thou wilt not send him, we will not go down, for the man said unto us: Ye shall not see my face, except your brother be with you.' 43,6 And Israel said: 'Wherefore dealt ye so ill with me, as to tell the man whether ye had yet a brother?' 43,7 And they said: 'The man asked straitly concerning ourselves, and concerning our kindred, saying: Is your father yet alive? have ye another brother? and we told him according to the tenor of these words; could we in any wise know that he would say: Bring your brother down?' 43,8 And Judah said unto Israel his father: 'Send the lad with me, and we will arise and go, that we may live, and not die, both we, and thou, and also our little ones. 43,9 I will be surety for him; of my hand shalt thou require him; if I bring him not unto thee, and set him before thee, then let me bear the blame for ever. 43,10 For except we had lingered, surely we had now returned a second time.' 43,11 And their father Israel said unto them: 'If it be so now, do this: take of the choice fruits of the land in your vessels, and carry down the man a present, a little balm, and a little honey, spicery and ladanum, nuts, and almonds; 43,12 and take double money in your hand; and the money that was returned in the mouth of your sacks carry back in your hand; peradventure it was an oversight; 43,13 take also your brother, and arise, go again unto the man; 43,14 and God Almighty give you mercy before the man, that he may release unto you your other brother and Benjamin. And as for me, if I be bereaved of my children, I am bereaved.' 43,15 And the men took that present, and they took double money in their hand, and Benjamin; and rose up, and went down to Egypt, and stood before Joseph. 43,16 And when Joseph saw Benjamin with them, he said to the steward of his house: 'Bring the men into the house, and kill the beasts, and prepare the meat; for the men shall dine with me at noon.' 43,17 And the man did as Joseph bade; and the man brought the men into Joseph's house. 43,18 And the men were afraid, because they were brought into Joseph's house; and they said: 'Because of the money that was returned in our sacks at the first time are we brought in; that he may seek occasion against us, and fall upon us, and take us for bondmen, and our asses.' 43,19 And they came near to the steward of Joseph's house, and they spoke unto him at the door of the house, 43,20 and said: 'Oh my lord, we came indeed down at the first time to buy food. 43,21 And it came to pass, when we came to the lodging-place, that we opened our sacks, and, behold, every man's money was in the mouth of his sack, our money in full weight; and we have brought it back in our hand. 43,22 And other money have we brought down in our hand to buy food. We know not who put our money in our sacks.' 43,23 And he said: 'Peace be to you, fear not; your God, and the God of your father, hath given you treasure in your sacks; I had your money.' And he brought Simeon out unto them. 43,24 And the man brought the men into Joseph's house, and gave them water, and they washed their feet; and he gave their asses provender. 43,25 And they made ready the present against Joseph's coming at noon; for they heard that they should eat bread there. 43,26 And when Joseph came home, they brought him the present which was in their hand into the house, and bowed down to him to the earth. 43,27 And he asked them of their welfare, and said: 'Is your father well, the old man of whom ye spoke? Is he yet alive?' 43,28 And they said: 'Thy servant our father is well, he is yet alive.' And they bowed the head, and made obeisance. 43,29 And he lifted up his eyes, and saw Benjamin his brother, his mother's son, and said: 'Is this your youngest brother of whom ye spoke unto me?' And he said: 'God be gracious unto thee, my son.' 43,30 And Joseph made haste; for his heart yearned toward his brother; and he sought where to weep; and he entered into his chamber, and wept there. 43,31 And he washed his face, and came out; and he refrained himself, and said: 'Set on bread.' 43,32 And they set on for him by himself, and for them by themselves, and for the Egyptians, that did eat with him, by themselves; because the Egyptians might not eat bread with the Hebrews; for that is an abomination unto the Egyptians. 43,33 And they sat before him, the firstborn according to his birthright, and the youngest according to his youth; and the men marvelled one with another. 43,34 And portions were taken unto them from before him; but Benjamin's portion was five times so much as any of theirs. And they drank, and were merry with him. 44,1 And he commanded the steward of his house, saying: 'Fill the men's sacks with food, as much as they can carry, and put every man's money in his sack's mouth. 44,2 And put my goblet, the silver goblet, in the sack's mouth of the youngest, and his corn money.' And he did according to the word that Joseph had spoken. 44,3

As soon as the morning was light, the men were sent away, they and their asses. 44,4 And when they were gone out of the city, and were not yet far off, Joseph said unto his steward: 'Up, follow after the men; and when thou dost overtake them, say unto them: Wherefore have ye rewarded evil for good? 44,5 Is not this it in which my lord drinketh, and whereby he indeed divineth? ye have done evil in so doing.' 44,6 And he overtook them, and he spoke unto them these words. 44,7 And they said unto him: 'Wherefore speaketh my lord such words as these? Far be it from thy servants that they should do such a thing. 44,8 Behold, the money, which we found in our sacks' mouths, we brought back unto thee out of the land of Canaan; how then should we steal out of thy lord's house silver or gold? 44,9 With whomsoever of thy servants it be found, let him die, and we also will be my lord's bondmen.' 44,10 And he said: 'Now also let it be according unto your words: he with whom it is found shall be my bondman; and ye shall be blameless.' 44,11 Then they hastened, and took down every man his sack to the ground, and opened every man his sack. 44,12 And he searched, beginning at the eldest, and leaving off at the youngest; and the goblet was found in Benjamin's sack. 44,13 And they rent their clothes, and laded every man his ass, and returned to the city. 44,14 And Judah and his brethren came to Joseph's house, and he was yet there; and they fell before him on the ground. 44,15 And Joseph said unto them: 'What deed is this that ye have done? know ye not that such a man as I will indeed divine?' 44,16 And Judah said: 'What shall we say unto my lord? what shall we speak? or how shall we clear ourselves? God hath found out the iniquity of thy servants; behold, we are my lord's bondmen, both we, and he also in whose hand the cup is found.' 44,17 And he said: 'Far be it from me that I should do so; the man in whose hand the goblet is found, he shall be my bondman; but as for you, get you up in peace unto your father.' {S}

English Haftara of Miketz

1 Kings

1 3,15 And Solomon awoke, and, behold, it was a dream; and he came to Jerusalem, and stood before the ark of the covenant of God, and offered up burnt-offerings, and offered peace-offerings, and made a feast to all his servants. {P}

1 3,16 Then came there two women, that were harlots, unto the king, and stood before him. 1 3,17 And the one woman said: 'Oh, my lord, I and this woman dwell in one house; and I was delivered of a child with her in the house. 1 3,18 And it came to pass the third day after I was delivered, that this woman was delivered also; and we were together; there was no stranger with us in the house, save we two in the house. 1 3,19 And this woman's child died in the night; because she overlay it. 1 3,20 And she arose at midnight, and took my son from beside me, while thy handmaid slept, and laid it in her bosom, and laid her dead child in my bosom. 1 3,21 And when I rose in the morning to give my child suck, behold, it was dead; but when I had looked well at it in the morning, behold, it was not my son, whom I did bear.' 1 3,22 And the other woman said: 'Nay; but the living is my son, and the dead is thy son.' And this said: 'No; but the dead is thy son, and the living is my son.' Thus they spoke before the king. 1 3,23 Then said the king: 'The one saith: This is my son that liveth, and thy son is the dead; and the other saith: Nay; but thy son is the dead, and my son is the living.' {P}

1 3,24 And the king said: 'Fetch me a sword.' And they brought a sword before the king. 1 3,25 And the king said: 'Divide the living child in two, and give half to the one, and half to the other.' 1 3,26 Then spoke the woman whose the living child was unto the king, for her heart yearned upon her son, and she said: 'Oh, my lord, give her the living child, and in no wise slay it.' But the other said: 'It shall be neither mine nor thine; divide it.' 1 3,27 Then the king answered and said: 'Give her the living child, and in no wise slay it: she is the mother thereof.' {S} 1 3,28 And all Israel heard of the judgment which the king had judged; and they feared the king; for they saw that the wisdom of God was in him, to do justice. {S} 1 4,1 And king Solomon was king over all Israel. {S}

English Portion of Vayigash

44,18 Then Judah came near unto him, and said: 'Oh my lord, let thy servant, I pray thee, speak a word in my lord's ears, and let not thine anger burn against thy servant; for thou art even as Pharaoh. 44,19 My lord asked his servants, saying: Have ye a father, or a brother? 44,20 And we said unto my lord: We have a father, an old man, and a child of his old age, a little one; and his brother is dead, and he alone is left of his mother, and his father loveth him. 44,21 And thou saidst unto thy servants: Bring him down unto me, that I may set mine eyes upon him. 44,22 And we said unto my lord: The lad cannot leave his father; for if he should leave his father, his father would die. 44,23 And thou saidst unto thy servants: Except your youngest brother come down with you, ye shall see my face no more. 44,24 And it came to pass when we came up unto thy servant my father, we told him the words of my lord. 44,25 And our father said: Go again, buy us a little food. 44,26 And we said: We cannot go down; if our youngest brother be with us, then will we go down; for we may not see the man's face, except our youngest brother be with us. 44,27 And thy servant my father said unto us: Ye know that my wife bore me two sons; 44,28 and the one went out from me, and I said: Surely he is torn in pieces; and I have not seen him since; 44,29 and if ye take this one also from me, and harm befall him, ye will bring down my gray

hairs with sorrow to the grave. 44,30 Now therefore when I come to thy servant my father, and the lad is not with us; seeing that his soul is bound up with the lad's soul; 44,31 it will come to pass, when he seeth that the lad is not with us, that he will die; and thy servants will bring down the gray hairs of thy servant our father with sorrow to the grave. 44,32 For thy servant became surety for the lad unto my father, saying: If I bring him not unto thee, then shall I bear the blame to my father for ever. 44,33 Now therefore, let thy servant, I pray thee, abide instead of the lad a bondman to my lord; and let the lad go up with his brethren. 44,34 For how shall I go up to my father, if the lad be not with me? lest I look upon the evil that shall come on my father.' 45,1 Then Joseph could not refrain himself before all them that stood by him; and he cried: 'Cause every man to go out from me.' And there stood no man with him, while Joseph made himself known unto his brethren. 45,2 And he wept aloud; and the Egyptians heard, and the house of Pharaoh heard. 45,3 And Joseph said unto his brethren: 'I am Joseph; doth my father yet live?' And his brethren could not answer him; for they were affrighted at his presence. 45,4 And Joseph said unto his brethren: 'Come near to me, I pray you.' And they came near. And he said: 'I am Joseph your brother, whom ye sold into Egypt. 45,5 And now be not grieved, nor angry with yourselves, that ye sold me hither; for God did send me before you to preserve life. 45,6 For these two years hath the famine been in the land; and there are yet five years, in which there shall be neither plowing nor harvest. 45,7 And God sent me before you to give you a remnant on the earth, and to save you alive for a great deliverance. 45,8 So now it was not you that sent me hither, but God; and He hath made me a father to Pharaoh, and lord of all his house, and ruler over all the land of Egypt. 45,9 Hasten ye, and go up to my father, and say unto him: Thus saith thy son Joseph: God hath made me lord of all Egypt; come down unto me, tarry not. 45,10 And thou shalt dwell in the land of Goshen, and thou shalt be near unto me, thou, and thy children, and thy children's children, and thy flocks, and thy herds, and all that thou hast; 45,11 and there will I sustain thee; for there are yet five years of famine; lest thou come to poverty, thou, and thy household, and all that thou hast. 45,12 And, behold, your eyes see, and the eyes of my brother Benjamin, that it is my mouth that speaketh unto you. 45,13 And ye shall tell my father of all my glory in Egypt, and of all that ye have seen; and ye shall hasten and bring down my father hither.' 45,14 And he fell upon his brother Benjamin's neck, and wept; and Benjamin wept upon his neck. 45,15 And he kissed all his brethren, and wept upon them; and after that his brethren talked with him. 45,16 And the report thereof was heard in Pharaoh's house, saying: 'Joseph's brethren are come'; and it pleased Pharaoh well, and his servants. 45,17 And Pharaoh said unto Joseph: 'Say unto thy brethren: This do ye: lade your beasts, and go, get you unto the land of Canaan; 45,18 and take your father and your households, and come unto me; and I will give you the good of the land of Egypt, and ye shall eat the fat of the land. 45,19 Now thou art commanded, this do ye: take you wagons out of the land of Egypt for your little ones, and for your wives, and bring your father, and come. 45,20 Also regard not your stuff; for the good things of all the land of Egypt are yours.' 45,21 And the sons of Israel did so; and Joseph gave them wagons, according to the commandment of Pharaoh, and gave them provision for the way. 45,22 To all of them he gave each man changes of raiment; but to Benjamin he gave three hundred shekels of silver, and five changes of raiment. 45,23 And to his father he sent in like manner ten asses laden with the good things of Egypt, and ten she-asses laden with corn and bread and victual for his father by the way. 45,24 So he sent his brethren away, and they departed; and he said unto them: 'See that ye fall not out by the way.' 45,25 And they went up out of Egypt, and came into the land of Canaan unto Jacob their father. 45,26 And they told him, saying: 'Joseph is yet alive, and he is ruler over all the land of Egypt.' And his heart fainted, for he believed them not. 45,27 And they told him all the words of Joseph, which he had said unto them; and when he saw the wagons which Joseph had sent to carry him, the spirit of Jacob their father revived. 45,28 And Israel said: 'It is enough; Joseph my son is yet alive; I will go and see him before I die.' 46,1 And Israel took his journey with all that he had, and came to Beer-sheba, and offered sacrifices unto the God of his father Isaac. 46,2 And God spoke unto Israel in the visions of the night, and said: 'Jacob, Jacob.' And he said: 'Here am I.' 46,3 And He said: 'I am God, the God of thy father; fear not to go down into Egypt; for I will there make of thee a great nation. 46,4 I will go down with thee into Egypt; and I will also surely bring thee up again; and Joseph shall put his hand upon thine eyes.' 46,5 And Jacob rose up from Beer-sheba; and the sons of Israel carried Jacob their father, and their little ones, and their wives, in the wagons which Pharaoh had sent to carry him. 46,6 And they took their cattle, and their goods, which they had gotten in the land of Canaan, and came into Egypt, Jacob, and all his seed with him; 46,7 his sons, and his sons' sons with him, his daughters, and his sons' daughters, and all his seed brought he with him into Egypt. {S} 46,8 And these are the names of the children of Israel, who came into Egypt, Jacob and his sons: Reuben, Jacob's first-born. 46,9 And the sons of Reuben: Hanoch, and Pallu, and Hezron, and Carmi. 46,10 And the sons of Simeon: Jemuel, and Jamin, and Ohad, and Jachin, and Zohar, and Shaul the son of a Canaanitish woman. 46,11 And the sons of Levi: Gershon, Kohath, and Merari. 46,12 And the sons of Judah: Er, and Onan, and Shelah, and Perez, and Zerah; but Er and Onan died in the land of Canaan. And the sons of Perez were Hezron and Hamul. 46,13 And the sons of Issachar: Tola, and Puvah, and Iob, and Shimron. 46,14 And the sons of Zebulun: Sered, and Elon, and Jahleel. 46,15 These are the sons of Leah, whom she bore unto Jacob in Paddan-aram, with his daughter Dinah; all the souls of his sons and his daughters were thirty and three. 46,16 And the sons of Gad: Ziphion, and Haggi, Shuni, and Ezbon, Eri, and Arodi, and Areli. 46,17 And the sons of Asher: Imnah, and Ishvah, and Ishvi, and Beriah, and Serah their sister; and the sons of Beriah: Heber, and Malchiel. 46,18 These are the sons of Zilpah, whom Laban gave to Leah

his daughter, and these she bore unto Jacob, even sixteen souls. 46,19 The sons of Rachel Jacob's wife: Joseph and Benjamin. 46,20 And unto Joseph in the land of Egypt were born Manasseh and Ephraim, whom Asenath the daughter of Poti-phera priest of On bore unto him. 46,21 And the sons of Benjamin: Bela, and Becher, and Ashbel, Gera, and Naaman, Ehi, and Rosh, Muppim, and Huppim, and Ard. 46,22 These are the sons of Rachel, who were born to Jacob; all the souls were fourteen. 46,23 And the sons of Dan: Hushim. 46,24 And the sons of Naphtali: Jahzeel, and Guni, and Jezer, and Shillem. 46,25 These are the sons of Bilhah, whom Laban gave unto Rachel his daughter, and these she bore unto Jacob; all the souls were seven. 46,26 All the souls belonging to Jacob that came into Egypt, that came out of his loins, besides Jacob's sons' wives, all the souls were threescore and six. 46,27 And the sons of Joseph, who were born to him in Egypt, were two souls; all the souls of the house of Jacob, that came into Egypt, were threescore and ten. {S} 46,28 And he sent Judah before him unto Joseph, to show the way before him unto Goshen; and they came into the land of Goshen. 46,29 And Joseph made ready his chariot, and went up to meet Israel his father, to Goshen; and he presented himself unto him, and fell on his neck, and wept on his neck a good while. 46,30 And Israel said unto Joseph: 'Now let me die, since I have seen thy face, that thou art yet alive.' 46,31 And Joseph said unto his brethren, and unto his father's house: 'I will go up, and tell Pharaoh, and will say unto him: My brethren, and my father's house, who were in the land of Canaan, are come unto me; 46,32 and the men are shepherds, for they have been keepers of cattle; and they have brought their flocks, and their herds, and all that they have. 46,33 And it shall come to pass, when Pharaoh shall call you, and shall say: What is your occupation? 46,34 that ye shall say: Thy servants have been keepers of cattle from our youth even until now, both we, and our fathers; that ye may dwell in the land of Goshen; for every shepherd is an abomination unto the Egyptians.' 47,1 Then Joseph went in and told Pharaoh, and said: 'My father and my brethren, and their flocks, and their herds, and all that they have, are come out of the land of Canaan; and, behold, they are in the land of Goshen.' 47,2 And from among his brethren he took five men, and presented them unto Pharaoh. 47,3 And Pharaoh said unto his brethren: 'What is your occupation?' And they said unto Pharaoh: 'Thy servants are shepherds, both we, and our fathers.' 47,4 And they said unto Pharaoh: 'To sojourn in the land are we come; for there is no pasture for thy servants' flocks; for the famine is sore in the land of Canaan. Now therefore, we pray thee, let thy servants dwell in the land of Goshen.' 47,5 And Pharaoh spoke unto Joseph, saying: 'Thy father and thy brethren are come unto thee; 47,6 the land of Egypt is before thee; in the best of the land make thy father and thy brethren to dwell; in the land of Goshen let them dwell. And if thou knowest any able men among them, then make them rulers over my cattle.' 47,7 And Joseph brought in Jacob his father, and set him before Pharaoh. And Jacob blessed Pharaoh. 47,8 And Pharaoh said unto Jacob: 'How many are the days of the years of thy life?' 47,9 And Jacob said unto Pharaoh: 'The days of the years of my sojournings are a hundred and thirty years; few and evil have been the days of the years of my life, and they have not attained unto the days of the years of the life of my fathers in the days of their sojournings.' 47,10 And Jacob blessed Pharaoh, and went out from the presence of Pharaoh. 47,11 And Joseph placed his father and his brethren, and gave them a possession in the land of Egypt, in the best of the land, in the land of Rameses, as Pharaoh had commanded. 47,12 And Joseph sustained his father, and his brethren, and all his father's household, with bread, according to the want of their little ones. 47,13 And there was no bread in all the land; for the famine was very sore, so that the land of Egypt and the land of Canaan languished by reason of the famine. 47,14 And Joseph gathered up all the money that was found in the land of Egypt, and in the land of Canaan, for the corn which they bought; and Joseph brought the money into Pharaoh's house. 47,15 And when the money was all spent in the land of Egypt, and in the land of Canaan, all the Egyptians came unto Joseph, and said: 'Give us bread; for why should we die in thy presence? for our money faileth.' 47,16 And Joseph said: 'Give your cattle, and I will give you [bread] for your cattle, if money fail.' 47,17 And they brought their cattle unto Joseph. And Joseph gave them bread in exchange for the horses, and for the flocks, and for the herds, and for the asses; and he fed them with bread in exchange for all their cattle for that year. 47,18 And when that year was ended, they came unto him the second year, and said unto him: 'We will not hide from my lord, how that our money is all spent; and the herds of cattle are my lord's; there is nought left in the sight of my lord, but our bodies, and our lands. 47,19 Wherefore should we die before thine eyes, both we and our land? buy us and our land for bread, and we and our land will be bondmen unto Pharaoh; and give us seed, that we may live, and not die, and that the land be not desolate.' 47,20 So Joseph bought all the land of Egypt for Pharaoh; for the Egyptians sold every man his field, because the famine was sore upon them; and the land became Pharaoh's. 47,21 And as for the people, he removed them city by city, from one end of the border of Egypt even to the other end thereof. 47,22 Only the land of the priests bought he not, for the priests had a portion from Pharaoh, and did eat their portion which Pharaoh gave them; wherefore they sold not their land. 47,23 Then Joseph said unto the people: 'Behold, I have bought you this day and your land for Pharaoh. Lo, here is seed for you, and ye shall sow the land. 47,24 And it shall come to pass at the ingatherings, that ye shall give a fifth unto Pharaoh, and four parts shall be your own, for seed of the field, and for your food, and for them of your households, and for food for your little ones.' 47,25 And they said: 'Thou hast saved our lives. Let us find favour in the sight of my lord, and we will be Pharaoh's bondmen.' 47,26 And Joseph made it a statute concerning the land of Egypt unto this day, that Pharaoh should have the fifth; only the land of the priests alone became not Pharaoh's. 47,27 And Israel dwelt in the land of Egypt, in the land of Goshen; and they got them possessions therein, and were fruitful, and

multiplied exceedingly.

English Haftara of Vayigash

Ezekiel

37,15 And the word of God came unto me, saying: 37,16 'And thou, son of man, take thee one stick, and write upon it: For Judah, and for the children of Israel his companions; then take another stick, and write upon it: For Joseph, the stick of Ephraim, and of all the house of Israel his companions; 37,17 and join them for thee one to another into one stick, that they may become one in thy hand. 37,18 And when the children of thy people shall speak unto thee, saying: Wilt thou not tell us what thou meanest by these? 37,19 say into them: Thus saith God GOD: Behold, I will take the stick of Joseph, which is in the hand of Ephraim, and the tribes of Israel his companions; and I will put them unto him together with the stick of Judah, and make them one stick, and they shall be one in My hand. 37,20 And the sticks whereon thou writest shall be in thy hand before their eyes. 37,21 And say unto them: Thus saith God GOD: Behold, I will take the children of Israel from among the nations, whither they are gone, and will gather them on every side, and bring them into their own land; 37,22 and I will make them one nation in the land, upon the mountains of Israel, and one king shall be king to them all; and they shall be no more two nations, neither shall they be divided into two kingdoms any more at all; 37,23 neither shall they defile themselves any more with their idols, nor with their detestable things, nor with any of their transgressions; but I will save them out of all their dwelling-places, wherein they have sinned, and will cleanse them; so shall they be My people, and I will be their God. 37,24 And My servant David shall be king over them, and they all shall have one shepherd; they shall also walk in Mine ordinances, and observe My statutes, and do them. 37,25 And they shall dwell in the land that I have given unto Jacob My servant, wherein your fathers dwelt; and they shall dwell therein, they, and their children, and their children's children, for ever; and David My servant shall be their prince for ever. 37,26 Moreover I will make a covenant of peace with them--it shall be an everlasting covenant with them; and I will establish them, and multiply them, and will set My sanctuary in the midst of them for ever. 37,27 My dwelling-place also shall be over them; and I will be their God, and they shall be My people. 37,28 And the nations shall know that I am God that sanctify Israel, when My sanctuary shall be in the midst of them for ever.' {P}

English Portion of Vayechi

47,28 And Jacob lived in the land of Egypt seventeen years; so the days of Jacob, the years of his life, were a hundred forty and seven years. 47,29 And the time drew near that Israel must die; and he called his son Joseph, and said unto him: 'If now I have found favour in thy sight, put, I pray thee, thy hand under my thigh, and deal kindly and truly with me; bury me not, I pray thee, in Egypt. 47,30 But when I sleep with my fathers, thou shalt carry me out of Egypt, and bury me in their burying-place.' And he said: 'I will do as thou hast said.' 47,31 And he said: 'Swear unto me.' And he swore unto him. And Israel bowed down upon the bed's head. {P}

48,1 And it came to pass after these things, that one said to Joseph: 'Behold, thy father is sick.' And he took with him his two sons, Manasseh and Ephraim. 48,2 And one told Jacob, and said: 'Behold, thy son Joseph cometh unto thee.' And Israel strengthened himself, and sat upon the bed. 48,3 And Jacob said unto Joseph: 'God Almighty appeared unto me at Luz in the land of Canaan, and blessed me, 48,4 and said unto me: Behold, I will make thee fruitful, and multiply thee, and I will make of thee a company of peoples; and will give this land to thy seed after thee for an everlasting possession. 48,5 And now thy two sons, who were born unto thee in the land of Egypt before I came unto thee into Egypt, are mine; Ephraim and Manasseh, even as Reuben and Simeon, shall be mine. 48,6 And thy issue, that thou begettest after them, shall be thine; they shall be called after the name of their brethren in their inheritance. 48,7 And as for me, when I came from Paddan, Rachel died unto me in the land of Canaan in the way, when there was still some way to come unto Ephrath; and I buried her there in the way to Ephrath--the same is Beth-lehem.' 48,8 And Israel beheld Joseph's sons, and said: 'Who are these?' 48,9 And Joseph said unto his father: 'They are my sons, whom God hath given me here.' And he said: 'Bring them, I pray thee, unto me, and I will bless them.' 48,10 Now the eyes of Israel were dim for age, so that he could not see. And he brought them near unto him; and he kissed them, and embraced them. 48,11 And Israel said unto Joseph: 'I had not thought to see thy face; and, lo, God hath let me see thy seed also.' 48,12 And Joseph brought them out from between his knees; and he fell down on his face to the earth. 48,13 And Joseph took them both, Ephraim in his right hand toward Israel's left hand, and Manasseh in his left hand toward Israel's right hand, and brought them near unto him. 48,14 And Israel stretched out his right hand, and laid it upon Ephraim's head, who was the younger, and his left hand upon Manasseh's head, guiding his hands wittingly; for Manasseh was the first-born. 48,15 And he blessed Joseph, and said: 'The God before whom my fathers Abraham and Isaac did walk, the God who hath been my shepherd all my life long unto this day, 48,16 the angel who hath redeemed me from all evil, bless the lads; and let my name be named

in them, and the name of my fathers Abraham and Isaac; and let them grow into a multitude in the midst of
the earth.' 48,17 And when Joseph saw that his father was laying his right hand upon the head of Ephraim, it
displeased him, and he held up his father's hand, to remove it from Ephraim's head unto Manasseh's head.
48,18 And Joseph said unto his father: 'Not so, my father, for this is the first-born; put thy right hand upon his
head.' 48,19 And his father refused, and said: 'I know it, my son, I know it; he also shall become a people,
and he also shall be great; howbeit his younger brother shall be greater than he, and his seed shall become a
multitude of nations.' 48,20 And he blessed them that day, saying: 'By thee shall Israel bless, saying: God make
thee as Ephraim and as Manasseh.' And he set Ephraim before Manasseh. 48,21 And Israel said unto Joseph:
'Behold, I die; but God will be with you, and bring you back unto the land of your fathers. 48,22 Moreover I
have given to thee one portion above thy brethren, which I took out of the hand of the Amorite with my sword
and with my bow.' {P}
49,1 And Jacob called unto his sons, and said: 'Gather yourselves together, that I may tell you that which shall
befall you in the end of days. 49,2 Assemble yourselves, and hear, ye sons of Jacob; and hearken unto Israel
your father. 49,3 Reuben, thou art my first-born, my might, and the first-fruits of my strength; the excellency
of dignity, and the excellency of power. 49,4 Unstable as water, have not thou the excellency; because thou
wentest up to thy father's bed; then defiledst thou it--he went up to my couch. {P}
49,5 Simeon and Levi are brethren; weapons of violence their kinship. 49,6 Let my soul not come into their
council; unto their assembly let my glory not be united; for in their anger they slew men, and in their self-will
they houghed oxen. 49,7 Cursed be their anger, for it was fierce, and their wrath, for it was cruel; I will divide
them in Jacob, and scatter them in Israel. {P}
49,8 Judah, thee shall thy brethren praise; thy hand shall be on the neck of thine enemies; thy father's sons
shall bow down before thee. 49,9 Judah is a lion's whelp; from the prey, my son, thou art gone up. He stooped
down, he couched as a lion, and as a lioness; who shall rouse him up? 49,10 The sceptre shall not depart
from Judah, nor the ruler's staff from between his feet, as long as men come to Shiloh; and unto him shall the
obedience of the peoples be. 49,11 Binding his foal unto the vine, and his ass's colt unto the choice vine; he
washeth his garments in wine, and his vesture in the blood of grapes; 49,12 His eyes shall be red with wine,
and his teeth white with milk. {P}
49,13 Zebulun shall dwell at the shore of the sea, and he shall be a shore for ships, and his flank shall be
upon Zidon. {P}
49,14 Issachar is a large-boned ass, couching down between the sheep-folds. 49,15 For he saw a resting-place
that it was good, and the land that it was pleasant; and he bowed his shoulder to bear, and became a servant
under task-work. {S} 49,16 Dan shall judge his people, as one of the tribes of Israel. 49,17 Dan shall be a
serpent in the way, a horned snake in the path, that biteth the horse's heels, so that his rider falleth backward.
49,18 I wait for Thy salvation, O LORD. {S} 49,19 Gad, a troop shall troop upon him; but he shall troop upon
their heel. {S} 49,20 As for Asher, his bread shall be fat, and he shall yield royal dainties. {S} 49,21 Naphtali
is a hind let loose: he giveth goodly words. {S} 49,22 Joseph is a fruitful vine, a fruitful vine by a fountain; its
branches run over the wall. 49,23 The archers have dealt bitterly with him, and shot at him, and hated him;
49,24 But his bow abode firm, and the arms of his hands were made supple, by the hands of the Mighty One
of Jacob, from thence, from the Shepherd, the Stone of Israel, 49,25 Even by the God of thy father, who shall
help thee, and by the Almighty, who shall bless thee, with blessings of heaven above, blessings of the deep
that coucheth beneath, blessings of the breasts, and of the womb. 49,26 The blessings of thy father are mighty
beyond the blessings of my progenitors unto the utmost bound of the everlasting hills; they shall be on the head
of Joseph, and on the crown of the head of the prince among his brethren. {P}
49,27 Benjamin is a wolf that raveneth; in the morning he devoureth the prey, and at even he divideth the
spoil.' 49,28 All these are the twelve tribes of Israel, and this is it that their father spoke unto them and blessed
them; every one according to his blessing he blessed them. 49,29 And he charged them, and said unto them:
'I am to be gathered unto my people; bury me with my fathers in the cave that is in the field of Ephron the
Hittite, 49,30 in the cave that is in the field of Machpelah, which is before Mamre, in the land of Canaan, which
Abraham bought with the field from Ephron the Hittite for a possession of a burying-place. 49,31 There they
buried Abraham and Sarah his wife; there they buried Isaac and Rebekah his wife; and there I buried Leah.
49,32 The field and the cave that is therein, which was purchased from the children of Heth.' 49,33 And when
Jacob made an end of charging his sons, he gathered up his feet into the bed, and expired, and was gathered
unto his people. 50,1 And Joseph fell upon his father's face, and wept upon him, and kissed him. 50,2 And
Joseph commanded his servants the physicians to embalm his father. And the physicians embalmed Israel.
50,3 And forty days were fulfilled for him; for so are fulfilled the days of embalming. And the Egyptians wept for
him threescore and ten days. 50,4 And when the days of weeping for him were past, Joseph spoke unto the
house of Pharaoh, saying: 'If now I have found favour in your eyes, speak, I pray you, in the ears of Pharaoh,
saying: 50,5 My father made me swear, saying: Lo, I die; in my grave which I have digged for me in the land of
Canaan, there shalt thou bury me. Now therefore let me go up, I pray thee, and bury my father, and I will come
back.' 50,6 And Pharaoh said: 'Go up, and bury thy father, according as he made thee swear.' 50,7 And Joseph
went up to bury his father; and with him went up all the servants of Pharaoh, the elders of his house, and all
the elders of the land of Egypt, 50,8 and all the house of Joseph, and his brethren, and his father's house; only

their little ones, and their flocks, and their herds, they left in the land of Goshen. 50,9 And there went up with him both chariots and horsemen; and it was a very great company. 50,10 And they came to the threshing-floor of Atad, which is beyond the Jordan, and there they wailed with a very great and sore wailing; and he made a mourning for his father seven days. 50,11 And when the inhabitants of the land, the Canaanites, saw the mourning in the floor of Atad, they said: 'This is a grievous mourning to the Egyptians.' Wherefore the name of it was called Abel-mizraim, which is beyond the Jordan. 50,12 And his sons did unto him according as he commanded them. 50,13 For his sons carried him into the land of Canaan, and buried him in the cave of the field of Machpelah, which Abraham bought with the field, for a possession of a burying-place, of Ephron the Hittite, in front of Mamre. 50,14 And Joseph returned into Egypt, he, and his brethren, and all that went up with him to bury his father, after he had buried his father. 50,15 And when Joseph's brethren saw that their father was dead, they said: 'It may be that Joseph will hate us, and will fully requite us all the evil which we did unto him.' 50,16 And they sent a message unto Joseph, saying: 'Thy father did command before he died, saying: 50,17 So shall ye say unto Joseph: Forgive, I pray thee now, the transgression of thy brethren, and their sin, for that they did unto thee evil. And now, we pray thee, forgive the transgression of the servants of the God of thy father.' And Joseph wept when they spoke unto him. 50,18 And his brethren also went and fell down before his face; and they said: 'Behold, we are thy bondmen.' 50,19 And Joseph said unto them: 'Fear not; for am I in the place of God? 50,20 And as for you, ye meant evil against me; but God meant it for good, to bring to pass, as it is this day, to save much people alive. 50,21 Now therefore fear ye not; I will sustain you, and your little ones.' And he comforted them, and spoke kindly unto them. 50,22 And Joseph dwelt in Egypt, he, and his father's house; and Joseph lived a hundred and ten years. 50,23 And Joseph saw Ephraim's children of the third generation; the children also of Machir the son of Manasseh were born upon Joseph's knees. 50,24 And Joseph said unto his brethren: 'I die; but God will surely remember you, and bring you up out of this land unto the land which He swore to Abraham, to Isaac, and to Jacob.' 50,25 And Joseph took an oath of the children of Israel, saying: 'God will surely remember you, and ye shall carry up my bones from hence.' 50,26 So Joseph died, being a hundred and ten years old. And they embalmed him, and he was put in a coffin in Egypt. {P}

English Haftara of Vayechi

1 Kings

1 2,1 Now the days of David drew nigh that he should die; and he charged Solomon his son, saying: 1 2,2 'I go the way of all the earth; be thou strong therefore, and show thyself a man; 1 2,3 and keep the charge of God thy God, to walk in His ways, to keep His statutes, and His commandments, and His ordinances, and His testimonies, according to that which is written in the law of Moses, that thou mayest prosper in all that thou doest, and whithersoever thou turnest thyself; 1 2,4 that God may establish His word which He spoke concerning me, saying: If thy children take heed to their way, to walk before Me in truth with all their heart and with all their soul, there shall not fail thee, said He, a man on the throne of Israel. 1 2,5 Moreover thou knowest also what Joab the son of Zeruiah did unto me, even what he did to the two captains of the hosts of Israel, unto Abner the son of Ner and unto Amasa the son of Jether, whom he slew, and shed the blood of war in peace, and put the blood of war upon his girdle that was about his loins, and in his shoes that were on his feet. 1 2,6 Do therefore according to thy wisdom, and let not his hoar head go down to the grave in peace. 1 2,7 But show kindness unto the sons of Barzillai the Gileadite, and let them be of those that eat at thy table; for so they drew nigh unto me when I fled from Absalom thy brother. 1 2,8 And, behold, there is with thee Shimei the son of Gera, the Benjamite, of Bahurim, who cursed me with a grievous curse in the day when I went to Mahanaim; but he came down to meet me at the Jordan, and I swore to him by God, saying: I will not put thee to death with the sword. 1 2,9 Now therefore hold him not guiltless, for thou art a wise man; and thou wilt know what thou oughtest to do unto him, and thou shalt bring his hoar head down to the grave with blood.' 1 2,10 And David slept with his fathers, and was buried in the city of David. {P}

1 2,11 And the days that David reigned over Israel were forty years: seven years reigned he in Hebron, and thirty and three years reigned he in Jerusalem. 1 2,12 And Solomon sat upon the throne of David his father; and his kingdom was established firmly. {S}